Applying Innovative Technologies in Heritage Science

George Pavlidis
Athena - Research and Innovation Center in Information, Communication, and Knowledge Technologies, Greece

A volume in the Advances in Religious and Cultural Studies (ARCS) Book Series

IGI Global
DISSEMINATOR OF KNOWLEDGE

Published in the United States of America by
IGI Global
Information Science Reference (an imprint of IGI Global)
701 E. Chocolate Avenue
Hershey PA, USA 17033
Tel: 717-533-8845
Fax: 717-533-8661
E-mail: cust@igi-global.com
Web site: http://www.igi-global.com

Library of Congress Cataloging-in-Publication Data

Names: Pavlidis, George, 1970- editor.
Title: Applying innovative technologies in heritage science / George Pavlidis, editor.
Description: Hershey, PA : Information Science Reference, [2020] | Includes bibliographical references and index. | Summary: "This book explores the ways in which science and technology are bridging the gap between science and the humanities"-- Provided by publisher.
Identifiers: LCCN 2019044158 (print) | LCCN 2019044159 (ebook) | ISBN 9781799828716 (hardcover) | ISBN 9781799828860 (paperback) | ISBN 9781799828723 (ebook)
Subjects: LCSH: Cultural property--Protection--Technological innovations. | Image processing--Digital techniques. | Three-dimensional imaging. | Augmented reality.
Classification: LCC CC135 .A66 2020 (print) | LCC CC135 (ebook) | DDC 363.6/90285--dc23
LC record available at https://lccn.loc.gov/2019044158
LC ebook record available at https://lccn.loc.gov/2019044159

This book is published in the IGI Global book series Advances in Religious and Cultural Studies (ARCS) (ISSN: 2475-675X; eISSN: 2475-6768)

British Cataloguing in Publication Data
A Cataloguing in Publication record for this book is available from the British Library.

For electronic access to this publication, please contact: eresources@igi-global.com.

Advances in Religious and Cultural Studies (ARCS) Book Series

Nancy Erbe
California State University-Dominguez Hills, USA

ISSN:2475-675X
EISSN:2475-6768

Mission

In the era of globalization, the diversity of the world and various cultures becomes apparent as cross-cultural interactions turn into a daily occurrence for individuals in all professions. Understanding these differences is necessary in order to promote effective partnerships and interactions between those from different religious and cultural backgrounds.

The **Advances in Religious and Cultural Studies (ARCS)** book series brings together a collection of scholarly publications on topics pertaining to religious beliefs, culture, population studies, and sociology. Books published within this series are ideal for professionals, theorists, researchers, and students seeking the latest research on collective human behavior in terms of religion, social structure, and cultural identity and practice.

Coverage

- Group Behavior
- Cross-Cultural Interaction
- Impact of Religion on Society
- Social Stratification and Classes
- Gender
- Politics and Religion
- Sociology
- Stereotypes and Racism
- Cultural Identity
- Globalization and Culture

IGI Global is currently accepting manuscripts for publication within this series. To submit a proposal for a volume in this series, please contact our Acquisition Editors at Acquisitions@igi-global.com or visit: http://www.igi-global.com/publish/.

The Advances in Religious and Cultural Studies (ARCS) Book Series (ISSN 2475-675X) is published by IGI Global, 701 E. Chocolate Avenue, Hershey, PA 17033-1240, USA, www.igi-global.com. This series is composed of titles available for purchase individually; each title is edited to be contextually exclusive from any other title within the series. For pricing and ordering information please visit http://www.igi-global.com/book-series/advances-religious-cultural-studies/84269. Postmaster: Send all address changes to above address.

Titles in this Series

For a list of additional titles in this series, please visit: www.igi-global.com/book-series

Fostering Collaborations Between African American Communities and Educational Istitutions
Patrice Wynette Jones (Embry-Riddle Aeronautical University, USA)
Information Science Reference • ©2020 • 260pp • H/C (ISBN: 9781799811817) • US $195.00

Developing Effective Communication Skills in Archaeology
Enrico Proietti (Ministry for Cultural Heritage and Activities and for Tourism, Italy)
Information Science Reference • ©2020 • 347pp • H/C (ISBN: 9781799810599) • US $195.00

Self-Organization of the Human Mind and the Transition From Paleolithic to Behavioral Modernity
Yury N. Kovalyov (Mykhailo Boichuk Kyiv State Academy of Decorative Applied Arts and Design, Ukraine) Nver M. Mkhitaryan (Institute of Renewable Energy, National Academy of Science of Ukraine, Ukraine) and Alexander Yu. Nitsyn (National Technical University "Kharkov Polytechnic Institute", Ukraine)
Information Science Reference • ©2020 • 478pp • H/C (ISBN: 9781799817062) • US $245.00

Understanding the Relationship Between Religion and Entrepreneurship
Khaled Tamzini (IHEC of Sousse, Tunisia) and Anis Ben Salem (ISG of Sousse, Tunisia)
Business Science Reference • ©2020 • 298pp • H/C (ISBN: 9781799818021) • US $235.00

Adapting Human Thinking and Moral Reasoning in Contemporary Society
Hiroshi Yama (Osaka City University, Japan) and Veronique Salvano-Pardieu (University of Tours, France)
Information Science Reference • ©2020 • 330pp • H/C (ISBN: 9781799818113) • US $175.00

Impacts of Globalization on Youth in the Developing World Emerging Research and Opportunities
Obediah Dodo (Bindura University, Zimbabwe) and Vincent Mabvurira (University of Zimbabwe, Zimbabwe)
Information Science Reference • ©2020 • 145pp • H/C (ISBN: 9781799819585) • US $170.00

Recent Social, Environmental, and Cultural Issues in East Asian Societies
Mika Markus Merviö (Kibi International University, Japan)
Information Science Reference • ©2020 • 298pp • H/C (ISBN: 9781799818076) • US $195.00

Projects That Fuel Women's Empowerment and Global Impact Emerging Research and Opportunities
Cassandra Sligh Conway (South Carolina State University, USA)
Information Science Reference • ©2020 • 160pp • H/C (ISBN: 9781799817147) • US $135.00

IGI Global
DISSEMINATOR OF KNOWLEDGE

701 East Chocolate Avenue, Hershey, PA 17033, USA
Tel: 717-533-8845 x100 • Fax: 717-533-8661
E-Mail: cust@igi-global.com • www.igi-global.com

Table of Contents

Detailed Table of Contents

Metric surveys have a key role in managing Cultural Heritage. They are needed for a wide range of activities like documentation, study, restoration, and valorization. The importance of the 3D description of objects is widely accepted considering costs/benefits ratio and the opportunities it offers. In recent years, laser scanning and digital photogrammetry offered new perspectives, widening the options in 3D CH recording. Scientific research tends to see their integration as the best approach to CH description. 3D surveys are offering extra opportunities respect to the traditional production of metric supports as 3D models are the ideal base for true 3D information systems and open the way to immersive virtual reality environments. Digital technologies provide new ways to collaborate, record excavations, and restore artifacts in such a way, they are transforming the way CH practitioners work. This chapter attempts to review the methods for 3D digitization that are today available and discuss the possible use of 3D models beyond the pure extraction of reliable and accurate measurements.

New techniques and methodological procedures, which would allow at a short time and at low cost for the identification of a new archaeological sites, were always in the interest of archaeologists. In addition, fast and accurate 3D modelling and documentation techniques were also always a hot research topic because they can help archeologists to document active excavation sites fast, thus helping them to advance the excavation in a timely manner. In this chapter, aerial and remote sensing archaeology issues will be analyzed, both as measuring tools for the documentation of existing archaeological structures as well as tools of archaeology prospection, which are based on the appearance of the reflection of covered structures in images (i.e., the so-called marks).

The interpretation of photos and the processing of Google Earth imagery that allowed the “random” discovery as a result of a non-systematical research of numerous marks of buried constructions in the wide area of the city of Larisa (Thessaly, Greece) is presented in this chapter. Additional data as aerial photographs over time, satellite images and the digital terrain model of the same area has been used. From the numerous marks, this chapter mainly focuses on three positions where the positive marks (soil marks or/and crop marks), circular or/and linear, reveal on a satisfying level covered construction of great dimensions. The ongoing research activity of the research team along with this research highlights the advantages of using Google Earth imagery in an attempt to “random” mark of unknown covered constructions, or, in the frame of a systematic survey of aerial and remote sensing archaeology, as additional and not exclusive source of information.

Recent trends in archaeological research dictate the incorporation of various analytical methods for dating, chemical/mineralogical characterization, morphological description, etc. of various excavation findings and landscapes to support and corroborate the archaeologists’ observations. Each method, when used individually, provides a different feedback, but once single studies are combined, the information produced can significantly contribute to the solution of the archaeological puzzle. Thus, numerous scientific data and metadata are produced creating large and complex scientific datasets. The use of common terminology and definitions to describe these data along with the establishment of a formal standardized structure any cultural heritage information could be mapped to would assure the credibility and durability of such scientific datasets. The chapter provides an overview of the types and formats of the scientific data/metadata produced in the archaeological research through the detailed presentation of the common practices used in pottery dating and provenance studies.

One of the most challenging tasks in cross reality environment simulations is the generation of realistic and attractive worlds. The continuous evolution of computer game industry has a dramatic effect on such tasks as younger generations have higher expectations and demands in terms of realism. Virtual, Augmented, and mixed reality-based museums allow the efficient dissemination of cultural heritage thesaurus and are considered a popular application domain for cross reality environments due to their broad appeal. One of their primary scopes is to enrich user experience by introducing intuitive means of interaction with artefacts while offering knowledge in a more pleasant way than most of the traditional approaches. This chapter focuses on the development aspects of realistic simulations of cross reality environments for cultural heritage applications. It covers aspects related to modern 3D graphics and game engines, 3D digitization, and modelling. It discusses on the combination of these technologies in order to produce realistic, pleasant, and educative environments.

Digital characters are software entities that look and act like real or imaginary creatures in a computer-generated environment. They are considered an important element of interactive digital heritage applications that can add significant value and increase user motivation and engagement. This chapter presents a review of the use of digital characters for communicating and disseminating cultural heritage. It explores the wide range of applications that make use of digital characters and attempts to identify how the characters are used, what are their main features, and how are they contributing to the overall cultural experience. The chapter includes an overview of current state of the art in digital character design and implementation approaches, a taxonomy about the usage of characters in cultural heritage applications, and a discussion about prospects and pitfalls of digital character technology for heritage dissemination.

Numerous software solutions implementing the structure-from-motion/multi-view stereo (SFM/MVS) 3D reconstruction approach have been made available over the last two decades. Hence, enabling the production of high quality, in terms of geometry and colour information, 3D objects using solely unordered image sequences depicting a static scene or objects from arbitrary viewpoints. Nowadays, SFM/MVS-based 3D reconstruction approaches constitute a popular solution in a variety of applications within many research domains including cultural heritage. However, as with all 3D reconstruction approaches, SfM/MVS has its limitations and applicability challenges. In this chapter, the authors attempt to provide a set of guidelines that are based on the important outcomes of published works that propose solutions to overcome some of the challenges introduced by non-friendly to SfM/MVS scenes or objects.

As an integral part of archaeology, archaeometry, employs standard laboratory techniques and ICT tools to examine and analyze art and archaeological materials. Most students involved with cultural heritage and Archaeology have a background in the arts or humanities and a minimal, if any, training in the principles and techniques of most natural and engineering sciences. Consequently, when choosing to be enrolled in an archaeometry course, an interdisciplinary field which also requires some background in applied sciences, cross reality labs can be the bridge between archaeology and its sub-disciplines, and "hard science." In this chapter, the authors focus on the use of virtual environments in the digital cultural heritage field, as well as on applications of cross reality laboratories in archaeometry. Finally, they present some evidence in favor of the simulations, pointing out that VR, AR, and MR labs could train, safely and efficiently, pre-service archaeometrists in the use of specialized laboratory apparatuses and help them take advantage of the full spectrum of modern laboratory tools.

Over the last few years, an increasing number of cultural sites, including museums, archaeological places, and historic cities, have adopted a wide range of interactive technologies to enhance the visitor (user) experience. This chapter presents a review of interactive systems for cultural heritage, selected from a total of 83 publications in 2012-2019, from the perspective of the methods employed for their empirical evaluation (i.e., the degree to which the system satisfies user goals and expectations). The review reports on several characteristics of interactive systems of CH including purpose, technology, content, and location of the interaction, and then emphasizes methods of empirical evaluation. The chapter provides discussion comparing to the results of the previous report, and outlook on particular challenges of interaction design and evaluation for CH.

Personalized software has been extensively used in museum guides and recommendation systems for tours because it provides added value to the interaction of the user with cultural heritage. However, this added value can only be confirmed through an evaluation experiment. Therefore, this chapter presents the indoor and outdoor personalized tours for exploring cultural heritage. More specifically, the chapter focuses on the methods used for personalization, the technology employed to improve interaction, and the evaluation experiments that have been implemented. The evaluation experiments are further categorized with respect to the method of evaluation and the criteria used. Finally, it provides a discussion on the main conclusions drawn from the researchers conducting evaluation experiments of the system performing indoor and outdoor tours for the exploration of cultural heritage.

Death is a great unifier, not only for one who is in grief but also those who have similar shared values (i.e., tourist demand for visiting death sites). In this sense, visitation to the death sites denotes its importance to people's lives. However, as types of death sites are distinctively different from one to another, death sites as tourist attraction remains a segmented target market. This chapter looks at some viewpoints for making death sites not only for a segmented target market, which leads to discourse of virtual dark tourism (VDT) formation. With sound branding coupled with augmented reality (AR) as tools to support the claims of virtual dark tourism, death sites, which are considered exclusive touristic market offerings, presumably could be consumed by more target markets. Several issues and direction for future research are discussed.

Preface

Cultural heritage is the repository of humanity's identity, a qualitative measure of peoples' progress in time. Cultural heritage is immensely rich in diversity, which reflects the richness of human civilization through the ages. It is, apparently, a deep source of knowledge, which it inherently encodes. In all its forms, tangible or intangible, cultural heritage has been recognized as a precious entity and significant efforts and funds have been allocated to its preservation, interpretation and safeguarding. Several sciences have contributed over the recent decades to this end. This contribution was so intense that the borders among sciences and the arts in this sector started to blur, formulating a domain referenced as 'Heritage Science'. This domain corresponds to a broad field of research and development that emerged to address multiple complex cultural heritage research questions with significant innovations. Such innovations have been focused on multiple facets, including digitization, documentation, analysis, description, interpretation, dissemination, reproduction, education, storytelling, sustainability and management.

Informatics has, arguably, a considerable effect on all domains of science, and has irreversibly transformed the way we experience the world. Apart from the broad term 'Heritage Science', other terms like 'Cultural Informatics', 'Digital Heritage' or 'Digital Humanities' have also been coined to express the bridging of informatics (and other exact sciences) with cultural heritage and the humanities in general, typically being used interchangeably, although with fundamentally different meanings. In addition, each of those terms has a dual, as it can be read from the side of the informatics or the side of the humanities, as either the application of informatics or a new form of human creation. For example, 'Digital Heritage' can either be the 'heritage of the digital creation' or the 'application of digital technologies in cultural heritage'. This book takes the second view and focuses on advancements of digital technologies and scientific applications that serve the study and preservation of cultural heritage.

There is today a vast number of innovative applications in Heritage Science, spanning the whole spectrum of challenges from digital documentation, optical 3D documentation, digital reconstruction and visualization of cultural heritage data, to applications like virtual exhibitions and museums, Virtual Reality, Augmented and Mixed Reality applications, gamification, game-based learning and serious games, narratives and storytelling, Natural Language Processing techniques, knowledge modeling and representation, language and lexical resources, Web/mobile/social networking and tourism applications, scientific tools for comparative study and academic training, digital archives, metadata, international standards and interoperability, big-data, open-data approaches and intellectual property rights, just to name the most prominent. The bibliography on those innovations is steadily growing and the advances are significant.

The success stories in the merging of multiple disciplines into Heritage Science creates an excitement; and the pleasant excitement is growing at the academic society, as a healthy community develops by an increasing number of researchers and students who have shown interest in this merging and started a long cross-disciplinary discussion. Nevertheless, this is not a surprise to those who observe closely the technological achievements coming from the use of Artificial Intelligence, who find it only natural to employ these techniques for the advancement of cultural heritage studies.

This book is a collection of innovations in various topics in Heritage Science over the recent years. It comprises of 14 chapters authored by distinguished researchers who have shared their experience and findings spanning across a wide range of applications. It may serve as a reference for the researchers and practitioners across the related disciplines in the general domain of Heritage Science. The book is naturally divided into four sections, covering topics of (a) optical, physical and chemical documentation and interpretation, (b) special innovations for the cultural heritage experts, (c) cases in dissemination and education and (d) future directions. Each section includes selected chapters that introduce respective aspects and present the current state of the art.

The first chapter titled ‘3D Documentation of Cultural Heritage: Design and Exploitation of 3D Metric Surveys’ discusses the future of 3D documentation of Cultural Heritage. The chapter presents how the evolution of digital technologies, their lowering costs, the diffusion of the 3D culture and skills among researchers and practitioners, makes it easy to foresee a ‘3D future’ in cultural heritage digitization. Furthermore, the chapter explores the wealth of options that stem from the availability of 3D data for management, visualization and dissemination.

The second chapter titled ‘Aerial and Remote Sensing Archaeology’ focuses on the application of aerial and remote sensing imagery for the identification, 3D mapping and documentation of archaeological sites. The chapter presents the latest advances in technology that enabled such applications and highlight the benefits in productivity, accuracy and resolution. As the authors of this chapter emphasize, further developments in satellite imagery are expected to provide more insight on cultural heritage sites and aid in the identification of underground structures sites.

The third chapter is titled ‘Google Earth Revisited: Case Studies at the Plain of Larissa (Thessaly, Greece)’ and explores the use of Google Earth as a useful tool for observing and studying already known archaeological sites; this study may bring benefits to other projects, such as those of the environmental protection or planning. Nevertheless, as the chapter argues, Google Earth cannot be described as a tool for archeology prediction, at least not one on which a research should be exclusively based on. The chapter takes a more practical approach and presents the benefits and arguments through specific case studies.

The fourth chapter is titled ‘Scientific Datasets in Archaeological Research Through Pottery Dating and Provenance Cases’ and focuses on the role of scientific reference datasets in the interpretation of the data in relation to an archaeological research question, as well as in the validation and repeatability of the research. The authors argue that these datasets exhibit large variability among the various research infrastructures that produced them, and an agreement on common definitions, purposes and structures as well as the establishment of standards is a requisite in order to bring together and integrate existing data infrastructures and to facilitate their accessibility and exploitation.

The fifth chapter titled ‘Exploiting Cross Reality Technologies for Cultural Heritage Dissemination’ discusses key techniques, approaches and technologies for developing realistic 3D virtual environments for cultural and educational purposes for all ages. The authors outline core concepts of dynamic processes in gaming environments, such as competitiveness, cooperation and dynamic feedback, along with innovations like smart tour guides, chat-bots and interactive entities. Furthermore, the authors argue that the ability to merge virtual elements within real environment in mixed reality applications, enables intuitive experience and better understanding of both tangible and intangible elements.

The sixth chapter is titled 'The Use of Digital Characters in Interactive Applications for Cultural Heritage' and attempts to present an overview of the technology of digital characters and their usage in cultural heritage applications. The chapter provides a review and some clarifications regarding the terminology in order to alleviate the ambiguity in the use of the relevant terms that still create confusion. After presenting the various modelling stages for creating digital characters and their interrelations the chapter introduces the notion of 'believability' and discusses about prospects and pitfalls of various design and technological approaches of digital characters, and concludes with current trends and open research challenges.

The seventh chapter is titled '3D Reconstruction Challenges Using Structure-From-Motion' and focuses on the challenges of a particularly successful 3D reconstruction method typically called SfM. Nowadays, SfM is commonly used for the digitization and 3D reconstruction of cultural heritage assets. The authors pinpoint the several cases in which the method may result erroneous data or even fail and present how those challenges can be overcome.

The eighth chapter titled 'Cross Reality Technologies in Archaeometry Bridge Humanities With "Hard Science"' explores how virtual labs can be exploited as preparatory tools for education in domains like Archaeometry, in cases in which laboratory training is crucial but laboratory equipment and infrastructures are scarce. The authors present case studies which provide insight on the success of such applications in students' education.

The ninth chapter is titled 'Methods and Practices for Assessing the User Experience of Interactive Systems for Cultural Heritage' and reports on a systematically selected sample of 83 publications on empirical evaluations of digital heritage. The chapter reports on the key features of interactive systems of cultural heritage in various aspects and provides comparative results using a previous relevant review as a reference. The study provides significant insight on the recent developments, as well as on emerging technologies, on the subject.

The tenth chapter titled 'Evaluation Experiments of Personalized Tours for Exploring Cultural Heritage' and focuses on the adaptation and personalization provided by recommendation systems in cultural heritage applications. The chapter explores the various approaches and presents evaluation results that although emphasize the positive effect of personalization in general, they highlight a skepticism that is based on the need for a considerable improvement of personalization to support the extra effort needed to incorporate personalization procedures.

The eleventh chapter is titled 'Virtual Dark Tourism: The Role of Sound Branding and Augmented Reality for Death Sites' and explores a particular type of cultural tourism the 'dark tourism' in death sites. It specifically focuses on the role of augmented reality and sound branding applications in signifying the exclusiveness of a site. The authors highlight the benefits but also identify challenges for future research directions.

The twelfth chapter titled 'Surfing Between Disciplines: Interdisciplinarity of Architectural Digital Heritage' presents how the study of architectural heritage is inherently interdisciplinary, due to the multifaceted nature of historical buildings. The chapter argues in favor of a cross-disciplinary dialog among the scholars using the principles of The London Charter and the example given by the Principles of Seville as useful references points. As digital heritage moves from physical to intangible, the cultural core tends to be forgotten. The chapter supports that digital technologies should be the enablers of important interdisciplinary approaches and computer-based visualization can be a compromise between measurement, modelling, rendering, culture, and interpretation.

The thirteenth chapter titled 'Toward Smart Heritage: Cultural Challenges in Digital Built Heritage' presents the new realm of mixed reality formed by the mixing of the reality with the digital heritage, the smart objects of the Internet of Things, the new forms of experience offered by the technologies of augmented and virtual reality and the ubiquity of computing with mobile devices. The chapter supports that in this new realm, the contrast between "physical reality" and "digital reality" ceases to exist; they become two kinds of real. The chapter also explores other aspects of this realm, like the "transparency" of digital phenomena and its impact on the conceptualization of objectivity, and highlights the cultural challenges in the digital heritage.

The fourteenth chapter is titled 'Ten Challenges for Digital Humanities and the Way Forward: Revisited From the Social Context' and focuses on the identification of challenges that are expected to have a significant impact on Digital Humanities in the following years. The authors support that the future technological developments need to be closely related and connected to existing or foreseen social challenges, the study of which would offer the ideal application area for new technologies. The chapter focusses on ten challenges of increased societal importance or our times and of which the social impact of Digital Humanities can be significant.

Chapter 1
3D Documentation of Cultural Heritage:
Design and Exploitation of 3D Metric Surveys

Eros Agosto
AdHoc 3D Solutions, Italy

Paolo Ardissone
AdHoc 3D Solutions, Italy

Leandro Bornaz
AdHoc 3D Solutions, Italy

Fabio Dago
AdHoc 3D Solutions, Italy

ABSTRACT

Metric surveys have a key role in managing Cultural Heritage. They are needed for a wide range of activities like documentation, study, restoration, and valorization. The importance of the 3D description of objects is widely accepted considering costs/benefits ratio and the opportunities it offers. In recent years, laser scanning and digital photogrammetry offered new perspectives, widening the options in 3D CH recording. Scientific research tends to see their integration as the best approach to CH description. 3D surveys are offering extra opportunities respect to the traditional production of metric supports as 3D models are the ideal base for true 3D information systems and open the way to immersive virtual reality environments. Digital technologies provide new ways to collaborate, record excavations, and restore artifacts in such a way, they are transforming the way CH practitioners work. This chapter attempts to review the methods for 3D digitization that are today available and discuss the possible use of 3D models beyond the pure extraction of reliable and accurate measurements.

DOI: 10.4018/978-1-7998-2871-6.ch001

INTRODUCTION

Cultural Heritage can be defined as artifacts, monuments or group of buildings of "*outstanding universal value from the point of view of history, art or science*" beside sites of "*outstanding universal value from the historical, aesthetic, ethnological or anthropological point of view*" (UNESCO, 1972). These sites have to face continuous atmospheric and anthropic attacks; they are often under threat from natural hazards (earthquakes, floods, fires), adverse environmental conditions, structural instability, increased tourism and development that raise the pressure they have to face, and they are most likely under-funded, and hence, inadequately documented and maintained. Their geometric documentation is of the highest importance as it is a necessary step to describe their as-it-is situation and also in order to build the base of a proper information management system; in the digital recording of Cultural Heritage the three-dimensional (3D) digitization of objects and monuments is a key issue. 3D digitization is now applicable to artifacts ranging from the smallest (e.g. small prehistoric findings) to the largest (e.g. buildings or entire historical sites), aiding researchers by providing them better resolution (sampled surface density) and improved accuracy. The needed acquisition time, and the available post-processing tools, are continuously improving. This spatial information forms not only an accurate record of these rapidly deteriorating sites, which are a legacy of the past and have to be saved for posterity, but also provides a comprehensive base dataset, by which site managers, archaeologists, and conservators can monitor sites and perform necessary restoration work to ensure their physical integrity. 3D models offer both the possibility to extract the needed metric information, and also the base for a wider exploitation for Cultural Heritage Information Systems, multimedia representations and reproductions (base for Cultural Heritage digital content).

Today, the available survey techniques have the potential to truly advance Cultural Heritage documentation, similar to photography at the end of the 19th century. Available digital solutions provide effective ways of exploiting 3D models. This chapter attempts to review them.

3D DIGITIZATION OF CULTURAL HERITAGE

3D digitization of Cultural Heritage has been attracting the attention of many researchers since long time and the literature about it is huge. Just considering the two last big innovations in the production of 3D models, the application of laser scanners to Cultural Heritage and the image matching approach or Structure from Motion (SfM) technique, many papers may be found.

Pieraccini et al. (2001), Pavlidis et al. (2007) or Agosto & Bornaz (2017) try to summarize most of the available methods for 3D digitization that can be applied to the digital recording of Cultural Heritage. Boehler et al. (2002) highlight the potentiality of Laser scanning instruments, that were mainly developed for industrial applications, for Cultural Heritage recording as well: in the vision of the authors this method would complement, and, in certain applications, replace currently existing methods. The advantages of laser scanning approach are evaluated against photogrammetry. Lichti and al. (2002), highlight the high acquisition rate, the relative high accuracy and high spatial density as the three key advantages of laser scanning adoption; besides, the authors, just like Kadobayashi et al. (2004) and Boehler et al. (2004), compare laser scanning and photogrammetry and their combined use to produce accurate and expressive models of Cultural Heritage objects and of the efficiency of the data processing pipeline; as a result, due to the great variety of Cultural Heritage objects, no single method is applicable to recording every subject of Cultural Heritage and hence there is a strong demand for a hybrid method that exploits several technologies. The authors also highlight that it is difficult to define a strict guideline in that sense and that practical experience and the accumulated know-how are essential. However photogrammetry is appreciated for the color information it has and the fact it eases the interpretation of 3D data. Eisenbess et al. (2006) compare Digital Surface Model (DSM) coming from laser scanning and digital photogrammetry, and highlight the comparable precision that can be achieved by using the two methods; the main difference is in the occlusions that the shooting positions may have. The integration of the two approaches is also highlighted by Beraldin (2004) as the most appropriate way to digital recording Cultural Heritage.

The integration between laser scanning and photogrammetry led to new survey products: Bornaz at al. (2002) invented the concept of Solid Image, that thanks to the new surveying methods is easily produced. Solid Image offers an easy access to 3D content by means of a simple 2D interface; while interacting with a common undistorted image, users can access the 3D coordinates of every pixel, and so to easily perform 3D measurements or digitization.

Also orthophotos take advantage of the fact that building a Dense Digital Elevation Model (DDEM) is at hand, so Dequal et al. (2001) invented the so called True Orthophotos, that offer a higher degree of fidelity and accuracy. True Orthohotos overcome the problems in large-scale orthoprojection due to the presence of many discontinuity lines (break-lines) and hidden areas, especially where complex architectural objects have to be represented. However, the trend in the integration of the two techniques, is that the geometric models come from laser scanning, whereas photogrammetry overlays an interpretation layer. The automation of the photogrammetric workflow had an incredible impact in the following years. Operators such as SIFT: Scale Invariant Feature Transform (Lowe, 2004) or SURF: Speed Up Robust Feature (Bay et al., 2006) offer a chance to digital photogrammetry to automatically identify tie points in different images; the following image matching problem is then solved by stereo matching (Hirschmuller, 2011) or by identifying the correspondences in multiple images (multi-view stereo – MVS) (Pierrot-Deseilligny et al., 2006), thus implementing the contemporary integrated Structure from Motion (SfM) technique (integrated in the sense that it includes the original SfM with dense multi-view 3D reconstruction). The SfM approach computes simultaneously both the relative projection geometry and a set of sparse 3D points by extracting corresponding image features from a set of overlapping photographs of a scene (Verhoeven et al, 2012). Thus, digital photogrammetry becomes a serious competitor of laser scanning also in the 3D geometric documentation of Cultural Heritage and many articles compare the precision of the 3D models coming from laser scanner and digital photogrammetry approach (e.g. Koutsoudis et al., 2014).

Digital photogrammetry has the advantage of the low hardware cost compared to laser scanning instruments, thus widening the application areas of digital recording; nowadays, a number of programmes, inexpensive and even open source or free of charge, carry out a near-automatic processing of data forestalling the need to rely on specific machines (e.g. Westoby et al., 2012). Even if best results are obtained with good sensors and lens, also almost inexpensive cameras prove to be usable in some context (e.g. geomorphology). Niederheiser et al. (2016) compared off the shelf digital photogrammetric suites and sensors in describing partially vegetated rock slopes; as expected, best results were related to good input images, so obtained using DSLR cameras. However, DSLR cameras are expensive compared to smartphone and other cheap cameras, which proved anyway to be able to give accurate results in the tests. As there are a number of bridge cameras on the market that fill the niche between the DSLRs and small hand-held digital cameras, offering good quality lenses and large sensors, they may offer a cheaper alternative to the more expensive DSLRs. For what concerns the tested photogrammetric suites, they showed different behaviors in relation to different site conditions, but results seemed mainly comparable.

One of the main limits of the a pure photogrammetric approach is the recording of homogeneous surfaces, where tie-point extraction fails because of the absence of identifying patterns. Koutsoudis et al. (2015) investigate noise function-based pattern (NFP) projection in the data collection phase to face this issue.

3D MODEL CREATION: METRIC DOCUMENTATION TECHNIQUES

The technologies for creating digital models of reality have undergone an impressive evolution. Although developed for industrial applications such as rapid prototyping and entertainment, these technologies are ideal for helping to preserve and restore Cultural Heritage. Today, most suitable techniques to 3D digitizing Cultural Heritage can be divided into active or passive techniques, according to the fact that they are both emitting a signal (laser beam) and recording its echoes, or just acquiring natural radiations. In the first group there's the laser scanning approach, whereas in the second there's the image based approach.

Each technique offers peculiar advantages, but both, that are widely used in production environments, are effective, offer high acquisition rates and an high degree of automation. These techniques seem to offer complementary advantages, as passive techniques takes advantage of low cost and easy to carry instruments, whereas laser scanner measurements are less influenced by the presence of vegetation in the scene or by homogeneous surfaces showing no evident patterns. As suggested by research trends, their integration seem the best approach to Cultural Heritage description.

Metric Documentation Techniques: Laser Scanning

A laser scanner automates the acquisition process, digitally sampling its field of view at a given resolution by point measurements and producing in this way a point cloud model of the surrounding scene. Distance measuring is performed in regular networks without the need for a reflector by means of an emitted laser beam or pattern. The acquisition rate is very high (range between 10000 pts/s to 500000 pts/s) making these kinds of instruments very productive compared to traditional ones and decreasing the fieldwork considerably. Laser scanners can be controlled by computers (using on-board interfaces, or remotely through Wi-Fi or LAN connections) and integrated with GPS measurements.

Laser scanners have a wide range of applications in Cultural Heritage documentation from small objects to large and complex sites. Their applications and capabilities are continuously developing. Real-time data acquiring in a real scale, high accuracy and high speed are among the major capabilities of laser scanners.

In contrast to image-based techniques, the surface form can cause fewer limitations in laser scanning acquisitions. In fact, laser scanners can provide better results in regards to detailed irregular objects. Despite the multitude of advantages, laser scanners, have however limitations too, the main of which are, besides the high cost of instruments, the need for skilled operators, the time-consuming post processing and the documentation of surfaces being reflective or with sharp edges (Rüther et al., 2003). Since water absorbs the rays near IR spectrum, while there is moisture on a surface, the reflection of laser beam cannot perform properly. Accordingly, rainy condition and moist surface affect the quality of the data acquisition and degrade the accuracy of the result.

In Cultural Heritage, laser scanning instruments can be categorized according to the surveying distance and the different kind of use of the emitted light.

Long-Medium Range 3D Scanners (LiDAR)

Long-Medium Range 3D Scanners are adopted in recording the general shape of large objects and surfaces with the aim of getting accurate metric information. These instruments are in fact robotic total stations that acquire data from the target at a high speed. The operating principle of these instruments is based on the two elements of distance and angle. They are useful for the topographic description of sites and buildings but don't offer a suitable accuracy for recording details of surfaces, decorations, inscriptions and relief scenes.

Long-medium range scanners use time-of-flight or laser-pulse based systems, in which a laser light is bounced off the target at a distance. A laser range finder calculates the distance to a surface by timing the round trip of a pulse of light using the known value for the speed of light. In Cultural Heritage documentation, long-medium range scanners are normally used in combination with close-range 3D scanners to generate models with both global metric accuracy and high resolution surface detail.

When a laser pulse is transmitted to the target, it might hit various obstacles, thus modern systems have the capability of recording at least two signals, first pulse and second pulse, or the full waveform. This characteristic differentiates active sensors from normal photogrammetry systems since obstacles (e.g. vegetation) can be better identified end eventually filtered.

Long-medium range 3D scanners have usually a minimum acquiring distance of about 1 meter.

When a long-medium range 3D scanner is used in Cultural Heritage the divergence of the laser ray have to be considered. The divergence value is an angular information that relates to the impact area of the laser beam on the object which value obviously depends on the laser-object distance. The measured distance can then be considered as the mean distance (among a number of measurements) between the laser and the impact area on the object. This must be taken into account in Cultural Heritage digitization in order to obtain the desired accuracy, according to the needed digitization scale. In addition, the material of the object and the incidence of the laser ray on the object have to be considered too. Depending on these aspects the acquisition noise might increase and change. To remove all the acquisition noise, a proper survey project have to be developed and specific algorithms and methods have to be adopted during the post-processing phase.

Close Range 3D Scanners

Close Range 3D Scanners (more than 8 cm and less than 1 m working distance) are used to record the shape and surface of objects in great detail. Close recording distance is usually associated with higher resolution. They are useful for scanning multi-featured surfaces, such as reliefs, decorations, column headers, muqarnases or pencil works, within the interior space of architectural works of art, recording shape and surface of sculptures and complex forms, along with the decay on surfaces.

The output has usually such a resolution and accuracy that can be used either for study using screen-based applications and/or for 3D printing and re-materialization for a range of purposes, including tactile objects for the blind and partially sighted, facsimile production and exhibition display.

These instruments are not suitable to record large structures for screen viewing. Close range scanning is usually slower than long-medium range scanning or photogrammetry.

Usually, these kinds of instruments are triangulation-based 3D laser scanners. They use a laser light and one or two cameras to record a subject. Through trigonometry, the distance of the object to the scanner can be calculated thus creating a precise map of the surface. Structured light scanners also use triangulation, but use projected patterns of light instead of a laser. Cameras record the projected patterns and calculate the distance of every point in the field of view. Close-range 3D scanning in its many variations is essential for recording 'at risk' heritage. To meaningfully document the past it is essential to be able to document not just the general shape but also the subtle details of the surface of the object.

Metric Documentation Techniques: Photogrammetry

Photogrammetry, the science of making measurements from photographs, is under a new popular age; it is spreading thanks to the low hardware cost and the software innovations that lead to an highly automated data processing workflow. Photogrammetry is suitable for the quick recording of vulnerable and inaccessible sites, besides the ideal way to obtain 3D information in situations where it is not possible to use 3D scanners (inaccessible locations, conflict zones), or when high-speed recording is required (scanning people, living organisms, liquids in movement). It has also good performance for the recording of translucent surfaces like alabaster and marble. Due to the composite nature of the image capture, color and form can be extracted from the data. The main limits for its application are represented by featureless, reflective and dark surfaces.

An ideal application field for this technique is the 3D documentation of archaeological excavations, because of its minimal hardware requirements and ease of use in all environments.

A related issue to this approach is the quality of the reconstruction, which may vary according to factors related to the object (texture, scale of features, and optical characteristics) or the environment (illumination, photo sharpness, and completeness of photographic coverage).

The great automation of the photogrammetric pipeline and the availability of software solution that offer an easy output production have intrinsic risks, as users need to have the needed experience and competence to critically evaluate the obtained results. In the perspective of the good quality of the obtained object description, a proper shooting design, that is tailored on the survey needs and features of the object, is crucial.

However those technologies may lead to an effective daily documentation of the excavation status, and in such a way 3D models replace the usual 2D images.

In photogrammetry, as the shooting distance roughly defines the survey scale, it becomes a classification criteria.

Close Range Photogrammetry

The highest resolution is given with the shortening of the shooting distance and that is the application field of close range photogrammetry. Usually cameras here are tripod-mounted. The shooting schema depends on the surveyed object, with the aim of acquiring all the images necessary for its 3D reconstruction. The shooting design has to set an adequate overlap between the images (e.g. 80%) in order to ensure adequate automatic detection of homologous points for the image orientation phase. In close range applications, usually a convergent shooting configuration is adopted, as it ensures to image possible hidden details. When details are seen in at least two images, then they can be 3D modeled. As in photogrammetry in general, the base-to-depth (B/D) ratio defines the precision of the results: small baselines offer more success chances for automatic photogrammetric procedures but decrease the accuracy of the final reconstruction. The dimensions, shape and morphology of the studied scene and the employed focal length (e.g. fish-eye lenses are very suggested for interiors), besides the desired survey scale, define the number of the necessary images. Close range photogrammetry provides 3D models of small objects, indoor spaces and architectural elements.

UAV Photogrammetry

Recent technological development and the consequent lowering of the costs have spread the use of Unmanned Autonomous Vehicles (UAV) also for survey and documentation purposes. Due again to the low hardware cost and limited weight, digital camera suits the payload capabilities of low cost UAVs. UAV operates without an on-board pilot and are an appropriate alternative to the classical manned aerial photogrammetry (Colomina et al., 2008). UAVs are categorized according to their weight, size, endurance or flying attitude. Generally speaking the system is composed of a light low-cost aerial vehicle, a digital camera and a Global Navigation Satellite System / Inertial Navigation System (GNSS/INS) for identifying the position and navigating of the system. Low-altitude flights proved their efficacy in the documentation and 3D modelling of Cultural Heritage and archaeological sites (e.g. Azzola et al., 2019). Panoramic images, Digital Surface Model (DSM), orthophotos, and three-dimensional models are obtained by pictures taken from UAV flights. The accuracy of the results depends on the features of the object, the shooting schema and distance. This non-intrusive system offers at least a couple of advantages; firstly, the fast image acquisition, and the consequent short interruption times, make it suitable for archaeological field-work (Eisenbeiß, 2009); secondly, UAVs provide the opportunity to survey inaccessible and/or dangerous areas, which cannot be accessed directly using other systems or piloted aerial systems (Everaerts, 2008). In contrast, the main problems UAVs face are the impact of wind, the vibration due to their low weight and the limited maximum load they can carry; obviously the description of vegetated sites and homogeneous surfaces remains problematic, due to the difficult identification of tie points within the photogrammetric pipeline and the parts of objects that are hidden and can't be seen in any image.

3D MODEL USE

Today 3D colored models are a complete survey product; it includes the whole geometric and radiometric data of objects, and can be exploited in a variety of ways. 3D models freeze in 3D a Cultural Heritage object at a timestamp, offering the chance to comfortably obtain the desired view or measure in the office. The phase of the identification of the significant points to be measured that was usually done by surveyors on the field, is here moved to the office work phase. Fieldwork is now quicker than in the past, even if it has however to be properly designed according to the desired scope and scale; a greater importance has now the office work phase, before and after the field activity, where most of the intelligence of the survey is due.

The importance of 3D models is widely accepted for the extraction of metric information, but they offer more exploitation opportunities.

Figure 1. Multi resolution 3D model from laser scanning, UAV and close range photogrammetry (AdHoc 3D, 2019)
Source: AdHoc 3D, 2019

They can be lead to produce traditional 2D plants and sections representations but they can also be used as inputs in Geographic Information Systems (GIS), Building Information Modeling (BIM) or Virtual Reality application (VR) and 3D printing systems to create physical replicas. The importance of 3D models is also already accepted for studying artworks, as investigations are carried out directly on digital replicas and may lead to new knowledge and insights. In the restoration perspective, having a 3D model created beforehand can be a valuable resource in order to make an accurate and successful intervention. For this reasons there are a number of organizations that are carrying out a process to create 3D models of valuable sites around the world. UNESCO created a list of "World Heritage Sites in Danger" in order to prioritize their conservation, whereas initiatives like Open Heritage aims at digitizing iconic, at risk or damaged monuments and to create the biggest database of 3D digital models in the world. Creating 3D models of cultural materials and heritage sites is a reliable and accurate mean to conserve these assets for the future (Pieraccini et al., 2001).

Beyond restoration and conservation, it is necessary to think about monitoring, as degradation is a progressive process. 3D models can help to detect changes in morphology and disposition of objects and structures to foresee problems and act on time.

3D models enable several types of analysis: comparative analysis of morphology, changes on structure, measuring distribution, architecture, textured, disposition. Non-invasive procedures to analyze, measure, archive and recreate artwork are particularly useful when working with fragile artworks, avoiding any physical contact (Guidi et al., 2004).

Besides, most 3D model-based applications in Cultural Heritage are related to visualization using various platforms and media: museum kiosks, tablet or desktop-based multimedia presentations or videos. New visualization technologies are of the highest importance in disseminating Cultural Heritage knowledge.

However, despite visualization's potential, the production of digital images or media is just a partial goal (Scopigno et al., 2011). The main challenge for a full exploitation of 3D models in Cultural Heritage lies in the creation of new 3D documentation and management systems or tools that exploit 3D models to assist Cultural Heritage practitioners and researchers, helping for example to assess conservation status or to plan and document restoration activities.

3D models offer the chance to watch Cultural Heritage from unusual or physically inaccessible points of view. Visualization is the first opportunity digital 3D models offer to Cultural Heritage, as they offer the possibility to produce images or videos in office, besides virtually exploring objects and sites. Visualization of 3D models can be offered in a static way, by images or predefined videos, or in a dynamic way, by environments in which it is possible to navigate or interact with the 3D model or having an immersive Virtual Reality experience, on desktop PC, tablet, museum kiosk or VR devices.

3D models make it possible to have access to the 3D coordinates of each point they are made of, besides 3D linear measurements and angle, area or volume computations. They also offer the chance to draw 3D vector elements to be used in CAD or BIM environments. 3D models allow also to derive classical 2D representations: plans, sections as vector elements (e.g. CAD drawings) or image views (metric: orthophotos as in Figure 2; distorted: Solid Image).

Digital 3D models let researchers study artworks at a higher zooming level than in real life, since they have virtual access to objects located far away, without the limitations of museum operating hours or access rights, exploiting the desired virtual point of view. Visual analysis that does not compromise the accuracy and quality of models are required for using digital models as replacements for printed material.

GIS and BIM Use

As GIS technology is a common working tool for all kind of experts involved in Cultural Heritage activities and as most of central and local authorities responsible for Cultural Heritage base their integrated information systems on GIS (Petrescu, 2007; Moscatelli et al., 2013), it is clear that 2D products coming from 3D digital recording can feed this managing tools. GIS can either mean desktop or web use (Agosto et al., 2007) or be closed/open source based (Agosto et al., 2011, Agosto, 2013). As 3D models are day by day commonly available and they have a richer informative content compared to traditional 2D geometric representations (map, sections), they are the ideal basis of real 3D GIS (Campanaro et al., 2016) and eventually of BIM thanks to the visualization and analysis of structures in the context of the natural and built environment they offer. The integration of BIM and GIS enables deeper insight for better decision making, communication, and understanding. By using BIM and GIS together with time information, it is possible to better understand the impacts of decisions before, during and after they are realized.

Figure 2. True orthophoto of the façade of a castle (AdHoc 3D, 2019)
Source: AdHoc 3D, 2019

3D Spatial Management Systems: Archeological Documentation and Restoration Management

Archaeology has been a pioneering field in the adoption of digital technologies for 3D documentation, as excavations require to rapidly document each stage of the destructive digging process, including its intermediate results and findings.

All archaeological excavations need to be graphically and photographically documented. A planimetric process, using an architectonical approach, is important in horizontal stratigraphy. Vertical stratigraphy and its documentation provide means to understand the sequence of occupations (Harris, 1989).

Advances in computing, the introduction of design programs and the implementation of photogrammetry have obviously greatly facilitated all archaeological processes, especially data collection and fieldwork, but the rapid rate of progress requires professionals to be constantly trained to be able to take advantage of the new possibilities given by technological improvements.

Archaeologists adopted database management technologies and then, later on, turned to Geographic Information Systems. Those systems are based on 2D or 2.5D spaces, which are an immediate derivation of the usual map-based representation.

As 3D documentation is becoming more easily available, the challenge is to turn them into 3D documentation systems; at present, very few projects target 3D documentation of the excavation and its findings. Ardissone et al. (2013) use 3D models as the basis for 3D documentation systems of archaeological digs or the management of restoration works. For what concerns archaeological digs, all the information (measurements, plotting, areas of interests, etc.) are organized according to their 3D position. The 3D database can be queried using attributes, geometric features or spatial position. Single context recording sheets can be filled and organized in a database, put in the correct location within the 3D model of the site, define their mutual relations and divide the different archaeological phases. The construction of the stratigraphic chart (Harris matrix) that represents archaeological relationships, in a 3D environment as well (matrix 3D) is then possible as shown in Figure 3.

Conservators and restorers have a tool to create relationships between the different approaches and descriptions of the same parts of the monument, i.e. between stratigraphic units or historical phases and architectural components and/or decay pathologies. Restorers are assisted to correctly compute surfaces and volumes. In this way, decay extension and intensity can be measured with high precision and with a high level of detail, for a correct time and costs estimation of each conservation step.

3D modeling opens interesting perspectives for researchers in using available historical material (e.g. photographs, drawings) to reassemble damaged or dismantled artifacts or reconstruct artworks that no longer exist. As mentioned, visual representations are not the final goal but a way to experiment and assess different reconstruction hypotheses.

3D Virtual Reality

Virtual Reality (VR) is an interactive computer-generated experience taking place within a simulated environment. It incorporates visual feedback to create an immersive environment that can be similar to the real world by taking advantage of input realistic 3D models as shown in Figure 4.

Current VR technology most commonly makes use of virtual reality headsets.

As 3D models can be exploited for in office analyses, VR offers the most immersive form of fruition; users can interact with the 3D model, navigating it by inside, but also getting the desired measures. VR can go beyond a pure visualization experience, where it is just possible to navigate a site, but becomes an effective working environment where it is possible to interact with the surrounding objects and their related information. There are available solutions where users can perform archaeological analyses by taking advantage of VR technology being immerse in a 3D realistic scenario and being able to insert, edit and manage pre defined templates of Units of Stratigraphy (US), Masonry Stratigraphic Unit (USM), and Units of Tomb (UT).

Similar solutions are available as real working tools in decay-management environments; users can interact in team and together virtually navigate a site and access the available information about the elements around them.

CONCLUSION

3D documentation of Cultural Heritage today is a wide spreading approach and it is easy to foresee it will be the tomorrow standard. The evolution of digital technologies, their lowering costs, the diffusion of the 3D culture and skills among researchers and practitioners, makes easy to argue that 3D models will play

Figure 3. 3D management system of an archeological dig – 3D matrix and 3D model (AdHoc 3D, 2019)
Source: AdHoc 3D, 2019

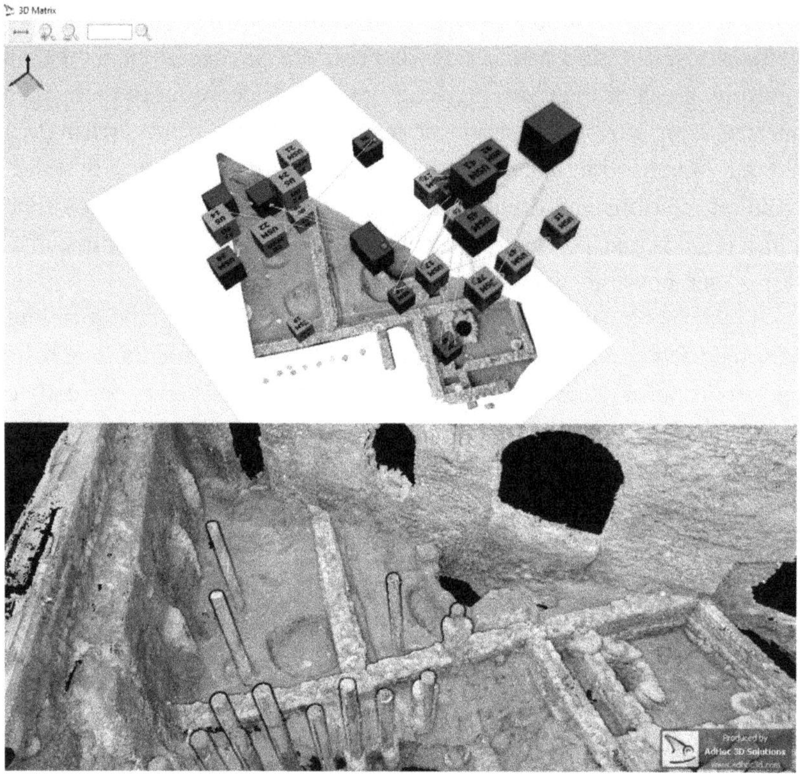

Figure 4. Use of a multi-resolution (medium and close range 3D scanning, close range photogrammetry) 3D model in a VR environment (AdHoc 3D, 2019)
Source: AdHoc 3D, 2019

a more and more important role in documenting Cultural Heritage, and will replace 2D photographic recording. In this paper we tried to summarize the main approaches for three-dimensional digitization available today, which can be applied to digital recording of Cultural Heritage, and to briefly present the main ways for their exploitation.

The use of 3D models goes beyond the pure extraction of metric supports for all the analyses and planning needs of Cultural Heritage sites and objects, but also becomes the base of pure 3D managing tools. In that sense proper 3D information managing systems and software solutions will be of the highest importance. Moreover, 3D models can both be exploited for visualization purposes and to enable immersive VR experience. VR then, can act both as a valorization way but also as a real working environment.

REFERENCES

Agosto, E. (2013). Vector-raster server-side analysis: a PostGIS benchmark. *Applied Geomatics, 5*(2), 177-184. DOI: doi:10.100712518-013-0104-x0

Agosto, E., Ardissone, P., & Rinaudo, F. (2007). GIS And Web-GIS, Cultural and Open Source Platforms: General Rules for Cultural Heritage Documentation. *ISPRS Archives, 36*(5), 625-630.

Agosto, E., & Bornaz, L. (2017). 3D Models in Cultural Heritage: Approaches for Their Creation and Use. *International Journal of Computational Methods in Heritage Science, 1*(1), 1–9. doi:10.4018/IJCMHS.2017010101

Agosto, E., Dalmasso, S., Pasquali, P., & Terzo, O. (2011). Ithaca worldwide flood alert system: the web framework. *Applied Geomatics, 3*(2). DOI: doi:10.100712518-010-0041-x

Ardissone, P., & Bornaz, L. (2013). A 3D information system for the documentation of archaeological excavations. In *Procedings of CIPA 2013.* Conference Strasbourg. doi:10.5194/isprsarchives-XL-5-W2-55-2013

Azzola, P., Cardaci, A., Mirabella Roberti, G., & Nannei, V. M. (2019). UAV photogrammetry for Cultural Heritage preservation modeling and mapping venetian walls of Bergamo. *The International Archives of the Photogrammetry, Remote Sensing and Spatial Information Sciences, 42*(W9), 45–50. doi:10.5194/isprs-archives-XLII-2-W9-45-2019

Bay, H., Tuytelaars, T., & Van Gool, L. (2006). Surf: Speeded up robust features. In Computer vision–ECCV 2006. Springer.

Beraldin, J.-A. (2004). Integration of Laser Scanning and Close-Range Photogrammetry - The Last Decade and Beyond. In *XXth International Society for Photogrammetry and Remote Sensing (ISPRS) Congress. Commission VII* (pp. 972-983). Istanbul, Turkey: Academic Press.

Boehler, W., Heinz, G., & Marbs, A. (2002). The potential of non-contact close range laser scanners for Cultural Heritage recording. In Surveying and documentation of Historic buildings-monuments sites: traditional and modern methods, Postdam, Germany

Boehler, W., & Marbs, A. (2002). 3D scanning instruments. *Proceedings of the CIPA WG 6 International Workshop on Scanning For Cultural Heritage Recording.*

Boehler, W., & Marbs, A. (2004). 3D Scanning and Photogrammetry for Heritage Recording: a Comparison. *Proc. of 12thInt. Conf. on Geoinformatics.*

Bornaz, L., & Dequal, S. (2003). A new concept: the solid image. *CIPA 2003 XIXth International Symposium.*

Campanaro, D., Landeschi, G., Dell'Unto, N., & Leander Touti, A. (2016). 3D GIS for cultural heritage restoration: A 'white box' workflow. *Journal of Cultural Heritage, 18*, 321–332. doi:10.1016/j.culher.2015.09.006

Colomina, I., Blázquez, M., Molina, P., Parés, M.E., & Wis, M. (2008). Towards a new paradigm for high-resolution low-cost photogrammetry and remote sensing. *IAPRS&SIS, 37*(B1), 1201-1206.

Dequal, S., & Lingua, A. (2001). True orthophoto for architectural surveys. *XVIII International Symposium of CIPA*, 269-276.

Eisenbeiß, H. (2009). *UAV photogrammetry* (Diss.). ETH No. 18515, Institute of Geodesy and Photogrammetry, ETH Zurich, Switzerland.

Eisenbess, H., & Zhang, L. (2006). Comparison of DSMS generated from mini UAV imagery and terrestrial laser scanner in a Cultural Heritage application. *ISPRS Commission V Symposium 'Image Engineering and Vision Metrology'.*

Everaerts, J. (2008). The Use of Unmanned Aerial Vehicles (UAVS) for Remote Sensing and Mapping. *IAPRS&SIS, 37*(B1), 1187-1192.

Guidi, G., Beraldin, J., & Atzeni, C. (2004). High-Accuracy 3-D Modeling of Cultural Heritage: The Digitizing of Donatello's "Maddalena". *IEEE Transactions on Image Processing, 13*(3), 370–380. doi:10.1109/TIP.2003.822592 PMID:15376928

Harris, E. (1997). *Principles of Archaeological Stratigraphy. Third print.* London: Academic Press.

Hirschmuller, H. (2011). Semi Global Matching – Motivation, Developments and Applications. Photogrammetric Week, 173-184.

Kadobayashi, R., Kochi, N., Otani, H., & Furukawa, R. (2004). Comparison and evaluation of laser scanning and photogrammetry and their combined use for digital recording of Cultural Heritage. Int. Arch. of PRS&SIS, 35(5).

Koutsoudis, A., Ioannakis, G., Arnaoutoglou, F., & Chamzas, C. (2015). Using noise function-based patterns to enhance photogrammetric 3D reconstruction performance of featureless surfaces. *Journal of Cultural Heritage, 16*(5), 664–670. doi:10.1016/j.culher.2015.01.008

Koutsoudis, A., Vidmar, B., Ioannakis, G., Arnaoutoglou, F., Pavlidis, G., & Chamzas, C. (2014). Multi-image 3D reconstruction data evaluation. *Journal of Cultural Heritage, 15*(1), 73–79. doi:10.1016/j.culher.2012.12.003

Lichti, D. D., Gordon, S. J., Stewart, M. P., Franke, J., & Tsakiri, M. (2002). Comparison of digital photogrammetry and laser scanning. In *Proc* (pp. 39–44). International Society for Photogrammetry and Remote Sensing.

Lowe, D. G. (2004). Distinctive Image Features from Scale-Invariant Keypoints. *International Journal of Computer Vision*, *60*(2), 91–110. doi:10.1023/B:VISI.0000029664.99615.94

Moscatelli, M., & Vallone, R. (2013). GIS as Tool for Cultural Heritage Management. Susteinable Tourism as driving force for cultural heritage sites development

Pavlidis, G., Koutsoudis, A., Arnaoutoglou, F., Tsioukas, V., & Chamzas, C. (2007). Methods for 3D digitization of cultural heritage. *Journal of Cultural Heritage*, *8*(1), 93–98. doi:10.1016/j.culher.2006.10.007

Petrescu, F. (2007). *The use of GIS technology in Cultural Heritage*. In *XXI International CIPA Symposium*, Athens, Greece.

Pieraccini, M., Guidi, G., & Atzeni, C. (2001). 3D digitizing of cultural heritage. *Journal of Cultural Heritage*, *2*(1), 63–70. doi:10.1016/S1296-2074(01)01108-6

Pierrot-Deseilligny, M., & Paparoditis, N. (2006). A multiresolution and optimization-based image matching approach: An application to surface reconstruction from SPOT5-HRS stereo imagery. *The International Archives of the Photogrammetry, Remote Sensing and Spatial Information Sciences*, *36*(1), w41.

Rüther, H., Mtalo, G., & Mngumi, E. (2003). 3D modelling of heritage sites in Africa. A case study in the world heritage site of Kilwa Kisiwani, Tanzania. *Proceedings CIPA XIXth International Symposium*, 175–180.

Scopigno, R., Callieri, M., Cignoni, P., Corsini, M., Dellepiane, M., Ponchio, F., & Ranzuglia, G. (2011). 3D models for Cultural Heritage: beyond plain visualization. IEEE Computer, 44(7), 48-55. DOI: doi:10.1109/MC.2011.196

UNESCO. (1972). *Recommendation concerning the Protection at National Level, of the Cultural and Natural Heritage*. Retrieved October 1, 2016, from http://whc.unesco.org/en/conventiontext/

Verhoeven, G., Taelman, D., & Vermeulen, F. (2012). Computer vision based orthophoto mapping of complex archaeological sites: The ancient quarry of Pitaranha (Portugal-Spain). *Archaeometry*, *54*(6), 1114–1129. doi:10.1111/j.1475-4754.2012.00667.x

Westoby, M. J., Brasington, J., Classer, N. F., Hambrey, M. J., & Reynolds, J. M. (2012). Structure-from-Motion photogrammetry: A low-cost, effective tool for geoscience applications. *Geomorphology*, *179*, 300–314. doi:10.1016/j.geomorph.2012.08.021

Chapter 2
Aerial and Remote Sensing Archaeology

Dimitris Kaimaris
Aristotle University of Thessaloniki, Greece

Charalampos Georgiadis
Aristotle University of Thessaloniki, Greece

Petros Patias
Aristotle University of Thessaloniki, Greece

Vasilis Tsioukas
Aristotle University of Thessaloniki, Greece

ABSTRACT

New techniques and methodological procedures, which would allow at a short time and at low cost for the identification of a new archaeological sites, were always in the interest of archaeologists. In addition, fast and accurate 3D modelling and documentation techniques were also always a hot research topic because they can help archeologists to document active excavation sites fast, thus helping them to advance the excavation in a timely manner. In this chapter, aerial and remote sensing archaeology issues will be analyzed, both as measuring tools for the documentation of existing archaeological structures as well as tools of archaeology prospection, which are based on the appearance of the reflection of covered structures in images (i.e., the so-called marks).

INTRODUCTION

Aerial and remote sensing imagery is being used for the documentation and 3d modelling of archaeological sites all over the world for the past decades. Furthermore, scientists are also using aerial and remote sensing imagery for the identification of potential buried archeological sites. The objective of this chapter is to familiarize the reader with the data, techniques and methodologies used for the 3d modelling, documentation and identification of archaeological sites using aerial and remote sensing imagery.

DOI: 10.4018/978-1-7998-2871-6.ch002

This objective is achieved by presenting an overview of the existing methodologies and by providing application examples that demonstrate the effectiveness of using aerial and remote sensing imagery in archaelogy applications.

BACKGROUND

The first aerial photographs of known archaeological sites were made in the early 20th century by a balloon, with the photographs of the Roman Market excavations in Rome in 1899 by the archaeologist Giacomo Boni, and of the Stonehenge in southern England by Captain Sharpe (Guerra & Pilot, 2000; Driver, 2004; Bewley, 2003). Aerial photographs with a camera tied on the belly of a dove (Renfrew, 1996) took place in 1913 during excavations in Sudan by Sir Henry Wellcome.

The First World War marked the beginning of aerial archaeology, using the aircraft as a platform for air photographing of archaeological remains at Mount Sinai by German aviators.

During the 1920s the English archaeologist O.G.S. Crawford, founder of Aerial Archaeology, accidentally observed the formations of covered Celtic constructions in black and white aerial photographs of the Windmill Hill area (England). He was the first to suggest that the covered structures can be observed on aerial photographs, when the conditions permit it. In 1928, he conducted the first, extensive at that time, systematic aerial photography in the Wessex region, emphasizing on the ability of air identification and mapping of covered archaeological remains (Doneus, 1996; Bewley, 2003).

A covered monument can be a ''compact structure'', e.g. the foundation of a building, or an 'open structure', for example an ancient trench. The interaction of covered monuments with the soil, or vegetation results in the appearance of traces. The types of traces and their intensity depend on the size, depth, and type of the covered monument, the air temperature, the soil, the amount of soil moisture, the type of soil coverage, the type of vegetation, the period and intensity of rainfall, etc. Therefore, different soil moisture and temperature, and, also, qualitative (height, density, color) and temperature difference in the vegetation are caused between the material covering the monument and the material on either side. These differences are recorded on aerial photographs, essentially revealing traces of covered structures (Figure 1).

In 1925, Antoine Poidebard, while presenting the identification of the ancient port in Lebanon, claimed that monuments at shallow depth beneath the sea can be detected in aerial photographs (Renfrew, 1996). In 1921-1922, Wells and McKinley mapped with the help of aerial photographs the monumental mounds of Cahokia near St. Louis (Illinois, USA). Reevers followed with the capture of vertical stereoscopic images in the same area. In 1930 new archaeological sites of the Mayas were identified from aerial photographs taken in Mexico by the Lindberghs (American Society for Photogrammetry and Remote Sensing, 1997).

After the Second World War systematic aerial archaeological researches were conducted both in Europe (mainly Italy, France, Austria, United Kingdom, Netherlands, Germany, Denmark, Sweden) and America (USA, Mexico, Canada) (American Society for Photogrammetry and Remote Sensing, 1997; Alvisi, 1963; American Society of Photogrammetry, 1983; Chevallier, 1963; Jalmain, 1963; Agache, 1963; Scollar, 1963; Brongers, 1963; Alfieri, 1963; Dassie, 1978). Consequently, the numerous detections of monuments, which were held in parallel with the evolution of imaging systems, led to the global acceptance of aerial archaeology in the early 1980s, as a basic archaeology prospection tool. The prolonged dry summers of the 1990s in England, allowed for the emergence of a large number of covered structures in Cherwell Valley Trail (England), North Oxford (Bewley, 2003; Featherstone, 1999).

Figure 1. Anatomy of traces (Kaimaris, 2006) Source: Kaimaris, 2006)

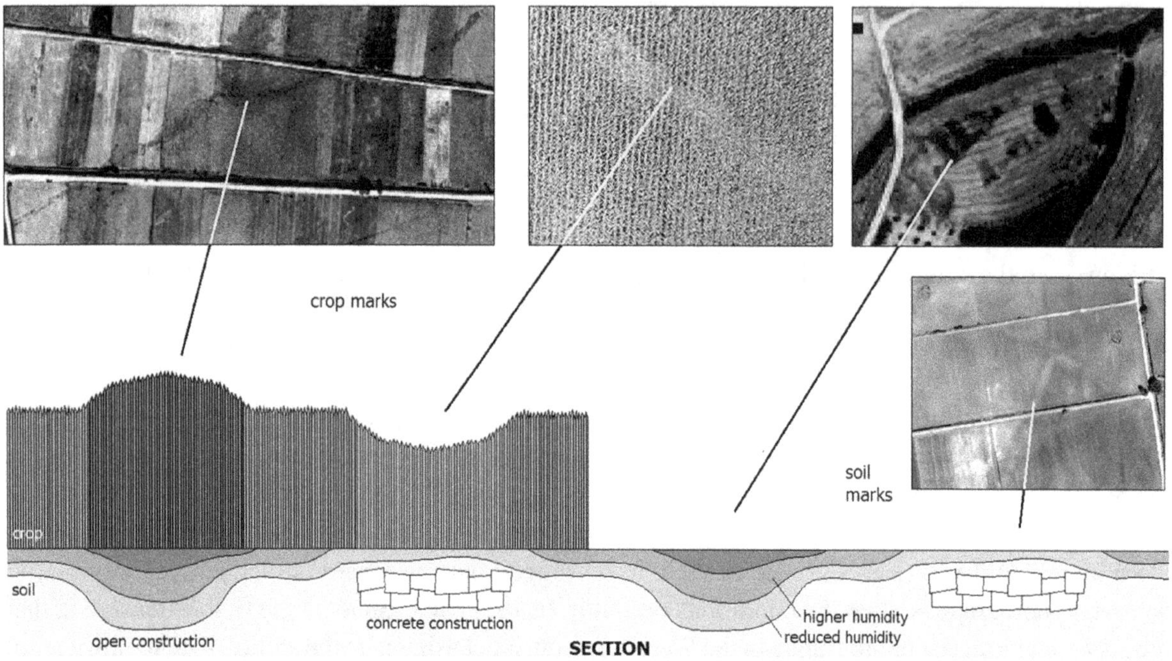

Today, Aerial Archaeology is focused on the research of new remote sensing sensors. The airborne Lidar sensor has made its appearance in archaeological applications, which through the "measurement" of small variations of the terrain of the earth's surface is able to reveal archaeological sites that are invisible to the naked eye (Bewley, 2003; Barnes, 2003; Kucukkaya, 2004). Hyperspectral sensors and thermal sensors are also used. Besides these, new platforms with sensors allow for easy, quick, and inexpensive collection of images of a site. Up to date several small platforms using motors (electric or thermal) for their movement have been utilized, such as the remote-controlled airplanes, helicopters, drones etc. (Abbeel, Coates & Ng, 2010; Miřijovský, Martínek & Brus, 2011; Kyoungah & Impyeong, 2011; Remondino, Barazzetti, Nex, Scaioni & Sarazzi., 2011). In many cases, they carry automatic navigation and programming systems. Besides those, there are platforms which do not use engines, such as the balloons.

Another source of information is satellite imagery. The use of satellite images and photos can be tracked back to 1965 when the first photographs of Earth were acquired by the astronauts of the Gemini 4 mission (Giardino, 2008). Archeologists started to use satellite images acquired from the Apollo 11 mission using multi spectral photos acquired as part of the S065 experiment (Giardino, 2008). Later on the archaeologists started to exploit every available satellite data for the identification of new or buried sites but also for their mapping. In the last 20 years with the introduction of very high resolution commercial satellite imagery a new tool is available for creating maps of high resolution (0.5 m) and also detecting hidden artefacts by using the multispectral information provided by the new satellites. Furthermore U.S.A. and Russia declassified some of their Intelligence satellite photographs (DISP) thus providing an additional tool for the documentation and identification of cultural heritage sites.

In the late 20th century, the appearance of image-capturing satellite systems of high spatial resolution has led in a new archaeological prediction technique (archaeology prospection), the Remote Sensing Archaeology.

High costs, low spatial resolution and lack of user-friendly software for satellite image processing were the main reasons of absence of studies of archaeological interest during the first years of remote sensing data (1960s).

During the early 1980s, the reduction of satellite images' cost, the improvement of their spatial resolution, the appearance of user-friendly software for their processing, combined with the increase in the supply of satellite imagery (panchromatic, multispectral and radar) have encouraged many researchers to use them either for the documentation of existing archaeological sites or for the detection of new covered archaeological remains. Using LANDSAT satellite images in 1983 an unknown city of Maya (600-900 AD) with twin pyramids was revealed and the location of the great ancient city Oxpemul, which was lost in the jungle after its discovery during the decade of 1930, was redefined (Renfrew, 1996). In 1986 a network of channels beneath the Arabian Desert in northwest Sudan (Hurtak, 1986) was revealed using LANDSAT and SIR-A images. Moreover, the unknown, until 1994, ancient city of Angkor of the 9th century BC was discovered in Cambodia, with the help of satellite images of SIR-C / X-SAR system (Fowler & Darling, 1998).

The substantial spatial and spectral improvement of satellite images from the late 1990s until today has helped archaeologists towards the interpretation of archaeological structures (Chen, Lasaponara & Masini, 2015; Tapete & Cigna, 2016; Savage, Levy & Jones, 2012). In remote sensing archaeology, besides the simple interpretation of the channels (PAN, R, G, B, NIR, etc.) in multi-spectral or hyperspectral images (700-800nm), indicators are used (image transformation), such as NDVI vegetation index and principal components analysis, for the exportation of new channels, suitable for interpretation (Kaimaris, 2006) and observation of traces. In particular, these processes visually improve what is already visible remotely. What is really important (as already mentioned in the case of aerial archaeology), is the determination of the optimal trace detection period in each study area.

MAIN FOCUS OF THE CHAPTER

The main focus of this chapter is to present case studies and examples that demonstrate the use of aerial and remote sensing imagery in the detection of and modelling of archaeological structures. Furthermore the available satellite data along with some satellite image processing methodologies and algorithms will be presented.

AERIAL IMAGERY DATA USAGE FOR THE DETECTION AND MODELLING OF ARCHAEOLOGICAL STRUCTURES

In this section three different indicative studies focusing on detecting and modelling archaeological structures are going to be presented. The case studies were implemented using three different sensor platforms, an unmanned helicopter, a balloon, and a hex-copter drone.

Modelling of the Prehistoric Lakeside Settlement of Dispilio (Kastoria, Greece)

The first study refers to the aerial photography and orthophoto production of the enclosure and the central trench of the prehistoric lakeside settlement of Dispilio (Kastoria, Greece). The part of the enclosure

Figure 2. The orthophoto map on the left (with grid 10 x 10 m.) of the central trench. The orthophoto map of the sane trench, a year later

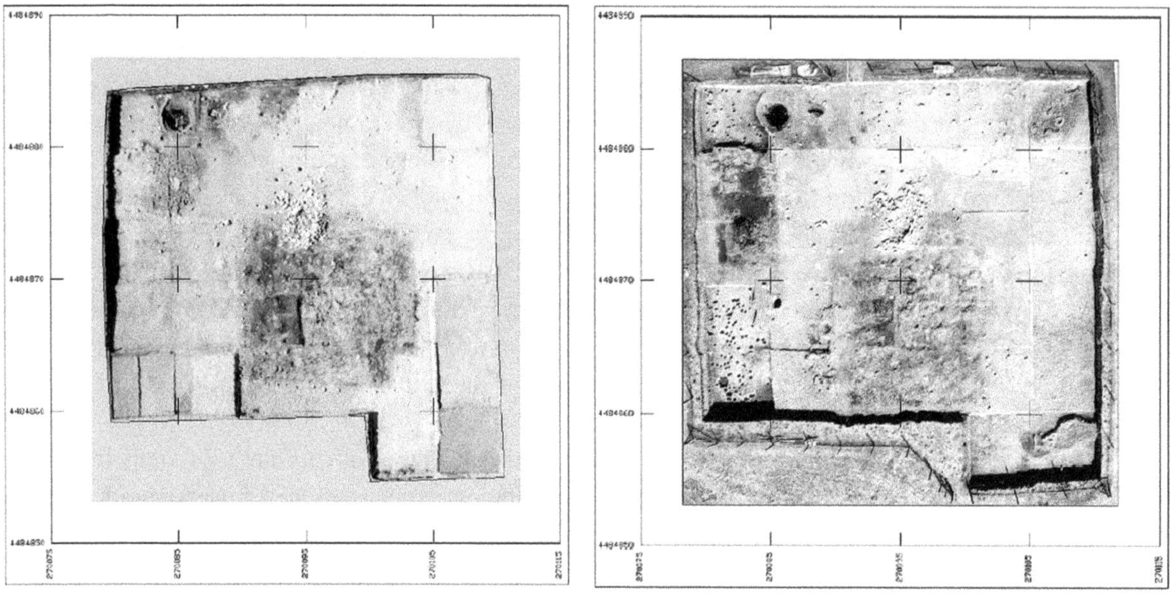

was 60 m. in length and 15 m. in width, while the central trench's dimension was 30 x 30 m. A remote controlled unmanned helicopter was used as the sensor-fitted platform for capturing aerial images. Its lifting capacity is 8 kg and lacks automatic take-off system, landing, planning and taking photogrammetric shots. Its length is 1.39 m., its width 0.15 m., helix opening 1.53 m. and weights 5.10 kg.

For this study a total of 195 aerial photos were acquired, 124 for the enclosure and 71 for the central trench. The flight height ranged from 6-50 m. (in exceptional cases it reached the minimum height of 2 m.), allowing for the capture of images with a spatial resolution of 2 to 17 mm respectively. From the existing trigonometric network, ground control points were measured in the field with referenced at the Greek Geodetic Reference System 1987 (EGSA '87). The ground control points were not realized on the ground with the use of predefined points before the aerial photography, but, afterwards, points were selected on digital pictures (e.g. stone features corners), which were then measured in the field. The accuracy of the generated ortho images of the western enclosure was approximately 4-5 cm, which determined the scale of 1: 200 of the produced orthophoto map .

Also, the accuracy of the respective ortho images of the central trench was approximately 1-2 cm, which allowed for the printing of the produced orthophoto map at a 1:50 scale (Figure 2).

One year later the production of orthophoto maps of the eastern and central trench in the same area was realized. The flight altitude of the unmanned drone helicopter ranged from 5-50 m, allowing for images with a spatial resolution of 2-17 cm respectively. 410 aerial photos were taken, 250 for the central trench and 160 for the eastern trench with the camera Canon EOS D400 10,1 Mp. Ground control points in EGSA '87 were measured from the existing network. At this case predefined ground control points were used in the form of tennis balls. The accuracy of the produced ortho images ranged from 1-2 cm for both trenches, giving the ability to produce maps with a scale of 1:50 (Figure 2 and 3).

Figure 3. The orthophoto maps (with grid of 10x10 m) of the eastern trench

Documentation of the Optimum Period for Trace Detection in the Philippi plain (Kavala, Greece)

This study is focused on the documentation of optimum period for trace detection in the Philippi plain (Kavala, Greece). At first, the optimum period for trace detection is determined based on crops (phenological cycle), type of soil cover and climatic-meteorological conditions prevailing in each study area. Afterwards, the documentation of the optimum period demands systematic and periodic image capturing throughout the year, in known positions of covered monuments within the study area. By evaluating the intensity of traces of known covered monuments throughout the year, the optimal trace detection period is rejected or eventually defined. The new images collected subsequently covering the study area, with acquisition dates within the defined optimum period, will lead to the identification of the largest possible number of new traces of potential covered archaeological structures.

Figure 4. Image acquisition dates (Kaimaris & Patias, 2014) Source: (Kaimaris & Patias, 2014)

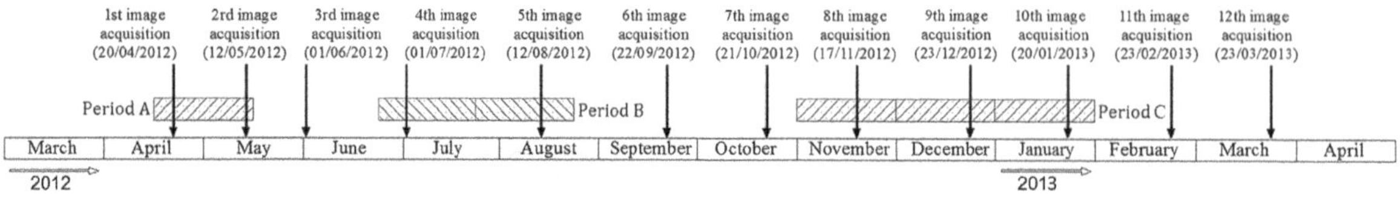

For the identification of the optimum period in the Philippi plain in two known locations of covered archaeological structures (Ancient Via Egnatia), an unmanned Balloon was constructed for the systematic acquisition of images during a year.

The balloon has a diameter of 2 m. When filled with helium (~ 5 m3), the balloon has a load capacity of 3.6 kg. It has four hooks, from which the image acquisition system is anchored. A rope, with a total length of 200 m, runs from the ground to the platform and is attached to one of these hooks.

The image acquisition system has a total weight of 1.24 kg (without the sensor). It consists of a base mounting suitable for any DSLR camera, camcorder, etc., with a weight of up to 1.5 kg. The digital camera Cannon EOS 20D was used for images acquisition. The cameras are embedded in the base mounting. The combined movement (servomechanisms actuation) of the four members (base, arm, vertical member and cross edge) allows the sensor to rotate 360°, horizontally and vertically. In this way, vertical, inclined, horizontal and oblique images of any target may be taken at any time.

The image acquisition system is constructed entirely of carbon fiber. A turbojet electric motor for controlling the mobility of the balloon is fitted to the vertical member.

The blueprint (dimensions, weights) of the image acquisition system's four members was designed in flight-simulation software that determined the lengths of the dependence ropes from the balloon hooks, and the position of the jet engine. This ensures a smooth flight and minimal vibrations during image acquisition.

The controller for the image acquisition system, the horizontal / vertical rotation sensor and the activation of the jet engine is mounted on the console of the ground station.

The pilot survey was launched in April 2012 and it was repeated in March 2013 (Figure 4-6). An 8Mpixel digital camera Canon EOS 20D was used as the imaging sensor.

3D Modelling of the Sanctuary of "Eukleia" Located in the Archaeological Site of Vergina, Greece

The third case study describes in detail the 3D modelling of the sanctuary of "Eukleia", located in Vergina, Greece using a state of the art hex copter drone (Figure 7).

The hex copter drone can fly using a completely automated mode or alternatively by using a remote control. Its equipment includes among others the batteries and a digital camera that are place in the spindle, and the ground station. The drone movements is realized through six propellers. The camera gimbal where the imaging sensors are placed can rotate in an arc of 180 degrees (± 90 degrees from nadir). In this study the Canon 1200D DSLR camera equipped with Canon EF-S 17-85mm f/4-5.6 IS USM lens was used for image acquisition. The camera has a 22.3 mm x 14.9 mm CMOS sensor and can acquire images with 18 MP resolution. The drone is equipped with the Wookong M of DJI autopilot, which incorporates a controller, IMU, and GPS. Its positioning accuracy is approximately ± 2m in the

Figure 5. a1: image acquisition 20/04/2012, a2: the position 1 of the Via Egnatia, width 6 m, b: image acquisition 12/05/2012, c: 01/06/2012, d: 12/08/2012, e: 22/09/2012, f: 21/10/2012, g: 17/11/2012, h: 23/12/2012, i: 20/01/2013, j: 23/02/2013 and k: 23/03/2013 (Kaimaris & Patias, 2014) Source: (Kaimaris & Patias, 2014)

horizontal plane and ± 0.5m in the vertical plane, while the angle measurement accuracy in all three axes ranges for 1 to 2 degrees (based on the specifications provide by the manufacturer). The drone has a lifting capacity of 2.5 Kgr, and its flying time ranges between 10 to 15 minutes.

The data acquisition campaign was realized in June of 2017 as part of a two week training course organized in the framework of the EC funded project HERITAG in the archeological site of Vergina, Greece. In total xxx images were captured from a height of approximately 40 m., following a flight plan designed with UgCS software (Figure 8). Three strips with a forward overlap of 80% and a side overlap

Figure 6. a1: image acquisition 20/04/2012, a2: the position 2 of the Via Egnatia, width 6 m, b: image acquisition on 01/06/2012, c: 01/07/2012, d: 12/08/2012, e: 22/09/2012, f: 21/10/2012, g: 17/11/2012, h: 23/12/2012, i: 20/01/2013, j: 23/02/2013 and k: 23/03/2013 (Kaimaris & Patias, 2014). Source: (Kaimaris & Patias, 2014)

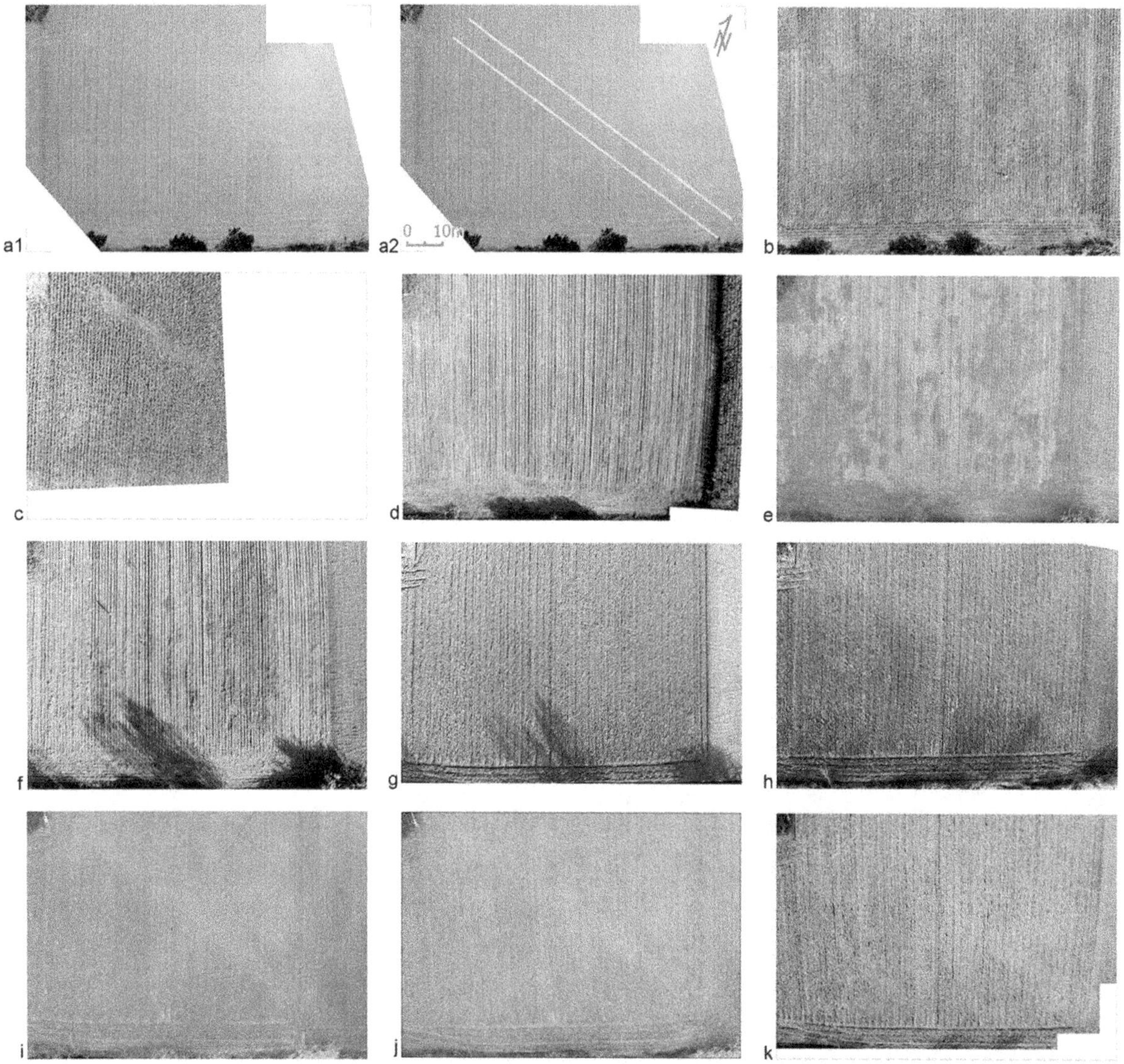

of 60% were realized acquiring images with a spatial resolution of 1 cm. In addition 8 Ground Control Points were measured using a dual frequency GNSS receiver with an accuracy of 1-3 cm.

The images were processed using the Agisoft Photoscan Professional software. The bundle solution yielded an error of 0.033m. The produced dense point cloud consisted of approximately 3.5 million points (Figure 9). Finally a Digital Surface Model (Figure 10) and an orthophoto (Figure 11) with a resolution of 1 cm were produced.

Figure 7. The hex copter used for data acquisition

REMOTE SENSING FOR ARCHAEOLOGY

In this section an overview of the application of remote sensing imagery in archaeology is going to be presented. At first the available satellite data that can be used in such applications are going to be presented, followed by an overview of basic satellite imagery processing techniques and methodologies. Finally, two examples are going to be presented that are using satellite imagery for the identification of potential buried archaeological sites and for modeling and documenting an archaeological excavation site.

Figure 8. The flight plan used for image acquisition

Figure 9. The produced dense point cloud

Figure 10. The produced digital surface model

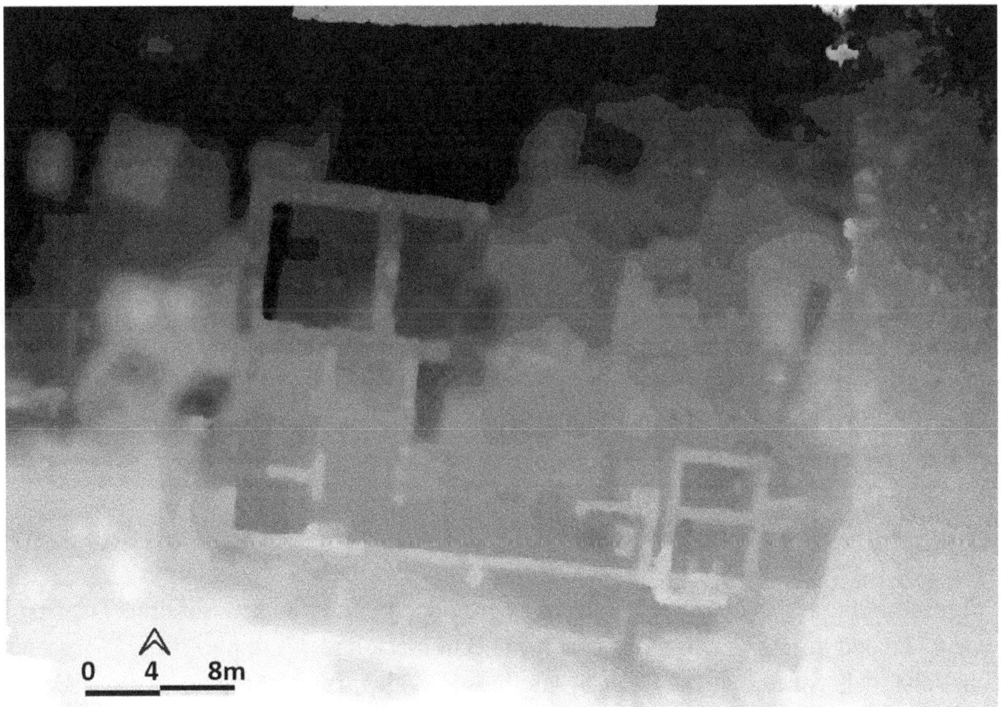

Figure 11. The produced orthophoto

Available Satellite Data

A brief overview of the available satellite data that can be used in archaeology is presented. Satellite sensors can be classified to passive or active, and panchromatic, multispectral or hyperspectral.

Declassified Intelligence Satellite Photographs (DISP)

On February 23, 1995 in accordance with Executive order 12951 more the 990,000 photographs taken by U.S intelligence satellites acquired from 1959 through 1980 were released in three separate occasions: February 1995 (Declass 1), September 2002 (Declass 3), and 2011 (Declass 3), (U.S. Geological Survey, 2008). The declassified images have a resolution spanning from 1 to 140 m. The declassified photographs were part of the following satellite systems (CORONA, ARGON, LANYARD, GAMBIT, HEXAGON). Detailed information about the DISP archive can be found in (Fowler, 2013). The DISP photographs can be purchased from the USGS site.

Optical and Multispectral Sensors

The first digital satellite earth observation data was provided by the Landsat mission. The first Landsat satellite was launched in 1972, with a resolution of 40 in black and white photos and 79 meters in the multispectral channels. Since then the Landsat satellites provide images of the Earth's surface. Currently data are acquired by the Landsat 7, and 8 satellites, while the Landsat 9 is scheduled to be launched in 2020(U.S. Geological Survey, 2016). Following Landsat the SPOT satellites, launched on 1986, provided a resolution of 10 m in panchromatic and 20 m in multispectral bands. The next step which introduced high resolution imagery was realized in 2000-2001 with the launch of the IKONOS and Quickbird satellites that provided sub meter resolution in the panchromatic and 4m, 2.5m in the multispectral respectively. Table 1 presents an overview of the available optical and multispectral satellite data.

It is obvious that with the introduction of the new very high resolution satellites such as World view 3 which will be able to deliver data with 0.25 m resolution in panchromatic and 1 m in multispectral a very powerful tool will be made available to the cultural heritage community not only for detection of archeological site but also for 3D mapping and modelling of them. Furthermore, most of the satellites have a revisit temporal resolution spanning from 1 to 10 days. Finally, optical satellite data can be used to produce Digital Elevation Models when image pairs are processed.

Radar Images

Besides the optical and multispectral satellite sensors one can also use radar satellite images for the detection of cultural heritage sites. Radar images have the advantage that can provide all weather data i.e. the can penetrate cloud cover. In addition, some of the bands used in radar satellites have the ability to penetrate specific types of ground up to 2-3 meters thus providing sub terrain images. Radar image are usually used for the production of high resolution DEMs. A list of available radar satellite systems is presented in table 2.

Table 1. Optical and multispectral satellites

Satellite	Launch Year	Resolution (m)	
		Panchromatic	Multi Spectral
World view 4	2016	0.3	1.2
KOMPSAT 3A	2015	0.55	2.2, 5.5
TripleSat	2015	0.8	3.2
Sentinel 2A	2015	10	10, 20, 60
SPOT 7	2014	1.5	6
World view 3	2014	0.3	1.2, 7.5, 30
Gaofen 2	2014	0.8	3.2
Landsat 8	2013	15	30
SkySat 1	2013	0.9	2
SkySat 2	2013	1.1	2
SPOT 6	2012	1.5	6
TH 01 Constellation	2012, 2012, 2015	2	10
Pleiades 1B	2012	0.5	2
KOMPSAT 3	2012	0.7	2.8
Pleiades 1A	2011	0.5	2
World view 2	2009	0.46	1.84
GeoEye	2008	0.46	1.84
RapidEYE	2008	5	5
EROS B	2006	0.7	-
ALOS	2006	2.5	10
CARTOSAT-1	2005	2.5	-
FORMOSAT 2	2004	2	8
SPOT 5	2002	2.5-5	10
Quickbird	2001	0.6	2.4
EROS A	2000	1.8	-
Landsat 7	1999	15	30
IKONOS	1999	1	4
ASTER	1999		15,30,90
SPOT 4	1998	-	-
SPOT 3	1993	10	20
SPOT 2	1990	10	20
SPOT 1	1986	10	20
Landsat 5	1984	30	30
Landsat 4	1982	30	30
Landsat 3	1978	40	79
Landsat 2	1975	40	79
Landsat 1	1972	40	79

Table 2. Radar satellite systems

Satellite	Launch year	Radar Band	Resolution
Sentinel 1B	2016	C	5
Sentinel 1A	2014	C	5
TanDEM-X	2010	X	12
RISAT 1	2010	C	1
TerraSAR-X	2007	X	up to 0.25
RADAR SAT2	2007	C	1
COSMO-Skymed	2007, 2007, 2008, 2010	X	1
Envisat	2002	C	30
SRTM	2000	C, X	30-90
RADAR SAT 1	1995	C	10
ERS 2	1995	C	30
SIR C/X SAR	1994	C, X	30
ERS 1	1991	C	30
SIR B	1984	L	15-45
SIR A	1981	L	15-45

Satellite Image Processing

When using multispectral and optical satellite data for the detection of potential archaeological sites different image processing techniques are used in order to enhance the images, to detect features, to apply filters and combine different bands. Image processing for detection of archaeological sites can include spectral indices, radiometric and spectral enhancement, Principal Component analysis, the tasseled cap algorithm, image filtering, edge detection, geospatial analysis, and classification, etc. In the following section some of these techniques will be analyzed.

Radiometric Enhancement

Radiometric enhancement helps to improve the visual characteristics of an image thus constituting photointerpretation an easier task. Radiometric enhancement is a pixel based operation, meaning that neighboring pixels are not influencing the operation. A detailed review of radiometric enhancement methods is presented in (Richards, 2013). Some of the radiometric enhancement techniques are the following:

- **Linear Contrast Modification**
- **Automatic Contrast Enhancement**
- **Histogram Equalization**
- **Histogram Matching**

The Tasseled Cap Transformation

The Tasseled Cap transformation is a linear transformation of multispectral data. It was first applied in Landsat MSS data by (Kauth & Thomas, 1976). They expressed the transformation using the following equation:

$$u = R^T x + r$$

where u is the transformed vector, x is the Landsat MSS signal vector, r is an offset vector and R is unitary matrix containing the transformation parameters.

The Tasseled Cap Transformation was also adapted for the TM (Crist, and Cicone, 1984; Crist, 1985; Crist & Kauth, 1986), and ETM+ (Huang, Wylie, Yang, Homer & Zylstra, 2002) Landsat sensor, for the IKONOS multispectral sensor (Horne, 2003), and the Quickbird multispectral sensor (Yarbrough, Easson & Kuszmaul, 2005).

Spectral Indices

Spectral Indices are spectral combinations of different remotely sensed bands. They are used to identify vegetation. In the application of detection of archaeological sites vegetation indexes can be used to enhance spots of areas that the vegetation has been influenced by the underground materials. Some of the spectral indices used in the detection of archeological sites include among others the following:

- **NDVI (Normalized Difference Vegetation Index)**
- **Green NDVI**
- **Albedo**
- **NVMI (Normalized Vegetation Moisture Index)**
- **NDWI (Normalized Difference Water Index)**

A detailed analysis of spectral indices can be found in (Lasaponara & Masini, 2012).

Principal Component Analysis

The principal Component analysis (PCA) is used for the transformation of a set of possible correlated variables in a set of linearly un-correlated ones. In the detection of potential archaeological sites is used for the creation of new images produced from multispectral data in order to enhance some image features thus making them more easily identified. A detailed definition of PCA can be found in (Richards, 2013). In general three steps are required for PCA (Richards, 2013):

- **Creation of the covariance matrix if the image**
- **Determination of the eigenvalues and eigenvectors**
- **Formulation of the components using the eigenvectors of the covariance matrix as the weighted coefficients**

Using remote sensing imagery for archaeology

Two different examples using remote sensing technology are going to be presented in this section. The first one studies the use of multispectral satellite images for the identification of potential buried archaeological sites, while the second one presents the 3D modelling of an active excavation using a multispectral camera mounted on a drone.

Using Multispectral Satellite Images to Identify Potential Buried Archeological Sites

An enhancement effort (no definition) of the optimal trace detection period utilizing archive satellite imagery was held during the remote sensing archaeology study in the Philippi plain (Kaimaris, 2006). After the amplification of time periods in new satellite QuickBird-2 images (captured within these time periods) of the study area, hundreds of new potentially covered archaeological structures (Figure 12) were identified.

3D Modelling and Documentation of an Excavation Site using a Multispectral Sensor

During the summer of 2019 three trenches were excavated in the archaeological site of Toumba. The site is managed by emeritus professor Stylianos Andreou member of the department of archaeology of the Aristotle University's school of history and archaeology. During the excavation the trenches were modelled and documented using a hex copter drone equipped with the sequoia parrot camera. The same drone that is described in the "3D modelling of the sanctuary of "Eukleia" located in the archaeological site of Vergina, Greece" section was used but with a different payload. During data acquisition the Parrot Sequoia multispectral camera was used to capture a total of 39 images from an average flying height of 9 m. The camera has a resolution of 16MP (4608x3456) for RGB image acquisition and resolution of 1.2 MP (1280x960) for the Green, Red, Red Edge, and Near Infrared bands. Furthermore 14 Ground Control Points (GCPs) were measured with an accuracy of approximately 2cm using a Leica TCR305 reflectorless total station. The images were processed using the Agisoft Metashape software. The photogrammetric processing was implemented at two stages. At the first stage the RGB images were processed, while during the second stage the multispectral images were processed. In both cases 11 GCPs were used. The RGB images processing yielded an error of 0.045 m, while the processing of the Multispectral images yielded an error of 0.023 m.

The processing of the RGB images resulted in the production of a point cloud with approximately 20 M points (Figure 13). The point cloud was used to produce a DSM with a resolution of 2 cm and an orthophoto with a resolution of 1 cm (Figure 14). The processing of the multispectral images resulted in the production of a point cloud with approximately1.5 M points (Figure 15). The point cloud was used to produce a DSM with a resolution of 2cm and an orthophoto with a resolution of 1 cm (Figure 16). Furthermore, the produced orthophoto was used to compute the NVDI index (Figure 17) and a thermal classification map based on the NIR band (Figure 18).

Figure 12. Negative grounds traces of covered structures. a. Satellite image QuickBird-2, NIR-G-B. b. PCA (PCA1-2-3). c. Trace imprinting (Kaimaris, 2006). Source: (Kaimaris, 2006)

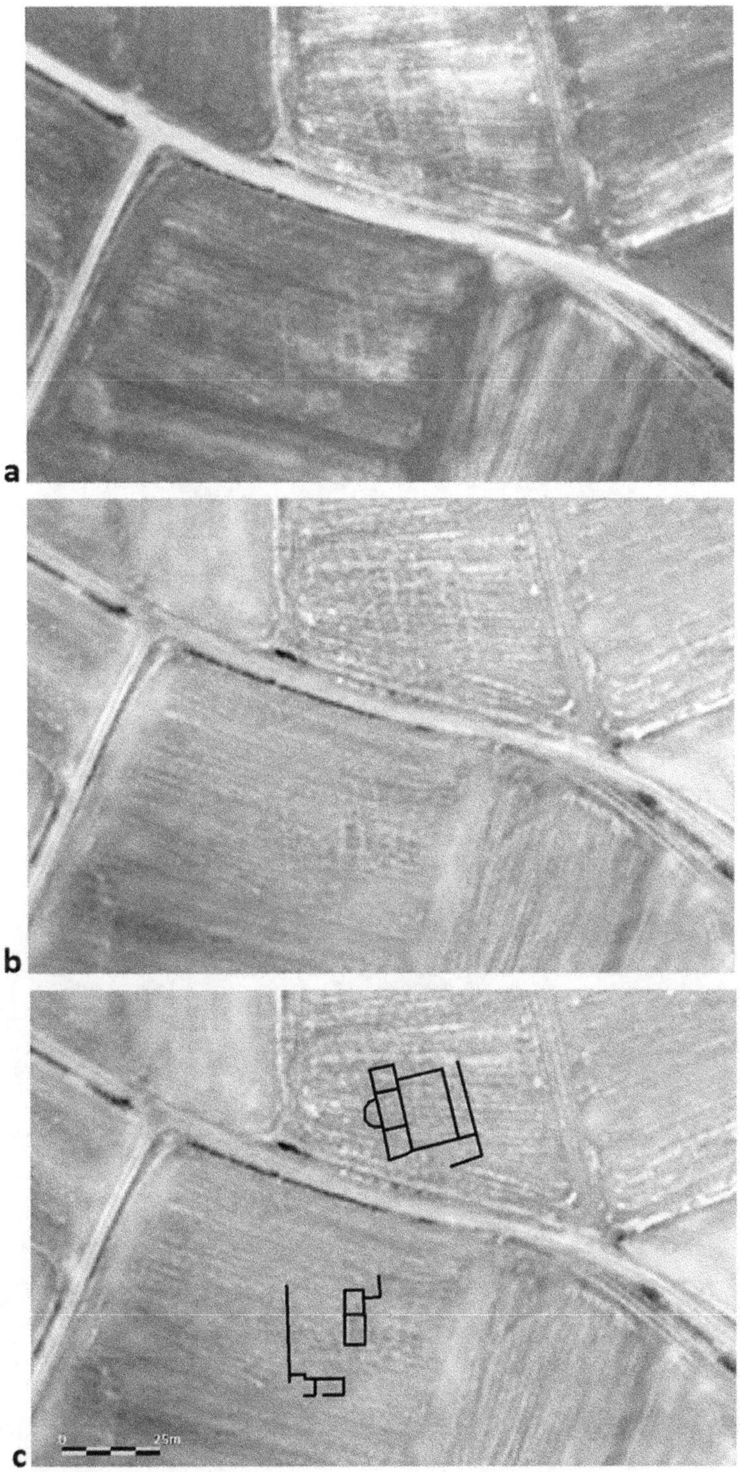

Figure 13. The RGB produced point cloud

Figure 14. The RGB produced orthophoto

Figure 15. The produced multispectral point cloud

Figure 16. The produced multispectral orthophoto

Figure 17. NDVI index

Figure 18. Thermal classification based on NIR band

CONCLUSION

In this chapter the authors presented and overview of the application of aerial and remote sensing imagery for the identification, 3D mapping and documentation of archaeological sites. During the last 10 years advances in the aerial platforms such as UAVs and the miniaturization of imaging and data acquisition sensors such as thermal, multispectral, LIDAR, IMU, GNSS has led to new paradigms of data acquisition, data processing and products. UAVs allow for the fast and accurate documentation of archaeological sites with up to sub-centimeter resolution depending on the used imaging sensors. Furthermore, new miniaturized sensors allow for the acquisition of multispectral data on relatively high resolution. On the other hand the introduction of coupled RTK-GNSS and IMU systems (still rather expensive as up to today) will lead to data acquisition schemes where the measurement of ground control points will not be required.

The use of remote sensing for archaeological applications practically started with the launch of the Landsat program. Remote sensing imagery can be used for both mapping and identification of new archeological sites. The new World View-3, and -4 satellites will provide data with a ground resolution of up to 25 cm, which is very adequate for the mapping of extensive sites. In addition, their multispectral sensor will offer a resolution of up to 1 m, providing thus a powerful tool for the identification of potential underground cultural heritage sites. Furthermore, the declassification of Intelligence satellite optical data with a sub-meter resolution, in some cases, offer a new tool to archaeologists to study historical images in regions that remote sensing data was not available before.

ACKNOWLEDGMENT

The image acquisition was conducted by the drone in Vergina during the summer school, which was organized within the frame of the research programme "Higher Education interdisciplinary Reform in Tourism management and Applied Geoinformation curricula-HERITAG" (561555-EPP-1-2015-1-ES-EPPKA2-CBHE-JP). The research programme was co-funded by the Erasmus+ programme of the European Union.

REFERENCES

Abbeel, P. C., Coates, C., & Ng, Y. A. (2010). Autonomous helicopter aerobatics through apprenticeship learning. *The International Journal of Robotics Research*, *29*(13), 1608–1639. doi:10.1177/0278364910371999

Agache, R. (1963). La prospection aerienne sur sols nus et l'inventaire archeoloque de la Somme. In *Archéologie Aérienne, Colloque International, 31/8-3/9/1963, S.E.V.P.E.N.* (pp. 49-58). Academic Press.

Alfieri, N. (1963). Topografia antica e aerofotografia a Spina. In *Archéologie Aérienne, Colloque International, 31/8-3/9/1963, S.E.V.P.E.N.* (pp. 155-160). Academic Press.

Alvisi, G. (1963). L' utilita dei vecchi rilemanti nella ricerca archeological. In *Archéologie Aérienne, Colloque International, 31/8-3/9/1963, S.E.V.P.E.N.* (pp. 277-281). Academic Press.

American Society for Photogrammetry and Remote Sensing. (1997). *Manual of photographic interpretation* (2nd ed.). Author.

American Society of Photogrammetry. (1983). *Manual of remote sensing* (2nd ed.; Vol. 2). Author.

Barnes, I. (2003). Aerial`Remote-sensing Techniques Used in the Management of Archaeological Monuments on the British Army's Salisbury Plain Training Area, Wiltshire, UK. *Archaeological Prospection*, *10*(2), 83–90. doi:10.1002/arp.197

Bewley, H. R. (2003). Aerial Survey for Archaeology. *The Photogrammetric Record*, *104*(18), 273–291. doi:10.1046/j.0031-868X.2003.00023.x

Chen, F., Lasaponara, R., & Masini, N. (2015). (in press). An Overview of Satellite Synthetic Aperture Radar Remote Sensing in Archaeology: From Site Detection to Monitoring. *Journal of Cultural Heritage*.

Chevallier, R. (1963). Detections aeriennes dans le Sud du department de l'Aisne. In *Archéologie Aérienne, Colloque International, 31/8-3/9/1963, S.E.V.P.E.N.* (pp. 95-108). Academic Press.

Crist, E. P. (1985). A TM tasseled cap equivalent transformation for reflectance factor data. *Remote Sensing of Environment*, *17*(3), 301–306. doi:10.1016/0034-4257(85)90102-6

Crist, E. P., & Cicone, R. C. (1984). A physically-based transformation of Thematic Mapper data the TM Tasseled Cap. *IEEE Transactions on Geoscience and Remote Sensing*, *GE-22*(3), 256–263. doi:10.1109/TGRS.1984.350619

Crist, E. P., & Kauth, R. J. (1986). The tasseled cap de-mystified. *Photogrammetric Engineering and Remote Sensing*, *52*, 81–86.

Dassie, J. (1978). *Manual d' archeologie aerienne*. Paris: Editions Technip.

Doneus, M. (1996). *Aerial Archive*. Retrieved October 2016, from http://www.univie.ac.at/Luftbildarchiv/

Driver, T. (2004). AARGnews. *AARGnews*, *28*, 6.

Featherstone, R., Horne, P., Macleod, D., & Bewley, R. (1999). Aerial Reconnaissance over England in Summer 1996. *Archaeological Prospection*, *6*(2), 47–62. doi:10.1002/(SICI)1099-0763(199906)6:2<47::AID-ARP113>3.0.CO;2-Y

Fowler, F. J. M., & Darling, P. (1998). Archaeological applications of imaging radar. *AARGnews*, *17*, 19–24.

Guerra, F., & Pilot, L. (2000). Historic Photoplanes. In IAPRS, Vol. XXXIII, Part B5 (pp. 611-618). Academic Press.

Horne, J. H. (2003). A Tasseled Cap Transform for IKONOS Images. *ASPRS Annual Conference Proceedings*.

Huang, C., Wylie, B., Yang, L., Homer, C., & Zylstra, G. (2002). Derivation of a tasselled cap transformation based on Landsat 7 at-satellite reflectance. *International Journal of Remote Sensing*, *23*(8), 1741–1748. doi:10.1080/01431160110106113

Hurtak, J. (1986). *Subsurface morphology and geoarchaeology revealed by spaceborne and airborne radar.* The Academy For Future Science. Retrieved October 2016, from http://www.affs.org/html/geo-archeology.html

Jalmain, D. (1963). Cinq années de prospection aérienne sur la Basée. In *Archéologie Aérienne, Colloque International, 31/8-3/9/1963, S.E.V.P.E.N.* (pp. 125-130). Academic Press.

Kaimaris, D. (2006). *Photogrammetric processing of digital images in the service of archaeological research: the localization of Via Egnatia from Amphipolis to Philippi* (Ph.D. thesis). Aristotle University of Thessaloniki, Greece.

Kaimaris, D., & Patias, P. (2014). A low-cost image acquisition system for the systematic observation of traces of buried archaeological structures. *GEOMATICA*, *68*(4), 299–308. doi:10.5623/cig2014-404

Kauth, R. J., & Thomas, G. S. (1976). The Tasselled Cap -- A Graphic Description of the Spectral-Temporal Development of Agricultural Crops as Seen by LANDSAT. *LARS Symposia.*

Kucukkaya, G. A. (2004). Photogrammetry and remote sensing in archeology. *Journal of Quantitative Spectroscopy & Radiative Transfer*, *88*(1-3), 83–88. doi:10.1016/j.jqsrt.2003.12.030

Kyoungah, C., & Impyeong, L. (2011). A UAV based close-range rapid aerial monitoring system for emergency responses. *Proceedings of the International Archives of the Photogrammetry, Remote Sensing and Spatial Information Sciences.*

Lasaponara, R., & Masini, N. (2012). Satellite Remote Sensing, A new tool for Archaeology. Springer Science & Business Media B.V. DOI doi:10.1007/978-90-481-8801-7

Marco, J. (2011). A history of NASA remote sensing contributions to archaeology. *Journal of Archaeological Science*, *38*(9), 2003–2009. doi:10.1016/j.jas.2010.09.017

Martin, J., & Fowler, F. (2013). Declassified Intelligence Satellite Photographs. In W. S. Hanson & I. A. Oltean (Eds.), Archaeology from Historical Aerial and Satellite Archives (pp. 47–66). Springer.

Miřijovský, J., Martínek, J., & Brus, J. (2011). Reconstruction of historical paths with using of small format aerial photography. *Proceedings of XXIIIrd International CIPA Symposium CTU.*

Remondino, F., Barazzetti, L., Nex, F., Scaioni, M., & Sarazzi, D. (2011). UAV photogrammetry for mapping and 3D modeling: current status and future perspectives. *Proceedings of the International Archives of the Photogrammetry, Remote Sensing and Spatial Information Sciences.*

Richards, J. A. (2013). *Remote Sensing Digital Image Analysis. An Introduction* (5th ed.). Springer Verlag Berlin Heidelberg. doi:10.1007/978-3-642-30062-2

Savage, H. S., Levy, E. T., & Jones, W. I. (2012). Prospects and problems in the use of hyperspectral imagery for archaeological remote sensing: A case study from the Faynan copper mining district, Jordan. *Journal of Archaeological Science*, *39*(2), 407–420. doi:10.1016/j.jas.2011.09.028

Scollar, I. (1963). Physical conditions tending to produce crop sites in the Rhinelad. In *Archéologie Aérienne, Colloque International, 31/8-3/9/1963, S.E.V.P.E.N.* (pp. 39-47). Academic Press.

Tapete, D., & Cigna, F. (2016). (in press). Trends and perspectives of space-borne SAR remote sensing for archaeological landscape and cultural heritage applications. *J. Archaeol. Sci. Rep.*

U.S. Geological Survey. (2008). Declassified intelligence satellite photographs. *U.S. Geological Survey Fact Sheet*, 2008–3054.

U.S. Geological Survey. (2016). Landsat-Earth observation satellites (ver. 1.1, August 2016). *U.S. Geological Survey Fact Sheet*, 2015–3081.

Yarbrough, L. D., Easson, G. & Kuszmaul J. S. (2005). QuickBird 2 tasseled cap transform coefficients: a comparison of derivation methods. *Pecora, 16*.

Chapter 3
Google Earth Revisited:
Case Studies at the Plain of Larissa (Thessaly, Greece)

Dimitris Kaimaris
Aristotle University of Thessaloniki, Greece

Petros Patias
Aristotle University of Thessaloniki, Greece

Olga Georgoula
Aristotle University of Thessaloniki, Greece

ABSTRACT

The interpretation of photos and the processing of Google Earth imagery that allowed the "random" discovery as a result of a non-systematical research of numerous marks of buried constructions in the wide area of the city of Larisa (Thessaly, Greece) is presented in this chapter. Additional data as aerial photographs over time, satellite images and the digital terrain model of the same area has been used. From the numerous marks, this chapter mainly focuses on three positions where the positive marks (soil marks or/and crop marks), circular or/and linear, reveal on a satisfying level covered construction of great dimensions. The ongoing research activity of the research team along with this research highlights the advantages of using Google Earth imagery in an attempt to "random" mark of unknown covered constructions, or, in the frame of a systematic survey of aerial and remote sensing archaeology, as additional and not exclusive source of information.

INTRODUCTION

The '' image '' of a covered monument from the soil or / and crop, embedded in the analogue or digital image, is the result of the interaction of the covered monument with the prementioned elements. This '' image '' is internationally called '' mark ''. The covered monument may be a '' solid construction '', e.g. the foundations of a building or an '' open construction '', e.g. an ancient ditch or an old stream (Figure

DOI: 10.4018/978-1-7998-2871-6.ch003

Figure 1. Anatomy of a mark (Kaimaris, 2006)

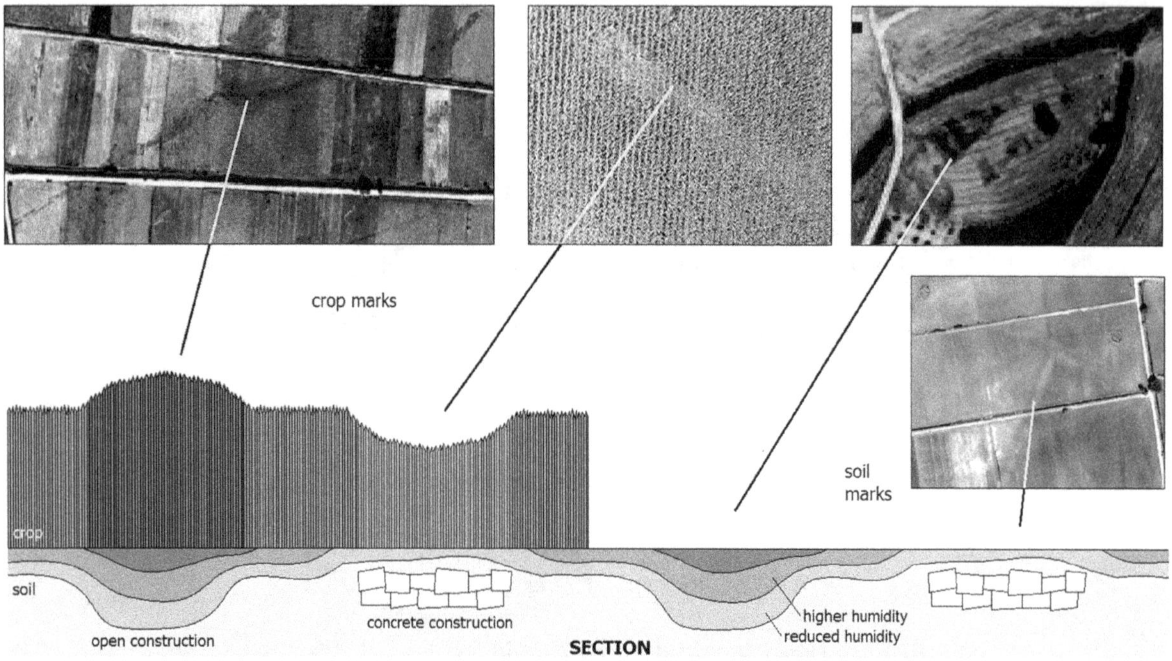

1). The result is, in the first case, the appearance of a negative soil or crop mark (light color or light gray in relation to the surroundings of the mark) and, in the second case, the appearance of a positive soil or crop mark (dark color or dark gray). The interaction of the covered monuments with the above elements (soil or crop) is very complex. The form of the event (kind of marks) and the intensity of its observation depend on dozens of factors, such as the type, size and depth of the covered monument, the amount of soil moisture, the temperature of the air, the soil, the type of cultivation or vegetation, the period and intensity of rainfall, the depth of the aquifer, etc. These factors cause, on the one hand, different soil moisture and temperature between the material covering the monument and the material on either side and, on the other hand, qualitative (height, density, color) and temperature difference between vegetation.

Thus, the amount of electromagnetic energy reflected or emitted by these materials (soil or vegetation) is different and is recorded by remote sensing systems (analogue photography, multispectral and panchromatic images, thermal images, etc.), allowing observations to be made on the '' images '' of the covered monuments (Kaimaris, 2006).

The tools for archaeologic forecasting are surface survey, historical sources, testimonies, field survey, historical map, aerial photography, satellite imagery and geophysical interruptions.

Google Earth (GE) can be characterized as a complementary and thus helping tool in the frame of a systematic survey of aerial and remote sensing archaeology (Kaimaris et al., 2011). More specifically, apart from the main use of GE imagery in archaeology, which is the observation and further study of known archaeological positions, in some occasions the imagery itself has led to a "random" tracing of unknown covered constructions.

For example, in the Philippi Plain (Macedonia, Greece) the editorial team is conducting systematic aerial and satellite archeology research since 2002. In 2011, during a periodic monitoring of the variation in the magnitude and number of traces of the covered ancient Via Egnatia and other laterally covered monuments, "random" were detected in GE light-colored linear marker images (Kaimaris et al., 2011), which show up on crops and on bare ground (soil). The marks (Figure 2) are 4-7m wide, ~ 5000m long and are located south of the Philippi Plain, between the ancient city of Philippi and the modern settlement of Antiphilippi. No markings or roads were observed at the mark positions on the historic maps of 1901, 1910, 1916, 1925 scale 1: 50,000 and 1: 200,000 and contemporary maps of 1980, scale 1: 5,000 and 1: 50,000. Therefore, they are not the "image" of a road of the early 20th century that was later covered by the ground. The mark may be the result of a covered fortification or a covered historic road that secured communication between the ancient city of Philippi and the settlement-locations that had developed in the area of the modern settlement of Antiphilippi.

On the other hand, there have been times when the GE imagery would not provide the researcher with enough information in areas where other tools of archaeology prospections (Figure 3), such as for example historic maps and aerial photographs, allowed the detection of interesting locations for further study (Kaimaris et al. 2011, Palmer 2005, Thomas et al. 2008, Myers and Camp 2010, Myers 2010, Cowley and Palmer 2009, Jia and Nie 2009, Micle et al. 2009, Jacobs 2013, Handwerk 2006, Kaimaris et al. 2018). This paper focuses on the "random" tracking of possible unknown large covered constructions via the use of GE. Subsequently, aerial photographs over time were gatherd and studied confirming our initial suspicions. Afterwards, the supply of a satellite image of specific date (Kaimaris 2006, Kaimaris 2012, Kaimaris and Patias 2015) followed and terrain of the study area was analyzed.

The collection of aerial photographs and satellite images over time are of major importance, and is one of the key components of the methodology of aerial and remote sensing archaeology, as far as covered structures tracking surveys are concerned. The continuous appearance of a mark over time confirms its presence and increases the likelihood of a covered construction. Otherwise, ie the presence of a mark in a single aerial photograph or satellite image, while it is absent in images over time, can lead to the conclusion that the mark might occur due to a covered construction and appeared due to special weather conditions (Featherstone et al., 1999), but it may also not be caused by a covered structure but by surface factors, such as, e.g. the geometry of the seed or the path of harvesting machines, etc.

STUDY AREA

The city of Larissa (Figure 4) is constructed on the riverside of Pineios River and is located in the center of the eastern part of Thessaly's plain, which is covered almost in full by the regional unit of Larissa. Meanwhile, its altitude from the sea level is 72m.

The regional unit's allocation of land is by 45,3% plain, 24,4% semi-mountainous and 30,3% mountainous. At the regional unit's north the following mountains are found: Karbounis, Titarow and Mount Olympus. At the regional unit's eastern part Mounts Kissavos and Maurovouni are found, sierra Antihasia is located at the northwest and a part of the sierra Othiros of the Narthakio mountain is located at the sounth of the municipality. The largest part of the plain area is shaped in the middle of the regional unit of Larissa and forms the plain of Larissa-Tyrnavos, one of the largest plain of the whole country. Its extent reaches 589 m2 and it covers its needs for water by Pineios River. The south part of the regional unity is covered by the plain of Farsala.

The Antiquities of Larissa is one of the Regional Offices of the Ministry of Culture and Sport. It is based in Larissa and its responsibility spans to the whole extent of the Regional Unit of Larissa. The period covered by the office's activities ranges from the prehistoric to the post-Byzantine period and the

Figure 2. Linear soil and / or crop marks on GE images, a. 2/5/2002, b. 24/11/2003 c. 9/4/2011. d. 14/5/2011, e. 22/4/2012, p. 18/3/2013 and g. 21/11/2017. h. The marks with red dashed line and the locations of the ancient city of Philippi and the modern settlement of Antiphilippi (Macedonia, Greece)

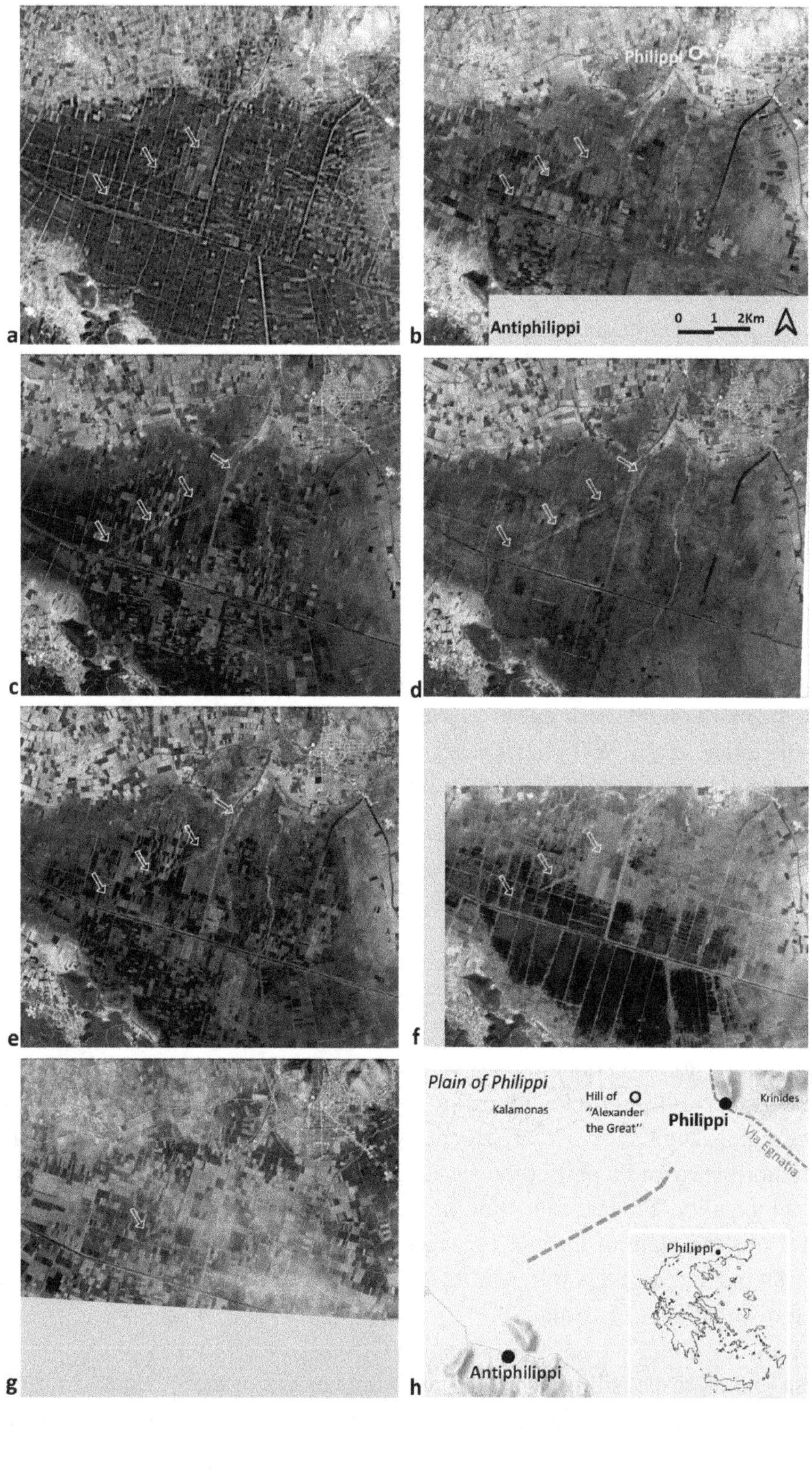

Figure 3. Plain of Philippi (Eastern Macedonia, Greece). a. Satellite image QuickBird-2, 02/05/2002 (personal ðle). Three ðrst channels (blue, green, red) of satellite image. Marks of Hippodamean System. b. Satellite image QuickBird-2, 23/11/2003, source: GE. True color. Accidentally marks. The satellite image date 02/05/2002 was a result of methodological process of Remote Sensing Archaeology.

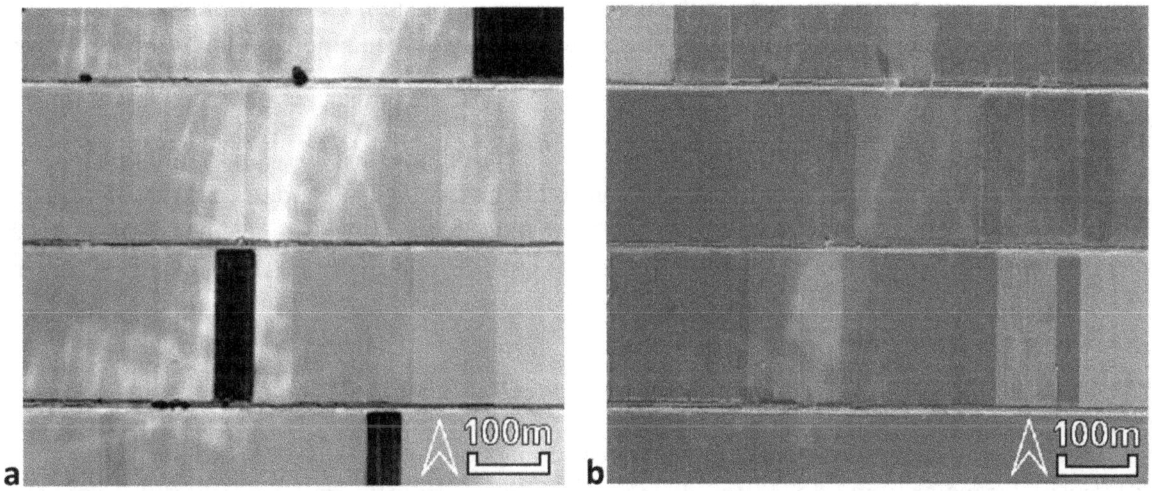

period of Ottoman rule. Its responsibilities included: detections of monuments, recording of memorials and any moving object, excavations, restoration works, monuments enhancement works and premises, maintenance of movable and immovable monuments, establishment of new museums and collections, organization of temporary exhibitions, organization of educational programs, cultural events and, lastly, organization of conferences.

Larissa is the capital of Thessaly and has been inhabited for almost 4.000 years. Archeological research proves that the city and its wider region is inhabited from the Paleolithic Era. During the ancient times, the city had its own coin. Hippocrates, the father of Medicine, lived and died in Larissa. In the 4th century BC, Larissa fought with another close city named Farsalo but due to this battle which was victorious for Larissa, the weakened army could not fight back to the invasion of the Macedonians (North Greece) under Philip II of Macedon in 344 BC. It remained under Macedonian control from 344 to 196 BC. During the Hellenistic period, horsemen from Larissa of the Great Alexander founded Larissa of Syria and Larissa of Arabia. In 197 BC Romans concurred the city. The 2nd century BC Eleftheria, a festival of the entire Thessaly in honor of Zeus Eleutherios, were introduced, which included horse races and literary, sports, etc. competitions. Afterwards, the city was under Byzantium and for the following centuries suffered repeated invasions. An era of peace and reorganization of the city followed by the Byzantine Emperor Basil II, who cared for the recovery of damaged fortresses of Thessaly. The decline that occurred in the 14th century facilitated the Ottoman domination. The Ottoman domination contributed to the economic decline of the area, resulting in the re-settlement of the population to on the mountains of Thessaly for greater security. In 1881 Thessaly was liberated by the Greek army and added to the Greek state. During World War II, the city was severely damaged by the Italian military aircraft bombing in 1941. Nowadays, Larissa is one of the largest Greek cities. The permanent population of the municipality (national census of 2011) reaches 162,591 inhabitants, with the permanent population of Larissa's Regional Unity reaching 284,325 inhabitants, making Larissa one of the largest cities in the country, and the largest in Thessaly. The city of Larissa has a population of 144,651 inhabitants and occupies an area of 19,000 acres (Wikipedia, 2016).

Southwest (~5Km) of the city of Larissa (Figure 4) GE images detected numerous marks. The detection was random and was conducted during the collection of GE images for the study of Larissa's urban area expansion. The experience of the editorial team on aerial and remote sensing archaeology allowed for the observation of weak marks, which otherwise would have been ignored. Thus, GE images were systematically studied and the existence of special marks of possible covered constructions of large dimensions were found.

The results of the photo-interpretation of images collected (GE, aerial photographs over time, satellite images, Table 1) are impressive, and impose the immediate archaeological cuts at specific locations. Three (3) of these marks will be presented, northeast of the settlement Mesoraxi (position A) and north-northeast of the settlement Eleytheres (positions B and C). These spots are not legislated Archaeological Positions.

DATA

For the study of aerial archeology in the study area aerial photographs of five (5) different dates and of different scale ranging from 1:15,000 to 1:42,000 were collected from the Hellenic Military Geographical Service (HMGS). Aerial photographs were digitized at 1200dpi and improved in contrast and brightness (no specific filter was used, but a regular correction in Photoshop was conducted). Also, orthophotographs of Kthmatologio S.A. were used, as well as the Digital Terrain Model (DTM) of the study area.

Through GE eight (8) image extracts belonging to six (6) different dates were collected. Finally, for the study of remote sensing archaeology a satellite image (pan sharpen) of the satellite system Pleiades was used. The data, that have been used, are presented in the Table 1.

STUDY OF DIGITAL TERRAIN MODEL

Utilizing the DTM (Figure 5-8) we come into the conclusion that the positions of the marks A and C are located on the top of hills. Especially the marks in position A follow the geomorphology of the area. At the southwest of position B no marks are being noted due to the intense contemporary human interventions. Additionally, it is quite obvious through the geomorphology of the area, that the marks in this position appear on a plateau of the hill.

DATA PROCESSING

The orthorectification of aerial photographs (Table 1) of HMGS was undertaken in Erdas Imagine 2014®. The orthophotographs of Kthmatologio S.A. (KT) were used for the determination of horizontal coordinates (X, Y, the Greek Geodetic Reference System 1987, GGRS87) of Ground Control Points (GCPs) and the DTM of KT was used to determine the elevation of GCPs. Taking into consideration the DTM of KT, orthophotographs were produced with horizontal accuracy up to ~ 2m (RMS). By the same process, simultaneously using the Rational Polynomia Coefficients (RPCs) of the satellite, the orthophotograph satellite image of the Pleiades system (PL) was produced with horizontal accuracy of 1.5m.

Figure 4. The position of Larissa city (Central Greece) in Greece, and the marks (marked in black color) in the wider study area. Positions A, B and C where marks of buried constructions which are presented in this project.

The same GCPs (keeping X and Y) were used for the affine transformation of the GE images. This procedure has enabled the production of rectified images of horizontal accuracy up to ~ 2.5m (RMS). All products were inserted in ArcMap 10.3.1®, under a common coordinate system (GGRS87), so that their comparison is possible.

The aim of the use of satellite Pleiades is to evaluate the possibilities that high resolution satellite image offers in the field of archaeological research. To facilitate the mark's identification and interpretation, the PCA transformation was applied on Pan-sharpened image. The three selected PC1, PC2 and PC3 bands have been used to produce Figures 9, 10 and 11.

Table 1. Data

Provider	Product	Spectral resolution	Spatial resolution (m)	Date	Availability
Hellenic Military Geographical Service (HMGS)	Arial photographs	BW	0.5-1.0	1945, 1960 1974 1976 18/06/1981	Not free
Google Earth (GE)	Images	RGB	0.5-1.0	03/05/2004 04/05/2010 27/04/2012 (a) 31/10/2012 (b) 20/03/2014 29/08/2015 19/03/2016 (a) 22/04/2016 (b) 31/05/2016 (c) 10/08/2017 (a) 22/09/2017 (b) 11/03/2019	Free
Kthmatologio S.A (KT)	Orthophotographs	RGB	0.5	2007-2009	Not free*
	Digital Terrain Model (DTM)	BW	5.0	2007-2009	
Pleiades (PL)	Satellite image	RGBNIR	0.5	01/05/2014	Not free

* Free donation of data from Kthmatologio S.A fro academic research.

Figure 5. The marks projected on the relief of the area as is described by the contour lines: a. position A, b. position B, c. position C.

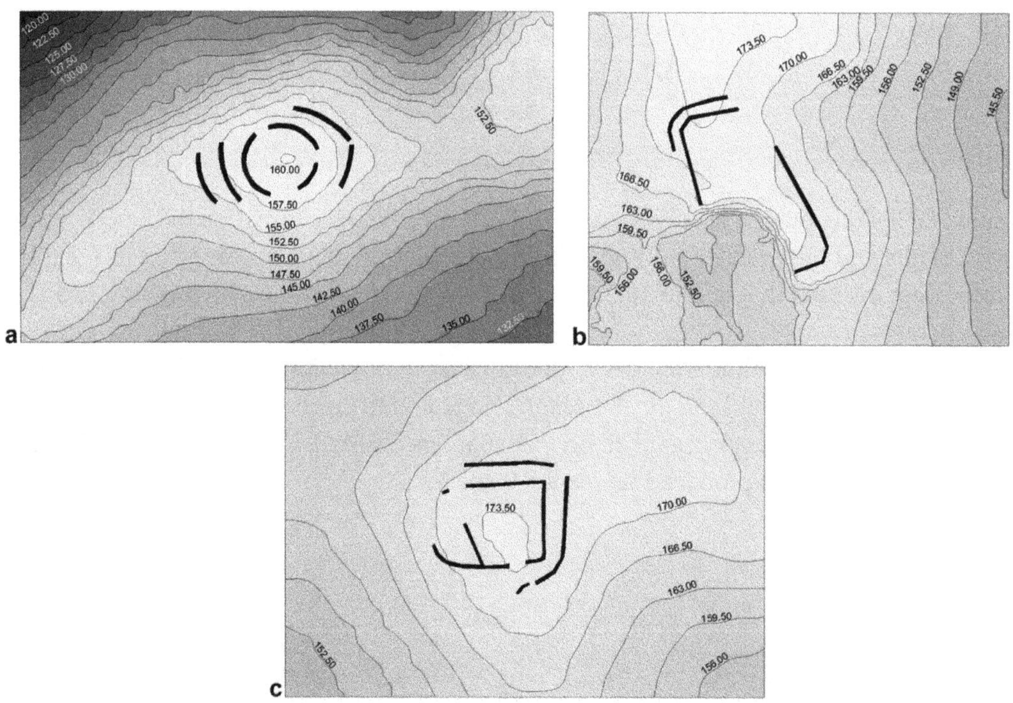

Figure 6. In position A: a. the 3D presentation of the DTM, b. the overlay of the GE 2010 on DTM.

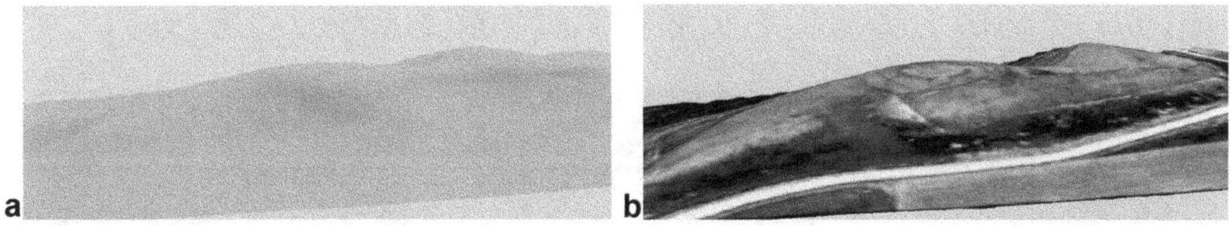

Figure 7. In position B: a. the 3D presentation of the DTM, b. the overlay of the GE 2010 on DTM.

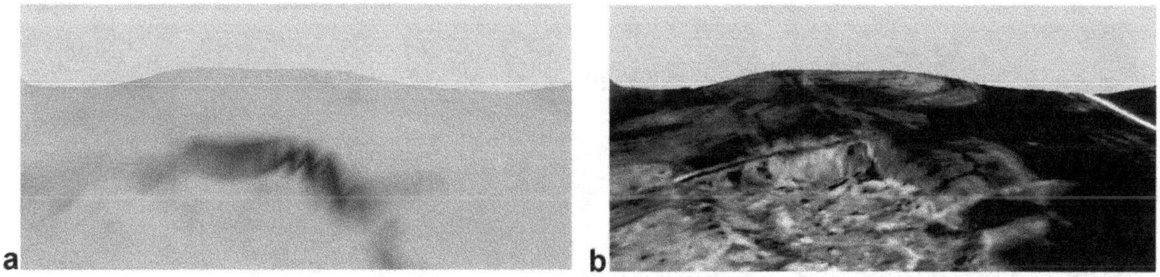

Figure 8. In position C: a. the 3D presentation of the DTM, b. the overlay of the GE 2010 on DTM.

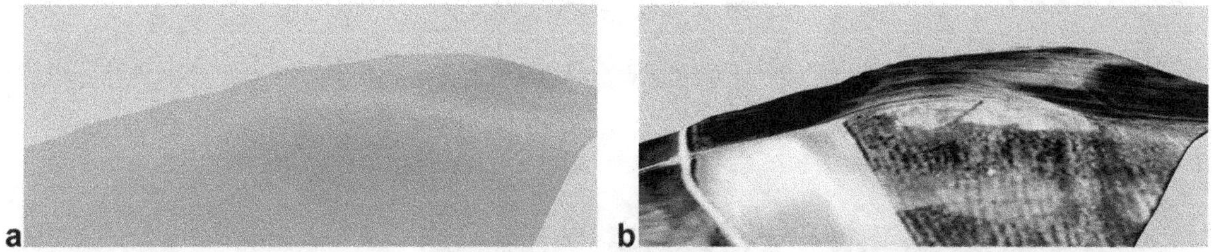

MARKS ON POSITIONS A, B AND C

In position A concentric positive (Kaimaris and Patias, 2015) circular marks (soilmarks or cropmarks in different images) with a diameter of 40 to 100m and width of 5 to 10m were detected (Figure 9). The marks show significant similarities with the marks of prehistoric covered ditches of Hanson's research (2014) or Neolithic covered ditches of the researches of Becker (1995), Kuzma et al. (1996), Doneus and Neubauer (1998), Luck and Eisenreich (1999), Löcker et al. (2009) and Campana et al. (2009). The similarities relate to their typology (circular structures), their size, the type of covered construction (tombs, as positive ie dark marks are identified), and the discontinuity of the positive marks which perhaps indicates the presence of passages to the interior of the circle. Finally, similar external concentric circles of positive marks are observed.

Figure 9. Concentric positive circular marks. Data: a. HMGS 1945, b. HMGS 1960, c. GE 2004, d. KT 2007-2009, e. GE 2010, f. GE 2012a, g. GE 2014, h. PL RGB 2014, i. PL Principal Component Analysis (PCA) 2014, j. GE 2015, k. GE 2016a, l. GE 2016b, m. GE 2016c, n. GE 2017a, o. GE 2019.

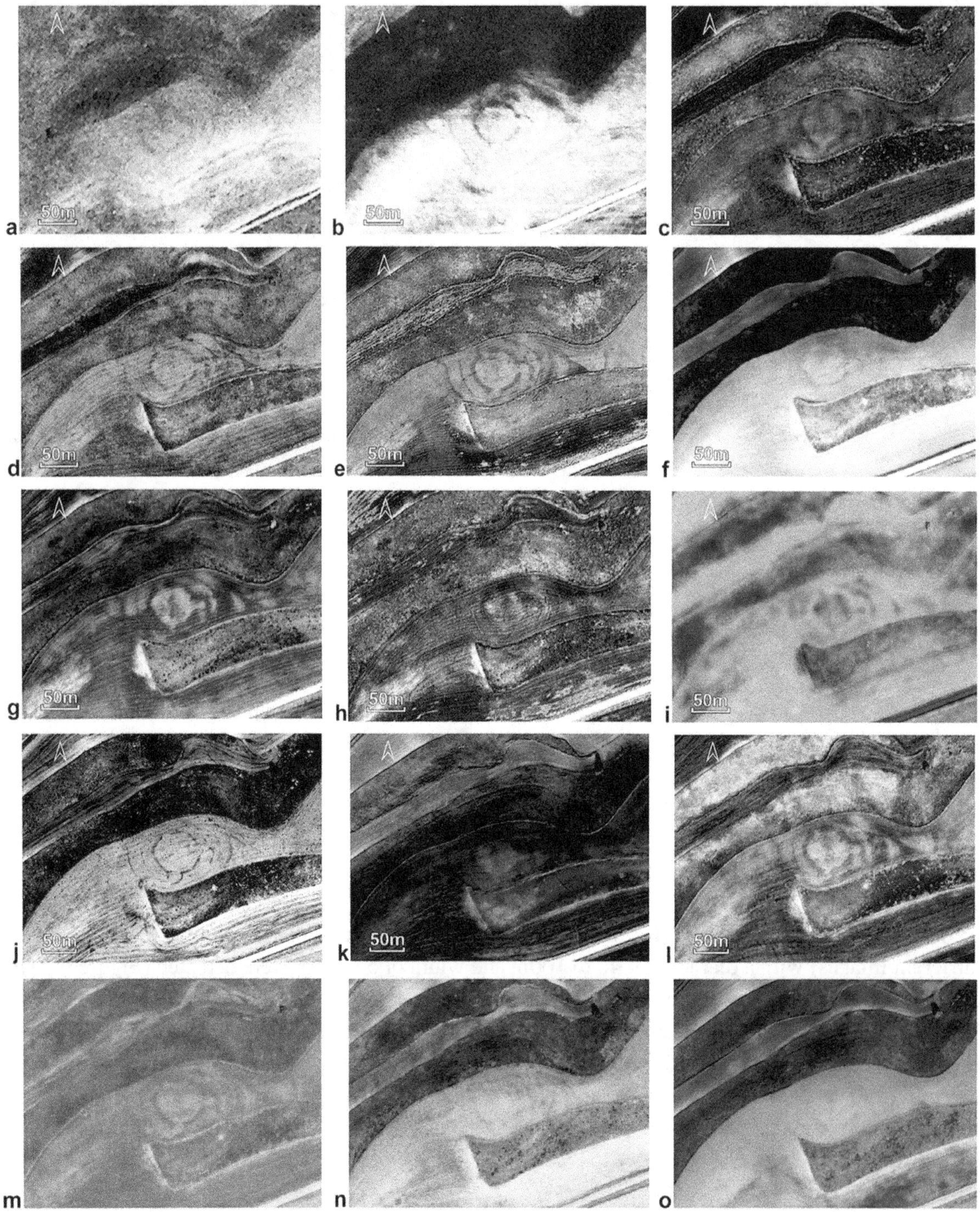

In position B positive, mainly linear cropmarks which reveal a covered construction of an almost orthogonal form of a 40x90m and width 3m (Figure 10) were detected. The marks show significant similarities with the marks of neolithic covered structures of the researches of Stanjek and Fassbinder (1995), Doneus and Neubauer (1998), Löcker et al. (2009) and Ceraudo (2013). The similarities relate to their typology (almost rectangular structures), the size, the type of covered construction (tombs, as positive ie dark marks are identified), and the repetitive parallel linear positive marks.

Similar traces with those of position B were detected at position C. They consist of positive marks (cropmarks), mainly linear, which reveal two successive covered constructions of almost rectangular form of 30x60m and 45x80m (Figure 11).

Figure 10. Positive, mainly linear marks which reveal a covered construction of an almost orthogonal form. Data: a. HMGS 1945, b. HMGS 1974, c. HMGS 1976, d. KT 2007-2009, e. GE 2010, f. GEP 2012a, g. PL RGB 2014, h. PL PCA 2014, i. GE 2016b.

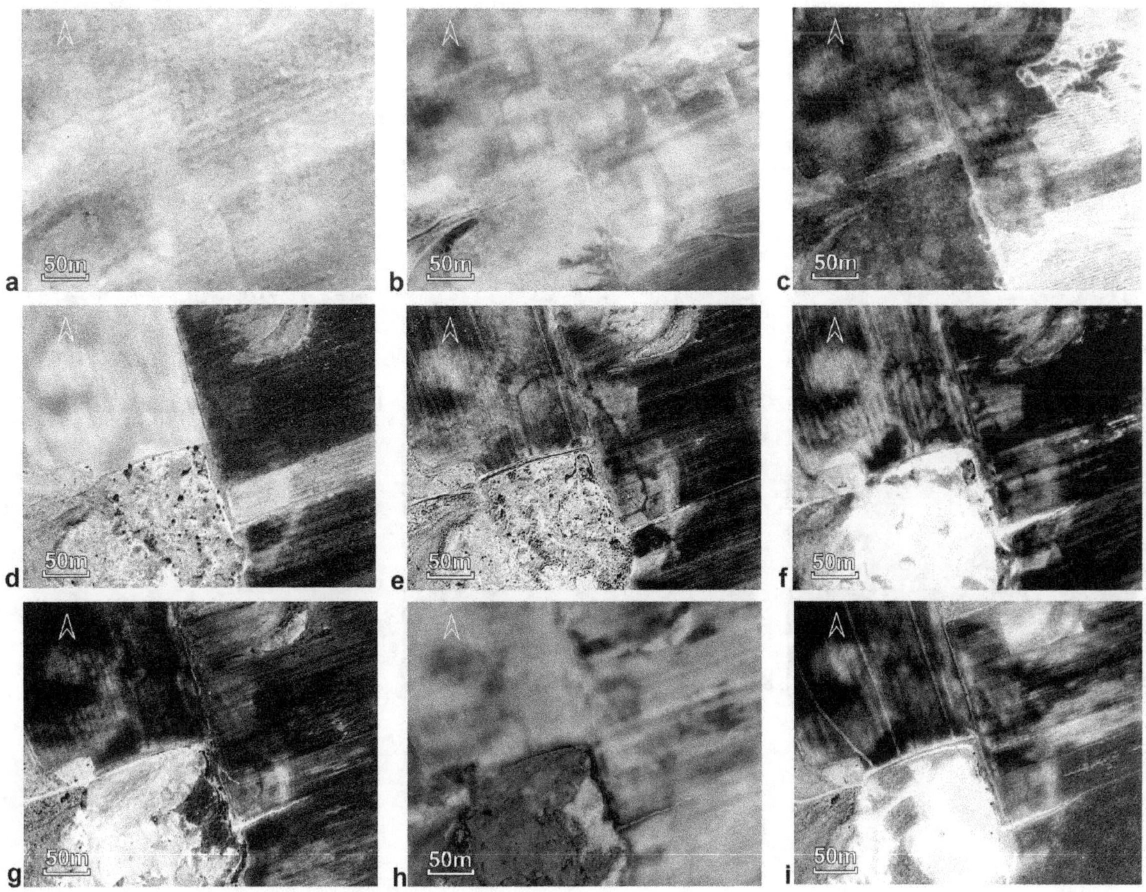

Figure 11. Positive, mainly linear marks. Data: a. HMGS 1945, b. KT 2007-2009, c. GE 2010, d. GE 2012a, e. GE 2012b, f. PL RGB 2014, g. PL NIRGB 2014, h. PL PCA 2014, i. GE 2016b, j. GE 2017a, k. GE 2017b.

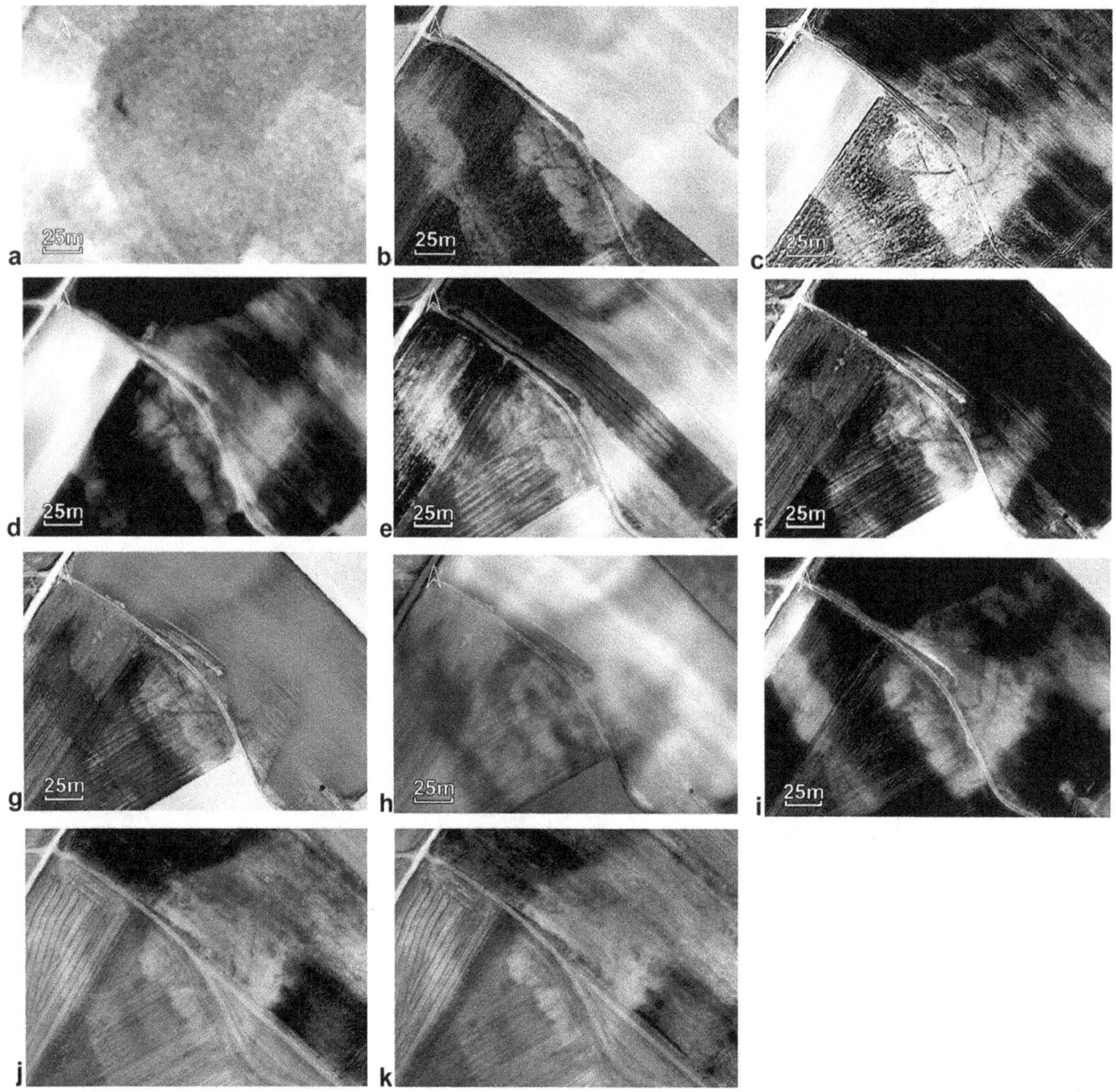

CONCLUSION

Google Earth is a useful tool for observing and studying already known archaeological positions and for the needs of other projects as of the environmental protection or planning, but cannot be described as a tool of archeology prediction on which a whole research should be exclusively based on. However, in some cases as this specific study, the motivation for further systematical research is given "randomly". The DTM revealed special information of great importance concerning the geomorphology of the positions' locations.

Thus, the research will be continued in a systematic way. Additional data as historical texts, maps, aerial photography, satellite imagery etc will be used. The methodological process of using tools of archeology prospection, as in other cases (Georgoula et al. 2003, Kaimaris et al. 2009, Kaimaris et al. 2012), will hopefully lead to safer conclusions about the nature of the marks. Finally, only archaeological excavations can allow the documentation and chronology of the marks, and, therefore, it is imperative to carry out excavation ditches, at least in the positions of the three (3) marks shown in this paper.

REFERENCES

Becker, H. (1995). From Nanotesla to Picotesla - a New Window for Magnetic Prospecting in Archaeology. *Archaeological Prospection, 2*, 217–228.

Campana, S., Dabas, M., Marasco, L., Piro, S., & Zamuner, D. (2009). Integration of remote sensing, geophysical surveys and archaeological excavation for the study of a Medieval Mound (Tuscany, Italy). *Archaeological Prospection, 16*(3), 167–176. doi:10.1002/arp.366

Ceraudo, G. (2013). *Aerial Photography in Archaeology*. Good Practice in Archaeological Diagnostics. doi:10.1007/978-3-319-01784-6_2

Cowley, D., & Palmer, R. (Eds.). (2009). *Education in aerial remote sensing for archaeology*. EAC/AARG.

Doneus, M., & Neubauer, W. (1998). 2D Combination of Prospection Data. *Archaeological Prospection, 5*(1), 29–56. doi:10.1002/(SICI)1099-0763(199803)5:1<29::AID-ARP92>3.0.CO;2-T

Featherstone, R., Horne, P., Macleod, D., & Bewley, R. (1999). Aerial Reconnaissance over England in Summer 1996. *Archaeological Prospection, 6*(2), 47–62. doi:10.1002/(SICI)1099-0763(199906)6:2<47::AID-ARP113>3.0.CO;2-Y

Georgoula, O., Kaimaris, D., Karadedos, G., & Patias, P. (2003, April). *Photogrammetry and Archaeology: A case study in the archaeological site of Philippoi in N.Greece*. Paper presented at the conference of the Computer Applications and quantitative methods in Archaeology, Vienna, Austria.

Handwerk, B. (2006). *Google Earth, Satellite Maps Boost Armchair Archaeology*, Available at: http://news.nationalgeographic.com/news/2006/11/061107-archaeology.html

Hanson, W. S. (2014). Aerial reconnaissance for archaeology. The West of Scotland, Glasgow Museums.

Jacobs, Q. J. (2013). *Ancient Monuments Placemarks*. Available at: http://www.jqjacobs.net/archaeo/sites/

Jia, P., & Nie, Y. (2009). *Remote sensing technique application in the research of ancient cities. A Case Study in Changhua Ancient City of Hainan Province*. Paper presented at the 30th Asian Conference on Remote Sensing, Beijing, China.

Kaimaris, D. (2006). *Photogrammetric processing of digital images in the service of archaeological research: the localization of Via Egnatia from Amphipolis to Philippi* (Doctoral Thesis). Interdisciplinary Postgraduate Studies Program Protection, preservation and restoration of cultural monuments, Aristotle University of Thessaloniki, Greece.

Kaimaris, D., Geogoula, O., Karadedos, G., & Patias, P. (2009). *Aerial and Remote sensing Archaeology in eastern Macedonia, Greece*. Paper presented at the conference of the CIPA XXII Symposium, Kyoto, Japan.

Kaimaris, D., Georgoula, O., Patias, P., & Stylianidis, E. (2011). Comparative analysis on the archaeological content of imagery from Google Earth. *Journal of Cultural Heritage*, *12*(3), 263–269. doi:10.1016/j.culher.2010.12.007

Kaimaris, D., Karadedos, G., Georgiadis, Ch., & Patias, P. (2018). Locating and Mapping the Traces of the Covered Ancient Theater of Amphipolis (Eastern Macedonia, Greece). *Heritage*, *1*(1), 306–319. doi:10.3390/heritage1020020

Kaimaris, D., & Patias, P. (2015). Systematic observation of the change of marks of known buried archaeological structures: Case study in the plain of Philippi, Eastern Macedonia, Greece. *Mediterranean Archaeology and Archaeometry*, *15*(20), 129–142.

Kaimaris, D., Patias, P., & Tsakiri, M. (2012). Best period for high spatial resolution satellite images for the detection of marks of buried structures. *The Egyptian Journal of Remote Sensing and Space Sciences*, *15*(1), 9–18. doi:10.1016/j.ejrs.2011.12.001

Kuzma, L., Hanzelyova, E., Rajtar, J., & Tlrpak, J. (1996). New results in aerial archaeology in Slovakia: Experience with reconnaissance, geophysical measurement and follow-up excavations. *Archaeological Prospection, 3*, 71-79.

Löcker, K., Nau, E., Neubauer, W., & Hinterleitner, A. (2009). Magnetic surveys of Early and Middle Neolithic settlements in Austria. *ArcheoSciences, revue d'archéométrie, 33*, 101-104.

Luck, E., & Eisenreich, M. (1999). Geophysical Prospection of Archaeological Sites in Brandenburg, Germany. *Archaeological Prospection*, *6*(3), 125–133. doi:10.1002/(SICI)1099-0763(199909)6:3<125::AID-ARP111>3.0.CO;2-U

Micle, D., Torok-Oance, M., & Maruia, L. (2009). The morpho-topographic and cartographic analysis of the archaeological site Cornes, ti "Iarcuri", Timis, County, Romania, using computer sciences methods (GIS and Remote Sensing techniques). *Anale. Computer Science*, *7*, 249–262.

Myers, A. (2010). Field work in the age of digital reproduction: A review of the potentials and limitations of Google Earth for archaeologists. *The SAA Archaeological Record*, *4*, 7–11.

Myers, A., & Camp, D. (2010). Google Earth and the ethics of remote sensing in archaeology. *World Archaeology*, *42*(3), 455–467. doi:10.1080/00438243.2010.498640

Palmer, R. (2005). Google Maps. *AARGnews*, *31*, 38–39.

Stanjek, H., & Fassbinder, J. (1995). Soil Aspects Affecting Archaeological Details in Aerial Photographs. *Archaeological Prospection*, *2*, 91–101.

Thomas, D., Kidd, F., Nikolovski, S., & Zipfel, C. (2008). The archaeological sites of Afghanistan in Google Earth. *AARGnews*, *37*, 22–30.

Wikipedia. (2016). *Larissa*. Available at: https://en.wikipedia.org/wiki/Larissa

Chapter 4
Scientific Datasets in Archaeological Research Through Pottery Dating and Provenance Cases

Nikolaos A. Kazakis
Athena – Research and Innovation Center in Information, Communication, and Knowledge Technologies, Greece

Nestor C. Tsirliganis
Athena – Research and Innovation Center in Information, Communication, and Knowledge Technologies, Greece

ABSTRACT

Recent trends in archaeological research dictate the incorporation of various analytical methods for dating, chemical/mineralogical characterization, morphological description, etc. of various excavation findings and landscapes to support and corroborate the archaeologists' observations. Each method, when used individually, provides a different feedback, but once single studies are combined, the information produced can significantly contribute to the solution of the archaeological puzzle. Thus, numerous scientific data and metadata are produced creating large and complex scientific datasets. The use of common terminology and definitions to describe these data along with the establishment of a formal standardized structure any cultural heritage information could be mapped to would assure the credibility and durability of such scientific datasets. The chapter provides an overview of the types and formats of the scientific data/metadata produced in the archaeological research through the detailed presentation of the common practices used in pottery dating and provenance studies.

DOI: 10.4018/978-1-7998-2871-6.ch004

INTRODUCTION

Archaeology aims towards the understanding of humankind. A further objective is the re-creation of the material culture, the reconstruction of the cultural past and the understanding of the lifeways of the people through the material remains of past societies. The above can considerably contribute to the better knowledge of the social, political, economic and cultural structure and evolution of ancient societies as well as their interactions within sites or regions (e.g. Rice, 1987; Tite, 2008).

In this endeavour the recent years, archaeology interacts increasingly with natural sciences and informatics to take advantage of the possibilities they offer and reduce the subjective element involved in the traditional approaches. The combined information from the various scientific disciplines allows the investigation of theories and interpretations that shed light on the human past and environment.

Numerous "components" of the archaeological research, such as Dating, Provenance and Dietary studies are leaning heavily on natural sciences and involve the use of advanced scientific methods applied on the archaeological finds. The information extracted from the materials using such methods produce a plethora of scientific data and metadata, which do not serve only as tools for answering individual archaeological questions, but also create large scientific reference datasets that allow the complete scientific documentation of the artifacts, environment and living beings of the past.

These datasets include data of various formats and types, while their metadata (e.g. experimental method, date of measurement etc) are essential for their evaluation and constructive use, especially when comparisons are attempted.

The present work provides an overview of the specifications of the scientific data and metadata produced in the archaeological research and their importance from a scientific point of view are discussed below, while a minimal simplified structure for such datasets is also proposed as a guideline towards standardization based mainly on best practices and procedures followed in scientific laboratories. The above is accomplished through the detailed presentation of the common practices in pottery dating and provenance studies, which can be considered as the most representative example of scientific data production in the archaeological research due to the large number of methods that can be involved and the variety of the obtained data.

APPROACHES IN THE ARCHAELOGICAL RESEARCH

Traditionally, the study of ancient artifacts was mainly focused on meticulous macroscopic observations by the archaeologists. Conclusions would be derived from their typology, decoration, iconography and chronology, based exclusively on stylistic considerations and aesthetic evaluation of the artifacts as well as their use, role and function. The above could also be complemented in some cases by available historic archive studies. In addition, evaluation of their characteristics would also shed light on the places (e.g. Attics or Corinthian pottery in ancient Greece) and the techniques of production (black-figure), the distribution, the trade routes, the organization and the contacts of the societies they created and exchange them.

In the late '50s, the term of Archaeometry was first introduced by Prof. C.F.C. Hawkes to refer to the use of methods and techniques coming from the natural sciences (physics, chemistry, mathematics, geology, geophysics, biology) and their application to archaeology as well as to art objects in order to provide solutions for specific questions and problems (Harding, 1994). The term today is expanded to include the computer technologies and their contribution to the study of the Cultural Heritage and is increasingly referred to as **Heritage Science**, which actually represents a modern and more sophisticated approach in the archaeological research.

Heritage Science can be regarded as the "forensics" in cultural investigations, since it seeks for information in retrospect trying to answer primary questions, like 'who', 'where', 'when' and 'how'. This is achieved through the amalgamation of several disciplines and the fusion of numerous scientific data that include (though not exclusively):

- § measurements of physicochemical parameters, properties and radiation of materials, environmental and biological samples
- § analyses of the composition of materials, environmental and biological samples
- § study of the 'structure' and form of materials, environmental and biological samples
- § assessment of physicochemical processes in materials, environmental and biological samples
- § spatial data
- § statistical data

In the case of artifacts, in particular, it is evident and widely accepted that the physical properties and composition are significant descriptive characteristics of both raw materials and the finished products (e.g. Buko, 1984). In the same respect, the manufacture techniques can characterize the appearance and functional capabilities of the finished object. As a result, various methods, simple or complex, destructive or non-destructive, qualitative or quantitative, can be employed to study the above features and provide information about the past of the archaeological finds. Any advanced method employed for such purposes is eligible to describe an artifact by objective, precise and replicable standards, free from aesthetic or subjective judgments common to art-historical appraisals. In parallel, they allow the definition of units of measurement or comparison that are standardized and independent of the context of observation. Thus, for a pot that could be described as "soft and poorly fired" for one cultural region and "hard and well fired" for another, a measured hardness of 5.0 in the Mohs' scale, and a firing temperature between 800 ^{o}C and 900 ^{o}C eliminates the ambiguity of the qualitative terms. It must be accentuated that the most important aspect of all these methods is that they yield a data base which can be used to relate material properties to human behavior and technology.

To this respect, very decisive is also the role of the digital technologies, which significantly contribute to the organization of the accumulated knowledge and set up new methodologies for analyzing the physicochemical properties of archaeological objects. Cultural databases, 3D digitization and reconstruction, as well as virtual reality, are used in order to make material remains more accessible and better understandable to both scholars and the general public. Last but not least, the Geographical Information Systems (GIS) introduced to archaeological studies since the late 20th century provides important information for matters such as trade routes, contacts, use and function etc, through the distribution of artifacts in place and time.

Scientific Datasets-Current Issues or Concerns

Large scientific datasets are frequently produced from several research infrastructures who serve the archaeological research analyzing the various archaeological finds using the latest instruments (Matsui et al., 2012). Yet, the straightforward comparison of data between different laboratories has remained problematic, despite the gradual improvement of the analytical techniques towards higher precision and accuracy. The above is attributed not only to technical reasons but also to the variable database formats used in the individual laboratories (Hein and Kilikoglou, 2012).

Scientists who support the archaeological research conducting measurements with advanced scientific methods usually adopt protocols and follow certain research paths, which however are not adequately and/or clearly documented, rendering the provenance of the extracted scientific data hard to determine. In addition, a different methodology can be followed by the various research installations making the interoperability of the scientific data almost impossible. In the same respect, the resulting scientific datasets, which may include data of various formats (e.g. numbers, spectra, charts) and types (e.g. raw data, calculation results), along with any metadata (e.g. experimental method, instrumentation, date), vary or contain inadequate information preventing their re-evaluation or use for comparison purposes.

The above is also reflected on the fact that in many case studies it has been preferable to undertake redundant new measurements of reference materials rather than accessing analytical data on the same material generated by another laboratory (Hein and Kilikoglou, 2012).

Availability and accessibility of scientific data could be a thorny issue, since in the archaeological community, scientific data (results) are not included in datasets in most cases, but they are presented in reports (for in-house or informal use) or similar documentation (Bisol et al., 2014). Thus, results may not be reproducible, not necessarily because of error, but because the data and/or metadata are absent or insufficient (e.g. Alsheikh-Ali et al., 2011; Freese, 2007), or even lost (Vines et al., 2014). In most datasets created for the needs of the Archaeological Research, only the archaeological observations are included (e.g. dimensions of the object, estimated period, stylistic properties etc), while the scientific data, which would actually confirm or help the archaeologists to build theories about the past (e.g. age, provenance), are completely absent making the re-evaluation of each analysis in the future, in light of new or emerging knowledge, virtually unfeasible. In the same respect, important metadata, such as instruments and methods used, measuring conditions and standards employed etc. are rarely available. As a result, dependable comparison between data of the same scientific investigation method, but of different techniques (e.g. different equipment) and/or re-estimation of the precision of the measurement are hardly attainable.

However, accessibility to data of other research infrastructures should not be such an issue at present, since digitization of data across all domains in academic research and scholarship (e.g. Carlson, 2006; Borgman, 2009) has made them available more easily and distributed more quickly than ever before (Strasser et al., 2014).

Summing up the above, the major current concerns of the scientific datasets produced in the archaeological research are the lack of efficiency and diffusion of the scientific data and the need for additional metadata, which would assure the reuse of the produced datasets, namely the re-evaluation of the samples and the inter-comparison of the results among various laboratories.

As Strasser et al. (2014) state, in order to fully take advantage of such heterogeneous data, a streamlined workflow for collection, organization and publication of data is needed. Data management, namely proper documentation, is required in order to assure the value of the scientific datasets over time thus allow the long-term storage, and easy discovery and access of the data.

STRUCTURE OF SCIENTIFIC DATASETS

Needs and Challenges

The efficient usage of a scientific dataset has several requirements that a user should take into consideration. The most important is that the user must get acquainted with the available scientific methods which are used to support the archaeological investigation of a particular problem and /or question. Knowledge and understanding of the principles, requirements and type of data produced by the various scientific methods is a prerequisite in order to be able to understand the structure of the database and the nuances of the data (i.e., 'read between the lines'). Secondly, in order to successfully tackle an archaeological problem, the user should also learn how to:

§ interpret laboratory results/scientific datasets from an archaeological point of view
§ manage and read beyond the data (metadata and paradata)
§ incorporate laboratory results/scientific datasets into the investigation of an archaeological problem
§ design archaeological projects that make use of scientific datasets

Several issues/challenges regarding the scientific datasets in the archaeological research also exist and should be confronted in order to optimize the availability, accessibility and interoperability of the scientific datasets. First of all, such scientific datasets should compose an inextricable part of each archaeological dataset rather than an independent set of additional information. Along with the archaeological observations (for instance condition of a finding, dimensions of an object, estimated period etc), all the available scientific data should also be recorded in order to create a complete 'identity' record for all archaeological findings or the environment, which should properly be updated after new analyses and/or findings.

Scientific datasets are not created only for in-house use, but also aim at corroborating the work of other researchers as well. However, the use of different terminology and definitions may create confusion to scientists of different scientific disciplines, which produce data for the archaeological research. Consequently, one of the keynote challenges is to agree on common terminology and definitions. Even the definition of the term *'data'* may confuse the scientific community. For example, in the case of the determination of the chemical composition of a ceramic artifact by means of X-ray Fluorescence Spectroscopy, some would regard the concentration of the elements as data, while others would consider the unprocessed information, namely the acquired (utterly qualitative) spectrum, as data!

To avoid any further confusion in the present document the term *'Data'* or *'Scientific Data'* refers to raw data, i.e., results of every measurement directly produced by the various scientific instruments without any intermediate calculations. Also the term *'metadata'* as is used here, unless explicitly mentioned otherwise, includes also the *'paradata'* related to a measurement.

Metadata and Paradata

There is seldom a perfect, complete and devoid of any ambiguities and/or outliers set of data. Consequently, to ensure that data is not misused, the assumptions and limitations affecting the creation of data must be fully documented, meaning that besides the acquired data, appropriate *metadata* and/or *paradata* should also be considered in a complete scientific dataset. Metadata allows a producer to describe a dataset fully so that users:

§ can understand the conditions, assumptions and limitations
§ evaluate the dataset's applicability for their intended use
§ efficiently use scientific datasets in their research (especially when comparisons are attempted)

Few examples of metadata that could or should be documented in a scientific dataset are given below:

§ laboratory, personnel who produced/created the data
§ date(s) when the measurements/analyses were done
§ experimental method/technique used
§ instrumentation used for the production of data
§ calibration method-data and standards used

In the same respect, paradata (a.k.a. operational parameters/conditions and procedure) can also be very important for the certification, assessment of limitations, and 'reproducibility' of the scientific datasets.

Documentation of all the above and their incorporation in a scientific dataset may be more significant for research purposes, such as:

§ to compare the results and/or re-estimate the precision of the measurement (e.g. instrument and/or method employed)
§ to repeat the experiment (e.g. protocols/conditions of the measurement)
§ to recalibrate the measurement (e.g. reference data and/or standards used)
§ to use exactly the same method/conditions for new samples in light of new/additional archaeological finds
§ to determine the provenance of the extracted data (spatiotemporal information, such as who, where and when the measurement was conducted)
§ to evaluate and certify the interoperability of the data

Metadata Standards

According to the above, the adoption of a metadata standard seems imperative in order to assure the credibility and durability of a scientific database, since it would encompass only the necessary data and metadata devoid of any excessive information. Furthermore, the database should be structured in a way that could be expanded towards different kinds of information in order to permit inter-comparison among different techniques, towards the implementation of multidisciplinary studies (Hein and Kilikoglou, 2012). A metadata standard should meet several requirements and define (ISO, 2003):

§ mandatory and conditional metadata sections and elements
§ a minimum set of metadata required to serve the full range of metadata applications (data discovery, determining data fitness for use, data access, data transfer, and use of digital data)
§ optional metadata elements – to allow for a more extensive standard description of the data, if required

§ a method for extending metadata to fit specialized needs, since numerous scientific methods are used as diagnostic tools in the various fields of the archaeological research (e.g. dating, provenance, dietary studies, gene studies etc.)

Implementation of a metadata standard in the scientific datasets produced in the archaeological research would have many benefits, since it would (ISO, 2003):

§ provide data producers with appropriate information to characterize their data properly
§ facilitate the organization and management of metadata
§ enable users to apply data in the most efficient way by knowing its basic characteristics
§ facilitate data discovery, retrieval and reuse. Users should be better able to locate, access, evaluate, purchase and utilize the data
§ enable users to determine whether data in a holding will be of use to them.

Agreement on common metadata standards is vital for the scientific community which serves the broader field of the archaeological research in order to bring together and integrate existing archaeological research data infrastructures and facilitate their accessibility and exploitation by researchers. A formal standardized structure that provides a common and extensible semantic framework that any cultural heritage information can be mapped to, should be established. Such a modeling of information will assure the credibility and durability of a scientific database, since it will encompass only the necessary data and metadata, which along with their interdisciplinary character should contribute to the creation of an integral archaeological research infrastructure.

In this respect, several ontologies/metadata standards are available, which are adopted for various natural sciences. Few examples are the DIF (Directory Interchange Format) (Olsen & Chiddo, 2008), used for exchanging information about scientific data sets primarily for earth sciences and the ISO 19100 series (especially ISO 19115) for geographic information metadata (ISO, 2003). In addition, the CIDOC-CRM is intended to promote a shared understanding of cultural heritage information by providing a common and extensible semantic framework that any cultural heritage information can be mapped to. However, CIDOC-CRM defines how cultural heritage information can be exchanged and how semantic relations can be arranged, but does not define what should be documented (Schröttner et al., 2012). The development of an extension to this (CIDOC-CRMsci) with modifications and improvements has being initiated in the framework of the ARIADNE project (FP7-INFRASTRUCTURES-2012-1-313193) (e.g. Doerr and Hiebel, 2014), with the aim to:

§ assure credibility and durability of datasets
§ maximize the info with minimum requirements
§ establish the use of common terminology and definitions
§ provide the common denominator for all sciences and studies involved (i.e., facilitate the interdisciplinary character)
§ facilitate the building of an integral archaeological research infrastructure

Metadata Standard in Scientific Datasets of Archaeological Research

As already discussed, contemporary archaeological research composes several scientific disciplines and incorporates different measurements and analyses conducted each one with its own identity and scientific background (e.g. isotope analysis, TL/OSL dating, DNA studies, composition analysis of organic samples or materials etc). To establish a 'universal' standard that covers all areas and their individual nuances and special details seems extremely complicated and difficult if not impossible. As an alternative, a common denominator should be found, namely the minimum required metadata fields and dataset structure in order to adequately record and describe all (most) possible (scientific) measurements that may be conducted to serve as tools for answering archaeological questions.

Table 1 presents the common metadata fields required (according to the authors' opinion) in a dataset, independently of the scientific field they originate from, in order to allow the verifiable accurate and efficient use, interoperability, comparison, update and reusability of these datasets. The Table is based on standard 'best practice' procedures (GLP, ISO) followed by scientific laboratories, as well as existent and accessible scientific datasets (web and publications). In addition, the Directory Interchange Format (DIF) (Olsen & Chiddo, 2008), which is an approved standard recommended for use in NASA Earth Science Data Systems and provides a metadata format used to create directory entries that describe scientific data sets, has also been taken into account with some necessary modifications.

The required metadata could be divided into three levels, Project level, Object level and Measurement level metadata. Each one provides different information. The project level metadata mainly refers to information related to the archaeological site under investigation (where the samples were collected). The object level metadata provide information (mainly archaeological) and description of every 'object' (or 'sample' in general) to be measured/analyzed. Finally, the measurement level metadata is related to all available information about the experimental/measuring procedure(s) including any post-measurement data treatment. Based on the above a project may include multiple measurements of several objects (samples) found (collected) in the same excavation site. Although the more metadata the better, in most cases a certain number of metadata is enough to establish their usability for future purposes.

It should be noted that the compilation of ***Table 1*** was heavily based on the information needed for pottery dating and provenance studies since these are usually more involved, can be conducted using various methodologies and measurement techniques, and the respective data, by the very nature of these studies, are most often used for comparisons while the augmentation of these datasets is a constant pursuit of the researchers involved. The metadata included in ***Table 1*** should be sufficient to cover most other cases. However, due to the multitude of methodologies and measurements used in archaeological studies and the continuous enrichment of those, thanks to the advancements in physical sciences, the possibility of some necessary additions cannot be excluded. As a result, at this stage, no attempt has been made to suggest/provide a schema that conforms to or is aligned with other established schemata or initiatives (DCMI, CIDOC-CRM). It is the authors' opinion that this Table should be first updated and streamlined to cover the needs of as many as possible scientific disciplines (or at least the most used) and then propose a final schema in accordance to internationally accepted standards.

Table 1. Metadata fields that should be filled when archiving scientific data

Field	Description	Field importance*
	Project level	
Name entry	Title of the data set described by metadata	M
Summary	Description of the data set along with the purpose of the data	M
Keywords	Keywords that are representative of the data set	M
Language	Language used in the preparation, storage and description of the data	D
Project name	Name of the project	M
Project date	Date the project started	M
Location	Geographical area, where the object(s)/sample(s) was (were) found/collected	M
Site geographical longitude	Longitude of the Location	D
Site geographical latitude	Latitude of the Location	D
	Object level	
Object/sample ID code	The inventory ID of the object/sample	M
Object/sample lab ID (if applicable)	The ID of the object/sample as registered by the laboratory performing the measurement (if different than above)	M
Object/sample lab date	Date the object/sample was delivered to the laboratory	M
Batch protocol number	The protocol number of the batch in which the object/sample belongs to	D
Excavation section	The section of the excavation site at which the object/sample was found/ collected	O
Area description	Description of the area/environment where the object/sample was found/ collected	M
Object/sample type	The type of the object/sample (e.g. soil, clay, sherd, pollen, seed, other)	M
Object/sample classification	The 'category' where the object/sample belongs to (taxon, vessel type etc. depending on the object/sample)	M/D (depending on the object/sample)
Object/sample dimensions (if applicable)	The dimensions of the object/sample	O
Object/sample description	Free text describing the object (form, condition, colors, texture, etc)	O
Object/sample picture	Picture of the object in tiff or jpg format	D
	Measurement level	
Type of analysis	Dating, chemical analysis etc.	M
Laboratory_ID	The laboratory at which the measurement was conducted and the data were collected	M
Personnel	The person (researcher) who conducted the analysis and can be contacted for more information about the data and metadata	O
Preparation method	Description of the preparation/pretreatment of the sample (cleaning, sieving, acid digestion etc)	M
Analytical method	The method was employed for the analysis (for instance, XRF or AAS or… for chemical analysis, C14 or thermoluminescence or dendrochronology or… for dating etc)	M
Technique	The specific technique used (for instance, flame or graphite furnace in elemental analysis with AAS or fine or coarse grain in TL dating)	M
Instrument(s)	Instrument(s) used for the measurement (brand name, model and serial number)	M

continued on following page

Table 1. Continued

Field	Description	Field importance*
Instrument(s) details	Other instrument details (especially those that are unique for the specific instrument (s) used)	D
Start measurement date	The date the measurement of the sample started	M
End measurement date	The date the measurement of the sample ended	M
Measurement protocol	Steps and operational conditions of the measurement (for instance the SAR protocol for dating using OSL)	M
Calibration method and standard materials/reference specimens	Calibration procedure and/or the standard materials/reference specimens used	M
Other conditions	Description of specific experimental conditions not stated explicitly elsewhere but can affect the measurement results (e.g. optical filters used in TL/OSL measurements)	M
Software (acquisition)	The specialized or commercial software used to acquire the data	O
Raw data	Original measured values without any mathematical treatment	M
Results	Results of the measurement following any necessary mathematical treatment of raw data	M
Error	The estimated error of the measurement	M
Methodology (alternatively software used)	Methodology or commercial software used to produce the results from the raw data	M
Additional files	Images, spectra or charts corroborating the interpretation of the results	O

*M: Mandatory (when applicable), D: Desirable, O: Optional

POTTERY DATING AND PROVENANCE STUDIES

To elaborate on the above and better realize the identity and complexity of scientific data in archaeological research and the need of a concise and complete set of metadata, the procedure followed during a pottery dating and provenance study are separately described in detail below.

Pottery in Scientific Studies

Selection of pottery in dating and/or provenance studies (and in the majority of the scientific studies assisting the archaeological research) seems more advantageous compared to any other material due to the features they exhibit, which allow the evaluation of their initial state and the extraction of valuable information from their composition (e.g. Padeletti and Fermo, 2010). More specifically:

- they have a long history of existence and can be found in great abundance virtually all over the world
- they exhibit remarkable resistance to weathering and erosion along with tolerance through time
- they are non-perishable, although they may break, fragments (sherds) are virtually indestructible
- they are usually heated up to high temperatures (700-800 °C) during their manufacture, which is a prerequisite for their dating using methods such as TL

- § pottery have virtually endless shapes and decorations and multiple functions, were commonly used in everyday life and easily transported.

As a result, the scientific study of pottery can provide valuable information regarding their manufacturing method, which can be described as "an additive process in which the successive steps are recorded in the final product". Thus, significant knowledge about the past can be gained since pottery manufacture, like any other productive technology, represents a point where a cultural system interacts directly with its surrounding socio-cultural and natural environment.

According to the above, pottery represents not only a category of useful containers, but also a simple and convenient means of:

- § dating sites
- § tracing trade patterns (local and long-distance trade arrangements)
- § studying ancient technology (resource selection, forming techniques, firing strategies)
- § investigating settlement patterns and demographic factors
- § studying a variety of social aspects (dietary habits, ceremonial or ritual activities etc.).

Objectives of Pottery Dating Studies

In most cases ceramic artifacts are traditionally dated based on their typological development. However, archaeologists also seek for an independent chronometry of the artifacts based on physicochemical measurements. Dating determines the "age" of the object, which is an ambiguous term, since it could suggest the age of formation of the material, the age of burial and/or the age of other events, such as heating or bleaching (Wagner, 1998). Thus, different dates are determined depending on the method applied, even for the same object. In general, pottery dating studies can have various scopes and can contribute to the:

§ *Chronometric Dating of Unknown or Corroded Ceramics*

In cases where ceramic artifacts are not decorated, painted or bearing any stylistic features, or when they are severely corroded due to the burial/environmental conditions (e.g. high humidity in a cave), the archaeological observation is not adequate or capable to determine the exact age of the pottery. Thus, an analytical method is needed for their chronometric dating (an age in years).

§ *Chronometric Dating and/or Cross Dating of Archaeological Sites*

Pottery is widely used as a tool in chronology building. Its abundance, easy transportability and numerous shapes and decorations render it an important probe for delineating stylistic changes through time and for tracing cultural relation. Thus, ceramic artifacts are commonly used for dating other things, such as construction episodes, burials, occupation layers, etc., by its associations (Rice, 1987).

In several cases pottery can be found among other archaeological finds, such as human remains. In such cases, cross dating of the ceramic finds and the human remains for example, which are dated separately, may offer more robust conclusions in an archaeological study.

§ *Dating of Natural Disasters or Historical Events*

Dating of the ceramic artifacts can also help to determine or corroborate the time of natural disasters or historical events, such as volcanic eruptions, earthquakes, a conflagration etc.

§ *Relative Dating/ Authenticity of Ceramic Artifacts*

A ceramic object can also be dated in order to determine whether the object itself is a genuine antiquity or a modern forgery. The above is one of the major concerns for museums and art historians.

Scientific Methods Used for Pottery Dating

Chronometric dating yields dates in absolute time, in either calendar years or calibrated years. There are several chronometric dating methods available to archaeologists for dating archaeological finds based on suitable time-dependent physical or chemical processes that lead to quantifiable changes in the characteristics or properties of the material. A further prerequisite to the age determination is the coincidence between an event and the start of a time-dependent process (e.g. time of firing of a ceramic object), which is considered the time zero. The dating procedure actually determines the time passed since that event and the time of measurement. Three such methods, of varying usefulness and applicability, exist for ceramic materials: Radiocarbon, Archaeomagnetic and Luminescence (Thermoluminescence-TL or Optically Stimulated Luminescence-OSL) dating, each based on different principles (Rice, 1987; Wagner, 1998) (***Table 2***).

All the above methods involve additional complementary measurements for calibration purposes or the evaluation of certain parameters, that produce a large amount of data. Luminescence dating is mostly used for pottery dating purposes, because it is an absolute dating method with relatively few limitations. Thus, luminescence dating will be described hereafter as the representative method in the archaeological research in order to elucidate the scientific data produced during a pottery dating study.

Table 2. Methods appropriate for dating ceramics

Dating method	*Based on*	*Time-zero*	*Limitations*
Radiocarbon	Remaining fraction of $^{12}C/^{14}C$ due to the radioactive decay of ^{14}C	"Death" of the organic material (disturbance of the ^{12}C to ^{14}C equilibrium)	Organic matter must be present in the ceramic (included in the temper or organic residue)
Archaeomagnetic	Remnant magnetism of heated ferromagnetic minerals	Last time the material was heated above the Curie point (material dependent)	The object must be in situ and undisturbed since the heating
Luminescence (TL or OSL)	Accumulation of trapped electrons and holes in the crystalline imperfections of the crystalline compounds of the clay due to low-level ionizing radiation from natural radioactivity.	Last heating for TL or last exposure to sunlight for OSL	Presence of suitable minerals in the clay, heating temperature >400 °C

Luminescence (TL, OSL) Dating of Pottery

Luminescence dating is based on the property of polycrystalline materials to store the energy receiving from environmental radioactivity for long periods and subsequently releasing it in the form of light when triggered by suitable means (heat in the case of Thermoluminescence-TL, light in the case of Optically Stimulated Luminescence-OSL). Ionizing radiation continuously ionizes atoms in the valence band and electrons are moving to the conduction while during de-excitation they are trapped in traps at various energy levels in the forbidden band where they remain for a long period. With a proper trigger (heat or light) they can be released, and combine with a hole giving up light. Obviously, the amount of light is proportional to the number of trapped electrons which in turn are proportional to the total amount of radiation the material has absorbed. Thus, measuring the emitted light during heating or exposure to light with a suitable wavelength of such a material one can determine the total amount of radiation (total dose) the material has received in time.

The total dose absorbed by a material, in dating, is called paleodose. Assuming a constant rate of dose absorbed per year, the age of the material can be estimated by ***Eq. 1*** (Aitken, 1985),

$$Age = \frac{paleodose}{annual\ dose} \tag{1}$$

The time zero of TL dating in archaeology is a definite event, the firing of the ceramic. This event resets the "TL (or OSL) clock" since any amount of energy stored up to that point is released in the process. After that the material is exposed once again to environmental radioactivity emitted by radio-active elements present in the clay itself and the surrounding environment (for instance burial soil) including cosmic rays and starts to accumulate energy once again and build up a new TL (OSL) signal.

In TL (or OSL) dating measurements, a ceramic sample is heated to a temperature up to 500 °C or higher (or stimulated by light of a specific wavelength) which causes this accumulated energy to be released resulting in a weak, but measurable light signal, which is measured by proper instrumentation. This provides a measurement of the paleodose (total absorbed dose).

The most common natural radioisotopes are the potassium-40 (K-40), and those occurring in the decay series of thorium (Th) and uranium (U). These radioisotopes have half-lives in the order of 10^9 years, which results in a constant radiation flux. Measurement of the alpha-, beta- and gamma-radiation of these isotopes provides a measure of their contribution to the total radiation flux and the dose rate the sample receives as a result.

Various environmental parameters, for instance humidity, affect the amount of dose that is finally absorbed by the sample per year (annual dose).

It is obvious that the TL (or OSL) measurement constitutes only a part of a complex process leading to an accurate and reliable dating of ceramics. Various measurements with several techniques should be conducted to get the correct age, producing a plethora of various-format data.

It should be noted that both OSL and TL can be used for dating well-fired objects, since heating at a high temperature resets the clock for both methods. On the other hand, pottery fired at low temperatures are not suitable for TL measurements since they may have not lost all their original geological (prior to firing) signal, which could lead to an erroneous age overestimation. However, OSL measurement under certain conditions, could still offer a good estimate of their age.

General Methodology in Pottery Dating Studies with Luminescence

The methodology followed during pottery dating studies with luminescence can be briefly described with the following steps:

- § a small fragment of a ceramic sherd is subjected to a special treatment (cleaning and removal of the outer surface, pulverization and sieving) in order to acquire grains of a certain size
- § next, depending on the specific technique used, a procedure is followed (Zimmerman, 1971) in order to isolate the "fine" grains (1-8 μm) and deposit them on aluminum disks ("fine grain" technique), or "coarse" grains (50-300 μm) are selected and treated by HF acid to remove their outer layer ("coarse grain" technique)
- § then, the luminescence (TL or OSL) signal is measured in order to determine the "paleodose",
- § complementary physicochemical measurements (laboratory and/or in situ) are made in order to assess the concentration of the radioactive isotopes present in the sherd and the burial soil (from the excavation site) as well as other environmental parameters (for instance water content of the sample) that lead to the estimation of the "annual dose"
- § finally, from the above measurement the age of the sherd is calculated along with its estimated error

The above process is illustrated in ***Figure 1***.

Procedures and Scientific Data Sources in Pottery Dating Studies Using Luminescence

Based on the above, luminescence dating encompasses several physicochemical measurements, which produce numerous data of various formats. Calculation of the age demands the estimation of both the paleodose and the annual dose, which in turn is accomplished by means of various physicochemical measurements on the clay body of the ceramic artifact and the surrounding soil of the excavation.

As already discussed, the paleodose in luminescence dating is determined using either TL or OSL. In both cases the main purpose is to determine the "*equivalent dose*", namely the artificial beta-dose which yields a TL or OSL signal equal to the natural one. The "*equivalent dose*" represents the total dose that has been stored in the clay matrix of the ceramic due to environmental radioactivity (radioisotopes in soil and clay, cosmic rays) since its manufacture (the firing procedure resets the "*clock*").

The estimation of the annual dose is a more complicated process since it requires the combination of various measurements in order to determine the contribution of the different radiation components (alpha, beta and gamma) to the total dose absorbed by the ceramic object in one year. These measurements aim to quantify (directly or indirectly) and calculate the *internal dose* (mainly alpha and beta components emitted by the main natural radionuclides ^{232}Th, ^{238}U, ^{235}U and ^{40}K and their daughter products present in the clay matrix) as well as the *external dose* (mainly beta and gamma radiation components from radionuclides in the surrounding environment). In most cases, both internal and external doses are estimated indirectly through the determination of the concentration of the natural radionuclides in the object and the surrounding soil. Various methods can be employed individually or combined for the above measurements, depending on the desired accuracy and the measured variable, the most common

Figure 1. Flow chart of the process for pottery luminescence dating

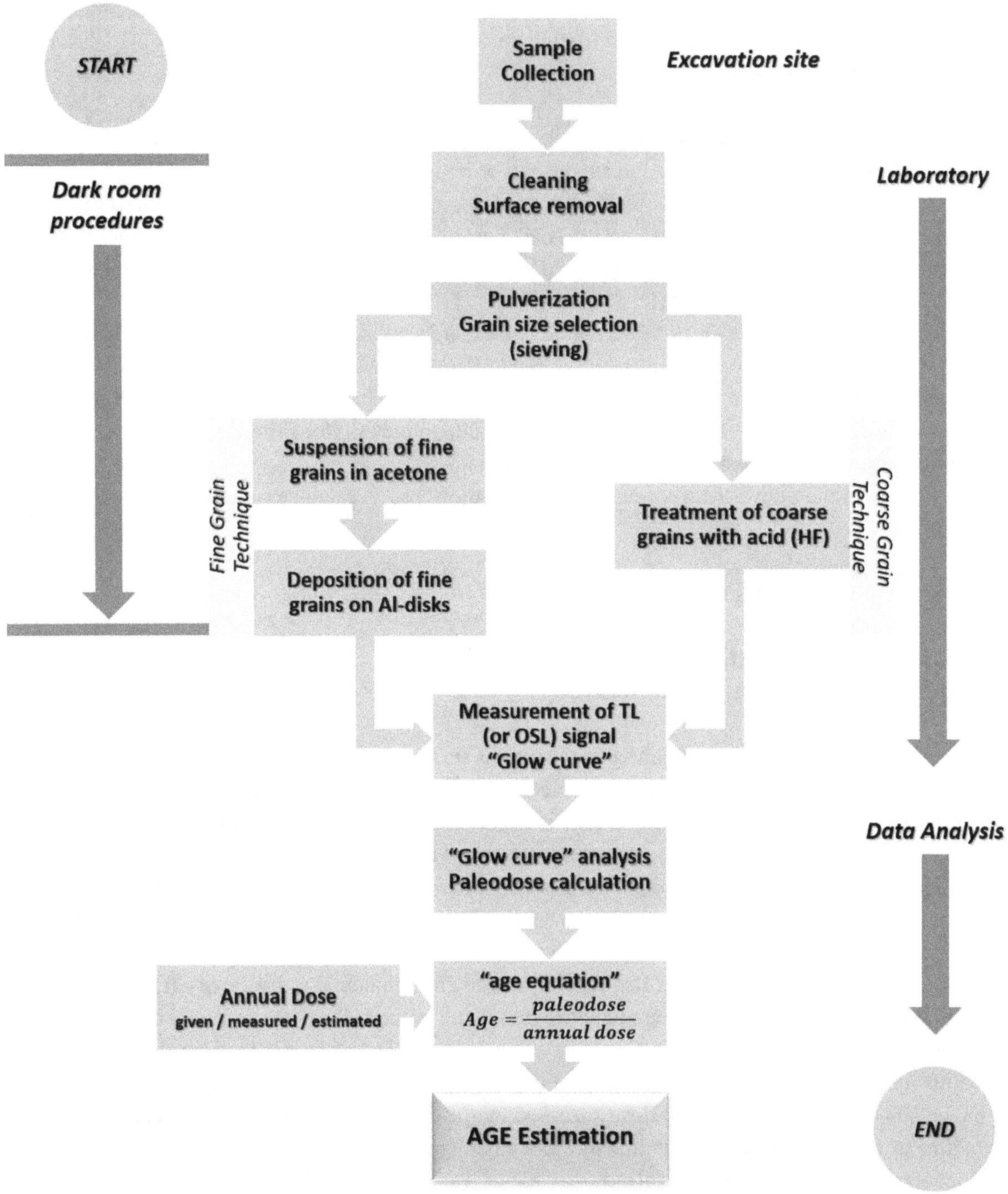

Table 3. Common instrumental physicochemical methods for the estimation of the internal and external dose in luminescence dating of ceramics.

Internal dose	*External dose*
X-ray fluorescence spectroscopy[1]	TL dosimetry (in situ)[6]
Atomic absorption spectrometry[1]	γ-ray spectroscopy (in situ)[7]
α-counting and α-spectroscopy[2]	γ-ray spectroscopy (laboratory)[7]
β-counting and β-spectroscopy[3]	β-counting and β-spectroscopy[8]
γ-ray spectroscopy[4]	X-ray fluorescence spectroscopy[9]
Neutron activation analysis[5]	Atomic absorption spectrometry[9]

of which are given in ***Table 3***. *Note*: The contribution of the *cosmic rays* to the total dose comprises in most cases only a few percent and is exclusively dependent on the geographical location of the excavation site and the depth of the sample location below the surface.

[1]total dose of K (indirectly)
[2]alpha-dose of Th and U and their daughter products
[3]beta-dose of K, Th and U and their daughter products
[4]gamma-dose of K, Th and U and their daughter products
[5]total internal annual dose (indirectly)
[6]total external annual dose
[7]gamma-dose of K, Th and U and their daughter products
[8]beta-dose of K, Th and U and their daughter products
[9]total dose of K (indirectly)

Objectives of Pottery Provenance Studies

A provenance study is one of the best examples of the synergy of various sciences and methodologies in archaeological studies (chemistry, physics, geology, petrography, mathematics, informatics, etc).

Provenance of ceramics, namely the answer to the question of where the artifacts were produced, is often a critical issue in archaeological studies, since it can illuminate various aspects of the civilization that produced them, such as trade routes and patterns, economic interactions between communities in a broader area and even of the technological level of an era. Using analytical methods several measurements are conducted to determine the chemical composition, physicochemical properties and structure of the materials along with the morphology and the physicochemical parameters of the excavation environment. The above, in conjunction with the statistical processing of the results, provide numerous important scientific data which represent a unique "fingerprint" for each artifact that can shed light on its origin, since featural variations between sources should be greater than within sources (Rice, 1987; Sterba et al., 2009; Tite, 2008).

Pottery provenance studies can have various scopes and the used methodology may involve additional steps or follow specific constrains. More specifically, provenance studies can aim at the (Kazakis & Tsirliganis, 2015):

§ *Identification of the Provenance of Ceramic Artifacts of Unknown Origin*

In such a case, the archaeological observation is not adequate to serve as a representative guide for the provenance study and consequently, the use of reference samples, namely samples of known provenance (ideally ceramics found at a workshop) is required.

§ *Classification of Ceramics of the Same Region*

In this case, the provenance study is conducted towards the identification of know-how and craftsmanship of certain production workshops in the same region or different geographical location. Such a successful study requires an adequate number of samples of each potential group in order to assure the credibility of the results.

§ *Confirmation of the Provenance of Ceramic Samples with "Suspected" Origin*

A pottery provenance study may also be employed to determine the origination of pottery which appears to have many stylistic similarities with major and "popular" ceramic categories with historically known production workshops (e.g. Attics in ancient Greece). Such a study can basically be regarded as an authenticity test, while it requires a reference group of the 'genuine' articles.

§ *Building Archaeological Databanks*

All scientific data produced during a pottery provenance study in conjunction with the archaeological data allow the full documentation of the ceramics studied and the creation of large archaeological reference datasets. As a result, new reference groups are produced, while existing ones can be expanded, improved and/or modified.

General Methodology in Pottery Provenance Studies

The methodology adopted during pottery provenance studies can be briefly described with the following steps:

§ a small fragment of a ceramic sherd is subjected to one or more laboratory analytical methods towards its qualitative and quantitative characterization and the identification of its unique fingerprint that allows its discrimination among others of different origin or its grouping with those exhibiting similar features

§ next, multivariate statistics are used to determine similarities and differences between the specimens, which ultimately lead to their classification into distinctive groups according to their provenance

§ final conclusions are usually reached with the juxtaposition of the laboratory/statistical and the archaeological data (primarily based on stylistic features)

Procedures and Scientific Data Sources in Pottery Provenance Studies

Besides the macroscopic visual observation of any stylistic properties on the under-study pottery, which is in principle carried out by archaeologists, several other laboratory scientific procedures are involved in pottery provenance studies which produce numerous data. Easily employed measurements of various physical properties of the clay, such as color (e.g. Munsell color system), density and hardness take place first, while more advanced approaches follow for the in-depth material characterization. The latter composes mainly the chemical analysis of the elemental bulk concentrations and the mineralogical investigation.

The *chemical analysis* is oriented towards the identification of the chemical elements constituting the ceramic fabric, present in major, minor or trace amounts, which could provide a unique chemical profile allowing ceramics made from the same raw materials to group together during the statistical analysis of the data. For this purpose, various methods can be employed (***Table 4***) (Kazakis & Tsirliganis, 2015) individually or in combination (two or more) in the same study in order to increase the validity of the results. Furthermore, in some cases one method may complement another, since accuracy and sensitivity of the various methods varies and in some cases they are element dependent. Consequently, one method may be used for the determination of the major elements, while a second one may be employed for the trace elements.

On the other hand, the *mineralogical investigation* aims at identifying the speciation of the geological components in the ceramic fabric and assessing the potential origin of the raw materials. Mineralogical study is focused on the analysis of the temper, which was added by potters in order to modify as desired the properties of the clay and the quality of the final product. The geological data and information acquired by such a study can increase knowledge regarding the selection and use of local and non-local resources by potters. As in the case of the chemical analysis, various methods can be employed for the mineralogical investigation of pottery, the most important of which are presented in ***Table 4***.

The above two approaches (chemical and mineralogical analysis) of ceramics characterization provide different kinds of scientific data which complement each other (Rice, 1987; Wilson, 1978). In most cases, the use of solely one of the above analyses is not adequate to determine with high certainty the provenance of the pottery studied (Mommsen, 2001; 2004). Chemical data alone do not identify fully the geological resources (raw materials) used, while petrographical analysis alone cannot account for possible phase transitions of the minerals due to the firing of the ceramics. As a result, the *state-of-the-art* in the

Table 4. Instrumental methods of chemical and mineralogical analysis of ceramics

Chemical analysis	***Mineralogical investigation***
Neutron activation analysis	Thin-section petrographic analysis
X-ray fluorescence spectroscopy	Scanning electron microscope
Atomic absorption spectrometry	X-ray diffraction
Electron microprobe analysis	
Proton-induced X-ray emission	
Scanning electron microscope + EDS/WDS	
Inductively coupled plasma-atomic emission spectroscopy-mass spectrometry	
Mossbauer spectroscopy	

provenance studies of ceramics dictates the adoption of an "*integrated*" approach, in which the above analyses are combined, while additional measurements of the microstructure and other physicochemical and mechanical properties of the pottery are more than desirable (e.g. Mirti et al., 1996; Moropoulou et al., 1995; Rice, 1987; Wilson, 1978). The amalgamation of all data obtained from the above scientific activities can offer the optimal characterization of ceramics which, aided by advanced specially tailored statistical methods (Principal Component Analysis or Hierarchical Cluster Analysis), will provide an accurate and distinct classification of ceramics leading to satisfactory, secure conclusions on their origin.

Scientific Data in Pottery Dating and Provenance Studies

According to the above, it is evident that both pottery dating and provenance studies combine many natural sciences which serve as detection tools to extract all possible underlying information that will promote the archaeological research. Regardless the approach adopted various scientific data are produced demanding different handling and processing. To elaborate on the above, ***Figure 2*** depicts various scientific data produced during a pottery dating and provenance study.

Figure 2 reflects the variety and complexity of the scientific data produced in general in the archaeological research, which can have:

§ Various ***formats***, such as numbers, spectra, diagrams, pictures, models and maps.
§ Various ***types***, such as raw data, calculation results, tables, plotted data and statistical data.

All the extracted data can be used either for a general approach to an archaeological problem or a 'customized' solution to a specific case. According to the above, the scientific datasets demand/involve a three-level interpretation (***Figure 3***):

§ *1st level → scientific interpretation (results-conclusions)*

In the 1st level, data/results are interpreted and evaluated strictly from a scientific point of view. Inspection of the various data (e.g. elemental concentration) and comparison between the values is made, allowing the extraction of conclusions, which do not have tangible meaning to the archaeologist, but provide the basis on which the 2nd level of interpretation will take place.

§ *2nd level → 'real life' meaning*

The 2nd level of interpretation involves the decoding of the scientific data and the conclusions of the 1st level into 'real life' meaning results. In this level, scientific data actually answer the archaeological problem and become of practical use.

§ *3rd level → implications for the specific archaeological problem*

In the final level of interpretation, the new knowledge gained by the acquired scientific data may induce implications for the specific archaeological problem and create new doubts and/or questions to the archaeologist (e.g. the "known" provenance of one or more ceramic samples may be put into question).

Figure 2. Example of scientific data produced during pottery dating and provenance studies

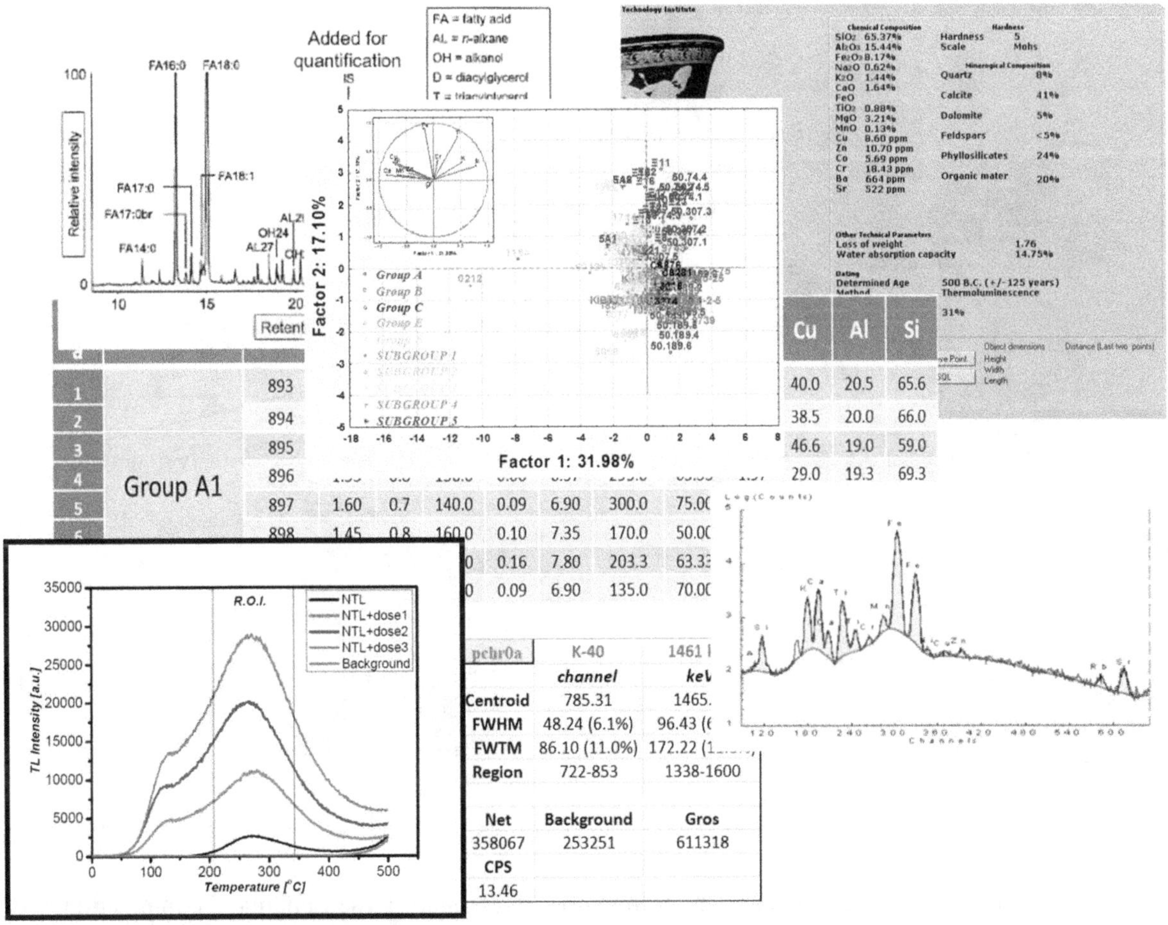

CASE STUDY: DATING AND STUDYING THE PROVENANCE OF POTTERY FOUND AT ANCIENT ABDERA (GREECE) SITE

Project Background/Scope

The site of Abdera, city of Democritos, was settled in the middle of the 7th century B.C. by colonists from Clazomenae and in 545 B.C. by the inhabitants of Teos. The site has undergone various changes during its history, from a prosperous city during the Roman period to a cemetery during the Byzantine period. According to the archaeologists, ceramics found in the site are both local and imported products, while their age may vary.

The scope of the project was twofold:

§ to date 25 ceramic objects (pottery) found in the archaeological site of ancient Abdera in Greece using Thermoluminescence

Figure 3. From the production of scientific data to their 2nd level interpretation.

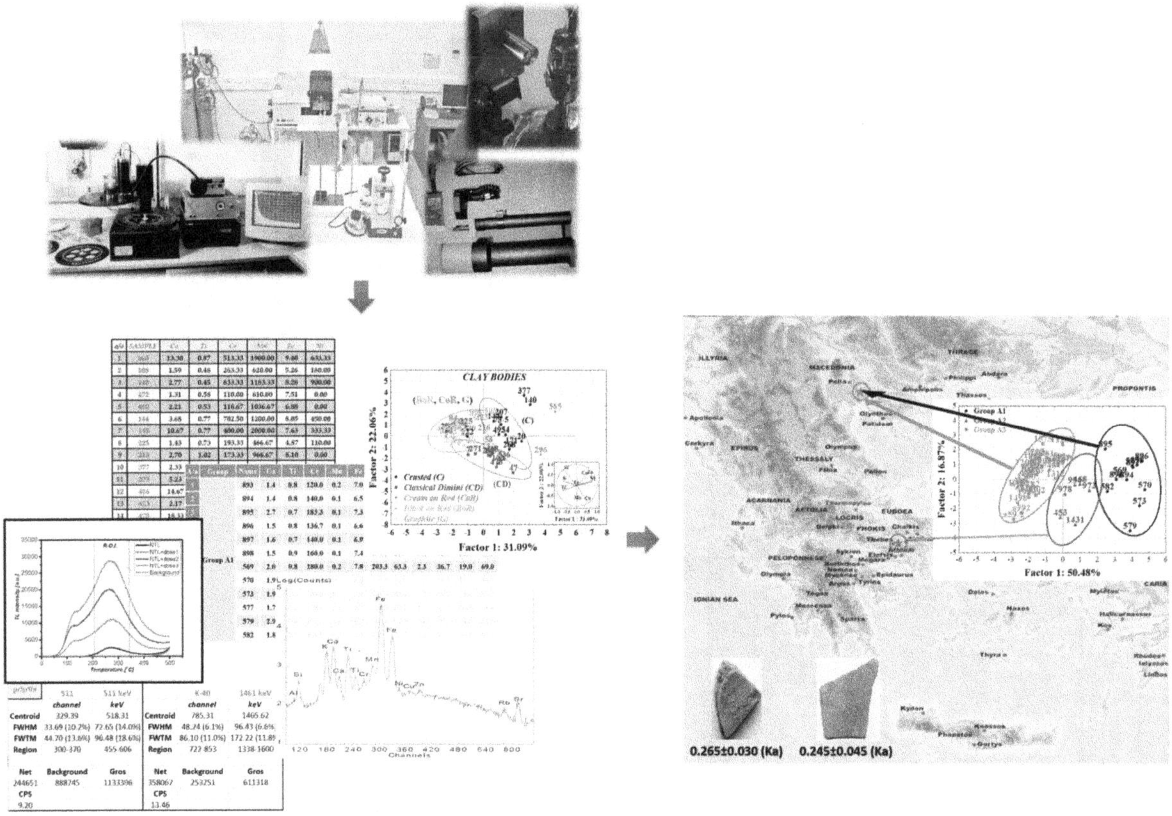

§ to study the provenance of the above ceramic objects comparing their chemical composition with reference material, namely pottery of known origin (local pottery originating from Abdera; 6 ceramic sherds in the present case).

Project Deliverables

Dating

For each object the age and the corresponding error were calculated following the established TL protocol along with all necessary complementary measurements as previously mentioned. The datasets which were selected for archival include:

§ Raw and converted in ASCII format TL-data file

§ Raw and converted in ASCII format data from every other measurement conducted for the estimation of the "annual dose" through the calculation of the radionuclide's concentration, namely from:

Ø Atomic Absorption Spectrometry (AAS) employed for the determination of ^{40}K concentration of both the objects (internal dose) and the soil (external dose)

Ø Alpha-radiation detection (thick source alpha particle counting) for both the objects (internal dose) and the soil (external dose) (determination of U and Th concentration)

Provenance

The chemical composition of each object (and that of the reference material) was determined by means of micro-XRF spectroscopy and the concentration of all major, minor and trace elements was calculated. Statistical analysis of the results shed light on their provenance. The datasets selected for archival encompass:

§ Raw and converted in ASCII format micro-XRF-data files (along with produced spectra)

Archival Metadata Example

In order to present an example of a complete metadata set, one of the analyzed objects was selected. Metadata of the Project level are filled once, since they refer to the archaeological site and are common for all objects of the project. On the other hand, the rest of the metadata (object and measurement level) are different for each object (in most cases the majority of the measurement-level metadata may also be common for all objects). All archived metadata are in given ***Table 5***.

CONCLUSION

Archaeology uses a variety of methods and tools to reconstruct the cultural past. Based on excavation finds, concerted efforts are made to shed light on the structure of the ancient societies, their environment and their socio-economical interactions. The above is mainly accomplished through the synergy of archaeology and various fields of natural sciences and informatics, which allow the extraction of information by means of advanced laboratory methods.

As a result, a plethora of scientific data (of various formats and types) and metadata are produced creating large and complex scientific datasets. The role of these datasets is twofold. First, they can be used either for a general approach to an archaeological problem or a 'customized' solution to a specific case. Secondly, they are very important in order to repeat an experiment, to validate the results in light of new measurements and allow comparison between different measurements.

However, such scientific reference datasets used in the archaeological research exhibit large variability among the various research infrastructures. Agreement on common definitions, purposes and structure as well as the establishment of standards regarding these scientific datasets is a requisite in order to bring together and integrate existing archaeological research data infrastructures and to facilitate their accessibility and exploitation by researchers.

In this respect, several ontologies/metadata standards are available, which are adopted for various natural sciences, however, the establishment of a 'universal' standard that would cover all disciplines is extremely complicated and difficult. As an alternative, a simplified dataset structure including the minimum required metadata fields is suggested in order to in order to allow the verifiable accurate and efficient use, interoperability, comparison, update and reusability of these datasets independently of the scientific field they originate. This structure was based on standard 'best practice' procedures followed by scientific laboratories, as well as existent and accessible scientific datasets (web and publications), while no attempt has been made at this point to provide a schema that conforms to or is aligned with other established schemata or initiatives.

Table 5. Metadata fields filled for the ancient Abdera project

Field	Entry
Project level	
Name entry	Dating and provenance_Ancient Abdera pottery
Summary	TL dating of 25 ceramic sherds (pottery) and study their provenance/comparison with 6 reference samples
Keywords	Ancient Abdera; TL; Dating; Provenance; m-XRF; AAS
Language	Greek
Project name	Ancient Abdera_2005
Project date	10 May 2005
Location	Site of Ancient Abdera, Greece
Site geographical longitude	40.934249
Site geographical latitude	24.975368
Object level	
Object/sample ID code	AB.ST.s(1)10
Object/sample lab ID (if applicable)	AA10
Object/sample lab date	15 May 2005
Batch protocol number	-
Excavation section	-
Area description	The object was found in a depth of 20 cm of relatively low moisture. No large objects (rocks etc) were found near it
Object/sample type	sherd
Object/sample classification	amphora
Object/sample dimensions (if applicable)	25 x 28 x 4 mm
Object/sample description	-
Object/sample picture	AB.ST.s(1)10.tiff
Measurement level 1	
Type of analysis	Dating (*paleodose estimation*)
Laboratory_ID	Laboratory of Archaeometry and Physicochemical Measurements, R.C. Athena
Personnel	Dr Nikolaos Kazakis
Preparation method	A piece of the sherd is removed. Then after removing few mm of the external layer, it is gently pulverized and then sieved.
Analytical method	Thermoluminescence
Technique	Fine grain
Instrument(s)	Riso TL/OSL reader (model TL/OSL-DA-15), S/N: RISO 105/00/10/b/OSL-B01-IR/830
Instrument(s) details	-
Start measurement date	1 June 2005
End measurement date	2 June 2005
Measurement protocol	Multiple aliquots
Calibration method and standard materials/ reference specimens	N/A

continued on following page

Table 5. Continued

Field	Entry
Other conditions	§ 16 aliquots were used § The Corning 7-59 & Pilkington HA-3 were used as optical filters
Software (acquisition)	Luminescence Analyst by RISO
Raw data	AA10_TL.bin
Results	AA10_TL.xls
Error	±8%
Methodology (alternatively software used)	Microsoft Excel
Additional files	-
Measurement level 2	
Type of analysis	Chemical analysis (*potassium concentration in the object*)
Laboratory_ID	Laboratory of Archaeometry and Physicochemical Measurements, R.C. Athena
Personnel	Dr Nikolaos Kazakis
Preparation method	A piece of the sherd is removed. Then after removing few mm of the external layer, it is gently pulverized. The powder is digested in appropriate acid mixture
Analytical method	Atomic Absorption Spectrometry
Technique	Flame
Instrument(s)	AAnalyst 800 Perkin Elmer, S/N: AS89582
Instrument(s) details	-
Start measurement date	6 June 2005
End measurement date	9 June 2005
Measurement protocol	Every sample was measured three times and after three samples the calibration curve was checked measuring a standard solution
Calibration method and standard materials/ reference specimens	6 solutions of different potassium concentrations were made / Potassium (K) standard, 1,000 μg/mL, in 5% HNO3 from Agilent
Other conditions	-
Software (acquisition)	WinLab32 for AA Analyst 800
Raw data	AA10_AAS_sherd-potassium.sif
Results	AA10_AAS_sherd-potassium.xls
Error	±3%
Methodology (alternatively software used)	Microsoft Excel
Additional files	-
Measurement level 3	
Type of analysis	Chemical analysis (*potassium concentration in the surrounding soil*)
Laboratory_ID	Laboratory of Archaeometry and Physicochemical Measurements, R.C. Athena
Personnel	Dr Nikolaos Kazakis
Preparation method	An amount of the soil of various grains pulverized. The powder is then digested in appropriate acid mixture
Analytical method	Atomic Absorption Spectrometry
Technique	Flame
Instrument(s)	AAnalyst 800 Perkin Elmer, S/N: AS89582
Instrument(s) details	-

continued on following page

Table 5. Continued

Field	Entry
Start measurement date	13 June 2005
End measurement date	17 June 2005
Measurement protocol	Every sample was measured three times and after three samples the calibration curve was checked measuring a standard solution
Calibration method and standard materials/ reference specimens	6 solutions of different potassium concentrations were made / Potassium (K) standard, 1,000 μg/mL, in 5% HNO3 from Agilent
Other conditions	-
Software (acquisition)	WinLab32 for AA Analyst 800
Raw data	AA10_AAS_soil-potassium.sif
Results	AA10_AAS_soil-potassium.xls
Error	±3%
Methodology (alternatively software used)	Microsoft Excel
Additional files	-
Measurement level 4	
Type of analysis	Alpha-radiation detection (*uranium and thorium concentration in the object*)
Laboratory_ID	Laboratory of Archaeometry and Physicochemical Measurements, R.C. Athena
Personnel	Dr Nikolaos Kazakis
Preparation method	A piece of the sherd is removed. Then after removing few mm of the external layer, it is pulverized. Then few grams of the grains are inserted in the special cell
Analytical method	Thick source alpha counting (TSAC)
Technique	ZnS(Ag) film detectors
Instrument(s)	ELSEC 7286 Low Level Alpha Counter, S/N: EL542A2
Instrument(s) details	-
Start measurement date	20 June 2005
End measurement date	23 June 2005
Measurement protocol	Measurement period was 3600 s and lasted 48 periods
Calibration method and standard materials/ reference specimens	Sand 109A
Other conditions	-
Software (acquisition)	Custom made
Raw data	AA10_AAS_sherd-U-Th.txt
Results	AA10_AAS_sherd-U-Th.xls
Error	±8%
Methodology (alternatively software used)	Microsoft Excel
Additional files	-
Measurement level 5	
Type of analysis	Alpha-radiation detection (*uranium and thorium concentration in the surrounding soil*)
Laboratory_ID	Laboratory of Archaeometry and Physicochemical Measurements, R.C. Athena
Personnel	Dr Nikolaos Kazakis
Preparation method	No special preparation. An amount of the soil of various grains is inserted in the special cell

continued on following page

Table 5. Continued

Field	Entry
Analytical method	Thick source alpha counting (TSAC)
Technique	ZnS(Ag) film detectors
Instrument(s)	ELSEC 7286 Low Level Alpha Counter, S/N: EL542A2
Instrument(s) details	-
Start measurement date	20 June 2005
End measurement date	23 June 2005
Measurement protocol	Measurement period was 3600 s and lasted 48 periods
Calibration method and standard materials/ reference specimens	Standard Sand 109A
Other conditions	-
Software (acquisition)	Custom made
Raw data	AA10_AAS_soil-U-Th.txt
Results	AA10_AAS_soil-U-Th.xls
Error	±8%
Methodology (alternatively software used)	Microsoft Excel
Additional files	-
Measurement level 6	
Type of analysis	Chemical analysis (*for provenance*)
Laboratory_ID	Laboratory of Archaeometry and Physicochemical Measurements, R.C. Athena
Personnel	Dr Nikolaos Kazakis
Preparation method	The external layer of the edge of the sherd, a few micrometres deep, was carefully removed from an area of 0.5–1.0 mm (diameter) from the surface using a drill
Analytical method	Micro-XRF
Technique	N/A
Instrument(s)	SPECTRO, COPRA model
Instrument(s) details	-
Start measurement date	27 June 2005
End measurement date	30 June 2005
Measurement protocol	N/A
Calibration method and standard materials/ reference specimens	Standard SARM69
Other conditions	-
Software (acquisition)	WinAxil by Canberra
Raw data	AA10_XRF.smp
Results	AA10_XRF.xls
Error	±8%-18%
Methodology (alternatively software used)	Microsoft Excel
Additional files	AA10_XRF.wax (spectrum)

Due to the multitude of methodologies and measurements used in archaeological studies the possibility of some necessary additions to the suggested structure cannot be excluded. These additions and the finalization of this structure with its compliance to international standards is an on-going work that requires the collaboration of specialized interested parties.

REFERENCES

Aitken, M. J. (1985). *Thermoluminescence Dating*. Orlando, FL: Academic Press.

Alsheikh-Ali, A., Qureshi, W., Al-Mallah, M. H., & Ioannidis, J. P. A. (2011). Public availability of published research data in high-impact journals. *PLoS One*, *6*(9), e24357. doi:10.1371/journal.pone.0024357 PMID:21915316

Bisol, G. D., Anagnostou, P., Capocasa, M., Bencivelli, S., Cerroni, A., Contreras, J., ... Boulton, G. (2014). Perspectives on Open Science and scientific data sharing: An interdisciplinary workshop. *Journal of Anthropological Sciences*, *92*, 179–200. PMID:25020017

Borgman, C. (2009). The digital future is now: A call to action for the humanities. *Digital Humanities Quarterly*, *3*(4).

Buko, A. (1984). Problems and research prospects in the determination of the provenance of pottery. *World Archaeology*, *15*(3), 348–365. doi:10.1080/00438243.1984.9979909

Carlson, S. (2006). Lost in a sea of science data. *The Chronicle of Higher Education*, *52*(42), A35.

Doerr, M., & Hiebel, G. (2014). *Developing common European archaeological concepts through extending the CIDOC CRM within ARIADNE*. Retrieved June, 2015, from http://www.ariadne-infrastructure.eu/content/download/1844/10313/version/1/file/CHNT-2013_04_GHiebel-MDoerr_cidoc-crm_archaeo-extensions_20131113.pdf

Freese, J. (2007). Replication standards for quantitative social science. *Sociological Methods & Research*, *36*(2), 153–172. doi:10.1177/0049124107306659

Harding, D. W. (1994). Charles Francis Christopher Hawkes 1905-1992. *Proceedings of the British Academy*, *84*, 323–344.

Hein, A., & Kilikoglou, V. (2012). ceraDAT-Prototype of a web-based relational database for archaeological ceramics. *Archaeometry*, *54*(2), 30–243. doi:10.1111/j.1475-4754.2011.00618.x

International Organization for Standardization. (2003). *ISO 19115: Geographic information - Metadata*. Retrieved June, 2015, from ftp://podaac.jpl.nasa.gov/misc/outgoing/ed/pre_2013/GHRSST_metadata/ISO%2019115%20.pdf

Kazakis, N. A., & Tsirliganis, N. C. (2015). Provenance of ceramics: Methods and Practices. In A. Sarris (Ed.), *Best Practices of GeoInformatic Technologies for the Mapping of Archaeolandscapes* (pp. 241–252). Oxford, UK: Archaeopress.

Matsui, Y., Gidding, A., Levy, Th. E., Kuester, F., & DeFanti, T. A. (2012). ArchaeoSTOR Map: Publishing Archaeological Geodata on the Web. *COM.Geo '12 Proceedings of the 3rd International Conference on Computing for Geospatial Research and Applications.* 10.1145/2345316.2345355

Mirti, P., Casoli, A., & Calzetti, L. (1996). Technology of production of fine pottery excavated on a western Greek site investigated by scanning electron microscopy coupled with energy-dispersive X-ray detection. *X-Ray Spectrometry, 25*(3), 103–109. doi:10.1002/(SICI)1097-4539(199605)25:3<103::AID-XRS151>3.0.CO;2-V

Mommsen, H. (2001). Provenance determination of pottery by trace element analysis: Problems, solutions and applications. *Journal of Radioanalytical and Nuclear Chemistry, 247*(3), 657–662. doi:10.1023/A:1010675720262

Mommsen, H. (2004). Short note: Provenancing of pottery-The need for an integrated approach? *Archaeometry, 46*(2), 267–271. doi:10.1111/j.1475-4754.2004.00156.x

Moropoulou, A., Bakolas, A., & Bisbikou, K. (1995). Thermal analysis as a method of characterizing ancient ceramic technologies. *Thermochimica Acta, 269-270*, 743–753. doi:10.1016/0040-6031(95)02570-7

Olsen, L., & Chiddo, C. (2008). *Directory Interchange Format (DIF) Standard.* Retrieved June, 2015, from https://earthdata.nasa.gov/files/ESDS-RFC-012v1.pdf

Padeletti, G., & Fermo, P. (2010). A scientific approach to the attribution problem of renaissance ceramic productions based on chemical and mineralogical markers. *Applied Physics. A, Materials Science & Processing, 100*(3), 771–784. doi:10.100700339-010-5689-x

Rice, P. M. (1987). *Pottery Analysis: A Sourcebook.* Chicago: The University of Chicago Press.

Schröttner, M., Havemann, S., Theodoridou, M., Doerr, M., & Fellner, D. W. (2012). A generic approach for generating cultural heritage metadata. *EuroMed'12 Proceedings of the 4th international conference on Progress in Cultural Heritage Preservation.* 10.1007/978-3-642-34234-9_23

Sterba, J. H., Mommsen, H., Steinhauser, G., & Bichler, M. (2009). The influence of different tempers on the composition of pottery. *Journal of Archaeological Science, 36*(7), 1582–1589. doi:10.1016/j.jas.2009.03.022

Strasser, C., Kunze, J., Abrams, S., & Cruse, P. (2014). DataUp: A tool to help researchers describe and share tabular data. *F1000 Research, 3*, 6. doi:10.12688/f1000research.3-6.v2 PMID:25653834

Tite, M. S. (2008). Ceramic Production, Provenance and Use-A Review. *Archaeometry, 50*(2), 216–231. doi:10.1111/j.1475-4754.2008.00391.x

Vines, T. H., Albert, A. Y., Andrew, R. L., Debarre, F., Bock, D. G., Franklin, M. T., ... Rennison, D. J. (2014). The availability of research data declines rapidly with article age. *Current Biology, 24*(1), 94–97. doi:10.1016/j.cub.2013.11.014 PMID:24361065

Wagner, G. A. (1998). *Age Determination of Young Rocks and Artifacts – Physical and Chemical Clocks in Quarternary Geology and Archaeology*. Berlin: Springer.

Wilson, A. L. (1978). Elemental Analysis of Pottery in the Study of its Provenance: A Review. *Journal of Archaeological Science*, *5*(3), 219–236. doi:10.1016/0305-4403(78)90041-9

Zimmerman, D. W. (1971). Thermoluminescent dating using fine grains from pottery. *Archaeometry*, *13*(1), 29–52. doi:10.1111/j.1475-4754.1971.tb00028.x

Chapter 5
Exploiting Cross-Reality Technologies for Cultural Heritage Dissemination

Chairi Kiourt
https://orcid.org/0000-0001-8501-8899
Athena – Research and Innovation Center in Information, Communication, and Knowledge Technologies, Greece

Helena G. Theodoropoulou
https://orcid.org/0000-0002-5896-0739
Athena – Research and Innovation Center in Information, Communication, and Knowledge Technologies, Greece

Anestis Koutsoudis
Athena – Research and Innovation Center in Information, Communication, and Knowledge Technologies, Greece

Jorgos Alexis Ioannakis
Athena – Research and Innovation Center in Information, Communication, and Knowledge Technologies, Greece

George Pavlidis
Athena – Research and Innovation Center in Information, Communication, and Knowledge Technologies, Greece

Dimitris Kalles
https://orcid.org/0000-0003-0364-5966
Hellenic Open University, Greece

ABSTRACT

One of the most challenging tasks in cross reality environment simulations is the generation of realistic and attractive worlds. The continuous evolution of computer game industry has a dramatic effect on such tasks as younger generations have higher expectations and demands in terms of realism. Virtual, Augmented, and mixed reality-based museums allow the efficient dissemination of cultural heritage thesaurus and are considered a popular application domain for cross reality environments due to their broad appeal. One of their primary scopes is to enrich user experience by introducing intuitive means of interaction with artefacts while offering knowledge in a more pleasant way than most of the traditional approaches. This chapter focuses on the development aspects of realistic simulations of cross reality environments for cultural heritage applications. It covers aspects related to modern 3D graphics and game engines, 3D digitization, and modelling. It discusses on the combination of these technologies in order to produce realistic, pleasant, and educative environments.

DOI: 10.4018/978-1-7998-2871-6.ch005

INTRODUCTION

Realistic simulation has a prominent role in Cultural Heritage (CH) dissemination (Kiourt, Pavlidis, Koutsoudis, & Kalles, 2017). Virtual museums are environments that host *synthetic* exhibitions created to tell the stories of real artefacts in a similar to a real museum visit but in with richer context and a wider range of interaction capabilities. In the context of a real museum, this is achieved by combining exhibits and information in a well-designed layout and presentation style (Lepouras & Vassilakis, 2004). The development of virtual museums is based on contemporary technologies such as real-time 3D computer graphics, spatial sound and Cross Reality that are used to deliver enriched virtual presence combined with a more vivid and enjoyable experience. Although each one of the previously mentioned technologies aim towards discrete goals, *realism* and *response time* are considered common. In addition, the continuous development of Web services and computer infrastructures complemented by the increasing availability of computer game development platforms (also known as *game engines*), contribute towards a continuous release of serious games in diverse fields including entertainment, cultural heritage, education, artificial intelligence, sociology, military and health systems (Breuer & Bente, 2010). In a sense, serious games can be considered as an efficient approach for blending domain specific activities, like in cultural heritage and education, with gaming. By utilizing contemporary visualization and simulation technologies, serious games enhance the user's experience through photorealistic interactive environments (Van Eck, 2006). This form of stimulation is considered to be one of the primary factors for a successful user engagement, in which playing, assumes the role of the driving force that promotes concentration in the activity process and user encouragement for further self-improvement. Stimulation is largely considered by the scientific community as an appropriate mechanism to achieve the desired results (Rogers, 1996).

Jacobson & Gillam (2012) define Virtual Heritage (VH) as "*the use of electronic media to recreate culture and cultural artifacts as they might have been or interpret them as they are today*". While Virtual Reality (VR), Augmented Reality (AR) and Mixed Reality (MR) technologies, are frequently adopted in the field of Virtual Heritage, their capabilities are much more dynamic and powerful, such as blending 3D visual reconstructed CH elements with the real environment (Desai, 2018) (Kolivand, El Rhalibi, Tajdini, Abdulazeez, & Praiwattana, 2018). VR/AR/MR technologies allows archaeologists and experts to study directly on site and gives the opportunity to the general public to explore immersively and interactively points of interest (Haydar, Roussel, Otmane, & Mallem, 2011) without coming into contact with the real exhibits (Van Krevelen & Poelman, 2010). This is considered to be one of the most important steps towards the dynamic dissemination of CH elements in a safe way and without time, financial and geographical restrictions. Cross Reality (XR) technologies can capture a visitor's attention by enhancing their satisfaction from the produced experience and by deepening his/her understanding for an exhibit (by revealing hidden unknown stories). This key point creates a positive active learning experience for the user (Dieck & Jung, 2017). Canciani et al (2016), report that AR is applied in CH domain for the last two decades. Its first appearance in the Archeoguide application (Vlahakis, et al., 2001), installed at Greece's Olympia archaeological site, simulating ancient life and reconstructing ruined elements. Since then, AR/MR technology has been applied in various CH derived case studies with promising results (Higgett, Chen, & Tatham, 2015) (Střelák, Škola, & Liarokapis, 2016) (Martínez, Casas-Yrurzum, Vidal-González, Vera, & García-Pereira, 2018) (Boboc, et al., 2019).

This chapter introduces and presents some of the most important factors that should be taken into account when building realistic simulations of CH with XR technologies for dissemination approaches that apply to all ages (children, adults and seniors). The chapter covers the following subjects: a) Primary computer graphics techniques for building virtual environments, b) Popular game engines, c) Creation of photorealistic virtual environments and assets, d) Dynamic interaction approaches, e) Gamification aspects in XR applications. The chapter concludes on commenting on the impact of XR technologies in CH while indicating key remarks and highlights.

EFFECTS FOR ENHANCED REALISM IN VIRTUAL REALITY ENVIRONMENTS

In order for the 3D virtual environment to be more realistic, some real-time image effects are being used, which significantly affect the quality and efficiency of the experience and do not impose any additional hardware requirements (Yang, Dong, Alelaiwi, & El Saddik, 2015). Often those image effects are named as *Screen Space effects*. It should be emphasized that by activating real-time image effects that are being recalculated for every pixel of every frame per second, the system exhibits high computational costs, which are only diminished by intelligent algorithms and the usage of sophisticated graphics hardware. A screen-space approach is one that involves 2D images of objects rather than the 3D geometry (Jonghyun, Jae-Hyun, Changwon, & Byoungho, 2013). Generally, a 3D object or scene is represented in terms of geometric primitives such as vertices, polygons, edges, and surface patches. Graphics algorithms directly operate on geometric-space (also referred to as object-space) data to produce a desired result. On the other hand, image-space algorithms first rasterize the 3D geometry into one or more 2D images, and then operate on the pixels of these images. The rasterization step discretizes the 3D scene into pixels as visible from a given viewpoint. Each pixel in the image thus represents a finite region of the scene. Therefore, all the information pertaining to that region required to perform the rendering can be stored at the corresponding pixel location in the image, such as 3D positions, surface normal vectors, etc. In the following paragraphs the main screen space effects that contribute to the realism of a simulation are being presented.

- **Lighting, Reflection and Ambient Occlusion**: Lighting is a method for calculating the shading of a 3D object, by using the intensity, direction and color of light that falls on it (Iones, Krupkin, Sbert, & Zhukov, 2003). Generally, nowadays, in almost all 3D environment developments tools, such as game engines, there are two types of lighting techniques: 1) *real-time lighting*, in which lighting is updated in every frame being displayed, 2) *baked lighting*, in which the lighting is pre-calculated and transform to a static lighting effect by being stored on the texture map of the objects, producing what is called a *light map*.
- **Depth of Field**: Depth of field (DoF) is the distance between the nearest and farthest objects in a scene that appear acceptably sharp in an image or 3D scene (Yu, Wang, & Yu, 2010; Demers, 2004). In computer graphics the simulation of DoF is a common post processing effect that simulates one of the most notable properties of a camera lens, the limited depth of focus. In real life, human eyes and a camera can only focus sharply on an object at a specific distance; objects nearer or farther from the camera will be somewhat out of focus.

In order to simulate the DoF effect a method has to approximate the blur that would happen as if the lens were real. Practical implementations of the DoF effect can be categorized in the following approaches:

- § Forward-mapped z-buffer techniques
- § Distributing traced rays across the surface of a (non-pinhole) lens
- § Rendering from multiple cameras (also accumulation-buffer technique)
- § Rendering multiple layers
- § Reverse-mapped z-buffer techniques
    - ◦ **Antialiasing:** In signal processing *antialiasing* refers to various techniques to tackle the problems of *aliasing* in a any sampled signal. In modern computer graphics applications, antialiasing is usually referenced as an image effect. The antialiasing image effect is calculated in real-time, which gives smoother appearance of the graphics based on the difference of colored areas of the image (Franklin, 1977; Bineta, 2013). It can be defined as a technique to minimize the distortion artifacts known as aliasing when showing a high-resolution image in a lower resolution display. Practically, antialiasing means removing signal components that have a higher frequency than those that can be properly resolved by the recording (or display) device (Franklin, 1977).
    - ◦ **Motion Blur:** *Motion blur* is the apparent streaking of rapidly moving objects in a still image or a sequence of images such as a movie or animation. During recording of a single image, motion blur appears as a capture of the motion of moving objects, which may occur either due to rapid movement or long exposure. Obviously, this effect is the result of limitations of the recording devices to freeze-capture fast moving objects, or even slow-moving objects but under long exposure requirements. Motion blur can take any of three forms, including (a) *linear blur*, which travels along a single direction to a specific extend, denoted by a strength and an angle, (b) *radial blur*, which is responsible for circular blurring effects around a center and can be defined by a radius and a strength, and (c) *zoom blur*, which represents a zooming in or out motion centered at a point on the image place defined by a center and a speed (the strength in this case).
    - ◦ **Particle Systems:** A *particle system* (Reeves, 1983) is a system of a large number of elementary graphics particles having a specific appearance, sharing a predetermined formation pattern and following specific rules, which can be used to represent fuzzy objects of processes otherwise difficult or impossible to represent by a single model. Such objects and processes include highly chaotic systems, natural phenomena or processes caused by chemical reactions, such as fire (Nguyen, Fedkiw, & Jensen, 2002), smoke (Huang, Gong, & Liang, 2015), explosions (Yngve, Obrien, & Hodgins, 2000), water (Foster & Fedkiw, 2001), ocean wave (Hinsinger & Neyret, 2002), clouds (Gardner, 1985), fogs, snow (Tan & Fan, 2011), dust (Jim, Xiadong, & Wegman, 1999), electricity, stars and galaxies. In essence, particle systems are used to realistically represent fluids and gasses, or in general, objects and processes with highly dynamic behavior. Instead of using geometric primitives, in these cases particle clouds are being used to render dynamically changing volumes. Stochastic processes are used to control those objects' shapes and appearance, adopting the paradigm of stochastic procedural modeling.

GAME ENGINES

Since the early 1990s when really appealing computer game graphics made their first appearance, game engines started to be used as tools in many scientific fields (Harrison, 2003; Craighead, Burke, & Murphy, 2008; Breuer & Bente, 2010). Nowadays, a common approach and trend in modern virtual world applications for various domains is to adopt the technology of game development, the game engines; a simple comparison of contemporary available game engines is included in the following paragraphs.

Game engines are integrated software suites that efficiently use 3D rendering pipelines, special data-structures and speed-up techniques for visualizing texture mapped 3D objects, scenes and 3D worlds in real-time with modern graphics and interaction capacities (Harrison, 2003). The choice of game engines for building dynamic realistic virtual, augmented and mixed reality environments was guided by the numerous possibilities and advantages offered by modern game engines and it is not limited to the presented game engines in this study (Lepouras & Vassilakis, 2004; Kiourt, et al., 2015a; Kiourt, et al., 2015b; Kiourt, Koutsoudis, & Pavlidis, DynaMus, 2016). Game engines are being extensively tested for usability and performance due to the strict requirements of contemporary games. The manufacturers and many computer game developers provide components, algorithms, tools, guides and source code, so that end-users can efficiently create new content. An extensive user support provided by large game development communities makes development platforms even more attractive. Most of the game engine functionalities are managed and exploited via a GUI, for the convenience of developers, providing a more efficient development framework when compared to virtual environment toolkits that often require additional effort to manually provide functionalities such as user interaction (Cowan & Kapralos, 2015), avatar behaviors, collision detection and management, audio management, avatar-based virtual environment interactions, embodied autonomous agents and many other properties (Lepouras & Vassilakis, 2004). Almost all modern game engines provide cross-platform development, which ensures their utilization over a diversity of platforms.

Nowadays, there is a wide selection of 3D game engines available for potential use (Lewis & Jacobson, 2008). In the following paragraphs we present the basics of some of the most popular contemporary game engines that are currently available, including *Unity*[1], *CryEngine*[2] and *Unreal*[3]. We have collected all major advantages and disadvantages regarding these game engines as discussed in (Craighead, Burke, & Murphy, 2008; Sillaurren & Aguirrezabal, 2012). *Unity* is a 2D/3D game engine, which offers a wide range of features and a user-friendly GUI. One of its main advantages is the cross-platform integration. Each application developed in Unity may be efficiently exported in nearly any available desktop and mobile platform composing a powerful game engine. It supports 3D content derived from popular 3D applications like Blender, 3DS Max, Maya, CINEMA 4D. It offers limited 3D modeling functionalities based on primitive shapes, although it provides better landscape modeling tools. In general, every 3D model needs to be created in a third-party application. However, Unity boasts a large 3D content library where a wide variety of objects can be downloaded for free or be purchased. The Unity engine provides animation mechanisms with real-time editor, particle engines with their own dedicated editor, AI Systems, dynamic lighting and shadowing, water effects, 2D game functionality, networking and multiplayer functionality, integrated physics system, terrain generation system, bitmap image effects, audio/music systems and scripting using C-sharp, JavaScript and Boo programming languages. The *CryEngine* (Craighead, Burke, & Murphy, 2008) is a product of *Crytek Studios* and it has been used by *Ubisoft Montreal* in 2004 to develop the game *Far Cry*. The engine supports a number of features such as a real-time editor with a rich tool arsenal that enable the development of realistic games. Most of its development components are managed through a sophisticated GUI that also integrates the CryEngine Sandbox world editing system. The engine supports a vast range of currently available platforms and it is continuously updated to provide export functionalities to new platforms. Licensed developers are offered with the complete source code and documentation for the whole engine and its accompanying tools. One of the primary advantages of CryEngine is the solid designer tool, by which complex meshes may be created. The *Unreal engine* (Craighead, Burke, & Murphy, 2008) was developed by *Epic Games* in C++. The engine supports high performance rendering, advanced animation features and high-quality dynamic lighting, environmental effects, particle system, blueprint visual scripting, C++ scripting, Virtual Reality, AI avatar system, terrain builder, physically-based rendering, UI, level building, animation, visual effects, physics, networking, and cross-platform development. One of the primary advantages of the engine is its powerful particle system that can handle up to one million particles real-time visualization.

DYNAMIC INTERACTION APROACHES

The dynamic (real-time) and realistic interaction with CH objects, is one of the most important elements for an effective dissemination. In order to improve the performance of the realistic simulation and in order to deliver information of higher quality in a more intuitive way to the end-users, studies have shown that the necessary equipment for XR systems are (Carmigniani, et al., 2011; Bekele, Pierdicca, Frontoni, Malinverni, & Gain, 2018):

- **Displays** (Organized into three categories):
    a) *Head-worn (Head-Mounted Display - HMD):* Use a display system paired with a headset representing the recently emerging wearable augmented reality devices technology (Werner, 2018). Although, such systems may be cost prohibitive and sometimes cumbersome, they have the advantage of allowing the user to fully interact with the application's features, since "*both users' hands are free*" (Tahoon, 2017). Additionally, such systems offer the video-see-through or optical see-through visualization approach (Zheng, 2015; Bekele, Pierdicca, Frontoni, Malinverni, & Gain, 2018; Desai, 2018; Carmigniani, et al., 2011). An HMD usually is equipped with calibrated cameras and build-in tracking systems based on accelometers, gyroscope, GPS, Bluetooth and Wi-Fi sensors, optical sensors, offering high levels of accuracy and precision on detecting the user's viewpoint και ότι άλλο (Tahoon, 2017; Margetis, Papagiannakis, & Stephanidis, 2019).
    b) *Handheld display* (Carmigniani, et al., 2011; Angelopoulou, et al., 2011; Casella & Coelho, 2013) (Angelopoulou, et al., 2011) corresponds to XR applications exploiting portable devices such as smartphones, tables, etc.. Such systems allow the user to simultaneously observe the real environment visualized in its "natural" and augmented state (Tahoon, 2017). These devices use video-see-through systems that combine digital cameras, inertial sensors, GPS and a portable display (Bekele, Pierdicca, Frontoni, Malinverni, & Gain, 2018) to merge virtual elements within the physical world (Berlino, Caroprese, La Marca, Vocaturo, & Zumpano, 2019).
    c) *Spatial AR (SAR)* implements either *Stationary display (optical projection system)* (Tahoon, 2017) or the emerging technology of *Holographic AR* (Microsoft Hololens[4] is such an example). *Stationary display (optical projection system)* (Carmigniani, et al., 2011) has the ability to

augment a large area and illustrate it to many people at the same time, allowing collaboration and restoring specific spatial attributes such as colors without touching the structure. Its operation is based on a set of video projection devices and desktop displays or advanced 3D spatial displays (Tahoon, 2017).

- **Computing Devices***:* Desktops, laptops and portables devices such as smartphones and tablets are being used to run the required XR systems. Considering the high computational demands (processing power, speed and memory capacity) (Carmigniani, et al., 2011), the need for a state-of-the-art hardware system is a prerequisite. Generally, mobile devices are considered to be the future of XR technology in CH. They combine high levels of portability due to their small size, build-in position and orientation tracking sensors, high-resolution displays and as with all similar computational devices they are continuously improved in terms of processing performance and memory size (Bekele, Pierdicca, Frontoni, Malinverni, & Gain, 2018).
- **Tracking Devices***:* Usually, the devices for the tracking camera pose procedure are sensors (electromagnetic, acoustic, inertial (accelerometer, gyroscope, magnetometer)) and cameras, operating independently or in a synergetic (hybrid) way (Bekele, Pierdicca, Frontoni, Malinverni, & Gain, 2018). Representative studies using various tracking devices are (Schnädelbach, et al., 2002; Seo, Kim, Park, & Park, 2010; Caggianese, Neroni, & Gallo, 2014).
- **Input Devices***:* According to Bekele et al. (2018) there is a wide range of devices that enable users to interact with a system include data gloves, gesture sensors (e.g. Leap Motion), wearable haptic sensors, gamepads, joysticks, mice, wands, microphones and touch screens. The input device approach that is going to be used in an AR/MR application is correlated to the previously selected system and visualization approach (display device). For instance, if the system is going to implement a Handheld Mobile Augmented Reality (MAR) application, the most applicable input device would be a touchscreen.

One of the crucial issues when introducing XR technology in the CH domain is the development of suitable techniques for intuitive human-computer interaction. Carmigniani, et al. (2011) and Bekele et al. (2018), organize interaction interfaces into the following:

- **Tangible**: implements direct manipulation of data through real objects. The interaction metaphor can be a physical input device, or the same real object that is being augmented.
- **Collaborative**: combines multiple display systems for multiple users to support shared activities, both remotely or collocated (Reitmayr & Schmalstieg, 2004; Carmigniani, et al., 2011).
- **Device Based**: are systems exploiting haptic, conventional devices (mouse, gamepad, joystick, wand, etc.) or sensor device-based interaction interfaces, allowing users to interact with the environment. Sensors based system exploit gestures, speech, and gaze in order to establish a more natural interaction process (Bekele, Pierdicca, Frontoni, Malinverni, & Gain, 2018) between users and the environment. Devices like Leap Motion give the opportunity to user to manipulate or interact with the virtual context by using hand gestures (Diaconescu, Popovici, & Popovici, 2019).
- **Hybrid**: are the interfaces which support the combination of different devices (conventional or sensors) and/or different interaction techniques for one or multiple users.

RECONSTRUCTION OF THREE-DIMENSIONAL (3D) ENVIRONMENTS

An integral part of a realistic simulation for CH applications is the environment, in the form of any cultural object, site, architectural complex, or any other form of tangible material object that conveys the story to be told. *Reconstruction* is the keyword for the creation of the 3D digital counterpart of a real-world cultural object. The reconstruction of 3D environments is based on two entirely distinctive methods: (a) *3D modeling* of objects, which is the process of developing a mathematical (graphical) representation of any 3D surface of an object via specialized software, such as Autodesk 3DS MAX, Blender; (b) *3D digitization* of objects, which is the process of capturing the shape and appearance of real objects using geometric and spectral measurements. In practice, in many cases those two methods are used in combination and the results are impressive (in terms of rendering realism).

3D modeling is an entirely digital process that takes places on a computer using specialized software. It requires high specialization in using such software, and, in particularly demanding applications – like in CH reconstruction – 3D modeling requires the participation of domain experts. *Obviously, 3D modeling is more of an artist's work, whereas 3D digitization is more of an engineer's work.* 3D digitization is a process of taking highly accurate measurements using specialized techniques and equipment. Its purpose is to get a highly accurate snapshot of reality, having CH frozen in time. In general, it has to be conducted by digitization experts, although in some cases, the automation provided makes it easier for non-experts to conduct a simple 3D digitization task. There are several techniques for the 3D digitization of CH thesaurus, each of which with its pros and cons (Pavlidis, Koutsoudis, Arnaoutoglou, Tsioukas, & Chamzas, 2007). The process of *3D digitalization* consists of two steps, the first step is to collect the data (images, distances, sizes, etc.), the second step is to analyze the collected data and develop the digital replicas via specialized algorithms. Nowadays the most common 3D digitalization techniques include a number of methods usually falling into two main categories, namely (a) light-dependent and (b) light-independent methods. The first category includes (i) active and (ii) passive methods. In summary, Table 1 presents a list of the contemporary 3D digitization methods. Pavlidis et al. (2007) summarized the various parameters involved in categorizing the cultural objects in three axes, namely the *size and shape*, *morphological complexity* and *diversity of materials*. Unfortunately, there is not a single 3D digitization method to fit all digitization projects.

Structure from motion or SfM (Schönberger & Frahm) is one of the most widely used technique, since it is one of the most efficient in terms of budget requirements solutions, which does not require mastering any highly specialized skills and equipment. A camera, a computer and a software application that can be open source, like Visual SFM[5], can produce incredibly realistic models, but the hardware requirements increase when the quality targeted and the size and complexity of the objects increase. Figure 1 depicts an example of a reconstruction using the SfM method for a typical CH 3D digitalization project; the blue rectangles represent the resolved camera sensor plane for each captured photograph, and the small black vectors help identify the orientation and direction of the camera in the actual 3D space, whereas the reconstructed 3D model is clearly visible.

Table 1. Summarized list of 3D digitization methods

Category	Method type	Method
Light-dependent methods	Active methods The light is emitted and is being detected by the digitization system	Laser triangulation
		Time-of-flight scanning (or LiDAR, LADAR, range scanning)
		Structured-light scanning
		Shape from Photometry
		Shape from Shading
		Shape from Shadow
		Tomography (of any kind)
		Speckle photography
		Holography
		Microscopy (of any kind)
	Passive methods The natural ambient light is being used by the digitization system	Photogrammetry
		Structure from Motion
		Shape from Silhouette
		Shape from Stereo
		Shape from Texture
		Shape from Focus (zooming)
Light-independent methods	Topographic methods	
	Empirical methods	
	Contact sensing methods	

GAMIFICATION

Developers and administrators of virtual museums have already started to realize the potential of new technologies for the development of edutainment content and services for their visitors (Bickmore, Pfeifer, & Schulman, 2011). In addition, gaming for educational purposes is a significant and active research domain (Brown & Vaughan, 2010; Nicholson, 2011; Nicholson, 2012). This has taken either the form of game-based learning or serious gaming. *Gamification* is the result of applying game mechanics into diverse domains, in order to engage users and enhance their knowledge and performance.

The importance of *playing* has been emphasized in many studies from various domains. According to Brown & Vaughan (2010), playing is an archetypical activity that arises from primordial biological structures existing even before the conscience or the capacity for speech; as Brown & Vaughan emphatically stated it is not something a person decides to do.

According to Nicholson (Nicholson, 2011; Nicholson, 2012), gamification is nothing more than the use of specific game design approaches and techniques in various environments, in order to attract people in problem solving and to enhance their contribution. Nicholson (Nicholson, 2011) shows the distinction between *Play* and *Game* using a "playful" mathematical approach,

$$Game = Play + Goals + Structure\,.$$

Figure 1. A typical result of the application of SfM for cultural heritage 3D digitization

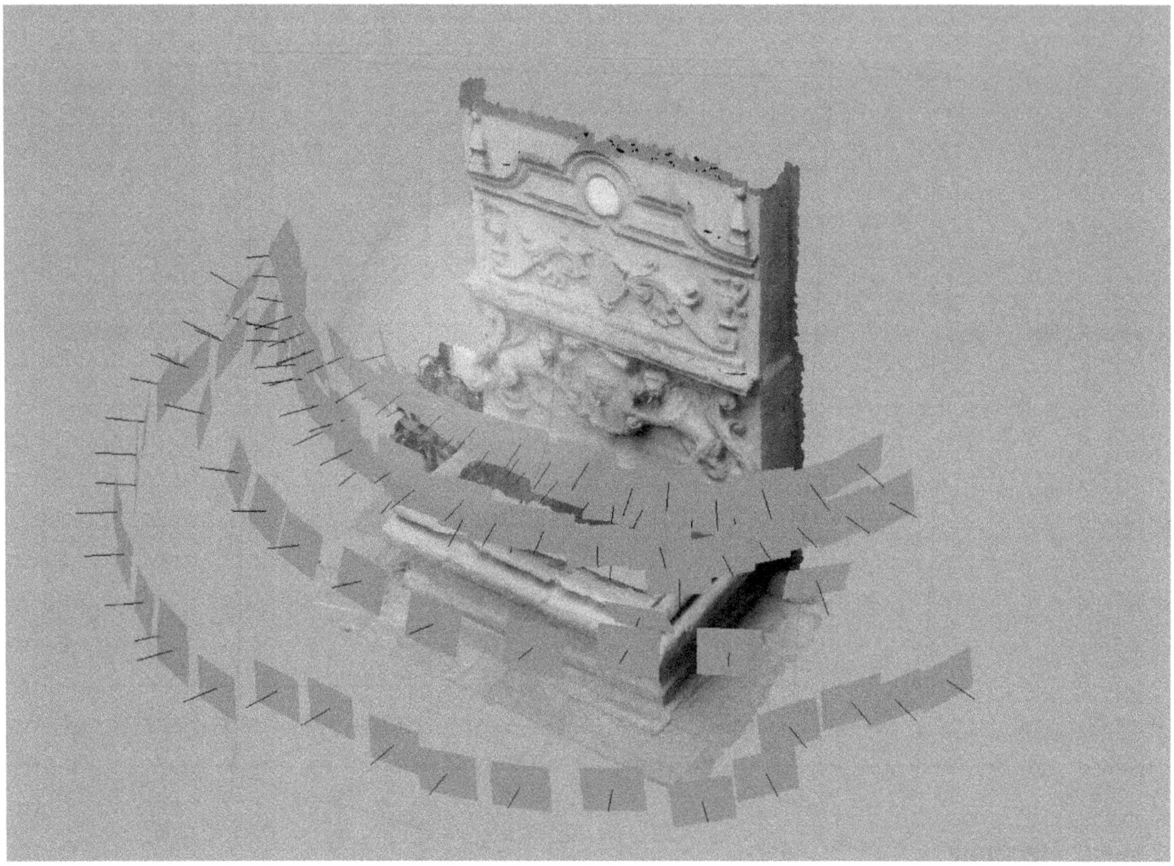

This equation tries to represent a gamification definition based on the meaning of the terms *game*, *play*, *goals* and *structure*. As in any equation, the terms may be rearranged, and interesting equations result, like,

$$Game - Play = Goals + Stucture\,.\,Play = Game - \left(Goals + Structure\right)$$

In the first variant, a *game without play* is not a play-centered activity and is largely used in gamification strategies like *BLAP* (Badges, Levels and Leaderboards, Achievements, and Points). A key strategy of meaningful gamification is represented in the second variant, in which by solving for *Play*, participants experience a true playful meaning in the underlying activity (Nicholson, 2012).

Gamification and its special application in education have a long history dating back to the 1980s. Today, with the advent of mature 3D technologies both in hardware and software implementations constitute a stable environment to successfully couple culture and education using technology and gaming as the catalysts. Various independent R&D efforts worldwide exploit this stable environment to deliver the next generation gamified virtual worlds for even more realistic and engaging CH simulations.

Cross reality technologies

Whereas a CH artefact is stored indoors or outdoors this is considered the main attribute that defines the type of the XR application (Bekele, Pierdicca, Frontoni, Malinverni, & Gain, 2018) (Carmigniani et al. (2011):

- Indoor implementations aim mostly at enhancing exhibits found in museums and other exhibition places. The give visitors the opportunity to interact with objects (Kolivand, El Rhalibi, Tajdini, Abdulazeez, & Praiwattana, 2018).
- In outdoor sites, reconstruction is the most common objective when applying XR in the CH domain, and system should be capable to handle weather and varying lighting conditions (depending on the time of day), environmental changes (change of position and orientation, occlusions and obstructions) (Kolivand, El Rhalibi, Tajdini, Abdulazeez, & Praiwattana, 2018) (Blanco-Pons, et al., 2019).

Numerous works utilize various XR technologies to provide solutions for history teaching and learning or to enhance actual museum visits. The notion of virtual museums and exhibitions has been introduced as an approach to overcome the limitations of the physical space and to provide a vivid experience to remote visitors (Tsichritzis & Gibbs, 1991). An overview of the available virtual museum technologies is presented in (Sylaiou, Liarokapis, Kotsakis, & Patias, 2009). The Augmented Representation of Cultural Objects (ARCO) (Wojciechowski, Walczak, White, & Cellary, 2004) was among the predominant efforts towards a dynamic virtual museum system accompanied by a 3D digitization technique to provide a framework to produce and exhibit 3D digital replicas of artifacts. ARCO was also, evaluated as an Augmented Reality Interface (ARIF) (Sylaiou, Mania, Karoulis, & White, 2010) by focusing on the user experience in relation to the technologies of ARCO. In 2004, Lepouras & Vassilakis (2004) presented the concept of creating virtual museums focused primarily on educational content and related services by using a game engine. This virtual exhibition space took advantage of the high visual quality of modern game engines. Pavlidis et al. (2006), proposed a Web-based 3D digital replicas management system with a dynamic virtual exhibition showroom. In addition, in (Pavlidis, Makarona, Arnaoutoglou, Koutsoudis, & Chamzas, 2008) a more advanced framework for digital museums has been presented, where a non-photorealistic digital replica of a real museum is used to demonstrate educational activities rather its actual exhibition, aiming at increasing the museum's visitors. Sookhanaphibarn & Thawonmas (2009) presented a 3D virtual museum developed in the Second Life 3D world engine. The virtual museum was equipped with an innovative intelligent guidance system that was able to provide a customized navigation route based on the visitors' preferences. In (Djaouti, Alvarez, Rampnoux, Charvillat, & Jessel, 2009) an interactive serious game is used for the promotion of a prehistoric heritage site. Anderson et al. (2010) reviewed the state-of-the-art of theories, methods and technologies utilized by serious games as CH promotion tools by showing case studies that exploit such technologies. Papastamatiou et al. (2010), presented a dynamic Web-based 3D e-shop system for commercial use, offering a WYSIWYG graphical user interface. Furthermore, Sillaurren & Aguirrezabal (Sillaurren & Aguirrezabal, 2012), presented 3DPublish, a content management system that was developed in Unity3D game engine and allowed the generation of dynamic 3D exhibitions. Furthermore, works like (Bellotti, Berta, Gloria, Dursi, & Fiore, 2012) focus on a generalization of the task-based learning theory in applications using smart mobile devices. In addition, Koutsoudis & Pavlidis (2011), proposed a novel approach for navigating within

Figure 2. Virtual Reality examples, left most image DynaMus, right most image MithTrek

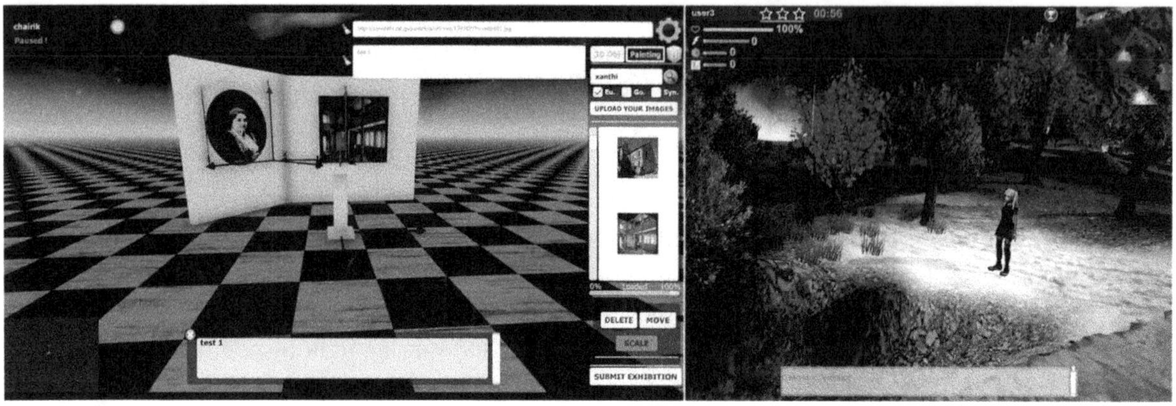

complex cultural scenes by exploiting content-based retrieval descriptors. Koutsoudis et al. (2012), proposed a content-based navigation framework for a virtual museum, based on metadata that describe the exhibits and thus providing a semantic similarity-based navigation. In (Doulamis, Liarokapis, Petridis, & Mialous, 2012) a serious game is proposed based on scenarios derived from the CH domain and attempts to enrich the player's knowledge by spreading a mystery in ancient times. In a more recent work (Bonis, Vosinakis, Andreou, & Panayiotopoulos, 2013) proposed a multi-user framework for virtual exhibitions that adapts to visitors' preferences. Recently, Kiourt et al. (2015a; Kiourt, et al., 2015b; Kiourt, Koutsoudis, & Pavlidis, 2016) have studied many aspects of interactive virtual museums mainly focusing on interactive 3D object exhibitions with dynamic open data content; the virtual museum was re-introduced as a cultural and educational tool that focuses on user-driven exhibitions. The leftmost image of Figure 2, depicts the DynaMus systems, in development mode, where the user creates its own environment with external resources. In (Kiourt & Markantonatou, 2018) a first person serious games was introduced focusing on Ancient Greek mythology and embedding a time-distorted history onto the present day's landscape in the center of the city of Athens. The game coupled the culture and education through an action/adventure gaming setting, right most image of Figure 2. Both systems, DynMus[6] and MythTrek[7], exploit the aforementioned technologies to enhance the realism of the environments focusing on more effective dissemination of CH.

In allmost all the aforementioned approaches, as in many other – a small list of virtual museums for educational purposes can be found at Sylaiou et al. (2009; Sylaiou, et al., 2016) – the main focus is to offer users pleasant and realistic virtual environments that try to simulate real museum conditions.

Augmented Reality (AR) is considered to be the technology that implements the act of superimposing digital objects (computer-generated graphics, images, models, text, etc.) onto real environments providing the user a composite view of both forms of reality (Brogni, Avizzano, Evangelista, & Bergamasco, 1999), (Haydar, Roussel, Otmane, & Mallem, 2011), (Panou, Ragia, Dimelli, & Mania, 2018), (Canciani, Conigliaro, Grasso, Papalini, & Saccone, 2016), (Higgett, Chen, & Tatham, 2015). Instead of replacing the real world with a virtual environment, Augmented Reality holds the ability to enrich the user experience by blending virtual components (objects etc) with the real environment (Tahoon, 2017), resulting a coexistance of virtual and real components in the same space (Kolivand, El Rhalibi, Tajdini, Abdulazeez, & Praiwattana, 2018), (Azuma, et al., 2001). Figure 3 depicts an example of AR application on CH elements. Information in the form of textual content (in Greek language) appear in

Figure 3. Augmented Reality examples based on smartphone technologies, the most top images present a single object description with specific points of interest, the bottom image presents specific points of interest in two objects at once.

front of replicas of two ancient pottery instances (Lekythos and Inochoe). The application exploits the object recognition feature of the Vuforia SDK[8] and the Unity3D game engine.

Mixed Reality (MR) focuses in the achievement of an ideal integration of both worlds (virtual and real), making the virtual objects spatially aware and responsive, behaving as if they were real (Fogliaroni, 2012). Thus, it is said that Mixed Reality can be considered as the evolution of Augmented Reality by adding visual and physical rules in the environment, which behave naturally. Considering those features, it can be stressed that the digital overlay and superimposition of information on user's immediate surround-

Figure 4. Mix Reality example based on low-cost equipment (smartphone and cardboard like glasses)

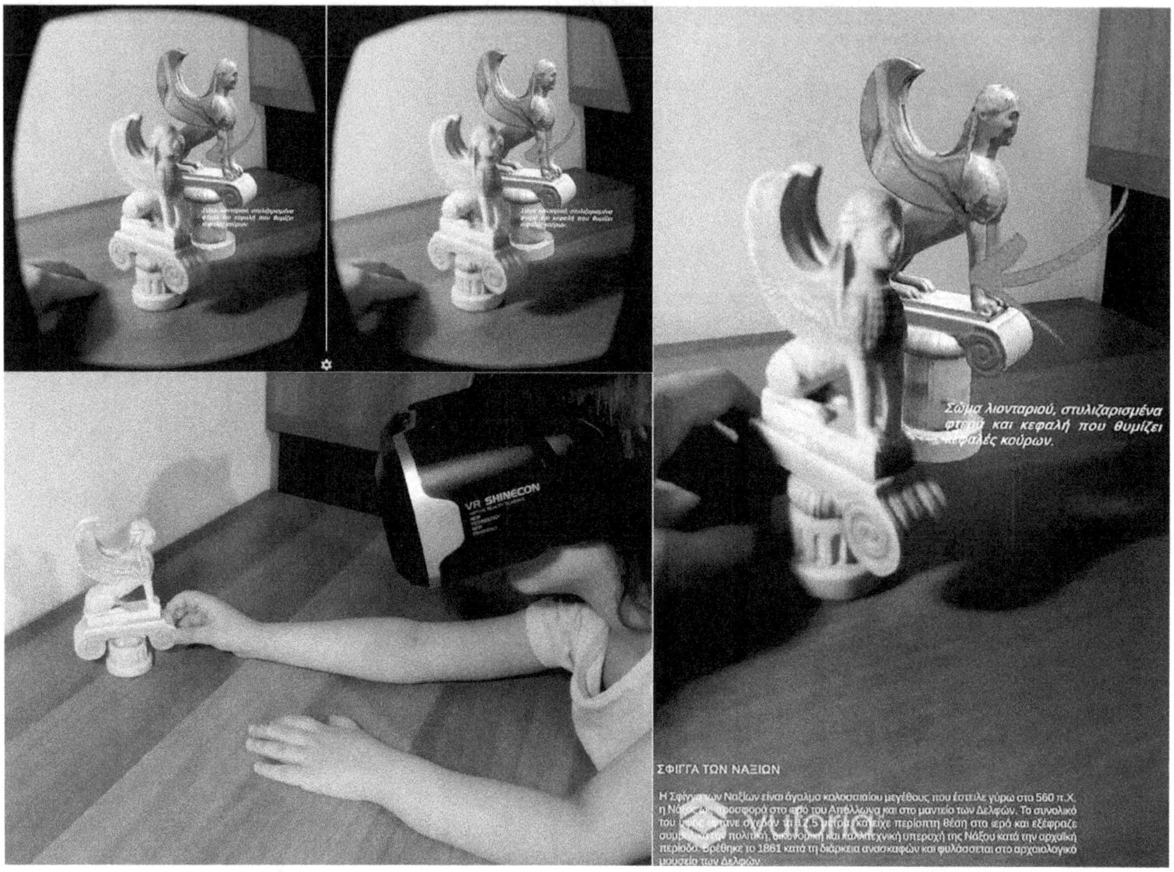

ings could have a significant value in interpreting, preserving, protecting and eventually disseminating surviving traces of the past referred to as CH. It is a fact that the presentation of inaccessible or past CH elements, usually is carried out through textual or audiovisual material or the process of reconstruction and simulation. The attempt to blend this material within real environment by exploiting AR/MR technology could lead to impressive learning experiences. Undoubtfully, preserving and disseminating world's historical elements, leads to the reevaluation of our own cultural identity and allows to pass it on to the next generations (Berlino, Caroprese, La Marca, Vocaturo, & Zumpano, 2019). Figure 4. depicts an example of MR application, where the user interacts with a real object (a replica of the sphinx) while the system presents additional information about the objects (in Greek language) as well as the 3D reconstructed model of a sphinx.

One of the biggest challenges in the area of 3D CH dissemination so far is the possibility of moving between two different dimensions: a virtual dimension and a physical dimension. The possibility of merging virtual and physical worlds is an idea that has been addressed from different points of view and disciplines, such as computer science, psychology, sociology, and even science fiction, among others. Nowadays, Cross Reality has several similar definitions with few differences, the most popular defined it as: a form of "*mixed reality environment that comes from the fusion of… ubiquitous sensor/actuator networks and shared online virtual worlds*", to encompass all of the possibilities of reality warping technology (Paradiso & Landay, 2009). Simply put, one may describe XR technologies as a combination of all reality technologies, including some additional tools (hardware, such as cameras, sensors, glasses, etc.) that enrich the interactivity between user and system.

Implementation of XR technologies in CH revealed the technical problems of registration (Brogni, Avizzano, Evangelista, & Bergamasco, 1999). Panou et al (2018), define registration as "*the degree to which 3D information is accurately placed and integrated as part of the real environment*". If the 3D content is not correctly aligned with the real object, then the AR experience cannot be sufficiently effective and "*the illusion that the two worlds coexist will be compromised*" (Azuma R., 1997). In order for the alignment to take place, the pose (position and orientation) of the viewer must be anchored in/to some point in the real-world using data from the tracking process in use. This point can be a physical object like an image marker or a ground control point in real world which can be determined using GPS or inertial tracking systems (Panou, Ragia, Dimelli, & Mania, 2018). System failures that affect the registration process can be divided into *Static* and *Dynamic* (Azuma R., 1997):

- *Static errors* are those arising from processes like calibration, tracking and modelling and cause registration errors even when there is no motion between the viewpoint and the objects of a scene.
- *Dynamic errors* occur because of system delays only when the user's viewpoint or the object to be augmented starts to move (Azuma R., 1997) (Zheng, 2015).

Several studies, work towards the development of a solutions for the probable registration issues. For instance, Gao et al. (2017) propose a method to increase AR marker-less registration stability and accuracy based on the Visual Simultaneous Localization and Mapping (V-SLAM), by generating three-dimensional map information (point cloud) in addition to the use of integrated camera poses on the registration of virtual objects. Furthermore, Wither et al. (2011) propose a radical approach of Augmented Reality, the ***Indirect AR***. The image where the virtual elements are superimposed is a previously captured panoramic image of the site instead of a live camera view. The user is not looking directly at the scene but instead is looking at an already acquired image of the environment merged with the virtual elements (Petrucco & Agostini, 2016). This results greater registration accuracy as the visible registration inconvenience, moves from inside the scene to the edge of the device screen. Because of the visual differentiation of a site (weather, lightning, shadows etc.), this method can be enhanced by selecting the image target from a set of different pre-captured images from different times of the day (Okura, Akaguma, Sato, & Yokoya, 2014).

The key feature of XR technology is to superimpose virtual data (information) on real world, allowing the user to experience a merged view of computed generated (synthetic) objects and physical environment. To accomplish this, viewer's pose tracking (three-dimensional position and orientation) of the viewer is a necessity. Bekele et al (2018), present three tracking methods:

- **Camera based tracking** mainly exploits the capabilities of a digital camera and can be implemented as: (Bekele, Pierdicca, Frontoni, Malinverni, & Gain, 2018).
  - *Marker-based technique* exploits a distinctive, easily recognized of a two-dimensional pre-defined image, placed in the physical world as marker, that can be recognized by a digital camera with the implementation of a specific computer vision algorithm (Bekele, Pierdicca, Frontoni, Malinverni, & Gain, 2018). Bekele et al (2018), pinpoint that this technique can be used both indoors and outdoors, however it is more suitable for indoor applications because

of the markers' fragility and regarding to the instability of the weather conditions and unpredictable human actions? (Bekele, Pierdicca, Frontoni, Malinverni, & Gain, 2018).

- *Marker-less technique* (or Visual-based tracking), exploits easily detectable geometric features (like lines, corners and edges) from the physical objects of a scene, to create a map of the object/environment visible to a camera (Siekański, Michoński, Bunsch, & Sitnik, 2018). Bekele et al (2018), introduced two distinctive types of marker-less tracking. To begin with, there is the *feature-based tracking* (Cucchiara & Del Bimbo, 2014), in which, the system needs to find a correspondence between 2D image features and their 3D world frame coordinates. In addition, there is the *model-based tracking* (Uchiyama & Marchand, 2012), which uses a CAD model or 2D templates of an object based on detected features such as lines, edges and primary shapes. Marker-less technique is applicable to both indoor and outdoor applications.
- *Infrared tracking* uses the position and orientation of IR markers (active or passive) to calculate in real time the pose of a target. Active markers periodically flash IR light, which is reflected back to the source, by the passive markers. This method has low latency, but it is not functional when IR source and reflector are not in line of sight (Bekele, Pierdicca, Frontoni, Malinverni, & Gain, 2018).

- **Sensor based tracking** techniques are based on a wide range of sensors, which can be organised in (Bekele, Pierdicca, Frontoni, Malinverni, & Gain, 2018):
  - *Electromagnetic tracking* exploits the intensity of the magnetic field between the base (transmiter and receiver) and a target, in different directions and orientations. Although this method is highly responsive and has low latency, it is prone to become unstable in non-stable environments (Bekele, Pierdicca, Frontoni, Malinverni, & Gain, 2018).
  - *Acoustic Tracking*, uses the speed of sound to determine the pose of a viewport. Sound travels from a target (emitter) to a sensor. The estimation of the pose is estimated using the travelling time of the sound.
  - *Inertial tracking* (Bekele, Pierdicca, Frontoni, Malinverni, & Gain, 2018) uses sensors like gyroscopes and accelerometers to calculate the pose of a given target.
- **Hybrid Tracking** has the potential to eliminate the technical failures of a tracking method when it is applied individually. Combining two or more tracking techniques of Camera and Sensor based categories, can lead to the required reliability (Reitmayr & Drummond, 2006) (Duguleana, Girbacia, Postelnicu, Brodi, & Carrozzino, 2016). Several studies, (Vlahakis, et al., 2002), (Miyashita, et al., 2008) (Barsanti, Caruso, Micoli, Rodriguez, & Guidi, 2015) indicate that hybrid tracking approaches (combined tracking methods that operate in a cooperative/synergistic way), the system becomes more accurate.

CONCLUSION

Realistic simulations of CH through XR systems for dissemination purposes are multidimensional and a cross-disciplinary processes. In this work we made an attempt to summarize most of the key techniques, approaches and technologies available today for developing realistic dissemination applications for cultural and educational purposes that aim to create pleasant and engaging XR environments that apply to all ages (children, adults and seniors). Contemporary efforts focus on various aspects including the representation of real-life environments, realistic simulation of human features, interactive interfaces in the world, realistic objects and dynamic environments. In addition, interest in terms of the dynamic processes in gaming environments focuses on competitiveness and cooperation and dynamic feedback. Virtual/Augmented/Mixed reality environments cannot and do not intend to replace real environments, either museums or anything else. They can be considered as reflections of physical environments either existing or fictitious, created for various reasons and goals. There are indications that if used complementarily and as extensions of physical environments they may be most effective in enhancing engagement with cultural heritage and education with all positive outcomes for a large variety of target groups, ranging from domain experts to kids at primary school.

Despite the fact that XR is considered to be a demanding technology because of the rigid requirements (hardware and software) in accurate alignment of the two worlds (real and computer generated), nevertheless it has the potential to present an effective and user-friendly alternative way in CH dissemination approaches. The ability to merge virtual elements within real environment, enables intuitive experience and better understanding of both tangible and intangible CH thesaurus. Blending computer generated virtual reconstruction of ruined, inaccessible or forgotten exhibits-elements with a real environment, completes the element's past-present puzzle and offers users the opportunity to preserve it and pass it on to next generations in the most possible complete way.

ACKNOWLEDGMENT

The present work was supported by the project "Computational Science and Technologies: Data, Content and Interaction/Technologies for Content Analysis in Culture", MIS code 5002437, co-financed by Greece and European Union in the framework of the Operational Programme "Competitiveness, Entrepreneurship and Innovation" 2014-2020.

REFERENCES

Anderson, E., McLoughlin, L., Liarokapis, F., Petridis, C. P., & Freitas, S. (2010). Developing serious games for cultural heritage: A state of the art review. *Virtual Reality (Waltham Cross)*, *14*(4), 255–275. doi:10.100710055-010-0177-3

Angelopoulou, A., Economou, D., Bouki, V., Psarrou, A., Jin, L., Pritchard, C., & Kolyda, F. (2011). Mobile Augmented Reality for Cultural Heritage. In N. Venkatasubramanian, V. Getov, & S. Steglich (Eds.), *Mobile Wireless Middleware, Operating Systems, and Applications. MOBILWARE 2011. Lecture Notes of the Institute for Computer Sciences, Social Informatics and Telecommunications Engineering* (Vol. 93). Berlin: Springer. doi:10.1007/978-3-642-30607-5_2

Azuma, R. (1997). A Survey of Augmented Reality. *Presence (Cambridge, Mass.)*, *6*(4), 355–385. doi:10.1162/pres.1997.6.4.355

Azuma, R., Baillot, Y., Behringer, R., Feiner, S., Julier, S., & MacIntyre, B. (2001). Recent advances in augmented reality. *IEEE Computer Graphics and Applications*, *21*(6), 34–47. doi:10.1109/38.963459

Barsanti, S., Caruso, G., Micoli, L., Rodriguez, M., & Guidi, G. (2015). 3D Visualization of Cultural Heritage Artefacts with Virtual Reality devices. *The International Archives of the Photogrammetry, Remote Sensing and Spatial Information Sciences*, *40*(5), 165–172. doi:10.5194/isprsarchives-XL-5-W7-165-2015

Bekele, M., Pierdicca, R., Frontoni, E., Malinverni, E., & Gain, J. (2018, March). A Survey of Augmented, Virtual, and Mixed Reality for Cultural Heritage. *ACM J. Comput. Cult. Herit. 11, 2. Article*, *7*, 36. doi:10.1145/3145534

Bellotti, F., Berta, R., Gloria, A., Dursi, A., & Fiore, V. (2012). A serious game model for cultural heritage. *ACM Journal on Computing and Cultural Heritage*, *5*(4), 17.

Berlino, A., Caroprese, L., La Marca, A., Vocaturo, E., & Zumpano, E. (2019). Augmented Reality for the Enhancement of Archaeological Heritage: a Calabrian Experience. *VIPERC, Visual Pattern Extraction and Recognition for Cultural Heritage Understanding Workshop.*

Bickmore, T., Pfeifer, L., & Schulman, D. (2011). Relational Agents Improve Engagement and Learning in Science Museum Visitors. In *Intelligent Virtual Agents: 10th International Conference* (pp. 55-67). Reykjavik, Iceland: Springer Berlin Heidelberg.

Bineta, M. (2013). Edge Based Antialiasing: Quality without Compromise. *International Journal of Engineering Science and Research Technology*, *2*(6), 1627–1631.

Blanco-Pons, S., Carrión-Ruiz, B., Duong, M., Chartrand, J., Fai, S., & Lerma, J. (2019). Augmented Reality Markerless Multi-Image Outdoor Tracking System for the Historical Buildings on Parliament Hill. *Sustainability*, *11*(4268). doi:10.3390u11164268

Boboc, R., Duguleană, M., Voinea, G.-D., Postelnicu, C.-C., Popovici, D.-M., & Carrozzino, M. (2019). Mobile Augmented Reality for Cultural Heritage: Following the Footsteps of Ovid among Different Locations in Europe. *Sustainability*, *11*(4), 1167. doi:10.3390u11041167

Bonis, B., Vosinakis, S., Andreou, I., & Panayiotopoulos, T. (2013). Adaptive virtual exhibitions. *DESIDOC Journal of Library and Information Technology*, *33*(3), 183–198. doi:10.14429/djlit.33.4604

Breuer, J., & Bente, G. (2010). Why so serious? On the relation of serious games and learning. *Journal for Computer Game Culture*, *4*(1), 7–24.

Brogni, A., Avizzano, C., Evangelista, C., & Bergamasco, M. (1999). Technological Approach for Cultural Heritage. PERCRO Scuola Superiore.

Brown, S., & Vaughan, C. (2010). *Play: How it changes the brain, Opens the Imagination, and Invigorates the Soul.* J P Tarcher/Penguin Putnam.

Caggianese, G., Neroni, P., & Gallo, L. (2014). Natural interaction and wearable augmented reality for the enjoyment of the cultural heritage in outdoor conditions. In *Augmented and virtual reality, international conference* (pp. 267–282). Springer International Publishing. doi:10.1007/978-3-319-13969-2_20

Canciani, M., Conigliaro, E., Grasso, M., Papalini, P., & Saccone, M. (2016). 3D Survey and augmented reality for cultural heritage. The case study of Aurelian Wall at Castra Praetoria in Rome. *XXIII ISPRS Congress- International Archives of the Photogrammetry, Remote Sensing and Spatial Information Sciences, XLI-B5*, 931-937. doi:10.5194/isprs-archives-XLI-B5-931-2016

Carmigniani, J., Furht, B., Anisetti, M., Ceravolo, P., Damiani, E. E., & Ivkovic, M. (2011). Augmented reality technologies, systems and applications. *Multimedia Tools and Applications, 51*(1), 341–377. doi:10.100711042-010-0660-6

Casella, G., & Coelho, M. (2013). Augmented heritage: situating augmented reality mobile apps in cultural heritage communication. *Proceedings of the 2013 International Conference on Information Systems and Design of Communication*, 138–140. 10.1145/2503859.2503883

Cowan, B., & Kapralos, B. (2015). A Survey of Frameworks and Game Engines for Serious Game Development. In *IEEE 14th International Conference on Advanced Learning Technologies*, (pp. 662-664). Athens, Greece: IEEE.

Craighead, J., Burke, J., & Murphy, R. (2008). Using the unity game engine to develop sarge: A case study. *Simulation Workshop at the International Conference on Intelligent Robots and Systems.*

Cucchiara, R., & Del Bimbo, A. (2014). Visions for augmented cultural heritage experience. *MultiMedia, IEEE, 21*(1), 74–82. doi:10.1109/MMUL.2014.19

Demers, J. (2004). Depth of field: A survey of techniques. GPU Gems, 23, 375–390.

Desai, N. (2018). Recreation of history using augmented reality. *ACCENTS Transactions on Image Processing and Computer Vision., 4*(10), 1–5. doi:10.19101/TIPCV.2017.39019

Diaconescu, C., Popovici, M.-I., & Popovici, D.-M. (2019). From Exploration of Virtual Replica to Cultural Immersion Through Natural Gestures. *First International Conference, VRTCH 2018*. 10.1007/978-3-030-05819-7_9

Dieck, T., & Jung, T. (2017). Value of Augmented Reality at Cultural Heritage SItes: A skakeholder approach. *Journal of Destination Marketing & Management*. doi:10.1016/j.jdmm.2017.03.002

Djaouti, D., Alvarez, J., Rampnoux, O., Charvillat, V., & Jessel, J. (2009). Serious games and cultural heritage: A case study of prehistoric caves. *15th International Conference on Virtual Systems and Multimedia*, 221–226. 10.1109/VSMM.2009.40

Doulamis, A., Liarokapis, F., Petridis, P., & Mialous, G. (2012). Serious Games for Cultural Applications. *Intelligent Computer Graphics*, 97–115.

Duguleana, M., Girbacia, F., Postelnicu, C., Brodi, R., & Carrozzino, M. (2016). Exploring Pisa Monuments Using Mobile Augmented Reality. *World Academy of Science, Engineering and Technology International Journal of Computer and Information Engineering, 10*(11).

Fogliaroni, P. (2012). Mixed Reality for Archeology and Cultural Heritage. *2nd Workshop on Computing Techniques for Spatio-Temporal Data in Archaeology and Cultural Heritage*. doi:10.4230/LIPIcs.COARCH.2018

Foster, N., & Fedkiw, R. (2001). Practical animation of liquids. In *Proceedings of ACM SIGGRAPH* (pp. 23-30). New York: ACM Press.

Franklin, C. (1977). The aliasing problem in computer-generated shaded images. *Communications of the ACM, 20*(11), 799–805. doi:10.1145/359863.359869

Gao, Q., Wan, T., Tang, W., & Chen, L. (2017). A stable and accurate marker-less augmented reality registration method. *2017 International Conference on Cyberworlds (CW)*, 41-47. 10.1109/CW.2017.44

Gardner, G. (1985). Visual simulation of clouds. *SIGGRAPH '85 Proceedings of the 12th annual conference on Computer graphics and interactive technique, 19*(3), 297–384.

Harrison, L. (2003). *Introduction to 3D Game Engine Design Using DirectX 9 and C*. Berkeley, CA: Apress. doi:10.1007/978-1-4302-0821-1

Haydar, M., Roussel, D., Otmane, S., & Mallem, M. (2011). Virtual and augmented reality for cultural computing and heritage: a case study of virtual exploration of underwater archaeological sites. *Virtual Reality, 15*(4), 311–327. doi:.hal00636621 doi:10.100710055-010-0176-4

Higgett, N., Chen, Y., & Tatham, E. (2015). A User Experience Evaluation of the use of Augmented and Virtual Reality in Visualising and Interpreting Roman Leicester 210AD (Ratae Corieltavorum). *Athens Journal of History, 2*(1), 7–22. doi:10.30958/ajhis.2-1-1

Hinsinger, D., & Neyret, F. (2002). Interactive animation of ocean waves. *Proceedings of ACM SIGGRAPH/Eurographics symposium on computer animation*, 161-166.

Huang, Z., Gong, G., & Liang, H. (2015). Physically-based smoke simulation for computer graphics: A survey. *Multimedia Tools and Applications, 74*(18), 7569–7594. doi:10.100711042-014-1992-4

Iones, A., Krupkin, A., Sbert, M., & Zhukov, S. (2003). Fast, Realistic Lighting for Video Games. *IEEE Computer Graphics and Applications, 23*(3), 54–64. doi:10.1109/MCG.2003.1198263

Jacobson, J., & Gillam, R. (2012). The Egyptian Oracle; Recreating Egyptian Religious Ceremony in Mixed Reality. *ACM Journal of Computing and Cultural Heritage*.

Jim, X., Xiadong, F., & Wegman, J. (1999). Real-time simulation of dust behavior generated by a fast traveling vehicle. *ACM Transactions on Modeling and Computer Simulation, 9*(2), 81–104. doi:10.1145/333296.333366

Jonghyun, K., Jae-Hyun, J., Changwon, J., & Byoungho, L. (2013). Real-time capturing and 3D visualization method based on integral imaging. *Optics Express, 21*(16), 18742–18753. doi:10.1364/OE.21.018742 PMID:23938790

Kiourt, C., Koutsoudis, A., Arnaoutoglou, F., Petsa, G., Markantonatou, S., & Pavlidis, G. (2015a). The 'Synthesis' Virtual Museum–an open virtual exhibition creation tool. *International Workshop on Virtual Archaeology: Museums & Cultural Tourism*.

Kiourt, C., Koutsoudis, A., Arnaoutoglou, F., Petsa, G., Markantonatou, S., & Pavlidis, G. (2015b). *A dynamic web-based 3D virtual museum framework based on open data*. Granada, Spain: Digital Heritage. doi:10.1109/DigitalHeritage.2015.7419589

Kiourt, C., Koutsoudis, A., & Pavlidis, G. (2016). DynaMus: A fully dynamic 3D virtual museum framework. *Journal of Cultural Heritage, 22*, 984–991. doi:10.1016/j.culher.2016.06.007

Kiourt, C., & Markantonatou, S. (2018). Intertwining Culture With Education Through Gamified Storytelling: The Case of "Myth Trek". *International Journal of Computational Methods in Heritage Science, 2*(1), 8–22. doi:10.4018/IJCMHS.2018010102

Kiourt, C., Pavlidis, G., Koutsoudis, A., & Kalles, D. (2017). Realistic Simulation of Cultural Heritage. *International Journal of Computational Methods in Heritage Science, 1*(1), 10–40. doi:10.4018/IJCMHS.2017010102

Kolivand, H., El Rhalibi, A., Tajdini, M., Abdulazeez, S., & Praiwattana, P. (2018). Cultural Heritage in Marker-Less Augmented Reality: A Survey. In D. Turcanu-Carutiu & R.-M. Ion (Eds.), Advanced Methods and New Materials for Cultural Heritage Preservation. Academic Press. doi:10.5772/intechopen.80975

Koutsoudis, A., Makarona, C., & Pavlidis, G. (2012). Content-based navigation within virtual museums. *Journal of Advanced Computing Science and Technology, 1*(2), 73–81. doi:10.14419/jacst.v1i2.135

Koutsoudis, A., & Pavlidis, G. (2011). Content-based search and retrieval within complex 3d scenes - an application to cultural heritage. *16th International Conference on Cultural Heritage and New Technologies.*

Lepouras, G., & Vassilakis, C. (2004). Virtual museums for all: Employing game technology for edutainment. *Virtual Reality (Waltham Cross), 8*(2), 96–106. doi:10.100710055-004-0141-1

Lewis, M., & Jacobson, J. (2008). Game engines in scientific research. *Communications of the ACM, 45*(1), 27–31.

Margetis, G., Papagiannakis, G., & Stephanidis, C. (2019). Realistic natural interaction with virtual statues in x-reality environments. *The International Archives of the Photogrammetry, Remote Sensing and Spatial Information Sciences, 42*(W11), 801–808. doi:10.5194/isprs-archives-XLII-2-W11-801-2019

Martínez, B., Casas-Yrurzum, S., Vidal-González, M., Vera, L., & García-Pereira, I. (2018). TinajAR: An Edutainment Augmented Reality Mirror for the Dissemination and Reinterpretation of Cultural Heritage. *Multimodal Technologies and Interaction., 2*(33). doi:10.3390/mti2020033

Miyashita, T., Meier, P., Tachikawa, T., Orlic, S., Eble, T., Scholz, V., ... Lieberknecht, S. (2008). An augmented reality museum guide. *Proceedings of the 7th IEEE/ACM International Symposium on Mixed and Augmented Reality*, 103–106.

Nguyen, D. Q., Fedkiw, R., & Jensen, H. W. (2002). Physically based modeling and animation of fire. *Transactions on Graphics, 21*(3), 721–728. doi:10.1145/566654.566643

Nicholson, S. (2011). Making the Gameplay Matter: Designing Modern Educational Tabletop Games. *Knowledge Quest, 40*(1), 60–65.

Nicholson, S. (2012). Strategies for meaningful gamification: Concepts behind transformative play and participatory museums. Presented at Meaningful Play 2012, Lansing, MI.

Okura, F., Akaguma, T., Sato, T., & Yokoya, N. (2014). Indirect augmented reality considering real-world illumination change. *Proceedings of the 2014 IEEE International Symposium on Mixed and Augmented Reality*. Retrieved September 10–12, 2014 10.1109/ISMAR.2014.6948453

Panou, C., Ragia, L., Dimelli, D., & Mania, K. (2018). An Architecture for Mobile Outdoors Augmented Reality for Cultural Heritage. *ISPRS International Journal of Geo-Information, 7*(12), 463. doi:10.3390/ijgi7120463

Papastamatiou, N., Alexandridis, T., Tsergoulas, K., Michopoulos, A., & Karadimas, N. (2010). Virtual reality applications with user interface for dynamic content development. *CEA'10 Proceedings of the 4th WSEAS international conference on Computer engineering and applications*, 201-206.

Paradiso, A., & Landay, A. (2009). Guest editors' introduction: Cross-reality environments. *IEEE Pervasive Computing, 8*(3), 14–15. doi:10.1109/MPRV.2009.47

Pavlidis, G., Koutsoudis, A., Arnaoutoglou, F., Tsioukas, V., & Chamzas, C. (2007). Methods for 3D digitization of Cultural Heritage. *Journal of Cultural Heritage, 8*(1), 93–98. doi:10.1016/j.culher.2006.10.007

Pavlidis, G., Makarona, C., Arnaoutoglou, F., Koutsoudis, A., & Chamzas, C. (2008). Museums In The Virtual World. *International Symposium Information and Communication Technologies in Cultural Heritage*, 16-18.

Pavlidis, G., Tsiafakis, N., Provopoulos, G., Chatzopolos, S., Arnaoutoglou, F., & Chamzas, C. (2006). Momi: A dynamic and internet-based 3d virtual museum of musical instruments. *Third International Conference of Museology.*

Petrucco, C., & Agostini, D. (2016). Teaching our cultural heritage using mobile augmented reality. *Je-LKS: Journal of e-Learning and Knowledge Society, 12*, 115-128. doi:10.20368/1971-8829/1180

Reeves, W. (1983). Particle Systems— A Technique for Modeling a Class of Fuzzy Objects. *ACM Transactions on Graphics, 2*(2), 91–108. doi:10.1145/357318.357320

Reitmayr, G., & Drummond, T. (2006). Going out: Robust model-based tracking for outdoor augmented reality. *Proceedings of the 2006 IEEE/ACM International Symposium on Mixed and Augmented Reality.*

Reitmayr, G., & Schmalstieg, D. (2004). Collaborative augmented reality for outdoor navigation and information browsing. *Proceedings of symposium location based services and telecartography.*

Rogers, A. (1996). *Teaching Adults*. Buckingham, UK: Open University Press.

Schnädelbach, H., Koleva, B., Flintham, M., Fraser, M., Izadi, S., Chandler, P., ... Rodden, T. (2002). The Augurscope: a mixed reality interface for outdoors. *Proceedings of the SIGCHI Conference onHuman Factors in Computing Systems*, 9-16. 10.1145/503376.503379

Schönberger, J. L., & Frahm, J. M. (n.d.). Structure-from-Motion Revisited. *The IEEE Conference on Computer Vision and Pattern Recognition (CVPR).*

Seo, B., Kim, K., Park, J., & Park, J. (2010). A tracking framework for augmented reality tours on cultural heritage sites. *ACM SIGGRPAH Conference*, 169-174. doi:10.1145/1900179.1900215

Siekański, P., Michoński, J., Bunsch, E., & Sitnik, R. (2018). CATCHA:Real-Time Camera Tracking Method for Augmented Reality Applications in Cultural Heritage Interiors. *ISPRS International Journal of Geo-Information, 7*(479). doi:10.3390/ijgi7120479

Sillaurren, S., & Aguirrezabal, P. (2012). 3d publish: A web-based solution for building dynamic 3d virtual museums. *International Journal of Heritage in the Digital Era, 1*(1_suppl), 147–152. doi:10.1260/2047-4970.1.0.147

Sookhanaphibarn, K., & Thawonmas, R. (2009). A content management system for user-driven museums in second life. *International Conference on CyberWorlds*, 185–189. 10.1109/CW.2009.58

Střelák, D., Škola, F., & Liarokapis, F. (2016). *Examining User Experiences in a Mobile Augmented Reality Tourist Guide*. doi:10.1145/2910674.2935835

Sylaiou, S., Liarokapis, F., Kotsakis, K., & Patias, P. (2009). Virtual museums, a survey and some issues for consideration. *Journal of Cultural Heritage, 4*, 520–528.

Sylaiou, S., Mania, K., Karoulis, A., & White, M. (2010). Exploring the relationship between presence and enjoyment in a virtual museum. *International Journal of Human-Computer Studies, 68*(5), 243–253. doi:10.1016/j.ijhcs.2009.11.002

Sylaiou, S., Mania, K., Paliokas, I., Pujol, L., Kilintzis, V., & Liarokapis, F. (2016). Exploring the educational impact of diverse technologies in online Virtual Museums. *International Journal of Arts and Technology.*

Tahoon, D. (2017). Simulating Egyptian Cultural Heritage by Augmented Reality Technologies. Case Study: Pyramids and Giza Plateau cultural heritage site, Egypt. *1st BUE Annual Conference & Exhibition - BUE ACE1-"Sustainable Vital Technologies in Engineering & Informatics".*

Tan, J., & Fan, X. (2011). Particle System Based Snow Simulating in Real Time. *3rd International Conference on Environmental Science and Information Application Technology ESIAT 2011*, 1244-1249. 10.1016/j.proenv.2011.09.199

Tsichritzis, D., & Gibbs, S. (1991). Virtual museums and virtual realities. *International Conference on Hypermedia and Interactivity in Museums*, 17-25.

Uchiyama, H., & Marchand, E. (2012). Object detection and pose tracking for augmented reality: Recent approaches. *18th Korea-Japan Joint Workshop on Frontiers of Computer Vision (FCV).*

Van Eck, R. (2006). Digital game-based learning: It's not just the digital natives who are restless. *EDUCAUSE, 41*(2), 16–30.

Van Krevelen, R., & Poelman, R. (2010). A Survey of Augmented Reality Technologies, Applications and Limitations. *International Journal of Virtual Reality, 9*(1).

Vlahakis, V., Ioannidis, M., Karigiannis, J., Tsotros, M., Gounaris, M., Stricker, D., ... Almeida, L. (2002, October). Archeoguide: An augmented reality guide for archaeolog sites. *IEEE Computer Graphics and Applications, 22*(5), 52–60. doi:10.1109/MCG.2002.1028726

Vlahakis, V., Karigiannis, J., Tsotros, M., Gounaris, M., Almeida, L., Stricker, D., ... Ioannidis, N. (2001). Archeoguide: First results of an augmented reality, mobile computing system in cultural heritage sites. *Proceedings of the 2001 Conference on Virtual Reality, Archeology, and Cultural Heritage, VAST '01*, 131. 10.1145/584993.585015

Werner, P. (2018). Review of Implementation of Augmented Reality into the Georeferenced Analogue and Digital Maps and Images. *Information, 10*(12). doi:10.3390/info10010012

Wither, J., Tsai, Y., & Azuma, R. (2011). Indirect augmented reality. *Comput. Graph, 35*(4), 810–822. doi:10.1016/j.cag.2011.04.010

Wojciechowski, R., Walczak, K., White, M., & Cellary, W. (2004). Building virtual and augmented reality museum exhibitions. *Proceedings of the ninth international conference on 3D Web technology*, 135-144. 10.1145/985040.985060

Yang, L., Dong, H., Alelaiwi, A., & El Saddik, A. (2015). See in 3D: State of the art of 3D display technologies. *Multimedia Tools and Applications, 75*(24), 17121–17155. doi:10.100711042-015-2981-y

Yngve, G., Obrien, J., & Hodgins, J. (2000). Animation explosions. In *Proceedings of ACM SIGGRAPH 2000 conference proceedings*. (pp. 29–36). ACM Press.

Yu, X., Wang, R., & Yu, J. (2010). Real-time depth of field rendering via dynamic light field generation and filtering. *Computer Graphics Forum, 29*(7), 2099–2107. doi:10.1111/j.1467-8659.2010.01797.x

Zheng, F. (2015). Spatio-Temporal Registration. In *Augmented Reality*. Chapel Hill, NC: University of North Carolina.

ENDNOTES

1 http://unity3d.com/

2 http://www.crytek.com/cryengine

3 https://www.unrealengine.com/

4 https://www.microsoft.com/en-us/hololens

5 http://ccwu.me/vsfm/

6 http://dynamus.ceti.gr

7 http://mythtrek.ipet.gr

8 https://developer.vuforia.com/

Chapter 6
The Use of Digital Characters in Interactive Applications for Cultural Heritage

Spyros Vosinakis
https://orcid.org/0000-0003-1735-4297
University of the Aegean, Greece

ABSTRACT

Digital characters are software entities that look and act like real or imaginary creatures in a computer-generated environment. They are considered an important element of interactive digital heritage applications that can add significant value and increase user motivation and engagement. This chapter presents a review of the use of digital characters for communicating and disseminating cultural heritage. It explores the wide range of applications that make use of digital characters and attempts to identify how the characters are used, what are their main features, and how are they contributing to the overall cultural experience. The chapter includes an overview of current state of the art in digital character design and implementation approaches, a taxonomy about the usage of characters in cultural heritage applications, and a discussion about prospects and pitfalls of digital character technology for heritage dissemination.

INTRODUCTION

Interactive applications built with novel technologies such as virtual worlds, augmented reality and serious games have the capacity to serve as dissemination and learning platforms for history, culture and archaeology (Anderson et al., 2010; Gaitatzes et al., 2001). They may offer affordances such as high-quality visualization of digital content, real-time simulation of realistic or imaginary environments, natural and intuitive user interactions, seamless blending of physical and virtual content, and single- or multi-user embodiment. These characteristics allow applications to represent existing or reconstructed cultural artifacts and places in high detail for local or remote visitors, enhanced by features such as the superimposition of associated descriptions and media. Added interactivity allows users to freely navigate

DOI: 10.4018/978-1-7998-2871-6.ch006

and explore the content, and provides engaging features such as interactive digital stories or mini-games related to the historical and cultural context of the subject. Applications of this kind not only let people closely observe reconstructed buildings or artifacts, but can also serve as a motivating means to supplement people's knowledge and increase their interest in culture.

Digital characters are an important element of this type of applications that can add significant cultural value and increase user motivation and engagement in various ways. Reconstructed buildings or cities feel empty, inanimate spaces without the presence of "living" digital humans moving and acting inside them. Furthermore, digital characters can recreate an appropriate context for cultural artifacts and monuments. They may demonstrate how a work of art or a building was constructed, how an object of the past was used for specific activities, they may wear proper clothes and accessories, perform a ritual inside a temple, etc. Even more important is the use of characters for presenting intangible aspects of cultural heritage. They could simulate the daily life and activities of ancient or lost cultures, and also re-enact theatrical plays, dances and other types of cultural performance. Finally, digital characters are also an engaging and natural form of user interface for this type of applications. A virtual human could assist users in navigating inside a large museum and probably present further information, it could discuss with users and answer their questions about the content they are experiencing, and it could also act as a tutor to test their knowledge in an engaging way through quizzes and mini-games.

There is a wide usage of digital characters in cultural heritage applications, but their functional characteristics have significant differences. Depending on the type and goals of each application, the characters have different design elements regarding their interface with humans, their interaction capabilities, their believability and their autonomy. Up to now these different manifestations have not been collected and documented in a systematic review. There are a number of older reviews about virtual humans and animated agents that offer a broad overview of design and implementation issues and research potentials, but they are not focused on the specific needs of cultural heritage applications (Luck & Aylett, 2000; Gratch et al., 2002; Kasap & Magnetat-Thalmann, 2008; Swartout et al., 2006). On the other hand, more recent reviews on virtual environments and serious games in cultural heritage are available in the bibliography. These, however, consider broader design aspects, such as the game genre and gameplay (Anderson et al., 2010; Mortara et al., 2014; Paliokas & Sylaiou, 2016; Bontchev, 2015), virtual museums and exhibitions (Sylaiou et al., 2009, Carmo & Claudio, 2013), or virtual and augmented reality technologies (Noh et al., 2009; Bekele et al., 2108), and do not specifically focus in digital characters. Finally, there is a recent review on virtual humans in cultural heritage ICT applications (Machidon et al., 2018), which categorizes the types of applications that use virtual humans and discusses their strengths and weaknesses. The current study aims to shed more light on the subject by reviewing and studying a number of design dimensions related to the use of digital characters and their affordances.

This paper explores the wide range of cultural heritage applications that make use of digital characters in order to identify how the characters are used, what are their main features, and how are they contributing to the overall cultural experience. The aim of the paper is twofold. First to inform designers of future digital heritage applications about the range of possible features and use cases to consider, if they decide to include digital characters in their prototypes. Second, to identify the positive aspects, drawbacks and critical issues of using digital characters in cultural heritage applications based on the existing works, in order to influence future research studies and prototypes. This review has been based on a thorough systematic study of recent scientific papers describing applications related to tangible or intangible cultural heritage, in which one or more digital characters of any type contribute significantly to the resulting application environment.

Table 1. Popular terms used to describe digital characters in the bibliography and their meaning

Term	Meaning
avatar	actions directly controlled by user
virtual human	realistic human look and motion
virtual crowd	virtual humans with crowd behavior
virtual actor	executes predefined action sequences (scripts)
virtual agent	decides on its actions
embodied conversational agent (ECA)	engages in dialogs with users
non-player character (NPC)	computer-controlled character in games
digital character	looks and acts like real or imaginary creature

The paper is structured as follows. Section 2 presents an overview of digital characters and their technology. Section 3 presents the current usage of digital characters in cultural heritage applications arranged in a set of dimensions identified during this study. Each of these dimensions is introduced and explained, and the possible solutions are presented using examples from existing applications. In Section 4 we present a broad discussion about our results and future perspectives. We identify prospects and pitfalls of digital character technology and their relation with cultural heritage, and propose future research dimensions. Finally, in Section 5 we present the conclusions of this study and summarize the important findings.

OVERVIEW OF DIGITAL CHARACTERS

Digital characters are software entities that look and act like real or imaginary creatures in a computer-generated environment. Obviously, this definition is so broad that includes implementations with very different characteristics, from simple animated props to sophisticated autonomous creatures. One can, therefore, find plenty of terms in the scientific bibliography that describe such characters. What seems however to be a common ground in all these approaches is the notion of believability; the resulting characters should behave so as to generate the illusion that they are 'alive' in the digital environment. This section presents terminology issues, an overview of the creation stages for digital characters, and a presentation of the concept of believability with respect to digital characters.

Terminology

The numerous terms used to describe digital characters is a possible source of confusion for scholars not familiar with this field. In this subsection we attempt to clarify this by introducing and explaining the most common of these terms found in scientific books and papers. The terms are summarized in Table 1.

The term *avatar* (Ducheneaut et al., 2009) is used to describe any digital character whose actions are directly or indirectly controlled by human users in a virtual environment or game. Note that the same term is also used in more generic cases to describe the graphical representation of a user in any online community, e.g. the icon or picture that represents a user in web-based forums and chat rooms.

Digital characters with realistic human look and motion are usually grouped under the term *virtual humans* (Swartout et al., 2006). The term is mostly used in virtual environments and simulations and is usually attributed to characters in which the emphasis is placed in various aspects of human body motion and dynamics.

Large groups of virtual humans that are able to perform coordinated motion and to exhibit crowd dynamics similar to that of a real human crowd are called *virtual crowd* (Pelechano et al., 2008).

Characters which execute a predefined sequence of actions are sometimes called *virtual actors* (Perlin & Goldberg, 1996). Usually these characters exhibit a standardized predictable behavior by performing some 'script', i.e. a sequence of locomotion or animation actions. The term is rarely used nowadays.

The term *virtual agent* is used to describe digital characters which take decisions on their own based on some artificial intelligence mechanism (Vosinakis & Panayiotopoulos, 2001). The term is based on intelligent agents (Woolridge & Jennings, 1995), an artificial intelligence structure for defining the behavior of autonomous systems.

Characters with sophisticated conversational abilities are described with the term *embodied conversational agents* (or ECAs) (Cassell, 2001). Their main function is to hold dialogs with users in natural language using text or speech.

Finally, the term *non-player character (or NPC)* has been introduced by the gaming community to describe any digital character included in a game except from the players' avatars (Nareyek, 2004). The term is nowadays found in a wider scope beyond games, possibly due to the fact that game engines are often used for developing serious games or even non-gaming applications (virtual worlds, simulations, etc).

In this review we adopt the term *digital characters*, which has a broader meaning and includes all the aforementioned types.

Modelling Stages

The creation of a digital character involves a number of stages that model the way it looks, behaves and takes decisions in the virtual environment. The stages are depicted in Figure 1.

The first stage is to construct the model of the body, hair and clothes. The characters' geometry can be either modelled using conventional 3D modelling software (e.g. 3ds Max) or, in the case of humans, combined with digitized data from real humans, such as photographs or full body scans (Lee et al., 2010; Luginbuhl et al., 2011).

The next stage is the definition of the moving parts of the character. It involves the creation of a 'skeleton' and the association of the skeleton's bones with the body geometry. The first process, also called rigging, is essential for animating the body. The skeleton includes the individual segments of the body, and the joints which define the rotation of these segments connected in a tree-like structure. The second process, called skinning, is required to define how the skeleton is associated with the human body mesh, so that the body deforms properly when one or more segments are moving (Gillies & Spanlang, 2010). Most 3D modelling programs and 3D engines today provide semi-automated support for this stage.

Once the skeleton is created, the character can move (parts of) its body based on one or more animation mechanisms. In most of the cases the animation is kinematic: the controller directly affects the joint rotations and the global position of the body. The animation data used by the digital characters can be: a) defined specifically by a designer as a set of 'key frames' that are automatically interpolated to generate the full motion, b) recorded from actors who perform the same motion using specialized motion capture

Figure 1. Modeling stages of digital characters

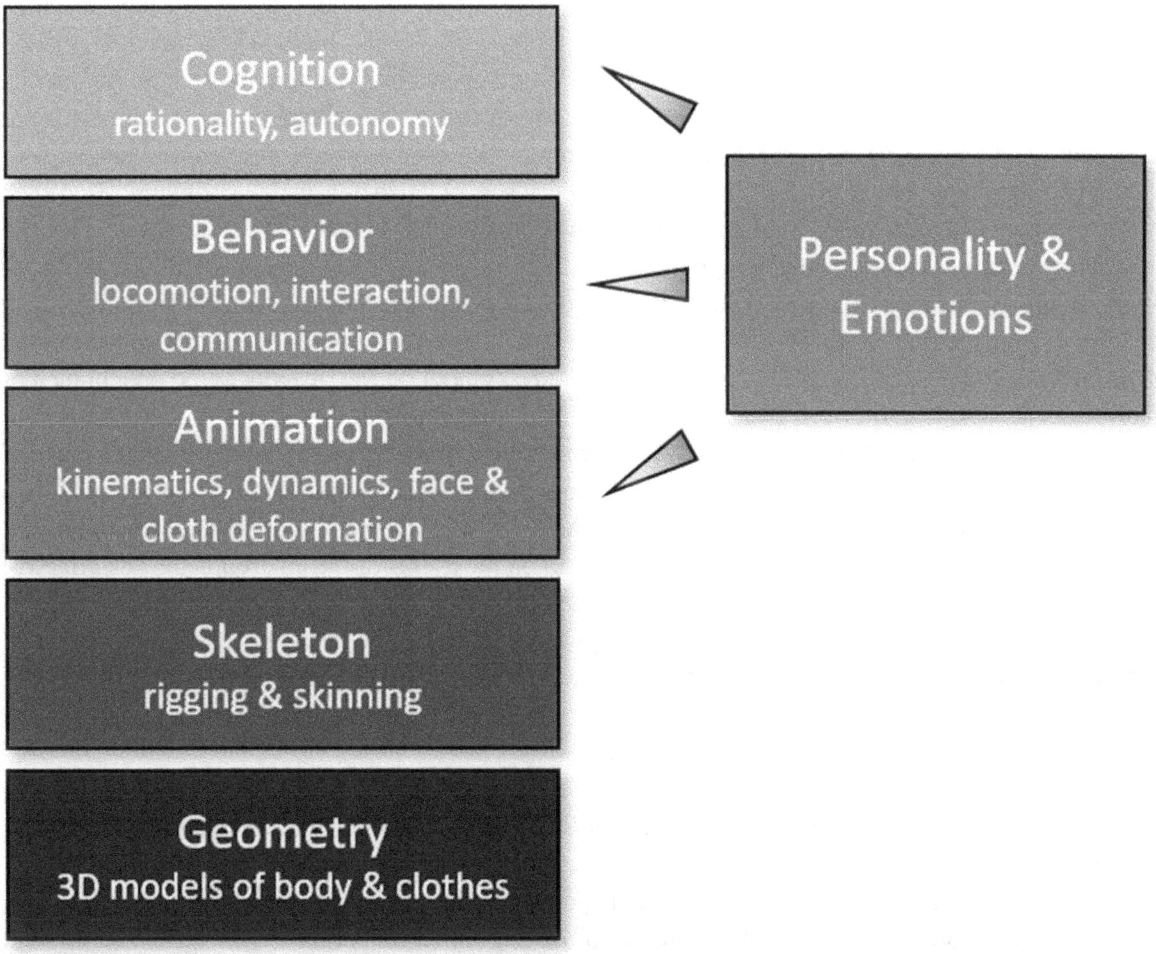

technology, or c) generated dynamically by a specific control mechanism to make the character respond to changes in the environment (Cavazza et al., 1998). In fewer cases, where the emphasis is placed in the accurate simulation of the human body, a dynamic approach is used: instead of directly controlling the body position and joint rotations, a controller generates forces in body muscles, and the resulting motion depends on their effect in the simulated environment, taking into account collision and friction with other elements (Brogan et al, 1998). Finally, some animation systems are able to generate various expressions of the character's face, or even to produce a natural-looking motion of the hair and clothes using morphing techniques that directly affect the 3D geometry of the character (Magnetat-Thalmann et al., 2004).

There are several levels of behavior that a digital character can exhibit. The most fundamental one is locomotion, i.e. the ability to move properly in the environment. Typical locomotion behavior includes algorithms for path finding (Bandi & Thalmann, 2000) and dynamic obstacle avoidance (Guy et al., 2010). In cases where multiple characters are present, crowd motion techniques are included as well to avoid congestions and unnatural behaviors (Ulicny & Thalmann, 2001). A more sophisticated level of behavior is the interaction of the agent with elements of the environment, e.g. to be able to grasp and hold objects. Inverse kinematics techniques are utilized to allow a character to dynamically reach its arm to a target spot (Tolani & Badler, 1996). Furthermore, some objects include semantic information about typical actions applied on them ('smart objects'), and agents may use this information to interact with them (Abaci et al., 2005). Finally, communication with other digital characters or humans is another ability which is often required. Communication may be based on free text in natural language or predefined set of answers. It involves not only the speech acts but also non-verbal communication such as body gestures, posture shifts and facial expressions (Cassel et al., 2004).

The next stage is the character's cognitive modeling, i.e. its ability to decide on its actions based on the status of the environment in order to pursue some given goals (Funge et al., 1999). In this case, techniques from the field of artificial intelligence and rational agents are being used, and the state of the environment and the agent's abilities are encoded in some symbolic form, usually based on a branch of mathematical logic, e.g. first-order logic.

Finally, an aspect which increases believability and makes characters more human-like is the use of personality and emotions (Magnetat-Thalmann & Kasap, 2009). Computational models from cognitive science, such as OCEAN (McCrae & John, 1992) and OCC (Ortony et al., 1990) have been employed to drive the characters' mood and emotional state based on the events of the environment. The affective state of a character may influence various other components described in the previous stages, such as its decision-making (cognition), the execution of typical behaviors, and even its facial expressions and body motions.

Designing and Assessing Believability

A key requirement for digital characters is *believability*, a rather complex concept that involves diverse design aspects and has led to equally diverse approaches of the matter. Before attempting to provide a definition for believability, it is important to distinguish the concept from *realism*, a close term that is, however distinct from believability. Realism refers to creating high fidelity reconstructions of the physical world. On the other hand, believability has to do with a digital character being consistent to essence of the entity it is supposed to embody, as well the coherence of this character within the world it is situated in.

An obvious and important aspect of believability is the visualization of the environment (Magnenat-Thalmann et al., 2005). Common sense would dictate that the more realistic the appearance of the character is made, the higher the degree of believability grows; however, this is not necessarily the case. As argued by Loyall & Bates (1997), realism is neither required, nor adequate to ensure believability. It is rather the consistency of the presentation in relation to the thematic context of the environment that leads to a greater degree of believability. As Mori (1970) has suggested in the well-known uncanny valley hypothesis, levels of realism beyond a certain threshold may seriously undermine the acceptance of the character as real by the audience and produce an awkward response, especially if other constituents of the total experience such as gaze and locomotion are lacking realism.

Believability, in the context of digital characters, has been defined by Bates (1994) as the ability on the part of the system to suspend the users' disbelief, by providing an illusion of life. Plainly put, believability in this case is about making the human user accept they are interacting with a living character, whose existence is consistent and coherent in the context of the virtual world it is situated in.

Extending beyond the strictly physical properties of the digital characters, it has been widely discussed that believability equally involves the character's behavior (Ortony, 2003). Works on behavioral believability are diverse in approach, depending on the particular viewpoint adopted: behavior as a way of expression of a character's internal state by communicative means such as gaze (Poel et al., 2009), facial expression (Sloan et al., 2009), gesture and posture (Corradini et al., 2004), or a synthesis of multiple means (Bevacqua et al., 2007). Believability also demonstrates a narrative aspect, both in terms of plot coherence and character expression (Ho & Dautenhahn, 2008). In terms of affect, the importance of emotion and personality has also been widely discussed (Lim & Aylett, 2007; Andre et al., 2000).

More recently Bogdanovych et al (2016) proposed a formal definition of believability of virtual agents as a synthesis of various factors including: appearance, personality, emotions, internal goals and beliefs, awareness of the environment, and behavior that changes over time.

Application In Cultural Heritage

The current study has been based on scientific papers found in well-known online bibliographic search engines. The initial search about digital characters (and related terms) and cultural heritage produced 112 results. These have been further filtered based on their relevance to cultural heritage, the contribution of digital characters to the application, the quality of the paper and the maturity of the work. Papers that have been found weak in one or more of these criteria or had a very vague / short description of the use and functionality of the digital character(s) in the application have been excluded.

The resulting papers were 67. These have been thoroughly studied in order to determine: a) what are the main design and implementation features of the digital characters, b) how do they contribute to the goals of the application and c) important design aspects and results. In some cases more than one papers were referring to the same project, focusing in different aspects or presenting small extensions. The unique

Table 2. Dimensions related to the usage of digital characters in heritage applications, their description and possible values

Name	Description	Values
Creation	How is the digital character created	manual, automated variations, reconstructed, user-created
Environment	The environment in which the character is embodied	virtual reality, augmented reality, mixed reality, public installation, augmented virtuality, robot
Interactivity	How does the user interact with the character	non-interactive, interactive, user-controlled
Capabilities	What can the digital character do in the environment	navigation, social, interaction with environment, interaction with other agents, complex
Believability	What kind of believability features does the character include	idle motion, facial animation, gaze, personality & emotions
Decision-making	How does the character decide on its actions	predefined, scripted, state machines, BDI
Function	What is the character's function in the context of the application	demonstrate, simulate, present, tutor, storytelling
Subject	What is the subject of the application that includes the character(s)	tangible heritage, ancient / lost cultures, intangible heritage, art, history

projects that we found in our study were 51. These include mature works that have been used and tested in real settings, as well as prototypes and case studies built for research purposes. It has been decided to include all of them in order to study a wider range of applications and to include any emerging trends.

As expected, our study revealed that there are numerous implementations and uses for digital characters in heritage applications. Based on our findings, we have identified eight different design aspects (or 'dimensions') related to the digital characters, and we have grouped and encoded the various solutions ('values') given in each one of them. The identified dimensions and their possible solutions are presented in the following subsections and summarized in Table 2.

Character Creation

The first dimension is about the possible approaches for generating the appearance of one or multiple digital character.

Digital heritage applications are sometimes in need of more than a few characters to populate the virtual environment. These could be citizens of a reconstructed city, visitors of a temple, etc., and in some applications their total number might be quite large. In such cases, it is useful to include mechanisms for semi-automatic creation of multiple characters instead of manually creating and configuring each one of them. Furthermore, a degree of variance in look and behavior is also desirable to avoid the non-realistic case where digital characters are all lookalikes.

The simplest approach to character creation is to follow the obvious, manual process: to have a library of character models as templates, and to manually introduce one or more instances of these models in the environment. In environments with a small number of digital characters, this approach is satisfactory. However, the downside for applications with plenty of characters is that either designers have to undergo the painstaking process of creating numerous individual models, or the environment will inevitably contain clones.

There are cases where more sophisticated, semi-automated approaches for character creation have been adopted. Based on some initial templates, a mechanism is able to produce variations or combinations, thus being able to introduce a large number of digital characters with different looks and in some cases also behavior. The digital crowd presented in the reconstructed ancient city of Pompeii (Thalmann et al., 2014) has been created from a small number of virtual human templates. Based on these templates, a mechanism could produce variations in shape, height, texture, colors, walking style and accessories to produce a relatively diverse crowd. In another project that simulates daily life in the reconstructed city of Uruk around 3000 BC (Trescak et al., 2014), a mechanism that creates variations in both look and behavior has been used. Initially, a base population of characters is created, where each character has its own body shape and clothing, motivational modifiers (such as hunger, thirst and energy rates) and personality traits. This information is encoded as a 'chromosome' that identifies the character. Then, an approach based on genetic algorithms is used to produce new unique characters by combining chromosomes from two 'parents'.

Another desired feature in some applications is to have a digitally reconstructed figure of an existing character, e.g. a historical figure, a painting etc. In a reconstruction of the daily life of John Calvin the Reformer (Arevalo et al., 2014), artists have based on past sketches, artistic representations and written descriptions of the historical figure to create the digital character's model and clothes. Inevitably, some interpretation from the part of the artists had to take place. In another project (Pietroni & Antinucci,

2010), an old painting came alive in 3D using animated characters and users could immerse into it. In that case the characters had to be created from their depiction in a single image. The production team used a high quality version of the painting and subdivided it into parts for texturing the character models. They created a 3D space depicting the painting's visual area and attempted to translate the 2D painting representation into the actual forms of characters and objects, as well as their placement on the 3D space. In the Qing-ming Festival project (Chen et al., 2012), users could have a personalized avatar embodied in the digital environment. The process included the automatic creation of a 3D face model based on a photo of the users, and then the manual customization of the avatar's appearance. Finally, in the AMICA project for learning the craft of printmaking (Carrozzino et al., 2016), the artisan's appearance is created from real video footage. Depth cameras have been used to capture the person's body and motion and isolate it from the surrounding environment, and the recorded data have been processed and re-inserted in a 3D environment forming an augmented virtuality experience.

Finally, in the Virtual STEM Buddies project, visitors themselves can create the digital character that will be embodied in the environment (Ball et al., 2019). In this project, two mini-games for children have been created and installed in a large-screen kiosk of a museum. The games include a pedagogical agent that interacts with the children while playing. The agent can be configured and adapted by the children: they can select the shapes and colors for various body parts, creating a unique appearance for the character.

Table 3 shows various approaches for character creation and indicative projects.

Environment

A second dimension regarding the use of digital characters in cultural heritage applications is the environment in which they are embodied.

The most frequent case is to have an environment which is totally computer-generated (virtual). The characters are part of the digital space, which possibly presents a place of cultural significance, such as reconstruction or an exhibition space. All the events take place within this environment and the user is probably also embodied there as avatar. The characters are aware of the objects and places in the 3D representation and they move and interact within that environment.

Table 3. Character creation approaches, indicative projects and their key features

Character creation	Indicative Project(s)	Key features
manual		
automated variations	Ancient Pompeii (Thalmann et al, 2014)	variations in shape, height, clothes and accessories
	City of Uruk - Unity (Trescak et al, 2014)	variations in look and behaviour using genetic algorithms
reconstructed	John Calvin the Reformer (Arevalo et al., 2014)	created based on past sketches and paintings
	The Rule Confirmation (Pietroni & Antinucci, 2010)	created from a painting
	Qing-ming Festival (Chen et al., 2012)	personalized avatar from user's photo and customization
	AMICA (Carrozzino et al., 2016)	created from video footage using depth cameras
user-created	Virtual STEM Buddies (Ball et al., 2019)	children create the character

In some mobile applications, the characters appear in an augmented environment, presented next to or on top of the real-world image coming from the camera of the device. Usually such systems are location-based, meaning that the behavior of the characters depend on where the user is standing and looking at, e.g. a character might refer to some content that exists in the physical space. As an example, in the prototype mobile tourist guide presented in (Doumanis, 2013) a digital character presents related cultural and historical information of a medieval castle based on the user's actual position. In another work, a mobile AR application features a digital character that acts as a virtual guide and presents the artifacts in a museum, pointing at specific targets of interest (Ghouaiel et al., 2016).

In fewer cases the characters are not simply superimposed on the real-world image, but also naturally blend with the physical environment giving the illusion that they are part of the real world. We refer to this type of applications as 'mixed-reality', because the goal is to efficiently combine the real setting with the digital content. Using these mixed-reality systems, which usually rely on high-end equipment, visitors of cultural sites are able to see both the physical environment around them and the digital characters being part of it and moving around. One of the first approaches of this kind was Archeoguide (Vlahakis et al., 2002), a system which offered personalized augmented reality tours of archaeological sites. While looking at the stadium, users could see digital characters dressed as ancient athletes competing in a race. In a more recent work (Pensyl et al., 2008), a mixed-reality system based on a low-cost tracking solution was installed in a public exhibition, and visitors could see a life-sized animated character naturally placed among physical artifacts of the room. Finally, in the 'Sanan seppa' application (Viinikkalla et al., 2016) a mixed reality environment is presented with the use of mobile devices: a number of short stories are recreated and displayed inside the physical space of a cathedral using animated characters. The characters are efficiently blended with the physical environment using markerless augmented reality technology.

Additionally, there are some hybrid cases, where a character is part of a digital application installed in a public space, such as a museum or exhibition, and interacts with the visitors. In these cases, the character is also context-aware, it may recognize new visitors and it may refer to places and objects located within the public space and discuss about them. As an example, Glas & Pelachaud (2015) present the design and prototype implementation of a digital character who greets and discusses with museum visitors about the contents of the exhibition.

Finally, there are two extra types of environments for digital characters that are worth mentioning. The first is the augmented virtuality environment presented in the AMICA project (Carrozzino et al., 2016), where the digital character is captured from real world footage of an artisan and inserted in the 3D space as part of the environment. The second is the use of a digital character as a moving robot in the physical environment of a museum to guide visitors. The MAVEN robotic virtual museum guide (Pang, 2018) is a telepresence robot presenting the animated body of a digital character and equipped with a depth sensor to understand human presence. It is embodied in a Robotics Research Center and is programmed to greet visitors, guide them to designated standpoints and present information about the environment.

Table 4 shows various environments of digital characters and indicative projects.

Table 4. Environments of digital characters, indicative projects and their key features

Environment	Indicative Project(s)	Key features
virtual		
augmented	Monemvasia-ECA (Doumanis, 2011)	mobile guide for visitors of a medieval castle
	MARTS (Ghouaiel et al., 2017)	mobile guide presenting exhibits in a museum
mixed reality	Archeoguide (Vlahakis et al., 2002)	digital athletes running in a real stadium
	Life-sized Avatar in Mixed Reality (Pensyl et al., 2008)	animated character placed among physical artifacts
	Sanan seppa (Viinikkalla et al., 2016)	short stories played by digital characters in a Cathedral
public installation	Avatar1:1 (Glas & Pelachaud, 2015)	digital character greets and discusses with museum visitors
augmented virtuality	AMICA (Carrozzino et al., 2016)	real-world captured person included in a 3D environment
robot	MAVEN virtual museum guide (Pang et al., 2018)	telepresence robot presenting a digital character, guides visitors and presents environment

Interactivity

Another feature considered important is the interaction possibilities between the digital character(s) and the user. We can distinguish three cases: non-interactive, interactive and user-controlled.

Non-interactive characters navigate and perform their actions regardless of any user activity. Their action sequences may be predefined by the designer, or dynamic (e.g. in the case of virtual crowd), but in all cases they are not affected by the presence of users. A large number of cultural heritage applications include non-interactive characters, and their primary role is to demonstrate some aspects or features of ancient cultures, to reenact significant events, or to portray famous people of the past. In the work of Arévalo et al. (2014), a historical person has been recreated as a digital character, and a reconstruction of a typical day in his life has been included in a non-interactive 3D simulation.

Interactive characters on the other hand can sense the presence of users and adapt their behavior accordingly. They may communicate with them using controlled or free-text dialogs, collaborate on some common task, present places or objects of interest, attack them in the context of some game, or even co-participate in a larger story. Most digital heritage applications and historical games are based on interactive characters. E.g. the role-playing game "Taiwan Epic Game", which aims to enhance player's cultural awareness about 19th century Southern Taiwan, includes a number of digital characters communicating and interacting with the players (Shih et al., 2015).

Finally, in a number of cultural heritage applications, the user him/herself is embodied through a digital character (avatar). In this case, the character's actions are directly controlled by the user. The character may be presented from a first- or third-person perspective and is usually controlled using standard input, such as keyboard and mouse. In some cases, the avatar control goes beyond traditional input to offer a more physical and intuitive experience, and the user's actions are naturally mapped into avatar motion. There have been virtual heritage projects that have adopted a kinesthetic approach supported by depth cameras or motion capture systems. In one case users control a digital character through their body movement using MS Kinect to perform a traditional Chinese shadow play (Shi et al., 2014). A more recent work for Chinese shadow play further explored the use of natural interaction devices as input for the digital characters, such as Leap Motion (Liang et al., 2016). In another case, users perform the movements of a traditional Japanese theatre using a full-body motion capture system, and their motion is performed in the virtual world of Second Life through animated avatars (Choi et al., 2010). A last input modality worth metntioning is the use of a brain-computer interface is used to control the player avatar. An existing history game (Roma Nova), which demonstrates aspects of daily life in ancient Rome, has been adapted to allow for controlling the avatar's movement and interaction by thought after some initial training (Vourvopoulos et al., 2012).

Table 5 shows various types of interactivity regarding digital characters and indicative projects.

Character Capabilities

The next dimension is about the capabilities of the digital characters in the environment and the kind of actions they can perform while they are inhibiting the digital world. Based on the proposed categorization, a character may have one or more of the following abilities: to navigate inside the environment, to socialize with users, to interact with the environment, to interact with other characters and to execute complex tasks.

Navigation is about moving around in the environment and/or reaching places of interest. This is a basic ability for any digital character to produce believable results. Cultural heritage applications involve reconstructed cities, stories, events, performances, etc. and all of them raise the need for characters to be able to walk around in predefined or dynamic paths. Digital characters usually include mechanisms for finding the shortest path in a complex environment and to dynamically avoid standing or moving obstacles. In cases where large crowds are depicted, individual characters should also be able to perform typical crowd behaviors, such as aligning, queuing, etc. In a reconstruction of the Ancient city of Pompeii the digital characters were able to plan their path to their target based on some desired behavior (e.g. buy bread), whilst dynamically avoiding inter-pedestrian collisions and slowing down to look at places of interest (Magnetat-Thalmann & Papagiannakis, 2010).

The ability of digital characters to discuss and socialize with users is another important feature for rich user interactions. The simplest case is to be able to talk to users with written or spoken language, e.g. present stories or information relevant to the context. A typical example is the work presented in (Schmidt et al., 2018) where a digital character with the appearance of an astronaut presented the story of the Apollo 11 mission from a first-person perspective. A more interesting extension is to support

Table 5. Interactivity types, indicative projects and their key features

Interactivity	Indicative Project(s)	Key features
non-interactive	John Calvin the Reformer (Arevalo et al., 2014)	presentation of a character's daily life
interactive	Taiwan Epic Game (Shih et al., 2015)	digital characters communicating and interacting with users
user-controlled	Piying (Shi et al., 2014), Digital Chinese Shadow Play (Liang et al., 2016)	users perform shadow play using natural interfaces (MS Kinect, Leap Motion, etc)
	Noh Play (Choi et al., 2010)	a full-body motion capture system maps user's motion to digital character
	Roma Nova - BCI (Vourvopoulos et al., 2012)	character controlled by thought using brain-computer interface

dialogues with users. Users would then be able to control the flow of information and get more personalized results. The dialogues may ask from users to select from predefined sets of answers or, preferably, to allow free text input in natural language. In the latter case, the user input could be either written or spoken. One has to note, however, that the use of free text in human – character dialogs might produce unnatural results and distort the flow of the application. Ikura, a serious game for understanding Japanese culture and etiquette (Froschauer et al., 2010), includes digital characters that talk to players and assists them through the learning process. They use a dialog system that lets the player interactively choose from a set of answers. On the other hand, the Roma Nova project (Panzoli et al., 2010), which presents a reconstruction of ancient Rome with virtual citizens and the Boston City Massacre History Experience (Novick et al., 2017), a VR application where users interact with historical characters, both use an ECA engine to allow for free text dialogues between the player and the citizens.

A more complex ability is to be able to interact with the environment. Digital characters sometimes need to grasp and use objects, to perform custom animations in specific circumstances, etc. To support these cases, the characters usually include an inverse kinematics mechanism, which provides the ability to apply custom rotations on their body joints in order to bring an end segment (hand or rarely foot) to a specific position, e.g. to place a character's hand on a specific object it needs to grasp. Furthermore, there are environments, which include 'smart objects', i.e. objects with embedded semantic information about the performance of specific actions on them (Abaci et al., 2005). E.g. a sword 'knows' how to be grasped and used, so when a character needs to perform such an action it retrieves this information from the object. In a virtual museum of computer science presented by Ieronutti & Chitaro (2007), a digital character acting as a guide was able to demonstrate the use of various types of equipment by interacting with the virtual objects.

In some projects the digital characters could also afford interactions between agents or even group interactions. One such example is the 'Weld Quay' project, where various scenarios for the interactions between different ethnic groups have been implemented (Lim et al., 2019). Agents could perform one-to-one interactions such as following a leader, chasing, negotiating, greeting, uploading and downloading goods, etc. Additionally, more complicated group interactions have been supported, such as soldiers marching side by side to welcome the traders or a captain catching a thief and bringing him to prison with the help of colleagues.

Finally, some characters are able to execute complex tasks by effectively combining the previously mentioned capabilities. E.g. they may participate in a game or story, which involves them moving around, discussing with other players, using objects of the environment, interacting with other characters, presenting aspects of the digital worlds, etc. In the reconstructed city of Uruk the digital characters apply actions such as locomotion, object use, gaze and user dialogs in order to execute complex tasks and demonstrate daily life activities (Bogdanovych et al., 2010).

Table 6 shows various capabilities of digital characters and indicative projects.

Believability Features

The next dimension concerns the characteristics especially designed to make digital characters more believable. As discussed before, there are a number of techniques and enhancements that may be used to enhance character believability. The most important of them found in digital heritage applications are: idle motion, facial animation, gaze control and personality.

Table 6. Digital character capabilities, indicative projects and their key features

Character capabilities	Indicative Project(s)	Key features
navigation	Ancient Pompeii (Magnetat-Thalmann & Papagiannakis, 2010)	characters plan path to target, avoid collisions, look at places of interest
social	Apollo 11 mission (Schmidt et al., 2018)	digital character presents a story
	Ikura (Froshauer et al., 2010)	dialogs, users chose from set of answers
	Roma Nova (Panzoli et al., 2010), Boston City Massacre History Experience (Novick et al., 2017)	dialogs in free text (speech)
interaction with environment	Virtual Museum of Computer Devices (Ieronutti & Chitaro, 2007)	interaction with objects of the environment
interaction with other agents	Weld Quay (Lim et al., 2019)	one-to-one and group interactions
complex	City of Uruk (Bogdanovych et al., 2010)	navigation, interaction between characters, use of objects, dialogs with user

A fundamental feature for believability is to have the character perform some idle motion when not doing anything else. Otherwise, the character might look inanimate and lifeless. Most modern systems currently support this feature and, generally, it is considered essential for achieving a basic level of believability. E.g. in the work of Egges et al. (2007), the digital characters perform idle animations based on balance shifting and continuous small posture variations.

A more sophisticated feature is the use of facial animation. Facial animation enhances the illusion that a character is talking and may also convey its thoughts and feelings. A lot of systems perform some random facial movement while talking. On the other hand, a more believable approach would be to have the mouth motion synchronize with the speech. This requires the selection of appropriate mouth animation based on the text and a good synchronization between the two. Furthermore, mouth animation may be blended with other facial expressions, which may further express their emotional state. In the virtual heritage game Solis' curse, a digital character plays with museum visitors a question-answering game using speech. When the character is speaking, a text-to-speech module generates the voice along with the associated visemes and temporal tags. A facial animation engine is then responsible for synchronizing the mouth movements with speech audio to generate more believable results (Neto et al., 2011).

The purposeful use of gaze direction also makes characters more lively and believable. E.g. looking at other characters / users passing by, looking at points of interest, shifting gaze while talking, etc. Digital characters acting as guides usually look at the users when speaking, e.g. in the virtual guide presented in (Carrozzino et al., 2018). Additionally, in the work of D. Thalmann (2014) on populating reconstructed cities with digital characters, a number of approaches regarding gaze control are presented and discussed. The characters are aware of objects, persons of interest, as well as the user, and they direct their gaze accordingly. Designers can also define interest points, which drive the attentional behavior of digital characters, thus making them more believable.

The incorporation of models for personality and emotions may also significantly contribute to the overall believability. There are already a few heritage applications, which include such characteristics. In the work of Vosinakis & Avradinis (2016) each digital character in a representation of the Ancient Agora of Athens had its own personality traits based on a hierarchy of needs. Individual differences in needs affected the prioritization of goals, and thus their behavior. In the reconstruction of the ancient city of Uruk (Trescak et al., 2014), the digital characters were based on the OCEAN model of personality, and each one of them had different values in the five personality traits: openness, conscientiousness, extroversion, agreeableness and neuroticism. Finally, an interesting believability feature for a digital character is the ability to recognize users' emotions. In the case of 'Lady Ada', an installation in an exhibition where a digitally reconstructed Lady Ada Byron greets visitors, the character includes an emotion recognition system based on movement analysis (Senecal et al., 2017). Visitors' motion is tracked using multiple depth cameras and analyzed in real time to produce an estimation of their emotional status. This is then being used to adapt the digital character's behavior accordingly.

Table 7 shows various believability features and indicative projects.

Decision-Making

One important feature of digital characters is the mechanism that controls their actions. The action selection may be partially defined by the designer and also dynamic, based on the setup and the events that take place in the environment. There are plenty of approaches for decision-making ranging from completely pre-defined action sequences to autonomous virtual agents.

The most simplified approach is to have characters perform pre-defined action sequences leaving little space for variation. In a number of applications, especially historical games, the characters included in the environment play a specific role, which may be part of a challenge. E.g. in the Fort Ross Virtual Warehouse project (Forte et al., 2012), the player has to complete some quests and to do so he needs to discuss and interact with digital characters. In these cases, the designer defines how the characters are introduced to the players and what types of interaction are supported. The advantage of this approach, is that the designer has complete control over the character's actions and may also include elements of style and personality that are appropriate for the narrative.

In other approaches, characters perform based on some 'script', which defines their dynamic behavior. A scripting language may be used to drive their actions, which is usually simpler and more high-level compared to general-purpose programming languages and, as such, more appropriate for prototyping, testing and improving a character's behavior. In the Virtual Agora of Athens project (Vosinakis et al.,

Table 7. Believability features, indicative projects and their key features

Believability features	project	key features
idle motion	Aspendos theatre in Minor Asia (Egges et al., 2007)	balance shifting, posture variations
facial animation	Solis' curse (Neto et al., 2011)	facial animation synchronizing mouth movements with speech audio
gaze	Virtual Gallery of Art Objects (Carrozzino et al., 2018)	character looks at the user when speeking
	Ancient Pompeii (Thalmann, 2014)	gaze at objects, persons of interest, user
personality & emotions	Virtual Agora (Vosinakis & Avradinis, 2016)	characters with personality traits affecting goal prioritization
	City of Uruk (Trescak et al., 2014)	characters based on OCEAN model of personality
	Lady Ada Byron (Senecal, 2017)	emotion recognition of users

2018), a scripting language for defining the agents' behavior has been introduced. It controls the sequence of actions that each character performs based on the elements that it senses in the environment and on its internal memory.

Another approach, quite common in games, is the use of finite state-machines (Nareyek, 2004). Designers define various behavioral states of the characters and conditional transitions between them. So, based on the perceived status of the environment a character either continues performing its present state (e.g. random walking in an area), or triggers a transition to switch to a new state (e.g. move towards the user). In the work of Popovici et al. (2011), state machines are used to drive the behavior of all animated entities, including characters, in a virtual environment that simulates the organization and activities of a Greek-Roman colony situated on a Black Sea coast. In another simulation presenting various ethnic groups in a trading port of Malaysia in the 1800s, the model for interactions between the groups has been based on state-machines (Lim et al., 2013). A similar approach is the use of behavior trees, i.e. a hierarchical structure describing an execution plan that includes nodes that control the flow and nodes that perform actions. This control mechanism has been used in the case of Lady Ada project (Senecal et al., 2017) to describe the execution logic of the tasks it can afford.

Finally, more sophisticated approaches based on intelligent agents may be used, such as the known Belief-Desire-Intention model (BDI). Characters maintain a set of beliefs about the environment based on their sensors, they have some generic desires, i.e. goals they would like to achieve, and based on predefined plans or some dynamic planning process, they form their intentions as the specific tasks to be performed next in order to fulfil their goals in the future. In the work of (Richards, 2012) the digital characters acting as virtual guides use BDI plans to respond to user queries. In the City of Uruk project (Bogdanovych et al., 2010; Trescak et al., 2014), the digital characters operate autonomously using a BDI architecture. They perform actions following a daily routine but can also dynamically alter their behavior based on the status of the environment.

Table 8 shows various decision-making mechanisms of digital characters and indicative projects.

Table 8. Decision-making approaches, indicative projects and their key features

Decision-making	Indicative Project(s)	Key features
predefined	Fort Ross Virtual Warehouse (Forte et al., 2012)	behaviour is defined by the designer
scripted	Virtual Agora (Vosinakis et al., 2018)	scripting language for programming agents' behaviour
state machines	ARéViMASCARET (Popovici et al., 2011)	state machines drive behaviour of all animeted entities
	Weld Quay (Lim et al., 2013)	state machines model the interactions between groups of characters
	Lady Ada Byron (Senecal, 2017)	behaviour trees
BDI	Virtual Guide of Saarlouis (Richards, 2012)	characters use BDI plans to respond to user queries
	CIty of Uruk (Bogdanovych et al., 2010)	characters operate autonomously using BDI architecture

General Function of the Character

The next category refers to the purpose of the character(s) in the digital or augmented environment: how do they contribute to the communication and dissemination of cultural heritage.

The first case is to have a character demonstrate something. E.g. to show how citizens used to look like, how an object is being used, how a ritual was performed, etc. Characters perform some activities, usually predefined, and the users are supposed to pay attention to their appearance and/or activities, and learn from observation. Typical examples of this approach include digital characters presenting aspects from their daily life, demonstrating some performance, or moving as crowd in some reconstructed area. In the work of Choi et al. (2010) digital characters demonstrate Japanese Traditional Performing Arts in the virtual world of Second Life, and in La Draga settlement project (Puig et al., 2019) a digital character portraying a Neolithic man performs an animation to demonstrate a simple construction using the appropriate tools.

An interesting extension of the above, is to have the character simulate something. In this case the character performs in a dynamic simulation environment, which may be possibly altered by users. Users may change the initial conditions and observe the results, or even participate in the environment themselves and take part in the activities. The characters should be aware of the environment and include proper decision mechanisms in order to be able to participate in the simulation. In the Virtual Agora of Athens (Vosinakis et al., 2018), the digital characters are simulating some aspects of life in the Agora (trading and rituals), and their behavior changes dynamically based on the status of the environment and the actions of other agents or the user (Figure 2).

A character may also be used as a presenter. Instead of demonstrating features, it could present places, artifacts or events, by pointing user's attention to specific content of the environment and offer interesting complementary information about it. It could present the contents of a museum, significant places or monuments in a reconstructed city, etc. In the digitally recreated town of Wolfenbuttel, a female character interactively presents the history of the town to visitors (Arnold et al., 2008). It responds to users'

Figure 2. Screenshots from Virtual Agora project (Vosinakis et al., 2018)

questions related to buildings and events in the town and offers virtual tours on demand. The typical use of digital characters acting as presenters is in the case of virtual guides in virtual or augmented reality applications (Ghouaiel et al., 2016; Carrozzino et al., 2018).

Characters may also act as tutors. They may introduce and explain new information and concepts and ask quizzes to the users to enhance and test their knowledge. In a learning environment providing history and cultural heritage information about Shandong Province in China, a digital character presented as a 'wise old man' gives clues to students to explore and discover relics in the virtual world (Wang et al., 2010). After that, the character asks questions to them about the related historical and cultural background and gives them rewards based on their success.

Finally, characters may be actors in a storytelling environment. In that case, the focus is not only on the demonstration of some features, but on a dramatic sequence of events, which is expected to capture users' attention and entertain them. Stories may be predefined or interactive. In the second case the user is also participating and may affect the outcome. This approach is usually found in historical games. E.g. in the popular series of games Assassin's Creed, the player has to carry out stealth assassinations during a historical event. It includes reconstructed locations, buildings and characters that provide rich historical details, and the player takes part in this story and carries out his/her mission (Spring, 2015).

Table 9 shows various functions of characters in the context of the digital heritage applications and indicative projects.

Subject

The final dimension is the subject of the applications that contain digital characters in the wider domain of culture. Our aim was to discover which are the areas of cultural heritage that are mostly supported by digital characters, and how are those characters contributing to the dissemination of heritage.

A significant number of projects were related to tangible heritage. In these cases, the focus is not on the characters themselves; they usually act as mediators between the user and the content. Therefore, it is common in these cases that the main function of the characters that are present is that of a virtual guide or presenter, as discussed in the previous subsection, e.g. see (Van Welbergen et al., 2006). The subject of focus may include buildings, places, collections in museums or exhibitions, or even clothes. In the latter case, the characters take the role of a 'virtual mannequin' (Martin & Mauriello, 2013).

Table 9. Character functions in the application, indicative projects and their key features

Function	project	key features
Demonstrate	Noh Play (Choi et al., 2010)	characters demonstrate performing arts
	La Draga settlement (Puig et al., 2019)	character demonstrates a construction
Simulate	Virtual Agora (Vosinakis et al., 2018)	simulate aspects of daily life and rituals
Present	Town of Wolfenbuttel (Arnold et al., 2008)	character presents history of the town to visitors
	Virtual Guides (Ghouaiel et al., 2016; Carrozzino et al., 2018)	presenting exhibits in virtual or real museums
Tutor	Virtual World of Shandong (Wang et al., 2010)	character motivates users to explore the environment, asks questions, gives rewards
Storytelling	Assassin's Creed series (Ubisoft) mentioned in (Spring, 2015)	characters participate in stories, provide historical details

Another equally popular subject is the presentation of ancient or lost cultures. The characters demonstate aspects of daily life and intangible heritage related to the cultures under consideration. In various projects, such as Archaeoguide (Vlahakis et al, 2002), Virtual Pompei (Magnetat-Thalmann & Papagiannakis, 2010) and City of Uruk (Bogdanovych et al., 2010), the digital characters imitate the appearance and behavior of ancient cultures and their role is to let visitors learn about those cultures through observation, exploration or active involvement.

Another subject that is also quite popular is performing arts, rituals and crafts, an area generally termed as intangible heritage. In this case, the characters are staging an act, performing a ritual or doing a craft, usually in a non-interactive way based on motion captured animations. The focus is not only on the appearance and behavior of individual characters, but also on the performance as a whole. Typical application examples include the reconstruction of the ancient Hellenistic theatre of Aspendos in Minor Asia, in which digital characters performed parts of ancient Greek dramas (Egges et al., 2007), the use of a digital character to represent a Morning Namaz Pray taking place in the 16th century restored Hagia Sophia edifice (Foni et al., 2007), and the immersive system to learn the craft of printmaking using captured motion from an artisan and a digital character as tutor (Carrozzino et al., 2016). Another notable example is the use of digital characters to reenact a traditional Chinese shadowplay (Shi et al., 2014; Liang et al., 2016). In this case, the characters are used as avatars and are controlled by users with natural interactions.

Digital characters have also been used in other forms of art, such as the reenactment of famous paintings. The role of the characters in this respect is to transform a still scene (a painting) to a lively environment. In the work of Chen et al. (2012) a famous Chinese painting presenting a riverside festival about 1000 years ago has been recreated as an animated 3D environment with digital characters. Users could navigate inside the environment and interact with the content. In another similar approach, a 13th century painting by Giotto has been recreated as a 3D environment with animated characters and users could freely navigate inside the scene using natural interactions (Pietroni & Antinucci, 2010).

History is another popular subject, mostly found in serious / historical games. Digital characters are employed to reenact known historical events, to portray famous persons, or simply to recreate the context of a specific historical period. In most cases the applications are interactive, and users have a role to play as well. E.g. The Fort Ross Virtual Warehouse project (Forte et al., 2012) is a game aiming to teach students about California history in an experiential way. The goal is to survive and prosper as a clerk at Fort Ross by learning and displaying historical, cultural and economic knowledge about the Fort.

Table 10 shows possible subjects of applications that include digital characters and indicative projects.

DISCUSSION

The various uses, design aspects and implemented features of digital characters in cultural heritage applications as described above raise a series of interesting observations and issues to consider.

The characteristics and functionality of digital characters largely depend on their role in the target application. If the application relies heavily on dialogs with the user, then the character(s) should emphasize this dimension and function as embodied conversational agents. They should include components for generating and maintaining dialogs, for synchronizing facial movements with speech, for performing non-verbal gestures, etc. In applications that focus on some character performance (e.g. a theatrical act, ritual or traditional dance), designers should consider using motion-capture technology to add more

Table 10. Subject of the application, indicative projects and their key features

Subject	project	key features
tangible heritage	Virtual Presenter (Van Welbergen et al., 2006)	presents museum exhibits
	Historic Costume Collection (Martin & Mauriello, 2013)	wears historic costumes
ancient / lost cultures	Archaeoguide (Vlahakis et al., 2002), Virtual Pompeii (Magnetat-Thalmann & Papagiannakis, 2010), City of Uruk (Bogdanovych et al., 2010)	characters imitate apperarance and behavior of ancient cultures
intangible heritage	Aspendos theatre in Minor Asia (Egges et al., 2007)	character performs ancient Greek dramas
	Hagia Sophia (Foni et al., 2007)	morning Namaz Pray in 16th century Hagia Sophia
	AMICA (Carrozzino et al., 2016)	craft of printmaking
	Piying (Shi et al., 2014), Digital Chinese Shadow Play (Liang et al., 2016)	traditional Chinese shadowplay
Art	Qing-ming Festival (Chen et al., 2012), the Rule Confirmation (Pietroni & Antinucci, 2010)	recreated painting with animated characters
History	Fort Ross Virtual Warehouse (Forte et al., 2012)	experiential learning of California history

'personality' to the digital human and make the motion more expressive. If the emphasis is in the user interactivity or in simulating some event, then the digital character should be able to cope with the unpredictability of the environment. The user interventions and/or the dynamic evolution of the simulated event will cause frequent changes in the setup of the environment, and the characters should be able to take these changes into account and act reasonably. Thus, it is more appropriate to use a virtual agent architecture in this case, so that the characters have a certain degree of autonomy in their reactions. Furthermore, as Eric Champion (2015) suggested, if these characters are demonstrating come lost or ancient culture, they should incorporate mechanisms to exhibit and recognize proper cultural behaviors. Finally, if a character is used as a presenter, it should be able to retrieve semantic information from the places and objects of cultural significance and to be able to summarize and present this information in a personalized manner, according to the visitors' interests and needs.

Designers should consider including elements that enhance visitor experience. As argued by Roussou (2008), storytelling is the best means to trigger abilities such as visitor interest, empathy and imagination, which are expected to lead to a successful entertainment experience of cultural heritage applications. Digital characters should have personality, they should be "as remarkable and unforgettable as humans" and they should tie well into story structures that fire the visitors' imagination. In applications that need to quickly capture the users' attention, e.g. public installations or edutainment apps for children, it is important to focus on the expressive side of digital characters, even by incorporating non-realistic elements, rather than striving for accuracy and realism. Elements such as facial expressions, motion-captured animations, and pre-defined dialogs and action sequences can enhance this side. Additionally, the inclusion of a background story and some funny incidents or dramatic events will probably contribute to the users' empathy and increase their engagement.

The choice between autonomy and predefined behavior seems to be a difficult dilemma. Autonomous characters are able to properly respond in a dynamic environment, and as such, they can support environments that are more interactive and exploratory. Users are free to interact with the characters in various ways; they may try out and experiment with different actions and observe the responses, and their activity can influence the evolution of the environment. Furthermore, autonomous agents are easily reused in similar applications. One could change or expand the scenario, or even create a similar scenario in an entirely different historical context, and still, most of the agents' components would be the same. On the other hand, the use of predefined actions and responses with a low degree of autonomy has other important benefits. One can easily control the flow of actions, the dialogs and the story. The designer can ensure that the resulting story is interesting, that the character is as expressive as needed, and it includes the desired elements of 'personality' to provide a remarkable user experience. It has thus been argued that digital characters should be better plot-driven than autonomous and intelligent, and that sometimes a completely emergent narrative can be obstacle to the aims of heritage applications (Champion, 2015).

As we have witnessed in a few cases, the role of digital characters in an application is not always distinct. Sometimes the same character may act as a presenter, a tutor or an actor. It may have to participate and act in some story, to have dialogs with the users, to present some elements of the environment, etc. Therefore, an interesting direction for future research is towards architectures that can effectively support multiple roles and easily switch between them. The levels of interaction framework by Panzoli et al. (2010) is a first step towards this aim. It proposes three distinct levels of interaction for digital characters, depending on their distance from the user: the living background, where the characters operate as part of the virtual crowd, the interaction level, where characters pay attention to the user and allow for some basic interactions with him, and the dialogue, where the user and character interact in natural language using text or speech. Unfortunately, little progress has been made from the introduction of this framework until now.

Another noteworthy feature that is currently emerging in digital heritage applications is the adoption of kinesthetic user interfaces. With the use of low-cost hardware (e.g. MS Kinect, Myo Armband or Leap Motion) users can directly control their avatar using natural hand gestures or even full-body motion. This affordance is mostly useful in public installations, to offer a more engaging and participatory user experience. In opens new possibilities, especially in the case of intangible heritage, as it lets users participate and imitate activities in a richer way compared to typical mouse-and-keyboard or touch interfaces (Koutsabasis & Vosinakis, 2016). An interesting future usage of these interfaces would be to have computer-controlled characters recognize and properly respond to facial expressions and non-verbal gestures of users, or even to evaluate their performance in the context of some cultural activity.

The augmentation of the physical environment with digital characters is another promising feature of virtual heritage applications that needs to be further exploited. The high-end technology that has been used in large projects such as Archeoguide (Vlahakis et al, 2002) in the previous decade is expensive, is associated with usability issues, and it certainly cannot be applied on a large scale. On the other hand, the more recent approach of mobile AR has other limitations. It may be accessible to everyone, but it has low tracking accuracy, especially in markerless environments. This will be possibly improved in the near future with the use of depth sensors that support automated mapping of a physical space, such as Google Tango and Structure Sensor. Furthermore, the typical screen size of a smartphone is quite limited to properly present an interesting scenery with animated digital characters. The size of the characters on screen will probably be too small to distinguish interesting elements of their appearance and behavior. The use of mobile devices with larger screens (tablets) might be preferable in that case.

Finally, the notable lack of standards and platforms for developing rich interactive digital characters is considered an important obstacle to the development of virtual heritage applications. Virtual worlds such as Second Life or its open-source alternative OpenSimulator would be a sufficient base platform for such applications, and it has already been used in projects such as the City of Uruk (Bodganovych et al.,

2010) and Virtual Agora (Vosinakis et al., 2018). However, nowadays they are not as popular as they used to be a decade ago, and their rendering, animation and physics quality is significantly lower compared to modern games and virtual environments. The use of powerful game engines such as Unity3D or Unreal Engine, which are available free of cost, is a better choice. However, being general-purpose engines, they provide only low-level support for constructing digital characters, such as triggering animations and pathfinding. Thus, it requires a lot of effort and programming experience to create characters with complex behavior in a virtual heritage environment.

CONCLUSION

This paper presented an overview of digital characters and their usage in cultural heritage applications. Initially, we attempted to collect the various terms used in the bibliography for digital characters and clarify their meaning, noticing that this multiplicity and ambiguity of terms is a possible source of confusion. Then, we presented the various modelling stages for creating a digital character and their interrelations, and we mentioned some common approaches and techniques related to these stages. We introduced and attempted to explain the notion of believability and its relation to digital characters, as this is an important design goal and assessment metric for them. After that we introduced eight dimensions related to the characteristics and function of digital characters in virtual heritage applications and for each one of them we provided a description of solutions found in the bibliography, along with typical examples. These results led to a discussion about prospects and pitfalls of various design and technological approaches of digital characters, current trends and open research challenges.

Based on the review and the discussion that followed, we can definitely acknowledge the significant contribution and importance of digital characters in heritage applications and their multiple manifestations in a variety of roles. It is therefore important for designers to be aware of the range of features, techniques and approaches related to the creation of digital characters, and their implications for the application and the user experience, so that they get the most out of this technology. This is even more crucial for intangible heritage, which seems to be underrepresented in today's applications, and is strongly connected with human presence and activity. Regarding, however, the maturity of current technology and the availability of tools and development platforms it seems that there is still road to be covered.

REFERENCES

Abaci, T., Ciger, J., & Thalmann, D. (2005). Planning with smart objects. WSCG 2005 (Short Papers), 25-28.

Anderson, E. F., McLoughlin, L., Liarokapis, F., Peters, C., Petridis, P., & de Freitas, S. (2010). Developing serious games for cultural heritage: A state-of-the-art Review. *Virtual Reality (Waltham Cross), 14*(4), 255–275. doi:10.100710055-010-0177-3

André, E., Klesen, M., Gebhard, P., Allen, S., & Rist, T. (2000). Integrating models of personality and emotions into lifelike characters. In *Affective interactions* (pp. 150–165). Springer Berlin Heidelberg. doi:10.1007/10720296_11

Arévalo, M., Cadi-Yazli, N., & Thalmann, N. M. (2014). Giving Life to John Calvin the Reformer. In *Euro-Mediterranean Conference* (pp. 526-535). Springer International Publishing. 10.1007/978-3-319-13695-0_52

Arnold, D. (2008). Tools for populating cultural heritage environments with interactive virtual humans. In *Open Digital Cultural Heritage Systems Conference* (p. 25). Academic Press.

Ball, C., Ahn, S. J., & Johnsen, K. (2019). Design and Field Study of Motion-based Informal Learning Games for a Children's Museum. In *2019 IEEE 5th Workshop on Everyday Virtual Reality (WEVR)* (pp. 1-6). IEEE. 10.1109/WEVR.2019.8809588

Bandi, S., & Thalmann, D. (2000). Path finding for human motion in virtual environments. *Computational Geometry, 15*(1-3), 103–127. doi:10.1016/S0925-7721(99)00046-2

Bates, J. (1994). The role of emotion in believable agents. *Communications of the ACM, 37*(7), 122–125. doi:10.1145/176789.176803

Bekele, M. K., Pierdicca, R., Frontoni, E., Malinverni, E. S., & Gain, J. (2018). A survey of augmented, virtual, and mixed reality for cultural heritage. *Journal on Computing and Cultural Heritage, 11*(2), 7. doi:10.1145/3145534

Bevacqua, E., Mancini, M., Niewiadomski, R., & Pelachaud, C. (2007) An expressive ECA showing complex emotions. *Proceedings of the AISB Annual convention, Workshop on Language, Speech and Gesture for Expressive Characters*, 208-216.

Bogdanovych, A., Rodríguez-Aguilar, J. A., Simoff, S., & Cohen, A. (2010). Authentic interactive reenactment of cultural heritage with 3D virtual worlds and artificial intelligence. *Applied Artificial Intelligence, 24*(6), 617–647. doi:10.1080/08839514.2010.492172

Bogdanovych, A., Trescak, T., & Simoff, S. (2016). What makes virtual agents believable? *Connection Science, 28*(1), 83–108. doi:10.1080/09540091.2015.1130021

Bontchev, B. (2015). Serious games for and as cultural heritage. *Digital Presentation and Preservation of Cultural and Scientific Heritage*, (5), 43-58.

Brogan, D. C., Metoyer, R. A., & Hodgins, J. K. (1998). Dynamically simulated characters in virtual environments. *IEEE Computer Graphics and Applications, 18*(5), 58–69. doi:10.1109/38.708561

Carmo, M. B., & Cláudio, A. P. (2013). 3D virtual exhibitions. *DESIDOC Journal of Library and Information Technology, 33*(3), 222–235. doi:10.14429/djlit.33.3.4608

Carrozzino, M., Colombo, M., Tecchia, F., Evangelista, C., & Bergamasco, M. (2018). Comparing Different Storytelling Approaches for Virtual Guides in Digital Immersive Museums. In *International Conference on Augmented Reality, Virtual Reality and Computer Graphics* (pp. 292-302). Springer. 10.1007/978-3-319-95282-6_22

Carrozzino, M., Lorenzini, C., Duguleana, M., Evangelista, C., Brondi, R., Tecchia, F., & Bergamasco, M. (2016). An immersive VR experience to learn the craft of printmaking. In *International Conference on Augmented Reality, Virtual Reality and Computer Graphics* (pp. 378-389). Springer. 10.1007/978-3-319-40651-0_30

Cassell, J. (2001). Embodied conversational agents: Representation and intelligence in user interfaces. *AI Magazine*, *22*(4), 67.

Cassell, J., Vilhjálmsson, H. H., & Bickmore, T. (2004). Beat: the behavior expression animation toolkit. In Life-Like Characters (pp. 163-185). Springer Berlin Heidelberg. doi:10.1007/978-3-662-08373-4_8

Cavazza, M., Earnshaw, R., Magnenat-Thalmann, N., & Thalmann, D. (1998). Motion control of virtual humans. *IEEE Computer Graphics and Applications*, *18*(5), 24–31. doi:10.1109/38.708558

Champion, E. (2015). Defining cultural agents for virtual heritage environments. *Presence (Cambridge, Mass.)*, *24*(3), 179–186. doi:10.1162/PRES_a_00234

Chen, S., Pan, Z., & Zhang, M. (2012). A virtual informal learning system for cultural heritage. In *Transactions on edutainment VII* (pp. 180–187). Springer Berlin Heidelberg. doi:10.1007/978-3-642-29050-3_16

Choi, W., Baker, D., Blazeby, M., Furukawa, K., Hachimura, K., & Beacham, R. (2010). Character Animation of Intangible Cultural Heritage in Second Life. *Proceedings of IEEEJ Image Electronics and Visual Computing Workshop.*

Corradini, A., Fredriksson, M., Mehta, M., Königsmann, J., Bernsen, N. O., & Johannesson, L. (2004). Towards believable behavior generation for embodied conversational agents. In *International Conference on Computational Science* (pp. 946-953). Springer Berlin Heidelberg. 10.1007/978-3-540-24688-6_121

Doumanis, I. (2013). *Evaluating humanoid embodied conversational agents in mobile guide applications* (Doctoral dissertation). Middlesex University.

Ducheneaut, N., Wen, M. H., Yee, N., & Wadley, G. (2009). Body and mind: a study of avatar personalization in three virtual worlds. *Proceedings of the SIGCHI Conference on Human Factors in Computing Systems (CHI '09)*, 1151–1160. 10.1145/1518701.1518877

Egges, A., Papagiannakis, G., & Magnenat-Thalmann, N. (2007). Presence and interaction in mixed reality environments. *The Visual Computer*, *23*(5), 317–333. doi:10.100700371-007-0113-z

Foni, A. E., Papagiannakis, G., Cadi-Yazli, N., & Magnenat-Thalmann, N. (2007). Time-Dependent Illumination and Animation of Virtual Hagia-Sophia. *International Journal of Architectural Computing*, *5*(2), 283–301. doi:10.1260/1478-0771.5.2.284

Forte, M., Lercari, N., Onsurez, L., Issavi, J., & Prather, E. (2012). The Fort Ross virtual warehouse project: a serious game for research and education. In *Virtual Systems and Multimedia (VSMM), 2012 18th International Conference on* (pp. 315-322). IEEE. 10.1109/VSMM.2012.6365940

Froschauer, J., Seidel, I., Gärtner, M., Berger, H., & Merkl, D. (2010). Design and evaluation of a serious game for immersive cultural training. In *Virtual Systems and Multimedia (VSMM), 2010 16th International Conference on* (pp. 253-260). IEEE. 10.1109/VSMM.2010.5665978

Funge, J., Tu, X., & Terzopoulos, D. (1999). Cognitive modeling: knowledge, reasoning and planning for intelligent characters. In *Proceedings of the 26th annual conference on Computer graphics and interactive techniques* (pp. 29-38). ACM Press/Addison-Wesley Publishing Co. 10.1145/311535.311538

Gaitatzes, A., Christopoulos, D., & Roussou, M. (2001). Reviving the past: cultural heritage meets virtual reality. In *Proceedings of the 2001 conference on Virtual reality, archeology, and cultural heritage* (pp. 103-110). ACM. 10.1145/584993.585011

Ghouaiel, N., Garbaya, S., Cieutat, J. M., & Jessel, J. P. (2016). Mobile Augmented Reality in Museums: Towards Enhancing Visitor's Learning Experience. *The International Journal of Virtual Reality, 17*(1), 21–31.

Gillies, M., & Spanlang, B. (2010). Comparing and evaluating real time character engines for virtual environments. *Presence (Cambridge, Mass.), 19*(2), 95–117. doi:10.1162/pres.19.2.95

Glas, N., & Pelachaud, C. (2015). User engagement and preferences in information-giving chat with virtual agents. In *Workshop on Engagement in Social Intelligent Virtual Agents (ESIVA)* (pp. 33-40). Academic Press.

Gratch, J., Rickel, J., André, E., Cassell, J., Petajan, E., & Badler, N. (2002). Creating interactive virtual humans: Some assembly required. *IEEE Intelligent Systems, 17*(4), 54–63. doi:10.1109/MIS.2002.1024753

Guy, S. J., Lin, M. C., & Manocha, D. (2010). Modeling collision avoidance behavior for virtual humans. In *Proceedings of the 9th International Conference on Autonomous Agents and Multiagent Systems* (vol. 2, pp. 575-582). International Foundation for Autonomous Agents and Multiagent Systems.

Ho, W. C., & Dautenhahn, K. (2008). Towards a Narrative Mind: The Creation of Coherent Life Stories for Believable Virtual Agents. Lecture Notes in Computer Science, 5208, 59-72.

Ieronutti, L., & Chittaro, L. (2007). Employing virtual humans for education and training in X3D/VRML worlds. *Computers & Education, 49*(1), 93–109. doi:10.1016/j.compedu.2005.06.007

Kasap, Z., & Magnenat-Thalmann, N. (2008). Intelligent virtual humans with autonomy and personality: State-of-the-art. In *New Advances in Virtual Humans* (pp. 43–84). Springer Berlin Heidelberg. doi:10.1007/978-3-540-79868-2_2

Koutsabasis, P., & Vosinakis, S. (2016). Adult and Children User Experience with Leap Motion in Digital Heritage: The Cycladic Sculpture Application. In *Euro-Mediterranean Conference* (pp. 350-361). Springer International Publishing. 10.1007/978-3-319-48496-9_28

Lee, S., Carlson, G., Jones, S., Johnson, A., Leigh, J., & Renambot, L. (2010). Designing an expressive avatar of a real person. *Lecture Notes in Computer Science, 6356*, 64–76. doi:10.1007/978-3-642-15892-6_8

Liang, H., Deng, S., Chang, J., Zhang, J. J., Chen, C., & Tong, R. (2016). Ontology-based interactive animation/game generation for Chinese shadow play preservation. In *2016 8th International Conference on Games and Virtual Worlds for Serious Applications (VS-GAMES)* (pp. 1-9). IEEE.

Lim, C. K., Cani, M. P., Galvane, Q., Pettre, J., & Talib, A. Z. (2013). Simulation of past life: Controlling agent behaviors from the interactions between ethnic groups. In *Digital Heritage International Congress (DigitalHeritage)*, 2013 (Vol. 1, pp. 589-596). IEEE. 10.1109/DigitalHeritage.2013.6743800

Lim, C. K., Tan, K. L., Zaidan, A. A., & Zaidan, B. B. (2019). A proposed methodology of bringing past life in digital cultural heritage through crowd simulation: A case study in George Town, Malaysia. *Multimedia Tools and Applications*, 1–37.

Lim, M. Y., & Aylett, R. S. (2007). Feel the difference: A Guide with Attitude! In *IVA 2007, LNAI 4722* (pp. 317–330). Berlin: Springer-Verlag. doi:10.1007/978-3-540-74997-4_29

Loyall, A. B., & Bates, J. (1997) Personality-rich believable agents that use language. *Proceedings of the First International Conference on Autonomous Agents*, 106–113. 10.1145/267658.267681

Luck, M., & Aylett, R. (2000). Applying artificial intelligence to virtual reality: Intelligent virtual environments. *Applied Artificial Intelligence*, *14*(1), 3–32. doi:10.1080/088395100117142

Luginbuhl, T., Delattre, L., & Gagalowicz, A. (2011). Towards the automatic generation of 3D photorealistic avatars using 3D scanned data. Lecture Notes in Computer Science, 6930, 192–203.

Machidon, O. M., Duguleana, M., & Carrozzino, M. (2018). Virtual humans in cultural heritage ICT applications: A review. *Journal of Cultural Heritage*, *33*, 249–260. doi:10.1016/j.culher.2018.01.007

Magnenat-Thalmann, N., & Kasap, Z. (2009). Modelling socially intelligent virtual humans. *International Conference on Virtual Reality Continnum and its Applications in Industry VRCAI.*

Magnenat-Thalmann, N., Kim, H. S., Egges, A., & Garchery, S. (2005) Believability and Interaction in Virtual Worlds. In *Proceedings of the 11th Intl. Multimedia Modelling Conference (MMM'05).* IEEE Computer Society. 10.1109/MMMC.2005.24

Magnenat-Thalmann, N., & Papagiannakis, G. (2010). Recreating Daily life in Pompeii. *Virtual Archaeology Review*, *1*(2), 19–23. doi:10.4995/var.2010.4679

Magnenat-Thalmann, N., Seo, H., & Cordier, F. (2004). Automatic modeling of virtual humans and body clothing. *Journal of Computer Science and Technology*, *19*(5), 575–584. doi:10.1007/BF02945583

Martin, K., & Mauriello, D. (2013). Motion and embodiment: 3D simulations for historic fashion. In *Digital Heritage International Congress (DigitalHeritage)*, 2013 (Vol. 2, pp. 329-332). IEEE. 10.1109/DigitalHeritage.2013.6744773

McCrae, R. R., & John, O. P. (1992). An introduction to the five-factor model and its applications. *Journal of Personality*, *60*(2), 175–215. doi:10.1111/j.1467-6494.1992.tb00970.x PMID:1635039

Mori, M. (1970). The Uncanny Valley. *Energy*, *7*(4), 33–35.

Mortara, M., Catalano, C. E., Bellotti, F., Fiucci, G., Houry-Panchetti, M., & Petridis, P. (2014). Learning cultural heritage by serious games. *Journal of Cultural Heritage*, *15*(3), 318–325. doi:10.1016/j.culher.2013.04.004

Nareyek, A. (2004). AI in computer games. *Queue*, *1*(10), 58. doi:10.1145/971564.971593

Neto, J. N., Silva, R., Neto, J. P., Pereira, J. M., & Fernandes, J. (2011). Solis' Curse-A Cultural Heritage game using voice interaction with a Virtual Agent. In *Games and Virtual Worlds for Serious Applications (VS-GAMES), 2011 Third International Conference on* (pp. 164-167). IEEE.

Noh, Z., Sunar, M. S., & Pan, Z. (2009). A review on augmented reality for virtual heritage system. In *International conference on technologies for E-learning and digital entertainment* (pp. 50-61). Springer. 10.1007/978-3-642-03364-3_7

Novick, D., Rodriguez, L., Pacheco, A., Rodriguez, A., Hinojos, L., Cartwright, B., ... Ponce, E. (2017). The Boston Massacre history experience. In *Proceedings of the 19th ACM International Conference on Multimodal Interaction* (pp. 499-500). ACM.

Ortony, A. (2003). On making believable emotional agents believable. In R. P. Trapple, P. (Ed.), Emotions in humans and artefacts. Cambridge, MA: MIT Press.

Ortony, A., Clore, G. L., & Collins, A. (1990). *The cognitive structure of emotions*. Cambridge University Press.

Paliokas, I., & Sylaiou, S. (2016). The Use of Serious Games in Museum Visits and Exhibitions: A Systematic Mapping Study. In *Games and Virtual Worlds for Serious Applications (VS-Games), 2016 8th International Conference on* (pp. 1-8). IEEE. 10.1109/VS-GAMES.2016.7590371

Pang, W. C., Wong, C. Y., & Seet, G. (2018). Exploring the use of robots for museum settings and for learning heritage languages and cultures at the chinese heritage centre. *Presence (Cambridge, Mass.), 26*(4), 420–435. doi:10.1162/PRES_a_00306

Panzoli, D. (2010). A level of interaction framework for exploratory learning with characters in virtual environments. *Intelligent Computer Graphics, 2010*, 123–143.

Pelechano, N., Allbeck, J. M., & Badler, N. I. (2008). Virtual crowds: Methods, simulation, and control. *Synthesis Lectures on Computer Graphics and Animation, 3*(1), 1–176. doi:10.2200/S00123ED1V01Y200808CGR008

Pensyl, W. R., Jernigan, D. K., Qui, T. C. T., Fang, H. P., & Ping, L. S. (2008). Large area robust hybrid tracking with life-size avatar in mixed reality environment: for cultural and historical installation. In *Proceedings of The 7th ACM SIGGRAPH International Conference on Virtual-Reality Continuum and Its Applications in Industry* (p. 9). ACM. 10.1145/1477862.1477874

Perlin, K., & Goldberg, A. (1996). Improv: A System for Scripting Interactive Actors in Virtual Worlds. *Proceedings of the 23rd Annual Conference on Computer Graphics and Interactive Techniques - SIGGRAPH '96*, (212), 205–216. 10.1145/237170.237258

Pietroni, E., & Antinucci, F. (2010). The Approval of the Franciscan Rule. Virtual Experience among the Characters of Giotto's Work. *Proceedings of the 11th International Symposium on Virtual Reality, Archaeology and Cultural Heritage VAST*.

Poel, M., Heylen, D., Nijholt, A., Meulemans, M., & Van Breemen, A. (2009). Gaze behaviour, believability, likability and the iCat. *AI & Society, 24*(1), 61–73. doi:10.100700146-009-0198-1

Popovici, D. M., Bogdan, C. M., Polceanu, M., & Querrec, R. (2011). Applying of an ontology based modeling approach to cultural heritage systems. *Advances in Electrical and Computer Engineering, 11*(3), 105–110. doi:10.4316/aece.2011.03017

Puig, A., Rodríguez, I., Arcos, J. L., Rodríguez-Aguilar, J. A., Cebrián, S., Bogdanovych, A., ... Piqué, R. (2019). Lessons learned from supplementing archaeological museum exhibitions with virtual reality. *Virtual Reality (Waltham Cross)*. doi:10.100710055-019-00391-z

Richards, D. (2012). Agent-based museum and tour guides: applying the state of the art. In *Proceedings of The 8th Australasian Conference on Interactive Entertainment: Playing the System* (p. 15). ACM. 10.1145/2336727.2336742

Roussou, M. (2008). The components of engagement in virtual heritage environments. *New Heritage: New media and cultural heritage*, 225-241.

Schmidt, S., Bruder, G., & Steinicke, F. (2018). *Effects of Embodiment on Generic and Content-Specific Intelligent Virtual Agents as Exhibition Guides*. ICAT-EGVE.

Sénécal, S., Cadi, N., Arévalo, M., & Magnenat-Thalmann, N. (2017). Modelling life through time: cultural heritage case studies. In *Mixed Reality and Gamification for Cultural Heritage* (pp. 395–419). Cham: Springer. doi:10.1007/978-3-319-49607-8_16

Shi, Y., Ying, F., Chen, X., Pan, Z., & Yu, J. (2014). Restoration of traditional Chinese shadow play-Piying art from tangible interaction. *Computer Animation and Virtual Worlds*, *25*(1), 33–43. doi:10.1002/cav.1530

Shih, J. L., Jheng, S. C., & Tseng, J. J. (2015). A simulated learning environment of history games for enhancing players' cultural awareness. *Interactive Learning Environments*, *23*(2), 191–211. doi:10.1080/10494820.2014.997249

Sloan, R. J. S., Cook, M., & Robinson, B. (2009). Considerations for believable emotional facial expression animation. In *Visualisation, 2009. VIZ'09. Second International Conference in* (pp. 61-66). IEEE. 10.1109/VIZ.2009.28

Spring, D. (2015). Gaming history: Computer and video games as historical scholarship. *Rethinking History*, *19*(2), 207–221. doi:10.1080/13642529.2014.973714

Swartout, W. R., Gratch, J., Hill, R. W., Hovy, E., Marsella, S., Rickel, J., & Traum, D. (2006). Toward Virtual Humans. *AI Magazine*, *27*(2), 96–108.

Sylaiou, S., Liarokapis, F., Kotsakis, K., & Patias, P. (2009). Virtual museums, a survey and some issues for consideration. *Journal of Cultural Heritage*, *10*(4), 520–528. doi:10.1016/j.culher.2009.03.003

Thalmann, D. (2014). Populating 3D Cities: A True Challenge. *Proceeding of the Electrical Engineering Computer Science and Informatics*, *1*(1), 1-10.

Thalmann, D., Maïm, B., & Maïm, J. (2014). Geometric Issues in Reconstruction of Virtual Heritage Involving Large Populations. In 3D Research Challenges in Cultural Heritage (pp. 78-92). Springer Berlin Heidelberg. doi:10.1007/978-3-662-44630-0_6

Tolani, D., & Badler, N. I. (1996). Real-time inverse kinematics of the human arm. *Presence (Cambridge, Mass.)*, *5*(4), 393–401. doi:10.1162/pres.1996.5.4.393 PMID:11539377

Trescak, T., Bogdanovych, A., & Simoff, S. (2014). City of Uruk 3000 BC: Using genetic algorithms, dynamic planning and crowd simulation to re-enact everyday life of ancient Sumerians. *Proceedings of the Simulation of the Past to Understand Human History Conference*.

Ulicny, B., & Thalmann, D. (2001). Crowd simulation for interactive virtual environments and VR training systems. In *Computer Animation and Simulation 2001* (pp. 163–170). Springer Vienna. doi:10.1007/978-3-7091-6240-8_15

Van Welbergen, H., Nijholt, A., Reidsma, D., & Zwiers, J. (2006). Presenting in virtual worlds: An architecture for a 3d anthropomorphic presenter. *IEEE Intelligent Systems*, *21*(5), 47–53. doi:10.1109/MIS.2006.101

Viinikkala, L., Yli-Seppälä, L., Heimo, O. I., Helle, S., Härkänen, L., Jokela, S., . . . Seppälä, K. (2016). Reforming the representation of the reformation: Mixed reality narratives in communicating tangible and intangible heritage of the protestant reformation in Finland. In *2016 22nd International Conference on Virtual System & Multimedia (VSMM)* (pp. 1-9). IEEE.

Vlahakis, V., Ioannidis, M., Karigiannis, J., Tsotros, M., Gounaris, M., Stricker, D., ... Almeida, L. (2002). Archeoguide: An augmented reality guide for archaeological sites. *IEEE Computer Graphics and Applications*, *22*(5), 52–60. doi:10.1109/MCG.2002.1028726

Vosinakis, S., & Avradinis, N. (2016). Virtual Agora: Representation of an Ancient Greek Agora in Virtual Worlds using Biologically-Inspired Motivational Agents. *Mediterranean Archaeology and Archaeometry*, *16*(5), 29–41.

Vosinakis, S., Avradinis, N., & Koutsabasis, P. (2018). Dissemination of Intangible Cultural Heritage using a Multi-Agent Virtual World. In *Advances in Digital Cultural Heritage* (pp. 197–207). Cham: Springer. doi:10.1007/978-3-319-75789-6_14

Vosinakis, S., & Panayiotopoulos, T. (2001). SimHuman: A platform for real-time virtual agents with planning capabilities. In *International Workshop on Intelligent Virtual Agents* (pp. 210-223). Springer Berlin Heidelberg. 10.1007/3-540-44812-8_17

Vourvopoulos, A., Liarokapis, F., & Petridis, P. (2012). Brain-controlled serious games for cultural heritage. In *Virtual Systems and Multimedia (VSMM), 2012 18th International Conference on* (pp. 291-298). IEEE. 10.1109/VSMM.2012.6365937

Wang, L., Guo, J. W., Yang, C. L., Zhao, H. S., & Meng, X. X. (2010). O3D-based game learning environments for cultural heritage online education. In *International Conference on Technologies for E-Learning and Digital Entertainment* (pp. 417-428). Springer Berlin Heidelberg. 10.1007/978-3-642-14533-9_43

Wooldridge, M., & Jennings, N. R. (1995). Intelligent agents: Theory and practice. *The Knowledge Engineering Review*, *10*(02), 115–152. doi:10.1017/S0269888900008122

Chapter 7
3D Reconstruction Challenges Using Structure-From-Motion

Anestis Koutsoudis
Athena – Research and Innovation Center in Information, Communication, and Knowledge Technologies, Greece

George Ioannakis
Democritus University of Thrace, Greece

Fotis Arnaoutoglou
Athena – Research and Innovation Center in Information, Communication, and Knowledge Technologies, Greece

Chairi Kiourt
https://orcid.org/0000-0001-8501-8899
Athena – Research and Innovation Center in Information, Communication, and Knowledge Technologies, Greece

Christodoulos Chamzas
https://orcid.org/0000-0003-4151-3200
Democritus University of Thrace, Greece

ABSTRACT

Numerous software solutions implementing the structure-from-motion/multi-view stereo (SFM/MVS) 3D reconstruction approach have been made available over the last two decades. Hence, enabling the production of high quality, in terms of geometry and colour information, 3D objects using solely unordered image sequences depicting a static scene or objects from arbitrary viewpoints. Nowadays, SFM/MVS-based 3D reconstruction approaches constitute a popular solution in a variety of applications within many research domains including cultural heritage. However, as with all 3D reconstruction approaches, SfM/MVS has its limitations and applicability challenges. In this chapter, the authors attempt to provide a set of guidelines that are based on the important outcomes of published works that propose solutions to overcome some of the challenges introduced by non-friendly to SfM/MVS scenes or objects.

DOI: 10.4018/978-1-7998-2871-6.ch007

Figure 1. Structure-from-Motion overview

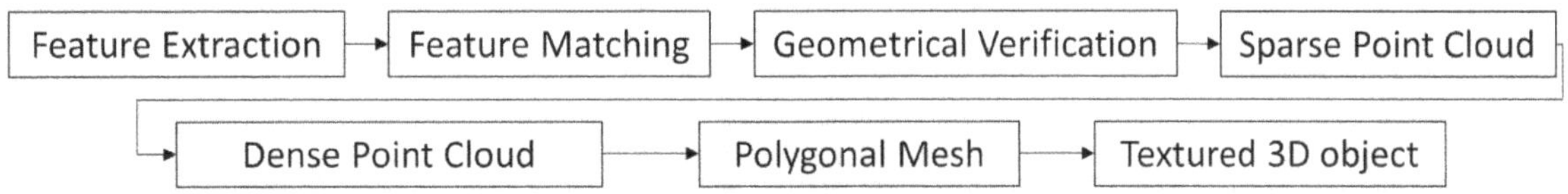

INTRODUCTION

Over the last decades the number of available 3D digital replicas is growing and constitute an integral part of many research domains including cultural heritage, Archaeology, Architecture, Medicine, etc. The key role for this fact is the progress achieved in 3D digitization systems coupled with the ongoing development of real-time 3D graphics. 3D digital replicas can be created through the usage of various methodologies ranging from multi-image photogrammetry (Structure-from-Motion -SfM/Multiple-View-Stereovision – MVS), Laser Triangulation to Structured Light. For the multi-image photogrammetry case, the existence of low-cost software solutions or open source libraries that implement the SfM/MVS pipeline, in combination with the minimum user intervention needs, enable their use as a black box solution. Moreover, its broad implementation relies also on the cost effectiveness in terms of hardware equipment, man-hours spent during the data collection phase and its relatively low background knowledge requirements. Additionally, as far as the generated 3D digital replica is concerned, its quality and accuracy in terms of geometry and texturing satisfies a vast range of 3D digitization projects (Koutsoudis et al., 2014).

Within the cultural heritage domain 3D reconstruction is considered as a common practice (Koutsoudis et al., 2012), an application domain that is very demanding in terms of geometrical and colour accuracy. 3D digital replicas can be used for dissemination and documentation purposes and constitute a valuable tool as well for archaeologists and conservators to conduct their studies. Europeana, the European commission's digital platform for Cultural Heritage (EUROPEANA), recognising the value of 3D digital replicas hosts a significant number of 3D items, ranging from small objects (e.g. a vase) to large scale objects (e.g. an architectural). Numerous European and national research and development projects exploiting the SfM approach (CARRARE; 3D-ICONS; 3D-COFORM), as well as independent initiatives have been conducted to enrich the digital libraries with high geometric accuracy 3D content.

The main scope of this chapter is to indicate challenges that the SfM/MVS approach is facing and subsequently to present significant published scientific works that confront and offer ways to handle the different limitations and drawbacks of the traditional SfM/MVS approach. Additionally, this work attempts to provide a framework to conduct SfM/MVS even in cases that normally are either unable to produce any 3D digital replica or the outcome fails to meet the requirements in terms of geometric accuracy.

Figure 2. SfM pipeline overview. Left: data collection, Middle: Image sequences and Right: 3D object

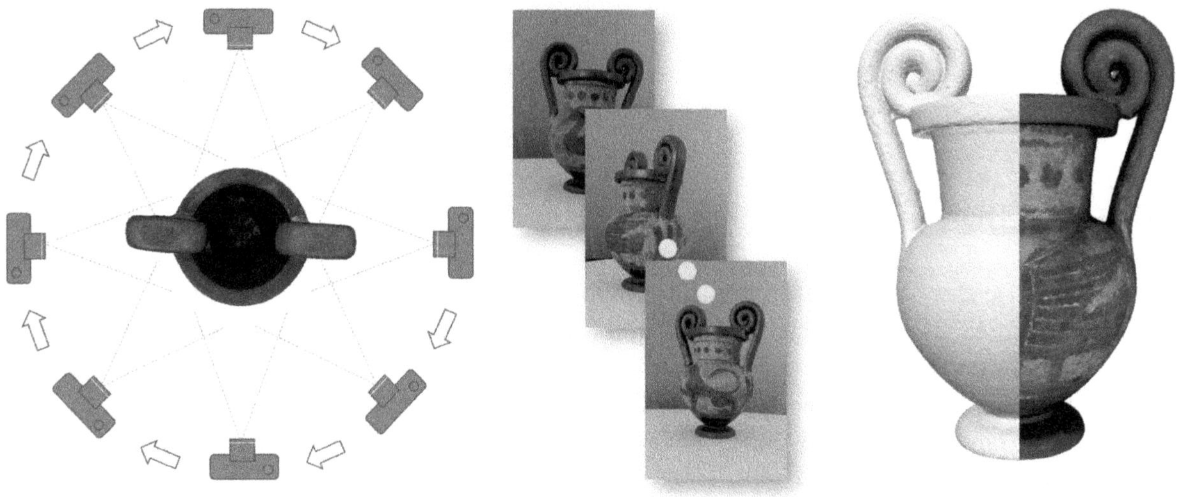

STRUCTURE-FROM-MOTION/MULTI-VIEW STEREO OVERVIEW

The SfM-MVS pipeline involves distinct phases such as image sequence collection, feature points extraction, matching of corresponding feature points among different images in overlapping areas and calculation of the extrinsic and intrinsic parameters of the camera (Cipolla, 2008). To improve the camera trajectory and thus minimize the projection error while preventing the error-built up of the camera tracking, bundle adjustment is implemented (Engels et al. 2006). SfM/MVS utilizes a set of unordered images, depicting a static scene or an object captured from arbitrary viewpoints that have a strong overlap with each other, to recover the camera parameters, to produce a sparse point cloud of the 3D scene followed by a dense point cloud which will ultimately be converted into a polygonal mesh (Figure 1 and 2).

Image Sequence Collection Phase

The phase is usually implemented using a digital camera. Sets of image sequences, that cover the surface of the object to be digitized, must be collected. Nevertheless, specific restrictions, during the image sequence collection, need to be addressed. Digital cameras carrying fixed lenses are favoured, however in case of zoom lenses, focal length should be set either to its minimal or maximal value. It is recommended to avoid lenses that have an ultra-wide field of view or fisheye lenses. Nonetheless, in cases where their usage is unavoidable, it is strongly recommended to perform a camera calibration and observe the lenses performance. As far as camera settings are concerned, it is preferable to use the lowest possible ISO value, because higher values introduce noise (random variation of brightness or colour information – electronic noise) to the image sequences. The same stands for high compression levels in JPG and colour information loss in PNG image file formats. On the other hand, optimum results are expected when using lossless TIFF images that are produced from RAW images.

Figure 3: Corresponding Point is identified in two sequential images. The intersection between the rays connecting the point (P) determines its location in the 3D space, where C stands for optical centres (or principal point) of the camera and P1', P2' the depiction of point P in Image1 and Image2 respectively

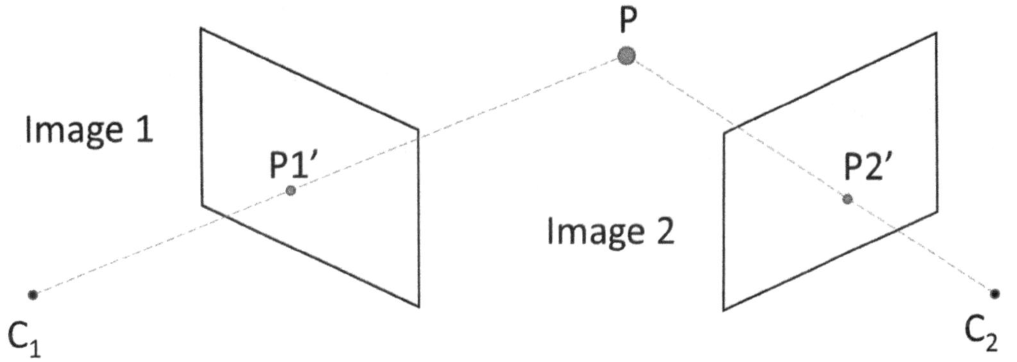

Sparse Point Cloud Generation

Computer vision has provided a breakthrough to photogrammetry by automating the 3D information extraction from images. More specifically, feature detection algorithms such as Scale-Invariant Feature Transform (SIFT) and Speeded Up Robust Features (SURF) can detect and describe local features (Lowe, 2004; Bay et al, 2008), that are later on matched across images. The workflow principal is depicted in Figure 3. These feature detection algorithms are robust against rotations, translations and scaling. The local features are used to determine overlapping areas of the scene among images; two key points are considered corresponding if they share a common description in different images. This process is performed for all local features of all images in a dataset. To define the true corresponding local features among images it is important to discard outliers, hence geometrical verification is performed using RANdom Sample Consensus (RANSAC) which was introduced by Fischler and Bolles (1981). Finally, bundle adjustment is performed in order to simultaneously refine the 3D coordinates of the sparse point cloud, the parameters of the relative motion, and the optical characteristics of the camera used to capture the image sequences.

Dense Point Cloud Generation

Multi-View Stereo (MVS) algorithms require prior knowledge in order to have a well posed 3D reconstruction problem. The generation of the dense point cloud relies on the estimated camera positions that where calculated in the bundle adjustment stage. Hence, every image must be accompanied by a corresponding camera model that describes the projection of each point from the 3D space onto the 2D space of an image. The camera model used within the MVS algorithms is the pinhole camera model, that is given through a *3x4* projection camera matrix (Furukawa and Hernández, 2015). The outcome of MVS algorithms is a highly detailed dense point cloud that constructs the geometry of the scene in a plausible manner.

Polygonal Mesh Generation

A 3D surface reconstruction from point samples is a research field within Computer Graphics that is thoroughly studied. It is a common fact that in practice several challenges arise while attempting to reconstruct a 3D surface from oriented points; non-uniform point sampling, noisy point position and normal vectors as well as misalignments that have occurred during the sparse point cloud generation. However, the better and well posed the outcome of the previous stages is, the better the 3D surface reconstruction methods can infer the underlying topology of the unknown surface and therefore accurately fit the dense point cloud (Kazhdan, 2006).

Texturing a 3D Digital Replica

The generation of a proper and plausible texture map for a 3D digital replica requires that illumination conditions did not significantly alter within the image sequence collection stage. Nevertheless, several image processing corrections can be performed to augment the outcome such as white balance and brightness calibration. However, the outcome, the 3D digital replica's texture map, is strongly related to the lighting conditions and thus it is recommended to consider performing the image collection under controlled environmental conditions. Nowadays, modern software solutions such as Agisoft Metashape and Reality Capture offer texture map processing functions to equalise lighting conditions that are visible on texture maps.

OVERCOMING SFM/MVS CHALLENGES

As aforementioned, a significant number of software solutions that implement SfM/MVS 3D reconstruction approach have been introduced over the last decades. It is a fact that SfM/MVS approach has a few requirements that are related to input data (image sequences) and need to be met. More specifically, the image collection phase should be performed, if possible, under controlled environmental conditions. Apart from the image sequence quality, the surface properties of the object being documented have to be approach-friendly attributes; high-frequency alterations in terms of colour and intensities and non-reflective are the major ones. In all other cases, it is most probable that the application of the SfM/MVS will produce 3D digital replicas that are erroneous in terms of geometric accuracy (noisy surfaces). A review of research works, introduced to the scientific community, that deal with challenges the SfM/MVS 3D reconstruction approach and provide a pipeline to overcome those is presented.

On Dealing with Featureless Surfaces

SfM/MVS belongs to the targetless photogrammetric family methods and therefore inevitably depends on the detection of strong local feature points on the surface of the object. SfM relies on correspondent feature point recognition to calculate the intrinsic and extrinsic parameters of the camera and thus determine the position and orientation of each image in 3D space. Hence, the generation of the initial sparse point cloud is highly coupled with the existence of local features on the surface of the object being captured. Objects with surfaces that are not SfM/MVS-friendly (no strong morphological features and low colour/intensity changes) result in poor feature detection and extraction algorithms' performance which inevitably affect the rest of the method's 3D reconstruction pipeline. Thus, the image quality and content play a key role in the feature extraction phase.

Gaiani et al. (2016) discuss on image content enhancement by utilizing Wallis filtering (Wallis, 1976), that had already proven its significant impact on the SfM/MVS approach (Baltsavias, 1991; Baltsavias, 1996; Remondino, 2008; MacDonald, 2014). The Wallis filter, that belongs to the digital image processing functions, enhances the contrast levels while flattening the varying exposure to achieve similar brightness among grey level values. Brightness values within local areas are adjusted, according to a user-defined mean value and standard deviation respectively. Its quality is related to the contrast expansion factor A and the brightness forcing factor B. A prerequisite is the accurate setting of the target mean and standard deviation to locally adjust areas with the user defined values. According to their experiments on three different datasets, the results led to the following considerations i) the number of the extracted tie points, which are points recognizable in the common content areas (overlap) of two or more images, is inversely proportional to the value of the parameter A, but the number of correct matches remains basically stable when varying A, which can be set to high values in order to reduce the processing time, ii) sensor size and window size are linearly related and the increase of the window size beyond the optimal size does not introduce any improvement in the number of matches or the number of extracted tie points, iii) increasing the user-defined standard deviation the number of tie points and correct matches increases substantially up to a specific value and then remains constant and iv) the optimum user-defined mean value lies within the range 100-150 and decreases afterwards. Finally, according to these considerations they derived the following optimum values for the filter parameters, the window size varies linearly from 41 for a 14Mpixel – to 24 for a 10MPixel sensor, the Contrast Expansion Constant parameter (A) was set to 0.8 while the brightness forcing factor (B) was set to 1 in cases where the image pixels' intensity mean value was lower than 150.

The in-house experiments revealed an average increase of 90% in the number of the extracted SURF features and an increase of corresponding SURF feature matches of 80% (geometrical verification was not performed) on the image sequences of the vase shown in Figure 4. Wallis filtering was performed using the executable written in C++ by D. Skarlatos (Wallis Filtering); indicative results are shown in Figure 4.

Figure 4. Wallis Filter implementation overview, accompanied by their histogram for every channel of the RGB colour space

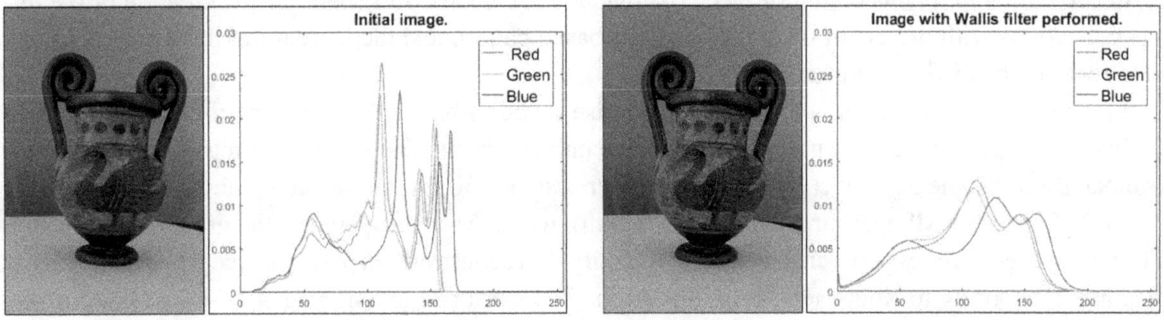

Figure 5. Overview of the setup and workflow

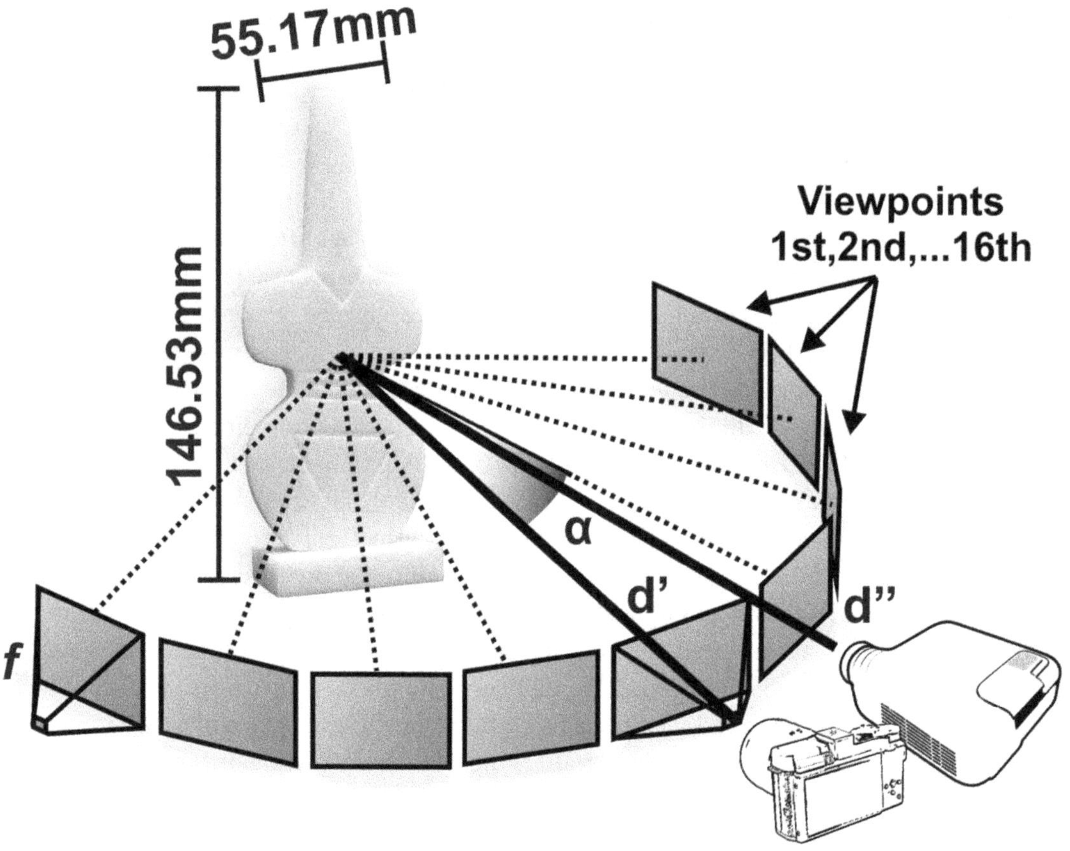

An efficient way to deal with the limitation and challenges introduced by featureless surfaces is proposed by Koutsoudis et al. (2015). In detail, the surface of an object being captured is artificially enriched with features with the aid of projecting noise function-based patterns (Figure 5). In such a manner, a higher accuracy 3D reconstruction is made possible in cases where the traditional SfM/MVS data collection would either completely fail to reconstruct a 3D object or result a poor 3D geometric accuracy.

The method affects the automation of the data collection phase as the noise function-based pattern should appear static on the object's surface and thus the introduction of partial 3D reconstruction alignments is inevitable. Evidently, the image collection phase time was increased due to the introduction of the proposed methodology to overcome the limitations of the SfM/MVS workflow that relied on the existence of feature points on the surface. To conclude, the time effort spent for the creation of the image collections with the use of the noise function-based pattern and the increase in the data processing time reflects the difficulty introduced.

In the experimental phase, a total of twelve noise function-based patterns were used and have been evaluated in terms of reconstruction performance enhancement. The twelve 3D reconstructions were compared against the 3D object produced by a laser scanner (50μm resolution on the Z axis and 100μm on the X, Y axes - RMS measurement error 6–10μm), which was considered as the ground truth model. The metric used in the experiments in order to quantify the reconstruction performance was the Hausdorff distance. According to Koutsoudis et al. (2014) the best performing noise function-based pattern was

Figure 6. Best performing grey scale bitmap rendition and intensity distribution histogram

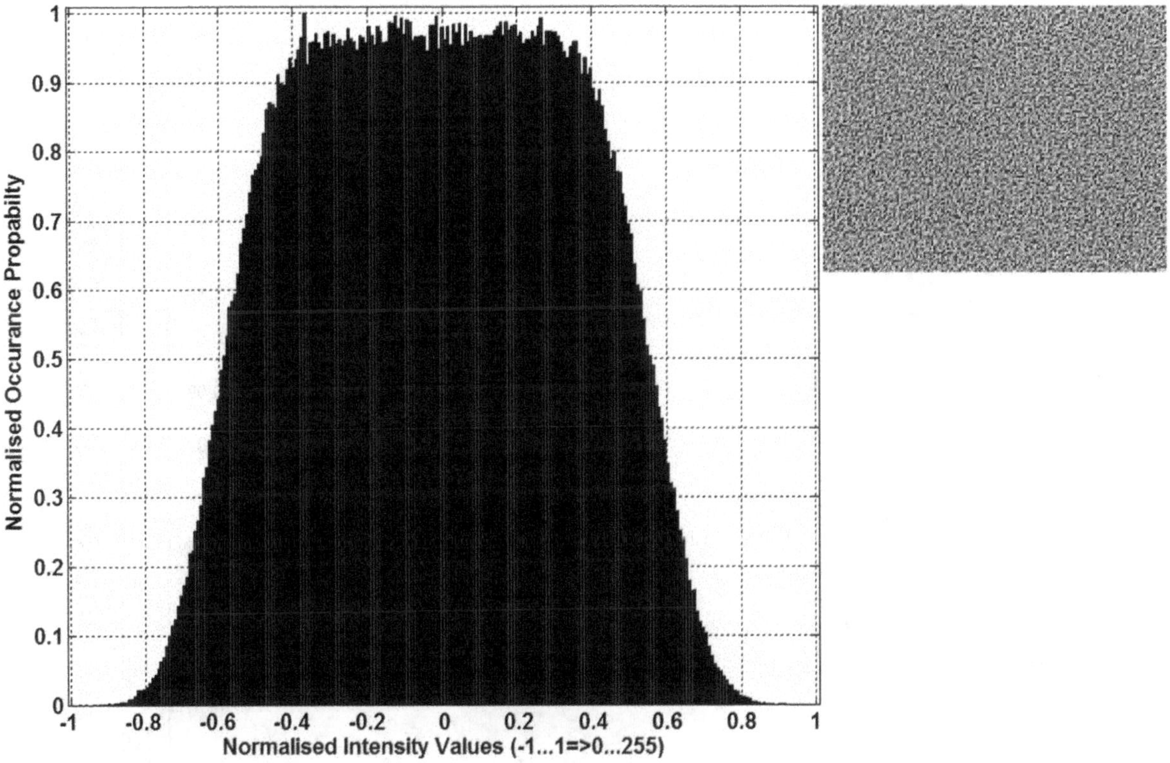

the Wavelet noise function (Figure 6 and Figure 7). The Hausdorff distance (Aspert et al., 2002), the mean distance and the standard deviation were the metrics calculated to quantify the surface deviation in comparison to the laser scanner data. The noise function-based patterns along with their documentation are publicly available at http://www.ceti.gr/~akoutsou/noisepatterns.rar.

Moreover, surfaces with monotone, repetitive or uniform visual texture represent a challenge as well for multi-image photogrammetry to reconstruct. Santoši et al. (2019) propose to overcome the lack of visual texture of surfaces through the projection of synthetical images based on digits of irrational numbers; pi, phi, e, sqrt2 and sqrt3 and numbers given by a random number generator. It is proven that the projection of synthetical images onto monotone and high reflexive surfaces leads to an improvement in its visual characteristics. The number of detected corresponding feature points significantly increases and therefore leads to an enhanced sparse point cloud.

The synthetic image produced using the irrational numbers of Pi (Class I – pi I), proved to be the best performing image in terms of accuracy verification (Santoši et al., 2019). The characteristics of that image are its small number of grey hues and its uniformly distributed histogram shape. Again, as in the case of projecting noise function-based patterns, the automation of the data collection phase is affected and thus the introduction of partial 3D reconstruction alignments is inevitable.

Figure 7. Mesh surface deviation comparison using the Hausdorff

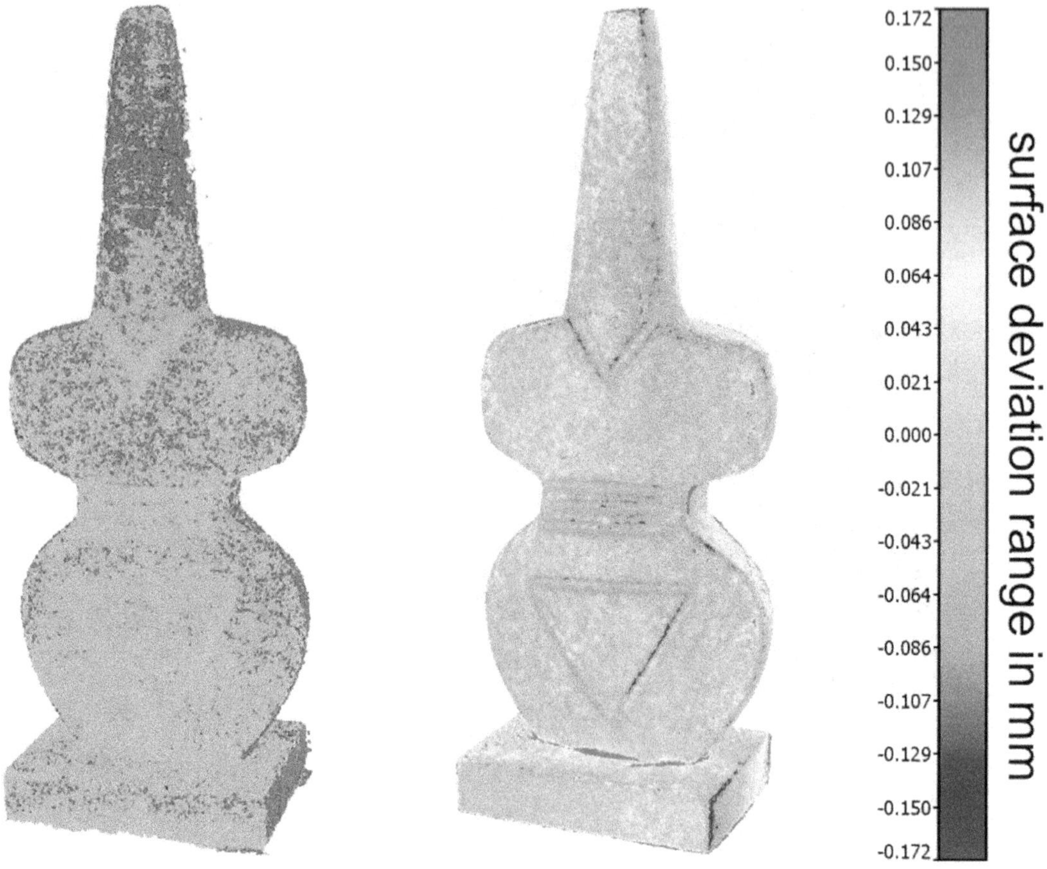

Table 1. Complete artefact 3D mesh comparison results (Koutsoudis et al., 2015)

	Hausdorff distance (*in mm*)	
	Mean Distance	**Std. Dev.**
Wavelet noise function-based pattern	0.0013	0.060
Original Surface	0.115	0.1

Dealing with Specular Surfaces

The Lambertian surface model, that ignores any specular highlights, is adopted by the SfM/MVS implementations. Hence, even in a completely controlled environment with respect to lighting and illuminations, it is a very challenging task to separate reflectance from a surface of a 3D object. However, using approaches that rely on photometric stereo it is possible to recover the shape from a given set of images depicting the object, that is captured under three varying (works also on unknown) illumination directions.

Photometric stereo techniques, introduced by Mallick et al. (2005), provide a framework to overcome the difficulties of reconstructing the shape of objects that have a specular surface. To achieve invariance from specular reflectance highlights, a data-dependent transformation of the RGB colour space. The approach relies on the SUV linear colour transformation and is capable of dealing with surfaces of arbitrary texture and provides a direct access to the underlying shape information. To validate the framework, Mallick et al. (2005), performed experiments on objects, of known shape, with varying material properties; spheres with varying specularity. For each sphere a set of four high dynamic range images were captured from a fixed viewpoint and under four different known illumination directions. A Macbeth colour checker (McCamy et al., 1976), which is a colour calibration target consisting of a cardboard-framed arrangement of 24 squares of painted samples, was also used to create the SUV image (colour calibration).

The experiments to overcome challenges introduced by specular surfaces were performed under the assumption that illumination is considered as constant over the whole surface. It is stated that the photometric stereo techniques can be furthermore enhanced through the usage of polarisation that enables the estimation of the light source colour locally. The direction of the light was known throughout the experimental validation; however, the approach can be extended to handle unknown lighting directions.

On Image Pre- Processing for SfM/MVS Optimisation

It is vital, for the SfM/MVS 3D reconstruction approach, to provide the maximum image dataset possible, since it relies on image content feature extraction. Hence, image pre-processing algorithms are capable of significantly enhancing the quality of the captured image sequences and thus aid the SfM/MVS approach to reconstruct more precisely the 3D scene.

Guidi et al. (2014) propose the usage of polarizing filters and HDR imaging to enhance the outcome of the SfM/MVS approach on objects that derive from the cultural heritage domain, that are typically not suitable for the approach. In their experiments, three images were captured from fixed viewpoints to ensure homogeneity in the image collection phase. This experiment was performed under four distinct shooting conditions; polarizing filter, no filter, no processing and HDR.

Polarising filters are broadly used by professional photographers. Their usage enables the diminishment of the strong sky luminance or the elimination of reflections introduced from glasses or stretches of water (Feininger, 1954). On the other hand, to capture the dynamic range of a scene with the aid of a digital camera, High Dynamic Range photo shooting was developed. This technique involves the combination of multiple images of the scene into a radiance map. These images were captured from the same viewpoint but with different exposure times. Experiments performed by Guidi et al. (2014) examined the impact of using both image pre-processing techniques (polarizing filters and HDR) on the SfM/MVS 3D reconstruction approach. The software solution used in their experiments was Agisoft Photoscan. Images were captured using a Canon 5D Mark II of 21 megapixels and a *50mm* lens on a tripod. The Ground Sampling Distance (Leachtenauer et al, 1997), which is a metric of resolution due to sampling, was below *<0.11mm* for all test objects. The HDR images were created in Adobe Photoshop using the function "merge to HDR pro". According to the analysis of their results, polarising filters do not enhance the procedure on objects with a metallic surface, since light reflections from metallic surfaces are not polarised and thus their highlighted areas remain unaffected. On the contrary, the use of polarising filters on ceramic objects increase the number of matching points, due to the fact that ceramic materials allow the electromagnetic waves to preserve their natural polarisation. The use of HDR imaging assists generally the matching process in cases where the dynamic range of highlights and dark parts is low. More specifically, it slightly improves the SfM/MVS 3D reconstruction on the tested ceramic objects and provides better results on metallic objects. Additionally, cross polarization, the usage of linear polarizing films in a predefined constellation (perpendicular to each other or in a custom order) and under controlled lighting conditions is considered a method that is able to cut-off reflections and therefore enhance the image sequence collection stage that subsequently results into an enhanced 3D reconstruction.

Also, according to a more recent research work (Gaiani et al, 2016) it is important to perform colour balancing to adjust colour channel intensities globally in an image to render it properly. Hence, consistency in the colour-to-grey transformation and faithful colour appearance is achieved. This pre-process step is vital for the feature extraction and feature matching task, that are based solely on the luminance channel. The proposed colour space, according to their work, is the Adobe-RGB as its wider and averts information loss of that may occur when using sRGB (for shadows ~25% luminance and for highlights ~75% luminance). In their work, the proposed approach is based on defining spectral sensitivities by exploiting colour targets (Hong, 2001). More specifically, they use a set of differently coloured samples measured with a spectrophotometer. The precise characterisation of any camera demands the recording of its output for all possible stimuli and comparing it with separately measured values for the same stimuli (Yaroslavsky, 1996). In fact, only a set of the total responses of the camera to representative stimuli is used to calibrate the camera for input stimuli that were not measured. This process is performed defining the transformation between measured CIExyz values and stored RGB values. In their work, they employed the target Macbeth ColourChecker in the image acquisition phase (McCamy, 1976). These captured images containing the Macbeth ColourChecker, are neutralized, balanced and properly exposed. Apart from colour balancing they perform an image denoising process that is an extended version of the CBM3D approach (Dabov, 2007). More specifically, each image of the dataset is coupled with a set of parameters based on the camera specifications, the ISO sensitivity and the colour stored profiles. According to their results, the image pre-processing methodology, which consists of colour balancing, image denoising and colour-to-grey transformation, is generally positively influencing the results of the automated photogrammetric pipeline.

On Choosing the Proper Acquisition Setup

The setup of the controlled environment for the data acquisition phase were evaluated through experimentations by Nikolov and Madsen (2016). More specifically, evaluations on the idea of using a turntable along with a given number of lighting sources. In their experiments, a bird bath was used as the experimental object, that is well performing in terms of 3D reconstruction. The underlying idea of the 3D reconstruction with respect to the setup of the environment is the determination of the impact on one hand of completely static lighting conditions in combination with a moving background and on the other hand a turntable and moving light sources. According to their results, static lighting conditions without the use of a turntable lead to a 3D reconstruction of higher geometric accuracy, lower mean and standard deviation values in comparison to the results produced by exploiting a turntable. Moreover, there is a difference in using one or multiple light sources. More specifically, when using one directional light source higher levels of noise is introduced which is an evident in the higher standard deviation values.

Table 2. Mean value (μ) in mm and standard deviation (σ) in mm² of the distance metric for the bird bath object for each of the tested software solutions (Nikolov and Madsen, 2016)

SfM/MVS software	No turntable	Turntable	
	Multiple lights (five bands)	One light (five bands)	Multiple lights (five bands)
	μ/σ	μ/σ	μ/σ
Context Capture	−7.167/13.289	N/A	N/A
Memento	−0.209/2.028	−0.366/2.148	-0.309/2.305
PhotoScan	−0.283/2.312	0.206/1.982	-0.167/1.159
Reality Capture	−0.031/0.284	N/A	N/A
3DF Zephyr	−0.039/0.584	−0.308/2.035	-0.165/0.922
Pix4D	−0.169/0.407	−5.023/12.401	0.061/1.674
Memento Offline	−0.105/1.355	−1.135/4.253	-0.114/1.552

On Extending the SfM/MVS Software Arsenal

Numerous SfM/MVS-based 3D reconstruction software packages have been made available in the last decade. Nikolov and Madsen (2016) performed benchmark scenarios under different lighting positions and image acquisition approaches to evaluate the performance of six popular software solutions. It is very crucial to choose the proper SfM/MVS software package, since each software has its advantages. The software packages which have been evaluated were Agisoft Photoscan (Now Metashape), Bentley Context Capture, Autodesk Memento Online/Offline, Reality Capture, 3Dflow 3DF Zephyr and Pix4D.

The experiments were performed on objects that were made of different materials and thus had different surface properties. All images were captured using the same DSLR camera; the Canon 6D using a *70-300mm* lens, at a resolution of *5472 x 3648* pixels. The image dataset was created in a controlled environment. All six objects were used to evaluate the reconstruction performance of the selected software solutions. The metrics used for the evaluation were the Hausdorff distance of the reconstructed model computed in relation to a ground truth 3D model and the local roughness. The local roughness metric, which is calculated using the Gaussian curvature and normalised to give proper weights to rough patches and smooth patches near edges, was introduced by Wang et al. (2012). The metric determines the visual quality of the mesh in terms of noise and over-smoothing. It is believed that there is a link between the mesh curvature and the perceived mesh quality and therefore the metric's calculation is based on the Gaussian curvature (Wang, 2012).

The roughness metric indicate that Pix4D, Memento Offline and Reality Capture introduce a significant amount of noise on the smoother parts of the test objects, while Memento Online, 3DF Zephyr and PhotoScan manage to capture most of the geometry details on the easier to reconstruct objects, without introducing noise. However, in test objects with generally smoother surfaces, uncertainty noise was introduced by Memento Offline, Reality Capture and Photoscan. The 3D reconstruction results are shown in Table 2.

CONCLUSION

Nowadays, SfM/MVS is commonly used within the cultural heritage domain. It is a common solution that reconstructs the photorealistic 3D geometry of different scale objects (movable and unmovable). The approach constitutes a viable solution for most the objects, nevertheless there are several occasions where the approach may produce erroneous data or even fail in reconstructing in an acceptable manner in terms of geometric accuracy. This work highlighted occasions where the SfM/MVS approach is driven at its limits and presented published works of overcoming such challenges. Nowadays there are several software solutions that implement SfM/MVS and thus we gathered a number of works that attempted to handle and overcome the reconstruction issues that are related to the object's nature (material, surface properties, etc.).

REFERENCES

Aspert, N., Santa-Cruz, D., & Ebrahimi, T. (2002). Mesh: Measuring errors between surfaces using the hausdorff distance. In *Multimedia and Expo, 2002. ICME'02. Proceedings. 2002 IEEE International Conference on* (Vol. 1, pp. 705-708). IEEE.

Baltsavias, E., Li, H., Mason, S., Stefanidis, A., & Sinning, M. (1996). Comparison of two digital photogrammetric systems with emphasis on DTM generation: Case study glacier measurement. *International Archives of Photogrammetry and Remote Sensing*, *31*, 104–109.

Baltsavias, E. P. (1991). *Multiphoto geometrically constrained matching* (Doctoral dissertation).

Bay, H., Ess, A., Tuytelaars, T., & Van Gool, L. (2008). Speeded-Up Robust Features (SURF). *Computer Vision and Image Understanding*, *110*(3), 346–359. doi:10.1016/j.cviu.2007.09.014

CARARE. (n.d.). Retrieved November 24, 2016 from the website: http://www.carare.eu

3D. COFORM. (n.d.). Retrieved November 24, 2016 from the website: http://3dcoform.eu

Dabov, K., Foi, A., Katkovnik, V., & Egiazarian, K. (2007). Color image denoising via sparse 3D collaborative filtering with grouping constraint in luminance-chrominance space. In *Image Processing, 2007. ICIP 2007. IEEE International Conference on* (Vol. 1, pp. I-313). IEEE.

Engels, C., Stewénius, H., & Nistér, D. (2006). Bundle adjustment rules. *Photogrammetric Computer Vision, 2*, 124-131.

EUROPEANA. (n.d.). Retrieved October 21, 2019 from the website: https://www.europeana.eu/

Feininger, A. (1954). *Successful photography*. Academic Press.

Fischler, A., & Bolles, R. (1981). Random Sample Consensus: A Paradigm for Model Fitting with Applications to Image Analysis and Automated Cartography. Comm. ACM, 24(6), 381–395. doi:10.1145/358669.358692

Furukawa, Y., & Hernández, C. (2015). Multi-View Stereo: A Tutorial. *Foundations and Trends in Computer Graphics and Vision*, *9*(1), 1–148. doi:10.1561/0600000052

Gaiani, M., Remondino, F., Apollonio, F. I., & Ballabeni, A. (2016). An advanced pre-processing pipeline to improve automated photogrammetric reconstructions of architectural scenes. *Remote Sensing*, *8*(3), 178. doi:10.3390/rs8030178

Guidi, G., Gonizzi, S., & Micoli, L. L. (2014). Image pre-processing for optimizing automated photogrammetry performances. *ISPRS Annals of the Photogrammetry. Remote Sensing and Spatial Information Sciences*, *2*(5), 145.

Hong, G., Luo, M. R., & Rhodes, P. A. (2001). *A study of digital camera colorimetric characterisation based on polynomial modelling*. Academic Press.

3D. ICONS. (n.d.). Retrieved November 24, 2016 from the website: http://3dicons-project.eu

Kazhdan, M., Bolitho, M., & Hoppe, H. (2006). Poisson surface reconstruction. *SGP '06 Proceedings of the fourth Eurographics symposium on Geometry processing*, 61-70.

Koutsoudis, A., Ioannakis, G., Vidmar, B., Arnaoutoglou, F., & Chamzas, C. (2015). Using noise function-based patterns to enhance photogrammetric 3D reconstruction performance of featureless surfaces. *Journal of Cultural Heritage*, *16*(5), 664–670. doi:10.1016/j.culher.2015.01.008

Koutsoudis, A., Stavroglou, K., Pavlidis, G., & Chamzas, C. (2012). 3dsse–a 3d scene search engine: Exploring 3d scenes using keywords. *Journal of Cultural Heritage*, *13*(2), 187–194. doi:10.1016/j.culher.2011.09.001

Koutsoudis, A., Vidmar, B., Ioannakis, G., Arnaoutoglou, F., Pavlidis, G., & Chamzas, C. (2014). Multi-image 3D reconstruction data evaluation. *Journal of Cultural Heritage*, *15*(1), 73–79. doi:10.1016/j.culher.2012.12.003

Leachtenauer, J. C., Malila, W., Irvine, J., Colburn, L., & Salvaggio, N. (1997). General image-quality equation: GIQE. *Applied Optics*, *36*(32), 8322–8328. doi:10.1364/AO.36.008322 PMID:18264373

Lowe, D. (2004). Distinctive Image Features from Scale-Invariant Keypoints. *International Journal of Computer Vision*, *60*(2), 91–110. doi:10.1023/B:VISI.0000029664.99615.94

MacDonald, L., Hindmarch, J., Robson, S., & Terras, M. (2014). Modelling the appearance of heritage metallic surfaces. *The International Archives of the Photogrammetry, Remote Sensing and Spatial Information Sciences*, *40*(5), 371–377. doi:10.5194/isprsarchives-XL-5-371-2014

Mallick, S. P., Zickler, T. E., Kriegman, D. J., & Belhumeur, P. N. (2005, June). Beyond lambert: Reconstructing specular surfaces using color. In *Computer Vision and Pattern Recognition, 2005. CVPR 2005. IEEE Computer Society Conference on* (Vol. 2, pp. 619-626). IEEE.

McCamy, C. S., Marcus, H., & Davidson, J. G. (1976). A color-rendition chart. *Journal of Applied Photographic Engineering*, *2*(3), 95–99.

Nikolov, I., & Madsen, C. (2016, October). Benchmarking Close-range Structure from Motion 3D Reconstruction Software Under Varying Capturing Conditions. In *Euro-Mediterranean Conference* (pp. 15-26). Springer International Publishing. 10.1007/978-3-319-48496-9_2

Ohdake, T., & Chikatsu, H. (2005). 3d modelling of high relief sculpture using image-based integrated measurement system. *The International Archives of the Photogrammetry, Remote Sensing and Spatial Information Sciences*, *36*(5), W17.

Remondino, F., El-Hakim, S., Gruen, A., & Zhang, L. (2008). Development and performance analysis of image matching for detailed surface reconstruction of heritage objects. *IEEE Signal Processing Magazine*, *25*(4), 55–65. doi:10.1109/MSP.2008.923093

Robertson, D. P., & Cipolla, R. (2009). *Structure from motion, Practical image processing and computer vision*. John Willey and Sons Ltd.

Santoši, Ž., Budak, I., Stojaković, V., Šokac, M., & Vukelić, Đ. (2019). Evaluation of synthetically generated patterns for image-based 3D reconstruction of texture-less objects. *Measurement*, 147.

Wallis, R. (1976). An approach to the space variant restoration and enhancement of images. *Proc. of symp. on current mathematical problems in image science, naval postgraduate school,* 329-340.

Wallis Filtering Implementation. (n.d.). Retrieved October 20, 2019 from the website: https://photogrammetric-vision.weebly.com/download-page.html

Wang, K., Torkhani, F., & Montanvert, A. (2012). A fast roughness-based approach to the assessment of 3D mesh visual quality. *Computers & Graphics*, *36*(7), 808–818. doi:10.1016/j.cag.2012.06.004

Yaroslavsky, L. P. (1996, October). Local adaptive image restoration and enhancement with the use of DFT and DCT in a running window. In *SPIE's 1996 International Symposium on Optical Science, Engineering, and Instrumentation* (pp. 2-13). International Society for Optics and Photonics. 10.1117/12.255218

Chapter 8
Cross-Reality Technologies in Archaeometry Bridge Humanities With "Hard Science"

Evgenia Paxinou
https://orcid.org/0000-0002-9910-8569
Hellenic Open University, Greece

Chairi Kiourt
https://orcid.org/0000-0001-8501-8899
Athena – Research and Innovation Center in Information, Communication, and Knowledge Technologies, Greece

Athanasios Sypsas
https://orcid.org/0000-0001-8301-4763
Hellenic Open University, Greece

Vasilis Zafeiropoulos
Hellenic Open University, Greece

Argyro Sgourou
Hellenic Open University, Greece

Dimitris Kalles
https://orcid.org/0000-0003-0364-5966
Hellenic Open University, Greece

ABSTRACT

As an integral part of archaeology, archaeometry, employs standard laboratory techniques and ICT tools to examine and analyze art and archaeological materials. Most students involved with cultural heritage and Archaeology have a background in the arts or humanities and a minimal, if any, training in the principles and techniques of most natural and engineering sciences. Consequently, when choosing to be enrolled in an archaeometry course, an interdisciplinary field which also requires some background in applied sciences, cross reality labs can be the bridge between archaeology and its sub-disciplines, and "hard science." In this chapter, the authors focus on the use of virtual environments in the digital cultural heritage field, as well as on applications of cross reality laboratories in archaeometry. Finally, they present some evidence in favor of the simulations, pointing out that VR, AR, and MR labs could train, safely and efficiently, pre-service archaeometrists in the use of specialized laboratory apparatuses and help them take advantage of the full spectrum of modern laboratory tools.

DOI: 10.4018/978-1-7998-2871-6.ch008

INTRODUCTION

The evolution of Information and Communication Technology (ICT) over the last decades, alters our lives and affects every domain of scientific research (Collins, & Halverson, 2018). In the field of Archaeology, ICTs are used in many areas but the deliberation about the way new technologies and the Internet affect the electronic processing and presentation of museum artifact collections and monuments, is still strong and already going on for about 20 years (Liritzis, Al-Otaibi, Volonakis, & Drivaliari, 2015). A popular adage mentions that *the 21st century archaeologists are no longer excavators* (Djindjian, 2015). Archaeologists play a key role in the difficult task of reconstructing the past and providing people with the necessary information about the civilizations of past societies. Digital tools have been employed in archaeology at every level. Their increased use facilitates the information processing and presentation, concerning the field investigation and the post excavation phase (Wilhelmson & Dell'Unto, 2015). The digital cultural heritage field, as major part of synchronous Archaeology, depicts to the end user all the information from excavation to the virtual representation, using ICT tools at every step. Musílek (2015) stated that archaeometry is the application of various scientific fields, like natural sciences and engineering, for exploring archaeological findings. The term archaeometry has appeared for the first time in the journal *Archaeometry* in Oxford in 1958. In the stage of archaeometry, laboratories are used in order to examine and analyze the archeological findings. As there should be a continuous interaction between the people managing the cultural heritage and the scientists, it is essential that both parties are aware of the potentials, each technique used for scientific investigation, can have. Unfortunately, in most countries the conventional academic differentiation between humanistic and scientific curricula in the educational institutions is the most important barrier to the exchange of competences between archaeology and science (Artioli, 2010). Most natural sciences students involved with cultural heritage have minimum training in the scientific principles and techniques they are about to use in an archaeometry lab. ICTs tools like Virtual Reality (VR) and Augmented Reality (AR) laboratories, could create an interface between these different disciplines and offer a deeper understanding for the science principles on which the operation of complicated laboratory equipment is based.

The objectives of the present study are at first, a presentation of studies concerning the use of virtual environments in digital cultural heritage field, secondly a brief review of virtual laboratories in Archaeometry and finally a proposal of how virtual laboratories can be a part of Archaeometry education based on the presentation of student's outcomes in educational scenarios where a VR laboratory application is involved.

BACKGROUND

The results of archeological excavations, the study of the findings and the available written sources, provide the bases of information concerning past cultures and places. Through archaeology, the history is synthesized and past cultures are comprehended (Balla, Pavlogeorgatos, Tsiafakis, & Pavlidis, 2014). The public is informed and educated in the past cultures using the data that the field experts, who work on preserving the cultural knowledge, present. Technology offers new methods to preserve and learn about ancient cultures (Bogdanovych, Rodriguez-Aguilar, Simoff, & Cohen, 2010). Furthermore, the archeological sites are fragile and disposed to possible causes of destruction. Thus, the original findings may be destroyed during an archeological site dig procedure (Forte, 2011). Making the digital representation of ephemeral places and objects, contributes to their preservation through time (Borba & Zuffo, 2016; Refsland, Ojika, & Addison, 2000). According to Wilhelmson and Dell'Unto (2015), digital tools have been employed in archaeology at every level. Their increased use provides researchers with additional instruments in order to reveal, elaborate, analyze and finally visualize almost all the data collected during the phases of field research and post excavation. Additionally, in the field of the research on site documentation and mapping, the development of digital tools such as the Geographic Information System (GIS), provides researchers with the necessary instruments to rebuild and visualize, the area of the excavation (Katsianis, Tsipidis, Kotsakis, & Kousoulakou, 2008). Liritzis, Al-Otaibi, et al. (2015) have suggested that the term "digital cultural heritage" can be used to denote the exploitation of effective digital tools in modern techniques which assist us to understand and at the same time explain the past. This term is used to specify the digital methods that are used in order to present the information concerning heritage within the appropriate historical context. Another term that is commonly used is the virtual archaeological heritage, or virtual heritage, and includes the visual simulations of the material culture (Roussou & Drettakis, 2003). Sanders (2008), claimed that virtual heritage tools create digital representations of the ancient world, offering many benefits by visualizing the past interactively and in three dimensions (3D). These tools contribute to the main purpose of virtual heritage, which is the reconstruction of cultural heritage environments, in order to present historic data, context and information, as accurate as possible in an engaging way (Addison, 2000). Moreover, virtual heritage plays an important role in comprehending cultural and natural history of past cultures, as the new technologies adopted, i.e. 3D, virtual reality serve the need for natural movement and the consciousness of three dimensions and realism (Kwon, Kim, Ahn, Ko, & Kim, 2001).

There are various virtual applications of digital cultural heritage, including virtual museums and exhibitions, serious games and virtual representations. According to Kiourt et al. (2017), *virtual museums have a prominent role in realistic simulations of Cultural Heritage.* They are virtual environments, often virtual replicas of the real ones, which host virtual exhibitions of artifacts, enabling the virtual visitors to get in touch with them in an enriched environment. The idea for virtual museums has been initiated as a solution to the problem of the physical space limitations and additionally as an opportunity for remote visitors to have a virtual tour (Tsichritzis & Gibbs, 1991). Several research and development works have led to a significant amount of projects relating to virtual museums and exhibitions, mainly for a particular cultural stakeholder (Kiourt, Koutsoudis, & Pavlidis, 2016). In Sylaiou, Liarokapis, Kotsakis and Patias (2009), virtual museum technologies are presented. Another approach concerning digital archaeology, is the virtual environments (cities, places, buildings etc.), which, apart from historic information, they include sociocultural information concerning the past cultures (Abdelmonem, Selim, Mushatat, & Almogren, 2017). These applications offer users the possibility to experience virtually reconstructed historic places as visitors.

Developers and administrators of virtual worlds have already started to realize the potential of new technologies for the development of edutainment content and services for their visitors (Bickmore, Pfeifer, & Schulman, 2011). In addition, gaming for educational purposes is a significant and active research domain (Brown & Vaughan, 2010; Nicholson, 2011, 2012; Seaborn & Fels, 2015). This has taken either the form of Game-Based Learning (GBL) or Serious Gaming (SG). Gamification (Seaborn & Fels, 2015) is the result of applying game mechanics into diverse domains, in order to engage users and enhance their knowledge and performance. The importance of the playing activity has been emphasized in many studies from various domains. According to Brown and Vaughan (2010), playing is an archetypical activity that arises from primordial biological structures existing even before the conscience or the capacity for speech; as Brown and Vaughan emphatically stated it is not something a person decides to do. Gamification is nothing more than the use of specific game design approaches and techniques in various environments, in order to attract people in problem solving and to enhance their contribution (Nicholson 2011, 2012). Gamification and its special application in education have a long history dating back to the 1980s. Today, the advent of mature 3D technologies both in hardware and software implementations constitute a stable environment to successfully couple culture and education by using technology and gaming as the catalysts. The evolution of ICT accompanied by the increasing availability of computer game development platforms (also known as game engines) has led to the continuous creation of several serious games in several scientific fields, including among others cultural heritage and education (Breuer & Bente, 2010).Various independent R&D efforts worldwide exploit this stable environment to deliver the next generation gamified virtual worlds for even more realistic and engaging cultural heritage simulations. These serious games can be used as an alternative approach to education in cultural heritage, as numerous works are used to enrich history education and actual museum visits (Kiourt et al., 2016). Another application in virtual heritage is the open virtual worlds, in which avatars represent users who they may interact with each other. As stated in Sequeira and Morgado (2013), virtual worlds like Second Life when used as a virtual museum environment can enrich the visiting experience by enabling the interaction between guides and visitors. Extending the virtual museum experience, researchers have reconstructed historical sites in Second Life using the benefits of its unique medium. According to Bogdanovych et al. (2010), virtual avatars can be used in order to integrate some of the knowledge aspects in the virtual heritage context. Thus, when avatars act as the ancient citizens, the virtual environment simulates the cultural preservation at a new level.

The production of documented virtual cultural heritage is based on four main phases process (Bruno et all., 2010), encompassing data collection (findings) via excavation on site, analysis of findings via archaeometry, digitization of the findings and finally presentation of the findings.

While archaeology is taught in Humanity University schools, it uses methods and techniques related to sciences, like physics, chemistry, geology, mathematics, computer science and others. Thus, the use of science laboratories is necessary in archaeometry education (Djindjian, 2015). Archaeometry laboratories have been established in many educational settings, like Universities and research centers worldwide, in order to serve the research and educational needs in the cognitive field of archaeometry in relation to the fields of science and humanities. Another term that describes the ICT application in Archaeometry is Cyber-archaeometry (Liritzis, Volonakis, Vosinakis, & Pavlidis, 2015), which is defined as the combination of using digital Information Technology (IT) techniques in order to simulate, restructure and manage archaeometric processes from the field of natural sciences with reference to the material culture, investigated variously with archaeometric methods, like dating, analysis, etc. According to Liritzis (2009), archaeometry is an interdisciplinary methodological approach for answering the "why, when, where" aspects of ancient (and not so ancient) findings, using technology, scientific instruments and measurements techniques. Scientific approaches in physics, chemistry, biology, geology, etc. contribute to interpreting the past, helping the archaeology scientists in their work (Pollard & Bray, 2007). Although archaeologists have exploited several tools and methods of the physical and chemical sciences, with the help of the respective scientists, for dating and analyzing archeological artifacts and materials (Glascock, Speakman, & Neff, 2007), their skills in using these tools and their ability to interpret their findings can surely be ameliorated as well as the skill of the students that focus in the area of archaeometry. Furthermore, as archaeometrists (scientists of natural sciences area) usually do not possess a broad overview of the used techniques there is a constant collaboration between them and the scientific side. XR environments could be a safe and economic way of giving archaeometrists and new students a little independence when they appear in their physical lab. The repetitive performance of the experiments under the instructions of the virtual applications, in combination with the technical information appeared in the simulation environments, can effectively prepare archaeometrists in using sensitive and expensive instruments in their lab without further help. Recent studies have shown that students who brought minimum or zero prior knowledge on the topic of science, and furthermore on the hands-on experience with lab apparatus, had high scores in science-concept tests and performed successfully quite difficult experiments when they used as preparation tools, VR educational applications (Paxinou et al., 2019).

It is undeniable that the familiarization with the lab instruments, and the ability to interpret research findings, can be achieved by the trial-and-error method, using the *real tools* in a real archaeometric lab. However, hands-on laboratories that provide experimentation using the real tools, require maintenance staff, materials, expendables and high cost equipment (Gomes & Bogosyan, 2009). Laboratories can be enriched with VR applications (Ma & Nickerson, 2006), creating a virtual lab environment, where learners use the virtual experimentation interface in order to conduct experiments (Kollöffel & de Jong, 2013). Furthermore, virtual laboratories support the educational process providing educational tools, which facilitate learning by highlighting significant information and removing unnecessary detail (Trundle & Bell, 2010). As stated in Jong, Linn, and Zacharia (2013), educators can adjust several characteristics of a simulation model, such as the materials or the time scale, in order to better clarify and look insight in certain phenomena or objects which would otherwise remain incomprehensible. Nevertheless, according to Liritzis et al. (2015), *the link connecting archaeology with the results but also the instrumentation and operation of archaeometrical methods has not been adequately developed.* Thus, since research on virtual laboratories in archaeology is evolving, the applications on this field are limited and new approaches will be developed in the next few years.

VIRTUAL LABORATORIES IN ARCHAEOMETRY

Laboratory sessions are essential in Natural Science courses in order to develop holistic and conceptual knowledge (Bernhard, 2010). In introductory courses in Archaeology, laboratories are used in order to teach students about archaeometry, in order to generate information about archeological findings (Donais, Whissel, Dumas, & Golden, 2009). As the techniques used in archaeology are related to Natural Sciences, students have to obtain some laboratory skills as a practical extension of the concepts taught. Not only the students have to be familiar with some specialized laboratory techniques but also, they have to master them as, in their professional life, they will handle and take care of unique and irreplaceable archaeological findings and in that sense, there won't be place for any mistakes.

According to Manhita et al. (2016) the use of physical and chemical techniques, contributes to the information gathering concerning the chemical composition of the findings, offering information on its origin and the production methods used. A common way for obtaining the laboratory skills is through the classical method that is performing several experimental exercises in a physical lab. Nowadays such a method is time consuming for the students and rather expensive for the educational institutions as the latter must update their laboratories with sensitive equipment and supply them with expensive consumables (Jong et al., 2013; Weller, 2004). Virtual laboratories are the new online educational trend for communicating to students practical skills of science (Paxinou et al., 2018). The use of virtual laboratories can enrich the science laboratories used in education, since, as stated in Gravier et al. (2008) and Ma and Nickerson (2006), the main benefits of using a virtual laboratory are:

- Increased availability, as virtual laboratories can be accessed at any time from any place.
- Cost savings, as *traditional* laboratories need equipment, consumables and maintenance staff.
- Improved accessibility, as people who might not be able to travel to physical laboratory premises, can access virtual laboratories.
- Reduced health of instruments damage hazards, from the use of dangerous materials or sensitive equipment.
- Safe environments including dangerous substances.
- Unlimited repeatability of the experiments, trial-and-error learning theory

These advantages have led researchers in various fields, like Archaeology and Natural Sciences to explore the possibilities of using virtual laboratories in educating trainees in archaeometry.

A cyber-archaeometry application is presented in the study by (Liritzis, Al-Otaibi, et al., 2015). The application consists of a 3D virtual laboratory with a petrographic microscope (also known as polarized light microscope). The petrographic microscope is used in petrology and optical mineralogy for the identification of rocks and minerals in thin sections with the purpose of extracting information about their origin and other properties. The user has access to the virtual lab through an internet browser; in it, the user, being guided by avatars, handles the various mechanical parts of the microscope and collects info about the specimens under examination. According to the authors, the virtual laboratory enables the inquiry learning approach, that is, it motivates students to discover knowledge via research.

In another study by Corrêa, Borba, Lopes, Zuffo, & Araujo (2017), apart from a virtual environment for the representation of a pre-historic archaeological site, three other virtual archaeometry tools have also been developed. These tools were used for users' interactions, like annotation, rock painting and artifact classification. In the same study, the users' opinions on the usage of virtual tools were surveyed and the authors stated that virtual tools should be improved so as to become a spontaneous application for archaeologists.

A virtual laboratory is used in another study (Burca et al., 2011), in order to plan and control diffraction measurements in archaeological research and art-historical object analysis. In order to construct the virtual diffraction instrument proposed in the study, a specific model of the instrument was first built. According to the authors, the proposed method using virtual instruments in the virtual laboratory environment, offers the archaeologists the ability to conveniently and rapidly characterize archaeological findings' features.

Getchell, Miller, Nicoll, Sweetman, and Allison (2010) developed a software application in order to educate future archaeologists, under the Laconia Acropolis Virtual Archaeology project. The project targeted to train archaeology students not only on the excavation of a historical site from a technical viewpoint, but also to deal with all aspects that they may face as archeologists, including funding, resource allocation, team management, etc. To do so, the students used a virtual archaeological site (in Second Life virtual world) in order to execute the excavation work. There was not a separate virtual laboratory, but students analyzed the findings using virtual tools in the archaeological site. Thus, the emphasis and work effort were put on a more realistic representation of the ancient site. Consequently, the produced expensive solutions were applicable for laboratory experiments and later for deployment as part of an exhibit of a real museum.

In Ontiveros, Macias, Berni, and Reynolds (2014), a web platform was developed in order to be conceived as a virtual laboratory enabling online work and collaboration and constant data update. The Virtual Laboratory interface could be presented in various languages and allowed free access to all the data and applications. The applications developed were related to administrative issues, such as user accounts, security subjects, etc. as well as to database topics, GIS-based engine and specific applications concerning archaeometric procedures.

Another-resource for education in archaeometry is the "Archaeometry" platform[1]. It is a web platform containing information on archaeometric procedures on the fields of Advanced Dating, The Art of Representation, The Art of Writing, Dreamtime, Rock Art Galleries, but it does not offer simulations of virtual laboratories for education in the specific fields.

SCIENCE COURSES- VR AND AR APPLICATIONS

According to Makransky, Thisgaard, and Gadegaard (2016), the success of performing experiments, depends basically on the students' preparation, as it increases her/his skill levels and the learning outcomes (Chandler & Sweller, 1991). Practicing new skills only once, and after a brief face-to-face tutorial, as it is the case in science courses that follow the traditional lab instruction method, can lead to superficial knowledge with low retention time (Paxinou et al., 2018b). On the other hand, it is time consuming and prohibitively expensive for institutions to let their students freely practice in a science lab. The expensive and sensitive laboratory equipment may be destroyed by the inexperienced learners' improper use. Thus, simulation is often a modern and convenient way for preparing students for their experiments (Wang et al., 2014), or professionals for the use of new coming laboratory apparatus (de Vries & May, 2019). Among other things, the simulation innovative applications provide: a) an information-rich and multiple representation environment (Hsu & Thomas, 2002), which is of crucial importance in archaeology, b) an immediate feedback about errors to the students that enables them to repeat easily and safely the exercises as many time as they wish, and finally c) students the opportunity to visualize seldom seen objects.

VR/AR/MR Educational Applications in Onlabs

Hellenic Open University (HOU) is an institution that is mastering the distance learning education. As it seeks new ways to communicate laboratorial skills to students, HOU has developed a VR laboratory application called Onlabs[2]. Onlabs provides a high level realistic environment as it simulates biology experiments like the microscopy procedure, the preparation of aqueous solutions and the protein electrophoresis. Through Onlabs and by using the mouse of a PC, the user navigates in the virtual laboratory, manipulates the various instruments and conducts particular experiments (Zafeiropoulos & Kalles, 2016). The current version of Onlabs provides three modes: the *Instruction Mode*, the *Evaluation Mode* and the *Experimental Mode*. When choosing the Instruction Mode, for example for the experiment of microscopy, the user performs, under written and oral instructions, a complete microscopy procedure of a test specimen. The procedure is divided into steps and for each step a written instruction appears at the top of the computer screen. By choosing the *Evaluation Mode* the user performs a complete microscopy without instructions. Through this mode she/he is also evaluated for her/his performance. The *Experimentation Mode* allows the user to perform a complete experiment without instructions and without evaluation. A screenshot of the Onlabs' virtual environment is presented in Figure 1.

Figure 1. A close-up of Onlabs-Experimental Mode

In parallel, additional elements, such as Augmented Reality and Mixed Reality – (AR/MR) elements, have recently enriched Onlabs towards the creation of a XR (VR/AR/MR) environment, making the use of this educational application a worthwhile educational experience. A collaboration between the HOU, the Research and Innovation Center in Information, Communication and Knowledge Technologies (Athena RC) and Omega Technology, a company experienced in Information Technologies, has led towards the development of the *XRLabs* platform[3]. XRLabs platform, whose name derives from the acronym of the research project, is an offspring of Onlabs. It is an innovative platform that combines web-based technologies, VR/AR/MR technologies and educational approaches for the remote preparation of students in laboratory experiments with realistic simulation environments. In more details, XRLabs is a platform that attempts to enhance the learning process by combining: a) the power of a digital literacy engine, b) the pedagogical benefits of the game-based learning with Serious Games, c) the interaction provided through the cross-platform systems with multiple players in a collaborative and/or competitive environment, and d) the augmented and mixed reality benefits that can contribute to *on the Job Training*. XRLabs is an ideal modern solution for students or professionals, who want to be trained in laboratory archaeometry exercises in privacy and at their own pace. Figure 2 presents a screenshot of the AR/MR elements of the XRLabs platform. Specifically, it depicts a 3D model of a microscope in a read desk, equipped with additional information that describes each part of the instrument. Each interactive part of the microscope has two different states. The first state activates additional text information about the part of the microscope and the part is highlighted with red texture, an example is shown in the left most image if Figure 2. The second state is when the part of microscope is manipulated by the user, the part is highlighted with green texture, the right most image of the Figure 2. In addition to that, two virtual

Figure 2. A close-up of augmented and mix reality elements of Onlabs through a mobile device

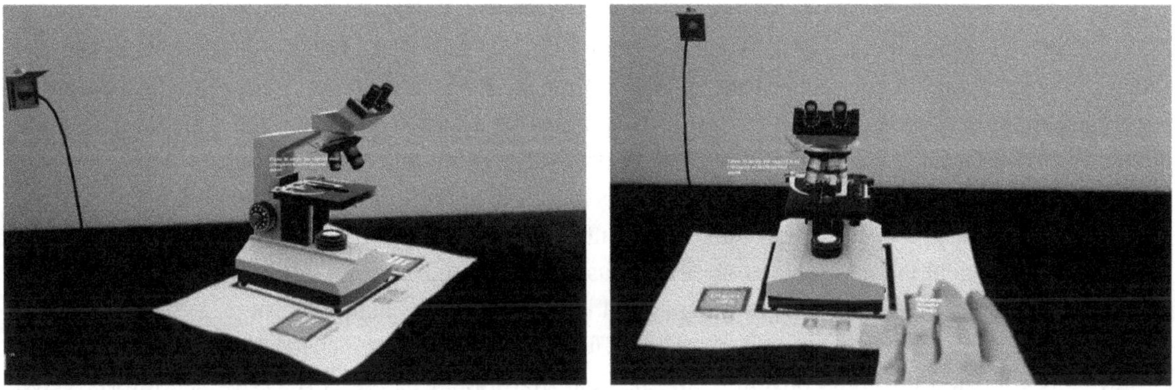

Figure 3. A stereoscopic view of AR/MR version of Onlabs for mobile devices equipped with cardboard glasses

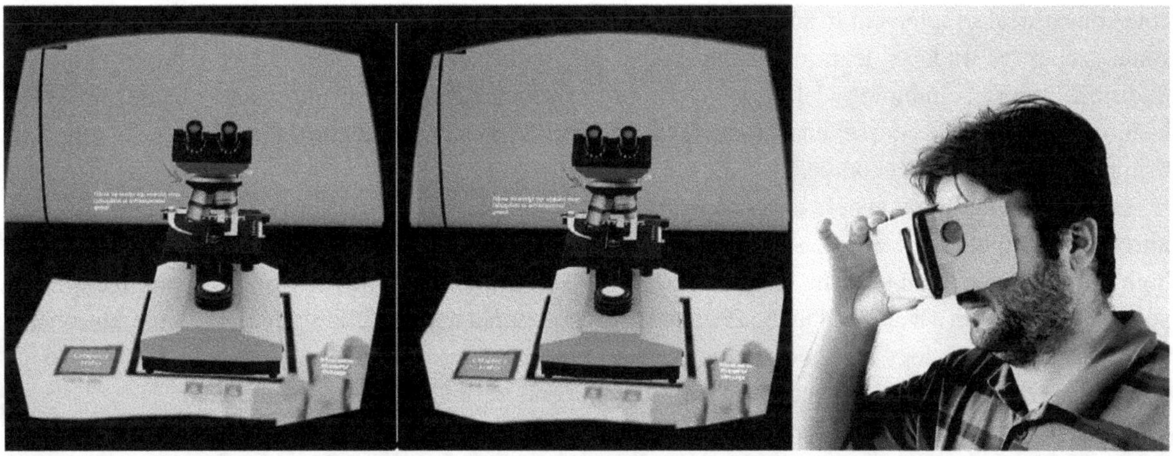

buttons are placed in the two sides of the microscope, which gives the ability to users to manipulate the active part of the microscope with simple hand gestures, as shown in the right most image of Figure 2 a human hand passes over the right virtual button. It should be stressed that the entire system is based on the smartphone's hardware, specifically on the single camera of the smartphone.

Figure 3, the left most image, shows an example of a stereoscopic view produced by the same system. Simply put, the user inserts its own smartphone, which has already installed the appropriate application, into the cardboard and automatically the AR and MR content appears in front of him, over the appropriate marker. While, by making hand gestures over the virtual buttons, the user interacts with the laboratory instrument. The right most image of Figure 3, depicts a cardboard usage by a user.

At this point it should be highlighted that AR/MR elements of Onlabs are not yet tested in educational scenarios, as the systems are under-construction without any stable version, but with many promising preliminary future results.

VR Environments and Learning Outcomes

VR and AR environments can serve as educational tools that can be embed in the learning process of science courses in higher education (Rutten, Van Joolingen, & Van Der Veen, 2012). Onlabs has already been used in several projects. In these projects, innovative educational scenarios were designed and interacting with Onlabs was part of the learning procedure in natural science courses (Paxinou et al., 2019, 2018a). In these studies Onlabs was used as an educational tool for communicating to students practical skills of science. By using Onlabs students were prepared for the microscopy experiment in their biology physical lab and their progress was assessed through written conceptual content Pre and Post tests. Students were always equally separated into cognitively balanced groups to be educated on their prescheduled microscopy experiment by different educational scenarios. The control group (C Group) was educated through conventional, classical, traditional methods (face-to-face tutorials, live demonstration of the microscopy procedure, PowerPoint slides, etc.), whereas the experimental group (VR Group) was educated by using supplementary, the virtual reality environment of Onlabs downloaded in a personal computer.

These studies provided some preliminary evidence that the incorporation of a VR lab in the educational procedure improves the quality of science education in institutions and that a VR lab can be a valuable educational supplement to students involved with science in general. Table 1 and Table 2 presents some data of the students' learning outcomes that denote the superiority of a VR application versus the traditional tutorials in biology laboratory courses for distance learning postgraduate students, enrolled in biology laboratory course, and graduate students in a Primary Education Department, enrolled in Computer and Education course.

In the first case study, where distance learning students from the HOU are involved, the Onlabs was introduced to them via a Skype session before their appearance in the wet lab. Onlabs prepared them both for the first written test, the Pre test, and for the performance of the microscopy experiment. This approach gave them a head start in the Pre test scores compared to their fellow students who traditionally just read only the biology text book to be prepared for their lab experiment. A tutorial was given to all students and a Post test assessed their progress, at the end of the learning procedure.

In the second case study, the sample was derived from the Primary Education Department in Patras University, in Greece. The VR Group was familiarized with Onlabs and practiced on microscopy under a tutor's instructions in the university computer lab, whereas the C Group just passively attended a demonstration of the microscopy experiment. Pre and Post tests were given appropriately to evaluate their performance during the learning process.

In order to verify the students' improvement and the correlation of the Pre and Post test scores, we applied a *k-means* clustering for both experimental sessions (C and VR Groups). After many repetitions of the clustering experiment, the fixed 4 classes gave the best result of the students based on their performance. These classes are schematically presented in Figure 4. For the following depiction we only used the data from the sample of the students in HOU. Every dot represents a student and its size depicts the student's progress based on her/his Pre and Post test scores. The range of the dots varies from -1.15 to 4.45 for the C Group, and -0.83 to 3.15 for the VR Group and it represents the different between the Pre and Post test score. We should highlight that, we set the re-runs of the *k-means* algorithm to 100 and the maximal iterations within each algorithm run to 300. Due to the small number of the students, the

Table 1. Averages and standard deviations of students' scores in written tests after the applied learning method, for C and VR Group

Postgraduate, Distance Learning Students	Pre test Score	Post test Score
C Group (*N*=36)	5.43±2.07	6.84±1.99
VR Group (*N*=31)	7.21±1.63	8.34±1.18
Graduate, Primary Education Students		
C Group (*N*=30)	5.65±1.25	6.52±1.31
VR Group (*N*=24)	5.63±1.32	7.39±1.18

Table 2. Percentage of students who had their scores increased, stabilized or dropped between the Pre and the Post test, in C and VR Group

Postgraduate, Distance Learning Students	% of students with increase in their score	% of students with stability in their score	% of students with reduction in their score
C Group (*N*=36)	86.1	2.8	11.1
VR Group (*N*=31)	83.9	9.7	6.4
Graduate, Primary Education Students			
C Group (*N*=30)	70	6.7	23.3
VR Group (*N*=24)	91.7	8.3	0

k-means configuration was good enough to show the best correlation between the students' performances associated to the experimental sessions. We tested the *k-means* algorithm with larger number of re-runs and maximal iteration but there was no difference in the result.

The Post-Test scores for the C Group were statistically significant higher than the Pre-Test scores (W=600,5, p<0,001). The Post-Test scores for the VR Group were also statistically significant higher than the Pre-Test scores (W=448,5, p<0,001). So, both educational methods led to improved learning outcomes but, according to Figure 4b, the familiarization with the microscopy topic via OnLabs gave a significant preliminary knowledge on the subject (green dots). Students were better prepared when they appeared in their wet lab. Finally, the Post-Test scores for the experimental group were statistically significant higher than the Post-Test scores for the control group, (U=773,5, p<0,005).

In Summary, when comparing VR teaching scenarios with traditional educational procedures, simulation environments provide students with benefits in terms of both conceptual understanding and practical skills (Brinson, 2015; Hoffler & Leutner, 2007). Simulation helped students understand the theory of microscopy and prepared them in a more efficient way for their wet lab. It connected theory and practice in the hands-on laboratory and helped students with zero or minimum science background to obtain higher scores and better experimental performance. Simulation creates a link between different professions and disciplines as it is presented in Figure 5.

Figure 4. Visualization of the change in students' scores from Pre to Post test. Distance Learning students in HOU who a) read the text biology book to be prepared for microscopy experiment, and b) used Onlabs to be prepared for their microscopy experiment

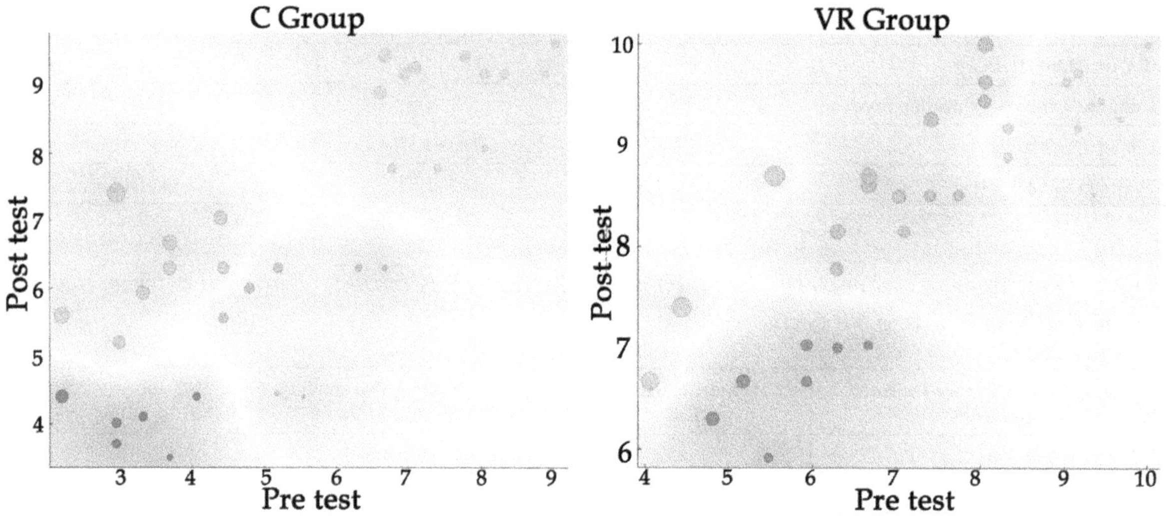

Figure 5. XR labs can be the bridge that facilitates the interface between different professions and disciplines

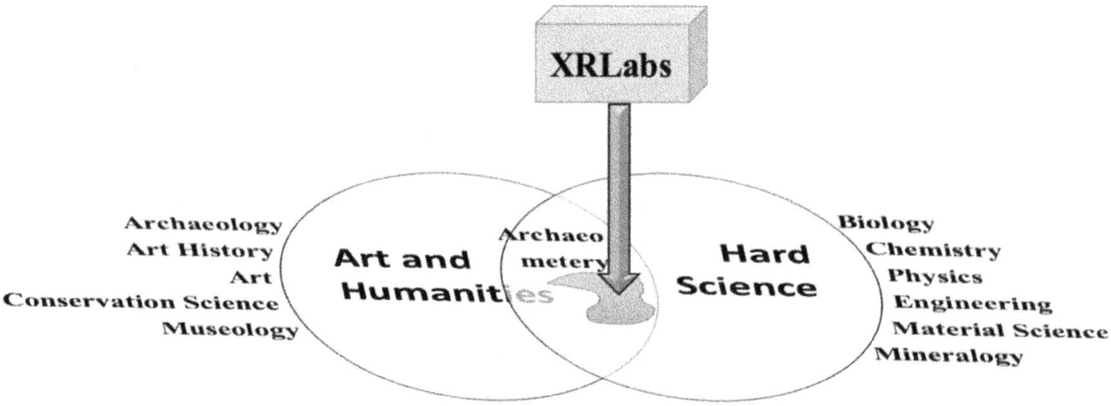

Archaeometry - VR and AR Applications

Students involved with Archaeometry courses attend laboratory science modules since, as archaeometrists they will be in the position of analysing and dating archaeological findings (Sypsas et al., 2019). They have to acquire basic, or sometimes, advanced knowledge on science issues. For example, they will definitely be challenged to operate a photonic microscope or a stereoscope to observe tiny structures. Although the majority of archaeometry students have a natural science background, everyday updated equipment and technology will shape their research. Therefore, these students have to overcome the practical difficulties and be familiarized with the digital age and its applications. Using VR and AR laboratories, students will be prepared for the laboratory sessions and they will get experience in using the laboratory instruments, avoiding possible damages of archaeological findings.

XR simulation laboratories could prepare archaeometrists for operating instruments for several analytical methods. For example, the analytical method of radiocarbon dating requires ability to operate a multi-counter system that calculates the concentration of the 14C, and thus the age of an archaeological object. This multi-counter system could be simulated through XR environment as a part of an educational activity, could help archaeometrists to handle later in the physical lab, the multitude of toggles and levers of the real system.

Furthermore, since the underwater archaeological sites and findings need *in situ* observation and examination, the virtual laboratories constitute an education tool for biology students. Moreover, the environmental marine conditions that affect these findings need to be examined by a biological point of view, in order to estimate the degradation biological factors that are involved (Fernández-Montblanc, Bethencourt, Izquierdo, & González-Duarte, 2014). Thus, the educational use of biology virtual laboratories could enrich marine archaeometric education. In this point we have to denote that the engagement with a virtual laboratory is limited and it is not equivalent with the original laboratory experiment (Hofstein & Mamlok-Naaman, 2007). It can serve as a tool for preparation and not as a replacement for the physical lab in its entirety (Makransky, Thisgaard & Gadegaard, 2016).

CONCLUSION

VR lab, like Onlabs, or XR environments, like XRLabs platform, could be a preparatory tool for education in Archaeometry, as it may enable virtual/augmented/mixed reality experimentation in processes involved in this field. It is proven that Onlabs is a very efficient supplementary educational tool for biology students. It could also help archaeometry students as Archaeometry education includes as well comprehension and familiarization with science laboratory technics. It is a promising tool that serve the ultimate purposes of institutions to save time and money and engage their students to the learning process by offering them up-to-date applications. Interactive cross-reality laboratories for archaeometry are convenient, safe, economic, rapid, flexible and user-friendly spaced educational tools that challenge, engage and prepare students for their real scientific experiment.

In the future, we plan to develop a fully dynamic cross reality environment, where educators will develop their own educational scenarios through 3D WYSIWYG (What You See Is What You Get) editor, with multiple interactive laboratory instruments. In addition to that, Artificial Intelligence instructors will guide both, educators and students. The entire systems will focus to open and linked data technologies in order to provide the opportunity to everyone to develop and share their own component (interactive laboratory instruments, educational scenarios etc.). Having regard this framework, we expect to provide a fundamental platform for laboratory training, for all levels of education (even for disabled people who don't have access to laboratories) focusing to the enhancement of daily international educational practice.

REFERENCES

Abdelmonem, M. G., Selim, G., Mushatat, S., & Almogren, A. (2017). Virtual Platforms for Heritage Preservation in the Middle East: The Case of Medieval Cairo. *Archnet-IJAR*, *11*(3), 28. doi:10.26687/archnet-ijar.v11i3.1404

Addison, A. C. (2000). Emerging trends in virtual heritage. *IEEE MultiMedia*, *7*(2), 22–25. doi:10.1109/93.848421

Artioli, G. (2010). *Scientific Methods and Cultural Heritage: An introduction to the application of materials science to Archaeometry and conservation science*. New York: Oxford University Press. doi:10.1093/acprof:oso/9780199548262.001.0001

Balla, A., Pavlogeorgatos, G., Tsiafakis, D., & Pavlidis, G. (2014). Recent Advances in Archaeological Modeling for Archaeological Research and Cultural Heritage Management. *Mediterranean Archaeology and Archaeometry*, *14*(4), 143–153.

Bernhard, J. (2010). Insightful learning in the laboratory: Some experiences from 10 years of designing and using conceptual labs. *European Journal of Engineering Education*, *35*(3), 271–287. doi:10.1080/03043791003739759

Bickmore, T., Pfeifer, L., & Schulman, D. (2011). Relational agents improve engagement and learning in science museum visitors. *Intelligent Virtual Agents*, *2011*, 55–67. doi:10.1007/978-3-642-23974-8_7

Bogdanovych, A., Rodriguez-Aguilar, J. A., Simoff, S., & Cohen, A. (2010). Authentic interactive reenactment of cultural heritage with 3D virtual worlds and artificial intelligence. *Applied Artificial Intelligence*, *24*(6), 617–647. doi:10.1080/08839514.2010.492172

Borba, E. Z., & Zuffo, M. K. (2016). *Replay! When past experiences are reassembled through virtual reality*. Academic Press.

Breuer, J. J., & Bente, G. (2010). Why so serious? On the relation of serious games and learning. *Eludamos (Göttingen)*, *4*(1), 7–24. doi:10.1177/1461444812450426

Brinson, J. R. (2015). Learning outcome achievement in non-traditional (virtual and remote) versus traditional (hands-on) laboratories: A review of the empirical research. *Computers & Education*, *87*, 218–237. doi:10.1016/j.compedu.2015.07.003

Brown, S., & Vaughan, C. (2010). Play: How it Shapes the Brain, Opens the Imagination, and Invigorates the Soul. J P Tarcher/Penguin Putnam.

Bruno, F., Bruno, S., De Sensi, G., Luchi, M. L., Mancuso, S., & Muzzupappa, M. (2010). From 3D reconstruction to virtual reality: A complete methodology for digital archaeological exhibition. *Journal of Cultural Heritage*, *11*(1), 42–49. doi:10.1016/j.culher.2009.02.006

Burca, G., James, J. A., Kockelmann, W., Fitzpatrick, M. E., Zhang, S. Y., Hovind, J., & Van Langh, R. (2011). A new bridge technique for neutron tomography and diffraction measurements. *Nuclear Instruments & Methods in Physics Research. Section A, Accelerators, Spectrometers, Detectors and Associated Equipment*, *651*(1), 229–235. doi:10.1016/j.nima.2011.01.096

Chandler, P., & Sweller, J. (1991). Cognitive Load Theory and the Format of Instruction. *Cognition and Instruction*, *8*(4), 293–332. doi:10.12071532690xci0804_2

Collins, A., & Halverson, R. (2018). *Rethinking education in the age of technology* (2nd ed.). New York: Teachers College Press.

Corrêa, A. G., Borba, E. Z., Lopes, R., Zuffo, M. K., & Araujo, A. (2017). *User Experience Evaluation with Arch a eometry Interactive Tools in Virtual Reality Environment*. Academic Press.

de Jong, T., Linn, M. C., & Zacharia, Z. (2013). *Physical and Virtual Laboratories in Science and Engineering Education*. Academic Press.

De Vries, L. E., & May, M. (2019). Virtual laboratory simulation in the education of laboratory technicians-Motivation and study intensity. *Biochemistry and Molecular Biology Education*, *47*(3), 257–262. doi:10.1002/bmb.21221 PMID:30748084

Djindjian, F. (2015). Computers and mathematics in archaeology, anatomy of an ineluctable success! *Concepts, Methods and Tools. Proceedings of the 42nd Annual Conference on Computer Applications and Quantitative Methods in Archaeology*, 1–6.

Donais, M. K., Whissel, G., Dumas, A., & Golden, K. (2009). Analyzing lead content in ancient bronze coins by flame atomic absorption spectroscopy. An archaeometry laboratory with nonscience majors. *Journal of Chemical Education*, *86*(3), 343–346. doi:10.1021/ed086p343

Fernández-Montblanc, T., Bethencourt, M., Izquierdo, A., & González-Duarte, M. M. (2014). Establishing the relationship between underwater cultural heritage deterioration and marine environmental factors. A comparative analysis of the Bucentaure and Fougueux sites. In M. A. Rogerio-Candelera (Ed.), *Science, Technology and Cultural Heritage* (pp. 53–58). Sevilla, Spain: CRC Press, Taylor & Francis Group.

Forte, M. (2011). Cyber-Archaeology : Notes on the simulation of the past. *Virtual Archaeology Review*, *2*(4), 7–18. doi:10.4995/var.2011.4543

Getchell, K., Miller, A., Nicoll, J. R., Sweetman, R. J., & Allison, C. (2010). Games methodologies and immersive environments for virtual fieldwork. *IEEE Transactions on Learning Technologies*, *3*(4), 281–293. doi:10.1109/TLT.2010.25

Glascock, M. D., Speakman, R. J., & Neff, H. (2007). Archaeometry at the University of Missouri Research Reactor and the provenance of obsidian artifacts in North America. *Archaeometry*, *49*(2), 343–357. doi:10.1111/j.1475-4754.2007.00305.x

Gomes, L., & Bogosyan, S. (2009). Current Trends in Remote Laboratories. *IEEE Transactions on Industrial Electronics*, *56*(12), 4744–4756. doi:10.1109/TIE.2009.2033293

Gravier, C., Fayolle, J., Bayard, B., Ates, M., & Lardon, J. (2008). State of the Art About Remote Laboratories Paradigms – Foundations of Ongoing Mutations. *International Journal of Online Engineering*, *4*(1), 19–25. Retrieved from http://www.online-journals.org/index.php/i-joe/article/view/480

Hoffler, T. N., & Leutner, D. (2007). Instructional animation versus static pictures: A Meta-analysis. *Learning and Instruction*, *17*(6), 722–738. doi:10.1016/j.learninstruc.2007.09.013

Hofstein, A., & Lunetta, V. N. (2004). The Laboratory in Science Education: Foundations for the Twenty-First Century. *Science Education, 88*(1), 28–54. doi:10.1002ce.10106

Hofstein, A., & Mamlok-Naaman, R. (2007). The laboratory in Science education: The state of the art. *Chemistry Education Research and Practice, 2*(8), 105–107. doi:10.1039/B7RP90003A

Hsu, Y. S., & Thomas, R. A. (2002). The impacts of a web-aided instructional simulation on science learning. *International Journal of Science Education, 24*(9), 955–979. doi:10.1080/09500690110095258

Katsianis, M., Tsipidis, S., Kotsakis, K., & Kousoulakou, A. (2008). A 3D digital workflow for archaeological intra-site research using GIS. *Journal of Archaeological Science, 35*(3), 655–667. doi:10.1016/j.jas.2007.06.002

Kiourt, C., Koutsoudis, A., & Pavlidis, G. (2016). DynaMus: A fully dynamic 3D virtual museum framework. *Journal of Cultural Heritage, 22*, 984–991. doi:10.1016/j.culher.2016.06.007

Kiourt, C., Pavlidis, G., Koutsoudis, A., & Kalles, D. (2017). Realistic Simulation of Cultural Heritage. *International Journal of Computational Methods in Heritage Science, 1*(1), 10–40. doi:10.4018/IJCMHS.2017010102

Kollöffel, B., & de Jong, T. (2013). Conceptual understanding of electrical circuits in secondary vocational engineering education: Combining traditional instruction with inquiry learning in a virtual lab. *Journal of Engineering Education, 102*(3), 375–393. doi:10.1002/jee.20022

Kwon, Y. M., Kim, I. J., Ahn, S. C., Ko, H., & Kim, H. G. (2001). Virtual heritage system: Modeling, database & presentation. Proceedings - 7th International Conference on Virtual Systems and Multimedia, VSMM 2001, 137–146. 10.1109/VSMM.2001.969665

Liritzis, I. (2009, Nov.). Archaeometry-Archaeometria a review. *History (London)*, 16–23.

Liritzis, I., Al-Otaibi, F. M., Volonakis, P., & Drivaliari, A. (2015). Digital technologies and trends in cultural heritage. *Mediterranean Archaeology and Archaeometry, 15*(3), 313–332. doi:10.5281/zenodo.33832

Liritzis, I., Volonakis, P., Vosinakis, S., & Pavlidis, G. (2015). Cyber-archaeometry from cyber-archaeology: new dynamic trends in archaeometric training and research. In *Virtual Archaeology (Methods and benefits). Second International Conference held at the State Hermitage Museum* (pp. 38–40). Saint Petersburg: The State Hermitage Publishers.

Ma, J., & Nickerson, J. V. (2006). Hands-on, simulated, and remote laboratories: A comparative literature review. *ACM Computing Surveys, 38*(3), 7, es. doi:10.1145/1132960.1132961

Makransky, G., Thisgaard, M. W., & Gadegaard, H. (2016). Virtual simulations as preparation for lab exercises: Assessing learning of key laboratory skills in microbiology and improvement of essential non-cognitive skills. *PLoS One, 11*(6), 1–11. doi:10.1371/journal.pone.0155895 PMID:27253395

Manhita, A., Dias, C., Martins, S., Costa, J., Teixeira, D., Costa, M., & Rocha, L. (2016). A new look into the archaeological materials from the Museum of Évora, Portugal–the case study of the Zambujeiro Dolmen. In *XIII CONFERENCIA INTERNACIONAL Antropologia* (pp. 212–228). Instituto Cubano de Antropologia.

Musílek, L. (2015). Archaeometry – an example of interdisciplinarity in engineering education. *Proceedings of 43rd SEFI Annual Conference 2015.*

Nicholson, S. (2011). Making gameplay matter: Designing modern educational tabletop games. *Knowledge Quest*, *40*(1), 60–65.

Nicholson, S. (2012). Strategies for meaningful gamification: Concepts behind transformative play and participatory museums. *Meaningful Play 2012*, (1999), 1–16.

Ontiveros, M. A. C., Macias, J. M., Berni, P., & Reynolds, P. (2014). lrcw.net: A web site with a virtual laboratory for the study of coarse and cooking wares in the late antique Mediterranean (http://www.lrcw.net/). In N. Poulou-Papadimitriou, E. Nodarou, & V. Kilikoglou (Eds.), *LRCW 4 Late Roman Coarse Wares, Cooking Wares and Amphorae in the Mediterranean: Archaeology and archaeometry. The Mediterranean: a market without frontiers* (Vol. 1, pp. 617–622). Publishers of British Archaeological Reports.

Paxinou, E., Karatrantou, A., Kalles, D., Panagiotakopoulos, C., & Sgourou, A. (2018a). *A 3D Virtual Reality Laboratory as a Supplementary Educational Preparation Tool for a Biology Course*. Retrieved from http://www.eurodl.org/?p=current&sp=brief&abstract=777

Paxinou, E., Panagiotakopoulos, C., Karatrantou, A., Kalles, D., & Sgourou, A. (2019). Implementation and evaluation of a 3D virtual reality biology lab vs conventional didactic practices in lab experimenting with the photonic microscope. *Biochemistry and Molecular Biology Education*. doi:10.1002/bmb.21307

Paxinou, E., Zafeiropoulos, V., Sypsas, A., Kiourt, C., & Kalles, D. (2018b). Assessing the Impact of Virtualizing Physical Labs. *27th EDEN Annual Conference*, 151-158.

Pollard, A. M., & Bray, P. (2007). A bicycle made for two? The integration of scientific techniques into archaeological interpretation. *Annual Review of Anthropology*, *36*(1), 245–259. doi:10.1146/annurev.anthro.36.081406.094354

Refsland, S. T., Ojika, T., Addison, A. C., & Stone, R. (2000). Virtual Heritage : Breathing New Life into Our Ancient Past. *IEEE MultiMedia*, *7*(2), 20–21. doi:10.1109/MMUL.2000.848420

Roussou, M., & Drettakis, G. (2003). Photorealism and Non-Photorealism in Virtual Heritage Representation. In A. Chalmers, D. Arnold, & F. Niccolucci (Eds.), *International Symposium on Virtual Reality, Archeology and Cultural Heritage* (p. 10). Brighton, UK: Academic Press.

Rutten, N., Van Joolingen, W. R., & Van Der Veen, J. T. (2012). The learning effects of computer simulations in science education. *Computers & Education*, *58*(1), 136–153. doi:10.1016/j.compedu.2011.07.017

Sanders, D. H. (2008). *Why do Virtual Heritage?* Retrieved from https://archive.archaeology.org/online/features/virtualheritage/

Seaborn, K., & Fels, D. I. (2015). Gamification in theory and action: A survey. *International Journal of Human-Computer Studies*, *74*, 14–31. doi:10.1016/j.ijhcs.2014.09.006

Sequeira, L. M., & Morgado, L. (2013). Virtual Archaeology in Second Life and OpenSimulator. *Journal of Virtual Worlds Research*, *6*(1), 3–7. doi:10.4101/jvwr.v6i1.7047

Sylaiou, S., Liarokapis, F., Kotsakis, K., & Patias, P. (2009). Virtual museums, a survey on methods and tools. *Journal of Cultural Heritage*, *10*(4), 520–528. doi:10.1016/j.culher.2009.03.003

Sypsas, A., Kiourt, C., Paxinou, E., Zafeiropoulos, V., & Kalles, D. (2019). The Educational Application Of Virtual Laboratories In Archaeometry. *International Journal of Computational Methods in Heritage Science*, *3*(1), 1–19. doi:10.4018/IJCMHS.2019010101

Trundle, K. C., & Bell, R. L. (2010). The use of a computer simulation to promote conceptual change: A quasi-experimental study. *Computers & Education*, *54*(4), 1078–1088. doi:10.1016/j.compedu.2009.10.012

Tsichritzis, D., & Gibbs, S. (1991). Virtual Museums and Virtual Realities. *International Conference on Hypermedia and Interactivity in Museums*, 17–25. Retrieved from http://dblp.uni-trier.de/rec/bibtex/conf/ichim/TsichritzisG91

Wang, C. Y., Wu, H. K., Lee, S. W. Y., Hwang, F. K., Chang, H. Y., Wu, Y. T., ... Lo, H. (2014). A Review of Research on Technology-Assisted School Science Laboratories. *Journal of Educational Technology & Society*, *17*(2), 17, 307–320.

Weller, J. M. (2004). Simulation in undergraduate medical education: Bridging the gap between theory and practice. *Medical Education*, *38*(1), 32–38. doi:10.1111/j.1365-2923.2004.01739.x PMID:14962024

Wilhelmson, H., & Dell'Unto, N. (2015). Virtual taphonomy: A new method integrating excavation and postprocessing in an archaeological context. *American Journal of Physical Anthropology*, *157*(2), 305–321. doi:10.1002/ajpa.22715 PMID:25720527

Zafeiropoulos, V., & Kalles, D. (2016). Performance Evaluation in Virtual Lab Training. In *Proceedings of the Online, Open and Flexible Higher Education Conference 2016* (pp. 455-468). Aarhus: EADTU.

ENDNOTES

1 http://www.archaeometry.org/

2 http://onlabs.eap.gr/

3 http://xrlabs.eu

Chapter 9
Methods and Practices for Assessing the User Experience of Interactive Systems for Cultural Heritage

Vasiliki Nikolakopoulou
https://orcid.org/0000-0001-6410-6697
University of the Aegean, Greece

Panayiotis Koutsabasis
https://orcid.org/0000-0003-0478-7456
University of the Aegean, Greece

ABSTRACT

Over the last few years, an increasing number of cultural sites, including museums, archaeological places, and historic cities, have adopted a wide range of interactive technologies to enhance the visitor (user) experience. This chapter presents a review of interactive systems for cultural heritage, selected from a total of 83 publications in 2012-2019, from the perspective of the methods employed for their empirical evaluation (i.e., the degree to which the system satisfies user goals and expectations). The review reports on several characteristics of interactive systems of CH including purpose, technology, content, and location of the interaction, and then emphasizes methods of empirical evaluation. The chapter provides discussion comparing to the results of the previous report, and outlook on particular challenges of interaction design and evaluation for CH.

INTRODUCTION

Digital Cultural Heritage (CH) is widely considered a new multidisciplinary research domain that incorporates methodologies from a wide range of disciplines and sectors. Expanding its initial purposes of preserving tangible and intangible heritage artefacts, such as archaeological sites, historic habitats,

DOI: 10.4018/978-1-7998-2871-6.ch009

human-made constructions and art, processes of craftsmanship and traditional practices through digitization and documentation, CH is now being disseminated in a broad universal manner and it is becoming accessible via contemporary digital technologies. In the last decade there has been an exploitation of interactive applications to enhance the (natural of virtual) experience of visitors at cultural institutions and sites. The digital landscape of interactive systems employed to improve the overall user experience (UX) and communicate aspects of CH is constantly increasing and diversifying.

Interactive applications in CH include: mobile applications and games, location-aware audio guides, VR/AR/MR (virtual/augmented/mixed reality) enabled technologies, online virtual worlds, multi-touch displays of ranging sizes and setups, and various types of interfaces that transcend CH content to the users. Researchers and practitioners in the digital CH domain intersect empirical methods and experience from computer science, human-computer interaction (HCI), exhibition design, museology, architecture, history, and archaeology, without this list of disciplines being exhaustive.

Consequently, empirical studies and evaluations of interactive systems in CH can inform the respective research community and at the same time be informed, since it is a continuously evolving domain that reflects on its own practices. A fortiori, a review of empirical evaluations that encloses interactive systems that have been evaluated during the recent years is needed in order to track current technological trends and update on possible shortcomings and limitations. This review paper expands and enhances the previous review of Koutsabasis (2017) and reports on a systematically selected sample of 83 publications from 2012-2019 (with 30 publications added to the sample of the first review). Furthermore, this paper draws conclusions comparing the findings of the previous review, informing on improvements and drawbacks that concern previously identified issues. Additionally, it provides a broader record of approaches, methods and new emerging technologies.

The structure of the paper is as follows: The next section presents background and related work on empirical evaluation methods outlining the dimensions of empirical evaluations, participant issues, types of evidence (data), place and time of evaluation, etc. Then, the paper reports on the systematic method of collection and processing of the sample of publications. The next section reports on results starting from the characteristics of the interactive systems examined: main purpose, main interactive technology/ interaction style, cultural content, and location of system use. Then it addresses the methods of empirical evaluation, namely: dimensions examined, general method, data collection methods (or techniques), participants, and finally comparative approaches. The next section discusses various issues stemming out of this review, also compared with the findings of the previous review, by acknowledging good practices, critically analyzing identified shortcomings of the current state of the art. The last section provides an outlook in the respected discussed areas.

BACKGROUND AND RELATED WORK

Empirical Evaluation of Interactive Systems

The evaluation of interactive systems has been extensively investigated in Human-Computer Interaction (HCI), which is an interdisciplinary field of computer science, psychology and design, "*concerned with the design, evaluation and implementation of interactive computing systems for human use and with the study of major phenomena surrounding them*" (Hewett et al. 1996). Evaluation in HCI is an activity that examines the degree to which an interactive system satisfies user goals and expectations (or more generally, the user perspective). According to MacDonald and Atwood (2013), "*evaluation has been a dominant theme in HCI for decades, but it is far from being a solved problem. As interactive systems and their uses change, the nature of evaluation must change as well*".

The principal epistemological standpoint to evaluation of interactive systems is empiricism, per which (Feldman, 2001) one can claim to have knowledge only when one has a true belief based on empirical evidence. Thus, empirical evaluations of interactive systems are dominant in contrast to those based on theory. An empirical evaluation yields knowledge by the direct or indirect observation of the UX; simply put, it employs users to interact with the system, while its results are derived by observation or experiment. Several methods of empirical evaluation have been analyzed in HCI textbooks (Dix et al. 2004; Cairns and Cox, 2008; Shneiderman and Pleasant, 2009) as well as in books with more specific framing about empirical evaluation of usability (Nielsen, 1994; Rubin and Chisnell, 2008) and the user experience (Sauro and Lewis, 2012; Albert and Tullis, 2013).

An indicative list of common empirical evaluation methods includes: observation (strategies), interview (strategies), focus groups, user testing (with respective protocols), field testing, field studies, questionnaires (instruments about usability in general or for particular technologies, as well as on other aspects of the UX; some of these tested for validity and reliability), surveys, diary studies and probes. Any empirical method has intrinsic advantages and disadvantages: they reach to conclusions, but with limited scope; they are useful, but error-prone; errors of one method may be corrected by applying another method; different methods must be combined so that intrinsic shortcomings of one method are corrected by the advantages of another.

An empirical evaluation is inherently a complex activity and requires careful planning and justified selection of respective methods and tools. Important factors to be considered for any empirical evaluation of an interactive system include:

- **The dimensions of the evaluation.** Many empirical evaluations of interactive systems examine their usability, i.e. "the extent to which a product can be used by specified users to achieve specified goals with effectiveness, efficiency, and satisfaction in a specified context of use" (ISO 9241). Over the last few years there is a shift towards a more holistic assessment of the UX, i.e. "a person's perceptions and responses that result from the use or anticipated use of a product, system or service" (ISO 9241). There are several other dimensions examined in empirical evaluations like accessibility, engagement, fun, learning effectiveness, presence, immersion, user acceptance, appreciation, etc.
- **The general approach of the evaluation.** Despite that each empirical evaluation is a unique case of method use and practice, if we think at a higher level of abstraction, each single case may be classified into one of a limited number of more general approaches that reflect the factors of purpose, data, place and time of an empirical evaluation (discussed in section Empirical Evaluation of Interactive Systems). Thus, at a more general line of thought, an evaluation approach may be classified *as a study or a test* based on some important criteria about the process followed, like: (a) if the approach allows users to explore and play with the system, or requires from them identical and instrumental (task-based) interactions; (b) if the approach does not include real-time user observation or monitoring by the evaluator or system; in contrast to a more rigorous test which would require this type of care; (c) if the approach allows users to interact with the system in a long period of time (e.g. a couple of hours) or at repeated intervals, in contrast to much shorter timeframes.

- **The participants (users).** Several considerations must be taken about participants, including their number (how many), profile (representativeness), availability, incentives, ethical issues of participation, etc. A thorough discussion is provided in Cairns and Cox (2008).
- **The purpose of the evaluation.** This may be generally classified into exploratory, formative or summative. Exploratory evaluations are often employed in research-through-design approaches (Zimmerman et al. 2010) to evaluate design concepts, highly innovative ideas or early prototypes. The purpose of a formative evaluation is to yield recommendations, corrections and comments about the interactive system, and it is typically conducted during the design and development process with a system under development, while summative evaluation can reach to conclusions about the quality of the UX and it is typically with the final system at the end of the process.
- **The data (evidence) of the evaluation.** This is generally divided into qualitative or quantitative. Qualitative data include (among others) observations, notes, comments, user reactions or responses, while quantitative data include various measures about the UX like for example task success, time to task, errors (and types of), responses in scaled statements (questionnaires), etc. Qualitative data can be processed so that they are presented in quantitative terms as well (e.g. frequencies, charts). A thorough approach to evaluation often requires the combination of qualitative and quantitative data.
- **The place of evaluation.** In general, these are the computer lab, the field or online. When evaluation occurs in the lab, an identical user testing procedure can be followed. When evaluation is conducted in the field (whatever this may be, like for example the city streets, the user's home or work environment, a museum or public place) the evaluation plan must be adapted to the particular context and situation, which evolves and changes between users; depending on the test plan it may be characterized as field study or field testing (more rigorous). When the evaluation is conducted online, behavioral and usage data (or analytics) are collected and processed through data logging. Online evaluations may be combined with either lab or field testing and field studies.
- **The time of evaluation.** Time may refer to system use or phases of the design process. The evaluation may be conducted before the user makes use of the system (exploratory, during design phase), during system use (with various kinds of observation and data logging, collecting qualitative observations and values for quantitative measures) and after system use (retrospectively with interviews, questionnaires, etc.).
- **Whether the evaluation is comparative or not**. Empirical evaluations may compare systems, e.g. a new system with the previous one, or an alternative. They may also compare the proposed system with another activity (e.g. compare learning through an app or via viewing a video), typically to measure learning. In addition, they may compare the UX of different user groups, e.g. 'experts'/'novices'; children/adults/older users, etc. Comparative empirical evaluations usually add further insight, since they present another point of reference upon which the results may be matched.

These characteristics of empirical evaluation explain why there is a wealth of respective methods and tools. They also imply that an evaluation of an interactive system may not be conducted with some sort of a recipe or a unified approach that fits any purpose, system, technology or user group. On the contrary, an empirical evaluation must be carefully planned with justified and complementary method use, as well as be conducted with rigor. It is currently unclear if these considerations are taken into account in evaluations of interactive systems in CH. A review of current practice is required as digital heritage systems emerge as a distinct class of interactive systems; it may contribute to a better understanding of good practices, shortcomings and areas of further research.

Other Related Reviews

There are no previous reviews of empirical evaluations of interactive systems in CH with the framing of this one. However, there are a few recent reviews that are relevant.

Kabassi (2016) presents a thorough review on evaluation experiments of the museums' websites aiming at making it easier for more museums to conduct such experiments. She includes both inspections and empirical methods in her review (nevertheless, inspections may account as empirical methods) and identifies several criteria for evaluation (in this paper these are called dimensions). She does not detail further into particular methods used but she presents an account for different types of web environments including virtual and mobile and emphasizes more on the dimensions employed for evaluation. In the current paper, interactive systems of CH are reviewed in contrast to museum web sites. Furthermore, this paper presents a wide range of issues about method use and it critically analyses current practice.

Paliokas and Sylaiou (2016) present a mapping study on modern museum gaming technologies and applications, with a focus on the use of serious games by the visitors during exhibition navigation and exploration of museum's cultural and educational content. Their review reports on game goals, purpose of use, scope, user acceptance and educational effectiveness. It does not focus on user-centered evaluation or particular evaluation methods used.

In addition, there are a few works that review specific technologies for disseminating CH like those of

- Neumüller et al. (2014) who argue for the need of multisensory experiences in museums and identify that 3D printing can be employed to enhance preservation, accessibility, research and education.
- Ravyse et al. (2016) review serious games for learning purposes and refer to several applications about CH,
- Malegiannaki & Daradoumis (2017) who review the educational and learning potentials of spatial games for CH.
- Bekele et al. (2018) who present a mapping study among the selection of augmented, virtual, and mixed reality technologies, and the general CH application areas in terms of suitability, appropriateness, and viability according to the purpose of use. Their study does not report on empirical evaluations of the presented technologies related either to human factors or aspects of user experience.

Last but not least, there are reviews about empirical evaluation methods and tools about the user experience like Bargas-Avila and Hornbæk (2011) and Alves et al. (2014). These works provide a critical analysis of evaluation methods use in research and practice regardless of particular applications. Despite they do not refer to CH systems per se, they provide useful conceptual framings about UX and empirical evaluation in general.

METHOD

The goal of this review is to systematically collect a representative sample, in more narrowed view than the previous one (Koutsabasis, 2017). In order to report on interactive systems in CH, in terms of their evaluating dimensions and methods used, a systematic approach to the selection of additional papers between the years 2017-2019 was followed, using the Quality of Reporting of Meta-Analyses (QUORUM) statement (Moher et al. 1999) which defines four major stages of a review report. The following schema (Figure 1) represent the selection process.

Step 1. Potential Publications for Retrieval and Initial Screening

Source selection. We selected to search for publications in the following important digital libraries: Google scholar, ACM digital library, IEEEXplore, Science direct, and Springer link.

Search queries. We used two more strict queries than the previous review: ("cultural heritage" + evaluation + interact), ("digital heritage" + evaluation + interact). The third query was used to help focusing only on interactive systems. Results were sorted 'by relevance', between years 2017-2019.

Retrieval. For each search engine we retrieved approximately 70 first results from the first query and 30 first results from the second query, as the latter's results were proportionally lesser than the former's ones.

Figure 1. (QUORUM) flow diagram of the screening method adopted in this review

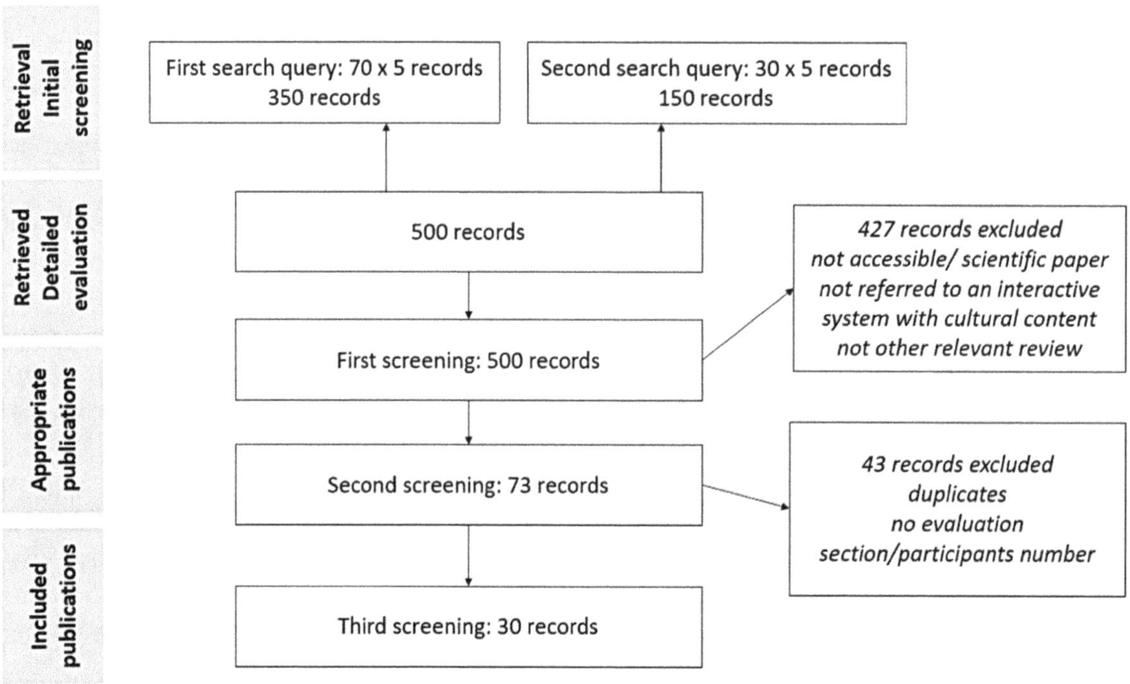

First screening criteria. A total of 500 search results were examined. The results for the second screening included (a) accessible scientific papers, that (b) referred to an interactive system with cultural content, (c) or it was another review relevant to this study. Search results were scanned based on their title, keywords, summary, and publication venue. From the total of 500 screened, 95 results met those criteria and included in the second step of the selection process.

Step 2. Publications Retrieved for Detailed Evaluation

Second screening criteria. In this phase, the papers were more thoroughly reviewed to (a) exclude duplicates and (b) identify if they contained an 'evaluation' section, reporting also on the number of participants and valid methods used. A total of 73 papers remained from this examination.

Step 3. Potentially Appropriate Publications for the Review

Third screening criteria. In this phase, papers were cross-examined in order to validate that each paper referred to a single system. Furthermore, papers were reviewed in further detail to ensure that they were empirical studies and that they included reasonably sufficient information about the evaluation, and also according to their citation's number. A total of 29 papers remained to be examined in detail.

Step 4. Publications Included for the Review

General characteristics of the selected sample. The publications included in the final step were added to the results of the previous review (Koutsabasis, 2017), providing us with a total number of 83 papers published in scientific journals (36/83) and conferences (46/83) (Table 1). The selected publications span along the 8-year period like this: 2012: 3 papers; 2013: 6 papers; 2014: 12 papers; 2015: 19 papers; 2016: 13 papers; 2017:10 papers; 2018: 14 papers; 2019: 7 papers. Regarding the sources of publication, most of the papers are published in journals and conferences of digital cultural heritage (45/83). There is also a considerable number of papers published in HCI/UX venues (21/83) and the rest (14/83) are published in other venues (e.g. learning, digital libraries, virtual reality, etc.).

Table 1. Papers selected for this review by academic publisher in journals and conferences

Journals	N	Conferences	N
ACM	19	ACM	16
Elsevier	7	IEEE	13
Taylor and Francis	2	by Springer	14
MIT Press	2	Other	4
Other	6		
Total	36	Total	47

Review process and data analysis. All the individual information concerning: purpose, technology, cultural content, location of system use, dimensions, general method, data collection methods, participants, comparative or not target groups addressed, dimensions of evaluation, methods and techniques used, participants (users), type of results, etc. were inserted in an MS Excel database for further statistical analysis, updating the number of charts and tables of the records of the previous review.

List of publications. Anagnostakis et al. 2016; Andreoli et al. 2016; Arends et al. 2012; Bellotti et al. 2012; Bellucci et al. 2015; Caggianese et al., 2018; Callaway et al. 2014; Camps-Ortueta et al., 2017; Chalvatzaras et al. 2014; Coenen et al. 2013; Correia et al. 2014; Creed et al. 2013; Di Franco et al. 2015; Diaz et al. 2014; Dimitropoulos et al., 2018; Duguleana et al. 2016; Fabola et al., 2017; Falvo, 2015; Fanini and Pagano, 2015; Fanini et al. 2015; Floch and Jiang 2015; Froschauer et al. 2013; Gaitanou et al. (2018); Georgiadi et al. 2016; Gkiti et al., 2018; Graf et al. 2015; Hai et al., 2018; Han et al. 2014; Hammady et al., 2018; Hu et al., 2017; Huang et al. 2013; Ijaz et al. 2016; Jones et al., 2019; Jylhä et al. 2015; Kassapakis et al. 2016; Katsouri et al. 2015; Kennedy et al. 2013; Koutsabasis and Vosinakis, 2016; Kyriakou & Hermon, 2019; Loizides et al. 2014; Lorenzini et al. 2015; Machidon et al., 2019; Madsen and Madsen, 2015; Maina and Suleman, 2015; Marshall et al. 2016; Marton et al. 2014; McCaffery et al. 2015; McGookin et al., 2019; Muntean et al., 2017; Nofal, Elhanafi, et al., 2018; Nofal, Reffat, et al., 2018; Not et al., 2019; O'Keefe and Benyon, 2015; O'Sullivan et al. 2014; Pagano et al., 2017; Panayiotou and Lanitis, 2016; Pereda, 2019; Philbin-Briscoe et al., 2017; Pietroni and Adami, 2014; Pollalis et al., 2018; Power et al., 2017; Pujol-Tost, 2019; Rennick-Egglestone et al. 2016; Reunanen et a; 2015; Rizvić and ; Roussou & Katifori, 2018; Schaper et al., 2018; Shin et al., 2017; Skalonjić 2015; Skowronski et al., 2018; Rojas et al. 2015; Rubino et al. 2015; Shih et al. 2015; Střelák et al. 2016; Sylaiou et al. 2015; van der Vaart and Damala, 2015; Vosinakis et al. (2018); Wang and Champion, 2012; Wang et al. 2014; Wu et al., 2017; Yelmi et al. 2016; Zamora-Musa et al., 2018.

RESULTS

Interactive Systems of Cultural Heritage

Main purpose. From the user perspective, the main purpose of the interactive systems examined (Table 2) was largely about to **explore a virtual or physical space or place** (virtual: 24,1% or 20/83; physical: 22,9% or 20/83), often by allowing interactions with selected virtual objects or physical points of interest (POIs) respectively, or explore both (3,6% or 3/83), frequently with physical computing and Tangible User Interfaces (TUIs). Virtual exploration often refers to a place or artifact that is no longer preserved, like for example in the work of McCaffery et al. (2015) on the 3D model of the lost township of Caen or the work of Vosinakis et al. (2018) on exploring the ancient agora of Athens (Figure 2); or is currently inaccessible like the work of Reunanen et al. (2015) who reconstructed a virtual wreck of the Vrouw Maria merchant ship that was discovered in 1999 but is still underwater; or is now replaced by another building as in the work of Fabola et al., (2017) who have virtually reconstructed a 19th century's fish curing yard. Physical exploration is mainly about mobile applications, which allow users to explore a cultural site outdoors or indoors. Exploration of both physical and virtual space of the user encompasses mutual examination and interaction of e.g. an interactive tangible replica and its virtually augmented audio-video feedback, as in the work of Dimitropoulos et al. (2018) where a physical and a digital model of traditional loom is designed to inform visitors on the early industrial weaving process.

A considerable number of systems allow the user to **play a game** (20,7% or 17/83). Several kinds of games were identified, like: educational games, e.g. a history game by Shih et al. (2015); location-based games, e.g. a pervasive role-playing game for introducing elementary school students to archaeology by Georgiadi et al. (2016, Figure 3); mobile games played indoors like "Gossip at Palace" (Rubino et al. 2015) which was designed with a mystery plot that requires the user to find a spy in an Italian historical residence; and a serious game like "The Seafarers" (by Philbin-Briscoe et al., 2017), that runs either on smart devices or desktop and familiarizes users with the trade routes in the Mediterranean sea during the Classical period.

Several systems offer various kinds of digital content presentation, or/and exploration in the case of **online exhibits and digital libraries**, to users (15,7% or 13/83). For example, in Graf et al. (2015) a mobile app presents users with a virtual museum that enables the connection between locally dispersed museums, collections and artifacts, while Creed et al. (2013) have developed multi-touch tables for exploring heritage content in public spaces. Most systems in this respect are about VR or AR presentations like the work of Madsen and Madsen (2016) who developed a handheld visual representation of a castle chapel ruin, whereas Caggianese et al. (2018) provided the visitors of National Archaeological

Figure 2. Exploring aspects of the ancient agora of Athens to discover how to make a ritual to the Gods (Vosinakis et al, 2018)

Figure 3. Screenshots of a pervasive outdoors game that introduces children to archaeology (Georgiadi et al, 2016)

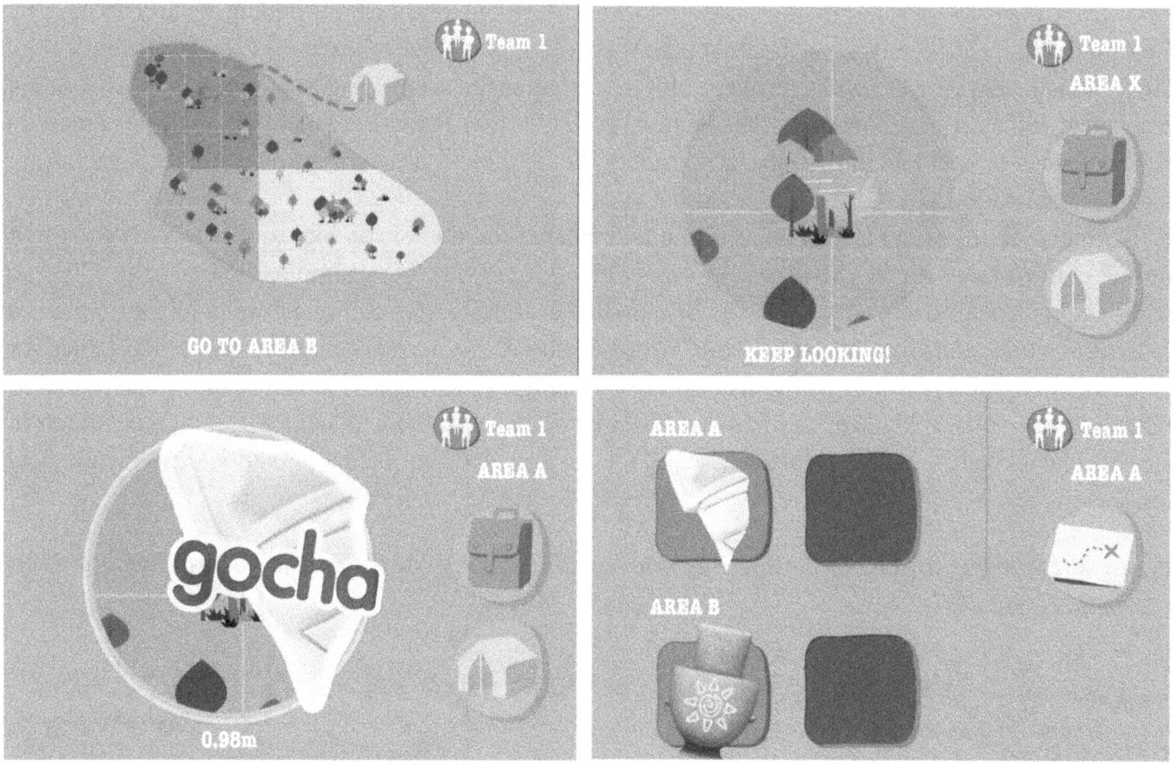

Museum of Naples with a gestured-based examination of a holographic model of a statue. Another case (Pereda, 2019), includes a different more inspired type of interaction in order to perform online searches in libraries (here, Europeana), using TUIs in the form of cubic tokens that help the user understand the process of Boolean searches.

A few systems (4.8% or 4/83) allow the user to **generate content online**, like tags (Arends et al. 2012) or annotations (Maina and Suleman, 2015).

Another distinct class of digital heritage systems is that of **simulating the (re)creation of digital artifacts** (3,6% or 3/83) for enhancing sensitization and learning of end-users, like the work of Correia et al. (2013) who allow users to recreate Portuguese medieval illuminations with pen-based interactions at an augmented book installation and the work of Koutsabasis and Vosinakis (2018) who invite museum visitors to make Cycladic figurines in an interactive kinaesthetic game.

Finally, a few systems present different kinds of **soundscapes**, like the work of Marshall et al. (2016) who present audio-based narratives for the trenches of World War I to visitors of a fortified camp and trenches located in the natural setting of the Italian Alps through a wearable system.

In relation to our previous review, these results show an **increase of physical exploration, leaving behind the *play (game)* purpose**, while there is also a new paradigm of exploration of both the physical and the virtual surroundings of the visitor. As will be latter discussed in more detail, this trend results from the wider employment of mobile Augmented Reality (AR) applications, TUIs and physical computing, that allows users to experience this type of hybrid exploration.

Table 2. Main purposes of the interactive systems examined.

Main purpose	N	%
Play (game)	17	20,7%
Exploration (virtual)	20	24,1%
Exploration (physical)	20	24,1%
Exploration (both)	13	15,7%
Digital content presentation	4	4,8%
User-generated content	3	3,6%
Simulate (creation)	3	3,6%
Soundscape	17	3,6%

Main interactive technology/interaction style. The main interactive technology of the systems examined (Table 3) was **3D game engines** (19,5%, 17/83), either as standalone PC-based applications (e.g. the work of Bellotti et al. (2012) who present an authoring framework of serious games for CII), or as immersive VR installations like the work of Andreoli et al (2016) present a VR Game for the urban reconstruction of ancient Salerno (Italy) and the work of (Fabola et al., 2017) who allows Timespan museum's (Scotland) visitors to examine -in contrast of present and past- a 19th century's fish curing yard that has now become the place of the current museum.

Several systems were based on **mobile technology**, which concerned various types of mobile apps (20,5%, 17/83) as well as mobile AR (9,6%, 8/83) like the work of Kasapakis et al. (2016) who implemented a mobile AR guide for the archaeological site of Knossos (in Crete, Greece), or in the work of Hammady et al. (2018) who use markerless AR to enhance thematic visits in Leeds City Museum and Egyptian Museum in Cairo.

VR systems were also combined with **kinesthetic interactions** (14,5%, 11/83), i.e. interactions that require from the user to make whole-body movements and mid-air gestures, like the work of Fanini and Pagano (2015) who present a Kinect-based interactive exploration of a 3D reconstruction of urban model of Bologna (Italy) during the Roman period; as well as bare-hand interactions (with the use of hand palm movements and gestures), like the work of Koutsabasis and Vosinakis (2016) who developed a Leap Motion enabled app that allows museum visitors to (re)create a Cycladic figurine. A similar 'mixture' of immersive installation is composed by AR wearables with natural user interaction via leap motion as in the work of (Kyriakou & Hermon, 2019), who confronts the concept of "do not touch" in museums by providing the user with 3D models of ancient artefacts.

Another emerging interactive technology includes **physical computing** (21%, 10/83), like the work of Anagnostakis et al. (2016) who describes a system that combines the tactual exploration of exhibit replicas using touch-sensitive audio descriptions with Arduino and touch gestures on a mobile device. Similar works using this type of technology can be found in works of Gkiti et al. (2018, Figure 4) and Hai et al. (2018) who enable user interaction on a wall's installation with conductive paint.

Other interactive technologies employed were **multi-touch displays** (6%, 5/83), like the work of Bellucci et al. (2015) who present a multi-touch see-through display screen that makes it possible to superimpose an overlay of digital information while observing the physical object behind the screen and to allow visitors to record their experience with the object. In another sense of multi-touch displays, the work of (Muntean et al., 2017) describes a digital tabletop that combines the selection of tangible heritage

Figure 4. Aspects of the i-wall installation which makes use of conductive ink and video mapping to present augmented information about a museum exhibit (Gkiti et al. 2018)

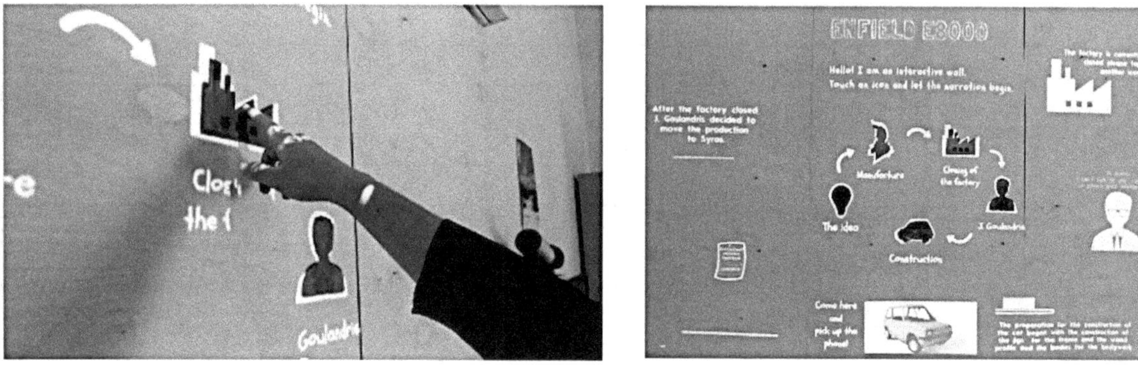

artefacts who, when enabled by two sensor rings, they display information on the tabletop concerning their interrelated intangible aspects. The remaining interactive technologies consist of **virtual worlds and multi-user virtual worlds** (6%, 5/83), wearable technology (3,6%, 3/83) like the work of Marshall et al. (2016), and location-based audio (3.6%, 3/83).

These results do not present many proportional differences with those of our previous review, apart from the change between *3D game engine*, who took first place against *Mobile* interaction technology. There is a small rise though in the use of VR technology, also accompanied by wearables in some cases, as well as in physical computing, regularly paired with TUIs. This reveals that the general trend is steady, still evolving and uncovering research findings that go deeper to their purpose of technological use in relation to various CH application areas (Bekele et al., 2018).

Table 3. Main interactive technologies and interaction styles of the systems examined (more than one for some systems)

Interaction technology / style	**N**	**%**
3D game engine	17	20,5%
Mobile	15	18,1%
Kinesthetic interaction	12	14,5%
Mobile AR	8	9,6%
VR	9	10,8%
Web	7	8,4%
Multi-touch display	5	6,0%
Physical computing	10	12,0%
Virtual World	5	6,0%
Location-based audio	3	3,6%
Wearable	3	3,6%
AR	4	4,8%

Cultural content. The cultural content of the systems examined (Table 4) was largely about **particular exhibits in a virtual or physical museum** (39,8%, 31/83). An example of conveying information about virtual exhibits is the work of Froschauer et al. (2013) who developed a 3D online learning game, ThIATRO, which places the player in an exhibition and communicates knowledge of art history concepts to the player. Two examples of physical exhibits as cultural content of interactive systems are the works of (Nofal, Elhanafi, Hameeuw, & Moere, 2018), who uses AR in front of an isolated museum artefact in order to virtually place it into its original historical context, and Van der Vaart and Damala (2015), who developed the Loupe, a handheld AR application that displays text-based information about a physical exhibit when the handheld is placed in front of it. Vice versa is the work of (Not, Cavada, Maule, Pisetti, & Venturini, 2019) who uses tangible replica of relic of WorldWar I to digitally augment its cultural content when the user interacts with it. Another example, is the work of (Schaper, Santos, Malinverni, Berro, & Pares, 2018) which is slightly different as it comprises elements of (virtual) exhibit in a cultural site and uses *World as Support* (WaS), an AR-related technology paradigm, to help children visualize missing cultural content of the place.

Many digital CH systems provide **3D models of a cultural site** (20,5%, 15/83) like the work of Ijaz et al. (2016) who have developed the ancient city of Uruk in virtual world technology (Second Life). With the same technology, the work of (Vosinakis, Avradinis, & Koutsabasis, 2018) have recreated a part of the ancient agora in Athens, and (Zamora-Musa, Vélez, & Paez-Logreira, 2018) have implemented elements of San Andre´s Island in the form of virtual heritage tour. In the same context, we find the work of (Pujol-Tost, 2019) who has developed a virtual reconstruction of the Neolithic site of Çatalhöyük (Turkey) in six different experimental versions.

Another considerable number of systems **allow users to identify POIs in urban cultural sites**, like the work of (Shin, Park, & Woo, 2017) who describe a metadata indexed mobile AR application that connects multiple POIs at Changdeokgung Palace (South Korea) through narrative- or search- based experience, as well as inside buildings of cultural value (15,7%, 12/83), like the work of Duguleana et al. (2016) who present a mobile application that allows outdoor exploration of the Leaning Tower of Pisa (Italy) and the nearby Cathedral and the Baptistery, throughout different periods of time. In addition, several systems present to the user some kind of fiction or plot (12%, 10/83), like DRAMATRIC (Callaway et al. 2014), which is a mobile presentation system that delivers hour-long dramas to small groups of museum visitors. More, in the study of (Pagano, Pietroni, & Cerato, 2017) cultural content is virtually presented to students in the form of narratives exploiting affordances of kinesthetic interaction.

Other types of cultural content identified include: **simulating the process of making** (4,8%, 4/83) e.g. ancient artifacts (e.g. Vosinakis et al. 2016) or the working progress of early industrial weaving process (Dimitropoulos et al., 2018; Figure 5); communicating sounds about the past (4,8%, 4/83; e.g. Fritsch et al. 2014, with Ekkomaten that provides an urban installation of access to an 18th century soundscape of Aarhus, Denmark, and the work of (Wu, Bryan-Kinns, Wang, Sheridan, & Xu, 2017) that delivers interactive music boxes of Chinese culture to locals and tourists, also informing on the cross-cultural design approach); content of important books (e.g. Wang et al. 2014, about the Analects by Confucius); and old photos (2,4%, 2/83) like the work of Han et al. (2014) who contribute to the enhancement of community awareness and participation in local heritage with a mobile application that reveals old photos of buildings and areas of a small city.

In comparison to the results of our previous review, we see no particular new trends. What seems to have been increased, is the exhibits in (virtual) museum, that shows a general preference in using interactive systems to digitally augment the cultural content of heritage artefacts in order to make them more accessible and understandable, employing new creative and vibrant means of interaction.

Location of system use. About half of systems examined were designed to be **used indoors** inside a museum or a cultural place (e.g. a historic building) (51,8%, 43/83), in some form of technological installation or a location-based mobile game. About a quarter of the systems (21,7%, 18/83) are meant to be used outdoors, like for example an urban cultural site. The remaining of them are either intended to be used from a **personal computer (PC)** (19,3%, 16/83), like a history game, or they can be used in more than one place (**smart devices** and desktops), or the place of use is unspecified (7,2%, 6/83).

These results do not indicate any remarkable difference from the results of our previous review. Those intended to be used by a PC may present an insignificant drop compared to the previous ones, but it is not clear enough to draw some conclusions.

Methods of Empirical Evaluation

Dimensions of empirical evaluations. A key issue in any empirical evaluation is about which dimensions of the UX are being evaluated. These dimensions should be expressed explicitly by researchers as the goals of each evaluation; however, this is not always the case. An empirical evaluation may be investigating more than one dimension (Table 5).

Figure 5. Simulating the industrial weaving process with Loom, a physical computing miniature installation with an outcome in the digital world (Dimitropoulos et al, 2018)

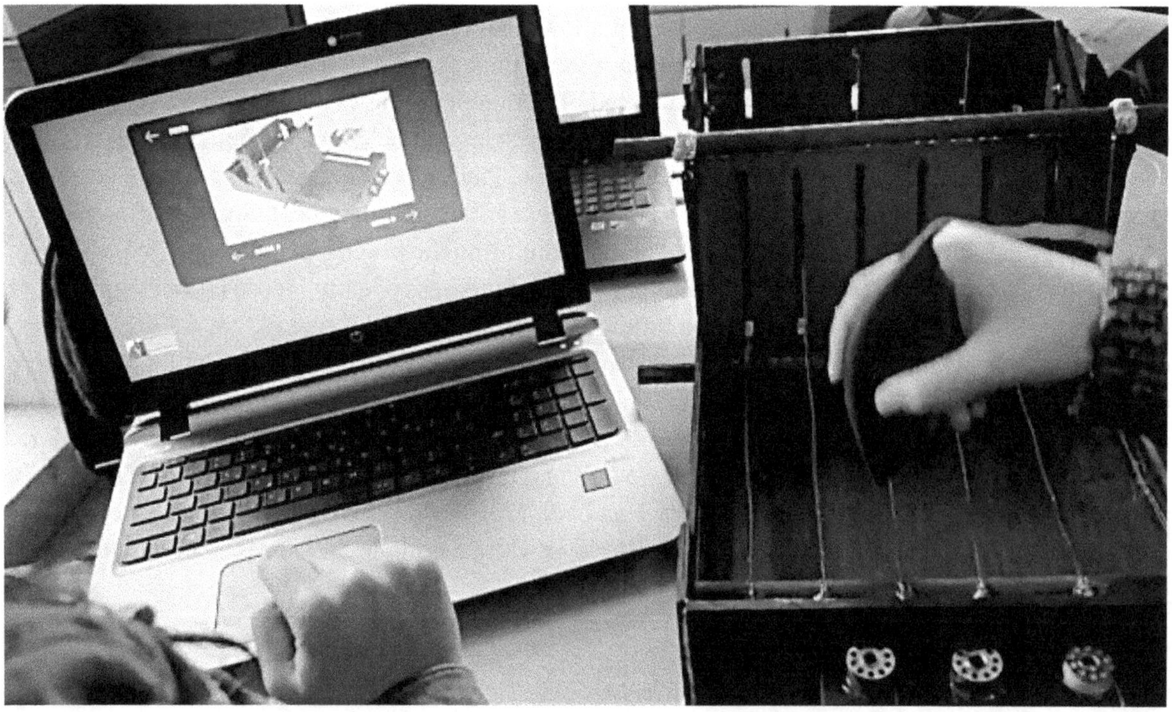

Table 4. Cultural content of the interactive systems examined.

Cultural content	N	%
Exhibits in (virtual) museum	32	39,8%
3D model of a cultural site	16	20,5%
Points of interest (both urban and indoors)	13	15,7%
Fiction with cultural content	10	12,0%
'Making of' process	4	4,8%
Sounds	4	4,8%
Books	2	2,4%
Old photos	2	2,4%

A lot of the systems examined identify **usability as a principal dimension of evaluation** (27/83). In general, usability involves both 'objective' and 'subjective' measures: the former are related to effectiveness and efficiency of use and the latter are about user satisfaction. An example of a usability evaluation that includes both types of measures is that of Reunanen et al. (2015), who have conducted a field usability test of their immersive installation where users could gesturally navigate around the wreck of Vrouw Maria. The test took place at the Finnish national museum and involved 23 users who were requested to complete certain tasks with the system; after the test they were interviewed about system usability. Likewise, (Kyriakou & Hermon, 2019) evaluated their wearable AR system with qualitative observation and post-tasks questionnaire in a field usability test, where visitors were asked to manipulate a number of 3D reconstructed ancient artefacts. The final test took place at the Leventis Museum in Nicosia (Cyprus), while there were also pre-tests in several venues (science festival, lab) and with various users (children, researchers, curators) before the final study. Nevertheless, **a considerable number of usability studies are dealing only with user satisfaction from system use** (27/83), which is referred in this paper as perceived usability. Perceived usability may be investigated with questionnaires and post-test interviews, usually after non-task-oriented use of the system; like for example in the work of Maina and Suleman (2015) who evaluate types of annotations (gamified or not) in digital collections of cultural heritage with questionnaires after system use or the work of (Hammady et al., 2018) who evaluate users' adoption of a mobile AR tour during visits in two museums, combining observation, post-visit interview and questionnaire.

A large number of systems examined are investigating **the UX in a general sense** of the term (28/83). These studies attempt to extend the scope of evaluation beyond usability to other experiential aspects of system use. **A few studies present a thorough investigation of UX**, which may also involve usability (i.e. they investigate both dimensions). For example, Jylhä et al. (2015) conducted a thorough comparative evaluation of their wearable interface for exploring urban POIs by assigning 12 users in two groups: a baseline group that used a mobile phone app and the test group that used the wearable app; they report on several significant issues like the usability of the interaction technique of the wearable interface, user reaction to cues, general UX issues and attention to surroundings. The work of (Roussou & Katifori, 2018) also examined aspects of UX combined with usability testing in a field evaluation with 53 users at the Acropolis museum (Athens), including methods like log data, observations with video recording, note-taking, and in-depth interviews. The evaluation involved exploration of the museum's exhibits through a mobile tour application and informs on several aspects of an interactive museum visit like flow in the narration presented by the app, play, wayfinding in physical space, personalization and social interaction. Other studies refer to **user experience from an educational point of view**, like the work of (Schaper et al., 2018) who investigates features of embodied exploration with AR to report on children's engagement and construction of meaning during the visit at a bomb shelter of Spanish Civil War, through an iterative design process with teachers and museum experts. Other studies follow **a non-instrumental approach to evaluating the UX,** for example Wang et al. (2014) conducted their user study during a local community event in Singapore, where the public had the opportunity to chat with the virtual Confucius; in this field study users were left to play with the system; at the end they completed a self-developed questionnaire that investigated particular aspects of the usability and UX with this system (e.g. if Confucius' replies are meaningful).

A considerable number of systems are evaluated upon **learning effects on users** (6,4%, 9/83). These works are typically organized into a comparative evaluation, like the work of Ijaz et al. (2016) who conducted an evaluation study of their proposed system (virtual world, city of Uruk) with three groups of students (n=20) who used the system in contrast to a book and a video. The work of (Pagano et al., 2017), also examines learning effectiveness in terms of attention, memorisation, and elaboration, through a comparative evaluation with high school students consisting of a Neutral Group (n=115), who follows pre-, guided, and virtual- visit experience with the proposed system (kinesthetic interaction with cultural content on big displays), and a Control group (n=115), who interacts only with the system (virtual visit) . Also, a comparative study between three TUIs, evaluates the communication of tacit knowledge among three different conditions of physical/touch-enabled navigation and physical/virtual representation of the entrance colonnade of Djoser Pyramid Comple. In addition, some systems investigate user engagement (7,1%, 10/83), although this is not always explicitly declared as such but with statements like 'increased conversations among groups of users' for the case of DRAMATRIC, a mobile presentation system that delivers hour-long dramas to small groups of museum visitor (Callaway et al. 2014); or 'usage time' for the case of the installation for the visualization of a 3D reconstruction of a castle chapel (Madsen and Madsen, 2016).

Many other dimensions of the UX are investigated to a lesser extent in empirical evaluations of interactive systems of CH. A considerable number of these dimensions is related to the value of the system for CH; either in a more general sense – i.e. appreciation (value): 6,4%, 9/83; for example in the work of Panayiotou and Lanitis (2016) on 3D animated paintings; or in more in-depth investigation terms, like the work of (Jones, Theodosis, & Lykourentzou, 2019) who use thematic coding and sentiment analysis to conclude with users' exploring profiles in relation to their appreciation of the CH system; or in more specific concepts, like the discussion of the concept of cultural awareness by Shih et al. (2015), who place users in a 2-hour play of a simulated-role playing game about the historical context of Southern Taiwan in the late nineteenth century based on the martial art novel "Xiao-Mao". They test whether users have gained aspects of cultural awareness with post-play interviews and questionnaire. Another example dealing with cultural awareness can be found in the work of (Skowronski et al., 2018) and the 'Blended Museum' approach, who encourages visitors to reflect on the destruction of Palmyra and sensitize awareness in a thematic interactive exhibit at the Braunschweigisches Landesmuseum. The designers implemented different information layers at the exhibits using VR, AR, and 3D printing to interpret replicas of the relics of the city, and tested the level of awareness of the visitors through the exploration of these layers. There are also works that deal with dimensions like cultural values, as in the work of (Muntean et al., 2017), and the work of (Pujol-Tost, 2019) who brings the concept of cultural presence into evaluation through a methodology of six distinct experimental conditions. Still, these studies are very few and examine these concepts from the perspective of certain technological paradigms, e.g. the concept of presence which is more related to virtual environments and VR technology. There is certainly a need to develop theoretical groundings of the impact of CH via using interactive systems in constructs that can be assessed in empirical studies.

Finally, **several empirical evaluations are dealing with issues that have not been widely investigated in other studies**, e.g. the recording of user behavior with physiological measurements (Falvo et al. 2015), recollection of POIs in a mobile urban guide (Chalvatzaras et al. 2014), fun or enjoyment – especially when children are the test users (e.g. Koutsabasis and Vosinakis, 2016), and so on.

Comparing to the dimensions of empirical evaluations examined in our previous review, a fluctuation has been identified in this review's results. It seems that **there is a balance between the dimensions of *user experience (overall)* and *usability***, while we also saw that there is a number of studies that inspect them both in their evaluation. In either way, this is an indication of their mutual consideration by a big number of research studies reviewed throughout this range of years. Additionally, we observe that the numbers of *perceived usability, engagement* and *appreciation (value)* have been increased. Last but not least, it is notable that the sum of all dimensions has reached the number of 142 (!), which means that there are a lot of dimensions appeared only once or twice. This could be an indication that there is a need of a more systematic approach in organizing research findings in the respective field and creating common ground of what is be evaluated, in order to inform future empirical studies.

The approach (general method) to empirical evaluation. As shown in (Table 6), about one quarter of the papers examined were evaluation studies (21/83); almost all of them were **field studies** like for example the work of Rubino et al. (2015) who integrated a location-based mobile game in the museum visit and evaluated visitors' behavior and learning by inviting them to play the game during their visit, or the work of (Caggianese et al., 2018) who installed a gesture-based interactive holographic projection in the museum and evaluated visitors' engagement and attractiveness of the system, or the work of (Roussou & Katifori, 2018) who systematically evaluated users'/ visitors' experience with mobile interactive tour among museum's exhibits. One study was longitudinal, that of Arends et al. (2012) who analyzed user

Table 5. The most frequently appeared dimensions of empirical evaluations of the interactive systems examined (some studies investigate more than one)

Dimensions of empirical evaluations	N	% out of total identified
User experience (overall)	28	19,9%
Usability	27	19,1%
Perceived usability (only)	12	8,5%
Learning	9	6,4%
Engagement	10	7,1%
Appreciation (value)	9	6,4%
User behavior	3	2,1%
Fun (enjoyment)	2	1,4%
Cultural awareness	3	2,1%
Attractiveness	3	2,1%

motivation (through logged data of their contributions) in an art folksonomy in a longitudinal study of eight users who used three versions of their platform in a total period spanning over a year.

Most approaches to the empirical assessment of digital heritage were **controlled tests** (75%, 61/83). Testing methods can be divided into those carried out in the computer lab (**laboratory tests**) or to those carried out in the field (**field tests**). The place of the test provides evaluators with further possibilities or imposes restrictions. In field tests, it is possible to employ real users on the fly (i.e. the visitors at a cultural site) as well as to have users interact in realistic context (about user cognitive state, time of day, lighting, noise, presence and interruptions of others, etc.) but on the other hand it may not be permitted for the evaluator to record user interactions (e.g. with video) or intervene to ask for clarifications. Each testing approach may be characterized as formative or summative depending on the type of data gathered.

Formative approaches mainly gather user opinions (e.g. about perceived usability) and qualitative observations by researchers, like the work of Lorenzini et al. (2015) who evaluate a VR-based videogame simulating an experiment of medical distillation in a medieval alchemy lab with having users play the game and then answer a questionnaire and provide a post-hoc interview, or the work of (Gaitanou et al., 2018) who iteratively evaluated their "escape room" system with physical computing components, by gathering opinions from a range of users: graduate designers, experts and professors, citizens and escape-rom funs, using video recording observations, questionnaire and post-game interviews.

In **summative approaches** conclusions are drawn based on measures of user performance or logged user actions, as in the case of (Zamora-Musa, Vélez, & Paez-Logreira, 2018) and remote evaluation of virtual heritage tour with standardized questionnaire and system's logging. In some cases of empirical evaluation, both types of data are employed; these cases are more comprehensive in their reporting, like for example the work of Koutsabasis and Vosinakis (2016) who perform an evaluation of a Leap Motion – enabled application that allows visitors of a museum to create (sculpt) a Cycladic figurine; the evaluation includes a familiarization phase in which users think-aloud and qualitative observations are made, and then a test phase in which performance measurements are collected with log data; at the end, test users filled-in a standardized questionnaire.

In contrast to our previous review, these results **show a shift toward empirical evaluations in the field**, as well as **a rise in both formative and summative tests, which provide richer and more prosperous research findings**. Furthermore, they contribute in informative future directions on surpassing shortcomings and limitations when applying interactive technologies in respect to human factors and users' experience in a real context of use.

The data collection methods (or techniques). At a further level of analysis, empirical studies can be examined on the basis of the particular data collection methods (or techniques) employed. Each empirical study may employ one or more data collection methods (Table 7). As discussed earlier on (section 2.1) **it is generally useful to employ more than one data collection methods in empirical studies**, in order to ensure that errors of one method are corrected – to some extent – by the application of another, that there are multiple data sources for each observation and that data are cross-examined.

In the empirical studies examined, there were six cases that made use of four data collection methods (7,2%), like for example the work of Loizides et al. (2014) who present the UX evaluation in virtual museums, by employing the data collection methods of a questionnaire (self-developed), post-hoc interviews, log data (about user actions) and concurrent think-aloud protocol that allowed users to provide feedback during interaction, or the work of (Nofal, Elhanafi, et al., 2018) who investigates architectural contextualization in a virtual exhibit by applying questionnaire (standardized), video recordings, pre-test interviews and sketches drawn by users in order to acquire richer results. Eighteen studies (20,7%)

Table 6. Approaches (general methods) of evaluation

Methods of evaluation	N	%
Studies	22	25,3%
-- Field study	21	24,4%
-- Longitudinal study	1	1,2%
Tests	61	74,5
-- Field testing	37	43,9%
-- -- Formative	22	25,6%
-- -- Summative	6	7,3%
-- -- Formative + summative	9	11,0%
-- Lab testing	24	30,6%
-- -- Formative	17	22,0%
-- -- Summative	4	4,9%
-- -- Formative + Summative	3	3,7%

employed three data collection methods, which is also comprehensive. However, there were many studies who made use of two (41%, 34/83) or only one (30,1%) method for data collection, which may be inadequate for a thorough evaluation of the UX.

If we look at the particular methods for data collection in (Table 8) that presents the most frequently identified, we see that **most studies employed some kind of a questionnaire**: many studies (49/83) employed a **self-developed questionnaire**, while 18 studies (18/83) adopted a **standardized questionnaire**, i.e. that has gone through the process of psychometric validation. For example, Andreoli et al. (2016) adopt the Presence Questionnaire to evaluate a VR Serious Game named HippocraticaCivitas-Game, in which users use head-mounted displays (HMDs) to navigate in a 3D model of the old town of Salerno (Italy).

Many studies included a **post-hoc interview** with users (27/83) and a similar number of studies employed observation, mainly with note-taking (14/83) or with video or audio recording (11/83). These methods are typical of an empirical evaluation and are required to cross examination and interpretation of findings from questionnaires, to some extent.

A considerable number of studies (mainly those that performed user testing) also included some kind of **log data** (15/83) about user actions and performance. For example, in the lab testing of vir-

Table 7. Number of data collection methods per empirical evaluation (for cross-examination)

N methods	N evaluations	%
4	6	7,2%
3	18	21,7%
2	34	41,0%
1	25	30,1%
Total:171 (4x6+3x18+2x34+1x25)	Total:83	100%

tual sculpting of a Cycladic figuring (Koutsabasis and Vosinakis, 2016) log data are recorded for task times (for three principal tasks of sculpting, smoothening and engraving) and types of errors (hitting on the statue, picking up wrong tools, etc.). In the study of (Caggianese et al., 2018), log data allowed researchers to inspect acceptability and attractiveness of the 'Head of Apollo of Omphalos' holographic model, exhibited at the museum for a period of almost four months. Some studies (7/83) employed the concurrent think-aloud protocol to allow users express their comments and feelings in free-form during interaction, like in the work of Correia et al. (2014) who organized a field test that encouraged users to think-aloud during the use their interactive installation that enabled them to reconstruct medieval illuminations of old books. Another study (Power et al., 2017) implemented the verbal protocol, where the users commented on their previous recorded interactions with system. Lastly, other data collection methods included physiological measurements, a visitor book and interaction analysis (between users in a collaborative scenario, in the work of Fritsch et al. (2014)).

In relation to our previous results in this section, we do not observe any critical differences. There is though, the *self-developed questionnaire* that prevails against the rest, with a number of studies informing on the questions employed.

The participants (users). The participants (users) of the empirical evaluations examined include **various groups** including students, adults of various ages, children, visitors at a cultural site of a museum, test users in the lab, tourists, families, blind people, etc. In addition, a notable number of studies included **CH professionals**, e.g. curators, either in the design process or the final evaluation or both.

Table 8. Most frequent methods (techniques) for data collection identified in empirical studies examined in a total of 168

Data collection methods	N	% out of total
Questionnaire (self-developed)	49	29,2%
Interview (post-hoc)	27	16,1%
Observation (note taking)	14	8,3%
Log data	15	8,9%
Questionnaire (standardized*)	18	10,7%
Observation (video/audio recording)	11	6,5%
Observations (general)	7	4,2%
Think-aloud (concurrent)	3	1,8%

** standardized questionnaires:*
SUS (System Usability Scale, Brooke (1996)) = 4;
AttrakDiff (Hassenzahl et al. 2006) = 2;
USE (Usefulness, Satisfaction, Ease of use; Lund (2001)) = 1;
HARUS (Handheld AR Usability Scale; Santos et al. 2008) = 1;
Presence questionnaire (Witmer and Singer, 1998) =1;
Fun toolkit (Read, 2008) = 1;
Aesthetics and perceived usability scale (Lavie and Tractinsky, 2004)= 1;
ARI (Augmented Reality Immersion) questionnaire (Georgiou and Kyza, 2017) = 1;
(SEQ) Single Ease Question (Sauro, 2012) = 1;
UEQ (User Experience Questionnaire, Laugwitz et al, 2009) = 2;
SUMI (Software Usability Measurement Inventory, Kirakowski and Corbett, 1993) = 1;
NASA TLX: Task Load Index (Hart and Staveland, 1988) = 1;
(MEC-SPQ) MEC Spatial Presence Questionnaire (Vorderer et al. 2004) = 1.

Some studies **focus on a particular user group**, like for example the work of (Power et al., 2017) who develops a system to reduce the effort of archaeologists with online archives, or the work of Rennick-Egglestone et al. (2016) who report on a field study of eight families (28 users in total) engaging with a bespoke tablet experience produced for a space science centre, or the work of Anagnostakis et al. (2016, Figure 6) who present a lab test of their tangible prototype system that enhances the accessibility of museum exhibits to visually impaired users, with the participation of ten users (2 blind, 4 visually impaired and 4 blindfolded). In the work of (Camps-Ortueta, Rodríguez-Muñoz, Gómez-Martín, & González-Calero, 2017), the developed mobile AR application is addressed to pairs of adult-child (8 pairs in total), exploring the effects of their shared interaction and collaboration while they are on a treasure hunt inside the Lazaro Galdiano Museum in Madrid. In some studies, it is not possible to provide an analytic account of the participants, since that there is inadequate information, or the groups are mixed.

Another aspect of the participants of the empirical studies examined is their number. In general, the (minimum) number of 'required' users in an empirical study has been widely debated in respective HCI literature. Off course, there is not a single answer to this question, however sometimes it is possible to estimate this number for the particular evaluation approach taken – for more discussion, see Tullis and Albert (2013), and Sauro and Lewis (2012). In (Table 9) the total number of users is outlined for the empirical studies examined. There **is a considerable number of studies that employed a rather large number of users** (+30 users, 35/83 studies, 42,2%) like for example the work of Yelmi et al. (2016) who report on a field study of their soundscape installation with data from 368 users (visitors at a museum), or the work of Graf et al. (2015) who report on a formative lab test with 147 participants (pupils) or the work of (Pagano et al., 2017) who included 230 high school students in their formative field-testing. At

Figure 6. Aspect of an evaluation session of the Orasis app that enhances accessibility of museum exhibits for the visually impaired (Anagnostakis et al. 2016)

a striking contrast, there is one study with a single blind participant (O' Sullivan et al. 2014), who provides useful feedback on an audio tactile map system for the exploration of digital heritage buildings by blind individuals – notably, there are serious difficulties in employing blind users for empirical studies.

Concerning participants, a considerable amount of empirical evaluations presented in the most recent publications (2017-2019) involved more CH professionals and experts, in contrast to the previous one. This indicates a notable turn in understanding the necessity of gaining insights and valuable feedback from experienced practitioners throughout the design process, as it was also stressed in the earlier review.

Comparative empirical evaluations. The last aspect of this review of empirical methods is about whether these evaluations are comparative or not (Table 10). About 1/5 of the works examined have performed some kind of a **comparative evaluation** (17/83, 20,5%).

Five cases involve **comparisons between user groups** like expert/novice users (e.g. Panayiotou and Lanitis, (2016) on 3D animated paintings) or between adults and children use of Leap Motion enabled application (Koutsabasis and Vosinakis, 2016; Figure 7) or between a neutral and a control group in order to assess aspects of learning effectiveness (Pagano et al., 2017). One study involves experimental comparison **among interaction styles** (Pollalis et al., 2018), and four studies present comparative evaluations **between interfaces**. For example, the work of Loizides et al. (2016) presents a user evaluation of art items using different virtual reality display systems. Also, the study of (Nofal, Reffat, Boschloos, Hameeuw, & Moere, 2018) implements three different types of TUIs into evaluation, each one delivering different kind of virtual cultural content to examine correlation between interaction features (input) and learning outcomes and cognitive effort (output) of users. Another three studies compare the UX of participants **between systems** (i.e. the introduced system and an alternative), like the work of Jylhä et al. (2015) who present a comparative field study of their proposed multimodal, wearable system for alerting the user of nearby recommended POIs to a visual mobile application. Finally, the study of Shih et al. (2015) investigated cultural awareness of students with **pre- and post-tests** (questionnaires), and the work of Pujol (2019) investigated features of cultural presence by evaluating the VR experience in a between-subjects experiment. In addition, unlike the abovementioned dedicated studies to comparative empirical evaluations on CH interactive systems, the work of (Caggianese et al., 2018) also included a pre-testing lab evaluation between two interaction techniques exploring a holographic projection system with Leap motion sensor, thus contributing in the general design-pattern implications of touchless user interfaces.

Table 9. Number of users (participants) in the studies examined

N of users (participants)	N	%
<10	7	8,4%
10-20	19	22,9%
20-30	16	19,3%
30+	35	42,2%
unspecified	6	7,2%

Figure 7. Aspect of a user test of Cycladic sculpture app, where a girl engraves a digital figurine with hand moves captured with the Leap motion sensor (Koutsabasis and Vosinakis, 2016)

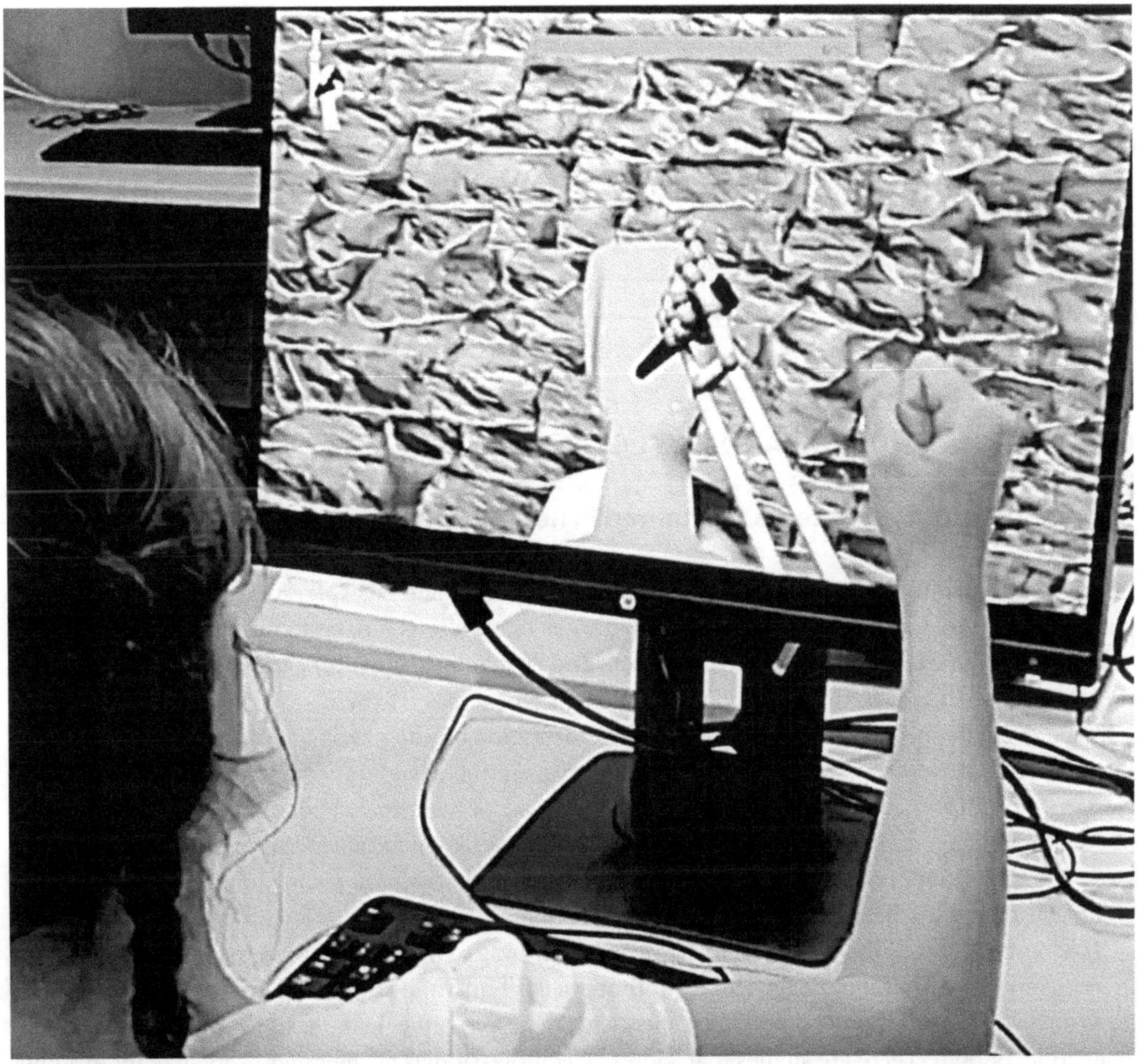

Although these results do not indicate any significant difference compared to the results of our previous review, **there is a steady amount of studies that employ comparative experimental conditions in their empirical evaluations**. Their findings are very fruitful in terms of providing other researchers in the field with helpful insights and future theoretical directions on the various technologies and interfaces examined relative to several CH-related issues, such as learning effectiveness, cultural presence, appropriateness of interaction style, and so forth.

Table 10. Comparative empirical evaluations of the systems examined

Comparative evaluation?	N	%
No	66	79,5%
Yes	17	20,5%
	6	35,3%
-- Between interfaces	3	17,6%
-- Between systems	5	29,4%
-- Between user groups	1	5,9%
-- Pre-test, post-test	1	5,9%
-- Between-subjects experiment	1	5,9%
-- Between interaction styles	1	5,9%

DISCUSSION, CRITIQUE AND OUTLOOK

On the Interactive Systems Examined, Their Purpose, Technology and Content

Most systems identified for this review were applications that promoted exploration of physical or virtual places. This type of emphasis of CH systems indicates that **there is a need to develop historically accurate and valid 3D models of places, artifacts and (when appropriate) activities**. Similar findings (Pujol-Tost, 2019) suggest that meaningful interactions are preferred to mere investment in photorealism. Interactions with objects and characters, the implementation of role playing and new means that foster learning effectiveness are some of the future directions in the design of virtual reconstructed cultural worlds. Some of the studies examined referred to the issue of historical validation and accuracy as part of their approach to design – for example to consult experts like in (Koutsabasis and Vosinakis, 2016)) – but few studies reported on these issues as an outcome of the evaluation. Only one study, the work of Floch and Jiang (2015), employed users and experts in their field test.

It is obvious that as the landscape of CH systems grows **to include CH professionals and experts in assessments of digital heritage can contribute to content validation**. We have found that there is a trend involve CH professionals, experts, teachers and professors, either in the design process, or in the final evaluation, or both. There are studies that address CH professionals as their end-users, like for example in the work of (Power et al., 2017) who address archaeologists, and studies that address general users and still consider curators and other related professionals, as in the work of (Skowronski et al., 2018), educators (Schaper et al., 2018), and other administrative staff, e.g. museum managers (Fabola et al., 2017), in their development and testing process. Related work in this respect is about co-designing with CH professionals, which is expected to materialize in particular design methods (e.g. Ciolfi et al. 2016).

Interactive systems in CH **employ diverse contemporary technologies**, mainly about 3D content, mobile technologies, VR/AR and kinesthetic control. It is very interesting and fruitful to see natural user interfaces employed in CH. More ideally, with the rise of use of TUIs and physical computing, researchers and designers are employing off-the-shelf low cost technological components to deliver smart interfaces combined with recent trends in entertainment and leisure activities, like the work of (Gaitanou et al., 2018) who adopt the concept of "escape-room" to a cultural visit at an old industrial site. This could be a considerable and affordable contribution for the exhibition design, especially in low budget museums and cultural sites. However, there is a temptation for researchers to promote the mastering and development of impressive interactive technologies overlooking cultural content and related aims and values for visitors. This danger has been identified by CH professionals (including curators and exhibition designers) in the survey of Maye et al (2014) in which they state that "*the design of interactive exhibitions should not be driven by the technology: interactive exhibitions should be designed with the core concept in mind; the concept could be formed around stories, themes, museum objects or experiences that the exhibition aims to portray*." Further research is required to identify whether this phenomenon arises in established digital exhibitions. However, in the recent studies reviewed, there is a delightful shift towards the abovementioned direction, and is becoming apparent by both the number of dimensions examined and the involvement of experts that provide feedback and reflection on the systems developed.

The **cultural content of interactive systems observed is quite diverse**, ranging from providing enhanced information about exhibits to the simulation of 'making of' (reconstructing, digitally) artworks and artifacts of cultural value as well as soundscapes. The cultural content of almost all interactive systems examined was apparently developed in the context of the respective projects. **Nevertheless, the possibilities of enabling access to larger volumes and types of cultural content are endless.** Notably, in contrast to our previous review, we have two systems reporting connection to well-known CH repositories like Europeana[1] in the works of (Machidon, Tavčar, Gams, & Duguleană, 2019; Pereda, 2019). There were also systems that made use of other online collections like the work of Maina and Suleman (2015) who examined annotations of content of the digital Bleek and Lloyd collection[2].

On the Dimensions of Empirical Evaluations of Systems Examined

The **overall UX and usability** are largely the primary 'lenses' for the evaluation of interactive systems in CH. This was expected, for several reasons with most important those related to the high-tech nature of systems and that these (systems) address end-users who may be – to a large extent – considered as 'novices' in terms of interaction styles and content. To evaluate the UX and usability of an interactive system is an important goal and it is a prerequisite to pursue deeper user impact. In addition, several studies have considered other dimensions for evaluation like **learning effectiveness, engagement, fun and attractiveness**. In the most recent corpus of publications, we identified more systems focused on dimensions of learning effectiveness, some of them using comparative studies that interpret more fruitful research results. Again, it is encouraging and refreshing to see that empirical evaluations are exploring particular aspects of the visitor experience in further detail.

However, these dimensions of empirical evaluations may also be found in other studies of UX, that are not concerned with CH (like for example in Bargas-Avila and Hornbæk, 2011). What seems to be missing in these 'lenses' of empirical evaluations is whether some kind of 'cultural value' is conveyed to the visitors. There was only one empirical evaluation (Muntean et al., 2017) that addressed the dimension of cultural values and employed a carefully planned interaction design approach (value sensitive design), between tangible and intangible heritage of the Musqueam culture, assessing visitors' sensitization and learning about these particular features. There are also other studies that incorporate dimensions related to CH, like the work of (Pujol-Tost, 2019) who addresses cultural presence, the work of (Wu et al., 2017) who design music boxes for cross-cultural experience, or the works of Shih et al. (2015) and (Skowronski et al., 2018) who examine cultural awareness. At last, do all these interactive systems help users reflect on the heritage of places, people and activities and draw analogies with today? Does interactive technology contribute to the sensitization of users about the value of preserving and learning about heritage? Do these systems help visitors interpret the messages conveyed from old situations into today's needs?

These questions are certainly not easy to answer, especially in short-term evaluation approaches. Additionally, it is perhaps premature to expect that interactive systems that have been recently introduced to CH may provide such an impact to visitors of a cultural site. On the other hand, these questions are about the essence of interactivity as it is approached in CH. In a similar vein, Papadimitriou (2012) remarks "*The ultimate goal of current museological research is interactivity. Quite often, however, "interactivity" in literature is meant in its strict technical sense, referring to various types of multimedia which communicate more effectively the messages of a given exhibition structure. Only rarely is this associated with a re-appraisal of curatorial practices and a reconsideration of conceptual attitudes towards the exhibits.*" Thus, it seems that there is still much theoretical work to be done on dimensions of empirical evaluations of interactive systems for CH; these systems are unique in purpose and they must convey meaningful interpretations for users and visitors.

On the Evaluation Approaches and Methods Employed

Most empirical evaluations of interactive systems in CH are planned and conducted as **user tests that may occur in the field or in the lab**. User tests may provide useful data; and it is therefore encouraging to see that an evidence-based approach followed. But user tests may not assess deeper impact of interactive technology on user learning, sensitization and re-appreciation of heritage.

Another interesting aspect of the general method employed in the studies examined is that a considerable number were conducted in the field, either as more general **field studies or as field testing** sessions. This is also an important trend in empirical evaluations in general (especially with regard to mobile UX) and perhaps empirical evaluation in CH is showing the way to transferring evaluation from the lab to the field. Field evaluations are contextual, which enhanced the validity of the process and results. In addition, in this review we have been introduced to studies that incorporated lab testing before the final evaluation and with several types of users, such as experts, curators, educators and so forth, usually to gather design requirements and fix certain usability issues.

Another interesting and emerging topic reported in this review, is the **recruitment of users/visitors to evaluate the applications**, especially when assessed in the field. While research encourages for more empirical studies on methods adopted from HCI, to be performed by or with more professionals and in 'real-work' environments, so less by chance, in CH contexts this direction seems not be a thoughtful choice or demands further investigation. Recruiting visitors to experience or assess CH content on purpose changes their original purpose of visit, which is something inherently connected with the visitor experience discussed in several museum and visitor studies (Csikszentmihalyi & Robinson, 1990; De Rojas & del Carmen Camarero, 2006; Falk, 2016; Falk & Dierking, 2018; Pekarik, Doering, & Karns, 1999; Tröndle, Greenwood, Kirchberg, & Tschacher, 2014). For example, pre-visit established motivation and intentions of visit are about to alter when the visitor is recruited to experience cultural heritage. For this reason, tangential opportunistic aspect of visit is introduced and evaluated in the work of (McGookin et al., 2019), opening another subfield of research and inquiry in empirical evaluations in the CH domain.

Regarding the particular methods for data collection, we have seen that most of them involved some type of **questionnaires and observation**. This is typical of UX evaluation as well; e.g. Bargas-Avila and Hornbæk (2011) also identify a large portion of UX studies to rest on these data collection methods.

If deeper assessments of the impact of CH are to be investigated, it is expected that new qualitative methods of inquiry will be invented, transferred or employed in the evaluation of interactive systems. Some design-oriented approaches have provided such attempts like the works of Yelmi et al. (2016) who employed workshops to assess aspects of their soundscape installation. Notably there is a grand challenge when employing qualitative and generative methods in evaluation: that of **balancing quality of findings with an evidence-based approach**. The results in this review, show a tendency in approaching this direction.

On Issues of Rigor in Conducting and Reporting on Empirical Evaluations

Despite that the papers examined were peer-reviewed and published in important journals and conferences, it was possible to identify several failures in the quality of reporting on empirical evaluations. For example, it is indicative that there were six studies that did not report on the number of users that participated in the evaluations (reported in Table 9, 'unspecified'), while even more studies did not provide sufficient user profile information. Another example of insufficient reporting is that some papers did not specify the questions in self-developed questionnaires. A considerable number of studies drew conclusions on the UX without specific references on the data employed. These issues are indicative of the quality of reporting in some studies, which needs to improve.

Limitations of this Review

Any literature review is limited. The sample of the works examined is the first and most important limitation. The query method employed has inevitably constrained the sample into ways that may not be easily assessed at the time of writing. Additionally, the selection of papers was conducted on august 2019, with the consequence that late 2019 papers have have appeared in search engines and digital libraries.

CONCLUSION

This paper reports on a systematically selected sample of 83 publications from 2012-2019 on empirical evaluations of digital heritage, expanding and enhancing the previous review of Koutsabasis (2017). The paper reports on the key features of interactive systems of CH in terms of purpose, interactive technology, cultural content, and location of the system use, as well as the main characteristics that every empirical evaluation addresses, such as dimensions examined, general method employed, data collection methods, participants, and whether the evaluation is comparative or not. In addition to the previous review, this study also draws comparisons between previous and recent results. Having identified the issues reported formerly, it provides further inquiry and analysis for significant differences in relation to these issues, it examines the possible causes of unaltered results, and finally suggests supplementary investigation by offering a broader view stemming from the records included in the study.

In general, the results show an advancement in the number of studies that have involved CH professionals, e.g. curators, archaeologists, in their empirical evaluations; an issue that was thoroughly discussed in the previous review. In addition, a general shift towards field studies and testing constitutes could promote more validity of the evaluation process and results. Could this be sufficient to act as an equilibrium between qualitative research methodologies and how they process and echoes their results? In either way, still needs more systematic approaches that will organize and evaluate these methodologies in distinct identifiable categories.

Concerning the dimensions of empirical evaluations of interactive systems in CH and in relation to our previous results, we observe no difference in the dimensions assessed in the recent studies. Aspects of cultural value, awareness, and presence could only be recognized in very few empirical evaluations. Evaluation studies that consider more qualitative dimensions and more related to general purposes of CH like learning effectiveness have been increased, and they are usually accompanied by comparative evaluations. Comparative evaluations represent a small number compared to the overall number of studies reviewed. So far, their employed methodologies could inform future studies and encourage further investigation that could be transferred in the evaluations of more 'inaccessible' aspects of CH, like the ones mentioned above.

Last but not least, we observed several emerging technologies like physical computing and TUIs, with studies that creatively exploit their cost-effective affordances turning interaction with CH content into a more inspired and engaging experience.

It seems that this new multidisciplinary research field is still at its infancy yet rapidly evolving. It is envisaged that researchers of digital heritage will be stimulated by the systems presented in this review, reflect on the issues identified, enrich their knowledge with state-of-the-art empirical evaluation and possibly re-think and improve their own work and practice.

REFERENCES

Albert, W., & Tullis, T. (2013). *Measuring the User Experience: Collecting, Analyzing, and Presenting Usability Metrics* (2nd ed.). Newnes.

Alves, R., Valente, P., & Nunes, N. J. (2014). The state of user experience evaluation practice. In *Proceedings of the 8th Nordic Conference on Human-Computer Interaction: Fun, Fast, Foundational* (pp. 93-102). ACM. 10.1145/2639189.2641208

Anagnostakis, G., Antoniou, M., Kardamitsi, E., Sachinidis, T., Koutsabasis, P., Stavrakis, M., ... Zissis, D. (2016). Accessible museum collections for the visually impaired: combining tactile exploration, audio descriptions and mobile gestures. In *Proceedings of the 18th International Conference on Human-Computer Interaction with Mobile Devices and Services Adjunct* (pp. 1021-1025). ACM. 10.1145/2957265.2963118

Andreoli, R., Corolla, A., Faggiano, A., Malandrino, D., Pirozzi, D., Ranaldi, M., ... Scarano, V. (2016, October). Immersivity and Playability Evaluation of a Game Experience in Cultural Heritage. In *Euro-Mediterranean Conference* (pp. 814-824). Springer International Publishing. 10.1007/978-3-319-48496-9_65

Arends, M., Froschauer, J., Goldfarb, D., Merkl, D., & Weingartner, M. (2012). Analysing user motivation in an art folksonomy. In *Proceedings of the 12th International Conference on Knowledge Management and Knowledge Technologies* (p. 13). ACM. 10.1145/2362456.2362473

Bargas-Avila, J. A., & Hornbæk, K. (2011). Old wine in new bottles or novel challenges: a critical analysis of empirical studies of user experience. In *Proceedings of the SIGCHI Conference on Human Factors in Computing Systems* (pp. 2689-2698). ACM. 10.1145/1978942.1979336

Bekele, M. K., Pierdicca, R., Frontoni, E., Malinverni, E. S., & Gain, J. (2018). A survey of augmented, virtual, and mixed reality for cultural heritage. *Journal on Computing and Cultural Heritage*, *11*(2), 7. doi:10.1145/3145534

Bellotti, F., Berta, R., De Gloria, A., D'ursi, A., & Fiore, V. (2012). A serious game model for cultural heritage. *Journal on Computing and Cultural Heritage*, *5*(4), 17. doi:10.1145/2399180.2399185

Bellucci, A., Diaz, P., & Aedo, I. (2015). A See-Through Display for Interactive Museum Showcases. In *Proceedings of the 2015 International Conference on Interactive Tabletops & Surfaces* (pp. 301-306). ACM. 10.1145/2817721.2823497

Brooke, J. (1996). SUS-A quick and dirty usability scale. *Usability Evaluation in Industry, 189*(194), 4-7.

Caggianese, G., Gallo, L., & Neroni, P. (2018). Evaluation of spatial interaction techniques for virtual heritage applications: A case study of an interactive holographic projection. *Future Generation Computer Systems*, *81*, 516–527. doi:10.1016/j.future.2017.07.047

Cairns, P., & Cox, A. L. (2008). *Research Methods for Human-Computer Interaction*. Cambridge University Press. doi:10.1017/CBO9780511814570

Callaway, C., Stock, O., & Dekoven, E. (2014). Experiments with mobile drama in an instrumented museum for inducing conversation in small groups. *ACM Transactions on Interactive Intelligent Systems*, *4*(1), 2. doi:10.1145/2584250

Camps-Ortueta, I., Rodríguez-Muñoz, J. M., Gómez-Martín, P. P., & González-Calero, P. A. (2017). Combining augmented reality with real maps to promote social interaction in treasure hunts. In CoSECivi (pp. 131–143). Academic Press.

Chalvatzaras, D., Yiannoutsou, N., Sintoris, C., & Avouris, N. (2014). Do you remember that building? Exploring old Zakynthos through an augmented reality mobile game. In *Interactive Mobile Communication Technologies and Learning (IMCL), 2014 International Conference on* (pp. 222-225). IEEE. 10.1109/IMCTL.2014.7011136

Ciolfi, L., Avram, G., Maye, L., Dulake, N., Marshall, M. T., van Dijk, D., & McDermott, F. (2016). Articulating Co-Design in Museums: Reflections on Two Participatory Processes. In *Proceedings of the 19th ACM Conference on Computer-Supported Cooperative Work & Social Computing* (pp. 13-25). ACM. 10.1145/2818048.2819967

Coenen, T., Mostmans, L., & Naessens, K. (2013). MuseUs: Case study of a pervasive cultural heritage serious game. *Journal on Computing and Cultural Heritage*, *6*(2), 8. doi:10.1145/2460376.2460379

Correia, N., Romão, T., Ricardo, A., Mota, T., Melo, M. J., Castro, R., ... Miranda, A. (2014). Design of an interactive experience with medieval illuminations: A journey into the beauty and meaning of medieval Portuguese manuscripts. *Journal on Computing and Cultural Heritage*, *7*(2), 13. doi:10.1145/2626289

Creed, C., Sivell, J., & Sear, J. (2013). Multi-touch tables for exploring heritage content in public spaces. In *Visual Heritage in the Digital Age* (pp. 67–90). Springer London. doi:10.1007/978-1-4471-5535-5_5

Csikszentmihalyi, M., & Robinson, R. E. (1990). *The art of seeing: An interpretation of the aesthetic encounter*. Getty Publications.

De Rojas, M. del C., & del Carmen Camarero, M. (2006). Experience and satisfaction of visitors to museums and cultural exhibitions. *International Review on Public and Non Profit Marketing*, *3*(1), 49.

Di Franco, P. D. G., Camporesi, C., Galeazzi, F., & Kallmann, M. (2015). 3d printing and immersive visualization for improved perception of ancient artifacts. *Presence (Cambridge, Mass.)*, *24*(3), 243–264. doi:10.1162/PRES_a_00229

Díaz, M. G. A., Toftedahl, M., & Svensson, T. (2014, December). The Mystery of Elin. Incorporating a City Cultural Program on History and Heritage into a Pervasive Game. In *Proceedings of the 2014 Conference on Interactive Entertainment* (pp. 1-10). ACM.

Dimitropoulos, A., Dimitropoulos, K., Kyriakou, A., Malevitis, M., Syrris, S., Vaka, S., ... Stavrakis, M. (2018). The loom: interactive weaving through a tangible installation with digital feedback. In *Digital Cultural Heritage* (pp. 199–210). Cham: Springer. doi:10.1007/978-3-319-75826-8_17

Dix, A., Finlay, J., Aboud, G. D., & Beale, R. (2004). *Human-Computer Interaction* (4th ed.). Pearson Education.

Duguleana, M., Brodi, R., Girbacia, F., Postelnicu, C., Machidon, O., & Carrozzino, M. (2016). Time-Travelling with Mobile Augmented Reality: A Case Study on the Piazza dei Miracoli. In *Euro-Mediterranean Conference* (pp. 902-912). Springer International Publishing. 10.1007/978-3-319-48496-9_73

Fabola, A., Kennedy, S., Miller, A., Oliver, I., McCaffery, J., & Cassidy, C., … Vermehren, A. (2017). A virtual museum installation for time travel. In *International Conference on Immersive Learning* (pp. 255–270). Springer. 10.1007/978-3-319-60633-0_21

Falk, J. H., & Dierking, L. D. (2018). *Learning from museums*. Rowman & Littlefield.

Falvo, P. G. (2015, September). Exhibit design with multimedia and cognitive technologies impact assessment on Luca Giordano, Raphael and the Chapel of the Magi in Palazzo Medici Riccardi, Florence. In *2015 Digital Heritage* (Vol. 2, pp. 525-532). IEEE.

Fanini, B., d'Annibale, E., Demetrescu, E., Ferdani, D., & Pagano, A. (2015). *Engaging and shared gesture-based interaction for museums the case study of K2R international expo in Rome. In 2015 Digital Heritage* (Vol. 1, pp. 263–270). IEEE.

Feldman, R. (2001). Evidence. In *The Cambridge Dictionary of Philosophy* (2nd ed.; pp. 293–294). Cambridge, UK: Cambridge University Press.

Floch, J., & Jiang, S. (2015). *One place, many stories digital storytelling for cultural heritage discovery in the landscape. In 2015 Digital Heritage* (Vol. 2, pp. 503–510). IEEE.

Fritsch, J., Breinbjerg, M., & Jensen, T. S. (2014). Designing interactive listening situations. In *Proceedings of the 26th Australian Computer-Human Interaction Conference on Designing Futures: the Future of Design* (pp. 31-40). ACM.

Froschauer, J., Merkl, D., Arends, M., & Goldfarb, D. (2013). Art history concepts at play with ThIATRO. *Journal on Computing and Cultural Heritage*, *6*(2), 7. doi:10.1145/2460376.2460378

Gaitanou, M., Charissi, E., Margari, I., Papamakarios, M., Vosinakis, S., Koutsabasis, P., ... Stavrakis, M. (2018). Design of an Interactive Experience Journey in a Renovated Industrial Heritage Site. In *Euro-Mediterranean Conference*, (pp. 150-161). Springer. 10.1007/978-3-030-01762-0_13

Georgiadi, N., Kokkoli-Papadopoulou, E., Kordatos, G., Partheniadis, K., Sparakis, M., Koutsabasis, P., ... Stavrakis, M. (2016). A pervasive role-playing game for introducing elementary school students to archaeology. In *Proceedings of the 18th International Conference on Human-Computer Interaction with Mobile Devices and Services Adjunct* (pp. 1016-1020). ACM. 10.1145/2957265.2963117

Georgiou, Y., & Kyza, E. A. (2017). The development and validation of the ARI questionnaire: An instrument for measuring immersion in location-based augmented reality settings. *International Journal of Human-Computer Studies*, *98*, 24–37. doi:10.1016/j.ijhcs.2016.09.014

Gkiti, C., Varia, E., Zikoudi, C., Kirmanidou, A., Kyriakati, I., Vosinakis, S., ... Koutsabasis, P. (2018). i-Wall: A Low-Cost Interactive Wall for Enhancing Visitor Experience and Promoting Industrial Heritage in Museums. In *Euro-Mediterranean Conference* (pp. 90–100). Springer. 10.1007/978-3-030-01762-0_8

Graf, H., Keil, J., Pagano, A., & Pescarin, S. (2015). *A contextualized educational museum experience connecting objects, places and themes through mobile virtual museums. In 2015 Digital Heritage* (Vol. 1, pp. 337–340). IEEE.

Hai, H., Lo, W. H., Ng, H. H., Brailsford, T., & O'Malley, C. (2018). Enhancing reflective learning experiences in museums through interactive installations. *Rethinking Learning in the Digital Age: Making the Learning Sciences Count*, *2*(2), 776–783.

Hammady, R., Ma, M., & Powell, A. (2018). User Experience of Markerless Augmented Reality Applications in Cultural Heritage Museums: 'MuseumEye'as a Case Study. In *International Conference on Augmented Reality, Virtual Reality and Computer Graphics* (pp. 349–369). Springer. 10.1007/978-3-319-95282-6_26

Han, K., Shih, P. C., Rosson, M. B., & Carroll, J. M. (2014). Enhancing community awareness of and participation in local heritage with a mobile application. In *Proceedings of the 17th ACM conference on Computer supported cooperative work & social computing* (pp. 1144-1155). ACM. 10.1145/2531602.2531640

Hart, S. G., & Staveland, L. E. (1988). Development of NASA-TLX (Task Load Index): Results of empirical and theoretical research. *Advances in Psychology*, *52*, 139–183. doi:10.1016/S0166-4115(08)62386-9

Hassenzahl, M., Burmester, M. Koller, F. (2006) AttrakDiff: Ein Fragebogen zur Messung wahrgenommener hedonischer und pragmatischer Qualität. *Mensch & Computer 2003*, 187-196.

Hewett, T. T., Baecker, R., Card, S., Carey, T., Gasen, J., Mantei, M., . . . Verplank, W. (1996). *ACM SIGCHI Curricula for Human-Computer Interaction*. Retrieved from http://old.sigchi.org/cdg/cdg2.html#2_1

Hu, X., Ho, E. M., & Qiao, C. (2017). Digitizing Dunhuang Cultural Heritage: A User Evaluation of Mogao Cave Panorama Digital Library. *Journal of Data and Information Science*, *2*(3), 49–67. doi:10.1515/jdis-2017-0014

Huang, C. H., & Huang, Y. T. (2013). An annales school-based serious game creation framework for taiwanese indigenous cultural heritage. *Journal on Computing and Cultural Heritage*, *6*(2), 9. doi:10.1145/2460376.2460380

Ijaz, K., Bogdanovych, A., & Trescak, T. (2016). Virtual worlds vs books and videos in history education. *Interactive Learning Environments*, 1–26.

ISO 9241. Ergonomics of Human-System Interaction. International Organization for Standardization.

Jones, C. E. K., Theodosis, S., & Lykourentzou, I. (2019). The Enthusiast, the Interested, the Sceptic, and the Cynic: Understanding User Experience and Perceived Value in Location-Based Cultural Heritage Games Through Qualitative and Sentiment Analysis. *Journal on Computing and Cultural Heritage*, *12*(1), 6. doi:10.1145/3297716

Jylhä, A., Hsieh, Y. T., Orso, V., Andolina, S., Gamberini, L., & Jacucci, G. (2015). A Wearable Multimodal Interface for Exploring Urban Points of Interest. In *Proceedings of the 2015 ACM on International Conference on Multimodal Interaction* (pp. 175-182). ACM. 10.1145/2818346.2820763

Kabassi, K. (2016). Evaluating websites of museums: State of the art. *Journal of Cultural Heritage*.

Kasapakis, V., Gavalas, D., & Galatis, P. (2016). Augmented reality in cultural heritage: Field of view awareness in an archaeological site mobile guide. *Journal of Ambient Intelligence and Smart Environments*, *8*(5), 501–514. doi:10.3233/AIS-160394

Katsouri, I., Tzanavari, A., Herakleous, K., & Poullis, C. (2015). Visualizing and assessing hypotheses for marine archaeology in a VR CAVE environment. *Journal on Computing and Cultural Heritage*, *8*(2), 10. doi:10.1145/2665072

Kennedy, S., Fawcett, R., Miller, A., Dow, L., Sweetman, R., Field, A., ... Allison, C. (2013, October). Exploring canons & cathedrals with open virtual worlds: The recreation of st andrews cathedral, st andrews day, 1318. In *Digital Heritage International Congress (DigitalHeritage)*, 2013 (Vol. 2, pp. 273-280). IEEE. 10.1109/DigitalHeritage.2013.6744764

Kirakowski, J., & Corbett, M. (1993). SUMI: The software usability measurement inventory. *British Journal of Educational Technology*, *24*(3), 210–212. doi:10.1111/j.1467-8535.1993.tb00076.x

Kirshenblatt-Gimblett, B. (2004). Intangible Heritage as Metacultural Production1. *Museum International*, *56*(1–2), 52–65. doi:10.1111/j.1350-0775.2004.00458.x

Koutsabasis, P. (2017). Empirical Evaluations of Interactive Systems in Cultural Heritage: A Review. *International Journal of Computational Methods in Heritage Science*, *1*(1), 100–122. doi:10.4018/IJCMHS.2017010107

Koutsabasis, P., & Vosinakis, S. (2016). Adult and Children User Experience with Leap Motion in Digital Heritage. In *The Cycladic Sculpture Application. In Euro-Mediterranean Conference* (pp. 350-361). Springer International Publishing.

Koutsabasis, P., & Vosinakis, S. (2018). Kinesthetic Interactions in Museums: Conveying Cultural Heritage by Making Use of Ancient Tools and (re-) Constructing Artworks. *Virtual Reality (Waltham Cross)*, *22*(2), 103–118. doi:10.100710055-017-0325-0

Kyriakou, P., & Hermon, S. (2019). Can I Touch This? Using Natural Interaction in a Museum Augmented Reality System. *Digital Applications in Archaeology and Cultural Heritage*, *12*, e00088. doi:10.1016/j.daach.2018.e00088

Laugwitz, B., Held, T., & Schrepp, M. (2008). Construction and evaluation of a user experience questionnaire. In *Symposium of the Austrian HCI and Usability Engineering Group* (pp. 63-76). Springer. 10.1007/978-3-540-89350-9_6

Lavie, T., & Tractinsky, N. (2004). Assessing dimensions of perceived visual aesthetics of web sites. *International Journal of Human-Computer Studies*, *60*(3), 269–298. doi:10.1016/j.ijhcs.2003.09.002

Loizides, F., El Kater, A., Terlikas, C., Lanitis, A., & Michael, D. (2014). Presenting cypriot cultural heritage in virtual reality: A user evaluation. In *Euro-Mediterranean Conference* (pp. 572-579). Springer International Publishing. 10.1007/978-3-319-13695-0_57

Lorenzini, C., Carrozzino, M., Evangelista, C., Tecchia, F., Bergamasco, M., & Angeletaki, A. (2015). *A Virtual Laboratory An immersive VR experience to spread ancient libraries heritage. In 2015 Digital Heritage* (Vol. 2, pp. 639–642). IEEE.

Lund, A. M. (2001). Measuring usability with the USE questionnaire. *Usability Interface*, *8*(2), 3–6.

MacDonald, C. M., & Atwood, M. E. (2013). Changing perspectives on evaluation in HCI: past, present, and future. In CHI'13 Extended Abstracts on Human Factors in Computing Systems (pp. 1969-1978). ACM. doi:10.1145/2468356.2468714

Machidon, O.-M., Tavčar, A., Gams, M., & Duguleană, M. (2019). CulturalERICA: A conversational agent improving the exploration of European cultural heritage. *Journal of Cultural Heritage*. doi:10.1016/j.culher.2019.07.010

Madsen, J. B., & Madsen, C. B. (2016). Handheld visual representation of a castle chapel ruin. *Journal on Computing and Cultural Heritage*, *9*(1), 6.

Maina, J. K. O., & Suleman, H. (2015, December). Enhancing Digital Heritage Archives Using Gamified Annotations. In *International Conference on Asian Digital Libraries* (pp. 169-179). Springer International Publishing. 10.1007/978-3-319-27974-9_17

Malegiannaki, I., & Daradoumis, T. (2017). Analyzing the educational design, use and effect of spatial games for cultural heritage: A literature review. *Computers & Education*, *108*, 1–10. doi:10.1016/j.compedu.2017.01.007

Marshall, M. T., Petrelli, D., Dulake, N., Not, E., Marchesoni, M., Trenti, E., & Pisetti, A. (2016). Audio-based narratives for the trenches of World War I: Intertwining stories, places and interaction for an evocative experience. *International Journal of Human-Computer Studies*, *85*, 27–39. doi:10.1016/j.ijhcs.2015.08.001

Marton, F., Rodriguez, M. B., Bettio, F., Agus, M., Villanueva, A. J., & Gobbetti, E. (2014). IsoCam: Interactive visual exploration of massive cultural heritage models on large projection setups. *Journal on Computing and Cultural Heritage*, *7*(2), 12. doi:10.1145/2611519

Maye, L. A., McDermott, F. E., Ciolfi, L., & Avram, G. (2014). Interactive exhibitions design: what can we learn from cultural heritage professionals? In *Proceedings of the 8th Nordic Conference on Human-Computer Interaction: Fun, Fast, Foundational* (pp. 598-607). ACM. 10.1145/2639189.2639259

McCaffery, J., Miller, A., Vermehren, A., & Fabola, A. (2015). *The Virtual Museums of Caen: A case study on modes of representation of digital historical content. In 2015 Digital Heritage* (Vol. 2, pp. 541–548). IEEE.

McGookin, D., Tahiroğlu, K., Vaittinen, T., Kytö, M., Monastero, B., & Vasquez, J. C. (2019). Investigating tangential access for location-based digital cultural heritage applications. *International Journal of Human-Computer Studies*, *122*, 196–210. doi:10.1016/j.ijhcs.2018.09.009

Moher, D., Cook, D. J., Eastwood, S., Olkin, I., Rennie, D., & Stroup, D. F. (1999). Improving the quality of reports of meta-analyses of randomised controlled trials: The QUOROM statement. *Lancet*, *354*(9193), 1896–1900. doi:10.1016/S0140-6736(99)04149-5 PMID:10584742

Muntean, R., Antle, A. N., Matkin, B., Hennessy, K., Rowley, S., & Wilson, J. (2017). Designing cultural values into interaction. In *Proceedings of the 2017 CHI Conference on Human Factors in Computing Systems* (pp. 6062–6074). ACM. 10.1145/3025453.3025908

Neumüller, M., Reichinger, A., Rist, F., & Kern, C. (2014). *3D printing for cultural heritage: Preservation, accessibility, research and education. In 3D Research Challenges in Cultural Heritage* (pp. 119–134). Springer Berlin Heidelberg. doi:10.1007/978-3-662-44630-0_9

Nielsen, J. (1994). *Usability Engineering*. Elsevier.

Nofal, E., Elhanafi, A. M., Hameeuw, H., & Vande Moere, A. (2018). Architectural Contextualization of Heritage Museum Artifacts Using Augmented Reality. *Studies in Digital Heritage*, *2*(1), 42–67. doi:10.14434dh.v2i1.24500

Nofal, E., Reffat, R., Boschloos, V., Hameeuw, H., & Moere, A. (2018). The Role of Tangible Interaction to Communicate Tacit Knowledge of Built Heritage. *Heritage*, *1*(2), 414–436. doi:10.3390/heritage1020028

Not, E., Cavada, D., Maule, S., Pisetti, A., & Venturini, A. (2019). Digital augmentation of historical objects through tangible interaction. *Journal on Computing and Cultural Heritage*, *12*(3), 18. doi:10.1145/3297764

O'Keefe, B., & Benyon, D. (2015). Using the blended spaces framework to design heritage stories with schoolchildren. *International Journal of Child-Computer Interaction*, *6*, 7–16. doi:10.1016/j.ijcci.2016.02.001

O'Sullivan, L., Picinali, L., Feakes, C., & Cawthorne, D. (2014). Audio tactile maps (atm) system for the exploration of digital heritage buildings by visually-impaired individuals-first prototype and preliminary evaluation. Forum Acusticum, Krakow, Poland.

Pagano, A., Pietroni, E., & Cerato, I. (2017). User experience evaluation of immersive virtual contexts: the case of the virtual museum of the Tiber Valley project. *International Conference on Education and New Learning Technologies*, 3–5. 10.21125/edulearn.2017.1735

Paliokas, I., & Sylaiou, S. (2016). The Use of Serious Games in Museum Visits and Exhibitions: A Systematic Mapping Study. In *Games and Virtual Worlds for Serious Applications (VS-Games), 2016 8th International Conference on* (pp. 1-8). IEEE. 10.1109/VS-GAMES.2016.7590371

Panayiotou, S., & Lanitis, A. (2016). Paintings Alive: A Virtual Reality-Based Approach for Enhancing the User Experience of Art Gallery Visitors. In *Euro-Mediterranean Conference* (pp. 240-247). Springer International Publishing. 10.1007/978-3-319-48974-2_27

Papadimitriou, N. (2012). Multiple Intepretations, Technological Applications and Public Interaction in Archaeological Museums in Europe. In M. Vaudetti, V. Minucciani, & S. Canepa (Eds.), *The Archaeological Musealization* (pp. 39–50). Torino, Italy: Multidisciplinary Intervention in Archaeological Sites for the Conservation, Communication and Culture.

Pekarik, A. J., Doering, Z. D., & Karns, D. A. (1999). Exploring satisfying experiences in museums. *Curator (New York, N.Y.)*, *42*(2), 152–173. doi:10.1111/j.2151-6952.1999.tb01137.x

Pereda, J. (2019). A TUI To Explore Cultural Heritage Repositories on The Web. In *Proceedings of the Thirteenth International Conference on Tangible, Embedded, and Embodied Interaction* (pp. 259–267). ACM. 10.1145/3294109.3301000

Philbin-Briscoe, O., Simon, B., Mudur, S., Poullis, C., Rizvic, S., Boskovic, D., … Skarlatos, D. (2017). A serious game for understanding ancient seafaring in the Mediterranean sea. In *2017 9th International Conference on Virtual Worlds and Games for Serious Applications (VS-Games)* (pp. 1–5). IEEE.

Pietroni, E., & Adami, A. (2014). Interacting with virtual reconstructions in museums: The Etruscanning Project. *Journal on Computing and Cultural Heritage*, *7*(2), 9. doi:10.1145/2611375

Pollalis, C., Minor, E. J., Westendorf, L., Fahnbulleh, W., Virgilio, I., Kun, A. L., & Shaer, O. (2018). Evaluating learning with tangible and virtual representations of archaeological artifacts. In *Proceedings of the Twelfth International Conference on Tangible, Embedded, and Embodied Interaction* (pp. 626–637). ACM. 10.1145/3173225.3173260

Power, C., Lewis, A., Petrie, H., Green, K., Richards, J., & Eramian, M. (2017). Improving archaeologists' online archive experiences through user-centred design. *Journal on Computing and Cultural Heritage*, *10*(1), 3. doi:10.1145/2983917

Pujol-Tost, L. (2019). Did We Just Travel to the Past? Building and Evaluating With Cultural Presence Different Modes of VR-Mediated Experiences in Virtual Archaeology. *Journal on Computing and Cultural Heritage*, *12*(1), 2. doi:10.1145/3230678

Ravyse, W. S., Blignaut, A. S., Leendertz, V., & Woolner, A. (2016). Success factors for serious games to enhance learning: A systematic review. *Virtual Reality (Waltham Cross)*, 1–28.

Read, J. C. (2008). Validating the Fun Toolkit: An instrument for measuring children's opinions of technology. *Cognition Technology and Work*, *10*(2), 119–128. doi:10.100710111-007-0069-9

Rennick-Egglestone, S., Brundell, P., Koleva, B., Benford, S., Roussou, M., & Chaffardon, C. (2016). Families and mobile devices in museums: Designing for integrated experiences. *Journal on Computing and Cultural Heritage*, *9*(2), 11. doi:10.1145/2891416

Reunanen, M., Díaz, L., & Horttana, T. (2015). A holistic user-centered approach to immersive digital cultural heritage installations: Case Vrouw Maria. *Journal on Computing and Cultural Heritage*, *7*(4), 24. doi:10.1145/2637485

Rizvić, S., & Skalonjić, I. (2015). *Reconstructing cultural heritage objects from storytelling. In 2015 Digital Heritage* (Vol. 2, pp. 221–226). IEEE.

Rojas, S. L., Oppermann, L., Blum, L., & Wolpers, M. (2014, November). Natural Europe educational games suite: using structured museum-data for creating mobile educational games. In *Proceedings of the 11th Conference on Advances in Computer Entertainment Technology* (p. 6). ACM. 10.1145/2663806.2663841

Roussou, M., & Katifori, A. (2018). Flow, staging, wayfinding, personalization: Evaluating user experience with mobile museum narratives. *Multimodal Technologies and Interaction*, *2*(2), 32. doi:10.3390/mti2020032

Rubin, J., & Chisnell, D. (2008). *Handbook of Usability Testing: How to Plan, Design, and Conduct Effective Tests*. John Wiley and Sons.

Rubino, I., Barberis, C., Xhembulla, J., & Malnati, G. (2015). Integrating a location-based mobile game in the museum visit: Evaluating visitors' behaviour and learning. *Journal on Computing and Cultural Heritage*, *8*(3), 15. doi:10.1145/2724723

Santos, M. E. C., Taketomi, T., Sandor, C., Polvi, J., Yamamoto, G., & Kato, H. (2014). A usability scale for handheld augmented reality. In *Proceedings of the 20th ACM Symposium on Virtual Reality Software and Technology* (pp. 167-176). ACM. 10.1145/2671015.2671019

Sauro, J. (2012). *10 things to know about the Single Ease Question (SEQ).* Retrieved from Measuring U: https://measuringu.com/seq10/

Sauro, J., & Lewis, J. R. (2012). *Quantifying the User Experience: Practical Statistics for User Research.* Elsevier.

Schaper, M.-M., Santos, M., Malinverni, L., Berro, J. Z., & Pares, N. (2018). Learning about the past through situatedness, embodied exploration and digital augmentation of cultural heritage sites. *International Journal of Human-Computer Studies*, *114*, 36–50. doi:10.1016/j.ijhcs.2018.01.003

Shih, J. L., Jheng, S. C., & Tseng, J. J. (2015). A simulated learning environment of history games for enhancing players' cultural awareness. *Interactive Learning Environments*, *23*(2), 191–211. doi:10.1080/10494820.2014.997249

Shin, J., Park, H., & Woo, W. (2017). Connecting the dots: Enhancing the usability of indexed multimedia data for AR cultural heritage applications through storytelling. In *Proceedings of the 15th International Workshop on Content-Based Multimedia Indexing* (p. 11). ACM. 10.1145/3095713.3095725

Shneiderman, B., & Pleasant, C. (2009). *Designing the User Interface* (5th ed.). Pearson Education.

Skowronski, M., Wieland, J., Borowski, M., Fink, D., Gröschel, C., Klinkhammer, D., & Reiterer, H. (2018). Blended Museum: The Interactive Exhibition Rebuild Palmyra? In *Proceedings of the 17th International Conference on Mobile and Ubiquitous Multimedia* (pp. 529–535). ACM. 10.1145/3282894.3289746

Střelák, D., Škola, F., & Liarokapis, F. (2016). Examining User Experiences in a Mobile Augmented Reality Tourist Guide. In *Proceedings of the 9th ACM International Conference on PErvasive Technologies Related to Assistive Environments* (p. 19). ACM.

Sylaiou, S., Mania, K., Liarokapis, F., White, M., Walczak, K., Wojciechowski, R., . . . Patias, P. (2015). Evaluation of a Cultural Heritage Augmented Reality Game. Cartographies of Mind, Soul and Knowledge.

Tröndle, M., Greenwood, S., Kirchberg, V., & Tschacher, W. (2014). An integrative and comprehensive methodology for studying aesthetic experience in the field: Merging movement tracking, physiology, and psychological data. *Environment and Behavior*, *46*(1), 102–135. doi:10.1177/0013916512453839

van der Vaart, M., & Damala, A. (2015). *Through the loupe: visitor engagement with a primarily text-based handheld AR application. In 2015 Digital Heritage* (Vol. 2, pp. 565–572). IEEE.

Vorderer, P., Wirth, W., Gouveia, F. R., Biocca, F., Saari, T., Jäncke, F., ... Klimmt, C. (2004). *MEC spatial presence questionnaire (MEC-SPQ): Short documentation and instructions for application.* Report to the European community, project presence: MEC (IST-2001-37661), 3.

Vosinakis, S., Avradinis, N., & Koutsabasis, P. (2018). Dissemination of Intangible Cultural Heritage using a Multi-Agent Virtual World. In *Advances in Digital Cultural Heritage* (pp. 197–207). Cham: Springer. doi:10.1007/978-3-319-75789-6_14

Vosinakis, S., Koutsabasis, P., Makris, D., & Sagia, E. (2016). A Kinesthetic Approach to Digital Heritage using Leap Motion: The Cycladic Sculpture Application. *8th International Conference on Games and Virtual Worlds for Serious Applications (VS-GAMES).* 10.1109/VS-GAMES.2016.7590334

Wang, L., & Champion, E. (2012). *Chinese culture approached through touch.* Virtual Systems in the Information Society.

Wang, X., Khoo, E. T., Nakatsu, R., & Cheok, A. (2014). Interacting with traditional Chinese culture through natural language. *Journal on Computing and Cultural Heritage*, *7*(3), 18. doi:10.1145/2597183

Witmer, B. G., & Singer, M. J. (1998). Measuring presence in virtual environments: A presence questionnaire. *Presence (Cambridge, Mass.)*, *7*(3), 225–240. doi:10.1162/105474698565686

Wu, Y., Bryan-Kinns, N., Wang, W., Sheridan, J. G., & Xu, X. (2017). Designing a Cross-Cultural Interactive Music Box through Meaning Construction. In *International Conference on Cross-Cultural Design* (pp. 241–257). Springer. 10.1007/978-3-319-57931-3_20

Yelmi, P., Kuşcu, H., & Yantaç, A. E. (2016). Towards a Sustainable Crowdsourced Sound Heritage Archive by Public Participation: The Soundsslike Project. In *Proceedings of the 9th Nordic Conference on Human-Computer Interaction* (p. 71). ACM. 10.1145/2971485.2971492

Zamora-Musa, R., Vélez, J., & Paez-Logreira, H. (2018). Evaluating learnability in a 3D heritage tour. *Presence (Cambridge, Mass.)*, *26*(4), 366–377. doi:10.1162/PRES_a_00305

Zimmerman, J., Stolterman, E., & Forlizzi, J. (2010). An analysis and critique of Research through Design: towards a formalization of a research approach. In *Proceedings of the 8th ACM Conference on Designing Interactive Systems* (pp. 310-319). ACM. 10.1145/1858171.1858228

ENDNOTES

1 http://www.europeana.eu/portal/en

2 http://lloydbleekcollection.cs.uct.ac.za/

Chapter 10
Evaluation Experiments of Personalized Tours for Exploring Cultural Heritage

Katerina Kabassi
https://orcid.org/0000-0003-4328-0084
Ionian University, Greece

ABSTRACT

Personalized software has been extensively used in museum guides and recommendation systems for tours because it provides added value to the interaction of the user with cultural heritage. However, this added value can only be confirmed through an evaluation experiment. Therefore, this chapter presents the indoor and outdoor personalized tours for exploring cultural heritage. More specifically, the chapter focuses on the methods used for personalization, the technology employed to improve interaction, and the evaluation experiments that have been implemented. The evaluation experiments are further categorized with respect to the method of evaluation and the criteria used. Finally, it provides a discussion on the main conclusions drawn from the researchers conducting evaluation experiments of the system performing indoor and outdoor tours for the exploration of cultural heritage.

INTRODUCTION

The exploration of cultural heritage has changed by the use of Information and Communication Technologies (ICTs). Visitors acquired easy access to cultural heritage regardless of place and time through the Internet. Additionally, even physical access to the cultural heritage in museums or outdoors changed significantly with the use of mobile guides. However, interaction with cultural heritage still encounters several problems. The vast amount of information presented in museums is often overwhelming to a visitor, making it difficult to select personally interesting exhibits (Ardissono et al. 2012). Indeed, as Jeong and Lee (2006) have noticed, visitors of museums may suffer physical and/or psychological fatigue during their long-lasting walking and focusing on exhibits. This often results in quitting the tour and feeling tiredness mainly due to the tediousness of the uninteresting exhibits.

DOI: 10.4018/978-1-7998-2871-6.ch010

Furthermore, museum visitors differ and their visit experience is composed of the physical, the personal, as well as the socio-cultural context, and identity-related aspects (Falk 2009). Therefore, it is really difficult for a museum to cover the interests and desires of all different users.

A solution to this problem may be given through the personalization of user experience. Indeed, since the first experiments of the late 90s, personalization applied to cultural heritage visits has been seen as a way to improve the overall visitor's experience (Not & Petrelli 2019). Petrelli et al. (1999) support that most museum visitors are willing to receive recommendations and assistance during their interaction with the exhibits. As a result, personalized guiding systems for museums (Vayanou et al. 2014; Katifori et al. 2014) or archaeological sites (Alexandridis et al. 2019) have been developed. This resulted in different recommendation systems have been used for personalizing interaction indoors or outdoors.

In this respect, personalization methods have been applied to adapt the route followed in a museum (LISTEN, PEACH, PIL, MNEMOSYNE, ec(h)o, Museum Wearable, etc.) or in a city (Cheverst et al., 2000, Fink and Kobsa 2002; Scherp & Boll 2004; Wakkary et al. 2009), the menus of a system (e.g. CHESS), the virtual reality route (e.g. MoMa), the text following an exhibit (PEACH, AmI, MyMuseum) etc. For this purpose, these systems use different user modeling techniques for acquiring and maintaining information about the users' interests, knowledge, and other characteristics.

Despite all these interesting approaches for personalizing cultural heritage, there are researchers that express concerns about the effectiveness of some of these approaches (e.g. Marty 2011). Indeed, as Lanir et al. (2011) point out it is not clear how reducing choice in terms of the number of content items that are presented to the visitor affects visitor behavior and satisfaction. This fact shows that personalization methods on their own are not enough for improving a cultural recommendation system or cultural website. Their effectiveness can only be confirmed through an evaluation experiment that is carefully examined and implemented.

Towards this direction, Hendrix (2010) supports that personalization methods should be evaluated based on their ability to meet user needs. Similarly, Bowen and Filippini Fantoni (2004) add that the personalization methods cost and this cost is only justified if it brings added value to the museum for a good percentage of museum visitors. This added value can only be confirmed through an evaluation experiment that is implemented with the participation of experts and/or users.

Evaluation of ubiquitous computing systems is extremely complex (Spasojevic and Kindberg, 2001) and there are only a few articles that focus only on the evaluation phase of a personalized system (Kadobayashi et al. 1998). Most evaluation experiments are part of a paper that presents both the personalization system and the evaluation experiment. Some of them use ad-hoc evaluation approaches borrowed from other better-established domains (Hatala & Wakkary 2005). As a result, Pechenizkiy & Calders (2007) try to attract attention to the problem of scientific evaluation of personalization. The importance, as well as the complexity of the evaluation of personalized software, is emphasized by Ardissono et al. (2012) in a review of personalization methods used in cultural heritage.

Taking into account the importance of recommendation system for personalizing indoor and outdoor tours in order to explore cultural heritage as well as the need and the difficulties in evaluating these systems, this paper presents the methods used for personalization in recommendation systems and the technology used. However, it mainly emphasizes in the systems that have been evaluated and provides a categorization of the experiments found in the literature with respect to the method used.

In view of the above the paper is structured as follows: Section 2 presents the recommendation system and the main user modeling methods that are used. The next two sections present the recommendation systems that provide individualized support in indoor and outdoor tours for the exploration of cultural heritage. Section 5 presents the new trends in this field focusing mainly on mobile technology and social networks for the personalization of tours and recommendations in cultural heritage. Section 6 presents the methods of evaluation and categorizes the evaluation experiment of recommendation systems in cultural heritage in three groups: Inspection method of evaluation, Empirical method of evaluation and Combination of the two methods. The last three sections present the discussion of the results of evaluation experiments analyzed in this paper, the future trends as well as the conclusions drawn by this work.

PERSONALIZATION IN CULTURAL HERITAGE

Recommendation Systems have been extensively used for personalizing interaction in cultural heritage. For this purpose, different personalization methods have been applied to adapt the interaction indoors in a museum (LISTEN, PEACH, PIL, MNEMOSYNE, ec(h)o, Museum Wearable, etc.) and outdoors in an archeological site (LOCUS, Archeoguide). Table 1 presents the systems that are presented in this paper and involves indoor tours for cultural heritage and Table 2 presents the systems for outdoor tours.

In such systems, there is the need to assess personalization from the perspective of the individual, the individual within a group, as well as the group or community as a whole (Smeaton & Callan 2005). The adaptation may take place for each individual user or on a group level e.g Museon (Van Dijk et al. 2012; 2014).

Personalization is based on different criteria that are maintained for the users on their user models. Personalization may be based on users' interests (e.g. Yu et al. 2008, Rutledge et al. 2006, etc.) or in many different characteristics (Zimmerman & Lorenz 2008). An important dimension that characterizes the users, deals with their emotions. Emotions influence user preferences. Therefore, researchers have already demonstrated how knowledge about emotions can be included in a recommendation process in different application areas (Aksenov et al. 2014). Lately, several systems have used affective reasoning for personalizing interaction in cultural heritage either indoors (Goren-Bar et al. 2011) or outdoors (Aksenov et al. 2014).

The collection of information about the user is conducted explicitly (e.g. AmI), implicitly (e.g. PEACH, CHIP) or combining both methods (Rousou et al. 2013, Munnelly et al. 2013). Explicit methods require that users explicitly state their preferences or specific characteristics. Implicit methods, on the other hand, are more common and less intrusive because they 'follow' the user during his/her visit in the museum and collects information about his/her interests, knowledge and other special characteristics without interrupting them. For this purpose, different kind of technology has been used e.g. cameras for users' emotions (Bandanov et al. 2011) or moves through the exhibition space (Hatala & Wakkary 2005). Indeed, as Not and Petrelli (2018) point out, a dynamic personalization needs an infrastructure to collect user data to feed the computational models of the current context and the visitor's interaction history. An interesting approach is proposed in MyMuseum, which provides a mechanism for the user to see how the information s/he receives is adapted to him/her and why (Bright et al. 2005).

The user model can be short-term (lasts as long as a visit) or long-term (lasts longer than a visit). A major change that came with the use of mobile phones while exploring cultural heritage, is the new lifelong user model (Kuflik et al. 2010), a user model that the user can carry in their mobile phone (Gerber et al, 2010; Kuflik and Poteriaykina, 2009, Patrarakis et al. 2016a; 2016b). The use of such a user model reduces the need for acquisition of the model on each visit.

A key issue in the personalization process is the initialization of the user model because it shows how quickly the system will start providing personalized interaction. A quite common method for the initialization of the user model is stereotypes (LISTEN, PEACH) or personas as called by Rousou et al. (2013). However, there are systems such as MUSE that do not make initialization of the user model.

As a representation method of the user model, the overlay method (e.g. ec(h)o, PEACH, PeVEP, CHIP, MUSE) and the feature-based method (e.g. Archeoguide, The Museum Wearable, LISTEN, UbiCicero) are the most commonly used. The overlay model describes user interests, knowledge, and other aspects in terms of the concepts represented in the domain ontology while the feature-based model represents user characteristics as a list of feature-value pairs (Ardissono et al. 2012).

INDOOR TOURS IN MUSEUMS

Roes et al. (2009) have identified four types of museum tours: human-guided tours, audio tours, online/virtual tours, and multimedia tours. A context-aware system for intelligent museum collects information of visitors and surroundings, recognizes visitors' purposes, and then assists visiting while striving to be minimally intrusive through this process (Satyanarayanan 2001). A visitor may enter the system by any device, desktop computer or mobile devices.

In an online interaction, a user may make personal digital collections. Such a way of personalization is proposed by several widely known museums such as the Musée du Louvre and the Virtual Museum of Canada. However, as Filippini Fantoni & Bowen (2007) have noticed, the development of these systems has not been particularly successful as users very often make their personal collections and abandon them without really using them. As a result, several researchers (Dowden & Sayre, 2009, Marty 2011) have examined new methods of personalization that could meet user needs in the online museum environment. Another way of interaction in an online museum is personalizing the interaction and navigation in a virtual museum (Sundar et al. 2015).

A lot of research energy has been put on personalizing interaction in the physical museum by using mobile technology (PEACH, UbiCicero, CHIP, PIL, etc.). An interesting example is the MUSE project (Bohnert et al. 2004), which personalizes the Dinosaur Walk exhibit area in the Melbourne Museum. A rather interesting and complete work on the subject of museum guides is the CHIP (Cultural Heritage Information Personalization) project, which demonstrates how Semantic Web technologies can be deployed to provide personalized access to digital museum collections. More specifically, CHIP personalizes the selection of artworks for the museum visitors based on their underlying semantic relations, e.g. related styles, artists, themes, or locations and the strength of the user interest in those semantically enriched properties (Roes et al. 2009).

Personalization may also take place on the multimedia level. The value of multimedia for a museum guide in order to simulate better the live experience is discussed by Proctor & Tellis (2003) who present an extended user study conducted at the Tate Modern in 2002. In this respect, there are some projects that have taken place in this direction. Multimedia personalization is proposed in the Multimedia Tour (Wilson 2004) and the InteractiveMuseum Guide (Bay et al. 2006).

Audio is a usual multimedia characteristic of a museum guide. Systems like HyperAudio (Petrelli et al. 2001) implement some reactive component but a general audio commentary was played each time the user visited a new location. In ec(h)o (Wakkary and Hatala 2006), on the other hand, the visitor's movement creates a dynamic soundscape of ambient sounds according to his/her initial selection of sound and

Table 1. Evaluated systems for indoor tours in cultural heritage

System		Where Adaptation is applied							
	System	Route/ Path/ Exhibits	Text	Images	Audio	Video	Virtual	Menus	Interface
Partarakis et al. (2016a), Patrarakis et al. (2016b)	AmI	x	x						x
Zimmerman & Lorenz (2008), Terrenghi & Zimmerman (2004)	LISTEN				x				
Hatala & Wakkary (2005)	ec(h)o				x				
Sundar et al. (2015)	MoMa						x		
Filippini-Fantoni (2003)	Museum Wearable				x	x			
Bonis et al. (2009)	PeVEP						x		
Garzotto et al. (2003; 2004)	MUSE					x	x		
Bohnert & Zukerman (2009) & Bohnert et al. (2005)	Melbourne Museum	x							
Bright et al. (2005)	MyMuseum	x	x						
Caus et al. (2008)	Hydra	x							
S. Hsi (2002)	Electronic Guidebook Exploratorium	x		x			x		
Fernie et al. (2012), Griffiths & Cal (2013)	PATHS	x							
Goren-Bar et al. (2005)	PEACH	x	x		x	x			
Kadobayashi et al. (1998)	Mediating Agent in the National Museum of Japanese History	x							
Karaman et al. (2016)	MNEMOSYNE			x		x			
Kuflik et al. (2011) & Lanir et al. (2011)	PIL		-	x	x			x	x
Marty (2011)	6 museums with digital collections	x							
Otegi et al. (2014)	PPR		x						
Pujol et al. (2013)	CHESS				x			x	
Van Hage et al. (2010) & Wang et al. (2008 & 2009) & Roes et al. 2009	CHIP	x							
Yu et al. (2009)	iMuseum		x	x	x	x			
Ghiani et al. 2009	UbiCicero			x	x	x			
Liarokapis & Sylaiou (2010), Liarokapis et al. (2008)	LOCUS	x					x		x

his/her distance from an exhibit. A quite interesting approach was presented in the Museum Wearable, developed for the MIT (Filippini-Fantoni 2003). The particular system gathered information about the museum visitor's preferences from their physical path and length of stops along with the museum exhibition and used this information to personalize the audiovisual narration to the visitor. The LISTEN project (Zimmerman & Lorenz 2008; Terrenghi & Zimmerman 2004) also provided presentations, adapted to the user's context taking into account the moves, position, and direction of the user while moving in an art exhibition. A different way of audio interaction in a museum is storytelling. For example, in the Acropolis museum, the personalization methods are performed in natural language generation as well as menus creation (Pujol et al. 2013)

PEACH (Stock et al., 2007) is another example of a system that proactively presents automatically generated adaptive video documentaries. A quite different approach is proposed by Lanir et al. (2013), who had developed a system that automatically generated a personalized post-visit video summary of a museum visit. Similarly, MNEMOSYNE (Karaman et al. 2016) personalized multimedia content delivery and providing visitors a personalized summary of their visit on a custom mobile application. A similar approach was also suggested in PIL, where the users were able to view and reflect on their experience as a group when sitting at a simulated "museum café" when they take a break or after the visit. PEACH, on the other hand, provided a personalized textual visit summary which also included suggestions on future activities.

OUTDOOR TOURS FOR THE EXPLORATION OF CULTURAL HERITAGE

Personalization techniques have also been used for recommendation systems that are used outdoors in a city or cultural sites. Outdoor personalized recommendations on the cultural heritage of a city are made by the GUIDE system (Cheverst et al., 2000), Gulliver's Genie (O'Hare & O'Grady 2003), WebGuide (WebGuide 2001, Fink and Kobsa 2002), Sightseeing4U (Scherp & Boll 2004) and COMPASS (Wakkary et al. 2009). Outdoor tours may also concern an archaeological site (e.g. Alexandridis et al. 2019).

Huang & Bian (2009) have developed a recommendation system for suggesting specific tourist attractions over the Internet. The proposed system combines a multi-criteria decision-making theory, the Analytic Hierarchy Process (AHP) (Saaty 1980), with a Bayesian network for finding over the Internet which is the tourist attraction that would interest the user interacting with the system. The personalization of specific touristic sites is also made in AVANTI (Fink et al. 1996, Fink et al. 1998). The specific system proposes sites and adapts the information provided to the user's interests and knowledge. Adaptation to a group's preferences on sightseeing destination is made by the INTRIGUE guide (Ardissono et al. 2003).

Personalized assistance to cultural site visitors is provided by ARCHEOGUIDE (Vlahakis et al. 2001). The system provides on-site help and Augmented Reality reconstructions of ancient ruins, based on the user's position and orientation in the cultural site, and real-time image rendering. It uses multi-modal user interfaces and personalizes the flow of information to its users' profile.

A quite interesting approach is proposed by Aksenov et al. (2014), who suggest that the composition of such a personalized cultural tour can be achieved by offering tourists a travel route recommendation tailored to their personal profiles that include three levels: 1) programming the tour, i.e. selecting a number of relevant POIs to be visited, 2) scheduling the tour, i.e. arranging the selected POIs into a suitable and meaningful sequence, in order to increase the cultural value of the tour, and 3) determining the tour's travel route, i.e. identifying a set of trips between the POIs that the tourist needs to perform in order to complete the tour.

Table 2. Systems for outdoor tours in cultural heritage

	System	Route/ Path/ Exhibits	Text	Images	Audio	Video	Virtual	Menus	Interface
Liarokapis & Sylaiou (2010), Liarokapis et al. (2008)	LOCUS	x					x		x
Cheverst et al. 2002	GUIDE	x	x						
Vlahakis et al. 2001	Archeoguide	x	x	x	x	X			
Kontogianni et al. 2018a	Prototype	x							
Alexandridis et al. 2019	Protoype	x	x						

TRENDS IN THE PERSONALIZATION IN CULTURAL HERITAGE

Recommendation systems may use different technologies in order to personalize interaction with cultural heritage. For this purpose, mobile technology has been extensively used for implementing recommendation systems for cultural heritage. This has been mainly used in outdoor tours for a path or sight recommendations. Indeed, mobile devices have been used for finding out information about the cultural sights of a city or even a whole country and have been used by Speta (García-Crespo et al. 2009) and Speta II (García-Crespo et al. 2010), PinPoint (Roth 2002), m-ToGuide prototype (Kamar 2003) and UMT(Yang & Marques, 2005).

More recent approaches include the use of personal mobile devices or Smartphones, which all visitors own and, therefore, is the easiest and sustainable solution. These devices are very popular lately and include various applications that collect data about the user and can be further used in order to personalize the interaction. These systems usually have a GPS that is utilized in order to locate users and provide information about heritage sites in their mobile phones (Dupuy 2014). The user's location can also be used to suggest a visiting "path" taking into consideration of users' location, the available Points Of Interest (POIs), the traveling distance and of course the user profile, e.g. the user's interests. A main advantage of Smartphones that older mobile phones did not have, is the availability of different sensors that establish a different mode of interaction between the user and its physical environment. Such sensors include Pedometer, step/activity counter, etc and could be used for the personalization of the interaction. Ardissono et al. (2012) focused on the different features that could be taken into account and concern the visitor, the heritage content and the space to personalize the interaction.

Smartphones provide a surprisingly large number of modalities for interaction between them and their environment (Bhargava & Agrawala 2016, Kontogianni et al. 2018b). Therefore, another main advantage of Smartphones is that these systems usually contain a wealth of information about their users since they use their personal mobile devices for interacting with multiple applications and social media platforms. When users interact with social media networks provide much information about their preferences, interests, personality, etc. based on their activities in the network. For example, they add or accept friends, check into locations, share articles or make posts.

Indeed, systems that have used Smartphones and information collected by the social media for a personalized recommendation for cultural heritage have been proposed by Kontogianni et al. (2018a) and Sansonetti et al. (2019). Kontogianni et al. (2018a) use data originating for the users' social networks about the users' personality as well as their interests in order to make recommendations. These data are collected implicitly without requiring the user's interaction and are further processed using a multi-criteria decision-making theory called AHP in order to combine this information and select the touristic destination that seems the most appropriate for the particular user. Sansonetti et al. (2019), on the other hand, propose a hybrid recommendation system in the artistic and cultural heritage area, which takes into account the activities on social media performed by the target user and her friends and takes advantage of linked open data sources. The latter use, dissimilarly to the system of Kontogianni et al. (2018a) that use different social networks, use only Facebook to analyze the content generated by the user and his/her friends and extract information about his/her user model. Both systems use this information to provide personalized suggestions in the surrounding area. What is really interesting in the approach in Sansonetti et al. (2019) is that it integrates collaborative filtering algorithms with semantic technologies in order to leverage linked open data sources such as DBpedia and Europeana.

A quite different and very interesting approach in personalizing cultural heritage path recommendation system is proposed by Alexandridis et al. (2019). The latter approach uses the data collected from actual visits to the archaeological sites of Gournia in Greece and Catalhoyuk in Turkey to make an analysis on visitors' movement pattern. More specifically, the particular approach tries to model the location using mean-shift clustering trained with actual user movement patters. The topic modeling is incorporated to formalize the implicit cultural heritage content, while first-order Markov models address the movement as a temporal transition aspect of the problem.

Another trend in personalizing cultural heritage includes digital augmentations that promise to provide an extended perception of the heritage space beyond its physical properties. For this purpose, systems (Damala et al. 2012; Pujol et al. 2013) use purpose-built sensors and algorithms commit to delivering interpretations adapted to the needs and preferences of the users (Ardissono et al. 2012).

However, the main problem with many of the above-mentioned approaches is that there are no reports about their evaluation. For example, Speta and Speta II have not been evaluated but used use cases instead.

METHODS OF EVALUATION

Evaluation is an important phase of software's life-cycle and the research areas of software engineering and human-computer interaction have paid a lot of attention in different aspects of this phase. Chiou et al. (2010), in a review of the literature between 1995-2006, analyze and categorize 83 articles of website evaluation in several domains. In the domain of museum, Kabassi (2017a) makes a state of the art on the evaluation experiments of museums' websites focusing on the methods and the criteria used in this kind of evaluation experiments. Nelson & Cohn (2015), in a review of the museum programs' and exhibitions' evaluations before 2013, report that 79% of the experiments use Interview, 60% observation and 55% survey for data collection. However, these reviews do not focus on personalized systems. A central research challenge in the evaluation of personalization is to evaluate the success of the personalized interaction and the acceptance of the personalization by the users.

Kabassi (2017b) was the first attempt in reviewing the evaluation experiments of personalized systems in cultural heritage. Generally, several categorizations of the proposed evaluation methods exist. For example, Lewis & Rieman (1994), as well as Davoli et al. (2005), distinguish methods to empirical and inspection methods, taking into account the participants of the experiment. Inspection methods are mainly conducted by experts. Several researchers have argued in favor of expert-based evaluations.

They focus on the advantages and mention that it is easier and cheaper compared to empirical methods (Reeves 1993; Karoulis et al. 2006). Furthermore, the correct choice of the experts would give reliable and valid results.

Empirical methods, on the other hand, are implemented with the participation of different categories of potential users of a museum's website. For the implementation of empirical methods direct observation, questionnaires and other techniques may be used for capturing the users' reactions and comments.

In view of the above, we have categorized the analyzed evaluation experiments of personalized systems in cultural heritage to two main groups: empirical methods, where real users participated (Table 3) and inspection methods where expert users participated (Table 4). Finally, there are some experiments that use a combination of the two methods (Table 5).

Empirical Methods

Generally, empirical methods are based on groups of end-users or museum visitors. These users are asked to access the software performing different tasks and their behavior is observed and/or their opinions are gathered. For this purpose, questionnaires (AmI, LISTEN, MyMuseum, PIL, LOCUS, CHIP, etc), Interview (Electronic Guidebook Exploratorium, GUIDE, CHESS, etc) and observation (GUIDE, Electronic Guidebook Exploratorium, GUIDE, etc.) are the main methods applied in empirical methods but questionnaires are the most commonly used. Some evaluation experiments involved several users (e.g Zimmerman & Lorenz 2008) while others were implemented with only a few participants (e.g. Bright et al. 2005, Hsi 2002).

In the case of personalized virtual guides, the most common evaluation method used is the empirical method. For example, Sundar et al. (2015) use questionnaires to evaluate the general characteristics of navigation in the virtual world by examining criteria such as orientation/navigability, interactivity, as well as customization/personalization. Similarly, Filippini-Fantoni (2003) uses the think-aloud method to evaluate a personalized virtual guide focusing on the interface, navigation, and access as well as the success of the personalization features.

A different kind of experiment is the one implemented by Ghiani et al. (2009), who have implemented an experiment where users had to perform certain tasks using two different versions of the same system, the personalized system and the standard system (no multi-device support, no adaptation, no RFID support). Similarly, Kuflik et al. (2011), during the PIL project, have used a non-adaptive version of the system and an adaptive version and compared them with respect of multimedia content preparation, user interface, user profiling, and group interaction. Kuflik et al. (2011) have implemented several evaluation experiments throughout the software's life cycle in order to improve the design of the final system. A number of user studies to evaluate the ideas underlying the many PEACH components and not the fully integrated system were designed by Stock et al. (2007). A summative evaluation of the personalized system is performed for the Electronic Guidebook Exploratorium (Hsi 2002).

Evaluation of a framework for the development of personalized software in cultural heritage is performed by using the framework to develop personalized software and then implementing a short experiment focussing on the success of suggestions (Bonis et al. 2009), adaptation (Caus et al. 2008), content and general technical issues.

Of course, there are recommendation systems that have not implemented yet an evaluation experiment but recognize the importance of an evaluation experiment and aim to plan one in the future. For example, Alexandridis et al. (2019) have implemented an offline evaluation that provides very encouraging results

Table 3. Empirical evaluations of recommendation systems for cultural heritage

System		Evaluation Tools						
		Questionnaire	**Interview**	**Observation**	**Certain tasks**	**Rating suggestions**	**Comparison of adaptive and non-adaptive system**	**Other**
Sundar et al. (2015)	MoMa		X	X				
Filippini-Fantoni (2003)	Museum Wearable	X		x				Think-aloud
Bonis et al. (2009)	PeVEP	X						
Garzotto et al. (2003; 2004)	MUSE	X				X		
Bright et al. (2005)	MyMuseum	x						
S. Hsi (2002)	Electronic Guidebook Exploratorium		X	x				
Fernie et al. (2012), Griffiths & Cal (2013)	PATHS			x	x			
Goren-Bar et al. (2005)	PEACH				x			
Kadobayashi et al. (1998)	Mediating Agent in the National Museum of Japanese History				X	x		
Karaman et al. (2016)	MNEMOSYNE	X						
Kuflik et al. (2011) & Lanir et al. (2011)	PIL	x		-			x	Log files
Marty (2011)	6 museums with digital collections				x			
Otegi et al. (2014)	PPR							Log files
Pujol et al. (2013)	CHESS		x	x				
Van Dijk et al. (2012; 2014)	Museon	x						
Van Hage et al. (2010) & Wang et al. (2008 & 2009) & Roes et al. 2009	CHIP	x						
Yu et al. (2009)	iMuseum		x					
Vlahakis et al. 2001	Archeoguide	x						
Ghiani et al. 2009	UbiCicero	X			x		X	

for their system. Although they have not implemented an experiment with real users or experts yet, they think that such an experiment is essential and plan to implement an empirical evaluation in the future as they conclude that this is the most suitable evaluation method for their system.

Inspection Method or Methods Without Users

In inspection methods, the experts have the central role and evaluate the website trying to spot errors and check several aspects of the website having careful attention to the user's point of view. There is a variety of inspection methods, using different types of guidelines, scenarios of use (Cuncliffe et al. 2001), etc. Liarokapis & Sylaiou (2010) have implemented an inspection method of LOCUS. During the life-cycle of LOCUS, some case studies were taking place involving human experts answering questionnaires, etc. Evaluation results for the above case studies have shown that both kiosk exhibitions and mobile guides have the power to provide personalized interaction. However, since the main scopus of an evaluation experiment of a personalized system is the success of the personalized process and the acceptability of the overall interaction, inspection methods are mainly combined with empirical methods while evaluating personalized software for cultural heritage.

Another way of evaluating a personalized in cultural heritage is simulating user behavior. In such evaluation experiments, user behavior was recorded and then simulated in order to allow experts to check the quality of the result of the personalization method. This method was applied to Museum Wearable and PEACH (Zancanaro et al. 2007). Similarly, during the evaluation of UbiquiTO (Cena et al. 2006), the interests of the users were predefined and then used them to evaluate system recommendations without letting the users evaluate the final product.

Combination of Two Methods

Taking into account the advantages and disadvantages of empirical and inspection methods, some evaluation experiments use both users and experts. For example, Hatala & Wakkary (2005) implement an empirical evaluation of the ec(h)o system in order to check whether the system performs the functions it was built for, based on the requirements specification. The inspection evaluation experiment focused on the depth of the content and meaningfulness of the interaction.

Combination of inspection and empirical method is also used in the evaluation experiment of AmI implemented by Partarakis et al. (2016a; 2016b). The expert-based evaluation experiment focuses on 'Usability' while the user-based evaluation experiment focuses on the overall user satisfaction, the quality of the provided information and the satisfaction regarding the interface provided by the system.

Table 4. Inspection Methods or methods without users for evaluating recommendation systems for cultural heritage

System		Evaluation Tools						
		Questionnaire	**Interview**	**Observation**	**Certain tasks**	**Rating suggestions**	**Comparison of adaptive and non-adaptive system**	**Other**
Liarokapis & Sylaiou (2010), Liarokapis et al. (2008)	LOCUS	x						
Bohnert & Zukerman (2009) & Bohnert et al. (2005)	Melbourne Museum						x	
Caus et al. (2008)	Hydra							

Table 5. Evaluations of recommendation systems for cultural heritage that use a combination of methods

System		Evaluation Tools						
		Questionnaire	**Interview**	**Observation**	**Certain tasks**	**Rating suggestions**	**Comparison of adaptive and non-adaptive system**	**Other**
Partarakis et al. (2016), Patrarakis et al. (2016)	AmI	X						
Zimmerman & Lorenz (2008), Terrenghi & Zimmerman (2004)	LISTEN	X						
Hatala & Wakkary (2005)	ec(h)o	X						
Cheverst et al. 2002	GUIDE		x	x				Walkthrough by experts

During the evaluation of LISTEN, three different evaluation experiments have taken place. In the first experiment, experts simulated the behavior of regular users in order to make a general evaluation of the system. In the second experiment, more emphasis was given on the improved user modeling process and the adaptation procedure while the third experiment was user-based and focused mainly on the acceptability of the system by real museum users.

DISUCSSION OF THE RESULTS OF THE EVALUATION EXPERIMENTS

The analysis of the evaluation experiments of personalized systems for cultural heritage revealed that the methods used may be divided into three main categories with respect to the users that participate in these experiments. As a result, the methods of evaluation have been divided into inspection methods and methods that simulated the behavior of real users (5 evaluations), empirical methods (22 evaluations) as well as methods where both real and expert users participate (4 evaluations).

The results of the evaluation experiments of different personalized systems in cultural heritage revealed how successful the personalized content delivery was and how successful the systems were in profiling the users interacting with these systems. In some cases, the users were largely supportive of the personalized interaction (Balwin et al 2011; Goren-Bar et al. 2005, Liarokapis et al. 2008). In other cases, the participants showed signs of not being used to the idea of scrutinizing the adaptation (Bright et al. 2005). There were evaluation experiments where the participants found the personalization fairly limited and quite superficial (Filippini-Fantoni 2003; Filippini-Fantoni & Bowen 2007). However, even the skeptical on the personalization admitted that the adapted information furthered their knowledge (Bright et al. 2005). In a minority of evaluation experiments, there was criticism concerning the use of stereotypes (Zimmerman &Lorenz 2008, Paternò & Mancini 1999).

In some cases, the users did not even notice that the user interface was personalized (Kuflik et al. 2011). But this can really be considered as an advantage because as Weibelzahl (2005) point out, good personalization should go unnoticed by the user who becomes aware of it only when there is a problem. Therefore, the desired effect is for personalized systems to be as less intrusive as possible. During the evaluation of CHESS, the users preferred to make their own choices through menus (rather than having the system deciding for them) due to their worry of missing out on something interesting (Pujol et al

2013). Indeed, an important issue in personalizing the interaction of the user with the cultural heritage is that the users should feel free to reject the system's recommendations and get on with their own choices.

Other experiments revealed that the usage of personalization features is confined better to certain categories of visitors such as young people, experts, teachers, students and frequent visitors (Filippini-Fantoni & Bowen 2007; Bright et al. 2005, Roes et al. 2009). However, the evaluation experiments do not conclude to the same categories of users. For example, Bright et al. (2005) as well as Terrenghi & Zimmerman (2004) support that the results of the personalization are more beneficiary for experts while Roes et al. (2009) and Van Hage et al. (2010) support that their system better helps novice users. This is probably due to the fact that these systems are very differently designed and use different personalization methods.

As a result, sometimes the results of the evaluation of the personalization system were used in order to improve the personalization process of a system (e.g. Ghiani et al. 2009, Kuflik et al. 2011). In other cases, different approaches for personalization have been compared. For example, Bohnert & Zuckerman (2009) compared the predictive performance of a memory-based nearest-neighbor collaborative ðlter, and a model-based approach utilizing the theory of Gaussian spatial processes. The results show that both models attain a higher predictive accuracy than a non-personalized baseline, with the second outperforming the first model.

Participants of some evaluation experiment enjoyed the incorporation and personalization of multimedia (Terrenghi & Zimmerman 2004, Pujol et al. 2013) or the incorporation of 3D objects (Bonis et al. 2009). We see that a new trend in the systems used in cultural heritage is personalizing multi-modal interaction and this was the issue of some evaluation experiments (e.g. Terrenghi & Zimmerman 2004, Liarokapis et al. 2008).

However, evaluation experiments also suffer from some drawbacks. For example, in the evaluation of the Marble Museum (Paternò & Mancini 1999), the usability problems were not distinguished from adaptivity issues. Furthermore, the small number of users participating in many of the evaluation experiments of personalized systems in cultural heritage is also an issue as it does not allow one to make strong conclusions.

FUTURE RESEARCH DIRECTIONS

The evaluation experiment is a critical phase of the software engineering life-cycle for any system and especially for personalized software that has to confirm that its mechanisms actually work and can successfully personalize to each user's characteristics. Lately, personalization techniques are employed in Smartphones and other mobile devices for navigating in cultural heritage. Mobile devices are very popular and include various applications that constantly collect data about the user. This information can be further used in order to personalize the interaction.

The need for evaluating the adaptive software of Smartphones and other mobile devices in cultural heritage is great. This study reveals that an evaluation experiment is a multi-dimensional and multi-criteria problem and, therefore, an evaluation framework that uses multi-criteria decision making theories could be very effective. Indeed, in the past, such frameworks have been developed for cultural heritage with the use of multi-criteria decision-making theories (Kabassi 2019). Generally, we see a trend for the use of multi-criteria decision making theories for evaluating cultural software (Kabassi & Martinis 2017; Kontogianni et al. 2018a; Kabassi 2019). However, these theories have not been used for developing an evaluation framework for personalized cultural software.

CONCLUSION

Different methods for adaptation and interaction, in general, could be effectively applied to personalize interaction in a museum (Antoniou and Lepouras 2010; Pujol et al. 2013), a virtual tour (Rajaonarivo et al. 2019), a city (Cheverst et al., 2000, Fink and Kobsa 2002; Scherp & Boll 2004; Wakkary et al. 2009) or an archeological site (Alexandridis et al. 2019). Except for method, different technologies have also been used to improve these tours. Especially, the mobile technology and the widespread of Smartphones have changed the way tourists are navigating outdoor and indoor. As a result, different recommendation systems have been implemented for improving and personalizing indoor and outdoor tours for exploring cultural heritage. However, recommendation systems can only confirm their usability and success if they are evaluated.

The evaluation experiments of personalized systems in cultural heritage are differentiated with respect to the method used, the number of participants, the criteria that are evaluated as well as the setting of the experiments. However, all experiments have a common goal, to test if the added value gained by the personalization of the interaction justifies the additional effort required for the development of these systems. The evaluation results revealed that there are researchers that are largely supportive of the personalized interaction (Balwin et al 2011; Goren-Bar et al. 2005, Liarokapis et al. 2008) and others that support that the personalization should be considerably improved to justify the extra effort of the incorporation of personalization procedures (Filippini-Fantoni 2003; Filippini-Fantoni & Bowen 2007). However, it is worth noticing that all evaluation experiments concluded that personalization improved the interaction of users with cultural heritage.

The implementation of these experiments is difficult and requires economical and staff resources. Therefore, the main problem identified in many of the experiments described in this paper is that many of these experiments involve a small number of participants. While small sample sizes are acceptable on multiphase usability projects (Petrie & Bevan 2009), a higher number of participants with diverse characteristics would have strengthened the statistical model and improved the generality of findings. Another problem of some evaluation experiments (e.g. Sylaiou et al. 2010) is that, although they have a satisfactory number of participants, these participants have similar characteristics (e.g. students of a specific department of a university).

REFERENCES

Aksenov, P., Kemperman, A., & Arentze, T. (2014). Toward personalized and dynamic cultural routing: A three-level approach. *Procedia Environmental Sciences*, *22*, 257–269. doi:10.1016/j.proenv.2014.11.025

Alexandridis, G., Chrysanthi, A., Tsekouras, G. E., & Caridakis, C. (2019). Personalized and content adaptive cultural heritage path recommendation: An application to the Gournia and Çatalhöyük archaeological sites. *User Modeling and User-Adapted Interaction*, *29*(1), 201–238. doi:10.100711257-019-09227-6

Ardissono, L., Goy, A., Petrone, G., Signan, M., & Torasso, P. (2003). Intrigue: Personalized recommendation of tourism attractions for desktop and handset devices. *Applied Artificial Intelligence*, *17*(8–9), 687–714. doi:10.1080/713827254

Ardissono, L., Kuflik, T., & Petrelli, D. (2012). Personalization in cultural heritage: The road travelled and the one ahead. *User Modeling and User-Adapted Interaction*, *22*(1-2), 73–99. doi:10.100711257-011-9104-x

Bagdanov, A. D., Del Bimbo, A., Landucci, L., & Pernici, F. (2011). MNEMOSYNE: Enhancing the Museum Experience through Interactive Media and Visual Profiling. In C. Grana & R. Cucchiara (Eds.), MM4CH 2011, CCIS 247, (pp. 39–50). Springer-Verlag Berlin Heidelberg.

Baldwin, T., Ye, P., Bohnert, F., & Zukerman, I. (2011). In Situ Text Summarisation for Museum Visitors. *25th Pacific Asia Conference on Language, Information and Computation*, 372–381.

Bay, H., Fase, B., & Van Gool, L. (2006). Interactive museum guide: Fast and robust recognition of museum objects. *Proceedings of the International Workshop on Mobile Vision.*

Bhargava, P., & Agrawala A.K. (2016). Modeling Users' Behavior from Large Scale Smartphone Data Collection. EAI Endorsed Trans. *Context-aware Systems & Applications, 3*(10).

Boehner, K., Thom-Santelli, J., Zoss, A., Gay, G., Hall, J. S., & Barrett, T. (2005). Imprints of Place: Creative Expressions of the Museum Experience. In *CHI 2005*. ACM.

Bohnert, F., & Zukerman, I. (2009). Non-intrusive Personalization of the Museum Experience. LNCS, 5535, 197–209.

Bonis, B., Stamos, J., Vosinakis, S., Andreou, I., & Panayiotopoulos, T. (2009). A Platform for Virtual Museums with Personalized Content. *Multimedia Tools and Applications*, *42*(2), 139–159. doi:10.100711042-008-0231-2

Bowen, J., & Filippini-Fantoni, S. (2004). Personalization and the Web from a Museum Perspective. In D. Bearman & J. Trant (Eds.), *Museums and the Web 2004: Selected Papers from an International Conference*, (pp. 63-78). Academic Press.

Bright, A., Kay, J., Ler, D., Ngo, K., Niu, W., & Nuguid, A. (2005). Adaptively Recommending Museum Tours. *Ubiquitous Computing, 7th International Conference on: Workshop: Smart Environments and their Applications to Cultural Heritage.*

Caus, T., Christmann, S., & Hagenhoff, S. (2008). Hydra – An Application Framework for the Development of Context-Aware Mobile Services. *LNBIP*, *7*, 471–481.

Cena, F., Console, L., Gena, C., Goy, A., Levi, G., Modeo, S., & Torre, I. (2006). Integrating heterogeneous adaptation techniques to build a flexible and usable mobile tourist guide. *AI Communications*, *19*(4), 369–384.

Cheverst, K., Mitchell, K., & Davies, N. (2002). The role of adaptive hypermedia in a context-aware tourist GUIDE. *Communications of the ACM*, *45*(5), 47–51. doi:10.1145/506218.506244

Chiou, W.-C., Lin, C.-C., & Perng, C. (2010). A Strategic Framework for Website Evaluation Based on a Review of the Literature from 1995-2006. *Information & Management*, *47*(5-6), 282–290. doi:10.1016/j.im.2010.06.002

Crespo, G. (2010). Intelligent Decision-Support Systems for e-Tourism: Using SPETA II as a Knowledge Management Platform for DMOs and e-Tourism Service Providers. *International Journal of Decision Support System Technology*, *2*(1), 36–48. doi:10.4018/jdsst.2010101603

Cuncliffe, D., Kritou, E., & Tudhope, D. (2001). Usability evaluation for museum web sites. *Museum Management and Curatorship*, *19*(3), 229–252. doi:10.1080/09647770100201903

Damala, A., Stojanovic, N., Schuchert, T., Moragues, J., Cabrera, A., & Gilleade, K. (2012). Adaptive augmented reality for cultural heritage: Artsense project. In M. Ioannides, D. Fritsch, J. Leissner, R. Davies, F. Remondino, & R. Caffo (Eds.), *Progress in Cultural Heritage Preservation* (pp. 746–755). Berlin: Springer. doi:10.1007/978-3-642-34234-9_79

Damala, A., Stojanovic, N., Schuchert, T., Moragues, J., Cabrera, A., & Gilleade, K. (2012). Adaptive augmented reality for cultural heritage: Artsense project. In M. Ioannides, D. Fritsch, J. Leissner, R. Davies, F. Remondino, & R. Caffo (Eds.), *Progress in Cultural Heritage Preservation* (pp. 746–755). Berlin: Springer. doi:10.1007/978-3-642-34234-9_79

Davoli, P., Mazzoni, F., & Corradini, E. (2005). Quality Assessment of Cultural Web Sites with Fuzzy Operators. *Journal of Computer Information Systems*, *46*(1), 44–57.

Dowden, R., & Sayre, S. (2009). Tear down the walls: The redesign of ArtsConnectEd. In J. Trant & D. Bearman (Eds.), *Museums and the Web 2009*. Toronto, CA: Archives & Museum Informatics. Retrieved from http://www.archimuse.com/mw2009/papers/dowden/dowden.html

Dupuy, A. (2014). Digital extension of the museum of marseilles towards a global museum built both in the real and the digital world. In N. Proctor & R. Cherry (Eds.), Museums and the Web. Academic Press.

Falk, J. (2009). *Identity and the Museum Visit Experience*. Walnut Creek, CA: Left Coast Press.

Fernie, K., Griffiths, J., Stevenson, M., Clough, P. D., Goodale, P., Agirre, E., & Bergheim, S. R. (2012). PATHS: Personalizing access to cultural heritage spaces. *Proceedings of 18th Int Conference on Virtual Systems and Multimedia (VSMM 2012)*, 469-474. 10.1109/VSMM.2012.6365960

Filippini-Fantoni, S. (2003). Personalization through IT in museums. *ICHIM 03: International Cultural Heritage Informatics Meeting*.

Filippini Fantoni, S., & Bowen, J. P. (2007). Bookmarking in museums: Extending the museum experience beyond the visit? In J. Trant & D. Bearman (Eds.), *Museums and the Web 2007*. Toronto: Archives & Museum Informatics. Retrieved from http://www.archimuse.com/mw2007/papers/filippini-fantoni/filippini-fantoni.html

Fink, J., & Kobsa, A. (2002). User Modeling for Personalized City Tours. *Artificial Intelligence Review*, *18*(1), 33–74. doi:10.1023/A:1016383418977

Garcia Cerspo, A., Chamizo, J., Rivera, I., Mncke, M., Colomo Palaciosm, R., & Gomez Berbis, J. M. (2009). SPETA: Social pervasive e-Tourism advisor. *Telematics and Informatics*, *26*(3), 306–315. doi:10.1016/j.tele.2008.11.008

Garzotto, F., Cinotti, T., & Pigozzi, M. (2003). Designing multi-channel web frameworks for cultural tourism applications: the MUSE case study. *Proceedings of the International Conference for Culture and Heritage Online 2003 on Museums and the Web.*

Garzotto, F., Salmon Cinotti, T., Raffa, G., Roffia, L., Muzii, R., Varlese, V., . . . Galasso, S. (2004). Evaluating Context-Aware Mobile Applications In Museums: Experiences from the MUSE Project. Proceedings Museums and the Web 2004.

Gerber, S., Pink, G., Fry, M., Kay, J., Kummerfeld, R., & Wasinger, R. (2010) PersonisJ: mobile, client-side user modelling. *User Modeling, Adaptation and Personalization.*

Ghiani, G., Paterno, F., Santoro, C., & Spano, L. D. (2009). UbiCicero: A location-aware, multi-device museum guide. *Interacting with Computers*, *21*(4), 288–303. doi:10.1016/j.intcom.2009.06.001

Goren-Bar, D., Graziola, I., Pianesi, F., Rocchi, C., Stock, O., & Zancanaro, M. (2005). I like it – Affective Control of Information Flow in a Personalized Mobile Museum Guide. *Proceedings of the CHI Workshop on Innovative Approaches to Evaluating Affective Interfaces.*

Griffiths, J. R., Goodale, P., Minelli, S., de Pollo, A., Agerri, R., Soroa, A., . . . Usher, T. (2013). *D5.1 Evaluation of the 1st PATHS Prototype.* Retrieved from http://www.paths-project.eu/eng/Resources/D5.1-Evaluation-of-the-1st-PATHS-Prototype

Hatala, M., & Wakkary, R. (2005). Ontology-Based User Modeling in an Augmented Audio Reality System for Museums. *User Modeling and User-Adapted Interaction*, *15*(3-4), 339–380. doi:10.100711257-005-2304-5

Hendrix, J. C. (2010). *Checking Out the Future: Perspectives from the Library* Community *on Information Technology and 21st Century Libraries.* ALA Office for Information Technology Policy Brief, No. 2. Available at: www.ala.org/ala/aboutala/offices/oitp/publications/policybriefs/ala_checking_out_the.pdf

Hsi, S. (2002). The Electronic Guidebook: A study of user experiences using mobile web content in a museum setting. *Proceedings of the IEEE International Workshop on Wireless and Mobile Technologies in Education.* 10.1109/WMTE.2002.1039220

Jeong, J. H., & Lee, K. H. (2006). The physical environment in museums and its effects on visitors' satisfaction. *Building and Environment*, *41*(7), 963–969. doi:10.1016/j.buildenv.2005.04.004

Kabassi, K. (2017a). Evaluating Websites of Museums: State of the Art. *Journal of Cultural Heritage*, *24*, 184–196. doi:10.1016/j.culher.2016.10.016

Kabassi, K. (2017b). Evaluation of Personalised Software in Cultural Heritage: An Exploratory Study. *International Journal of Computational Methods in Heritage Science*, *1*(1), 41–57. doi:10.4018/IJCMHS.2017010103

Kabassi, K. (2019). *Evaluating Museum Websites Using a Combination of Decision-Making Theories. Journal of Heritage Tourism.* Taylor & Francis Online. doi:10.1080/1743873X.2019.1574301

Kabassi, K., & Martinis, A. (2017) Multi-Criteria Decision Making in the Evaluation of the Thematic Museums' Websites", Springer Proceed. *Proceedings of the 4th International Conference on "Innovative Approaches to Tourism and Leisure: Culture, Places and Narratives in a Sustainability Context".*

Kadobayashi, R., Nishimoto, K., Sumi, Y., & Mase, K. (1998). Evaluation of mediating agents that personalize museum exhibitions. *Proceedings of the Ninth International Workshop on Database and Expert Systems Applications* 10.1109/DEXA.1998.707447

Kamar, A. (2003). *Mobile tourist guide (m-ToGuide).* Deliverable 1.4, Project Final Report. IST2001-36004.

Karaman, S., Bagdanov, A. D., Landucci, L., D'Amico, G., Ferracani, A., Pezzatini, D., & Del Bimbo, A. (2016). Personalized multimedia content delivery on an interactive table by passive observation of museum visitors. *Multimedia Tools and Applications*, *75*(7), 3787–3811. doi:10.100711042-014-2192-y

Karoulis, A., Sylaiou, S., & White, M. (2006). Usability Evaluation of a Virtual Museum Interface. *Informatica*, *17*(3), 363–380.

Katifori, A., Karvounis, M., Kourtis, V., Kyriakidi, M., Roussou, M., Tsangaris, M., ... Pujol, L. (2014). Chess: personalized storytelling experiences in museums. In A. Mitchell, C. Fernández-Vara, & D. Thue (Eds.), *Interactive Storytelling* (pp. 232–235). Springer International Publishing.

Kontogianni, A., Kabassi, K., & Alepis, E. (2018a). Designing a Smart Tourism Mobile Application: User Modelling through Social Networks' User Implicit Data. *Springer Lecture Notes in Computer Science series*, 148-158.

Kontogianni, A., Kabassi, K., Virvou, M., & Alepis, A. (2018b). Smart Tourism through social network user modeling: a literature review. *9th International Conference on Information, Intelligence, Systems and Applications*. 10.1109/IISA.2018.8633633

Kuflik, T., & Poteriaykina, K. (2009). User Model on a Key. *Hypertext*, *2009*, 371–372.

Kuflik, T., Stock, O., Zancanaro, M., Gorfinkel, A., Jbara, S., Kats, S., Sheidin, J. & Kashtan, N. (2011). A Visitor's Guide in an "Active Museum": Presentations, Communications, and Reflection. *ACM Journal of Computing and Cultural Heritage*, *3*(3) article 11.

Lanir, J., Kuflik, T., Wecker, A. J., Stock, O., & Zancanaro, M. (2011). Examining proactiveness and choice in a location-aware mobile museum guide. *Interacting with Computers*, *23*(5), 513–524. doi:10.1016/j.intcom.2011.05.007

Lanir, J., Kuflik, T., Zolantz, I., & Lanzet, U. (2013). Personalized video summary of a museum visit. AI* HCI@ AI* IA.

Lewis, C., & Rieman, J. (1994). *Task-eentered User Interface Design: A Practical Introduction*. Boulder, CO: University of Colorado.

Liarokapis, F., & Sylaiou, S. (2010). Experiencing Personalized Heritage Exhibitions through Multimodal Mixed Reality Interfaces. In *Proceedings, of the 5th International Workshop on Ubiquitous and Collaborative Computing (iUBICOM '10), In conjunction with the 24th BCS Conference on Human Computer Interaction (HCI 2010)*. University of Abertay.

Liarokapis, F., Sylaiou, S., & Mountain, D. (2008). Personalizing Virtual and Augmented Reality for Cultural Heritage Indoor and Outdoor Experiences. *Proceedings of the 9th International Symposium on Virtual Reality, Archaeology and Cultural Heritage*, 55-62.

Marty, P. F. (2011). My lost museum: User expectations and motivations for creating personal digital collections on museum websites. *Library & Information Science Research*, *33*(3), 211–219. doi:10.1016/j.lisr.2010.11.003

Munnelly, G., Hampson, C., Lawless, S., & Conlan O. (2013). The CULTURA Portal - Exploring Cultural Treasures. *TPDL Workshops*, 155-158.

Nelson, A. G., & Cohn, S. (2015). Data Collection Methods for Evaluating Museum Programs and Exhibitions. *Journal of Museum Education*, *40*(1), 27–36. doi:10.1080/10598650.2015.11510830

Not, E., & Petrelli, D. (2018). Blending customisation, context-awareness and adaptivity for personalised tangible interaction in cultural heritage. *International Journal of Human-Computer Studies*, *114*, 3–19. doi:10.1016/j.ijhcs.2018.01.001

Otegi, A., Agiree, E., & Clough, P. (2014). Personalized PageRank for Making Recommendations in Digital Cultural Heritage Collections. *Proceeding JCDL '14 Proceedings of the 14th ACM/IEEE-CS Joint Conference on Digital Libraries*, 49-52.

Partarakis, N., Antona, M., & Stephanidis, C. (2016a). Adaptable, Personalizable and Multi User Museum Exhibits. Curating the Digital, Springer Series on Cultural Computing, 167-179

Partarakis, N., Antona, M., Zidianakis, E., & Stephanidis, C. (2016b). Adaptation and content personalization in the context of multi user museum exhibits. *Proceedings of the 1st Workshop on Advanced Visual Interfaces for Cultural Heritage (AVI*CH 2016)*, 1621.

Paternò, F., & Mancini, C. (1999). Designing web user interfaces adaptable to different types of use. *Proceedings of the International Conference for Culture and Heritage Online 1999 on Museums and the Web*. Retrieved from http://www.archimuse.com/mw99/papers/paterno/paterno.html

Pechenizkiy, M., & Calders, T. (2007). A Framework for Guiding the Museum Tours Personalization. *Proceedings of the Workshop on Personalized Access to Cultural Heritage (PATCH'07)*, 11-28.

Petrelli, D., & Not, E. (2005). User-centred design of flexible hypermedia for a mobile guide: Reflections on the hyperaudio experience. *User Modeling and User-Adapted Interaction*, *15*(3–4), 303–338. doi:10.100711257-005-8816-1

Petrelli, D., & Not, E. (2019). Empowering cultural heritage professionals with tools for authoring and deploying personalised visitor experiences. *User Modeling and User-Adapted Interaction*, *29*(1), 64–120. doi:10.100711257-019-09224-9

Petrelli, D., Not, E., Sarini, M., Stock, O., Strapparava, C., & Zancanaro, M. (1999). HyperAudio: Location-Awareness +Adaptivity. *Proceeding of Conference on Human Factors in Computing Systems*, 21-22.

Petrelli, D., Not, E., Zancanaro, M., Strapparava, C., & Stock, O. (2001). Modelling and adapting to context. *Personal and Ubiquitous Computing*, *5*(1), 20–24. doi:10.1007007790170023

Petrie, H., & Bevan, N. (2009). The Evaluation of Accessibility, Usability and User Experience. In C. Stephanidis (Ed.), The Universal Access Handbook, (pp. 10-20). Boca Raton, FL: CRC Press.

Proctor, N., & Tellis, C. (2003). *The State of the Art in Museum Handhelds in 2003, Museums and the Web*. Retrieved from http://www.archimuse.com/mw2003/papers/proctor/proctor.html

Pujol, L., Katifori, A., Vayanou, M., Roussou, M., Karvounis, M., Kyriakidi, M., . . . Ioannidis, Y. (2013). From personalization to adaptivity - Creating immersive visits through interactive digital storytelling at the Acropolis Museum. In J.A. Botνa & D. Charitos (Eds.), *Workshop Proceedings of the 9th International Conference on Intelligent Environments*. (pp. 541-554). Academic Press.

Reeves, T. C. (1993). Evaluating technology-based learning. In G. M. Piskurich (Ed.), *The ASTD Handbook of Instructional Technology* (pp. 15.1–15.32). New York: McGraw-Hill.

Roes, I., Stash, N., Wang, Y., & Aroyo, L. (2009). A Personalized Walk through the Museum: The CHIP Interactive Tour Guide. *CHI, 2009*, 3317–3322.

Roth, J. (2002). Context-aware web applications using the pinpoint. In *IADIS International Conference WWW/Internet 2002*. IADIS Press.

Rousou, M., Katifori, A., Pujol, L., Vayanou, M., & Rennick-Egglestone, S. (2013). A Life of Their Own: Museum Visitor Personas Penetrating the Design Lifecycle of a Mobile Experience. *CHI 2013 Extended Abstracts*, 547-552.

Rutledge, L., Aroyo, L., & Stash, N. (2006). Determining user interests about museum collections. *Proceedings of the 15th International Conference on World Wide Web (WWW'06)*, 855–856. 10.1145/1135777.1135912

Saaty, T. L. (1980). *The analytic hierarchy process*. New York, NY: McGraw-Hill.

Sansonetti, G., Gasparetti, F., Micarelli, A., Cena, F., & Gena, C. (2019). Enhancing cultural recommendations through social and linked open data. *User Modeling and User-Adapted Interaction, 29*(1), 121–159. doi:10.100711257-019-09225-8

Satyanarayanan, M. (2001). Interview on Mobile and Pervasive Computing. *IEEE Distributed Systems Online, 2*(6).

Scherp, A., & Boll, S. (2004). Generic support for personalized mobile multimedia tourist applications. *ACM Multimedia 2004 - proceedings of the 12th ACM International Conference on Multimedia,* 178-179.

Spasojevic, M., & Kindberg, T. (2001). Evaluating the CoolTown User Experience. *Ubicomp'01 Workshop: Evaluation Methodologies for Ubiquitous Computing*. Retrieved from http://zing.ncsl.nist.gov/ubicomp01/papers/Exploratorium-UbicompPosition.pdf

Stock, O., Zancanaro, M., Busetta, P., Callaway, C., Krüger, A., Kruppa, M., ... Rocchi, C. (2007). Adaptive, intelligent presentation of information for the museum visitor in PEACH. *User Modeling and User-Adapted Interaction, 17*(3), 257–304. doi:10.100711257-007-9029-6

Sundar, S., Go, E., Hyang-Sook, K., & Zhang, B. (2015). Communicating Art, Virtually! Psychological Effects of Technological Affordances in a Virtual Museum. *International Journal of Human-Computer Interaction, 31*(6), 385–401. doi:10.1080/10447318.2015.1033912

Terrenghi, L., & Zimmerman, A. (2004). Tailored Audio Augmented Environments for Museums. *IUI '04 Proceedings of the 9th international conference on Intelligent user interfaces*, 334-336.

Van Dijk, B., Lingnau, A., & Kockelkom, H. (2012). Measuring Enjoyment of an Interactive Museum Experience. ICMI'12.

Van Dijk, B., Lingnau, A., Vissers, G., & Kockelkom, H. (2014). Individual and Collaborative Personalization in a Science Museum. In Playful User Interfaces, Gaming Media and Social Effects. Springer Science+Business Media Singapore.

Van Hage, W. R., Stash, N., Wang, Y., & Aroyo, L. (2010). Finding Your Way through the Rijksmuseum with an Adaptive Mobile Museum Guide. In ESWC 2010: The Semantic Web: Research and Applications. Springer-Verlag Berlin Heidelberg

Vayanou, M., Katifori, A., Karvounis, M., Kourtis, V., Kyriakidi, M., Roussou, M., ... Pujol, L. (2014). Authoring personalized interactive museum stories. In A. Mitchell, C. Fernández-Vara, & D. Thue (Eds.), *Interactive Storytelling* (pp. 37–48). Springer International Publishing.

Vlahakis, V., Karigiannis, J., Tsotros, M., Gounaris, M., Almeida, L., Stricker, D., . . . Ioannidis, N. (2001). Archeoguide: first results of an augmented reality, mobile computing system in cultural heritage sites. *VAST '01 Proceedings of the 2001 conference on Virtual reality, archaeology, and cultural heritage*, 131-140.

Wakkary, R., & Hatala, M. (2006). ec(h)o: Situated play in a tangible and audio museum guide. *Proceedings of the 6th Conference on Designing Interactive systems*, 281–290. 10.1145/1142405.1142448

Wakkary, R., Hatala, M., Muise, K., Tanenbaum, K., & Budd, J. (2009). Kurio: a museum guide for families. *Proceedings of 3rd International Conference on Tangible and Embedded Interaction*, 215–222.

Wang, Y., Stash, N., Aroyo, L., Gorgels, P., Rutledge, L., & Schreiber, G. (2008). Recommendations based on semantically enriched museum collections. *Journal of Web Semantics, 6*(4), 283–290. doi:10.1016/j.websem.2008.09.002

Wang, Y., Stash, N., Sambeek, R., Schuurmans, Y., Aroyo, L., Schreiber, G., & Gorgels, P. (2009). Cultivating Personalized Museum Tours Online and On-Site. *Interdisciplinary Science Reviews, 34*(2–3), 139–153. doi:10.1179/174327909X441072

WebGuide. (2001). *WebGuide: A City Guide for the internet. European Media Lab.* Retrieved from http://www.eml.org/english/research/deepmap/deepgis/webguide.html

Weibelzahl, S. (2005). Problems and pitfalls in evaluating adaptive systems. In Adaptable and Adaptive Hypermedia Systems, (pp. 285–299). IRM Press.

Wilson, G. (2004). Multimedia tour programmer at Tate Modern. *Proceedings of Museums and the Web.*

Yang, Y., & Marques, N. C. (2005). User group profile modeling based on user transactional data for personalized systems. Lect. Notes Comput. Sci., 3808, 337–347. doi:10.1007/11595014_34

Yu, Z., Zhou, X., Yu, Z., Hyuk Park, J., & Ma, J. (2008). iMuseum: A scalable context-aware intelligent museum system. *Computer Communications*, *31*(18), 4376–4382. doi:10.1016/j.comcom.2008.05.004

Zancanaro, M., Kuflik, T., Boger, Z., Goren-Bar, D., & Goldwasser, D. (2007). Analyzing museum visitors' behavior patterns. In C. Conati, K. F. McCoy, & G. Paliouras (Eds.), Lecture Notes in Computer Science: Vol. 451. *User Modeling* (pp. 238–246). Heidelberg, Germany: Springer.

Zimmerman, A., & Lorenz, A. (2008). LISTEN: A user-adaptive audio-augmented museum guide. *User Modeling and User-Adapted Interaction*, *18*(5), 389–416. doi:10.100711257-008-9049-x

Chapter 11
Virtual Dark Tourism:
The Role of Sound Branding and Augmented Reality for Death Sites

Maximiliano Emanuel Korstanje
University of Palermo, Buenos Aires, Argentina

Handayani Bintang
https://orcid.org/0000-0002-3324-7486
Independent Researcher, Indonesia

ABSTRACT

Death is a great unifier, not only for one who is in grief but also those who have similar shared values (i.e., tourist demand for visiting death sites). In this sense, visitation to the death sites denotes its importance to people's lives. However, as types of death sites are distinctively different from one to another, death sites as tourist attraction remains a segmented target market. This chapter looks at some viewpoints for making death sites not only for a segmented target market, which leads to discourse of virtual dark tourism (VDT) formation. With sound branding coupled with augmented reality (AR) as tools to support the claims of virtual dark tourism, death sites, which are considered exclusive touristic market offerings, presumably could be consumed by more target markets. Several issues and direction for future research are discussed.

INTRODUCTION

In the post-modern society, the life expectancy was expanded creating new benefits and opportunities for aging citizens. The bio-technology which was systematically applied to the life expectancy and the war-fare enhanced the quality of life in global cities while changing the disposition of subject to death. As Phillip Aries (1975) puts it, technology made the life safer though the figure of death became wilder. The same in other terms, postmodernism domesticated indeed the death expanding the life expectancy –in comparison to Middle Age- while potentiating its psychological effects in society. In the book *The Rise of Thana Capitalism and Tourism,* Korstanje (2016) argues convincingly that lay-tourists look to

DOI: 10.4018/978-1-7998-2871-6.ch011

gaze "the other´s death" in order to reinforce their own sentiment of supremacy and narcissism. They feel that after all, they belong to the "privilege class". This explains why dark tourism has situated as an emerging and growing segment over the recent years (Lennon & Foley, 2000; Stone 2006; Stone & Sharpley 2008). Quite aside from this and the attention given to dark tourism, Virtual Dark Tourism (VDT) still remains in its infancy. Technology often potentiates and declines dark tourist destinations. To some extent, VDT derives from the notion of Virtual reality (VR) and Augmented Reality (AR) as two key forces towards the enrichment of sound branding. Despite of studies on AR and VR in Tourism Destination and Mobile phone context has been discussed in the literature (see Cheong, 1995; Julier, Lanzagorta, Baillot, Rosenblum, Feiner, Hollerer & Sestito, 2000; Vlahakis, Karigiannis, Tsotros, Gounaris, Almeida, Stricker & Ioannidis, 2001; Fritz, F., Susperregui & Linaza, 2005;Marimon, Sarasua, Carrasco, Álvarez, Montesa, Adamek, ... & Gascó, 2010; Kounavis, Kasimati & Zamani, 2012; Yovcheva, Buhalis & Gatzidis, 2012; Linaza, Marimón, Carrasco, Álvarez, Montesa, Aguilar & Diez, 2012; Han, Jung & Gibson, 2013;Tussyadiah, Wang & Jia, 2017; Tussyadiah, 2017), much remains to be explored in the case of VDT. The specialized literature suggests that AR as well as VDT combines element of interactions which often mediate between the virtual tourist and the visited landscape. Most probably, this new emerging segment substantially changes the essence of classic tourism (Alimamy, Deans & Gnoth, 2017). In this token, Wilkinson (2010), and Stone (2006) debate to what extent death-related sites are not only formed by attraction-driven but also by tourist-demand forces. The emotional theory –e.g. Sound Branding (Westermann, 2008; Robinson, 2014; Doucleff, 2012; Yang & Lee, 2009; Zangwill, 2004; Yang & Lee, 2004; Sloboda, 1999; Kivy, 1991) occupies a central position in the configuration of tourist experience as well as the co-values created in the dark sites. Specifically, AR revolves around incorporation of digital elements into the physical world through technology gives interactivity and enhances the physical world by adding elements such as textual content, URL links, video and audio into previously static objects (Vaughan-Nichols, 2009). Further, the difference between AR and VR is that VR fully replaces the physical world with another world whereas AR retains the existing world but with additional information (Alimamy, Deans & Gnoth, 2017). However, the intertwined variables of VDT in the context of development of Death sites, proliferation of ICT e.g. AR and Sound Branding seem to be limited in the literature.

This study presents the role of Sound branding and AR on the development of death sites i.e. Trunyan cemetery. It is suggested that Sound Branding coupled with AR offers liminal opportunities in giving brand image to death sites. Not only it may enrich the identity of death sites as premium market offerings, which would make the experience co-creation more applicable but also it offers death sites to be consumed by larger market share, without lessen death sites' profile as attraction-driven and/or without lessen its exclusiveness of "darkness" attributed to death sites. The discussion is oriented to widely validate that shared values can be harnessed by applying Sound branding in general and/or by a certain song specifically. Utilising the narrative of dark themed songs, this study examines the core musical melody and lyrics, coupled with AR as tourism drivers. In order to draw the link among the song, VR, AR, and the death sites profile, this study is guided by social constructionist research philosophy, coupled with Semiology and Compositional interpretation, the analysis offers valuable clues to position sites built around the narratives of death. Carl-Frank Westermann (2008) reminds that sounds have a direct impact on human emotions while Robinson (2014) stresses on the interplay on emotion and music. However, far from being conclusive, the connection of emotion and music is subject to a great controversy. Some studies have indicated that music has nothing to do with emotion (Zangwill 2004; Kivy 1991; Sloboda, 1999; Doucleff 2012; Yang & Lee 2004; 2009). This begs the question to what extent sound branding may be applied to dark sites?

LITERATURE REVIEW: SOUND BRANDING IN DARK TOURISM SPECTRUM

Originally, anthropology and ethnology pivoted in the study of music and its impact in the culture. Musicology revealed not only how our hopes and fears can be represented by music but also its direct correlation with the economic production (Merriam & Merriam, 1964; Juslin & Slodoboda, 2001; Vila 2014). For a long time, the role of sound in the branding process was systematically neglected by specialists (Westermann 2008), though recent investigation proved the opposite. The process of sound branding offers a fertile ground towards the formation of common values, identity and imagined landscapes (He, Jin, Xiong, Chen, Sun & Zhao, 2008). A song of Adele (2011) for instance is used for teaching English in Indonesia context (e.g. Jati, 2014). Particularly, it aims to "improve listening comprehension, reading, guessing, and composition skills" (Murphey, 1992; Duff and Maley, 2007). As past studies suggest that certain features of music are consistently associated with producing strong emotions in listeners, combined with heartfelt lyrics and a powerhouse voice, hence these structures can send reward signals to our brains that rival any other pleasure (Doucleff, 2012).

Adapting contemporary theory of branding in general and theory of personification and/or impression management on the death sites particularly, Handayani, Ivanov & Korstanje (2016) indicate that the development design should be revolved around philosophical views of Smart tourism coupled with Slow tourism. In this respect, development design of death sites is accordingly based on emotional and unique selling propositions (Kotler, Armstrong, Saunders & Wong (1999). This is in line with past studies that suggest for selecting sound branding for market offerings, is aimed to develop sound creations that are derived from the details of brand values and that characterize the brand (Westermann, 2008). Ther

Therefore, the selection of Sound which refers to music should be applied in line with the philosophy of Smartness and Slow tourism. While Smart tourism indicates application of ICT in supporting the supply aspects of attractions and destination attributes (Gretzel, Sigala, Xiang & Koo, 2015; Neuhofer, Buhalis & Ladkin, 2015) and/or encourages the co-creation shared values e.g. User-Generated Content (UGC) (Arriga & Levina, 2008; Gretzel, Fesenmaier, Lee & Tussyadiah, 2010), Slow tourism advocates the use of Sound branding should be in line with "right speed" i.e. the tempo of travel slowly and locally (Honoré, 2009; Dickinson & Lumsdon; 2010; Caffyn, 2009: Oh, Assaf & Baloglu, 2014). In this token, while proliferation of ICTs can be interpreted as the used of AR, the term of "right speed" i.e. the tempo of travel slowly and locally can be interpreted as "right tempo" of Sound branding that is used to characterize the type of death sites and its shared values. Technically, the Sound branding i.e. certain song(s) to be selected is the one that denotes the "darkness" elements of circle of life. As Handayani & George (2016) put it, people learn to (re)live the goodness of being alive, being vulnerable, being happy and being sad. Presumably these are the most intriguing aspects of life that becomes commodification that may (may not) be useful to be revelation and contemplation for human being. With this view point, the use of Sound branding can be optimized, not only for the purposes of satisfying tourist's needs and want but also most importantly is for the creative design making death sites to be able to be consumed by larger market shares without making it is less exclusive. This explains why Sound branding could sharpen brand image and may enhance recognition on "darkness" elements (e.g. sorrowfulness) attributed to Death Sites. Therefore, interpretation of the selected song(s) should be indicating meanings that can be interpreted as for instance the word of "home" denotes not only a place where a man can be rested (sleep, eat, and do activities comfortably) but also can be signifying "a grave" where a man is rested for good. Doubtlessly, this interpretation of the word "Home" would also emerge as conflicted perceived reality which is subjected to individual shared values who is gazing at death, which is framed based on frame of reference and framework of experiences. Therefore, the gap between "us" and "them" emerged as its reality perceived by the host-community and the guest(s).

Robinson (2014) acknowledges that the act of listening music coincides with the needs to grasp its harmonic, melodic and rhythmic structure or form. Consequently, a song that is selected for the death sites must be in line with the "darkness" elements of identity and images attributed to its profile. Contemporary music to represent "darkness" elements of identity and images attributed to death sites profile normally utilising orchestra, as depicted in horror movie. Research seems to be limited on how the death sites development to be designed coupled with the ICT proliferation (i.e. indicated in Smart tourism) and philosophy of "right speed" experiences advocated by Slow tourism (i.e. to travel slowly and locally). Consequently, the crucial questions to be answered are: (1) what kind of target market that needs Sound as enrichment for experiencing death sites? (2) to what extent the importance of Sound branding relevant to death sites?; (3) what does Sound branding do?

The intertwined relationship among ICT, music, emotion, and the spectrum of Sound branding emerged as inevitable phenomenon, it lays foundations on the tendency that people post-modern society engages actively with high-technology. No less true that real-time interaction with their significant others is existed. Worries of this nature ushered Kozinets (2015) into the thesis that in the years to come branding process rests on the need of searching truth as the main ontological project of the lay-citizen. To put this slightly in bluntly, the search for natural culture implies the movement towards the genuine existence of the self. In addition, he suggests that relational matters much as people are looking for authenticity, the authentic selves. It involves our relationship to one another and our relationship to what we find to be the World around us. Interpersonal communication according to theory of human communication revolves around delivering the message rightly i.e. the message is received but what is most important, a correct re-codification of the meaning of the message as mutually-interpreted by either parties, which means by encoder and decoder. This can be evaluated accordingly based on the feedback phases. As a result of this, interpersonal communication also denotes the importance of relationships built as effect of the successful feedback and/or the message is received rightly (Griffin, 2011).

The above noted point raises a more than interesting question, what is the intersection of virtual tourism and the augmented reality?

THE AUGMENTED REALITY

In practical terms, Augmented Experience is interpreted as the sound sharpens brand image and enhances recognition of death sites, and is derived CGC activities. Importantly, CGC serves as trigger for circular communication among visitors in the virtual sphere i.e. CGM, sharing their shared values by exposing their feelings to others about their post-visitation to the death sites. Somewhere between the lights, the towers, the pleasurably activities, people are looking for experience something different from human communication and interaction. The act of travel not only ignites an ancient rite of passage, vulnerating the epistemological borders of the known, but also needs from the alterity to reach what Dean Maccannell dubbed as *staged authenticity* (MacCannell, 1976). In this respect, some critical voices brought the problem of alienation into the foreground (Xue, Manuel-Navarrete & Buzinde, 2014). Some emergent study-cases evince that when tourism is adopted in an unregulated manner, the risks the branding process turns in negative effects for locals such as gentrification, discriminative practices or resentment against tourists, are higher than in those cases, where tourism couples with other stronger industries (Korstanje 2012; Skoll & Korstanje, 2014). Doubtless, the formation of authenticity, which is vital for the configuration of heritage, plays a vital role in offering to strangers a spectacle which is externally designed to meet their hopes and ideological expectances (Korstanje 2012; Tzanelli, 2016). In this token, Rickly-Boyd (2012, p.273) has widely discussed how the sense of authenticity conforms the postmodern world of consumption. She believes that although not unified in approach, postmodernists do not consider inauthenticity a problem and, therefore, engage concepts such as ''hyperreality'' and ''simulacra''. The hyperreal is a simulated experience that fulfils the desire for the ''real'' (Eco, 1986), while simulacra is the increasing representation of the hyperreal with signs (Baudrillard, 1983). Lash and Urry (1993) -in their seminal book *Economies of Signs and Space*- alert on the immediacy of a new modernity where signs and a reflexive aesthetics prevail. The late-capitalism was succeeded in reformulating the means of production towards more abstract forms. The signs not only denote certain type of production but also connect the self with a broader (sensible) space. Hence, the well-famous "tourist gaze" reformulates a new –moulded- self who are in quest of expropriating spaces which are visually commoditized. In this respect, tourism -which is a force born in the modernity- reorganize two contrasting forces (labour and leisure) into a coherent product. This means that spaces are consumed according to an aesthetic and preceding sign that gives value to them. The same can be very well applied to the configuration of nature as well as the position of the self in the enviroment. The dark product seems to be a novel way of domesticating the uncertainty in order for the social trauma to be replicated continuously to be finally commoditized in a cultural spectacle. As depicted implicitly in the lyrics of "Company of Strangers" (Third Eye Blind, 2016) truth be told, initially people wants a robot but a robot (indeed) could not be able to push away the emptiness, thus strangers may (not may) be able to fill a void. More so, as theory of dark tourism puts it, the shift of people liking non-light attractions such as visitation from "light tourism" market offerings e.g. natural beauties and/or man-made attractions to macabre sites (Korstanje & George, 2015). It is argued that this tendency of people shifting their needs and wants from visiting natural and/or man-made attractions into macabre sites is as for the purpose of "anticipation for death". Dark tourism places or shrines are systematically designed to disseminate an ethical message to community. In this sense, current studies suggest that understanding death leads to discourse about thanatology which shed the light on human interpretation and acceptance to death (Korstanje, 2014; Handayani & Korstanje, 2016; Handayani, Ivanov & Korstanje, 2016). Although, this trend does not cover big market shares in as market offerings, research points out that this trend potentially could be not only the attraction-driven but also it may be emerge as a tourist-demand (Korstanje & Handayani, 2016; Wilkinson, 2010; Stone, 2006). This could be an indication of how "death sites" potentially associated with dark virtual tourism, and branded "darkness" attributed on the death sites as the new form of religiosity. Further, it may also explain why darkness elements attributed to negativity is not simply stimulate negative behaviour. Likely, the experience would shift the feelings of lonely in crowded places, strengthens the interpersonal relationship with significant others, and be more humanist, as Marshmello (2016) puts it "I'm so alone, Nothing feels like home, I'm so alone, Trying to find my way back home to you...". Take this issue of loneliness to the extreme level, Blink-182 in their song titled "Adam's Song" (1999) in first verse i.e.

" You'll be sorry when I'm gone" and in verse 3 last line " Please tell mom this is not her fault" these verses denote loneliness and a man relationship with his significant other, followed by contemplation as depicted in [Chorus:] "The world was wide, too late to try, The tour was over we'd survived, I couldn't wait till I got home, To pass the time in my room alone". Some arguments support this claim indicates that: (1) man comes to this world from and to death (Korstanje, 2014); (2) proposition that denotes the dependency of self to other´s suffering creating a vicious circle that empirical research has not revealed; (3)authenticity visiting macabre sites generate feelings for contemplation and self-awareness (Handayani & Korstanje, 2016; Handayani & George, 2016).

Generally, the induction of applied-research into death sites encourages it to be consumed by (certain) publics (Handayani & Korstanje, 2016; Handayani & George, 2016). It is not only because of the death sites attached with "darkness" attributes and its strong personality of its hospitality attributes but also most importantly is because death sites accessibility which arguably makes it authentic, is also considered as dilemmatic issues that interpreted as "(un)met" expectation that leads to e-complains and/or e-reviews (see the study of Handayani & George, 2016a; Handayani & George, 2016b). This kind of phenomenon of authentic branded experience indicates inevitable sacrificing and more effort, as JIKES Ft. Nori (2013) analogically observed, "fly everywhere that you can't reach". However, as debate on the death sites as attraction-driven cannot be for all segmented target market, hence there is a need to support (not support) this claim. Whatever the case it may be, adapting Westermann (2008) point of view to support claims that argued for death sites to be able to be consumed by larger market, Sound branding which revolves around a sonic brand can be further examined. As stated, Sound assists people understanding and even the features of music are consistently associated with producing strong emotions in listeners, combined with heartfelt lyrics and a powerhouse voice, hence these structures can send reward signals to our brains that rival any other pleasure (Doucleff, 2012). Further, Westermann suggests that a sonic brand requires an underlying story that is so compelling that people enjoy and take pride in telling it. It must also be a story that others understand, enjoy hearing and respond to with enthusiasm. Müllensiefen and Baker (2015) suggest two techniques to assess the fit between pieces of music and a given brand: the Brand Music Matrix and the Semantic Differential, which each of these align an effective sonic signature. Their work indicates that sonic signature aligns positive values of brand; it would lead to properties of music and target audience, whereas properties of music (mutually) lead to target audience, and vice versa. In other words, comprehensible uniqueness of death sites can be used as brand-sound connotation represents "darkness" elements attributed to death sites. For that reason, sound branding process begins by examining and selecting the sonic equivalents of brand values, coupled with specific technology e.g. Wayfinding (Baker, 2016) or Geotag (Chung, Tyan & Han, 2016). Wayfinding e.g. which includes signage landmarks, area lighting, open sight lines to key buildings, pedestrian nodes, landscaping and pageantry could be designed along with the mobile apps and GPS systems. This would also in line with the value co-creator of tourism experience as a song being shared would be the brand-sound connotation represents "darkness" elements attributed to death sites. On the other hand, Geotag could be useful; as research on enhancement of Smart Tourism experience through Geotag suggests positive relationships between tourist's readiness and Geotag ease of use. Further, Geotag ease of use and Geotag enjoyment influence its use of intention.

Specific studies indicate that development of death sites aims to enrich the tourists experience and to give brand image to death sites (e.g. Trunyan Cemetery). As Trunyan Cemetery exploration mainly focuses on how to enrich the tourists' experience, how visitation to death sites influence tourist "life-world", and how its "darkness" attributes give brand image to death sites (Handayani & Korstanje, 2016;

Handayani, Ivanov & Korstanje, 2016), much still remains to be explored. There seems to be lack of study aimed to design death sites e.g. Trunyan Cemetery as "virtual" touristic market offerings. Death Sites, where the dead body would be rested in peace for good, is defined as last destination (a home) for the man. A home is just like for the living one, it categorically refers to a place where s/he is not feeling lonely (The Cinematic Orchestra, 2007), it says home is where your heart is (Green Day, 2004). Likewise, anthropologically speaking the sense of *a home* is just outside there where the dead bodies would find peace, rest their bones & lay their head, and a place where the heart is set in stone, where the future and the past are buried, as found in songs titled "Home" by Gabrielle Aplin Lyrics (2013). Presumably, this song would not only emerge as leading intro for "dark virtual" tour to the death sites i.e. Trunyan cemetery but also it sharpens brand image and enhances recognition on darkness" elements (e.g. sorrowfulness) attributed to Death Sites. Sound branding in this sense would play role as mixed emotion of witnessing unique propositions of death sites and emotional propositions offered by "darkness" elements of Trunyan cemetery, as a home for dead bodies. More so, Sound branding would accelerate the tourists' feelings for contemplation and self-reflection as previous studies indicated (e.g. Handayani & Korstanje, 2016; Handayani & George, 2016).

DESIGN OF THE STUDY

In this study we pursue the clue left long time ago by constructionist research philosophy which reminds that the uses of songs as stimuli for engagement and experience have been researched especially Pop songs (see Jakubowski, Farrugia & Stewart (2016). However, much still remains to be explored e.g. research that utilises other kinds of genre i.e. Rock or Punk Rock. Dark themed songs are analysed by compositional interpretation and semiology. Semiology and discourse analysis on the narrative of dark themed songs (i.e. "Company of Strangers" By Third Eye Blind, "Home". Gabrielle Aplin, "Adam's Song" by Blink-182, "Jesus of Suburbia" by Green Day, "Alone" by Marshmello, "Lets Fly Away" by Jikes (Ft. Nori) Pt.2 (NCS Release) become the basis of most arguments advanced here. Systematic search of meaning is imperative in interpreting qualitative data analysis (Hatch, 2002; Ngulube, 2015). In this vein, Ngulube (2015) points out that qualitative data analysis involves the identification, examination, comparison and interpretation of patterns and themes. Further, a case study is set as a research design which focuses on the narrative of dark themed songs. A case study investigates a contemporary phenomenon in depth and within its real-life context (Yin, 2013). Further, Yin (2013) suggests that case study as a research method allows investigator to retain the holistic and meaningful characteristics of real-life event.

Technically, methods for narrative of dark themed songs analysis consist of compositional interpretation and semiology. While compositional interpretation is analysed accordingly by looking at aspects of lyrics and sound, semiology as method technically is used to gain a detailed and precise insight into the meaning carried by the dark themed songs. As semiology mentioned semiotics as tool for interpretation, semiotics in general can be defined as study of sign and codes. Moriarty (2005) points out that signs are used in producing, conveying, and interpreting messages and the codes that govern their use. In the terms of Monaca (2000) which originally coined by Ferdinand de Saussure, sign systems within the language that could be derived from movie can be analysed as a language. Having this in mind, sign systems within the lyrics and melody of the song can be analysed as language. Semiology addresses the way in which the various elements of the text work together and interact with our culture knowledge to generate meaning (Stokes, 2012). Further, Stokes points out the key semiotics is how the producer of an image makes it mean something and how we, as readers, get meaning out. With this viewpoint, it is expected that the storytelling framework was used with the purpose of unveiling how the death sites and hospitality attributes on dark themed songs positions itself in a larger narrative.

SETTING OF THE STUDY: TRUNYAN CEMETERY

Located on the edge of Lake Batur in northern Bali, the cemetery is where people from the nearby village of Kuban bring their dead to rest on top of the ground. The only dead allowed here are those who passed away because of old age or sickness brought on by old age, not those who died through accident or any other tragic cause e.g. being murdered. The site can only be reached by boat, a small fleet of which awaits visitors at the end of a wooden jetty overlooked by the stunning Mount Batur. Crossing the lake to Trunyan takes between 20 and 30 minutes and upon arrival a small huddle of men awaits the boats. The cemetery is small and seems to be poorly maintained, but what indicates the importance of this final resting place is the great number of human skulls lined up on stone-shelves (Gower, 2010; Morton, 2014).

Trunyan village was the only area of Bali not conquered by the Majapahit emperors, which means that the empire's traditions, culture and belief structures did not influence the village (ANTARA TV, 2013). This may be an indication of why rituals of shared values in Trunyan cemetery are different from other classical types of Balinese cremation. The uniqueness of this ritual lies in not burying the body, but merely placing it under the tree named Teruyan (Teru Menyan) . This tree has a strong scent, and the people of Trunyan village believe that it diminishes the smell from the dead body (Sutika, 2014). In the cemetery, under the teruyan trees, the bodies of the deceased are just covered in cloth and rudimentary bamboo cages. These cages are flimsy and practically leave the body open to the elements. The bodies left out in the open will of course decompose, and the potential for unwelcome odours and even health concerns is real. The presence of a banyan tree, described as a holy tree, seems to stand guard protecting the cemetery. Its leaves carpet the ground and presumably this is part of the way in which the tree keeps the area free from unwelcome odours. In addition, once the the bodies of the deceased are decomposed; old bones will be moved stone shelves, to make way for new ones. This sacred ritual profoundly indicates the shared values which distinguish the people of Trunyan from other Balinese and their cultural rituals for dealing with the death of family members. The Trunyan ritual denotes the mixed aspects of spirituality and religion with the cultural heritage.

DISCUSSION

Technology in Tourism

Studies on dark tourism in general and/or dark sites in particular with proliferation of ICT e.g. VR is associated with interdisciplinary and/or multidisciplinary studies. More so, it have gained significant scholarly and practitioner attention. The interconnection of dark sites with many domains of studies, e.g. technological innovations could enhance visitation experiences. VR which is defined as Computer-mediated multisensory experience could serve to facilitate access into dimensions e.g. tourist sites that differ from our own (Cheong, 1995; Tussyadiah, Wang & Jia, 2017). Tussyadiah, Wang and Jia (2017) specifically suggest that VR environment contributes significantly to spatial presence, that persuasiveness of VR is also found as spatial presence positively affects post VR attitude change towards tourism destination. In addition, research also indicates that VR can be augmented with various sensory stimulations i.e. sight, sound, and touch, altogether with their respected feedback (Cheong, 1995). This explains the interconnection between VR and AR In line with that, Linaza, Marimón, Carrasco, Álvarez, Montesa, Aguilar, and Diez (2012) indicate that AR in the context of Tourism Business and Mobile phone Application aimed to enrich tourist experience through precise and tailored way, especially in terms of surrounding of the area they are visiting. Further, they point out that AR systems share 3 characteristics i.e. (1) combination of real and virtual object in the real world; (2) interactivity and interaction in real-time; (3) registration and alignment of virtual and physical objects with each other in 3D. With this in mind, development of dark sites e.g. in the case of Trunyan cemetery in Bali can be designed along with these VR and AR.

VR which can be augmented with various sensory stimulations i.e. sight, sound, and touch can be applicable for death sites development. This could be the potential response for the urge on more exploration which calls the possibility for death sites (i.e. as one of dark tourism forms) to be marketable without degrading the values attributed with its profile (Handayani, Ivanov & Korstanje, 2017). This way, future research which is aimed for making death sites remains to be exclusive market offerings but can be consumed for more market shares (Handayani & George, 2017a; Handayani & George, 2017b). In this sense, VR which can be augmented by sensory stimulations e.g. sound, in the case of tourist site development explains on how visitation experience can be enhanced, and how the co-creation of computer-generated image on a tourist's view of the surrounding (e.g. the cemetery) can be harnessed. Therefore, studies into Sound branding in the context of tourist sites in general and death sites (e.g. the cemetery) in particular could be applied as it may offer liminal opportunities in giving brand image to death sites.

Even though for a long time the role of Sound in the branding spectrum was neglected over visual forms of expression, only recently the role of sounds, music and voice attracted greater interest for both academic work and practitioner (Westermann, 2008). As much as research have been attempting to expand the role of sounds branding on market offerings' identity and images, the role of sound branding on the development of death sites received less attention. As past studies suggest that certain features of music are consistently associated with producing strong emotions in listeners, combined with heartfelt lyrics and a powerhouse voice, hence these structures can send reward signals to our brains that rival any other pleasure (Doucleff, 2012). Adapting contemporary theory of branding in general and theory of personification and/or impression management on the death sites particularly indicate that the development design should be revolved around philosophical views of Smart tourism coupled with Slow tourism (e.g. Handayani, Ivanov & Korstanje, 2017). While Smart tourism indicates application of ICT in supporting the supply aspects of attractions and destination attributes (Gretzel, Sigala, Xiang & Koo, 2015; Neuhofer, Buhalis & Ladkin, 2015) and/or encourages the co-creation shared values e.g. User-Generated Content (UGC) (Arriga & Levina, 2008; Gretzel, Fesenmaier, Lee & Tussyadiah, 2010), Slow tourism advocates "right speed". In this sense, the use of Sound branding on death sites should be in line with "right speed" i.e. the tempo of travel slowly and locally (Honoré, 2009; Dickinson & Lumsdon; 2010; Caffyn, 2009: Oh, Assaf & Baloglu, 2014). Specifically, while proliferation of ICTs can be interpreted as the used of AR, the term of "right speed" i.e. the tempo of travel slowly and locally can be interpreted as "right tempo" of Sound branding that is used to characterize the type of death sites and its shared values. Technically, the Sound branding i.e. certain selected song(s) is the one that denotes the "darkness" elements of circle of life. As Handayani & George (2017b) put it, people learn to (re)live the goodness of being alive, being vulnerable, being happy and being sad. Presumably these are the most intriguing aspects of life that becomes commodification that may (may not) be useful to be revelation and contemplation for human being (Handayani & George, 2017a). With this view point, the use of Sound branding can be optimized, not only for the purposes of satisfying tourist's needs and want but also most importantly is for the creative design making death sites to be able to be consumed by larger market shares without making it is less exclusive. In addition, development design of death sites should also be based on emotional and unique selling propositions (Kotler, Armstrong, Saunders & Wong (1999). This is in line with past studies that suggest for selecting Sound Branding for market offerings, is aimed to develop sound creations that are derived from the details of brand values that characterizes the brand (Westermann, 2008). Carl-Frank Westermann (2008) points out that Sound not only has a direct impact on human emotion but Sound also sharpens brand image of market offerings and enhances recognition. Likely, sound branding which is defined as a song used in branding spectrum i.e. combination of creative melody and deep meaningful lyrics sang by singer, also is labelled as music, is not only used for optimizing and enriching identities attributed to the content of market offerings, but also it plays role as core essence for personification attributed to the leading brand, accelerates positioning at certain category.

Research suggests that the relationship between music, emotion, and the proliferation of ICT is among the most contentious issues in the philosophy of Music (Robinson, 2014; Doucleff, 2012). Studies indicate pros and cons whether Music in itself has to do (has nothing to do) with emotion (Zangwill, 2004; Kivy, 1991). Research also suggests that music can elicit thrills and chills when it "(teases) structural expectancies" by "repeatedly creating and resolving tensions." (Sloboda, 1999). Further, formalists agree that great music can elicit emotions of admiration or excitement when its melodic, harmonic and rhythmic structure are appraised as beautiful and well-crafted (Kivy, 1991). Research that combines these three variables i.e. music, emotion, and ICT revolve around large online music databases, identifying lyrical text of songs for specific emotion (Yang & Lee, 2004; Yang & Lee, 2009; Doucleff, 2012). Su & Fung (2013) point out that a computational Music Emotion Classification (MEC) system able to greatly enhance user experience with music, as well as contribute to more effective music data storage and management for music service providers. Further, studies denote MEC systems adopt one of two approaches—knowledge-based (Meyers, 2007; Hu, Chen & Yang, 2009) and statistical (Laurier, Grivolla & Herrera, 2008; Hu & Downie, 2010; Mihalcea & Strapparava, 2012; He, Jin, Xiong, Chen, Sun & Zhao 2008; Yang, Lin, Cheng, Liao, Ho & Chen, 2008; Van Zaanen & Kanters, 2010). It is also noted that the future of the intertwined relationships among Technology in general (ICT particularly), consumer behaviour and Digital Marketing revolve around the uses of mobile augmented reality and computer vision (Hidden creative, 2010). Indeed, this proliferation of ICT is depicted as innovation phenomenon of technology e.g. Google Glasses, Augmented Reality (AR) in contact lenses, sun glasses with AR, Microsoft HoloLens (Mackie, 2016), and Smart shoes. Presumably this innovation phenomenon of technology could be useful and may applicable for design context of death sites development.

Most probably, Sound branding would not only useful for enrichment identity and images of death sites but also it (1) may strengthen positioning of the death sites as attraction-driven; (2) could give another spectrum of exclusiveness of death sites to be consumed by other kinds of targeted market, without making its premium brand images less exclusive. Coupled with adaptation of SmartPhone Apps and AR, application of sound branding may merge as evidence for proposition which advocates death sites is one of Virtual Dark Tourism (VDT) forms that not only signifies as attraction-driven but also as tourist-demand. With this in mind, the process of experiencing and experience that suggested by Gnoth & Matteucci (2014) as Tourism Experience Model (TEM) would be enriched. This explains the proposition that suggests the ''understanding'' of experiences is often submerged in unwieldy supply models couched in behaviouristic stimulus-response theories (Crouch and Ritchie, 1999). Further, Gnoth & Matteucci (2014) defined tourists' experiencing as ''the conflux of, what is sensually perceived, how it is processed, and how it is retained in the resulting experience'' whereby the experience implicates the self in its being, change and growth. Therefore, the statement that set as the research problem is how do dark themed songs coupled with AR as tourism drivers significance for designing death sites i.e. Trunyan cemetery in Bali. As the argument given, utilizing the narrative of dark themed songs, this research proposal would examine the core musical melody and lyrics, coupled with AR on the death sites. Therefore, the study variables discussed in this statement of the problem is proposed to be further explored.

SOUNDS AS EMOTIONAL CONNECTION AND REAL-TIME CO-CREATION EXPERIENCE

In an age of immediacy over longevity, perhaps what is most impressive about death sites' emergence intertwined with Sound branding and AR is how distinctive it all feels. As mentioned, narrative of dark themed songs analysis consist of compositional interpretation and semiology, thus this section aims to explore how sound is Sound branding for the dark sites. In this sense, the crucial question is not about what is Sound branding role on the death sites development but importantly it should explore the extent on how sound is Sound Branding for the dark sites. Westermann (2008) suggests that that tendency of people cannot stop hearing and fact that when it comes to delivering messages, sound has an advantage over visuals. Further, he indicates that auditory dimension absorbs information more quickly and allows us to find our bearings at an unconscious level. In line with that, Müllensiefen and Baker (2015, 2013) denote that music tracks may have effects on brand perception that they can represent the imaged character built by a brand.

Bearing this in mind, hence the influence of Sound on the death sites serves as added values which works along with AR as visualization that links "shared values" of ritual performed in the cemetery, coupled with the topography and its host community characteristics. However, this proposition should be tested properly as "shared values" of ritual performed in the cemetery is considered sacred not only for the dead bodies but also more importantly because the topography and its host community characteristics, coupled with its shared values is sacred as well.

Research into Trunyan cemetery as the sacred site of the dead intertwined with the ICTs proliferation suggests that experience visiting death sites should be fundamentally designed based on the principle of Smart and Slow tourism (Handayani, 2017; Handayani, Ivanov & Korstanje, 2016). Further, detail of innovation of technology proposed for the death sites suggest for designing Wayfining and Smart shoes as for response on the demand for customised "death sites" as market offerings and demand for comfy premium services & hospitality, and sites accessibility (see Handayani, Ivanov & Korstanje, 2016). For that reasons, same application should be designing death sites with the total concerns for not only to be responsive with the tourists demand but also most importantly should put effort for keeping the death sites as "attraction-driven". In such a case, no less true is that interpretation of song (as form of Sound branding) relies on its characteristic of auditory dimension, which serves as a way for tourists to absorb information more quickly and allows them to find their bearings at an unconscious level as Prof. Carl-Frank Westermann suggested. On the other hand, the development of AR for the death sites design focuses on imposing a computer-generated image on a tourist's view of the surrounding the cemetery. It serves as a composite view of the dead and its images of the rituals that most likely embedded with cultural heritage. Again, this kind of design setting have to be properly developed with total concern of not making the death sites as generic market offerings, but must be focus on how to design it along with technology of AR combined with auditory sound as tool for augmenting the co-experience of the VDT, as tool for sharpening brand image and enhances recognition of "darkness" elements attributed to the death sites.

As mentioned, Sound branding to be proposed for death sites revolves around the combination of three variables i.e. music, emotion, and ICT which designed deliberately for large online music databases which also able to identifying lyrical text of songs for specific emotion. In this case, the narrative of dark themed songs e.g. "Jesus of Suburbia" by Green Day could be used to depict the "darkness" elements attributed to the death sites' profile. Although, Trunyan Cemetery in Bali is somehow difficult to be categorically included in the terms of Thanatourism coined by past studies, the song "Jesus of Suburbia" which embedded with multiple verses that may represent "darkness" elements attributed to the death sites' profile. As attached in the lyrics (see appendix), the verses of part 2: "City of the Damned" of the song reflects tragedy of the 7/11 which wakes up global citizens of terror on the one hand and stimulate people to be self-aware. Likewise, Aplin Lyrics (2013) "home", second verse says "With every small disaster, I'll let the waters still, Take me away to some place real…" it advocates people for contemplation, leading to the self-reflection of the meaning of life, purpose of life, and the meaning of "death". Further, MEC system which able to greatly enhance user experience with music and to contribute to more effective music data storage and management for music service providers could be used for AR death sites' attributes. In this sense, it would generate personalized experience on visitation to the death sites. With this in mind, it is expected Sound that is used for death sites context would enhance recognition and sharpens brand image as indicated by past studies e.g. Westermann (2008).

CONCLUSION

This study has looked at some viewpoints for consuming death-sites as not only for segmented target market but it paves the ways for the rise of a new epistemology in dark tourism studies. With Sound branding, coupled with proliferation of ICT that proposes AR as tools to support the claims of VDT, death sites which signifies its exclusiveness as touristic market offerings could be consumed by the orchestration of more targeted markets. More so, the role of Sound branding coupled with AR in this study is believed could enhance recognition and sharpens brand image of the death sites. In the years to come, some misunderstandings and limitations should be tackled off. Even though, this study has shown some evidences for supporting claims for VDT, this study leaves several issues that urge for further research. First and foremost, a follow-up research aimed for testing this claim must be done. Secondly, another type(s) of deaths sites from other place need to be applied as it could indicate its relevance for implementing this notion. Lastly, preliminary design for prototype of death sites for Trunyan Cemetery, Bali as a form of VDT could be delivered the kind of experiences that sampled by non-virtual tourist is designed based on interactive mobile application. In this sense, the design could be done in three phases i.e. (1) initial system that is designed as Database contains data from various media, including text, voice, video, etc. At this first stage, a Trunyan Cemetery profiles will be implemented as the pilot project; (2) to emerge the Database into Big Data; (3) development of knowledge based system. This system will transform Big Data into more adaptive system.

REFERENCES

Adele. (2011). *Someone Like You*. Retrieved 27 November 2016, from http://www.azlyrics.com/lyrics/adele/someonelikeyou.html

Alimamy, S., Deans, K. R., & Gnoth, J. (2017). Augmented Reality: Uses and Future Considerations in Marketing. In Leadership, Innovation and Entrepreneurship as Driving Forces of the Global Economy (pp. 705-712). Springer International Publishing.

Aplin, G. (2013). *Home*. Retrieved 27 November 2016, from http://www.azlyrics.com/lyrics/gabriel-leaplin/home.html

Ariès, P. (1975). *Western attitudes toward death: from the Middle Ages to the present* (Vol. 3). Baltimore, MD: John Hopkins University Press.

Arriga, M., & Levina, N. (2008). *Social dynamics in online cultural fields*. Paper presented at the 29th International Conference on Information Systems (ICIS'08), Paris, France.

Baker, B. (2016, April 27). What Does Wayfinding Add to City Branding? *Small City Branding Around the World*. Retrieved 27 April 2016, from http://citybranding.typepad.com/city-branding/2016/04/what-does-wayfinding-add-to-city-branding.html

Baudrillard, J. (1983). Simulations. New York: Semiotext(e).

Blink-182. (1999). *Adam's Song*. Retrieved 27 November 2016, from http://www.azlyrics.com/lyrics/blink182/adamssong.html

BrandSound. (2016). *Insights on Music in Brand Communication*. Retrieved 27 November 2016, from http://www.brand-sounds.com/wordpress/

Caffyn, A. (2009, Sept.). The Slow Route to New Markets. *Tourism Insights*.

Cheong, R. (1995). The virtual threat to travel and tourism. *Tourism Management*, *16*(6), 417–422. doi:10.1016/0261-5177(95)00049-T

Chung, N., Tyan, I., & Han, H. (2016). Enhancing the smart tourism experience through geotag. *Information Systems Frontiers*, 1–12.

Crouch, G. I., & Ritchie, J. R. B. (1999). Tourism, competitiveness, and social prosperity. *Journal of Business Research*, *44*(3), 137–152. doi:10.1016/S0148-2963(97)00196-3

Day, G. (2004). *Jesus of Suburbia*. Retrieved 7 November 2015, from http://www.azlyrics.com/lyrics/greenday/jesusofsuburbia.html

Dickinson, J. E., & Lumsdon, L. (2010). *Slow travel and tourism*. New York: Earthscan. doi:10.4324/9781849776493

Doucleff, M. (2012). Anatomy of a Tear-Jerker Why does Adele's "Someone Like You" Make Everyone Cry? Science has Found the Formula. *The Wall Steet Journal, 11*, 201–206.

Duff, A., & Maley, A. (2007). *Literature*. Oxford, UK: Oxford University Press.

Eco, U. (1986). *Travels in hyperreality*. London: Picador.

Fritz, F., Susperregui, A., & Linaza, M. T. (2005). Enhancing cultural tourism experiences with augmented reality technologies. *6th International Symposium on Virtual Reality, Archaeology and Cultural Heritage (VAST)*.

Gnoth, J., & Matteucci, X. (2014). A phenomenological view of the behavioural tourism research literature. *International Journal of Culture, Tourism and Hospitality Research, 8*(1), 3–21. doi:10.1108/IJCTHR-01-2014-0005

Gonzalez, M. (2013). *Top 5 Augmented Reality Apps!* Retrieved 27 November 2016, from https://www.youtube.com/watch?v=NqUSfjTSLyo

Gretzel, U., Fesenmaier, D. R., Lee, Y. J., & Tussyadiah, I. (2010). Narrating travel experiences: the role of new media. *Tourist experience: Contemporary perspectives*, 171.

Gretzel, U., Sigala, M., Xiang, Z., & Koo, C. (2015). Smart tourism: Foundations and developments. *Electronic Markets, 25*(3), 179–188. doi:10.100712525-015-0196-8

Griffin, E. A., & McClish, G. A. (2011). *A first look at communication theory*. Boston: McGraw-Hill.

Han, D. I., Jung, T., & Gibson, A. (2013). Dublin AR: implementing augmented reality in tourism. In Information and communication technologies in tourism 2014 (pp. 511-523). Springer International Publishing. doi:10.1007/978-3-319-03973-2_37

Handayani, B. (2017). *Going to the dark sites with intention: Construction of niche tourism*. Academic Press.

Handayani, B., & George, B. (2017a). An Analysis of Online User Reviews of the Death sites. In *Gazing at Death: Dark Tourism as an Emergent Horizon of Research*. Nova Science Publishers.

Handayani, B., & George, B. (2017b). Dark Tourism as Quasi-Suicide: A Case Study of The Sea of Trees. In *Gazing at Death: Dark Tourism as an Emergent Horizon of Research, 2017*. Nova Science Publishers.

Handayani, B., Ivanov, S., & Korstanje, M. E. (2017). Smart tourism for dark sites: The sacred site of the dead, Trunyan cemetery. In *Gazing at Death: Dark Tourism as an Emergent Horizon of Research, 2017*. Nova Science Publishers.

Handayani, B., & Korstanje, M. E. (2016a). Isle of the Dead: A Study of Trunyan Cemetery. Bali: Academic Press.

Handayani, B., & Korstanje, M. E. (2016b). *Place Brand Authenticity in Social Media Interaction: A Postmodern Perspective*. Academic Press.

Hatch, J. A. (2002). *Doing qualitative research in education settings*. Suny Press.

He, H., Jin, J., Xiong, Y., Chen, B., Sun, W., & Zhao, L. (2008, December). Language feature mining for music emotion classification via supervised learning from lyrics. In *International Symposium on Intelligence Computation and Applications* (pp. 426-435). Springer Berlin Heidelberg. 10.1007/978-3-540-92137-0_47

Hidden Creative. (2010). *The Future of Augmented Reality*. Retrieved 27 November 2016, from https://www.youtube.com/watch?v=tnRJaHZH9lo&spfreload=10

Honoré, C. (2009). *In praise of slow: How a worldwide movement is challenging the cult of speed.* Vintage Canada.

Hu, X., & Downie, J. S. (2010, June). Improving mood classification in music digital libraries by combining lyrics and audio. In *Proceedings of the 10th annual joint conference on Digital libraries* (pp. 159-168). ACM. 10.1145/1816123.1816146

Hu, Y., Chen, X., & Yang, D. (2009, August). *Lyric-based Song Emotion Detection with Affective Lexicon and Fuzzy Clustering Method.* ISMIR.

Jakubowski, K., Farrugia, N., & Stewart, L. (2016). Probing imagined tempo for music: Effects of motor engagement and musical experience. *Psychology of Music, 44*(6), 1274–1288. doi:10.1177/0305735615625791

Jati, A. (2014). Using Adele's "Someone Like You" to Teach Verbs Tenses and Passive Forms. *PAROLE: Journal of Linguistics and Education, 3*(2), 76-83.

Jikes, N. (2013). *Lets Fly Away*. Retrieved 15 July 2015, from https://www.musixmatch.com/lyrics/JIKES-feat-Nori-Jikes-Nori/Lets-Fly-Away

Julier, S., Lanzagorta, M., Baillot, Y., Rosenblum, L., Feiner, S., Hollerer, T., & Sestito, S. (2000). Information filtering for mobile augmented reality. In *Augmented Reality, 2000.(ISAR 2000). Proceedings. IEEE and ACM International Symposium on* (pp. 3-11). IEEE. 10.1109/ISAR.2000.880917

Juslin, P. N., & Sloboda, J. A. (2001). *Music and emotion: Theory and research.* Oxford, UK: Oxford University Press.

Kivy, P. (1991). *Music alone: Philosophical reflections on the purely musical experience*. Cornell University Press.

Korstanje, M. (2012). Reconsidering cultural tourism: An anthropologist's perspective. *Journal of Heritage Tourism, 7*(2), 179–184. doi:10.1080/1743873X.2011.639883

Korstanje M (2014). Conceptual discussion of dark tourism: suffering, egoism and the depersonalization of death. *Globalization of tourism, opportunities and challenges.*

Korstanje, M. E. (2011). Influence of history in the encounter of guests and hosts. *Anatolia, 22*(2), 282–28. doi:10.1080/13032917.2011.597991

Korstanje, M. E. (2016). *The Rise of Thana Capitalism and Tourism.* Abingdon, UK: Routledge. doi:10.4324/9781315457482

Korstanje, M. E., & George, B. (2015). Dark Tourism: Revisiting Some Philosophical Issues. *Ereview of Tourism Research, 12*, 127–136.

Korstanje, M. E., & Handayani, B. (2016). Gazing at Death. *Dark Tourism as an Emergent Horizon of Research.*

Kotler, P., Armstrong, G., Saunders, J., & Wong, V. (1999). *Principles of marketing* (2nd ed.). Editura Prentice Hall.

Kounavis, C. D., Kasimati, A. E., & Zamani, E. D. (2012). Enhancing the tourism experience through mobile augmented reality: Challenges and prospects. *International Journal of Engineering Business Management, 4*, 10. doi:10.5772/51644

Kozinets, R. V. (2015). The Post-Human Future of Brands. *Strong Brands, Strong Relationships*, 149-158.

Krentzman, A. R. (2013). *What Is Spirituality?* Retrieved 15 July 2015, from University of Minnesota, Center for Spirituality and Healing and Charlson Meadows website: http://www.takingcharge.csh.umn.edu/enhance-your wellbeing/purpose/spirituality/what-spirituality

Kress, G. R., & Van Leeuwen, T. (1996). *Reading images: The grammar of visual design.* Psychology Press.

Lash, S. M., Urry, S. L. J., & Urry, J. (1993). *Economies of signs and space* (Vol. 26). London: Sage.

Laurier, C., Grivolla, J., & Herrera, P. (2008, December). Multimodal music mood classification using audio and lyrics. In *Machine Learning and Applications, 2008. ICMLA'08. Seventh International Conference on* (pp. 688-693). IEEE. 10.1109/ICMLA.2008.96

Lennon, J. J., & Foley, M. (2000). *Dark tourism.* London: Cengage Learning EMEA.

Linaza, M. T., Marimón, D., Carrasco, P., Álvarez, R., Montesa, J., Aguilar, S. R., & Diez, G. (2012). Evaluation of mobile augmented reality applications for tourism destinations. In *Information and Communication Technologies in Tourism 2012.* Wien: Springer-Verlag. doi:10.1007/978-3-7091-1142-0_23

MacCannell, D. (1976). *The tourist: A new theory of the leisure class.* Berkeley, CA: University of California Press.

Mackie, J. (2016). *Microsoft HoloLens Review, mind blowing Augmented Reality?* Retrieved 15 July 2015, from https://www.youtube.com/watch?v=ihKUoZxNClA

Marimon, D., Sarasua, C., Carrasco, P., Álvarez, R., Montesa, J., Adamek, T., & Gascó, P. (2010). *MobiAR: tourist experiences through mobile augmented reality.* Barcelona, Spain: Telefonica Research and Development.

Marshmello. (2016). *Alone.* Retrieved 27 November 2016, from http://www.azlyrics.com/lyrics/marshmello/alone.html

Menninger, K. A. (1938). *Man against himself.* New York: Harcourt, Brace.

Merriam, A. P., & Merriam, V. (1964). *The anthropology of music.* Evanston, IL: Northwestern University Press.

Meyers, O. C. (2007). *A mood-based music classification and exploration system* (Doctoral dissertation). Massachusetts Institute of Technology.

Mihalcea, R., & Strapparava, C. (2012, July). Lyrics, music, and emotions. In *Proceedings of the 2012 Joint Conference on Empirical Methods in Natural Language Processing and Computational Natural Language Learning* (pp. 590-599). Association for Computational Linguistics.

Monaco, J. (2000). *How to read a film: the world of movies, media, and multimedia: language, history, theory*. Oxford University Press.

Moriarty, S. (2005). Visual semiotics theory. Handbook of visual communication: Theory, methods, and media, 8, 227-241.

Müllensiefen, D., & Baker, D. J. (2015, October). Music, Brands, & Advertising: Testing What Works. In Audio Branding Yearbook 2014/2015 (pp. 31-52). Nomos Verlagsgesellschaft mbH & Co. KG.

Müllensiefen, D., Davies, C., & Dossman, L. (2013, May). Implicit and Explicit Effects of Music on Brand Perception in TV Ads. In Audio Branding Academy Yearbook 2012/2013 (pp. 139-155). Nomos Verlagsgesellschaft mbH & Co. KG. doi:10.5771/9783845243559-139

Murphey, T. (1992). *Music and Songs*. Oxford, UK: Oxford University Press.

Neuhofer, B., Buhalis, D., & Ladkin, A. (2015). Smart technologies for personalized experiences: A case study in the hospitality domain. *Electronic Markets*, *25*(3), 243–254. doi:10.100712525-015-0182-1

Ngulube, P. (2015). Qualitative data analysis and interpretation: systematic search for meaning. In Addressing Research Challenges: Making Headway for Developing Researchers. Mosala-MASEDI Publishers & Booksellers.

Oh, H., Assaf, A. G., & Baloglu, S. (2014). Motivations and goals of slow tourism. *Journal of Travel Research*, *55*(2), 205–219. doi:10.1177/0047287514546228

Ramkissoon, H., & Uysal, M. (2014). Authenticity as a value co-creator of tourism experiences. *CABI*, 113-124.

Rickly-Boyd, J. M. (2012). Authenticity & aura: A Benjaminian approach to tourism. *Annals of Tourism Research*, *39*(1), 269–289. doi:10.1016/j.annals.2011.05.003

Robinson, J. (2014). *How Music Grabs the Emotions*. Retrieved 27 November 2016, from Emotion Researcher ISRE's Sourcebook for Research on Emotion and Affect, website: http://emotionresearcher.com/how-music-grabs-the-emotions/

Rose, G. (2016). *Visual methodologies: An introduction to researching with visual materials*. London: Sage Publication.

Skoll, G. R., & Korstanje, M. (2014). Urban heritage, gentrification, and tourism in Riverwest and El Abasto. *Journal of Heritage Tourism*, *9*(4), 349–359. doi:10.1080/1743873X.2014.890624

Sloboda, J. A. (1999). Music: Where cognition and emotion meet. *The Psychologist*, *12*, 450–455.

Stokes, J. (2012). *How to do media and cultural studies*. Sage Publications.

Stone, P. (2006). A dark tourism spectrum: Towards a typology of death and macabre related tourist sites, attractions and exhibitions. Tourism: An Interdisciplinary. *International Journal (Toronto, Ont.), 54*(2), 145–160.

Stone, P., & Sharpley, R. (2008). Consuming dark tourism: A thanatological perspective. *Annals of Tourism Research, 35*(2), 574–595. doi:10.1016/j.annals.2008.02.003

Su, D., & Fung, P. (2013, October). These words are music to my ears: Recognizing music emotion from lyrics using AdaBoost. In *Signal and Information Processing Association Annual Summit and Conference (APSIPA), 2013 Asia-Pacific* (pp. 1-4). IEEE.

The Cinematic Orchestra. (2007). *To build a home*. Retrieved 27 November 2016, from http://www.azlyrics.com/lyrics/cinematicorchestra/tobuildahome.html

Third Eye Blind. (2016). *Company of Strangers*. Retrieved 27 November 2016, from http://www.azlyrics.com/lyrics/thirdeyeblind/companyofstrangers.html

Tussyadiah, I. P. (2017). Technology and Behavioral Design in Tourism. In *Design Science in Tourism* (pp. 173–191). Springer International Publishing. doi:10.1007/978-3-319-42773-7_12

Tussyadiah, I. P., Wang, D., & Jia, C. H. (2017). Virtual Reality and Attitudes Toward Tourism Destinations. In *Information and Communication Technologies in Tourism 2017* (pp. 229–239). Cham: Springer. doi:10.1007/978-3-319-51168-9_17

Tzanelli, R. (2016). *Thanatourism and Cinematic Representations of Risk: Screening the End of Tourism* (Vol. 176). Abingdon, UK: Routledge. doi:10.4324/9781315624105

Van Zaanen, M., & Kanters, P. (2010, August). Automatic Mood Classification Using TF* IDF Based on Lyrics. In ISMIR (pp. 75-80). Academic Press.

Vaughan-Nichols, S. J. (2009). Augmented Reality: No Longer a Novelty? *Computer (Long Beach, Calif.), 42*(12), 19–22.

Vila, P. (2014). *Music and Youth Culture in Latin America*. Oxford, UK: Oxford University Press. doi:10.1093/acprof:oso/9780199986279.001.0001

Vlahakis, V., Karigiannis, J., Tsotros, M., Gounaris, M., Almeida, L., Stricker, D., ... & Ioannidis, N. (2001). Archeoguide: first results of an augmented reality, mobile computing system in cultural heritage sites. *Virtual Reality, Archeology, and Cultural Heritage, 9*.

Westermann, C. F. (2008). Sound Branding and Corporate Voice–Strategic Brand Management Using Sound. In *Usability of Speech Dialog Systems* (pp. 147–155). Springer Berlin Heidelberg. doi:10.1007/978-3-540-78343-5_7

What, I. A. B. (2016a). *Audio Branding Academy*. Retrieved 27 November 2016, from http://audio-branding-academy.org/aba/knowledge/what-is-audio-branding/

What, I. A. B. (2016b). Retrieved 27 November 2016, from http://www.soundbranding.com/

Wilkinson, P. F. (2010). Review of "The darker side of travel: The theory and practice of dark tourism", by Sharpley and Stone. *e-Review of Tourism Research, 8*(1).

Xue, L., Manuel-Navarrete, D., & Buzinde, C. N. (2014). Theorizing the concept of alienation in tourism studies. *Annals of Tourism Research, 44*, 186–199. doi:10.1016/j.annals.2013.10.001

Yang, D., & Lee, W. S. (2004, October). *Disambiguating Music Emotion Using Software Agents* (Vol. 4). ISMIR.

Yang, D., & Lee, W. S. (2009, December). Music emotion identification from lyrics. In *Multimedia, 2009. ISM'09. 11th IEEE International Symposium on* (pp. 624-629). IEEE. 10.1109/ISM.2009.123

Yang, Y. H., Lin, Y. C., Cheng, H. T., Liao, I. B., Ho, Y. C., & Chen, H. H. (2008, December). Toward multi-modal music emotion classification. In *Pacific-Rim Conference on Multimedia* (pp. 70-79). Springer Berlin Heidelberg.

Yin, R. K. (2013). *Case study research: Design and methods*. Sage Publications.

Yovcheva, Z., Buhalis, D., & Gatzidis, C. (2012). Overview of smartphone augmented reality applications for tourism. *e-Review of Tourism Research, 10*(2), 63–66.

Zangwill, N. (2004). Against emotion: Hanslick was right about music. *British Journal of Aesthetics, 44*(1), 29–43. doi:10.1093/bjaesthetics/44.1.29

Chapter 12
Surfing Between Disciplines:
Interdisciplinarity of Architectural Digital Heritage

Stefano Brusaporci
https://orcid.org/0000-0002-8505-7895
L'Aquila University, Italy

ABSTRACT

The aim of the chapter is to reflect on how ICT and digital tools and methodologies influence the study of architectural heritage, favouring interdisciplinary interactions. First, the chapter analyses the characteristics of digital heritage from real built contents in relation with the general concept of heritage. Then, it discusses the communicative characteristics of 3-D digital models and the related issues, common among the different disciplines. Finally, it presents the peculiar aspects of architectural heritage and the building information modeling applied to architectural heritage as a specific kind of digital procedure naturally born for this kind of heritage. In conclusion, it highlights new trends and points out issues in transdisciplinary temptations.

INTRODUCTION

Reflecting on the concept of "Digital Heritage", Pescarin (2016) highlights a double approach based on 'tracks' and 'themes', respectively referred to the words "digital" and "heritage". The "digital" approach includes the following 'tracks': 1) Digitization and Acquisition, 2) Computer Graphics and Interaction, 3) Analysis and Interpretation, 4) Theory, Methodologies, Preservation and Standards, 5) Digital Heritage Projects and Applications. While the "heritage" approach includes five 'themes' according to UNESCO classification: a) Built Heritage from monuments to archaeological sites, cities, and landscapes, b) Culture & Traditions from folklife to languages, crafts, song and dance, c) Museums & Collections from movable objects to the museums, d) Libraries & Archives documentary heritage from books to audiovisual and e) Art & Creativity from digital / new media art to creative digital and online culture (p.1-2). Interesting are her conclusions: She highlights the role of the 'human dimension' and the

DOI: 10.4018/978-1-7998-2871-6.ch012

importance of "narrativity", realized with different kind of outputs: "Which trends can be recognized, looking at this overlapping area, which is Digital Heritage, through presented projects and demonstrations? One of the first element to appear is the position of the 'human dimension', considered more and more a key element. Heritage professionals necessities are better taken into consideration, from digital projects early stages; end users, such as visitors of museums, tends to be involved in some cases during the planning phase. The 'wow' effect of ICT technologies for heritage researchers, practitioners and curators is now diminishing, while the sustainability of digital projects and their effectiveness as referred to a specific goal, in constantly increasing. The role of design and co-creation is emerging [...], filling the gap among audience, developer and heritage curator. The role of 'narrativity' is also considered as important as the coding, for the success of a digital heritage project [...]. Mixed digital outputs (i.e. serious games including short movies, VR immersive applications that includes passive and active moments, etc.) are experimenting different levels of user interaction and involvement, while trying at the same time to find and define new communication styles and approaches, since the traditional proved to be unsatisfactory [...]. Finally, most of the projects have demonstrated a high interest toward the quality of user involvement, a topic currently under investigation from different perspectives" (p.3). The lesson are two: Designers and users are the heart of the process and the most important role is not played by amazing and photorealistic images but by "narrativity", that is photorealism could be important but the cultural involvement is essential.

Previously, in 1999, in the UNESCO's *World Heritage Magazine*, Stone described "Virtual Heritage" as "the utilization of technology for interpretation, conservation and preservation of Natural, Cultural and World Heritage" (Stone 1999). According to this definition, 'virtual heritage' is not in opposition to traditional one – it does not substitutes cultural heritage in a virtual dimension – but it is a tool for heritage interpretation, presentation and conservation. Virtual heritage and cultural heritage live together.

Afterwards, from the publication of the *Charter on the Preservation of the Digital Heritage* (UNESCO, 2003) many pages have been written on the concept of "Digital Heritage". The Charter explains: "The digital heritage consists of unique resources of human knowledge and expression. It embraces cultural, educational, scientific and administrative resources, as well as technical, legal, medical and other kinds of information created digitally, or converted into digital form from existing analogue resources. Where resources are "born digital", there is no other format but the digital object. Digital materials include texts, databases, still and moving images, audio, graphics, software and web pages, among a wide and growing range of formats" (Art.1).

Today there is the awareness that technologies cannot be seen as mere aid instruments for surveying or visualization, but they favour a development of research methodologies for knowledge, understanding, interpretation, presentation, and conservation. Computer-based visualization takes ever more importance, according to the line of visual computing, i.e. the analysis technique based on the visual representation of data. It favors the study of large amount of data, and of complex systems of heterogeneous data (textual, visual, audio, etc.). Those data can derive from various kinds or phenomena, also from non-visual ones. In fact, visual computing consists in the representation of multi-dimensional digital environments, where there is a complex interaction of an elevated number of agents simulating different kinds of data and information. The images of data provide information and through the manipulation of the images, we can observe, interact with, compute and control the data and the information, and create new knowledge (Card, Mackinlay, & Shneiderman, 1999).

As a consequence of the diffusion of digital visualization, derives the interest in this subject by many disciplines, in particular those interested in built heritage: humanities scholars – especially ones involved in museography (Parry, 2010. Cameron & Kenderdine, 2010) –, archaeologists (Frischer, 2008; Lake, 2014), architects (Docci, 2005; Gaiani, 2006; Calabi, 2013; Tamborrino, 2014), and in general scholars of history (Weller, 2012) have begun to work and reflect on digital heritage derived from tangible artefacts.

The complexity of heritage issues requires the involvement of interdisciplinary teams, made by scholars of different fields: Historians, humanities, museographers, archaeologists, architects, engineers, experts of ICT, etc. Additionally, new matters arise from digital heritage. The common use of the same digital instruments and applications promotes the intersection of disciplines. Therefore, according to digital heritage characteristics of inter-disciplinarity and/or trans-disciplinarity, the digital heritage has become the subject of dissimilar categories of researchers, for unlike purposes, with diverse levels of engagement. At the same time, scholars work together on the same object. Conferences and journals on digital heritage grow up. Undoubtedly, interdisciplinarity is an important aspect, which can promote results of particular value and high levels of innovation. However, the ever strict collaboration between different scholars requires the definition of ontologies, thesauri, and glossary useful to allow their collaboration. The common use of the same digital instruments and applications promotes the intersection of disciplines, and in practice, very often the scholars are tempted by hazardous trespassing in other fields. Nevertheless, the crossing of the walls is useful – rather necessary – for a cultural updating and enrichment, but these intrusions require maximum critical awareness (Brusaporci, 2016).

Ross Perry (2003) underlines how the diffusion of digital tools poses disciplinary, cultural, methodological, and operative issues to the academics. In fact "[...] disciplines typically preserve their own canon of key works, their own common grammar of research questions, as well as core sets of methodologies and even shared protocols of publishing. Offering identity, community and intellectual equipment to their members, scholars, academic disciplines remain, in effect, the tribes of scholarship". But, at the same time, "There are, after all, no core sets of methodologies at the centre of digital heritage, no routine forms of evidence or data". Moreover "Instead of a 'discipline' digital heritage is, rather, an 'agora'". That is digital heritage is a field where academics, scholars, intellectuals, etc. meet each other, collaborate, learn something from each other mutually, steal ideas, create intuitions, and where they get in and get out with the greatest freedom: "[…] ebbing and flowing of the expertise dawn into its domain; rather than being permanently resident, experts might only pass through the agora of digital heritage, as and when expertise becomes relevant" (Perry, 2003, pp. v-vi).

The Internet favours the meeting between disciplines. For example, web sites like Academia.edu and ResearchGate consent a constant and instantaneous knowledge sharing among scholars. What happens on the Web is explained by Weinberger (2011), when he describes the "Echo Chambers": "Knowledge has always needed communities to flourish. Communities need walls so that they can let in the right amount of diversity, even if too frequently they err on the side of homogeneity. Now the Net has made community walls semi-permeable. The transparency of the Net lets outsiders look in and insiders look out" (p. 85).

But Ramsay (2013), arguing on Digital Humanities, highlights something true for the whole Digital Heritage world: "Digital Humanities is not some airy Lyceum. It is a series of concrete instantiations involving money, students, funding agencies, big schools, little schools, programs, curricula, old guards, new guards, gatekeepers, and prestige. It might be more than these things, but it cannot not be these things" (p. 240).

Figure 1. 3D Scanning of the medieval church of St. Cipriano (Carapelle Calvisio, IT)

THE CONCEPT OF HERITAGE

UNESCO defines Cultural Heritage as “the legacy of physical artifacts and intangible attributes of a group or society that are inherited from past generations, maintained in the present and bestowed for the benefit of future generations”[1]. It ratifies the inescapable importance and interconnection of tangible and intangible characteristics of cultural heritage.

The Burra Charter (ICOMOS, 2013) puts together tangible and intangible aspects in “Place” defining: “Place means a geographically defined area. It may include elements, objects, spaces and views. Place may have tangible and intangible dimensions” (p.2). About “Places”, Silberman (2016) asks the following question: “How can such sweeping, all-inclusive definitions – attempting to cover all material, immaterial, objective, and subjective aspects of heritage places – possibly capture their irreducible essence? How can we identity the distinctive characteristic of heritage places without endlessly extending the list of specific material forms and subjective associations a heritage place may possess? At a time when officially recognized heritage types are splintering into distinct regional, ethnic, and religious variants [...], when the UNESCO World Heritage list has exceeded a thousand inscribed properties all said to possess Outstanding Universal Value [...], when the possession and control of cultural heritage resources have become symbols of political legitimacy, no single physical definition of a heritage place seems capable of capturing the thoroughly fragmented reality of cultural heritage in the twenty-first century. Thus focusing on process, rather than object, may be a more useful approach” (p.30).

Silberman highlights the difficulty in heritage definition, and the complexity in heritage identification. Elsewhere he comments different characteristic from which the investiture as heritage has derived: Official monuments with outstanding historical or artistic significance; Religious places; Places of civic manifestation, symbol of resistance or freedom, or on the opposite (or in parallel) of state power; Heritage places as entertainment venue; heritage places as reaction to change, related to self-perception and memory of communities. (Silberman, 2016, pp.29-40). Therefore, the lesson is that it is important to reflect on the process of heritage defining, rather than on authored outlining.

The UNESCO *World Heritage Cultural Landscape* (2009) fixes the concept of culture as cornerstone for "Landscape" definition, according to an interpretative line, which tends to integrate both tangible and intangible values into the landscape idea. What pointed out by the *Convention for the Safeguarding of Intangible Cultural Heritage* (UNESCO, 2003), recurs in all its relevance: Heritage is constantly recreated by communities. Not only intangible heritage, but also tangible heritage because it is the outcome of the secular and continuous interaction of anthropic action and use with nature. It suggests a bottom-up process to merge the traditional authoritative role of experts with participative approaches. This method could be useful to point out the cultural changing dynamics.

In conclusion, cultural issues are nodal characteristics of the present era of globalization, mass communication and content production (Schafer 2014).

The *Convention for the Safeguarding of Intangible Cultural Heritage* (UNESCO, 2003) expands the concepts of heritage – and therefore of conservation – from material manifestations, such as monuments and objects, to living expressions and to traditions transmitted during centuries. In practice, the distinction between tangible and intangible heritage replaces the one between cultural and natural heritage. Because the dualism tangible/intangible involves natural and cultural without any division. "The "intangible cultural heritage" means the practices, representations, expressions, knowledge, skills – as well as the instruments, objects, artefacts and cultural spaces associated therewith – that communities, groups and, in some cases, individuals recognize as part of their cultural heritage" (Art.2). It highlights the importance of "individuals", and not only of "people" or of "inhabitants", narrowing even more the "circle" of heritage making. Tangible elements (objects, spaces) are included in this kind of heritage. The text of the *Convention on Intangible Heritage* specifies that "This intangible cultural heritage, transmitted from generation to generation, is constantly recreated by communities and groups in response to their environment, their interaction with nature and their history, and provides them with a sense of identity and continuity, thus promoting respect for cultural diversity and human creativity". It undermines the traditional concept of heritage as monolithic object, and it suggests that we have to take into account that heritage is something changing.

The *Nara Document on Authenticity* (UNESCO, 1994) focuses on protection and enhancement of "Cultural Diversity" and "Heritage Diversity". It says "All cultures and societies are rooted in the particular forms and means of tangible and intangible expression which constitute their heritage, and these should be respected" (Art.7). This call for the 'intangible' was made to include non-European cultures, but today it is renewed by participative culture challenges.

The *Faro Convention* (Council of Europe, 2005) puts at the center the "community": It says that Cultural heritage is "a group of resources inherited from the past which people identify, independently of ownership, as a reflection and expression of their constantly evolving values, beliefs, knowledge and traditions. It includes all aspects of the environment resulting from the interaction between people and places through time"; and define 'Heritage Community' as "people who value specific aspects of cul-

Figure 2. View of the sectioned point cloud St. Cipriano (Carapelle Calvisio, IT)

tural heritage which they wish, within the framework of public action, to sustain and transmit to future generations" (p.2).

Therefore, the focus shift from heritage definition to the process of heritage making. Silberman and Purser (2012) say: "This whole hearted acceptance of re-creation and adoption as essential part of heritage significance places a new emphasis on process rather than product". It is a new idea of people centered heritage, "distinct from older, static conceptions of heritage as unambiguous, expert-defined and needing protection from the forces of change" (p.13). This approach gives to people an active and ineludible role in making sense of heritage and of sites. They are the main actors of interpretation. Heritage making becomes a social activity of interpretation, and according to a postmodern line, the discourse on interpretation defines the content. From this point of view, heritage looks like a "performance".

According to this context, communicative and participative opportunities given by digital devices and ICT could favor these cultural processes. Follows the necessity to reflect on the characteristics of digital heritage from real contents and on the issues posed by 3-D models and computer based visualization.

NEW MODALITIES OF COMMUNICATION

The communicative flow offered by the iconic text of the 3-D digital model, associated with the easy manipulability and the ability to be questioned, makes it a powerful and smart interface for information accessing and analysis. Unlike the textual structures, the model presents a simultaneously way of communication. It can work according through frames, operated with zooming, intersections, transparency, spatial and temporal skips. This flow finds in the three-dimensional architecture of the model its own structuring logic. The digital model provides new methods, timing, and spatial characteristics of visualization: The observer can freely navigate the model, and zoom it; he can proceed in a continuous way or skipping; he can enter the realm of the model, measuring, questioning, and dissecting it. In addition, the more innovative aspect is, perhaps, that the same model can be experienced at the same time in different ways (to the limit in infinite ways). Not only because it can be projected and sectioned as you desire, but also because it can be graphically represented in many ways (wireframe, shaded, textured, etc.) in parallel views from multiple points of view (Brusaporci, 2015b).

New technologies bring into question not only the traditional perception of the physical space of the architectural heritage and its relation with the mental space of the observer, but they disarticulate this relationship, with multiple interactive and simultaneous visualizations of different nature, accompanied by the moving and transformation of the "significant".

Focusing on architectural heritage, the representation is the first and more important tool for architectural heritage's study and communication, because visualization allows the scholars to "see" their ideas, make them experienceable, verify them, and – consequently – to change and improve their concepts, and share them. Architectural surveying is based on a historical-critical process, where data and information are summarized through graphical models (Docci & Maestri, 2009). Substantially digital tools move the representation in a three-dimensional space, that is in a space similar to the architectural one. And the 3-D model is a smart interface for the gathering, computing, sharing, and communication of the huge mass of information accompanying the architecture. Moreover, 3D modelling favours a heuristic process, because the modellers check and modify the results of the modelling procedures according to an iterative process of reading / understanding / communication of the architectural artefact's characteristics and values (Brusaporci, 2015a)

3-D architectural heritage models favour the development of historical-critical analysis, realized in the three-dimensional digital space (for example metrological, proportional, constructive analysis). In the 3-D re-constructions of architectural shape, from the raw data of point clouds, a special reflection should be done on the critical comprehension, interpretation, and definition of the design willingness of the author – and at the same time pointing out the irregularities –, with attention to the formal and geometrical principles intended according to the historical and technological context of the building.

Another consideration concerns the role that the digital models are taking over time: No more only an "aesthetic" simulation of reality – i.e. a representative image of a visual perception – but they are becoming "complex model": They are interactive models, manipulable, interrogable, and navigable. They allow new ways of visualization and new modalities to data and information access. In this way, the digital model should be a sort of "master model" both for architectural visualization and building's data and information's visualization. This complex informative model offers new non-linear narrative ways, collecting the whole knowledge, communication and design process (Brusaporci, 2015b).

It's limitative to consider modelling only a virtual construction of the geometric and spatial characteristic of the building: The modelling act also involves the numerous and heterogeneous information about the building. Data, metadata, paradata (Brusaporci, 2017b), and information are the core of the model: 3-D models and databases are two sides, and the modelling process has to involve both of them. The 3-D model's semantization and the "granularity" of its components are important aspects for the correlation with the informative model (Murray, 2012; Apollonio, 2012; Gaiani, 2012). This complex informative model offers new non-linear narratives, favouring the knowledge, communication and design.

INTERDISCIPLINARITY RECOMMENDATIONS IN COMPUTER BASED VISUALIZATION

From the very beginning of the Seventies, the archaeology has immediately looked carefully to the possibilities offered by computer modelling. It is a research path that, beginning from the purpose of digital representations as an effective tool for three-dimensional representation (Forte & Siliotti, 1996), developed towards the use of computer graphics for scientific research (Frischer, 2008). Hence, it has resulted in the need to define appropriate procedural protocols (Nicolucci, 2012).

How technology and digital simulation bring to new methodologies is evident in the work of Maurizio Forte. In particular, since 2000 he has proposed an eco-systemic approach for the archaeological research, called "Cyber-Archaeology" (Forte, 2000. Forte, 2008), based on a knowledge model realized through interactions and feedback in a virtual reality environment: It is an informative model with non-linear learning and communication processes, and, at the same time, a methodological instrument for scientific and cultural contents validation. Therefore, the VR has an epistemological computational role, according to a cybernetic model with a progressive information growth, where the observer and the observed contemporaneously interact in the same world. "Information" and "Relations" guide and enrich the model in a dynamic way. Forte highlights how the cybernetic model is a real informative model instead the informatics ones that only develops techniques of data computing (Forte, 2008 p.4).

According to the examples, it is evident how digital tools favour a new methodological approach in the archaeological study, strongly based on an interdisciplinary work.

In 2009, The London Charter (http://www.londoncharter.org/) aimed "to establish principles for the use of computer based visualization methods and outcomes in the research and communication of cultural heritage" (p.4). It arises from the consideration that "While computer-based visualisation methods are now employed in a wide range of contexts to assist in the research, communication and preservation of cultural heritage, a set of principles is needed that will ensure that digital heritage visualisation is, and is seen to be, at least as intellectually and technically rigorous as longer established cultural heritage research and communication methods. At the same time, such principles must reflect the distinctive properties of computer-based visualisation technologies and methods" (p.2).

The document is addressed to different academic, educational, curatorial and commercial domains, and it has the purpose to define principles of general validity in the use of digital visualization. Six principles are enunciated: 1. Implementation; 2: Aims and Methods; 3: Research Sources; 4: Documentation; 5: Sustainability; 6: Access.

Here – focusing on the concept of disciplinarity / interdisciplinarity – it is worth dwelling on the first principle: The Implementation. Assuming that "the principles of the London Charter are valid wherever computer-based visualisation is applied to the research or dissemination of cultural heritage", it is enunciated that "Each community of practice, whether academic, educational, curatorial or commercial, should develop London Charter Implementation Guidelines that cohere with its own aims, objectives and methods" (p. 5). This is of particular importance because in a document expressly with an interdisciplinary perspective, the first principle refers to a set of disciplinary specifications. The general principles are interdisciplinary: "for the use of computer-based visualisation methods in relation to intellectual integrity, reliability, documentation, sustainability and access" (p.2). But disciplinary are the specific declinations. In fact, the principle of Implementation also says: "Every computer-based visualisation heritage activity should develop, and monitor the application of, a London Charter Implementation Strategy" (p. 5). And the concept of "implementation" specifics relations that should exist between scholars of different fields when collaborate together: "And in collaborative activities, all participants whose role involves either directly or indirectly contributing to the visualisation process should be made aware of the principles of the London Charter, together with relevant Charter Implementation Guidelines, and to assess their implications for the planning, documentation and dissemination of the project as a whole." (p.5). Therefore, the Charter calls for all fields of research to provide guidelines as strict scientific methodological reference, also to favour the correlation between different scholars.

According to the principle of "Implementation" of The London Charter, in 2012 the "Principles of Seville - International Principles of Virtual Archaeology" have been realized to propose guidelines for archaeology (http://www.arqueologiavirtual.com/carta/?page_id=12).

The Principles of Seville recognize the recommendations of The London Charter and, at the same time, propose new and specific disciplinary purposes. Referring to the archaeological heritage, the document enunciates the following eight principles: 1. Interdisciplinarity; 2. Purpose; 3. Complementarity; 4. Authenticity; 5. Historical rigour; 6. Efficiency; 7. Scientific transparency; 8. Training and evaluation. These principles reflect the ones of The London Charter. Also, here there are numerous interesting elements for scholars of architecture.

We point out how in The London Charter the first principle calls for a disciplinary reflection and specification (top-down), while now the first principle of Seville focuses on interdisciplinarity (bottom-up): "Any project involving the use of new technologies, linked to computer-based visualisation in the field of archaeological heritage, whether for research, documentation, conservation or dissemination, must be supported by a team of professionals from different branches of knowledge". And going on: "Given the complex nature of computer-based visualization of archaeological heritage, it cannot be addressed only by a single type of expert but needs the cooperation of many specialists (archaeologists, computer scientists, historians, architects, engineers etc.)". And: "A truly interdisciplinary work involves the regular and fluid exchange of ideas and views among specialists from different fields. Work divided into watertight compartments can never be considered interdisciplinary even with the participation of experts from different disciplines" (p. 5).

It is evident how the discussed matters are common to all the disciplines where 3-D modelling of real contents – both restitutive models and interpretative or reconstructive models, for example from findings – plays an important role for visual computing and communication.

ARCHITECTURAL HERITAGE

Architectural heritage has some important characteristics. A building shapes from a relationship between "built" and "voids", masses and details; it's the synthesis of materials, surfaces, constructive systems, spaces able to accommodate human activities, last but not least aesthetic characteristics. All defined through continuous processes of modification and transformation over time. Therefore, a building witnesses cultures and events over time until today.

The building system plays a prominent role, as static reason of existence of the architectural artefact, and witnesses of the architectural and constructive cultures occurred in the past: It is the "support" of the building and its physical reference. The surveying, comprehension, and "re-construction" of the building's system require a critical reflection, in particular because usually it is not directly visible and not totally experienceable – except in the case of ruin –: It has to be studied and represented according to direct and indirect analysis.

Figure 3. Point could of St. Cipriano, internal view (Carapelle Calvisio, IT)

In architecture, constructive and aesthetic characteristics sustain the building's ability to satisfy the necessity to be used – both from a spatial and environmental point of view –. The use implies continuous processes of transformation and adaptation. Finally yet importantly, a very important issue is the study of the spatial context, because it is an essential element of each specific building. In particular, recalling the concept that an historical centre can be intended as a "sylloge" of architectures, each building has both its own historical and aesthetic values and urban ones – constantly changing – rising from the relationship with other surrounding buildings.

Scholars of architecture have various kinds of archival documents, ancient and recent, often scattered in several archives: Graphical and textual archival data on the yard, the building, and its transformations, on the different players (designers, builders, contractors, etc.); bibliographies and biographies; different kinds of drawings, such as previous surveys, paintings, etc.; photographs; surveying data (preliminary surveying sketches, field notebooks, measures, point clouds, etc.); 2D and 3D interpretative models; comparative, metrological, proportional, historical, structural, energetic analysis, and on degradation and materials analysis; reports, calculations, and project elaborations. Moreover, the architectural analysis requires the study of other works of the same author and of the same workers, and of buildings of the same age and of the same architectural culture. Data, information, and considerations arising from the critical interpretation made by surveyors and scholars may be added to this information core. The virtual re-construction of non-more existing buildings or of past configurations, or of projects not realized – critically made according to the historical documents and/or to the traces still existing –, favour the historical-critical analysis of the architectural and cultural events. The historical "dimension" of the building requires its study also considering the architectural theories of the past – preserved by treatises and manuals –, original writings and drawings, and recent and past critical studies (Brusaporci, 2015a).

In 1983 the XXI Congress of History of Architecture was held in Rome, organized by the Centro di Studi per la Storia dell'Architettura [Centre for the Study of the History of Architecture] and by the Istituto dell'Enciclopedia Italiana [Institute of the Italian Encyclopaedia]. In particular, the paper titled "Autonomia della Storia dell'Architettura" [Autonomy of the History of Architecture] by Gianfranco Spagnesi (1984) is really interesting: Spagnesi starts from a disciplinary reflection on the study of history in the architectural field: "we must reaffirm the autonomy of architectural history [...] especially the identification of an own field of investigation, studied with own tools, that cannot be confused with ones of other historical disciplines". Then "If history is always equivalent to knowledge, the History of Architecture has to be the knowledge of the physical built space made by men, i.e. the current reality" (p.7). The fact is that an architectural heritage bases its ontology precisely on the fact of being a building equipped with a story. Therefore, its total study, and then its visualization, cannot evade its historicity and therefore the study of its history.

The first important aspect is the subject of knowledge: the "physical built space". The wording "physical space" recalls the study of the space according to its geometries, functions, but also to architectural elements, materials, illumination and perception. The adjective "built" points out that an artefact must be studied – first of all – as a tangible heritage, made by specific constructive techniques, witnesses of the protagonists and architectural cultures occurred over time. Therefore, the study of designers, technologies, yards, workers assumes further significance. This does not exclude other kinds of studies – intangible heritage – that can favourably accompany the study of the "built" because architectural heritage makes immanent and tangible social, cultural, and historical aspects of people that built and transformed it in the past, and that currently lives it.

The second aspect to note is the emphasis on the concept of "current reality": the study of the history for an architectural artefact aims to analyse the existent building. Compared to archaeology, the viewpoint is reversed: Not the re-construction of no more existing artefacts (usually from existing remains), – obviously underlining the importance of the findings –. The History of Architecture is the analysis of a temporal sequence of events that led to the current state. In fact, Spagnesi highlights: "only the "current reality" can be known, the contemporary one, through the analysis of the causes that determined it" (p.7). Spagnesi concludes: "The knowledge of reality is the critical synthesis of the judgments of values referred to the singles historical moments" that conduced to the current situation (p.10). That is the study of the past configurations aims to the understanding of the values of the current artefact.

It's interesting a definition of heritage given by Silberman (2008), and his parallel consideration on the concept of past: "Heritage is an ever-changing array of objects and symbols, a complex mosaic of artefacts, images, monuments, and customs that demand our attention and demand that we give some meaning to them". While "The Past – in contrast to heritage – is one of the most virtual of the realities we be to content with. It is an untouchable phantom: a once lived reality that survives only in fragments and can be experienced only in retrospect" (p.18). This last remark recalls the archaeological experiences primarily aimed at the re-construction of a no longer existing past from the findings. In the architectural field, heritage has a different quality of immanence and physicality, compared with archaeological remains. The aim of the historical representations of a building is the study of actual values, and it isn't only the re-discovering of values today no more existing: Compared to archaeology, the critical perspective of the historical reconstruction is inverted. Therefore, in archaeology the study of history is first a path toward the past, in architecture a way to the present, and therefore to the project: A project of conservation that involves the "image" of the building, its systems, its everyday use. (Brusaporci, 2014. Brusaporci, 2017a).

Figure 4. Point could of the catacombs St. Vittorino (L'Aquila, IT)

ARCHITECTURAL HERITAGE BUILDING INFORMATION MODELING

Building Information Modelling is a process that place the 3-D model at the centre of the design process. The model is a tool for project development, a shared and interoperable interface between the various professionals involved: The BIM is interdisciplinary by definition, because involves professional experts of civil engineering, architecture, technological systems, restoration.

The concept of Information is central and related to model's components made by 3-D objects semantically defined as elements of the constructive system. Therefore, they represent both geometrical features, materials aspects, and structural, energetic, economic characteristics. Differently from CAD objects, they are not general volumes, but they are walls, floors, windows, doors, etc. Consequently, they are pre-defined by libraries, i.e. these components are standardized. Recently, numerous studies have focused on the application of BIM to architectural heritage. However, numerous problems are matter of investigation (Garagnani, 2015; Dore & Murphy, 2015; Garagnani, 2013; Apollonio, Gaiani & Zheng, 2012; Centofanti & Brusaporci, 2012; Murphy, McGovern, & Pavia, 2011; Brusaporci & Maiezza, 2016; Brusaporci, Maiezza & Tata, 2018).

A first reflection concerns the modelling of historical buildings. The current surveying technologies based on 3-D laser-scanning and digital photogrammetry permit the acquisition of significant amount of metric data, in very short times. Once you get the point clouds, three essential questions are posed: First, the issues related to procedures for the derivation of 3-D models from point clouds; Secondly, the problems of 3-D definition not only according to external shape but also to internal and intrinsic material and constructive aspects; Thirdly – perhaps the more complex problem from a conceptual point of view –, the BIM model is made by parametrized and standardized objects, uploaded from libraries, while every historic building is the synthesis of processes of modification and stratification during time, and its components are realized – in most cases – with craft practices. That is the matters is how reconcile the unique character of historical architecture, with parametric 3D objects from typed libraries.

Considering the Historic Building Information Modelling (HBIM) approach, the architectural elements are parametrized according to historical manuals and treatises. This semi-automatic procedure is founded on plug-in that uses libraries of historic architectural building components and algorithms – based on the classic proportions and on architectural rules – that combine automatically the library items. Subsequently, the operator alters the parameters and refines the model by matching with surveying data (Dore & Murphy, 2015). It is also possible the importation of complex geometric shapes – for example NURBS – trying to overcome the deficiencies of BIM software in surface modelling (Oreni et al. 2014).

In parallel with the problem of modelling, a second important reflection on the implementation and management of information related to the model arises: The BIM database, as designed for new buildings realization, does not fully support the vastness and heterogeneity of information necessary for the documentation and computing of architectural heritage. The specificity, heterogeneity and multiplicity of information requires the creation of appropriate databases, able to record, manage, analyse, and correlate more complex information than one traditionally offered by BIM on the market (for example archival data and documents, such as historical and recent drawings, reports, photos, etc., but also various kinds of studies, investigations and diagnostics). A solution is offered by the use of a Relational Database Management System that is a more extensive database in which insert the BIM model and its information. This research line is the so-called Built Heritage Information Modelling (B(H)IM) aiming to integrate 3-D BIM models with a knowledge system based on ontologies (Simeone et al., 2014).

Provocatively, someone suggests that BIM should favour the end of drawing and the end of the role of the Architect, substituted by a team of architects, engineers, builders, producers, and stakeholders (Scheer 2014; Sacchi, 2015). From a conceptual point of view, it may be true, but when the BIM is applied to architectural heritage, the role of historical scholar is unavoidable. Recently, studies highlight how the HBIM process is substantially different from the traditional BIM one: the BIM was naturally born for new building design, instead HBIM deals with an inductive knowledge process of existing buildings. Therefore, issues of "transparency" (see The London Charter, 2009) and the "realiability" of the model compared to the real content are essential (Maiezza, 2019).

FUTURE RESEARCH LINES: PARTICIPATIVE HERITAGE

The participatory approaches (Jenkins, 2009) are based on interactive and bidirectional media, where sharing and individual collaboration enable and strengthen the diffusion and adhesion to participatory cultures. The result is a strong creative tension, with an interpretative cooperation, rooted on an open-ended process of updating and on skill development for sources, accessing, creative reworking and distribution. The phenomena of "collective intelligence" rises (Levy, 1994): It is based on a multitasking cognitive approach that is on continuous experiences and successive approximations. Follows that the culture-making configures no more like a linear process but as a complex evolving discourse. In the networked society, consumers have become active content producers, and the distinction between scholar(s), modeler(s) and user(s) blends, according to new kind of media.

Jenkins (2009) says that participative culture is at least a "cultural matter" and not only a "technological problem": "The importance of culture's complex relationship with technology is why we focus [...] on the concept of participatory cultures rather than on interactive technologies, inter-activity is a property of the technology, while participation is a property of culture. Participatory culture is emerging as the culture adsorbs and responds to the explosion of new media technologies that make it possible

Figure 5. Point could of the catacombs St. Vittorino (L'Aquila, IT).

for average consumers to archive, annotate, appropriate, and recirculate media content in powerful new ways" (p.8). Jenkins defines "participatory culture" as "a culture with relatively low barriers to artistic expression and civic engagement, strong support for creating and sharing creations, and some type of informal mentorship whereby experienced participants pass along knowledge to novices. In a participatory culture, members also believe their contributions matter and feel some degree of social connection with one another" (p. xi). In particular, the following skills underlies the participative culture: Affiliation, Expression, Collaborative problem solving, Circulation. New skills follow: Play, Performance, Simulation, Appropriation, Multitasking, Distributed cognition, Collective intelligence, Judgment, Transmedia navigation, Networking, Negotiation.

Murray, in her famous book *Hamlet on the Holodeck* (1997), points out four essential proprieties of digital environments: They are Procedural, Participatory, Spatial and Encyclopedic. And focusing on the aesthetics of the medium, she highlights the importance of immersion, agency, and transformation. Manovich in *The Language of New Media* (2001) states five basic principles of new media: Numerical representation, Modularity, Automation, Variability, Transcoding.

All these aspects have repercussions on the cultural heritage field: On the ways of access and fruition, on heritage meaning and value making, on heritage interpretation and presentation, etc.

In addition, the public space for participatory culture changes: The Internet and Social media favor the meeting and discussion, in particular within dedicated groups of discussion – the so-called "eco chambers" – populated by people with similar interests. These are "spaces of affinity" where shared ideas and cultures grow and diffuse. They are not cultural laissez faire spaces, but they are ruled by complex balances: The "Posts", the "I Like", the answers and comments, not least the authoritative role of group managers. The control is complex and based on group admins, on senior followers opinions, on member reactions.

Participation could also be a research methodology. For example there are many experiences based on Agent-based Modeling (Wurzel, Kowarik, & Reschreiter, 2015), such as the "Lost Frontiers" Project Web Site (https://lostfrontiers.teamapp.com/).

How digital simulation brings to new methodologies is evident in the work of Forte: In particular he proposed an eco-systemic approach for the archaeological research, called "Cyber-Archeology" (Forte, 2000), based on a knowledge model realized through the interaction and feedback in a virtual reality environment: It is an informative model with non-linear learning and communication processes, and, at the same time, a methodological instrument for scientific and cultural contents validation. In this way, the VR has an epistemological computational role, according to a cybernetic model with a progressive information growth, where the observer and the observed contemporaneously interact in the same world. "Information" and "Relations" guide and enrich the model in a dynamic way. Forte highlights how the cybernetic model is a real informative model instead the informatics ones that only develops techniques of data computing (Forte, 2008 p.4).

The effective participation of people – that is of non-disciplinary experts – could foresee scenarios characterized by interdisciplinarity. However, practically these modalities of participation aren't in a laissez-faire environments, but into systems where experts, scholars, professionals that defines interaction modalities, admins, and senior followers play a very important role.

CONCLUSION

The study of architectural heritage has a vocation for interdisciplinary, because historical buildings are multifaceted artefacts.

The field of architecture is long time facing with the digital technologies, but they have changed and are still changing the "modus operandi" of surveying, visualization, data archiving, analysis, and communication (Brusaporci, 2015b).

In particular the scientific community interested in architectural heritage should develop a debate on principles and procedures for computer based visualization of historical (but also contemporary) buildings.

The principles of The London Charter, and the example given by the Principles of Seville, are useful references point for the architectural field. In fact, considering the interdisciplinary context of many researches, the sharing of principles of general validity should be advantageous in heterogeneous groups and favour the "conversation" between scholars.

Thus, a definition of disciplinary ontologies in the "digital dimension" of architecture should be useful. And similarly, the drafting of a glossary – already proposed in The London Charter and in the Seville Principles –: it should be a disciplinarily vocabulary useful to be understood in the interdisciplinary arena. If the development of Principles for computer based visualization of architectural heritage should be significant, many research lines – mainly carried on by scholars involved in interdisciplinary studies – are focused on the definition of Procedures. They are guidelines, based on methodologies and workflows, to define a scientific, critical and verifiable process. And they allow the collaboration of scholars of different fields (for example see Benedetti, Gaiani, & Remondino, 2010).

In conclusion, we cite the interesting the debate on the relationship between Humanities and digital technologies (Gold, 2012; Terras, Nyhan, Vanhoutte, 2013). And we'd like to mention Ramsay (2013) once again: "[…] no discipline can survive without actively engaging with disciplinary questions. Not because there are definitive answers. Least of all because it's important to alienate people. But simply because without those questions, we cede the answer to institutions eager to oblige people who are paying attention. Personally, I think Digital Humanities is about building things." (pp. 240-241).

Embraceable is the claim for a deep cultural debate, instead of a recurrent interest restricted on tools and computing, made by Koh (2015). She highlights: "[…] champion the new wave of digital humanities: one which has humanistic questions at its core".

In architecture, digital heritage moves from a physical content, therefore the technological issues on measurement, modelling, and rendering are substantial, but the critical and cultural core cannot be forgotten. Because computer-based visualization is ever a compromise between measurement, modelling, rendering, culture, and interpretation. In conclusion, digital technologies favour important interdisciplinary approaches. We don't believe in "multi-disciplinarity" intended as critic to specialization, or in "trans-disciplinarity" as ability of the scholar to "morph" into other fields. But scholars should learn from each other, paying attention to purposes, with a wise critical approach, aware of their methodologies and of the peculiar characteristics of their field of interest.

REFERENCES

Apollonio, F. I. (2012). *Architettura in 3D*. Milano: Bruno Mondadori.

Apollonio, F.I., Gaiani, M., & Zheng, S. (2012). BIM-based modeling and data enrichment of classical architectural buildings. *SCIRES-IT*, *2*(2).

Benedetti, B., Gaiani, M., & Remondino, F. (2010). *Modelli digitali 3D in archeologia: il caso di Pompei*. Pisa: Scuola Normale Superiore Pisa.

Brusaporci, S. (2014). Issues of Historic Town Surveying: Visualizing Urban Values. *SCIRES.IT, 4*(2), 63-80.

Brusaporci, S. (2015 a). The Representation of Architectural Heritage in the Digital Age. In M. Khosrow-Pour (Ed.), Encyclopedia of Information Science and Technology, Third Edition (pp. 4195-4205, VI). Hershey, PA: IGI Global. doi:10.4018/978-1-4666-5888-2.ch412

Brusaporci, S. (2015 b). On Visual Computing for Architectural Heritage. In S. Brusaporci (Ed.), *Handbook of Research on Emerging Digital Tools for Architectural Surveying, Modeling, and Representation* (pp. 94–123). Hershey, PA: IGI Global. doi:10.4018/978-1-4666-8379-2.ch003

Brusaporci, S. (2016). Swimming in the Liquid Age: A Disciplinarily Reflection on Computer-Based Visualization of Architectural Heritage. In G. Amoruso (Ed.), *Handbook of Research on Visual Computing and Emerging Geometrical Design Tools* (pp. 1–24). Hersey, PA: IGI Global. doi:10.4018/978-1-5225-0029-2.ch001

Brusaporci, S. (2017a). *Digital Innovations in Architectural Heritage Conservation: Emerging Research and Opportunities*. Hersey, PA: IGI Global. doi:10.4018/978-1-5225-2434-2

Brusaporci, S. (2017b). The Importance of Being Honest: Issues of Transparency in Digital Visualization of Architectural Heritage. In A. Ippolito (Ed.), *Handbook of Research on Emerging Technologies for Architectural and Archaeological Heritage* (pp. 66–93). Hersey, PA: IGI Global. doi:10.4018/978-1-5225-0675-1.ch003

Brusaporci, S., & Maiezza, P. (2016). Re-Loading BIM: Between Spatial and Database Information Modeling for Architectural Heritage Documentation. In F. Felip Miralles, J. Gual Ortí, M. Cabeza González, & C. García-García (Eds.), *Dibujar, Construir, Sonar. Investigaciones en torno a la expresion grafica aplicada a la edificacion* (pp. 835–847). Valencia: Tirant Lo Blanch.

Brusaporci, S., Maiezza, P., & Tata, A. (2018). A Framework for Architectural Heritage HBIM Semantization and Development. *The International Archives of the Photogrammetry, Remote Sensing and Spatial Information Sciences*, *42*, 179–184. doi:10.5194/isprs-archives-XLII-2-179-2018

Calabi, D. (Ed.). (2013). *Built City, Designed City, Virtual City, The Museum of the City*. Roma: CROMA.

Cameron, F., & Kenderdine, S. (Eds.). (2010). *Theorizing digital cultural heritage: a critical discourse*. Cambridge, MA: MIT Press.

Card, S. K., Mackinlay, J., & Shneiderman, B. (Eds.). (1999). *Readings in Information Visualization: Using Vision to Think*. San Francisco, CA: Morgan Kaufmann.

Centofanti, M., & Brusaporci, S. (2012). Architectural 3D modeling in historical buildings knowledge and restoration processes. In C. Gambardella (Ed.), *Less More architecture design landscape*. Naples: La Scuola di Pitagora.

Council of Europe. (2005). *Framework Convention on the Value of Cultural Heritage for Society*. Retrieved on September, 25, 2019 from http://www.coe.int/t/dg4/cultureheritage/heritage/Identities/default_en.asp

Docci, M. (Ed.). (2005). *Metodologie innovative integrate per il rilievo dell'architettura e dell'ambiente*. Roma: Gangemi.

Docci, M., & Maestri, D. (2009). *Manuale di rilevamento architettonico e urbano*. Rome: Laterza.

Dore, C., & Murphy, M. (2015). Historic Building Information Modelling (HBIM). In S. Brusaporci (Ed.), *Handbook of Research on Emerging Digital Tools for Architectural Surveying, Modeling, and Representation* (Vols. 1–2). Hershey, PA: IGI Global. doi:10.4018/978-1-4666-8379-2.ch007

Forte, M. (2000). About Virtual Archaeology: Disorders, Cognitive Interactions and Virtuality. In Virtual Reality in Archaeology (pp. 247-263). Oxford, UK: BAR International Series S843 (Archaeopress).

Forte, M. (2008). Introduzione. In M. Forte (Ed.), La Villa di Livia. Un percorso di realtà virtuale (pp.1-36). Roma: "L'Erma" di Bretschneider.

Forte, M., & Siliotti, A. (Eds.). (1996). *Virtual Archaeology. Re-creating Ancient Words*. New York: Harry N. Abrams.

Frischer, B. (2008). From digital illustration to digital heuristic. In B. D. Frischer (Ed.), *Beyond illustration: 2d and 3d Digital Technologies As Tool for Discovery in Archaeology*. Oxford, UK: British Archaeological Reports.

Gaiani, M. (2006). Un viaggio attraverso gli strumenti e i metodi di produzione del progetto di disegno industriale nell'epoca della progettazione digitale totale. In M. Gaiani (Ed.), *La rappresentazione riconfigurata* (pp. 23–57). Milano: Poli.Design.

Gaiani, M. (2012). Towards a critical rethinking of the theory of surveying following the advent of digital media. In L. Carlevaris & M. Filippa (Eds.), *In Praise of Theory. The fundamentals of the disciplines of representation and survey* (pp. 375–381). Roma: Gangemi.

Garagnani, S. (2013). Building Information Modeling and real world knowledge: a methodological approach to accurate semantic documentation for the built environment. In Proceedings of Digital Heritage 2013 (vol. 1, pp. 489-496). Marseille: IEEE. doi:10.1109/DigitalHeritage.2013.6743788

Garagnani, S. (2015). Semantic Representation of Accurate Surveys for the Cultural Heritage: BIM Applied on the Existing Domain. In S. Brusaporci (Ed.), *Handbook of Research on Emerging Digital Tools for Architectural Surveying, Modeling, and Representation* (pp. 292–310). Hershey, PA: IGI Global. doi:10.4018/978-1-4666-8379-2.ch009

Gold, M. K. (Ed.). (2012). *Debates in the Digital Humanities.* University of Minnesota Press.

ICOMOS. (2013). *Charter for Places of Cultural Significance.* Retrieved on September, 25, 2019 from http://australia.icomos.org/publications/charters/

Jenkins, H. (2009). *Confronting the Challenges of Participatory Culture: Media Education for the 21st Century.* Cambridge, MA: MIT. doi:10.7551/mitpress/8435.001.0001

Koh, A. (2015, April 19). A Letter to Humanities: DH Will Not Save You. *Hybridpedagogy.*

Lake, M. W. (2014). Trends in Archaeological Simulation. *Journal of Archaeological Method and Theory, 21*(2), 258–287. doi:10.100710816-013-9188-1

Maiezza, P. (2019). As-Built Reliability in Architectural HBIM Modeling. *The International Archives of the Photogrammetry, Remote Sensing and Spatial Information Sciences, 42*(W9), 461–466. doi:10.5194/isprs-archives-XLII-2-W9-461-2019

Manovich, L. (2001). *The Language of New Media.* Cambridge, MA: The MIT Press.

Murphy, M., McGovern, E., & Pavia, S. (2011). Historic building information modelling - adding intelligence to laser and image based surveys. *The International Archives of the Photogrammetry, Remote Sensing and Spatial Information Sciences, 38*(W16).

Murray, J. (1997). *Hamlet on the Holodeck. The Future of Narrative in Cyberspace.* Cambridge, MA: The MIT Press.

Murray, J. H. (2012). *Inventing the Medium. Principles of Interaction Design as a Cultural Practice.* Cambridge, MA: The MIT Press.

Nicolucci, F. (2012). Setting Standards for 3D Visualization of Cultural Heritage. In *Paradata and Transparency in Virtual Heritage* (pp. 23–36). Farnham: Ashgate Publishing.

Oreni, D., Brumana, R., Della Torre, S., Banfi, F., Barazzetti, L., & Previtali, M. (2014). Survey turned into HBIM: The restoration and the work involved concerning the Basilica di Collemaggio after the earthquake (L'Aquila). *ISPRS Annals of the Photogrammetry. Remote Sensing and Spatial Information Sciences, 2*(5), 267–273.

Parry, R. (Ed.). (2010). *Museums in a Digital Age.* Abingdon, UK: Routledge.

Perry, R. (2003). Foreword. Digital Heritage: Agora and Agility. In E. Ch'ng, V. Gaffney, & H. Chapman (Eds.), *Visual Heritage in the Digital Age* (pp. v–vii). New York: Springer-Verlag.

Pescarin, S. (2016). Digital Heritage into Practice. *SCIRES-IT*, *6*(1), 1–4.

Principles of Seville. (2012). Retrieved on September, 25, 2019, from http://smartheritage.com/seville-principles/seville-principles

Ramsay, S. (2013). Who's In and Who's Out. In M. Terras, M. Nyhan, & E. Vanhoutte (Eds.), *Defining Digital Humanities* (pp. 239–241). Farnham: Ashgate.

Schafer, D. P. (2014). *The Age of Culture*. Rock's Mills Press.

Silberman, N. (2008). Chasing the Unicorn? The Quest for Essence in Digital Heritage. In Y. E. Kalay, T. Kvan, & J. Affleck (Eds.), *New Heritage* (pp. 81–91). Abington, UK: Routledge.

Silberman, N. (2016). Heritage places: Evolving conceptions and changing forms. In W. Logan, M. N. Craith, & U. Kockel (Eds.), *A Companion to Heritage Studies*. London: Wiley-Blackwell.

Silberman, N., & Purser, M. (2012). Collective memory as affirmation: People-centered cultural heritage in a digital age. In E. Giaccardi (Ed.), *Heritage and Social Media: Understanding heritage in a Participatory Culture* (pp. 13–29). Abingdon, UK: Routledge.

Simeone, D., Cursi, S., Toldo, I., & Carrara, G. (2014). B(H)IM – Built Heritage Information Modelling. Extending BIM to historical and archaeological heritage representation. In E. Mine Thompson (Ed.). *Fusion, Proceedings of the 31nd International Conference on Education and research in Computer Aided Architectural Design in Europe:* Vol. 1. *eCAADe: Conferences 1* (pp. 613-622). Newcastle upon Tyne, UK: Northumbria University.

Spagnesi, G. (1984). Autonomia della Storia dell'architettura. In G. Spagnesi (Ed.), *Storia e restauro dell'architettura* (pp. 7–10). Roma: Istituto della Enciclopedia Italiana Treccani.

Stone, R. J. (1999, Nov.). Virtual heritage. *UNESCO World Heritage Magazine*, 18-20.

Tamborrino, R. (Ed.). (2014). *Digital Urban History: Telling the History of the City in the Age of ICT Revolution*. Roma: Croma.

Terras, M., Nyhan, J., & Vanhoutte, E. (Eds.). (2013). *Defining Digital Humanities: A Reader*. Farnham: Ashgate.

The London Charter. (2009). Retrieved on September, 25, 2019, from http://www.londoncharter.org/

UNESCO. (1994). *The Nara Document on Authenticity*. Retrieved on September, 25, 2019, from whc.unesco.org/document/9379

UNESCO. (2003). *Charter on the Preservation of the Digital Heritage*. Retrieved on September, 25, 2019, from http://portal.unesco.org/en/ev.php-URL_ID=17721&URL_DO=DO_TOPIC&URL_SECTION=201.html

UNESCO. (2009). *World Heritage Cultural Landscape*. Retrieved on September, 25, 2019, from http://whc.unesco.org/en/culturallandscape/

Wurzel, G., Kowarik, K., & Reschreiter, H. (Eds.). (2015). *Agent-based Modeling and Simulation in Archeology*. Cham: Springer. doi:10.1007/978-3-319-00008-4

KEY TERMS AND DEFINITIONS

3D Modeling: Realization of a system of information based on and referred to a model in the virtual 3-D space. The model is made by digital solids and/or surfaces, able to simulate the characteristics of an object. The 3-D model can rise from physical objects (according to a "reverse modeling" process) or directly assembling 3-D digital forms. 3-D modeling includes the modeling of the scene, lights, cameras, textures, using both 2-D (for example background images or the so called "impostor billboards") and 3D elements. The characteristics of the 3-Ds are related to the ones of the object and to the aims of the representation. A model could present a photorealistic image or both iconic and symbolic representations.

Architectural Heritage: The UNESCO 1972 World Heritage Convention indicates as cultural heritage monuments, group of buildings and sites, outstanding universal value from the point of view of history, art or science. In the modern theory by Brandi, the qualities of a cultural heritage are the historical and the aesthetic values. An historical building is a complex system of spaces, volumes, materials, surfaces, constructive aspects, actual and past functions and configurations, degradation, etc. The whole is the result of a continuous historical process of modification and transformation. An architectural heritage can be interpreted as an "artifact", where its elements are witnesses of the cultures, actors, and of events occurred during the life of the building. In the study of architectural heritage is fundamental the archival analysis.

BIM: Building information modeling is a process about the whole lifecycle of a building, from project, to construction, maintenance, management and dismantlement. BIM is based on the realization of the 3-D models, where the digital elements are constructive objects (walls, floors, windows, etc.) uploaded from predefined parametrized libraries. The objects relate to a database with the design information that allow structural, energetic, economic, timing, computing. BIM involves the architectural, civil engineering, and plant aspects, and it favors the interoperability between professionals that work on the same model. BIM rises for new building design, but its application to historic architectures (the so called HBIM) presents numerous matters, because it is difficult to reconcile the unique character of historical architecture made with artisan procedures, with parametric 3D objects from standardized libraries and typed databases; interesting solutions rises from the integration of BIM procedures with Visual Programming Language.

Semantization: Logical division of digital model's components and of related information according to their meaning. In architectural heritage models, the semantization can be realized "a-posteriori" (reverse modeling processes) or "a-priori" (for example Constructive Solid Geometry processes).

Virtual Reality: It bases on a total-body immersion in a computer-generated environment. Perceptions derives from digital information and, although the synthetic environment often follows laws different from real word ones, the user has a psychological involvement and lives it like a real experience.

Visual Computing: Technique of analysis based on the visual representation of large amount of data. Those data can derive from various kinds or phenomena, also from non-visual ones. Visual computing consists in the representation of three-dimensional digital environments, where there is a complex interaction of an elevated number of agents simulating different kinds of data and information. The images provide information and through images, the user can observe, interact with, compute and control data and information, and create new knowledge.

ENDNOTE

1 Retrieved on September 25, 2019 from http://www.unesco.org/new/en/cairo/culture/tangible-cultural-heritage/

Chapter 13
Toward Smart Heritage:
Cultural Challenges in Digital Built Heritage

Stefano Brusaporci
https://orcid.org/0000-0002-8505-7895
L'Aquila University, Italy

ABSTRACT

The concept of cultural heritage has evolved over time. In relation to a context where digital technologies and ICT are changing our everyday lives and the way to visualize, experience, and think, the growth of digital heritage poses new issues in the conceptual and operative relationship with real contents. The chapter reflects on the concept of tangible heritage, presents issues in heritage digitalization, and highlights the new relationships that the real dimension and the digital sphere of heritage establish, according to advanced frontiers of mixed heritage. Pressing topics are the matters of interpretation and presentation of heritage, the transparency of digital communication, and the participation of people in cultural content through digital content production, sharing, re-elaboration.

INTRODUCTION: DIGITAL BUILT HERITAGE

The growing of computing capabilities, the development of Information and Communication Technologies, the opportunity offered by digital heritage for different purposes, and the diffusion of non-expensive – often free – software and apps of easy use has made digital tools ever more affordable for everyone and used indifferently and simultaneously in dissimilar research fields. Consequently, there is a constant ever rising of digital products, and a wide overlapping and mixing of tools, methodologies, and research object and aims made by different kind of scholars, such as computer scientists, topographers, surveyors, archaeologists, architects, engineers.

The *Charter on the Preservation of the Digital Heritage* (UNESCO, 2003a), points out that the Digital Heritage is not something special, out of the ordinary, but it is a 'Common Heritage'. It can be constituted by: "cultural, educational, scientific and administrative resources, as well as technical, medical and other

DOI: 10.4018/978-1-7998-2871-6.ch013

kinds of information created digitally, or converted into digital form from existing analogue resources. It includes different kinds of products such as texts, databases, images, audio, graphies, software and web pages". In particular, the Charter claims for maintenance, management, and access.

In 1999, on UNESCO's "World Heritage Magazine", Stone defined Virtual Heritage as: «the utilization of technology for interpretation, conservation and preservation of Natural, Cultural and World Heritage» (Stone, 1999).

Unlike Stone's definition of Virtual Heritage, in the *Charter* the Digital Heritage tends to assume an independent connotation and value. This qualification of digital heritage is favored by the diffusion of digital products and by the growth of tools, technologies, and methodologies that today are ineludible and pervasive for each field.

The digital objects assume a new meaning of "real", but in digital heritage from real contents, conceptually this real meaning cannot be related with the physical content, from which it derives. In this kind of digital heritage, there is not visualization without a prior reality and, in a philological study of a digital model, we cannot forget its real reference from whom it is born. Therefore, the issues related to data and information grow to include the relationship with history and materiality.

A double condition of the digital model of built heritage descends: On one side the 'relation with the reality', on the other side its 'digital nature'. The wording "heritage" implies that the digital resources presents own values, but indirectly related to the physical content.

As pointed out by Digital Heritage Charter (UNESCO, 2003a), we can see the digital historical objects independently by human creativity, according to a status of object in its own right. Being a critical product of a creative-interpretative act, the model is a knowledge contribution and, therefore, it becomes a new document: Centofanti (2010) writes: "The representative and restitutive model of an architectural heritage is an integral part of historical knowledge and an autonomous text that can be subjected to further analysis and interpretations. Indeed the model provides a series of useful information on the architectural significant [...]. In turn, the model lends itself to be historicized and studied no more, and not only for its relationship with the presented object, but as a document itself in relation to the historical and cultural context that produced it" (p.47). Moreover, being equipped with values, digital heritage has to be safeguarded. Therefore, we remember the recommendations of the Charter on Digital Heritage (UNESCO, 2003a) about the guarding against loss of heritage, the need for action, in particular related to the lifecycle of information, and the development of strategies and policies.

ON TANGIBLE HERITAGE

A deep reflection on heritage conservation and protection moved from the rise of a critical consciousness of the past. At the beginning, it originated from the archaeological findings of XVIII century, and it has grown especially from the XIX century – let us remember the works of Viollet Le-Duc in France e John Ruskin in England –, with important consequences in the culture, documents and laws of different countries. Without retracing the well-known history of conservation and protection, it is useful to develop the discourse from the consideration made in the second half of the XX century.

The *Convention for the Protection of Cultural Property in the Event of Armed Conflict* (1954), adopted soon after the WWII, is the first international treaty on heritage safeguarding with a worldwide vocation. It focuses on the protection of cultural heritage in the event of armed conflict and "It covers ammovable and movable cultural heritage, including monuments of architecture, art or history, archaeological sites, works of art, manuscripts, books and other objects of artistic, historical or archaeological interest, as well as scientific collections of all kinds regardless of their origin or ownership". Heritage is intended as a material artifact with evidence of culture. The wording "Cultural Property", to define heritage, has a "legal" suggestion, influenced by the French concept of "bien culturel". "Bien" recalls the idea of "value", here not in an economic sense, but referred to historical, formal and cultural characteristics of the work of art. Somehow, "property" evokes the idea of belonging, affiliation and identity, namely the "historical value". Similarly, the Anglo-Saxon "heritage" remembers that artifacts are a legacy, embodying the story and witnessing the past cultures.

The UNESCO *Convention Concerning the Protection of the World Cultural and Natural Heritage* (1972, aka *World Heritage Convention*) distinguishes between "cultural heritage" and "natural heritage":

"Art. 1 For the purpose of this Convention, the following shall be considered as 'cultural heritage':

- monuments: architectural works, work s of monumental sculpture and painting, elements or structures of an archaeological nature, inscriptions, cave dwellings and combinations of features, which are of out standing universal value from the point of view of history, art or science;
- groups of buildings: groups of separate or connected buildings which, because of their architecture, their homogeneity or their place in the landscape, are of outstanding universal value from the point of view of history, art or science;
- sites: works of man or the combined works of nature and man, and areas including archaeological sites which are of outstanding universal value from the historical, aesthetic, ethnological or anthropological point of view.

Art. 2 For the purposes of this Convention, the following shall be considered as 'natural heritage':

- natural features consisting of physical and biological formations or groups of such formations, which are of outstanding universal value from the aesthetic or scientific point of view;
- geological and physiographical formations and precisely delineated areas which constitute the habitat of threatened species of animals and plants of outstanding universal value from the point of view of science or conservation;
- natural sites or precisely delineated natural areas of outstanding universal value from the point of view of science, conservation or natural beauty."

They are all tangible heritage, and the definition of "site" puts together the work of nature and man. With regard to this, the *Operational Guidelines for the Implementation of the World Heritage Convention* (UNESCO, 2015) offers the definition of "Mixed Cultural and Natural Heritage" (Art 46).

However, the concept of Heritage has extended more and more over time. In particular consequently to the *Convention for the Safeguarding of Intangible Cultural Heritage* (UNESCO, 2003b), the distinction between kinds of heritage, has moved from "natural"/"cultural"/"work of art" to the dualism between "tangible" and "intangible" heritage. The intangible heritage "means the practices, representations, expressions, knowledge, skills". For example: oral traditions and expressions, including language as a vehicle of the intangible cultural heritage; performing arts; social practices, rituals and festive events; knowledge and practices concerning nature and the universe; traditional craftsmanship (Art.2).

As ratified by the *The Venice Charter* (ICOMOS, 1964) for the architectural field, the consciousness that buildings and sites are not isolated but intrinsically related to the "context" – word referred not only to the physical but also cultural surroundings – has suggested to study them in physical, social, cultural, economic and environmental terms. This led to a new way of thinking and to new conservation strategies based on the idea that a site cannot be simply identified with a border, but – at the same time – it is necessary to bear in mind of people that live the site and of activities that takes place.

Over the years, two lines of heritage concept have developed in the direction of a substantial convergence: On one hand, there has been the expansion of the heritage concept from monuments, to their context, to the landscape; On the other hand, there has been the widening of the concept of site to the environment, intended as a whole. Similarly, in the ecological filed, there has been the extension of the idea of safeguarding from the biotype or endangered species, to the whole ecosystem. This process is evident examining the documents on landscape, where the idea changes from an aesthetic perception to the current one given by the *European Landscape Convention* (Council of Europe, 2000).

With reference to international documents on heritage, four related phenomena can be highlighted:

- The extension of the concept of heritage to involve intangible aspects;
- The shift of the focus from the idea of "property" – as object individually identifiable and definable – to the more general one of "culture" (that suggest different ways of heritage definition);
- The rise of processes for heritage definition ever more based on participation, and less and less on authoritative approaches;
- The diffusion of the concept of Landscape (cultural landscape, urban landscape, etc.) to include the complexity of the phenomena and to engage and gather the subjects involved.

Finally yet importantly, the Digital Heritage rises: the *Charter for the preservation of the Digital Heritage* (UNESCO, 2003a) defines it as a cultural expression of human work. Therefore, it creates new legacy. In particular, digital works from physical heritage could be significant ways for heritage interpretation, communication, and protection.

In conclusion, the concept of heritage is ever and ever wider and more complex. The definition of heritage is a cultural matter, where the relationship between tangible, intangible, and digital is an open issue.

The *Convention for the Safeguarding of Intangible Cultural Heritage* (UNESCO, 2003b) expands the concepts of heritage – and therefore of conservation – from material manifestations, such as monuments and objects, to living expressions and to traditions transmitted during centuries. In practice, the distinction between tangible and intangible heritage replaces the one between cultural and natural heritage. Because the dualism tangible/intangible involves natural and cultural without any division. "The "intangible cultural heritage" means the practices, representations, expressions, knowledge, skills – as well as the instruments, objects, artefacts and cultural spaces associated therewith – that communities, groups and, in some cases, individuals recognize as part of their cultural heritage" (Art.2). It highlights the importance of "individuals", and not only of "people" or of "inhabitants", narrowing even more the "circle" of heritage making. Tangible elements (objects, spaces) are included in this kind of heritage. The text of the *Convention on Intangible Heritage* specifies that "This intangible cultural heritage, transmitted from generation to generation, is constantly recreated by communities and groups in response to their environment, their interaction with nature and their history, and provides them with a sense of identity and continuity, thus promoting respect for cultural diversity and human creativity". It undermines the traditional concept of heritage as monolithic object, and it suggests that we have to take into account that heritage is something changing.

Figure 1. Digital surveying of St. Giovanni Convent (Lucoli, IT)

The *Nara Document on Authenticity* (UNESCO, 1994) focuses on protection and enhancement of "Cultural Diversity" and "Heritage Diversity". It says "All cultures and societies are rooted in the particular forms and means of tangible and intangible expression which constitute their heritage, and these should be respected" (Art.7). This call for the 'intangible' was made to include non-European cultures, but today it is renewed by participative culture challenges.

The *Faro Convention* (Council of Europe, 2005) puts at the center the "community": It says that Cultural heritage is "a group of resources inherited from the past which people identify, independently of ownership, as a reflection and expression of their constantly evolving values, beliefs, knowledge and traditions. It includes all aspects of the environment resulting from the interaction between people and places through time"; and define 'Heritage Community' as "people who value specific aspects of cultural heritage which they wish, within the framework of public action, to sustain and transmit to future generations" (p.2).

Therefore, the focus shift from heritage definition to the process of heritage making. Silberman and Purser (2012) say: "This whole hearted acceptance of re-creation and adoption as essential part of heritage significance places a new emphasis on process rather than product". It is a new idea of people centered heritage, "distinct from older, static conceptions of heritage as unambiguous, expert-defined and needing protection from the forces of change" (p.13). This approach gives to people an active and ineludible role in making sense of heritage and of sites. They are the main actors of interpretation. Heritage making becomes a social activity of interpretation, and according to a postmodern line, the discourse on interpretation defines the content. From this point of view, heritage looks like a "performance".

The *Landscape Convention* (Council of Europe, 2000) defines Landscape as "an area, as perceived by people, whose character is the result of the action and interaction of natural and/or human factors" (p.9). Interesting is the wording "as perceived by people", that puts the focus on cultural aspects. At the same time, it is constituted both by human elements integrated to the landscape, and natural anthropic object.

The expression Cultural Landscape rises in all its importance from the UNESCO *World Heritage Cultural Landscapes* (2009). The concept of Cultural Landscape was originally diffused by the geographer Carl Sauer with his work *Morphology of Landscape* (1925), where he correlated physical and cultural phenomena. The UNESCO *Operational Guidelines for the Implementation of the World Heritage Convention* (2015) says: "Cultural landscapes are cultural properties and represent the 'combined works of nature and of man' [...]. They are illustrative of the evolution of human society and settlement over time, under the influence of the physical constraints and/or opportunities presented by their natural environment and of successive social, economic and cultural forces, both external and internal" (Art 47).

The *World Heritage Cultural Landscape* (UNESCO, 2009) specifies: "The very notion of landscape is highly cultural", where the "term "cultural" has been added to express the human interaction with the environment and the presence of tangible and intangible cultural values in the landscape" (p.17). Moreover, "Landscape interpretation and cultural landscape go together, for both are about ideas and meanings, concepts and interpretations, dynamics and dialogues" (p.22). The Landscape is a complex and integrated system, resulting from processes of modification and transformation occurred – and currently occurring – over time. Tangible and intangible correlate, sometime they blurs. Furthermore, the idea of ever changing heritage – rising from the definition of intangible heritage – is appropriate also for tangible heritage. Because its matter is in continuous changing. This changing can be related to natural events but to people's life, how it is understood and used, and consequently how men action upon it. Shortly, how people moved by culture changes the Landscape. Intangible shapes the tangible, and tangible inspire the intangible. Tangible and intangible are related, mirroring each other.

The role of Memory is very important: "Landscapes also exist in people's memories and imaginations and are linked to place names, myths, rituals and folklore. In people's minds there is rarely a clear distinction between the visible and invisible – or tangible and intangible – components of the landscapes. Stories and myths endow landscapes with meanings transcending the directly observable and thereby help to create people's 'mental maps', or awareness of place". Therefore, "Cultural landscapes can be seen as the repository of collective memory" (UNESCO, 2009, p.22).

In the past, the idea of Place was related to the idea of "monument", at least intended according to its perceptive relation with the surrounding context. Also remembering the *Recommendation concerning the Safeguard and Contemporary Role of Historic Areas* (UNESCO, 1976), environments are intended as defined places, circumscribed, through an authoritative decision, made by experts.

The concept of Place was usual in the Seventies and Eighties. The works of Christian Norberg-Schulz (1979) are well known, and well-known is his use of the Latin expression "genius loci". He focuses on the study of the environment perception and symbolization as essential component of architecture. Key is the "meaning of place", made according to a phenomenological and qualitative reading of architectures and environments. The Place is described as the sum of "space" and "character": the "space" – the perception field – is given by the three-dimensional place's elements, while "character" is defined by the general atmosphere.

The Burra Charter (ICOMOS, 2013), speaking on Place, puts together tangible characteristics (a place is "a geographically defined area" that "may include elements, objects, spaces and views") with intangible ones (a place "may have tangible and intangible dimensions)" (p.2). Defining the expression

Figure 2. Point cloud of St. Giovanni Convent (Lucoli, IT)

"Cultural significance", it says that it "means aesthetic, historic, scientific, social or spiritual value for past, present or future generations. Cultural significance is embodied in the place itself, its fabric, setting, use, associations, meanings, records, related places and related objects" (p.2). It roots the intangible upon the tangible. Moreover, a Place "may have a range of values for different individuals or groups" (p.2) that is the interpretation, values, and meaning of a place can vary for different groups of people and cultures.

The merging of natural and anthropic, and of tangible and intangible, is definitive in the notion of "Urban Landscape". The *Recommendation on the Historic Urban Landscape* (UNESCO, 2011) defines it as: "the urban area understood as the result of a historic layering of cultural and natural values and attributes, extending beyond the notion of "historic centre" or "ensemble" to include the broader urban context and its geographical setting" (Art.8). In particular, the Art.9 says: "This wider context includes notably the site's topography, geomorphology, hydrology and natural features, its built environment, both historic and contemporary, its infrastructures above and below ground, its open spaces and gardens, its land use patterns and spatial organization, perceptions and visual relationships, as well as all other elements of the urban structure". The urban area is intended as the result of an historical stratification of values and both cultural and natural characteristics that extends beyond the notion of historical center to include a wider spatial, historical, and cultural background". The Art. 9 adds: "It also includes social and cultural practices and values, economic processes and the intangible dimensions of heritage as related to diversity and identity". Tangible and Intangible are both considered, where tangible is the physical expression of intangible; it is the outcome and witness of a complexity of relationships, and intangible is a fundamental aspect.

Figure 3. Sectioned view of the point cloud of St. Giovanni Convent (Lucoli, IT)

According to the definition of Urban Landscape, here there are not natural or anthropic aspect, although mixed, but the Anthropic becomes Natural, and vice versa the Natural definitely Anthropic. Natural merges with Historical. Nevertheless, we should consider another translation of concepts: Natural and Anthropic blur, and the everyday life comes into play.

DIGITALIZING HERITAGE

The digital technologies of laser scanning, digital photogrammetry, and photo-modeling have produced a changing in the traditional architectural surveying process (Bianchini, 2014), in particular with a partial inversion. Architectural survey aims to the understanding and communication of the values of the building, through the analysis, selection, synthesis, and graphitization of the real work (Docci & Maestri, 2009). Traditionally, the process is articulated according to the following steps: 1) the preliminary documental research; 2) the drafting of sketches to analyze the building, to understand its characteristics, and to design the surveying project; 3) the measuring; 4) the restitution, i.e. the realization of drawings. In particular, the sketches are a graphical tool for the "reading" of the architectural document and they aim to the discretization of the architectural continuum with the individualization and selection of the significant elements of the building. This is a first critical act made by the surveyor. In the traditional drawing, the ongoing relation between mind and hand produces directly the message, while nowadays the technology operates a filtering, requiring a double transliteration. In architectural surveying, the relationship between the real and the model is more articulated than in the traditional process, because the partial inversion of the traditional procedure: The phase of measurements is anticipated, producing a digital cast of the whole building, and translating the critical contribution of the surveyor in the post-processing. In the practice of digital survey, the referent is only to be ideally represented by the existing building, in fact replaced by the point cloud or mesh data. The process of transliteration becomes even more complex: Reality - Bit - Raster - Mind - Bit - Raster. The modeler has to play in the jungle of the measures, critically reconstructing the underlying architectural concept (i.e. the real reference).

Currently, the architectural heritage knowledge process is based on remote sensing, where instruments play a leading role. They can offer measures in number, density and accuracy unthinkable until some time ago. However, the reality that they present is, in some ways, less complete than the one that we can know directly: The information provided by the tools is more accurate on what they say (metrical data), but it is less rich for what they cannot tell us. The problems of measurement and topography are fundamental (Andrews, 2009), but they are not sufficient in the analysis of complex historicized organisms, like the architectural heritage. Point clouds are raw data, per se they are not a critic interpretation; not differently, the textured mesh surfaces automatically derived by structure from motion applications. "The existing reference articles are not a critical review of the chain of 'measure, drawing and visualization' [...] but a series of a-critical and dogmatic models that define a series of requisites defined 'a priori' certainly commensurable with each other, but they are difficult to be applied in different contexts. Moreover, they do not usually refer to the qualities of the real object, but they refer to the capacity of a certain instrument or a certain technology" (Gaiani, Benedetti & Apollonio, 2011).

Fundamentally, digital sensing instruments operate in an uncritical way, "shooting" measures in an area of the space, according to a pre-defined grid, and getting data not related to the buildings geometry and to its spatial, formal, and constructive characteristics. Although the surveyor has a preliminary role in defining the views and density of remote sensing, we can say that his act of critical analysis is transposed in the post-processing step. Simplifying, in the digital age the surveying process can be summarized into two actions: "measure" and "drawing" – or rather "modeling" – (Gaiani, 2012a), according to the well-known process of "reverse modeling".

Therefore, the issue of architectural heritage surveying becomes conceptually correlated with digital modeling. Another aspect breaks with the tradition: the restitutions are no more made by two-dimensional drawings but by a 3D model, from which – eventually but not necessarily – you can derive 2D illustrations.

The matters related to digital surveying are essential. They are about: The measurements tools, methodologies and data (point clouds); the modeling process (noise reduction, uniforming, smoothing, decimating point clouds, interpolating meshes, filling holes, texturing, CSG / B-Rep / Mesh / Image Based representations, the semantization of the model, LODs, etc.); the kind of software; the database organization; the visualization tools, etc. In addition, we cannot forget: The historical research; the metrological, proportional, comparative and typological studies; the analysis of the constructive components, etc. Because the surveying process is a critical, iterative, and articulate workflow, where the aim is the wise representation of built characteristics. Therefore, a first consideration on transparency follows: the digitalizing and computing processes and tools have to be declared, in relation to the real heritage and its documents.

Cameron (2010) reflects on the theme of cultural heritage digitization, highlighting the different nature, origin, and content of digital heritage: Deciding what to digitize, modeling, and visualize means to take an active action of decoding and interpretation of the work, i.e. to choose what is meaningful, according to a "process of selective canonization" (p.57). Last but not least the fourth dimension of built heritage: how it modified and transformed during its life. It requires the realization of reconstructive models of past configurations. Not only to understand past characteristics and values, but to know how it arrived to actuality, and because currently it has its actual characteristics.

In built heritage, there is not visualization without a prior reality (Ch'ng & Gaffney, 2013) and in a philological study of the model we cannot forget its real reference from whom it was born. According to this aspect, the model's "aura", "materiality", and "genius loci" are related to (and gain strength from) the ones of the real building. Therefore, a digital object, built from material heritage (real thing,

Figure 4. Internal view of the point cloud of St. Giovanni Convent (Lucoli, IT)

drawings, historical descriptions, etc.), and finalized to re-present a reality, has an inalienable conceptual characteristic: It cannot be completely intended separately from its reference (physical, historical, cultural, etc.), unless it loses its sense and it is transformed into something else.

In the age of industrialization and mechanical serial production, Benjamin (1936) expressed its concern with regard to the technological reproducibility of the work of art, dangerous for the concepts of centrality, aura, material and historical authenticity of the artifact.

Nowadays, the problem has taken a critical aspect: There is not a problem of model's mimesis of the reality, but the question of the capability of the digital model to describe the reality raises. Because the digital reproduction is not a replacement.

However, the consideration and the principles placed by Benjamin are still useful: The "hic et nunc" refers to a gnosiological problem of relationship between digital representation and reality, while the "aura" addresses the problems of re-production of the aesthetical and historical values of the heritage and of his context. It is simple to image how the model can re-present the aesthetical values through the simulation of the perceptible image. But, if the model is built through a stratification of 3D diachronic sections, therefore the model can also "contain" the historic values, ever with the foresight to declare, for each one, the critical degree of the hypothesis and the sources – documental or derived from surveying – (Brusaporci, Centofanti, Continenza & Trizio, 2012; De Luca, Bussayarat, Stefani, Véron & Florenzano, 2011; Brusaporci, 2015b).

Cameron (2010) argues that the digital object, interpreted according to a post-modernist epistemology, becomes a sign, and it resurrects the effectual and physical reality of the object. Rather, it is not only a sign of the reality but also an instrument for the reality. Like the reality, the digital work has its own historical and aesthetical qualities, being the result of a human activity. The digital object does not aim to "appropriate" of the aura of the reality, but to interpret it: "The real object is not under threat but acts as an alibi for the virtual" (p.58).

INTERPRETATION AND PRESENTATION

Interpretation and presentation are a fundamental part of the overall process of cultural heritage conservation. The ICOMOS *Charter for the Interpretation and Presentation of Cultural Heritage Sites* (2008) arises from the concept that "stress the importance of public communication as an essential part of the larger conservation process (variously describing it as "dissemination," "popularization," "presentation," and "interpretation"). They implicitly acknowledge that every act of heritage conservation – within all the world's cultural traditions – is by its nature a communicative act" (p.2).

Therefore, the Charter presents the following definitions:

- Interpretation: "refers to the full range of potential activities intended to heighten public awareness and enhance understanding of cultural heritage site. These can include print and electronic publications, public lectures, on-site and directly related off-site installations, educational programmes, community activities, and ongoing research, training, and evaluation of the interpretation process itself." (p.4).
- Presentation: "more specifically denotes the carefully planned communication of interpretive content through the arrangement of interpretive information, physical access, and interpretive infrastructure at a cultural heritage site. It can be conveyed through a variety of technical means, including, yet not requiring, such elements as informational panels, museum-type displays, formalized walking tours, lectures and guided tours, and multimedia applications and websites." (p.4).

A very important role is played by "Interpretive infrastructures": They "refer to physical installations, facilities, and areas at, or connected with a cultural heritage site that may be specifically utilised for the purposes of interpretation and presentation including those supporting interpretation via new and existing technologies" (p.4).

The Charter offers seven cardinal principles on which Interpretation and Presentation should be based:

- Principle 1: Access and Understanding: Interpretation and presentation programmes should facilitate physical and intellectual access by the public to cultural heritage sites
- Principle 2: Information Sources: Interpretation and presentation should be based on evidence gathered through accepted scientific and cholarly methods as well as from living cultural traditions
- Principle 3: Attention to Setting and Context: The Interpretation and Presentation of cultural heritage sites should relate to their wider social, cultural, historical, and natural contexts and settings
- Principle 4: Preservation of Authenticity: The Interpretation and presentation of cultural heritage sites must respect the basic tenets of authenticity in the spirit of the Nara Document (1994).
- Principle 5: Planning for Sustainability: The interpretation plan for a cultural heritage site must be sensitive to its natural and cultural environment, with social, financial, and environmental sustainability among its central goals
- Principle 6: Concern for Inclusiveness: The Interpretation and Presentation of cultural heritage sites must be the result of meaningful collaboration between heritage professionals, host and associated communities, and other stakeholders
- Principle 7: Importance of Research, Training, and Evaluation: Continuing research, training, and evaluation are essential components of the interpretation of a cultural heritage site

The Australia ICOMOS *Charter for Places of Cultural Significance* (*The Burra Charter*, 2013), says: "1.17 Interpretation means all the ways of presenting the cultural significance of a Place" (p.3). In addition, it explains: "Interpretation may be a combination of the treatment of the fabric (e.g. maintenance, restoration, reconstruction); the use of and activities at the place; and the use of introduced explanatory material".

The "Practice Note_Interpretation" of *The Burra Charter* is expressly dedicate to interpretation. It underlines the importance of: Making Inventories, Defining the audience; Developing interpretation policy; Defining key interpretive themes and stories; Establish interpretation methods and techniques; Systematic implementation (p.4-6).

The presented "Key principles" are noteworthy:

1. "Facilitate understanding and appreciation of cultural heritage sites and foster public awareness and engagement in the need for their protection and conservation.
2. Communicate the meaning of cultural heritage sites to a range of audiences through careful, documented recognition of significance, through accepted scientific and scholarly methods as well as from living cultural traditions.
3. Safeguard the tangible and intangible values of cultural heritage sites in their natural and cultural settings and social contexts.
4. Respect the authenticity of cultural heritage sites, by communicating the significance of their historic fabric and cultural values and protecting them from the adverse impact of intrusive interpretive infrastructure, visitor pressure, inaccurate or inappropriate interpretation.
5. Contribute to the sustainable conservation of cultural heritage sites, through promoting public understanding of, and participation in, ongoing conservation efforts, ensuring long-term maintenance of the interpretive infrastructure and regular review of its interpretive contents.
6. Encourage inclusiveness in the interpretation of cultural heritage sites, by facilitating the involvement of stakeholders and associated communities in the development and implementation of interpretive programs.
7. Develop technical and professional guidelines for heritage interpretation and presentation, including technologies, research, and training. Such guidelines must be appropriate and sustainable in their social contexts." (p.2)

Interpretation is strictly related to knowledge and understanding. Therefore, conservation – and consequently presentation, communication, engagement, maintenance and enhancement – is founded on interpretation.

Reflections on Interpretation and Presentation have a long tradition. One of the more important reference is Tielden (1957). In his *Interpreting Our Heritage* starts from a dictionary definition: It's "An educational activity which aims to reveal meanings and relationship through the use of original objects, by firsthand experience, and by illustrative media, rather than simply to communicate factual information" (p.8).

Nevertheless, Tielden offers two brief concepts of Interpretation, useful for the interpreter, for his private use and his contact with the public (p. 8):

- Interpretation is the revelation of a larger truth that lies behind any statement of fact;
- Interpretation should capitalize mere curiosity for the enrichment of the human mind and spirit.

From hence, Tielden proposes six principles:

"I. Any interpretation that does not somehow relate what is being displayed or described to something within the personality or experience of the visitor will be sterile.
II. Information, as such, is not Interpretation. Interpretation is revelation based upon information. But they are entirely different things. However, all interpretation includes information.
III. Interpretation is an art, which combines many arts, whether the material presented are scientific, historical or architectural. Any art is in some degree teachable.
IV. The chief aim of Interpretation is not instruction, but provocation.
V. Interpretation should aim to present a whole rather than a part, and must address itself to the whole man rather than any phase.
VI. Interpretation addressed to children (say, up to the age of twelve) should not be a dilution of the presentation to adults, but should follow a fundamentally different approach. To be at its best it will require a separate program" (p. 9).

Interpretation and Presentation are not issues to be faced after the overall process of knowledge, but they are strategies for conservation and for knowledge and understanding.

Moreover, when we recur to participative approaches, where the authoritative role of the scholar collaborate with the one of inhabitants – i.e. with people who constitute, build, transform, and give meaning to the heritage itself –. Interpretation and Presentation acquire a wider meaning and purpose: From an educational to a cultural function oriented to everybody involved in the heritage conservation, both for knowledge and planning.

Figure 5. Digitalization as virtual casting: inside a wall of St. Giovanni Convent (Lucoli, IT)

TRANSPARENCY

Pointing out the attention on the archaeological field – interested in digital heritage derived from physical contents – from the very beginning of the Seventies, it has immediately looked carefully to the possibilities offered by computer modeling: It is a research path that, beginning from the purpose of digital representations as an effective tool for three-dimensional representation (Forte & Siliotti, 1996), developed towards the use of computer graphics for scientific research (Frischer, 2008).

In the book "The Virtual Representation of the Past" (Greengrass & Hughes, 2008), transparency is one of the fundamental issues, and in the different chapters the problem related to the representation of "when", "where", and "what" recurs. In particular Beacham (2008) focuses on transparency and paradata, as crucial topic "if 3D visualization is to 'mature' as a research method and acquire widespread acceptance within subject communities" (p. 172).

Of particular interest are the "Guides to Good Practice" by Archaeology Data Service and Digital Antiquity (2013), that highlights main contents in archiving digital works on archeology. From these research lines grows a methodological reflection, in particular focused on the philological transparency of digital visualization (Huvila, 2013).

On 'transparency', cornerstones are The London Charter and the Principles of Seville, that deal with issues related to "Research Sources", "Documentation", "Authenticity", and "Historical Rigor" of computer-based visualization of cultural and archaeological heritage. And they find in paradata an important tool to reach transparency.

The London Charter (2009) defines paradata for cultural heritage as: «Information about human processes of understanding and interpretation of data objects. Examples of paradata include descriptions stored within a structured database of how evidence was used to interpret an artefact, or a comment on methodological premises within a research publication. It is closely related, but somewhat different in emphasis, to "contextual metadata", which tend to communicate interpretations of an artefact or collection, rather than the process through which one or more artefacts were processed or interpreted» (p. 13). Paradata configures as a sort of metadata useful to the philological reconstruction of the modeling process (Denard, 2012). In this way The London Charter defines "Intellectual transparency" as: «The provision of information, presented in any medium or format, to allow users to understand the nature and scope of "knowledge claim" made by a computer-based visualization outcome» (p.12). The concept of paradata accompanies the one of "scientific transparency", following the ambition to shun the seduction of some photorealistic computer based visualizations, and to declare the scientific fundaments, reasons, and reflections from which the digital representation derives.

The Principles of Seville (2012) say: «All computer-based visualization must be essentially transparent, i.e. testable by other researchers or professionals, since the validity, and therefore the scope, of the conclusions produced by such visualization will depend largely on the ability of others to confirm or refute the results obtained» (p.8). The principle of transparency has been widely developed in the archaeological field, where the digital reconstruction of artifacts (in their ancient configuration) is largely based on indirect information, comparative analysis, interpretative hypothesis.

In 2012 a publication titled "Paradata and Trasparency in Virtual Heritage" renovates the debate on transparency (Bentkowska-Kafel, Denard, Baker 2012). This is necessary requisite because: «Digital technologies offer flexible analytical tools, both sensory and semantic, for the study and representation of the past, but the digital techniques – it is argued here – are only useful and valid if interpretative frameworks and processes are published», therefore the need to «emphasize the importance of reliably, documenting the process of interpretation of historical materials and hypotheses that arise in the course of the research». From here descend the use of paradata: «[...] the term borrowed from other disciplines that rely on recording information processes. Paradata document the process of interpretation so that the aims, contexts and reliability of visualization methods and their outcomes can be properly understood» (p.1).

And «Paradata may be seen as a digital equivalent to "scholia", as well as an addition to the traditional critical apparatus for describing the process of reasoning in scholarly research» (p.2).

In this way paradata is a sort of "comments" and "explanations" that refer the choices made in visualizing raw-data (i.e. the "documents") and describe the critical interpretations.

Although the archaeological experience rises from the necessity of computer based visualization of ancient heritage, it is an important lesson in our on line state. A claim for Transparency is very important and urgent now, in our constant dimension of "digitality" melt into reality (Brusaporci, 2017b).

MIXED HERITAGE

Since the advent of computer graphic, "modeling" and "rendering" are the subsequent steps that bring the digital model to his epiphany. The model is constitutively made by an orderly succession of bits that uniquely describe data, information, i.e. the characteristics and relationships of virtual elements: The model can be written and read, in a text format – but not in its true form of machine language –. Although in the process of raster transcription the model manifests itself, in all its characteristics. Therefore, the model has a dual nature: It is a "signans", which has to be conducted to the true icon of the "signatum", through a "materialization of the conventionalization processes, on which the synthetic icon bases to come to exist" (Colombo 1995, 105).

The diffusion of economic and increasingly powerful CPU and memories, coupled with ICT and Real Time Rendering and Interactive applications have made different kinds of mixed realities an active instrument of information processing for knowledge, interpretation, presentation, and conservation.

Figure 6. Internal view of the point cloud of St. Menna Church (Lucoli, IT)

In particular, they allow the collecting of information in the same way in which the mind accumulates them, i.e. preferring a spatial knowledge rather than an intellectual one, differently than the traditional alphabetical organization. Because the shaded and textured visualization of the 3-D model in real time rendering and the model's manipulation favor the simultaneity of ideation and elaboration. It is a working knowledge, and according to De Kerckove (1991), it allows a "sensory remapping".

The role of visualization in heritage has changed during last years: Visualization is no more a mere product but it is an interpretation research and exploration learning process pf data acquisition and processing, interpretation, modeling, simulation, and visualization of different kind of products, according to a so called "secondary digital product revolution" (Ch'ng, Gaffney, & Chapman, 2014).

The inherent aesthetic quality of each medium is inescapable (book, radio, tv, etc.): "A stirring narrative in any medium can be experienced as a virtual reality because our brains are programmed to tune into stories with an intensity that can obliterate the world around us" (Murray 1997, 98). In synthetic images, the greatest temptation is the aesthetic for its own sake, and the real question is on the point of balance between "quantity" (of details, of information, of photorealism) vs "quality". That is how complete must be a simulation of the real, i.e. how much information (and what kind) the visualization has to contain to be a tool for knowledge, interpretation, and presentation. At the same time the seduction can also be intellectual, losing into a universe of concatenated information.

At the dawn of the digital age, Baudrillard (1976) foreshadowed that reality was under the threat of simulations: They could be more convincing of the real and consequently the viewers could be no longer able to distinguish the replica from the reality". The end of the real would have generated a paradoxical: The rise of the "Hyperreality", i.e. the more real than reality.

In the Eighties Baudrillard underlined that the instantaneous proximity of the things would have caused the world's transparency for excessive visibility. Hence his idea of "Obscenity": When everything becomes immediately visible, transparent, and then coded and transmitted, the illusion ceases to exist. The Baudrillard's cry of alarm is that we are no longer in the drama of alienation, but we are in the ecstasy of communication (Baudrillard, 1987).

The idea of Obscenity may be used to evoke the new approach of the scholar towards the digital model and its visualization: No more an aesthetic perspective to synthetic images, but an "anatomical" attitude, rather addressed to the complexity of modeling – 'modeling' interpreted in the broadest sense –, i.e. to the articulation and interaction of data. Largely, in the current participative and interactive culture, the enchantment for the computer graphics ended: Now the attention of the researcher – but often also of the user – moves from the observation of synthesis renders – eventually printed on photographic paper – to the interactive working interface, where models are processed. This is the place where visual computing is an "obscene" interrelation and interpretation of data and where there is a live interaction with and between them. In this place, data becomes information, and information becomes knowledge. An important consequence follows: The focus shifts from model to modeling.

Therefore, the digital "master model" – that is the one on which the modeler works in the graphical interface of modeling software and from which derivers the representations – gets a particular importance. The approach of "New Realism" (Ferraris, 2012), can be also referred to digital built heritage: Consciously, virtuality is observed in its essence, it is unveiled: Not a hoax but a mechanism for multiple simulations/visualizations of reality. The model is a "sign" that, at the same time, plays as "signifier" or "meaning". Reality re-acquires more and more importance.

According to the current disenchanted approach of scholars and users to digital visualization, we have new communication strategies and new relationships with the medium. Considering the reflection on "Mediation" made by Bolter and Grusin (1999), let us consider the double logic of "Immediacy" and of "Hypermediacy" of media in our culture: On one hand, virtual reality, 3-D graphics, and graphical interfaces favor the logic of transparent immediacy, that is "[…] the user is no longer aware of confronting a medium, but instead stands in an immediate relationship to the contents of that medium" (p. 24). On the other hand, media multiplies itself and "The multiple representations inside the windows (text, graphies, video) create a heterogeneous space, as they compete for the view's attention. Icons, menus, and toolbars add further layers of visual and verbal meaning. […] Unlike a perspective painting or three-dimensional computer graphic, this windowed interface does not attempt to unify the space around any one point of view. Instead, each text window defines its own verbal, each graphic window its own visual, point of view […] The multiplicity of windows and the heterogeneity of their contents mean that the user is repeatedly brought back into contact with the interface, which she learns to read just as she would read any hypertext. She oscillates between manipulating the windows and examining their contents, just as she oscillates between looking at a hypertext as a texture of links and looking through the links to the textual units as language" (p. 32-33).

The digital representation of an architectural model requires the visualization of 3-D elements and data together. The first – according to their built nature – can be experienced by spatial images, while the second by multiple media windows. They are not alternative but integrated, aiming to a critical and efficient communication. Windows re-mediates the model and "Where immediacy suggests a unified visual model space, contemporary hypermediacy offers a heterogeneous space, in which representation is conceived of not as window on to the world, but rather as 'windowed' itself – with windows that open on to other representations or other media" (Bolter & Grusin, 1999, 34). This is the visualization environment offered by "complex master models": The medium is not only – and no more – a pretty and charming photorealistic representation of a synthetized reality, but an "obscene" (because absolutely transparent) decomposition of the "system choreography" and of information. The model is not any more hidden behind the interface but it shows itself – and in the case of augmented reality, it is related to reality –.

Expressions like "Virtual Reality" (VR) – first used by Sutherland in 1965 – has become common. The VR is based on a total-body immersion in a computer-generated environment: User's perceptions are produced from digital information. Although the synthetic environment often follows laws different from the real word ones, the user has a psychological involvement and lives it like a real experience. Another wording is "Augmented Reality" (AR) – or also "Enhanced Reality" or "Enriched Reality" –. It consists on the superimposition of digital information on user's perceptions. It is ever more diffused thanks by ICT because onerous computational digital visualization are not entrusted to the device (tablet and smartphone – the last one also used as new kind of head mounted displays –) but data (video, audio, windows, text) are only transmitted in real time (Brusaporci, Ruggieri, Sicuranza, & Maiezza, 2017). In VR external perceptions are limited as much as possible, while in AR they are fundamental, because the communication roots on them.

Analyzing the interfaces for visualization, Milgram and Kishino (1994) coin the expression "Mixed Reality" (MR): It describes the "virtual continuum" between only-real and completely virtual environment perception, identifying six classes of hybrid states, with the aim to define a taxonomy to distinguish between different technological requirements. Of particular interest are the observations on the relationship between real and virtual, according to visualization modalities and image quality (p.6-7). In particular, the definition of "direct viewing" and "non-direct viewing" is interesting, because it is

Figure 7. Internal view of the point cloud of St. Menna Church (Lucoli, IT)

not referred to a distinction between real objects and virtual objects, but to what "looks real" (derived from reality or synthetized or both of them). In this way, recalling the concept of AR, these two aspects integrates, because a digital image (also non-photorealistic) is correlated to images from reality. Therefore, the device mediates the perception of reality. In the MR, another interesting idea is the "Extent of Presence Methapor", related to the perception quality, that is to the level of "presence feeling" of the user in the represented environment.

PARTICIPATIVE HERITAGE

The line of Cultural Heritage naturally inserts in the most recent reflections on participative heritage. The *World Heritage Cultural Landscape* says: "The intangible cultural heritage is traditional and living at the same time. It is constantly recreated and mainly transmitted orally. It is difficult to use the term authenticity in relation to intangible cultural heritage; some experts advise against its use in relation to living heritage" (UNESCO 2009, p.27). This in line with the *Convention for the Safeguarding of Intangible Cultural Heritage* (UNESCO, 2003b) that underlines that intangible heritage is "recreated by people".

The Internet, ICT, web application, and smartphone – that allow us to be in a constant on-line state – favors an open access discourse on heritage and on its values. At the same time, the open-ended flux between people influences the process of heritage memory, identity, and authenticity definition (Brusaporci, 2017a).

Therefore, the concept of "collective memory" underlies the one of participative heritage (Silberman & Puser, 2012). Collective memory is the formation of a shared identity, defined by the continuous interactions, in particular made possible by social networks.

Giaccardi (2012) highlights that heritage meaning is "the result of repeated and ongoing interactions in the lived world of ordinary people" (p.2). According to the idea of heritage making related the cultural "public sphere", – i.e. to the interactions of people that create, maintain, or transform heritage – the role of digital technologies is ever and ever important: "Today mobile and ubiquitous technologies are accelerating these changes by enabling users to participate, spontaneously and continuously, in activities of collection, preservation and interpretation of digitized heritage content and new digitally mediated forms of heritage practice" (Giaccardi, 2012, p.2). The Internet and Social Media allow the interactive and continuous practice of remembering and of memory sharing and definition.

The ICT development has made the new ways of media communication ubiquitous: VR, AR etc. are no more available only in technological laboratories or on home console, but on our smart devices, always with us. Moreover, The Internet and Social Media has allowed participative multidirectional approaches. Consequently, in the current "Participatory Culture" (Jenkins 2009. Jenkins, 2006), the distributed knowledge and the collective intelligence processes favor the collecting, scanning, and mixing of data and information, and the comparison between different points of view to achieve a common goal. This opens to advanced strategies and processes for heritage understanding, interpretation, presentation, and conservation.

The multi-directional communication relationship amplifies the traditional two-directional line of data transmission according to new experiences of participative culture. But an experienced approach requires to focus on the cultural aspects: Jenkins (2009) specifies that the questions posed by participatory culture are basically cultural and not just technological issues, because it is important to focus on the concept of participation rather than on interactive technologies. In fact, participation is a distinctive feature of social media and it makes possible for the average user (or maybe it is better to say for the "universal user") to store, exchange, re-elaborate, and re-circulate media contents according to innovative methods, instantaneous, wherever you are. Therefore, Jenkins indicates how participatory culture is characterized by: relatively low barriers for artistic expression and civic involvement, the ease creating and sharing content, informal characteristics of "tutoring" where participants transmit acquired skills and knowledge.

It follows that the "public space" of meeting and dialogue changes (Silberman, 2016): the Internet and social media favor relations and discussions, especially within interest groups populated by users with similar interests. Contrary to how one might think, they are not laissez faire spaces, but they are governed by complex relationships: "post" and "I like", questions – answers – comments, votes, members' reactions, opinions of senior followers, last but not least the authoritative role of site and groups managers.

All this renews the relationship with the world around us – people, heritage, landscapes, etc. –according to interaction and collaboration principles and not of substitution of reality by virtuality.

SMART HERITAGE

The dissemination and development of ICT makes it possible to transmit information pervasively and ubiquitously, favoring an interrelation between information and environment.

Conceptually the realization of a Smart City starts from the possibility of an automatic control and processing of data in order to have useful information for the management of the multiple aspects of the city. This approach, also intended in cultural terms, prefigures scenarios strongly marked by technology (Mitchell, 1995).

Our age is characterized by a "cultural" approach to the environment that surrounds us (Schafer, 2014). This combines with the inclusiveness of the concepts underlying the idea of Cultural Landscape (UNESCO, 2009) and Place (ICOMOS, 2013). At the same time, the spread and development of ICT make information transmission pervasive, available in every place and for every user, and immerse the society and the artifacts in the so-called info-sphere (European Commission, 2015). Furthermore, ICTs give everyone the opportunity to interact in a personal, continuous and multidirectional manner, strengthening a process of people-centered cultural heritage (Silberman & Puser, 2012). Therefore, the discourse on smart cities is also shifting from purely technological issues to cultural ones (Dustdar, Nastić, & Šćekić, 2017) highlight how according to the traditional vision of Smart Cities, the Citizen plays a passive role, and ICT and the infrastructure systems act as tools for infrastructure planning and management, collecting and analyzing data, prefiguring and optimizing the use of services. They propose a new vision called collective smart", referred to the concept of "cyber-human smart city", rooted on the active interaction of people, local business, authorities and stakeholders. In this way, a Smart City value-driven is defined: "This effectively transforms the role and broadens the involment and opportunities of citizen-stakeholders, but also promote the ICT from passive infrastructure to an active participant shaping the ecosystem" (p.3). The concept of "value" takes on a central role and, to all effects, ICT and infrastructure become tools for the construction of an "ecosystem" where the inhabitants play a leading role in defining the values. It follows that this concept of "value", referred to society in general, and to cultural heritage in particular, and more precisely to the places and buildings of the historic city, needs a careful consideration. Gaiani, Martini, and Apollonio (Gaiani, Martini, & Apollonio, 2017) focus on study of the impact of Smart City technologies in the field of cultural heritage. The reflection presented by the authors builds on the consideration of diffusion and density of Widepread Built Heirtage in the European context, and on the need to guarantee its conservation, visibility and accessibility both from a physiscal and intellectual point of view, also for the purpose of favoring the enhancement of local economies and citizens identities. To this end, the authors identify the following main issues: The lack of "guiding information system"; problems in the use of ICT specifically dedicated to the issues posed by Built Heritage; the lack of specific cognitive capabilities (of perception, comprehension and use) for a smart interaction of common users with smart built hertiage, for example by 3-D interfaces. "ICT could increase the visibility and accessibility of 'cultural DNA' that shaped the actual appearance of our cities and our territory and enhance the related cultural production, aiding in conservation and exploitation [...] transforming Cultural Items into Smart Cultural Objects (SCO), meant as sources and recipients of advanced information applied to 'Built Cultural Heritage" (p. 219). Therefore, the meeting between ICT and Cultural Heritage facilitates a cultural turn, in relation to which a Smart City becomes able to innovate its development dynamics in a cultural sense and in a sustainability perspective.

CONCLUSION

With augmented reality, information matches on real objects. At the same time – also thanks to Internet of Things – objects have become cyber-objects, or better, smart-objects, and therefore digital heritage. The screen (smartphones, tablets, VR goggles, oculus rift, google glass, etc.) re-news the potentialities of virtual: It comes to life with the real and thanks to the reality. Because is the reality that empower the virtuality.

The Mitchell's concept of "iconic panic" highlights how images seem to come alive, cloning and multiplying indefinitely, out of control. Follows the sensation that images can animate and become real, or better "be real" (Cometa, 2017). Moving from Mitchell's reflections, in our participative and interactive on-line social system where information continuously develop – and where the time vector comes into play overbearingly, according to a vertiginous flow –, current phenomena of "mixed reality" could amplify the iconic panic process. The taking life of images becomes all the more important in augmented reality environments, where images "marry" reality and accompany us continuously and in a ubiquitous way, without leaving us alone.

In this sense, the Mitchell's idea evolves: We have a new kind of images, where the real objects cloned in advanced images through the visors become alive. However, these will not be a frightening experiences, because recalling the concept of "uncanny valley" (or "eeriness valley") by Masahiro Mori (1970), images of Augmented Reality don't change the nature of objects but superimpose – in a visual way – a different kind of "life". In this way objects become so called smart objects, and the virtual offers new potentialities (Lévy, 1995). Also the Mitchell's "cloning" process changes: The diffusion of 3-D printing shows that every image can become physical and real, possibly printed ad infinitum; but they are in scale simulacra that don't substitute the original but recall it.

With the explosive growth and diffusion of digital technologies, the status of novelty, aroused by modeling and visualizing advanced tool for architectural heritage, can be said to be exceeded, and by now, their application in the study of historical architecture has become common and daily. In particular, the spread of digital media, based on non-alphabetical forms of communication, has made "natural" the visual and non-linear approach of visual computing techniques. At the same, the nihilistic postmodern approach has left the room for a new neo-realist perspective, where the perceivable data is back to be a useful tool for a critical knowledge of reality, and for models analysis, design and validation. From this point of view, the contrast between "physical reality" and "digital reality" ceases to exist: They are two kinds of real that collaborates for the study, protection, and exploitation of architectural heritage. Indeed, with 3-D Printing and Augmented Reality technologies, the real-virtual circle is closes.

Meanwhile, another phenomenon has taken hold: the risk of aestheticization for its own sake – a "Dionysian impetus" of "absolute appear" to quote Purini (2003, p.95) – gives way to the disenchanted sight of the observer/practitioner. The "transparency" of digital phenomena means also "coolness", "objectivity", and therefore "analysis". The "obscene" sight of the scholar and of the everyday user combines with new forms of simultaneous intelligence: "mutatis mutandis" a sort of "savage mind" (Lévi Strauss, 1962), with the use-bricoleur who works with computerized visual information, and where visual data – from both "physical" and "digital" related realities – are used according to their ability to produce a continuous network of knowledge. With this in mind, the integration between digital models and database models for built heritage seems successful, and the Informative Model aims to be a new kind of tool for computing the world complexity, with new visual, intuitive, and participatory experiences.

REFERENCES

Andrews, D. (Ed.). (2009). Metric Survey Specification for Cultural Heritage. Swindow: English Heritage.

Archeology Data Service, & Digital Antiquity. (2013). *Guides to Good Practice*. Retrieved January 05, 2018, from http://guides.archaeologydataservice.ac.uk/

Baudrillard, J. (1976). *L'echange symbolique et la mort*. Paris: Gallimard.

Baudrillard, J. (1987). *L'autre par lui-même: Habilitation*. Paris: Editions Galilée.

Beacham, R. (2008). 'Oh, to Make Boards to Speak! There is a Task!' Toward a Poetics of Paradata. In M. Greengrass & L. Hughes (Eds.), The Virtual Representation of the Past (pp. 171-178). Farnham: Ashgate.

Benjamin, W. (1936). Das Kunstwerk im Zeitalter seiner technischen Reproduzierbarkeit. *Zeitschrift für Sozialforschung*.

Bentkowska-Kafel, A. D., & Baker, D. (Eds.). (2012). Paradata and Transparency in Virtual Heritage. Farnham: Ashgate Publishing.

Bianchini, C. (2014). Survey 2.0: new technologies, new equipment, new surveyors? In P. Giandebiaggi & C. Vernizzi (Eds.), *Italian Survey & International Experiences* (pp. 763–768). Roma: Gangemi.

Bolter, J. D., & Grusin, R. (1999). *Remediation – Understanding New Media*. Cambridge, MA: MIT Press.

Brusaporci, S. (2015 a). On Visual Computing for Architectural Heritage. In S. Brusaporci (Ed.), *Handbook of Research on Emerging Digital Tools for Architectural Surveying, Modeling, and Representation* (pp. 94–123). Hershey, PA: IGI Global. doi:10.4018/978-1-4666-8379-2.ch003

Brusaporci, S. (2015 b). The Representation of Architectural Heritage in the Digital Age. In M. Khosrow-Pour (Ed.), Encyclopedia of Information Science and Technology, Third Edition (pp. 4195-4205, VI). Hershey, PA: IGI Global. doi:10.4018/978-1-4666-5888-2.ch412

Brusaporci, S. (2017a). *Digital Innovations in Architectural Heritage Conservation: Emerging Research and Opportunities*. Hershey, PA: IGI Global; doi:10.4018/978-1-5225-2434-2

Brusaporci, S. (2017b). The Importance of Being Honest. In 3D Printing: Breakthroughs in Research and Practice (pp. 333-360). Hershey, PA: IGI Global.

Brusaporci, S., Centofanti, M., Continenza, R., & Trizio, I. (2012). Sistemi Informativi Architettonici per la gestione, tutela e fruizione dell'edilizia storica. In *ATTI 16ª Conferenza Nazionale ASITA 2012* (pp. 315–322). Vicenza: ASITA.

Brusaporci, S., Ruggieri, G., Sicuranza, F., & Maiezza, P. (2017). Augmented Reality for Historical Storytelling. The INCIPICT Project for the Reconstruction of Tangible and Intangible Image of L'Aquila Historical Centre. *Proceedings*, *1*(9), 1083. doi:10.3390/proceedings1091083

Cameron, F. (2010). Beyond the Cult of the Replicant. In F. Cameron & S. Kenderdine (Eds.), Theorizing digital cultural heritage: a critical discourse (pp. 49-76). Cambridge, MA: MIT Press.

Centofanti, M. (2010). Della natura del modello architettonico. In S. Brusaporci (Ed.), *Sistemi informativi integrati per la tutela, la conservazione e la valorizzazione del patrimonio architettonico e urbano* (pp. 43–54). Roma: Gangemi.

Ch'ng, E., Gaffney, V., & Chapman, H. (Eds.). (2013). Visual Heritage in the Digital Age. London: Springer.

Ch'ng, E., & Gaffney, V. L. (2013). Seeing Things: Heritage Computing, Visualization and the Arts and Humanities. In E. Ch'ng, V. Gaffney, & H. Chapman (Eds.), Visual Heritage in the Digital Age (pp. 1-14). London: Springer.

Colombo, F. (1990). *Ombre sintetiche*. Napoli: Liguori.

Cometa, M. (2017). Prefazione all'edizione italiana. In W. J. T. Mitchell (Ed.), *Pictorial Turn* (pp. 9–39). Milano: Raffaello Cortina Editore.

Council of Europe. (2000). *European Landscape Convention*. Retrieved on September 25, 2019 from https://rm.coe.int/1680080621

Council of Europe. (2005). *Framework Convention on the Value of Cultural Heritage for Society*. Retrieved on September 25, 2019 from https://www.coe.int/en/web/conventions/full-list/-/conventions/treaty/199

De Kerckove, D. (1991). *Brainframes. Technology, Mind and Business*. Utrecht: Bosh & Keuning.

De Luca, L., Bussayarat, C., Stefani, C., Véron, P., & Florenzano, M. (2011). A semantic-based platform for the digital analysis of architectural heritage. *Computers & Graphics*, *2*(35), 227–241. doi:10.1016/j.cag.2010.11.009

Denard, H. (2012). A New Introduction to The London Charter. In *Paradata and Transparency in Virtual Heritage* (pp. 57–72). Farnham: Ashgate Publishing.

Docci, M., & Maestri, D. (2009). *Manuale di rilevamento architettonico e urbano*. Rome: Laterza.

Dustdar, S., Nastić, S., & Šćekić, O. (2017). *Smart Cities. The Internet of Things, People and Systems*. Cham: Springer International Publishing.

European Commission. (2015). *The Onlife Manifesto – Being Human in a Hyperconnected Era*. Retrieved on September 25, 2019 from https://ec.europa.eu/digital-single-market/sites/digital-agenda/files/Manifesto.pdf

Ferraris, M. (2012). *Manifesto del nuovo realismo*. Roma, Bari: Laterza. doi:10.26530/OAPEN_617573

Forte, M., & Siliotti, A. (Eds.). (1996). *Virtual Archaeology. Re-creating Ancient Words*. New York: Harry N. Abrams.

Frischer, B. (2008). From digital illustration to digital heuristic. In B. D. Frischer (Ed.), *Beyond illustration: 2d and 3d Digital Technologies As Tool for Discovery in Archaeology*. Oxford, UK: British Archaeological Reports.

Gaiani, M. (2012). Towards a critical rethinking of the theory of surveying following the advent of digital media. In L. Carlevaris & M. Filippa (Eds.), *In Praise of Theory. The fundamentals of the disciplines of representation and survey* (pp. 375–381). Roma: Gangemi.

Gaiani, M., Benedetti, B., & Apollonio, F. I. (2011). Teorie per rappresentare e comunicare i siti archeologici attraverso modelli critici. *SCIRES-IT*, *1*(2), 33–70.

Gaiani, M., Martini, B., & Apollonio, F. I. (2017). A Framework for a Smart Cultural City. In M. Ceccarelli, M. Cigola, & G. Recinto (Eds.), *New Activities For Cultural Heritage* (pp. 217–227). Cham: Springer International Publishing. doi:10.1007/978-3-319-67026-3_24

Giaccardi, E. (2012). Introduction: reframing Heritage in a participatory culture. In E. Giaccardi (Ed.), *Heritage and Social Media: Understanding Heritage in a Participatory Culture* (pp. 1–10). Abingdon, UK: Routledge. doi:10.4324/9780203112984

Greengrass, M., & Hughes, L. (Eds.). (2008). *The Virtual Representation of the Past*. Farnham: Ashgate.

Huvila, I. (2013). The Unbearable Complexity of Documenting Intellectual Processes: Paradata and Virtual Cultural Heritage Visualisation. *Human IT*, *12*(1), 97–110.

ICOMOS. (1964). *International charter for the conservation and restoration of monuments and sites.* Retrieved on September 25, 2019 from http://www.icomos.org/charters/venice_e.pdf

ICOMOS. (2008). *Charter for the Interpretation and Presentation of Cultural Heritage Sites*. Retrieved on September 25, 2019 from http://icip.icomos.org/downloads/ICOMOS_Interpretation_Charter_ENG_04_10_08.pdf

ICOMOS. (2013). *The Burra Charter*. Retrieved on September 25, 2019 from http://portal.iphan.gov.br/uploads/ckfinder/arquivos/The-Burra-Charter-2013-Adopted-31_10_2013.pdf

Jenkins, H. (2006). *Convergence Culture: Where Old and New Media Collide*. New York: NY University Press.

Jenkins, H. (2009). *Confronting the Challenges of Participatory Culture: Media Education for the 21st Century*. Cambridge, MA: MIT. doi:10.7551/mitpress/8435.001.0001

Lévi Strauss, C. (1962). *La pensée sauvage*. Paris: Plon.

Lévy, P. (1995). *Qu'est-ce que le virtuel?* Paris: Editions La Découverte.

Milgram, P., & Kishino, F. (1994). A taxonomy of mixed reality visual displays. *IEICE Transactions on Information and Systems*, *E77-D*, 12, 1321–1329.

Mitchell, W. J. (1996). *City of Bits*. Cambridge, MA: MIT Press.

Mori, M. (1070). 不気味の谷現象 [On the Uncanny Valley]. *Enerugi*, *7*(4), 33–35.

Murray, J. H. (1997). *Hamlet on the Holodeck*. Cambridge, MA: The MIT Press.

Principles of Seville. (2012). Retrieved on September 25, 2019 from http://smartheritage.com/seville-principles/seville-principles

Purini, F. (2003). Digital divide. In L. Sacchi & M. Unali (Eds.), *Architettura e cultura digitale* (pp. 87–96). Milano: Skira.

Schafer, D. P. (2014). *The Age of Culture*. Oakville: Rock's Mills Press.

Silberman, N., & Purser, M. (2012). Collective memory as affirmation: People-centered cultural heritage in a digital age. In E. Giaccardi (Ed.), *Heritage and Social Media: Undestanding heritage in a Participatory Culture* (pp. 13–29). Abingdon, UK: Routledge.

Stone, R. J. (1999, Nov.). Virtual heritage. *UNESCO World Heritage Magazine*, 18-20.

The London Charter. (2009). Retrieved on September 25, 2019 from http://www.londoncharter.org/

Tielden, F. (1957). *Interpreting Our Heritage*. Chapel Hill, NC: University of North Carolina Press.

UNESCO. (1954). *Convention for the Protection of Cultural Property in the Event of Armed Conflict*. Retrieved on September 25, 2019 from http://portal.unesco.org/en/ev.php-URL_ID=13637&URL_DO=DO_TOPIC&URL_SECTION=201.html

UNESCO. (1972). *Convention Concerning the Protection of the World Cultural and Natural Heritage*. Retrieved on September 25, 2019 from http://whc.unesco.org/en/conventiontext/

UNESCO. (1976). *Recommendation concerning the Safeguard and Contemporary Role of Historic Areas*. Retrieved on September 25, 2019 from http://portal.unesco.org/en/ev.php-URL_ID=13133&URL_DO=DO_TOPIC&URL_SECTION=201.html

UNESCO. (1994). *The Nara Document on Authenticity*. Retrieved on September 25, 2019 from whc.unesco.org/document/9379

UNESCO. (2003a). *Charter on the Preservation of the Digital Heritage*. Retrieved on September 25, 2019 from http://portal.unesco.org/en/ev.php-URL_ID=17721&URL_DO=DO_TOPIC&URL_SECTION=201.html

UNESCO. (2003b). *Convention for the Safeguarding of Intangible Cultural Heritage*. Retrieved on September 25, 2019 from https://ich.unesco.org/en/convention

UNESCO. (2009). *World Heritage Cultural Landscape*. Retrieved on September 25, 2019 from http://whc.unesco.org/en/culturallandscape/

UNESCO. (2011). *Recommendation on the Historic Urban Landscape*. Retrieved on September 25, 2019 from http://whc.unesco.org/en/activities/638

UNESCO. (2015). *Operational Guidelines for the Implementation of the World Heritage Convention*. Retrieved on September 25, 2019 from http://whc.unesco.org/en/guidelines/

Ware, C. (2000). *Information Visualization: Perception for Design*. San Francisco, CA: Morgan Kaufmann.

KEY TERMS AND DEFINITIONS

Augmented Reality: Superimposition of digital information on observer's perceptions of reality. In VR external perceptions are limited as much as possible, in AR they are fundamental, because the computer-generated images roots on the vision of the real world.

Interpretation: The ICOMOS *Charter for the Interpretation and Presentation of Cultural Heritage Sites* (2008) says that interpretation: "refers to the full range of potential activities intended to heighten public awareness and enhance understanding of cultural heritage site. These can include print and electronic publications, public lectures, on-site and directly related off-site installations, educational programmes, community activities, and ongoing research, training, and evaluation of the interpretation process itself."

Mixed Reality: In 1994 Milgram and Kishino coined the expression "Mixed Reality" (MR) to describe the "virtual continuum" between only real and completely virtual environment perception. Analyzing the interfaces for visualization, they identified six classes of hybrid states. Their aim is to define a taxonomy to distinguish between different technological requirements.

Paradata: It can be generically referred to the process by which the survey data are collected. In particular, paradata is a kind of metadata focused on the use of data, and moreover it describes the transformation of data during their "inter-use" in participatory systems. According to the definition presented by *The London Charter* (2009) – focused on its use in 3D computer-based visualizations – paradata is:

"Information about human processes of understanding and interpretation of data objects. Examples of paradata include descriptions stored within a structured dataset of how evidence was used to interpret an artefact, or a comment on methodological premises within a research publication. It is closely related, but somewhat different in emphasis, to "contextual metadata", which tend to communicate interpretations of an artefact or collection, rather than the process through which one or more artefacts were processed or interpreted."

Participatory Culture: It is "a culture with relatively low barriers to artistic expression and civic engagement, strong support for creating and sharing creations, and some type of informal mentorship whereby experienced participants pass along knowledge to novices. In a participatory culture, members also believe their contributions matter and feel some degree of social connection with one another". In particular, the following skills underlies the participative culture: Affiliation, Expression, Collaborative problem solving, Circulation. New skills follow: Play, Performance, Simulation, Appropriation, Multitasking, Distributed cognition, Collective intelligence, Judgment, Transmedia navigation, Networking, Negotiation" (Jenkins, 2009).

Presentation: The ICOMOS *Charter for the Interpretation and Presentation of Cultural Heritage Sites* (2008) defines explains that presentation: "more specifically denotes the carefully planned communication of interpretive content through the arrangement of interpretive information, physical access, and interpretive infrastructure at a cultural heritage site. It can be conveyed through a variety of technical means, including, yet not requiring, such elements as informational panels, museum-type displays, formalized walking tours, lectures and guided tours, and multimedia applications and websites."

Transparency: In computer-based visualization, it consists in the statement of sources and of the degree of reliability of the virtual re-constructions. From a methodological point of view, it makes the digital model testable by other professionals. In the built heritage field, the concept has been developed in archaeology where 3D models are realized to reconstruct ancient configurations. In The *London Charter*'s Glossary (2009), there is a definition of "Intellectual transparency": It is "The provision of information, presented in any medium or format, to allow users to understand the nature and scope of "knowledge claim" made by a computer-based visualization outcome."

Chapter 14
Ten Challenges for Digital Humanities and the Way Forward:
Revisited From the Social Context

Stella Markantonatou
Athena – Research and Innovation Center in Information, Communication, and Knowledge Technologies, Greece

Simon Donig
University of Passau, Germany

George Pavlidis
Athena – Research and Innovation Center in Information, Communication, and Knowledge Technologies, Greece

Thomas Gees
Institut Digital Enabling, Berner Fachhochschule, Switzerland

Adamantios Koumpis
Institut Digital Enabling, Berner Fachhochschule, Switzerland

ABSTRACT

In a previous article, the authors came up with a list of what they considered 10 challenges that would define the area of digital humanities at large and their evolution in the next years. However, in the almost two years that have passed since the publication of that paper, they are now able to see the need for relating the challenges for digital humanities with what one may characterize as socially relevant topics by means of outlining 10 challenges where the digital humanities can make a social impact. This chapter does that.

DOI: 10.4018/978-1-7998-2871-6.ch014

INTRODUCTION

Digital Humanities are, unjustly at some extent, regarded as an application of Computer Science in Humanities or vice versa, the application-oriented equivalent of Humanities with the assistance of computer technologies.

In this respect. there is a need for the people who feel like or identify themselves as 'digital humanists' to define a roadmap that will provide them the means to implement an ambitious agenda. The term 'digital humanist' denotes a person involved in cross-disciplinary work related to or including humanities studies and Computer Science, and is rather not convincing, probably, not attractive either – as the term 'computer scientist' might have been a couple of decades ago. The aim of the enterprise is to prove the functionality and the value that Digital Humanities can bring to Humanities, eventually upgrading the former from the status of a 'servant discipline' of the latter, or on the other hand, to totally diffuse and embed the former within the latter and cancel the need for the adjective 'digital'.

In a previous article (Pavlidis, Markantonatou, Donig, & Koumpis, 2018), we came up with a list of what we considered as ten challenges that would define the domain of Digital Humanities at large and their evolution in the next years. In the almost two years that have passed since the publication of that paper, we are now able to see the need for relating the challenges for Digital Humanities with what one may characterize as socially relevant topics by means of outlining ten challenges where the Digital Humanities can make a social impact.

THE CHALLENGES

The difference between the aforementioned original paper and the current one is that while in the first we took a *top-down approach* by axiomatically defining some guiding principles – which by the way still believe they are all holding and are still valid, we now are able to see and admit that the impact that such an approach has is very limited. So based on this, we now suggest a *bottom-up approach* that will pay special attention to needs and problem areas where Digital Humanities can be what people call a *game-changer*. So in the following paragraphs, we list these newly formulated challenges, which we aspire to help spark a dialogue in the academic and the research communities.

Challenge 1: Fake news

There is a wide field for open-ended, high-risk research in the area of fake news. One may, for example, consider the case of a broad multilingual corpus for training and testing Natural Language Processing tools for computing veracity. Such a research action could build on existing research infrastructures and cutting-edge Natural Language Processing components that are already developed and are based on e.g. hybrid knowledge-based and/or deep learning approaches for text analytics and cross lingual aspect-oriented sentiment analysis. Research in this context would demonstrate in real world settings several yet-not-met goals such as:

a) back testing and historical processing for detection of fake news in the past for a variety of online media – much of which may refer to archived news reports and blogs, social media, etc.;
b) capabilities to detect emergence of fake news patterns in near real time mode;

c) based on (a) and (b), to propose an early and weak signals detector for identifying potential fake news spots in online media, blogs, Facebook, Twitter accounts, etc. given historical records of content exchanges and news reporting / content presentation styles.

Challenge 2: Hate speech

Hate speech is, similar to fake news, a phenomenon that has been a rather hot and coming topic. While we don't need to claim it is a desideratum, it is easy to identify that research in this field can at a great extent profit from methods and research in Digital Humanities. Addressing the challenge is only possible by joining forces; only a concerted action that would include experts, practitioners and scientists from the domain of Digital Humanities would exhibit increased possibilities of success. The generic contribution of the Digital Humanities could be related, amongst others, to the development and the validation of tools for use by institutional users (public authorities) as well as news and media organisations and individuals (citizens) offering an enhanced ability to monitor online hate speech, while also providing all the necessary hate speech analytics that can support the users in taking all the necessary, as well as the immediate actions for blocking the hate speech contributors.

In such a context we see the involvement of members of the Digital Humanities academic community as a natural development of existing research in the area, thus helping create interdisciplinary groups with results that shall have a long-lasting and high impact to the society, as in the case of the Online Hate Index Research Project at Berkeley University[1]. In this context we see also the involvement of journalists and media as an important add-on that will help preserve the integrity of their professions, while the inclusion of law enforcement authorities shall allow the latter to get access to state of the art methods and tools in their fight against hate speech.

Challenge 3: Radicalisation

Radicalisation does not start in an Internet forum or in a closed Facebook group – this is where it may end up, unless it will have found its way towards a terrorist action. Radicalisation may start as early as at school – in the classroom, as a result of rigid formal or loosely defined informal structures supported or tolerated by the setting; it also starts at home, again as result of interaction patterns between the parents or in the communications of them with the children. Same also may start in the neighbourhoods or in any group activity where people may have the opportunity to meet and exchange views, opinions and ideas.

No doubt that it is a complex phenomenon: there are multiple shades of radicalisation, and different signals and trends in society that can eventually sum up and result or evolve into radicalisation incidents, and especially for the current Zeitgeist, where a right-wing and nationalist tide is rising all across Europe and globally. This tide not only undermines the founding principles of democratic governance but is also a threat to the strength and safety of the welfare and prosperity of the citizens for all individual countries.

Again, the role of Digital Humanities is exceptionally critical as it can provide this holistic approach that is necessary, and which may help bridge the various aspects of radicalisation that have been studied separately.

Challenge 4: Political Correctness

While the term as such is not as recent, with appearances also in the 1930s, it started having an increased presence in media coverage and bibliography. We may need to refer to the seminal work of Allan Bloom in 'The Closing of the American Mind' (Bloom, 2008) that set the stage (and at some extent also the agenda) for the debate about political correctness in the North American higher education in the last decades of the 20th century.

Nowadays, we may all agree that same as with the first three aforementioned challenges, political correctness is neither right nor left. Whoever would see this as a symptom of cultural pessimism, connecting it to a process of irreversible decline may find traces of influence by libertarian political philosophy. While some recent writings (Internet Safety 101, 2019) aim to correct a common popular misrepresentation of libertarianism as unreservedly supporting private persons, whatever their situation or behaviour, with a carefully engineered intellectual argumentation, there is still a long shadow in the means and the ends of political correctness as such, especially when we may see how it can act as a fire accelerator for the three previously mentioned challenges.

Political correctness may be a core challenge of our societies (how can we be just and inclusive towards all our members) but can also develop damaging dynamics. Digital Humanities can offer these tools and methods that will help take a more self-reflective stance by making it a research topic. For example, one could seek to research such closure processes by large scale text-mining and distant reading approaches combined with close reading and historicizing.

Challenge 5: Storytelling

Language is at the core of what makes us human. Man is not alone a *homo ludens* or a *homo faber* but a *homo narrans*. Narrating and story-telling dates thousands of years back to the nights our ancestors as in the campfire folklore were sharing stories, while also decorating their caves with wall pictures may be seen as offering exactly the mediatization that the modern human finds in several aspects of multimodality. Language, in this respect, is at the core of our collective memory, engrained in religion. Memory and narrating form the heart of the imagined communities such as nation states, as identified by the work of Benedict Anderson (Anderson, 2006).

Nowadays, stories are an important part of a nation's identity: people use stories to internalize their values and concurrently to externalize their fears and wishes. Same is the case also for commercial companies and organisations that need to invent or reinvent their history, process it in retrospect to find some handles that will help them move on. The very same is also the case with start-ups that need to come up with convincing 'elevator pitches', where a CEO or a founder provides in a few minutes a combination of aspirations, goals and scenarios that may convince financiers and investors to support their venture. Here, again, it is the face value of a story that matters. The implications of this are easy to foresee, given the impact storytelling can have on falsifying memories, influencing ideologies or fostering fake news and hate speech, each of which relates to some other of the identified challenges here. What we see here as a challenge is that researching narratology is an endeavour that Digital Humanities can contribute jointly with Computer Linguistics, Semiotics, Communication Science and History.

Challenge 6: Authenticity

The quality of being authentic is having more than one dimensions and interpretation levels. It is not only how persons perceive, 'invent' and present themselves in the digital and the social media, but also affects the very nature of content: a speech by Obama that is a result of deepfake (Parkin, 2019) is only the start of a new era, taking into account also the fact that the hurdle for creating deepfakes increases significantly (Schwartz, 2018). In an analogy, the supposedly 'Hitler Diaries' ('Hitler-Tagebücher') were 'discovered' and appeared in the German news magazine Stern back in 1983 and were also, on request by the British 'The Sunday Times' authenticated for their originality by the historian Hugh Trevor-Roper (Harris, 1986).

A core issue – though not the only one – here is what the role of Digital Humanities in authenticating information could be, apart from being a watchful and critical eye of the public.

Challenge 7: Memory

Memory – either as a notion related to what we nowadays would refer to as collective memory relates to the idea of a shared space of stories or histories, related to a social group. Such a collective memory is important for the sustainment of the group's identity. The basic idea has been documented back in the 50s by Halbwachs (Halbwachs, 1992) and is at a great extend affected by fiction. The latter depends, as we very well know, on imagination – and for this there are many famous quotes – we would prefer to refer only to Thomas Mann's 'What a glorious gift is imagination, and what satisfaction it affords!' (Mann, 1992) and slightly paraphrase it to *what a dangerous gift imagination is, and what consequences it brings*. Here again we need to set the stage by introducing two concepts: this of a memory institution and that of an institutional memory:

- ***Memory institutions*** are defined as organization expected to maintain a repository of public knowledge. This is a generic term used for institutions such as libraries, archives and museums, but nowadays, may also refer to digital libraries and digital repositories which may serve as memories for our societies or the mankind at large. As it is easy to understand, such institutions are increasingly considered as a part of a documentation and information science perspective. Next to the concept of a memory institution it is useful to have a look to the concept of institutional memory.
- ***Institutional memory:*** though this concept does not exist, we coin it here, aiming to define or actually design an intermediate level between the group as a whole (collective memory) and the individual or its family (communicative memory). The concept may also be extended or adapted to describe different forms of collective memory e.g. for an enterprise, having their own archive, archivists, memory policy (what gets and published where) etc. To this process, the individual and its immediate peers form a 'communicative memory', which is in a constant process of exchange with the – relatively fictious – collective memory that is represented by mediatisations of memory that are essentially driven by mass media and social media in our days.

In light of the above, institutional memory may be regarded as a collective set of facts, concepts, experiences and ideas held by a group of people. We expect this to transcend the individual level and reflect a collective memory hi(story) aspect that reflects an ongoing transmission of memories between members of a group. Elements of institutional memory may be found not only at the national level but also in companies, professional, religious or political groupings, etc. and by extension in any cultural appearance or phenomena.

In a world with few absolute truths it is about reconciling memory of different groups, communities, nations that now increasingly happens in the the digital sphere, where they clash and may easily lead to toxic situations. The role of Digital Humanities could be that of a mediator, fostering and presenting memory in new ways.

That said, there is always a risk with institutional memories, as these may be encouraged or manipulated to preserve a certain *ideology* (on this see Challenge 8), and to this aim they can be manipulated to serve specific aims or goals. To stay to a relatively safe area of examples, our parents may remain the heroes of our childhood as we may consciously and deliberately choose to foster positive memories from them. However, it is not uncommon that we may again choose to make use only of some selective negative memories we have with them to ground some later events.

We humans need to provide an interpretation for what happens around us, usually in the form of narratives. And we are ready to accept that narratives reflect the subjectivity of the individuals that transmit them, but what about the case of events that are either results of a deliberate falsification process, which either omits events that have taken place or introduces new ones that have been invented?

The Battle of Marathon – Did It (N)Ever Happen?

Let us have a look in the history of human kind and choose a battle that related to what in many schools is still taught as the first invasion of Europe by some non-European tribe: the battle of Marathon. As it took place about 2500 years before our time, we can make some hypotheses that will project to the future. It doesn't need to be a very distant future from now, so we don't need to travel 2500 years. We can still make our point with a projection of about 100 or 150 years ahead of today.

We can safely assume that in 100 or 150 years all the information will reside in electronic form, so there may be no need to keep books in the form we still have today. And we may also assume that people will not need to keep electronic information in their hard disks, same as most of us still do today. What we may nowadays expperience with online services may be taken as a safe basis for foreseeing a future where people may not need to store information in any other form than on the Cloud, and may be able to dynamically retrieve it on demand.

There is no need to think about conspiracy theories and that some evil hand manipulates history: back to the battle of Marathon, imagine now that all information related to it gets erased – not gradually like a human brain suffering from dementia may lose information but instantly: all 'entries' that related to content and information related to the battle of Marathon are now void. Or refer to some other battle. It doesn't need to be the battle of Gettysburg – it can still be some battle that took place in Greece – but not with the Persians. Like for instance the battle of Chaeronea. It is still a battle but was amongst the Greeks – so there were no 'evil' Persians invading Greece and thus also Europe.

The point we want to make with the above hypothetical example is that collective and institutional memories are – same as the individual human ones – more fragile than we tend to think. It is in this respect a challenge for Digital Humanists to find really robust means to preserve them and their integrity as much unaffected by human or other interventions. It may be highly probable that climate change or some other reason will affect or destroy more than individual humans aimed to.

Challenge 8: Ideologies

We shouldn't elaborate here on the etymology of the term, derived from the composite Greek word *ιδεολογία* from two components: idea (*ιδέα*) and logos (word - *λόγος*). However, it is useful to mention a relevant term that appears in the Greek language, namely *ιδεοληψία*. Unfortunately, no one uses the term *ideolepsy* or, as one would expect it to appear in German, *Ideolepsie*. The relevant term in English is *obsession* related with a certain ideology. So, something similar to the case when the toxicity values in some ideology go far beyond the 'normal' – this is where one may use the term ideolepsy.

Internet and the Word Wide Web are for sure a cradle of ideologies (and ideolepsies). Still, the digital humanists may ignore the big picture and what happens out there, preferring to concentrate, as one would also expect from a scientist or a researcher, to the study of cases. Such a sterilization of a social process may usually lead us to false results, by e.g. leaving out parameters of the problem or emphasizing on providing the right answers, even though there is no prior control on how valid the questions we ask are. A recent debate in the German political scene initiated by the ex-president of the country on the limits of tolerance and the need to keep the dialogue with the far righters open, can be seen as such a live use case (Joachim Gauck, 2019).

Taking a rather post-Marxist perspective as presented in (Castoriadis, 1991), in the arena of ideologies both the base and the superstructure model refer to one and the same, namely ideas. So, where a Marxist textbook example base refers to production and its relations and modes of production, while superstructure refers to the dominant ideology (religious, legal, political systems), when dealing with ideas, both base and superstructure can be measured in the same unit or 'traded' with the same currency, namely this of ideas.

As one would expect, ideologies as a challenge, are closely related and relevant to other challenges presented here such as radicalisation (challenge 3), hate speech (challenge 2) and fake news (challenge 1). As expected, they also use memories as ground (challenge 7) and storytelling as a means to its any ends (challenge 5). In this respect, and while it is part of the other dimensions mentioned, it still very much transports the idea of a 'false' consciousness. Its relevance to the Digital Humanities relates to contemporary developments also in the area of Artificial Intelligence (AI) that relate to algorithm transparency, ethical aspects and responsibility for application of AI and other fields.

Challenge 9: Ethics (and beyond)

We are all aware about the arguments about privacy in the digital age and how this is challenged by the use of e.g. deepfakes. What is necessary here is to discuss both ethical considerations in research as well as generally come up with a new assessment of what privacy and the digital self are and the contribution that Digital Humanities can deliver in this context. As an example, we can take the case of pornography: the Web is full of porn in all forms, including videos, pictures, talks. There have been attempts to quantify the amount of porn – some estimates report a 30% (Internet Safety 101, 2019), but, as expected, this figure only offers an estimate of the memory space taken by porn content and does not contain the relative itemisation of such content with respect to other 'genres' or types of content.

What one should examine, given the rise of violence in pornographic content (Internet Safety 101, 2019), is to recognize the drivers that help to the sustainment of this genre, by means of studying pornographic content as such and trying to infer from the type of the content the needs that this content meets and satisfies.

A central postulate to be supported with evidence from an experimental investigation is that humans watch pornographic content mainly in the format of videos, because this makes them feel like watching some form of religious-like ritual that involves carnal interactions that are transformed or reflecting some type of transcendental and metaphoric value for themselves as individuals and for their lives. This thesis is in contrast to the mainstream conceptualisation and which relates consumption of porn content as an expression of mental or emotional instability, as a result of depression, or some other 'disease' or perversion.

The interactions and impact of porn on fake news (Challenge 1) and hate speech (Challenge 2) as well as to Authenticity (Challenge 6) is easy to identify and has been recognized also by the media. This may again create a 'lethal cocktail' that may transform the nature of our realities and our lives in a multitude of ways. And it is also easy to foresee the emergence of radicalisation (Challenge 4) and political correctness (Challenge 5) tendencies that will also act as catalyst not only in the specific area (porn) but to great parts of the value systems of our societies.

Challenge 10: Working with more than one of the challenges

Similar to the debate about climate and weather, where the former relates to long-term patterns and the latter to short-term conditions, all previously presented challenges may be studied separately. However, to increase the impact of one's research contributions, we need to study and take into account the interactions that several social phenomena bring, as a result of these interactions. In brief, this means that studying, for example, the challenge posed by hate speech separately from the other challenges, may still provide us with results, but their value will be significantly lower than in case we have co-studied hate speech with respect to all other challenges.

CONCLUSION

In this chapter an attempt was made to identify and highlight challenges that are expected to have a significant impact on Digital Humanities in the following years.

We are aware that there are many discussions about the use of big data analytics and the use of neural networks and artificial intelligence for solving certain problems in a variety of fields, including, amongst others, this of Digital Humanities. One mistake we make, though, when considering the case of Digital Humanities, which appears also wherever the term digital accompanies some noun, is that we tend to think that *digital means virtual*. This is not the case. Great parts of development and growth in Digital Humanities may come from areas that relate to hardware for Artificial Intelligence or what is currently called 'Edge AI'. Whatever the future will bring, there is a need to keep all developments closely related and connected to existing or foreseen social challenges.

It is this co-study of the challenges that will offer an ideal application area for all new technologies, as it may offer a wide field for stress-testing not only the computational power but also the robustness and consistency of several of these technologies, while also providing useful results that would have been otherwise impossible to acquire if one follows traditional research paths.

REFERENCES

Anderson, B. (2006). *Imagined communities: Reflections on the origin and spread of nationalism*. Verso books.

Bloom, A. (2008). *Closing of the American mind*. Simon and Schuster.

Castoriadis, C. (1991). *Philosophy, Politics, Autonomy: Essays in Political Philosophy*. New York: Oxford University Press.

Halbwachs, M. (1992). *On collective memory*. University of Chicago Press.

Harris, R. (1986). *Selling Hitler: The Extraordinary Story of the Con Job of the Century* (1st ed.). New York: Pantheon.

Internet Safety 101. (2019). *Enough Is Enough: Pornography*. Retrieved October 15, 2019, from Internet Safety 101 website: https://enough.org/stats_porn_industry

Joachim Gauck. (2019). *Altbundespräsident wirbt für "erweiterte Toleranz in Richtung rechts."* Retrieved October 15, 2019, from https://www.zeit.de/politik/deutschland/2019-06/joachim-gauck-nationalismus-toleranz

Mann, T. (1992). *Confessions of Felix Krull, confidence man: The early years*. Vintage.

Parkin, S. (2019). The rise of the deepfake and the threat to democracy. *The Guardian, 22*. Retrieved from https://www.theguardian.com/technology/ng-interactive/2019/jun/22/the-rise-of-the-deepfake-and-the-threat-to-democracy

Pavlidis, G., Markantonatou, S., Donig, S., & Koumpis, A. (2018). Ten Challenges for Digital Humanities and the Way Forward. *International Journal of Computational Methods in Heritage Science*, *2*(1), 1–7. doi:10.4018/IJCMHS.2018010101

Schwartz, O. (2018). You thought fake news was bad? Deep fakes are where truth goes to die. *The Guardian*. Retrieved from https://www.theguardian.com/technology/2018/nov/12/deep-fakes-fake-news-truth

ENDNOTE

1 https://dlab.berkeley.edu/landing-page/online-hate-index-scalable-detection-online-hate-speech

Compilation of References

Abaci, T., Ciger, J., & Thalmann, D. (2005). Planning with smart objects. WSCG 2005 (Short Papers), 25-28.

Abbeel, P. C., Coates, C., & Ng, Y. A. (2010). Autonomous helicopter aerobatics through apprenticeship learning. *The International Journal of Robotics Research, 29*(13), 1608–1639. doi:10.1177/0278364910371999

Abdelmonem, M. G., Selim, G., Mushatat, S., & Almogren, A. (2017). Virtual Platforms for Heritage Preservation in the Middle East: The Case of Medieval Cairo. *Archnet-IJAR, 11*(3), 28. doi:10.26687/archnet-ijar.v11i3.1404

Addison, A. C. (2000). Emerging trends in virtual heritage. *IEEE MultiMedia, 7*(2), 22–25. doi:10.1109/93.848421

Adele. (2011). *Someone Like You.* Retrieved 27 November 2016, from http://www.azlyrics.com/lyrics/adele/someone-likeyou.html

Agache, R. (1963). La prospection aerienne sur sols nus et l'inventaire archeoloque de la Somme. In *Archéologie Aérienne, Colloque International, 31/8-3/9/1963, S.E.V.P.E.N.* (pp. 49-58). Academic Press.

Agosto, E. (2013). Vector-raster server-side analysis: a PostGIS benchmark. *Applied Geomatics, 5*(2), 177-184. Doi:10.100712518-013-0104-x0

Agosto, E., Ardissone, P., & Rinaudo, F. (2007). GIS And Web-GIS, Cultural and Open Source Platforms: General Rules for Cultural Heritage Documentation. *ISPRS Archives, 36*(5), 625-630.

Agosto, E., Dalmasso, S., Pasquali, P., & Terzo, O. (2011). Ithaca worldwide flood alert system: the web framework. *Applied Geomatics, 3*(2). Doi:10.100712518-010-0041-x

Agosto, E., & Bornaz, L. (2017). 3D Models in Cultural Heritage: Approaches for Their Creation and Use. *International Journal of Computational Methods in Heritage Science, 1*(1), 1–9. doi:10.4018/IJCMHS.2017010101

Aitken, M. J. (1985). *Thermoluminescence Dating.* Orlando, FL: Academic Press.

Aksenov, P., Kemperman, A., & Arentze, T. (2014). Toward personalized and dynamic cultural routing: A three-level approach. *Procedia Environmental Sciences, 22*, 257–269. doi:10.1016/j.proenv.2014.11.025

Albert, W., & Tullis, T. (2013). *Measuring the User Experience: Collecting, Analyzing, and Presenting Usability Metrics* (2nd ed.). Newnes.

Alexandridis, G., Chrysanthi, A., Tsekouras, G. E., & Caridakis, C. (2019). Personalized and content adaptive cultural heritage path recommendation: An application to the Gournia and Çatalhöyük archaeological sites. *User Modeling and User-Adapted Interaction, 29*(1), 201–238. doi:10.100711257-019-09227-6

Alfieri, N. (1963). Topografia antica e aerofotografia a Spina. In *Archéologie Aérienne, Colloque International, 31/8-3/9/1963, S.E.V.P.E.N.* (pp. 155-160). Academic Press.

Alimamy, S., Deans, K. R., & Gnoth, J. (2017). Augmented Reality: Uses and Future Considerations in Marketing. In Leadership, Innovation and Entrepreneurship as Driving Forces of the Global Economy (pp. 705-712). Springer International Publishing.

Alsheikh-Ali, A., Qureshi, W., Al-Mallah, M. H., & Ioannidis, J. P. A. (2011). Public availability of published research data in high-impact journals. *PLoS One*, *6*(9), e24357. doi:10.1371/journal.pone.0024357 PMID:21915316

Alves, R., Valente, P., & Nunes, N. J. (2014). The state of user experience evaluation practice. In *Proceedings of the 8th Nordic Conference on Human-Computer Interaction: Fun, Fast, Foundational* (pp. 93-102). ACM. 10.1145/2639189.2641208

Alvisi, G. (1963). L' utilita dei vecchi rilemanti nella ricerca archeological. In *Archéologie Aérienne*, *Colloque International, 31/8-3/9/1963, S.E.V.P.E.N.* (pp. 277-281). Academic Press.

American Society for Photogrammetry and Remote Sensing. (1997). *Manual of photographic interpretation* (2nd ed.). Author.

American Society of Photogrammetry. (1983). *Manual of remote sensing* (2nd ed.; Vol. 2). Author.

Anagnostakis, G., Antoniou, M., Kardamitsi, E., Sachinidis, T., Koutsabasis, P., Stavrakis, M., ... Zissis, D. (2016). Accessible museum collections for the visually impaired: combining tactile exploration, audio descriptions and mobile gestures. In *Proceedings of the 18th International Conference on Human-Computer Interaction with Mobile Devices and Services Adjunct* (pp. 1021-1025). ACM. 10.1145/2957265.2963118

Anderson, B. (2006). *Imagined communities: Reflections on the origin and spread of nationalism.* Verso books.

Anderson, E., McLoughlin, L., Liarokapis, F., Petridis, C. P., & Freitas, S. (2010). Developing serious games for cultural heritage: A state of the art review. *Virtual Reality (Waltham Cross)*, *14*(4), 255–275. doi:10.100710055-010-0177-3

André, E., Klesen, M., Gebhard, P., Allen, S., & Rist, T. (2000). Integrating models of personality and emotions into lifelike characters. In *Affective interactions* (pp. 150–165). Springer Berlin Heidelberg. doi:10.1007/10720296_11

Andreoli, R., Corolla, A., Faggiano, A., Malandrino, D., Pirozzi, D., Ranaldi, M., ... Scarano, V. (2016, October). Immersivity and Playability Evaluation of a Game Experience in Cultural Heritage. In *Euro-Mediterranean Conference* (pp. 814-824). Springer International Publishing. 10.1007/978-3-319-48496-9_65

Andrews, D. (Ed.). (2009). Metric Survey Specification for Cultural Heritage. Swindow: English Heritage.

Angelopoulou, A., Economou, D., Bouki, V., Psarrou, A., Jin, L., Pritchard, C., & Kolyda, F. (2011). Mobile Augmented Reality for Cultural Heritage. In N. Venkatasubramanian, V. Getov, & S. Steglich (Eds.), *Mobile Wireless Middleware, Operating Systems, and Applications. MOBILWARE 2011. Lecture Notes of the Institute for Computer Sciences, Social Informatics and Telecommunications Engineering* (Vol. 93). Berlin: Springer. doi:10.1007/978-3-642-30607-5_2

Aplin, G. (2013). *Home.* Retrieved 27 November 2016, from http://www.azlyrics.com/lyrics/gabrielleaplin/home.html

Apollonio, F.I., Gaiani, M., & Zheng, S. (2012). BIM-based modeling and data enrichment of classical architectural buildings. *SCIRES-IT*, *2*(2).

Apollonio, F. I. (2012). *Architettura in 3D*. Milano: Bruno Mondadori.

Archeology Data Service, & Digital Antiquity. (2013). *Guides to Good Practice*. Retrieved January 05, 2018, from http://guides.archaeologydataservice.ac.uk/

Ardissone, P., & Bornaz, L. (2013). A 3D information system for the documentation of archaeological excavations. In *Procedings of CIPA 2013*. Conference Strasbourg. doi:10.5194/isprsarchives-XL-5-W2-55-2013

Ardissono, L., Goy, A., Petrone, G., Signan, M., & Torasso, P. (2003). Intrigue: Personalized recommendation of tourism attractions for desktop and handset devices. *Applied Artificial Intelligence, 17*(8–9), 687–714. doi:10.1080/713827254

Ardissono, L., Kuflik, T., & Petrelli, D. (2012). Personalization in cultural heritage: The road travelled and the one ahead. *User Modeling and User-Adapted Interaction, 22*(1-2), 73–99. doi:10.100711257-011-9104-x

Arends, M., Froschauer, J., Goldfarb, D., Merkl, D., & Weingartner, M. (2012). Analysing user motivation in an art folksonomy. In *Proceedings of the 12th International Conference on Knowledge Management and Knowledge Technologies* (p. 13). ACM. 10.1145/2362456.2362473

Arévalo, M., Cadi-Yazli, N., & Thalmann, N. M. (2014). Giving Life to John Calvin the Reformer. In *Euro-Mediterranean Conference* (pp. 526-535). Springer International Publishing. 10.1007/978-3-319-13695-0_52

Ariès, P. (1975). *Western attitudes toward death: from the Middle Ages to the present* (Vol. 3). Baltimore, MD: John Hopkins University Press.

Arnold, D. (2008). Tools for populating cultural heritage environments with interactive virtual humans. In *Open Digital Cultural Heritage Systems Conference* (p. 25). Academic Press.

Arriga, M., & Levina, N. (2008). *Social dynamics in online cultural fields.* Paper presented at the 29th International Conference on Information Systems (ICIS'08), Paris, France.

Artioli, G. (2010). *Scientific Methods and Cultural Heritage: An introduction to the application of materials science to Archaeometry and conservation science.* New York: Oxford University Press. doi:10.1093/acprof:oso/9780199548262.001.0001

Aspert, N., Santa-Cruz, D., & Ebrahimi, T. (2002). Mesh: Measuring errors between surfaces using the hausdorff distance. In *Multimedia and Expo, 2002. ICME'02. Proceedings. 2002 IEEE International Conference on* (Vol. 1, pp. 705-708). IEEE.

Azuma, R. (1997). A Survey of Augmented Reality. *Presence (Cambridge, Mass.), 6*(4), 355–385. doi:10.1162/pres.1997.6.4.355

Azuma, R., Baillot, Y., Behringer, R., Feiner, S., Julier, S., & MacIntyre, B. (2001). Recent advances in augmented reality. *IEEE Computer Graphics and Applications, 21*(6), 34–47. doi:10.1109/38.963459

Azzola, P., Cardaci, A., Mirabella Roberti, G., & Nannei, V. M. (2019). UAV photogrammetry for Cultural Heritage preservation modeling and mapping venetian walls of Bergamo. *The International Archives of the Photogrammetry, Remote Sensing and Spatial Information Sciences, 42*(W9), 45–50. doi:10.5194/isprs-archives-XLII-2-W9-45-2019

Bagdanov, A. D., Del Bimbo, A., Landucci, L., & Pernici, F. (2011). MNEMOSYNE: Enhancing the Museum Experience through Interactive Media and Visual Profiling. In C. Grana & R. Cucchiara (Eds.), MM4CH 2011, CCIS 247, (pp. 39–50). Springer-Verlag Berlin Heidelberg.

Baker, B. (2016, April 27). What Does Wayfinding Add to City Branding? *Small City Branding Around the World.* Retrieved 27 April 2016, from http://citybranding.typepad.com/city-branding/2016/04/what-does-wayfinding-add-to-city-branding.html

Baldwin, T., Ye, P., Bohnert, F., & Zukerman, I. (2011). In Situ Text Summarisation for Museum Visitors. *25th Pacific Asia Conference on Language, Information and Computation*, 372–381.

Ball, C., Ahn, S. J., & Johnsen, K. (2019). Design and Field Study of Motion-based Informal Learning Games for a Children's Museum. In *2019 IEEE 5th Workshop on Everyday Virtual Reality (WEVR)* (pp. 1-6). IEEE. 10.1109/WEVR.2019.8809588

Balla, A., Pavlogeorgatos, G., Tsiafakis, D., & Pavlidis, G. (2014). Recent Advances in Archaeological Modeling for Archaeological Research and Cultural Heritage Management. *Mediterranean Archaeology and Archaeometry, 14*(4), 143–153.

Baltsavias, E. P. (1991). *Multiphoto geometrically constrained matching* (Doctoral dissertation).

Baltsavias, E., Li, H., Mason, S., Stefanidis, A., & Sinning, M. (1996). Comparison of two digital photogrammetric systems with emphasis on DTM generation: Case study glacier measurement. *International Archives of Photogrammetry and Remote Sensing, 31*, 104–109.

Bandi, S., & Thalmann, D. (2000). Path finding for human motion in virtual environments. *Computational Geometry, 15*(1-3), 103–127. doi:10.1016/S0925-7721(99)00046-2

Bargas-Avila, J. A., & Hornbæk, K. (2011). Old wine in new bottles or novel challenges: a critical analysis of empirical studies of user experience. In *Proceedings of the SIGCHI Conference on Human Factors in Computing Systems* (pp. 2689-2698). ACM. 10.1145/1978942.1979336

Barnes, I. (2003). Aerial `Remote-sensing Techniques Used in the Management of Archaeological Monuments on the British Army's Salisbury Plain Training Area, Wiltshire, UK. *Archaeological Prospection, 10*(2), 83–90. doi:10.1002/arp.197

Barsanti, S., Caruso, G., Micoli, L., Rodriguez, M., & Guidi, G. (2015). 3D Visualization of Cultural Heritage Artefacts with Virtual Reality devices. *The International Archives of the Photogrammetry, Remote Sensing and Spatial Information Sciences, 40*(5), 165–172. doi:10.5194/isprsarchives-XL-5-W7-165-2015

Bates, J. (1994). The role of emotion in believable agents. *Communications of the ACM, 37*(7), 122–125. doi:10.1145/176789.176803

Baudrillard, J. (1983). Simulations. New York: Semiotext(e).

Baudrillard, J. (1976). *L'echange symbolique et la mort*. Paris: Gallimard.

Baudrillard, J. (1987). *L'autre par lui-même: Habilitation*. Paris: Editions Galilée.

Bay, H., Fase, B., & Van Gool, L. (2006). Interactive museum guide: Fast and robust recognition of museum objects. *Proceedings of the International Workshop on Mobile Vision.*

Bay, H., Tuytelaars, T., & Van Gool, L. (2006). Surf: Speeded up robust features. In Computer vision–ECCV 2006. Springer.

Bay, H., Ess, A., Tuytelaars, T., & Van Gool, L. (2008). Speeded-Up Robust Features (SURF). *Computer Vision and Image Understanding, 110*(3), 346–359. doi:10.1016/j.cviu.2007.09.014

Beacham, R. (2008). 'Oh, to Make Boards to Speak! There is a Task!' Toward a Poetics of Paradata. In M. Greengrass & L. Hughes (Eds.), The Virtual Representation of the Past (pp. 171-178). Farnham: Ashgate.

Becker, H. (1995). From Nanotesla to Picotesla - a New Window for Magnetic Prospecting in Archaeology. *Archaeological Prospection, 2*, 217–228.

Bekele, M., Pierdicca, R., Frontoni, E., Malinverni, E., & Gain, J. (2018, March). A Survey of Augmented, Virtual, and Mixed Reality for Cultural Heritage. *ACM J. Comput. Cult. Herit. 11, 2. Article, 7*, 36. doi:10.1145/3145534

Bellotti, F., Berta, R., De Gloria, A., D'ursi, A., & Fiore, V. (2012). A serious game model for cultural heritage. *Journal on Computing and Cultural Heritage, 5*(4), 17. doi:10.1145/2399180.2399185

Bellotti, F., Berta, R., Gloria, A., Dursi, A., & Fiore, V. (2012). A serious game model for cultural heritage. *ACM Journal on Computing and Cultural Heritage*, *5*(4), 17.

Bellucci, A., Diaz, P., & Aedo, I. (2015). A See-Through Display for Interactive Museum Showcases. In *Proceedings of the 2015 International Conference on Interactive Tabletops & Surfaces* (pp. 301-306). ACM. 10.1145/2817721.2823497

Benedetti, B., Gaiani, M., & Remondino, F. (2010). *Modelli digitali 3D in archeologia: il caso di Pompei*. Pisa: Scuola Normale Superiore Pisa.

Benjamin, W. (1936). Das Kunstwerk im Zeitalter seiner technischen Reproduzierbarkeit. *Zeitschrift für Sozialforschung*.

Bentkowska-Kafel, A. D., & Baker, D. (Eds.). (2012). Paradata and Transparency in Virtual Heritage. Farnham: Ashgate Publishing.

Beraldin, J.-A. (2004). Integration of Laser Scanning and Close-Range Photogrammetry - The Last Decade and Beyond. In *XXth International Society for Photogrammetry and Remote Sensing (ISPRS) Congress. Commission VII* (pp. 972-983). Istanbul, Turkey: Academic Press.

Berlino, A., Caroprese, L., La Marca, A., Vocaturo, E., & Zumpano, E. (2019). Augmented Reality for the Enhancement of Archaeological Heritage: a Calabrian Experience. *VIPERC, Visual Pattern Extraction and Recognition for Cultural Heritage Understanding Workshop*.

Bernhard, J. (2010). Insightful learning in the laboratory: Some experiences from 10 years of designing and using conceptual labs. *European Journal of Engineering Education*, *35*(3), 271–287. doi:10.1080/03043791003739759

Bevacqua, E., Mancini, M., Niewiadomski, R., & Pelachaud, C. (2007) An expressive ECA showing complex emotions. *Proceedings of the AISB Annual convention, Workshop on Language, Speech and Gesture for Expressive Characters*, 208-216.

Bewley, H. R. (2003). Aerial Survey for Archaeology. *The Photogrammetric Record*, *104*(18), 273–291. doi:10.1046/j.0031-868X.2003.00023.x

Bhargava, P., & Agrawala A.K. (2016). Modeling Users' Behavior from Large Scale Smartphone Data Collection. EAI Endorsed Trans. *Context-aware Systems & Applications, 3*(10).

Bianchini, C. (2014). Survey 2.0: new technologies, new equipment, new surveyors? In P. Giandebiaggi & C. Vernizzi (Eds.), *Italian Survey & International Experiences* (pp. 763–768). Roma: Gangemi.

Bickmore, T., Pfeifer, L., & Schulman, D. (2011). Relational Agents Improve Engagement and Learning in Science Museum Visitors. In *Intelligent Virtual Agents: 10th International Conference* (pp. 55-67). Reykjavik, Iceland: Springer Berlin Heidelberg.

Bickmore, T., Pfeifer, L., & Schulman, D. (2011). Relational agents improve engagement and learning in science museum visitors. *Intelligent Virtual Agents*, *2011*, 55–67. doi:10.1007/978-3-642-23974-8_7

Bineta, M. (2013). Edge Based Antialiasing: Quality without Compromise. *International Journal of Engineering Science and Research Technology*, *2*(6), 1627–1631.

Bisol, G. D., Anagnostou, P., Capocasa, M., Bencivelli, S., Cerroni, A., Contreras, J., ... Boulton, G. (2014). Perspectives on Open Science and scientific data sharing: An interdisciplinary workshop. *Journal of Anthropological Sciences*, *92*, 179–200. PMID:25020017

Blanco-Pons, S., Carrión-Ruiz, B., Duong, M., Chartrand, J., Fai, S., & Lerma, J. (2019). Augmented Reality Markerless Multi-Image Outdoor Tracking System for the Historical Buildings on Parliament Hill. *Sustainability, 11*(4268). doi:10.3390u11164268

Blink-182. (1999). *Adam's Song*. Retrieved 27 November 2016, from http://www.azlyrics.com/lyrics/blink182/adams-song.html

Bloom, A. (2008). *Closing of the American mind.* Simon and Schuster.

Boboc, R., Duguleană, M., Voinea, G.-D., Postelnicu, C.-C., Popovici, D.-M., & Carrozzino, M. (2019). Mobile Augmented Reality for Cultural Heritage: Following the Footsteps of Ovid among Different Locations in Europe. *Sustainability, 11*(4), 1167. doi:10.3390u11041167

Boehler, W., Heinz, G., & Marbs, A. (2002). The potential of non-contact close range laser scanners for Cultural Heritage recording. In Surveying and documentation of Historic buildings-monuments sites: traditional and modern methods, Postdam, Germany

Boehler, W., & Marbs, A. (2002). 3D scanning instruments. *Proceedings of the CIPA WG 6 International Workshop on Scanning For Cultural Heritage Recording.*

Boehler, W., & Marbs, A. (2004). 3D Scanning and Photogrammetry for Heritage Recording: a Comparison. *Proc. of 12thInt. Conf. on Geoinformatics.*

Boehner, K., Thom-Santelli, J., Zoss, A., Gay, G., Hall, J. S., & Barrett, T. (2005). Imprints of Place: Creative Expressions of the Museum Experience. In *CHI 2005*. ACM.

Bogdanovych, A., Rodríguez-Aguilar, J. A., Simoff, S., & Cohen, A. (2010). Authentic interactive reenactment of cultural heritage with 3D virtual worlds and artificial intelligence. *Applied Artificial Intelligence, 24*(6), 617–647. doi:10.1080/08839514.2010.492172

Bogdanovych, A., Trescak, T., & Simoff, S. (2016). What makes virtual agents believable? *Connection Science, 28*(1), 83–108. doi:10.1080/09540091.2015.1130021

Bohnert, F., & Zukerman, I. (2009). Non-intrusive Personalization of the Museum Experience. LNCS, 5535, 197–209.

Bolter, J. D., & Grusin, R. (1999). *Remediation – Understanding New Media*. Cambridge, MA: MIT Press.

Bonis, B., Stamos, J., Vosinakis, S., Andreou, I., & Panayiotopoulos, T. (2009). A Platform for Virtual Museums with Personalized Content. *Multimedia Tools and Applications, 42*(2), 139–159. doi:10.100711042-008-0231-2

Bonis, B., Vosinakis, S., Andreou, I., & Panayiotopoulos, T. (2013). Adaptive virtual exhibitions. *DESIDOC Journal of Library and Information Technology, 33*(3), 183–198. doi:10.14429/djlit.33.4604

Bontchev, B. (2015). Serious games for and as cultural heritage. *Digital Presentation and Preservation of Cultural and Scientific Heritage*, (5), 43-58.

Borba, E. Z., & Zuffo, M. K. (2016). *Replay! When past experiences are reassembled through virtual reality*. Academic Press.

Borgman, C. (2009). The digital future is now: A call to action for the humanities. *Digital Humanities Quarterly, 3*(4).

Bornaz, L., & Dequal, S. (2003). A new concept: the solid image. *CIPA 2003 XIXth International Symposium.*

Bowen, J., & Filippini-Fantoni, S. (2004). Personalization and the Web from a Museum Perspective. In D. Bearman & J. Trant (Eds.), *Museums and the Web 2004: Selected Papers from an International Conference*, (pp. 63-78). Academic Press.

BrandSound. (2016). *Insights on Music in Brand Communication.* Retrieved 27 November 2016, from http://www.brand-sounds.com/wordpress/

Breuer, J. J., & Bente, G. (2010). Why so serious? On the relation of serious games and learning. *Eludamos (Göttingen), 4*(1), 7–24. doi:10.1177/1461444812450426

Breuer, J., & Bente, G. (2010). Why so serious? On the relation of serious games and learning. *Journal for Computer Game Culture, 4*(1), 7–24.

Bright, A., Kay, J., Ler, D., Ngo, K., Niu, W., & Nuguid, A. (2005). Adaptively Recommending Museum Tours. *Ubiquitous Computing, 7th International Conference on: Workshop: Smart Environments and their Applications to Cultural Heritage.*

Brinson, J. R. (2015). Learning outcome achievement in non-traditional (virtual and remote) versus traditional (hands-on) laboratories: A review of the empirical research. *Computers & Education, 87*, 218–237. doi:10.1016/j.compedu.2015.07.003

Brogan, D. C., Metoyer, R. A., & Hodgins, J. K. (1998). Dynamically simulated characters in virtual environments. *IEEE Computer Graphics and Applications, 18*(5), 58–69. doi:10.1109/38.708561

Brogni, A., Avizzano, C., Evangelista, C., & Bergamasco, M. (1999). Technological Approach for Cultural Heritage. PERCRO Scuola Superiore.

Brooke, J. (1996). SUS-A quick and dirty usability scale. *Usability Evaluation in Industry, 189*(194), 4-7.

Brown, S., & Vaughan, C. (2010). Play: How it Shapes the Brain, Opens the Imagination, and Invigorates the Soul. J P Tarcher/Penguin Putnam.

Brown, S., & Vaughan, C. (2010). *Play: How it changes the brain, Opens the Imagination, and Invigorates the Soul.* J P Tarcher/Penguin Putnam.

Bruno, F., Bruno, S., De Sensi, G., Luchi, M. L., Mancuso, S., & Muzzupappa, M. (2010). From 3D reconstruction to virtual reality: A complete methodology for digital archaeological exhibition. *Journal of Cultural Heritage, 11*(1), 42–49. doi:10.1016/j.culher.2009.02.006

Brusaporci, S. (2014). Issues of Historic Town Surveying: Visualizing Urban Values. *SCIRES.IT, 4*(2), 63-80.

Brusaporci, S. (2015 a). The Representation of Architectural Heritage in the Digital Age. In M. Khosrow-Pour (Ed.), Encyclopedia of Information Science and Technology, Third Edition (pp. 4195-4205, VI). Hershey, PA: IGI Global. doi:10.4018/978-1-4666-5888-2.ch412

Brusaporci, S. (2017b). The Importance of Being Honest. In 3D Printing: Breakthroughs in Research and Practice (pp. 333-360). Hershey, PA: IGI Global.

Brusaporci, S. (2015 b). On Visual Computing for Architectural Heritage. In S. Brusaporci (Ed.), *Handbook of Research on Emerging Digital Tools for Architectural Surveying, Modeling, and Representation* (pp. 94–123). Hershey, PA: IGI Global. doi:10.4018/978-1-4666-8379-2.ch003

Brusaporci, S. (2016). Swimming in the Liquid Age: A Disciplinarily Reflection on Computer-Based Visualization of Architectural Heritage. In G. Amoruso (Ed.), *Handbook of Research on Visual Computing and Emerging Geometrical Design Tools* (pp. 1–24). Hersey, PA: IGI Global. doi:10.4018/978-1-5225-0029-2.ch001

Brusaporci, S. (2017a). *Digital Innovations in Architectural Heritage Conservation: Emerging Research and Opportunities.* Hersey, PA: IGI Global. doi:10.4018/978-1-5225-2434-2

Brusaporci, S. (2017b). The Importance of Being Honest: Issues of Transparency in Digital Visualization of Architectural Heritage. In A. Ippolito (Ed.), *Handbook of Research on Emerging Technologies for Architectural and Archaeological Heritage* (pp. 66–93). Hersey, PA: IGI Global. doi:10.4018/978-1-5225-0675-1.ch003

Brusaporci, S., Centofanti, M., Continenza, R., & Trizio, I. (2012). Sistemi Informativi Architettonici per la gestione, tutela e fruizione dell'edilizia storica. In *ATTI 16ª Conferenza Nazionale ASITA 2012* (pp. 315–322). Vicenza: ASITA.

Brusaporci, S., & Maiezza, P. (2016). Re-Loading BIM: Between Spatial and Database Information Modeling for Architectural Heritage Documentation. In F. Felip Miralles, J. Gual Ortí, M. Cabeza González, & C. García-García (Eds.), *Dibujar, Construir, Sonar. Investigaciones en torno a la expresion grafica aplicada a la edificacion* (pp. 835–847). Valencia: Tirant Lo Blanch.

Brusaporci, S., Maiezza, P., & Tata, A. (2018). A Framework for Architectural Heritage HBIM Semantization and Development. *The International Archives of the Photogrammetry, Remote Sensing and Spatial Information Sciences, 42*, 179–184. doi:10.5194/isprs-archives-XLII-2-179-2018

Brusaporci, S., Ruggieri, G., Sicuranza, F., & Maiezza, P. (2017). Augmented Reality for Historical Storytelling. The INCIPICT Project for the Reconstruction of Tangible and Intangible Image of L'Aquila Historical Centre. *Proceedings, 1*(9), 1083. doi:10.3390/proceedings1091083

Buko, A. (1984). Problems and research prospects in the determination of the provenance of pottery. *World Archaeology, 15*(3), 348–365. doi:10.1080/00438243.1984.9979909

Burca, G., James, J. A., Kockelmann, W., Fitzpatrick, M. E., Zhang, S. Y., Hovind, J., & Van Langh, R. (2011). A new bridge technique for neutron tomography and diffraction measurements. *Nuclear Instruments & Methods in Physics Research. Section A, Accelerators, Spectrometers, Detectors and Associated Equipment, 651*(1), 229–235. doi:10.1016/j.nima.2011.01.096

Caffyn, A. (2009, Sept.). The Slow Route to New Markets. *Tourism Insights.*

Caggianese, G., Gallo, L., & Neroni, P. (2018). Evaluation of spatial interaction techniques for virtual heritage applications: A case study of an interactive holographic projection. *Future Generation Computer Systems, 81*, 516–527. doi:10.1016/j.future.2017.07.047

Caggianese, G., Neroni, P., & Gallo, L. (2014). Natural interaction and wearable augmented reality for the enjoyment of the cultural heritage in outdoor conditions. In *Augmented and virtual reality, international conference* (pp. 267–282). Springer International Publishing. doi:10.1007/978-3-319-13969-2_20

Cairns, P., & Cox, A. L. (2008). *Research Methods for Human-Computer Interaction.* Cambridge University Press. doi:10.1017/CBO9780511814570

Calabi, D. (Ed.). (2013). *Built City, Designed City, Virtual City, The Museum of the City.* Roma: CROMA.

Callaway, C., Stock, O., & Dekoven, E. (2014). Experiments with mobile drama in an instrumented museum for inducing conversation in small groups. *ACM Transactions on Interactive Intelligent Systems, 4*(1), 2. doi:10.1145/2584250

Cameron, F. (2010). Beyond the Cult of the Replicant. In F. Cameron & S. Kenderdine (Eds.), Theorizing digital cultural heritage: a critical discourse (pp. 49-76). Cambridge, MA: MIT Press.

Cameron, F., & Kenderdine, S. (Eds.). (2010). *Theorizing digital cultural heritage: a critical discourse.* Cambridge, MA: MIT Press.

Campanaro, D., Landeschi, G., Dell'Unto, N., & Leander Touti, A. (2016). 3D GIS for cultural heritage restoration: A 'white box' workflow. *Journal of Cultural Heritage, 18*, 321–332. doi:10.1016/j.culher.2015.09.006

Campana, S., Dabas, M., Marasco, L., Piro, S., & Zamuner, D. (2009). Integration of remote sensing, geophysical surveys and archaeological excavation for the study of a Medieval Mound (Tuscany, Italy). *Archaeological Prospection, 16*(3), 167–176. doi:10.1002/arp.366

Camps-Ortueta, I., Rodríguez-Muñoz, J. M., Gómez-Martín, P. P., & González-Calero, P. A. (2017). Combining augmented reality with real maps to promote social interaction in treasure hunts. In CoSECivi (pp. 131–143). Academic Press.

Canciani, M., Conigliaro, E., Grasso, M., Papalini, P., & Saccone, M. (2016). 3D Survey and augmented reality for cultural heritage. The case study of Aurelian Wall at Castra Praetoria in Rome. *XXIII ISPRS Congress- International Archives of the Photogrammetry, Remote Sensing and Spatial Information Sciences, XLI-B5*, 931-937. doi:10.5194/isprs-archives-XLI-B5-931-2016

CARARE. (n.d.). Retrieved November 24, 2016 from the website: http://www.carare.eu

Card, S. K., Mackinlay, J., & Shneiderman, B. (Eds.). (1999). *Readings in Information Visualization: Using Vision to Think*. San Francisco, CA: Morgan Kaufmann.

Carlson, S. (2006). Lost in a sea of science data. *The Chronicle of Higher Education, 52*(42), A35.

Carmigniani, J., Furht, B., Anisetti, M., Ceravolo, P., Damiani, E. E., & Ivkovic, M. (2011). Augmented reality technologies, systems and applications. *Multimedia Tools and Applications, 51*(1), 341–377. doi:10.100711042-010-0660-6

Carmo, M. B., & Cláudio, A. P. (2013). 3D virtual exhibitions. *DESIDOC Journal of Library and Information Technology, 33*(3), 222–235. doi:10.14429/djlit.33.3.4608

Carrozzino, M., Colombo, M., Tecchia, F., Evangelista, C., & Bergamasco, M. (2018). Comparing Different Storytelling Approaches for Virtual Guides in Digital Immersive Museums. In *International Conference on Augmented Reality, Virtual Reality and Computer Graphics* (pp. 292-302). Springer. 10.1007/978-3-319-95282-6_22

Carrozzino, M., Lorenzini, C., Duguleana, M., Evangelista, C., Brondi, R., Tecchia, F., & Bergamasco, M. (2016). An immersive VR experience to learn the craft of printmaking. In *International Conference on Augmented Reality, Virtual Reality and Computer Graphics* (pp. 378-389). Springer. 10.1007/978-3-319-40651-0_30

Casella, G., & Coelho, M. (2013). Augmented heritage: situating augmented reality mobile apps in cultural heritage communication. *Proceedings of the 2013 International Conference on Information Systems and Design of Communication*, 138–140. 10.1145/2503859.2503883

Cassell, J., Vilhjálmsson, H. H., & Bickmore, T. (2004). Beat: the behavior expression animation toolkit. In Life-Like Characters (pp. 163-185). Springer Berlin Heidelberg. doi:10.1007/978-3-662-08373-4_8

Cassell, J. (2001). Embodied conversational agents: Representation and intelligence in user interfaces. *AI Magazine, 22*(4), 67.

Castoriadis, C. (1991). *Philosophy, Politics, Autonomy: Essays in Political Philosophy*. New York: Oxford University Press.

Caus, T., Christmann, S., & Hagenhoff, S. (2008). Hydra – An Application Framework for the Development of Context-Aware Mobile Services. *LNBIP, 7*, 471–481.

Cavazza, M., Earnshaw, R., Magnenat-Thalmann, N., & Thalmann, D. (1998). Motion control of virtual humans. *IEEE Computer Graphics and Applications, 18*(5), 24–31. doi:10.1109/38.708558

Cena, F., Console, L., Gena, C., Goy, A., Levi, G., Modeo, S., & Torre, I. (2006). Integrating heterogeneous adaptation techniques to build a flexible and usable mobile tourist guide. *AI Communications, 19*(4), 369–384.

Centofanti, M. (2010). Della natura del modello architettonico. In S. Brusaporci (Ed.), *Sistemi informativi integrati per la tutela, la conservazione e la valorizzazione del patrimonio architettonico e urbano* (pp. 43–54). Roma: Gangemi.

Centofanti, M., & Brusaporci, S. (2012). Architectural 3D modeling in historical buildings knowledge and restoration processes. In C. Gambardella (Ed.), *Less More architecture design landscape*. Naples: La Scuola di Pitagora.

Ceraudo, G. (2013). *Aerial Photography in Archaeology*. Good Practice in Archaeological Diagnostics. doi:10.1007/978-3-319-01784-6_2

Ch'ng, E., & Gaffney, V. L. (2013). Seeing Things: Heritage Computing, Visualization and the Arts and Humanities. In E. Ch'ng, V. Gaffney, & H. Chapman (Eds.), Visual Heritage in the Digital Age (pp. 1-14). London: Springer.

Ch'ng, E., Gaffney, V., & Chapman, H. (Eds.). (2013). Visual Heritage in the Digital Age. London: Springer.

Chalvatzaras, D., Yiannoutsou, N., Sintoris, C., & Avouris, N. (2014). Do you remember that building? Exploring old Zakynthos through an augmented reality mobile game. In *Interactive Mobile Communication Technologies and Learning (IMCL), 2014 International Conference on* (pp. 222-225). IEEE. 10.1109/IMCTL.2014.7011136

Champion, E. (2015). Defining cultural agents for virtual heritage environments. *Presence (Cambridge, Mass.)*, *24*(3), 179–186. doi:10.1162/PRES_a_00234

Chandler, P., & Sweller, J. (1991). Cognitive Load Theory and the Format of Instruction. *Cognition and Instruction*, *8*(4), 293–332. doi:10.12071532690xci0804_2

Chen, F., Lasaponara, R., & Masini, N. (2015). (in press). An Overview of Satellite Synthetic Aperture Radar Remote Sensing in Archaeology: From Site Detection to Monitoring. *Journal of Cultural Heritage*.

Chen, S., Pan, Z., & Zhang, M. (2012). A virtual informal learning system for cultural heritage. In *Transactions on edutainment VII* (pp. 180–187). Springer Berlin Heidelberg. doi:10.1007/978-3-642-29050-3_16

Cheong, R. (1995). The virtual threat to travel and tourism. *Tourism Management*, *16*(6), 417–422. doi:10.1016/0261-5177(95)00049-T

Chevallier, R. (1963). Detections aeriennes dans le Sud du department de l'Aisne. In *Archéologie Aérienne, Colloque International, 31/8-3/9/1963, S.E.V.P.E.N.* (pp. 95-108). Academic Press.

Cheverst, K., Mitchell, K., & Davies, N. (2002). The role of adaptive hypermedia in a context-aware tourist GUIDE. *Communications of the ACM*, *45*(5), 47–51. doi:10.1145/506218.506244

Chiou, W.-C., Lin, C.-C., & Perng, C. (2010). A Strategic Framework for Website Evaluation Based on a Review of the Literature from 1995-2006. *Information & Management*, *47*(5-6), 282–290. doi:10.1016/j.im.2010.06.002

Choi, W., Baker, D., Blazeby, M., Furukawa, K., Hachimura, K., & Beacham, R. (2010). Character Animation of Intangible Cultural Heritage in Second Life. *Proceedings of IEEEJ Image Electronics and Visual Computing Workshop*.

Chung, N., Tyan, I., & Han, H. (2016). Enhancing the smart tourism experience through geotag. *Information Systems Frontiers*, 1–12.

Ciolfi, L., Avram, G., Maye, L., Dulake, N., Marshall, M. T., van Dijk, D., & McDermott, F. (2016). Articulating Co-Design in Museums: Reflections on Two Participatory Processes. In *Proceedings of the 19th ACM Conference on Computer-Supported Cooperative Work & Social Computing* (pp. 13-25). ACM. 10.1145/2818048.2819967

Coenen, T., Mostmans, L., & Naessens, K. (2013). MuseUs: Case study of a pervasive cultural heritage serious game. *Journal on Computing and Cultural Heritage*, *6*(2), 8. doi:10.1145/2460376.2460379

Collins, A., & Halverson, R. (2018). *Rethinking education in the age of technology* (2nd ed.). New York: Teachers College Press.

Colombo, F. (1990). *Ombre sintetiche.* Napoli: Liguori.

Colomina, I., Blázquez, M., Molina, P., Parés, M.E., & Wis, M. (2008). Towards a new paradigm for high-resolution low-cost photogrammetry and remote sensing. *IAPRS&SIS, 37*(B1), 1201-1206.

Cometa, M. (2017). Prefazione all'edizione italiana. In W. J. T. Mitchell (Ed.), *Pictorial Turn* (pp. 9–39). Milano: Raffaello Cortina Editore.

Corradini, A., Fredriksson, M., Mehta, M., Königsmann, J., Bernsen, N. O., & Johannesson, L. (2004). Towards believable behavior generation for embodied conversational agents. In *International Conference on Computational Science* (pp. 946-953). Springer Berlin Heidelberg. 10.1007/978-3-540-24688-6_121

Corrêa, A. G., Borba, E. Z., Lopes, R., Zuffo, M. K., & Araujo, A. (2017). *User Experience Evaluation with Arch a eometry Interactive Tools in Virtual Reality Environment.* Academic Press.

Correia, N., Romão, T., Ricardo, A., Mota, T., Melo, M. J., Castro, R., ... Miranda, A. (2014). Design of an interactive experience with medieval illuminations: A journey into the beauty and meaning of medieval Portuguese manuscripts. *Journal on Computing and Cultural Heritage, 7*(2), 13. doi:10.1145/2626289

Council of Europe. (2000). *European Landscape Convention.* Retrieved on September 25, 2019 from https://rm.coe.int/1680080621

Council of Europe. (2005). *Framework Convention on the Value of Cultural Heritage for Society.* Retrieved on September 25, 2019 from https://www.coe.int/en/web/conventions/full-list/-/conventions/treaty/199

Council of Europe. (2005). *Framework Convention on the Value of Cultural Heritage for Society.* Retrieved on September, 25, 2019 from http://www.coe.int/t/dg4/cultureheritage/heritage/Identities/default_en.asp

Cowan, B., & Kapralos, B. (2015). A Survey of Frameworks and Game Engines for Serious Game Development. In *IEEE 14th International Conference on Advanced Learning Technologies*, (pp. 662-664). Athens, Greece: IEEE.

Cowley, D., & Palmer, R. (Eds.). (2009). *Education in aerial remote sensing for archaeology.* EAC/AARG.

Craighead, J., Burke, J., & Murphy, R. (2008). Using the unity game engine to develop sarge: A case study. *Simulation Workshop at the International Conference on Intelligent Robots and Systems.*

Creed, C., Sivell, J., & Sear, J. (2013). Multi-touch tables for exploring heritage content in public spaces. In *Visual Heritage in the Digital Age* (pp. 67–90). Springer London. doi:10.1007/978-1-4471-5535-5_5

Crespo, G. (2010). Intelligent Decision-Support Systems for e-Tourism: Using SPETA II as a Knowledge Management Platform for DMOs and e-Tourism Service Providers. *International Journal of Decision Support System Technology, 2*(1), 36–48. doi:10.4018/jdsst.2010101603

Crist, E. P. (1985). A TM tasseled cap equivalent transformation for reflectance factor data. *Remote Sensing of Environment, 17*(3), 301–306. doi:10.1016/0034-4257(85)90102-6

Crist, E. P., & Cicone, R. C. (1984). A physically-based transformation of Thematic Mapper data the TM Tasseled Cap. *IEEE Transactions on Geoscience and Remote Sensing, GE-22*(3), 256–263. doi:10.1109/TGRS.1984.350619

Crist, E. P., & Kauth, R. J. (1986). The tasseled cap de-mystified. *Photogrammetric Engineering and Remote Sensing, 52*, 81–86.

Crouch, G. I., & Ritchie, J. R. B. (1999). Tourism, competitiveness, and social prosperity. *Journal of Business Research, 44*(3), 137–152. doi:10.1016/S0148-2963(97)00196-3

Csikszentmihalyi, M., & Robinson, R. E. (1990). *The art of seeing: An interpretation of the aesthetic encounter.* Getty Publications.

Cucchiara, R., & Del Bimbo, A. (2014). Visions for augmented cultural heritage experience. *MultiMedia, IEEE, 21*(1), 74–82. doi:10.1109/MMUL.2014.19

Cuncliffe, D., Kritou, E., & Tudhope, D. (2001). Usability evaluation for museum web sites. *Museum Management and Curatorship, 19*(3), 229–252. doi:10.1080/09647770100201903

Dabov, K., Foi, A., Katkovnik, V., & Egiazarian, K. (2007). Color image denoising via sparse 3D collaborative filtering with grouping constraint in luminance-chrominance space. In *Image Processing, 2007. ICIP 2007. IEEE International Conference on* (Vol. 1, pp. I-313). IEEE.

Damala, A., Stojanovic, N., Schuchert, T., Moragues, J., Cabrera, A., & Gilleade, K. (2012). Adaptive augmented reality for cultural heritage: Artsense project. In M. Ioannides, D. Fritsch, J. Leissner, R. Davies, F. Remondino, & R. Caffo (Eds.), *Progress in Cultural Heritage Preservation* (pp. 746–755). Berlin: Springer. doi:10.1007/978-3-642-34234-9_79

Dassie, J. (1978). *Manual d' archeologie aerienne.* Paris: Editions Technip.

Davoli, P., Mazzoni, F., & Corradini, E. (2005). Quality Assessment of Cultural Web Sites with Fuzzy Operators. *Journal of Computer Information Systems, 46*(1), 44–57.

Day, G. (2004). *Jesus of Suburbia.* Retrieved 7 November 2015, from http://www.azlyrics.com/lyrics/greenday/jesusofsuburbia.html

de Jong, T., Linn, M. C., & Zacharia, Z. (2013). *Physical and Virtual Laboratories in Science and Engineering Education.* Academic Press.

De Kerckove, D. (1991). *Brainframes. Technology, Mind and Business.* Utrecht: Bosh & Keuning.

De Luca, L., Bussayarat, C., Stefani, C., Véron, P., & Florenzano, M. (2011). A semantic-based platform for the digital analysis of architectural heritage. *Computers & Graphics, 2*(35), 227–241. doi:10.1016/j.cag.2010.11.009

De Rojas, M. del C., & del Carmen Camarero, M. (2006). Experience and satisfaction of visitors to museums and cultural exhibitions. *International Review on Public and Non Profit Marketing, 3*(1), 49.

De Vries, L. E., & May, M. (2019). Virtual laboratory simulation in the education of laboratory technicians-Motivation and study intensity. *Biochemistry and Molecular Biology Education, 47*(3), 257–262. doi:10.1002/bmb.21221 PMID:30748084

Demers, J. (2004). Depth of field: A survey of techniques. GPU Gems, 23, 375–390.

Denard, H. (2012). A New Introduction to The London Charter. In *Paradata and Transparency in Virtual Heritage* (pp. 57–72). Farnham: Ashgate Publishing.

Dequal, S., & Lingua, A. (2001). True orthophoto for architectural surveys. *XVIII International Symposium of CIPA*, 269-276.

Desai, N. (2018). Recreation of history using augmented reality. *ACCENTS Transactions on Image Processing and Computer Vision., 4*(10), 1–5. doi:10.19101/TIPCV.2017.39019

Di Franco, P. D. G., Camporesi, C., Galeazzi, F., & Kallmann, M. (2015). 3d printing and immersive visualization for improved perception of ancient artifacts. *Presence (Cambridge, Mass.), 24*(3), 243–264. doi:10.1162/PRES_a_00229

Diaconescu, C., Popovici, M.-I., & Popovici, D.-M. (2019). From Exploration of Virtual Replica to Cultural Immersion Through Natural Gestures. *First International Conference, VRTCH 2018*. 10.1007/978-3-030-05819-7_9

Díaz, M. G. A., Toftedahl, M., & Svensson, T. (2014, December). The Mystery of Elin. Incorporating a City Cultural Program on History and Heritage into a Pervasive Game. In *Proceedings of the 2014 Conference on Interactive Entertainment* (pp. 1-10). ACM.

Dickinson, J. E., & Lumsdon, L. (2010). *Slow travel and tourism*. New York: Earthscan. doi:10.4324/9781849776493

Dieck, T., & Jung, T. (2017). Value of Augmented Reality at Cultural Heritage SItes: A skakeholder approach. *Journal of Destination Marketing & Management*. doi:10.1016/j.jdmm.2017.03.002

Dimitropoulos, A., Dimitropoulos, K., Kyriakou, A., Malevitis, M., Syrris, S., Vaka, S., ... Stavrakis, M. (2018). The loom: interactive weaving through a tangible installation with digital feedback. In *Digital Cultural Heritage* (pp. 199–210). Cham: Springer. doi:10.1007/978-3-319-75826-8_17

Dix, A., Finlay, J., Aboud, G. D., & Beale, R. (2004). *Human-Computer Interaction* (4th ed.). Pearson Education.

Djaouti, D., Alvarez, J., Rampnoux, O., Charvillat, V., & Jessel, J. (2009). Serious games and cultural heritage: A case study of prehistoric caves. *15th International Conference on Virtual Systems and Multimedia*, 221–226. 10.1109/VSMM.2009.40

Djindjian, F. (2015). Computers and mathematics in archaeology, anatomy of an ineluctable success! *Concepts, Methods and Tools. Proceedings of the 42nd Annual Conference on Computer Applications and Quantitative Methods in Archaeology*, 1–6.

Docci, M. (Ed.). (2005). *Metodologie innovative integrate per il rilievo dell'architettura e dell'ambiente*. Roma: Gangemi.

Docci, M., & Maestri, D. (2009). *Manuale di rilevamento architettonico e urbano*. Rome: Laterza.

Doerr, M., & Hiebel, G. (2014). *Developing common European archaeological concepts through extending the CIDOC CRM within ARIADNE*. Retrieved June, 2015, from http://www.ariadne-infrastructure.eu/content/download/1844/10313/version/1/file/CHNT-2013_04_GHiebel-MDoerr_cidoc-crm_archaeo-extensions_20131113.pdf

Donais, M. K., Whissel, G., Dumas, A., & Golden, K. (2009). Analyzing lead content in ancient bronze coins by flame atomic absorption spectroscopy. An archaeometry laboratory with nonscience majors. *Journal of Chemical Education*, *86*(3), 343–346. doi:10.1021/ed086p343

Doneus, M. (1996). *Aerial Archive*. Retrieved October 2016, from http://www.univie.ac.at/Luftbildarchiv/

Doneus, M., & Neubauer, W. (1998). 2D Combination of Prospection Data. *Archaeological Prospection*, *5*(1), 29–56. doi:10.1002/(SICI)1099-0763(199803)5:1<29::AID-ARP92>3.0.CO;2-T

Dore, C., & Murphy, M. (2015). Historic Building Information Modelling (HBIM). In S. Brusaporci (Ed.), *Handbook of Research on Emerging Digital Tools for Architectural Surveying, Modeling, and Representation* (Vols. 1–2). Hershey, PA: IGI Global. doi:10.4018/978-1-4666-8379-2.ch007

Doucleff, M. (2012). Anatomy of a Tear-Jerker Why does Adele's "Someone Like You" Make Everyone Cry? Science has Found the Formula. *The Wall Steet Journal*, *11*, 201–206.

Doulamis, A., Liarokapis, F., Petridis, P., & Mialous, G. (2012). Serious Games for Cultural Applications. *Intelligent Computer Graphics*, 97–115.

Doumanis, I. (2013). *Evaluating humanoid embodied conversational agents in mobile guide applications* (Doctoral dissertation). Middlesex University.

Dowden, R., & Sayre, S. (2009). Tear down the walls: The redesign of ArtsConnectEd. In J. Trant & D. Bearman (Eds.), *Museums and the Web 2009*. Toronto, CA: Archives & Museum Informatics. Retrieved from http://www.archimuse.com/mw2009/papers/dowden/dowden.html

Driver, T. (2004). AARGnews. *AARGnews*, *28*, 6.

Ducheneaut, N., Wen, M. H., Yee, N., & Wadley, G. (2009). Body and mind: a study of avatar personalization in three virtual worlds. *Proceedings of the SIGCHI Conference on Human Factors in Computing Systems (CHI '09)*, 1151–1160. 10.1145/1518701.1518877

Duff, A., & Maley, A. (2007). *Literature*. Oxford, UK: Oxford University Press.

Duguleana, M., Girbacia, F., Postelnicu, C., Brodi, R., & Carrozzino, M. (2016). Exploring Pisa Monuments Using Mobile Augmented Reality. *World Academy of Science, Engineering and Technology International Journal of Computer and Information Engineering, 10*(11).

Duguleana, M., Brodi, R., Girbacia, F., Postelnicu, C., Machidon, O., & Carrozzino, M. (2016). Time-Travelling with Mobile Augmented Reality: A Case Study on the Piazza dei Miracoli. In *Euro-Mediterranean Conference* (pp. 902-912). Springer International Publishing. 10.1007/978-3-319-48496-9_73

Dupuy, A. (2014). Digital extension of the museum of marseilles towards a global museum built both in the real and the digital world. In N. Proctor & R. Cherry (Eds.), Museums and the Web. Academic Press.

Dustdar, S., Nastić, S., & Šćekić, O. (2017). *Smart Cities. The Internet of Things, People and Systems*. Cham: Springer International Publishing.

Eco, U. (1986). *Travels in hyperreality*. London: Picador.

Egges, A., Papagiannakis, G., & Magnenat-Thalmann, N. (2007). Presence and interaction in mixed reality environments. *The Visual Computer*, *23*(5), 317–333. doi:10.100700371-007-0113-z

Eisenbeiß, H. (2009). *UAV photogrammetry* (Diss.). ETH No. 18515, Institute of Geodesy and Photogrammetry, ETH Zurich, Switzerland.

Eisenbess, H., & Zhang, L. (2006). Comparison of DSMS generated from mini UAV imagery and terrestrial laser scanner in a Cultural Heritage application. *ISPRS Commission V Symposium 'Image Engineering and Vision Metrology'.*

Engels, C., Stewénius, H., & Nistér, D. (2006). Bundle adjustment rules. *Photogrammetric Computer Vision, 2*, 124-131.

European Commission. (2015). *The Onlife Manifesto – Being Human in a Hyperconnected Era*. Retrieved on September 25, 2019 from https://ec.europa.eu/digital-single-market/sites/digital-agenda/files/Manifesto.pdf

EUROPEANA. (n.d.). Retrieved October 21, 2019 from the website: https://www.europeana.eu/

Everaerts, J. (2008). The Use of Unmanned Aerial Vehicles (UAVS) for Remote Sensing and Mapping. *IAPRS&SIS, 37*(B1), 1187-1192.

Fabola, A., Kennedy, S., Miller, A., Oliver, I., McCaffery, J., & Cassidy, C., … Vermehren, A. (2017). A virtual museum installation for time travel. In *International Conference on Immersive Learning* (pp. 255–270). Springer. 10.1007/978-3-319-60633-0_21

Falk, J. (2009). *Identity and the Museum Visit Experience*. Walnut Creek, CA: Left Coast Press.

Falk, J. H., & Dierking, L. D. (2018). *Learning from museums*. Rowman & Littlefield.

Falvo, P. G. (2015, September). Exhibit design with multimedia and cognitive technologies impact assessment on Luca Giordano, Raphael and the Chapel of the Magi in Palazzo Medici Riccardi, Florence. In *2015 Digital Heritage* (Vol. 2, pp. 525-532). IEEE.

Fanini, B., d'Annibale, E., Demetrescu, E., Ferdani, D., & Pagano, A. (2015). *Engaging and shared gesture-based interaction for museums the case study of K2R international expo in Rome. In 2015 Digital Heritage* (Vol. 1, pp. 263–270). IEEE.

Featherstone, R., Horne, P., Macleod, D., & Bewley, R. (1999). Aerial Reconnaissance over England in Summer 1996. *Archaeological Prospection*, *6*(2), 47–62. doi:10.1002/(SICI)1099-0763(199906)6:2<47::AID-ARP113>3.0.CO;2-Y

Feininger, A. (1954). *Successful photography*. Academic Press.

Feldman, R. (2001). Evidence. In *The Cambridge Dictionary of Philosophy* (2nd ed.; pp. 293–294). Cambridge, UK: Cambridge University Press.

Fernández-Montblanc, T., Bethencourt, M., Izquierdo, A., & González-Duarte, M. M. (2014). Establishing the relationship between underwater cultural heritage deterioration and marine environmental factors. A comparative analysis of the Bucentaure and Fougueux sites. In M. A. Rogerio-Candelera (Ed.), *Science, Technology and Cultural Heritage* (pp. 53–58). Sevilla, Spain: CRC Press, Taylor & Francis Group.

Fernie, K., Griffiths, J., Stevenson, M., Clough, P. D., Goodale, P., Agirre, E., & Bergheim, S. R. (2012). PATHS: Personalizing access to cultural heritage spaces. *Proceedings of 18th Int Conference on Virtual Systems and Multimedia (VSMM 2012)*, 469-474. 10.1109/VSMM.2012.6365960

Ferraris, M. (2012). *Manifesto del nuovo realismo*. Roma, Bari: Laterza. doi:10.26530/OAPEN_617573

Filippini Fantoni, S., & Bowen, J. P. (2007). Bookmarking in museums: Extending the museum experience beyond the visit? In J. Trant & D. Bearman (Eds.), *Museums and the Web 2007*. Toronto: Archives & Museum Informatics. Retrieved from http://www.archimuse.com/mw2007/papers/filippini-fantoni/filippini-fantoni.html

Filippini-Fantoni, S. (2003). Personalization through IT in museums. *ICHIM 03: International Cultural Heritage Informatics Meeting*.

Fink, J., & Kobsa, A. (2002). User Modeling for Personalized City Tours. *Artificial Intelligence Review*, *18*(1), 33–74. doi:10.1023/A:1016383418977

Fischler, A., & Bolles, R. (1981). Random Sample Consensus: A Paradigm for Model Fitting with Applications to Image Analysis and Automated Cartography. Comm. ACM, 24(6), 381–395. doi:10.1145/358669.358692

Floch, J., & Jiang, S. (2015). *One place, many stories digital storytelling for cultural heritage discovery in the landscape. In 2015 Digital Heritage* (Vol. 2, pp. 503–510). IEEE.

Fogliaroni, P. (2012). Mixed Reality for Archeology and Cultural Heritage. *2nd Workshop on Computing Techniques for Spatio-Temporal Data in Archaeology and Cultural Heritage*. doi:10.4230/LIPIcs.COARCH.2018

Foni, A. E., Papagiannakis, G., Cadi-Yazli, N., & Magnenat-Thalmann, N. (2007). Time-Dependent Illumination and Animation of Virtual Hagia-Sophia. *International Journal of Architectural Computing*, *5*(2), 283–301. doi:10.1260/1478-0771.5.2.284

Forte, M. (2000). About Virtual Archaeology: Disorders, Cognitive Interactions and Virtuality. In Virtual Reality in Archaeology (pp. 247-263). Oxford, UK: BAR International Series S843 (Archaeopress).

Forte, M. (2008). Introduzione. In M. Forte (Ed.), La Villa di Livia. Un percorso di realtà virtuale (pp.1-36). Roma: "L'Erma" di Bretschneider.

Forte, M., Lercari, N., Onsurez, L., Issavi, J., & Prather, E. (2012). The Fort Ross virtual warehouse project: a serious game for research and education. In *Virtual Systems and Multimedia (VSMM), 2012 18th International Conference on* (pp. 315-322). IEEE. 10.1109/VSMM.2012.6365940

Forte, M. (2011). Cyber-Archaeology : Notes on the simulation of the past. *Virtual Archaeology Review*, *2*(4), 7–18. doi:10.4995/var.2011.4543

Forte, M., & Siliotti, A. (Eds.). (1996). *Virtual Archaeology. Re-creating Ancient Words.* New York: Harry N. Abrams.

Foster, N., & Fedkiw, R. (2001). Practical animation of liquids. In *Proceedings of ACM SIGGRAPH* (pp. 23-30). New York: ACM Press.

Fowler, F. J. M., & Darling, P. (1998). Archaeological applications of imaging radar. *AARGnews*, *17*, 19–24.

Franklin, C. (1977). The aliasing problem in computer-generated shaded images. *Communications of the ACM*, *20*(11), 799–805. doi:10.1145/359863.359869

Freese, J. (2007). Replication standards for quantitative social science. *Sociological Methods & Research*, *36*(2), 153–172. doi:10.1177/0049124107306659

Frischer, B. (2008). From digital illustration to digital heuristic. In B. D. Frischer (Ed.), *Beyond illustration: 2d and 3d Digital Technologies As Tool for Discovery in Archaeology.* Oxford, UK: British Archaeological Reports.

Fritsch, J., Breinbjerg, M., & Jensen, T. S. (2014). Designing interactive listening situations. In *Proceedings of the 26th Australian Computer-Human Interaction Conference on Designing Futures: the Future of Design* (pp. 31-40). ACM.

Fritz, F., Susperregui, A., & Linaza, M. T. (2005). Enhancing cultural tourism experiences with augmented reality technologies. *6th International Symposium on Virtual Reality, Archaeology and Cultural Heritage (VAST).*

Froschauer, J., Seidel, I., Gärtner, M., Berger, H., & Merkl, D. (2010). Design and evaluation of a serious game for immersive cultural training. In *Virtual Systems and Multimedia (VSMM), 2010 16th International Conference on* (pp. 253-260). IEEE. 10.1109/VSMM.2010.5665978

Froschauer, J., Merkl, D., Arends, M., & Goldfarb, D. (2013). Art history concepts at play with ThIATRO. *Journal on Computing and Cultural Heritage*, *6*(2), 7. doi:10.1145/2460376.2460378

Funge, J., Tu, X., & Terzopoulos, D. (1999). Cognitive modeling: knowledge, reasoning and planning for intelligent characters. In *Proceedings of the 26th annual conference on Computer graphics and interactive techniques* (pp. 29-38). ACM Press/Addison-Wesley Publishing Co. 10.1145/311535.311538

Furukawa, Y., & Hernández, C. (2015). Multi-View Stereo: A Tutorial. *Foundations and Trends in Computer Graphics and Vision*, *9*(1), 1–148. doi:10.1561/0600000052

Gaiani, M. (2006). Un viaggio attraverso gli strumenti e i metodi di produzione del progetto di disegno industriale nell'epoca della progettazione digitale totale. In M. Gaiani (Ed.), *La rappresentazione riconfigurata* (pp. 23–57). Milano: Poli.Design.

Gaiani, M. (2012). Towards a critical rethinking of the theory of surveying following the advent of digital media. In L. Carlevaris & M. Filippa (Eds.), *In Praise of Theory. The fundamentals of the disciplines of representation and survey* (pp. 375–381). Roma: Gangemi.

Gaiani, M., Benedetti, B., & Apollonio, F. I. (2011). Teorie per rappresentare e comunicare i siti archeologici attraverso modelli critici. *SCIRES-IT*, *1*(2), 33–70.

Gaiani, M., Martini, B., & Apollonio, F. I. (2017). A Framework for a Smart Cultural City. In M. Ceccarelli, M. Cigola, & G. Recinto (Eds.), *New Activities For Cultural Heritage* (pp. 217–227). Cham: Springer International Publishing. doi:10.1007/978-3-319-67026-3_24

Gaiani, M., Remondino, F., Apollonio, F. I., & Ballabeni, A. (2016). An advanced pre-processing pipeline to improve automated photogrammetric reconstructions of architectural scenes. *Remote Sensing*, *8*(3), 178. doi:10.3390/rs8030178

Gaitanou, M., Charissi, E., Margari, I., Papamakarios, M., Vosinakis, S., Koutsabasis, P., ... Stavrakis, M. (2018). Design of an Interactive Experience Journey in a Renovated Industrial Heritage Site. In *Euro-Mediterranean Conference*, (pp. 150-161). Springer. 10.1007/978-3-030-01762-0_13

Gaitatzes, A., Christopoulos, D., & Roussou, M. (2001). Reviving the past: cultural heritage meets virtual reality. In *Proceedings of the 2001 conference on Virtual reality, archeology, and cultural heritage* (pp. 103-110). ACM. 10.1145/584993.585011

Gao, Q., Wan, T., Tang, W., & Chen, L. (2017). A stable and accurate marker-less augmented reality registration method. *2017 International Conference on Cyberworlds (CW)*, 41-47. 10.1109/CW.2017.44

Garagnani, S. (2013). Building Information Modeling and real world knowledge: a methodological approach to accurate semantic documentation for the built environment. In Proceedings of Digital Heritage 2013 (vol. 1, pp. 489-496). Marseille: IEEE. doi:10.1109/DigitalHeritage.2013.6743788

Garagnani, S. (2015). Semantic Representation of Accurate Surveys for the Cultural Heritage: BIM Applied on the Existing Domain. In S. Brusaporci (Ed.), *Handbook of Research on Emerging Digital Tools for Architectural Surveying, Modeling, and Representation* (pp. 292–310). Hershey, PA: IGI Global. doi:10.4018/978-1-4666-8379-2.ch009

Garcia Cerspo, A., Chamizo, J., Rivera, I., Mncke, M., Colomo Palaciosm, R., & Gomez Berbis, J. M. (2009). SPETA: Social pervasive e-Tourism advisor. *Telematics and Informatics*, *26*(3), 306–315. doi:10.1016/j.tele.2008.11.008

Gardner, G. (1985). Visual simulation of clouds. *SIGGRAPH '85 Proceedings of the 12th annual conference on Computer graphics and interactive technique, 19*(3), 297–384.

Garzotto, F., Salmon Cinotti, T., Raffa, G., Roffia, L., Muzii, R., Varlese, V., . . . Galasso, S. (2004). Evaluating Context-Aware Mobile Applications In Museums: Experiences from the MUSE Project. Proceedings Museums and the Web 2004.

Garzotto, F., Cinotti, T., & Pigozzi, M. (2003). Designing multi-channel web frameworks for cultural tourism applications: the MUSE case study. *Proceedings of the International Conference for Culture and Heritage Online 2003 on Museums and the Web.*

Georgiadi, N., Kokkoli-Papadopoulou, E., Kordatos, G., Partheniadis, K., Sparakis, M., Koutsabasis, P., ... Stavrakis, M. (2016). A pervasive role-playing game for introducing elementary school students to archaeology. In *Proceedings of the 18th International Conference on Human-Computer Interaction with Mobile Devices and Services Adjunct* (pp. 1016-1020). ACM. 10.1145/2957265.2963117

Georgiou, Y., & Kyza, E. A. (2017). The development and validation of the ARI questionnaire: An instrument for measuring immersion in location-based augmented reality settings. *International Journal of Human-Computer Studies*, *98*, 24–37. doi:10.1016/j.ijhcs.2016.09.014

Georgoula, O., Kaimaris, D., Karadedos, G., & Patias, P. (2003, April). *Photogrammetry and Archaeology: A case study in the archaeological site of Philippoi in N.Greece.* Paper presented at the conference of the Computer Applications and quantitative methods in Archaeology, Vienna, Austria.

Gerber, S., Pink, G., Fry, M., Kay, J., Kummerfeld, R., & Wasinger, R. (2010) PersonisJ: mobile, client-side user modelling. *User Modeling, Adaptation and Personalization.*

Getchell, K., Miller, A., Nicoll, J. R., Sweetman, R. J., & Allison, C. (2010). Games methodologies and immersive environments for virtual fieldwork. *IEEE Transactions on Learning Technologies*, *3*(4), 281–293. doi:10.1109/TLT.2010.25

Ghiani, G., Paterno, F., Santoro, C., & Spano, L. D. (2009). UbiCicero: A location-aware, multi-device museum guide. *Interacting with Computers*, *21*(4), 288–303. doi:10.1016/j.intcom.2009.06.001

Ghouaiel, N., Garbaya, S., Cieutat, J. M., & Jessel, J. P. (2016). Mobile Augmented Reality in Museums: Towards Enhancing Visitor's Learning Experience. *The International Journal of Virtual Reality*, *17*(1), 21–31.

Giaccardi, E. (2012). Introduction: reframing Heritage in a participatory culture. In E. Giaccardi (Ed.), *Heritage and Social Media: Understanding Heritage in a Participatory Culture* (pp. 1–10). Abingdon, UK: Routledge. doi:10.4324/9780203112984

Gillies, M., & Spanlang, B. (2010). Comparing and evaluating real time character engines for virtual environments. *Presence (Cambridge, Mass.)*, *19*(2), 95–117. doi:10.1162/pres.19.2.95

Gkiti, C., Varia, E., Zikoudi, C., Kirmanidou, A., Kyriakati, I., Vosinakis, S., ... Koutsabasis, P. (2018). i-Wall: A Low-Cost Interactive Wall for Enhancing Visitor Experience and Promoting Industrial Heritage in Museums. In *Euro-Mediterranean Conference* (pp. 90–100). Springer. 10.1007/978-3-030-01762-0_8

Glas, N., & Pelachaud, C. (2015). User engagement and preferences in information-giving chat with virtual agents. In *Workshop on Engagement in Social Intelligent Virtual Agents (ESIVA)* (pp. 33-40). Academic Press.

Glascock, M. D., Speakman, R. J., & Neff, H. (2007). Archaeometry at the University of Missouri Research Reactor and the provenance of obsidian artifacts in North America. *Archaeometry*, *49*(2), 343–357. doi:10.1111/j.1475-4754.2007.00305.x

Gnoth, J., & Matteucci, X. (2014). A phenomenological view of the behavioural tourism research literature. *International Journal of Culture, Tourism and Hospitality Research*, *8*(1), 3–21. doi:10.1108/IJCTHR-01-2014-0005

Gold, M. K. (Ed.). (2012). *Debates in the Digital Humanities.* University of Minnesota Press.

Gomes, L., & Bogosyan, S. (2009). Current Trends in Remote Laboratories. *IEEE Transactions on Industrial Electronics*, *56*(12), 4744–4756. doi:10.1109/TIE.2009.2033293

Gonzalez, M. (2013). *Top 5 Augmented Reality Apps!* Retrieved 27 November 2016, from https://www.youtube.com/watch?v=NqUSfjTSLyo

Goren-Bar, D., Graziola, I., Pianesi, F., Rocchi, C., Stock, O., & Zancanaro, M. (2005). I like it – Affective Control of Information Flow in a Personalized Mobile Museum Guide. *Proceedings of the CHI Workshop on Innovative Approaches to Evaluating Affective Interfaces.*

Graf, H., Keil, J., Pagano, A., & Pescarin, S. (2015). *A contextualized educational museum experience connecting objects, places and themes through mobile virtual museums. In 2015 Digital Heritage* (Vol. 1, pp. 337–340). IEEE.

Gratch, J., Rickel, J., André, E., Cassell, J., Petajan, E., & Badler, N. (2002). Creating interactive virtual humans: Some assembly required. *IEEE Intelligent Systems*, *17*(4), 54–63. doi:10.1109/MIS.2002.1024753

Gravier, C., Fayolle, J., Bayard, B., Ates, M., & Lardon, J. (2008). State of the Art About Remote Laboratories Paradigms – Foundations of Ongoing Mutations. *International Journal of Online Engineering*, *4*(1), 19–25. Retrieved from http://www.online-journals.org/index.php/i-joe/article/view/480

Greengrass, M., & Hughes, L. (Eds.). (2008). *The Virtual Representation of the Past.* Farnham: Ashgate.

Gretzel, U., Fesenmaier, D. R., Lee, Y. J., & Tussyadiah, I. (2010). Narrating travel experiences: the role of new media. *Tourist experience: Contemporary perspectives*, 171.

Gretzel, U., Sigala, M., Xiang, Z., & Koo, C. (2015). Smart tourism: Foundations and developments. *Electronic Markets, 25*(3), 179–188. doi:10.100712525-015-0196-8

Griffin, E. A., & McClish, G. A. (2011). *A first look at communication theory*. Boston: McGraw-Hill.

Griffiths, J. R., Goodale, P., Minelli, S., de Pollo, A., Agerri, R., Soroa, A., . . . Usher, T. (2013). *D5.1 Evaluation of the 1st PATHS Prototype*. Retrieved from http://www.paths-project.eu/eng/Resources/D5.1-Evaluation-of-the-1st-PATHS-Prototype

Guerra, F., & Pilot, L. (2000). Historic Photoplanes. In IAPRS, Vol. XXXIII, Part B5 (pp. 611-618). Academic Press.

Guidi, G., Beraldin, J., & Atzeni, C. (2004). High-Accuracy 3-D Modeling of Cultural Heritage: The Digitizing of Donatello's "Maddalena". *IEEE Transactions on Image Processing, 13*(3), 370–380. doi:10.1109/TIP.2003.822592 PMID:15376928

Guidi, G., Gonizzi, S., & Micoli, L. L. (2014). Image pre-processing for optimizing automated photogrammetry performances. *ISPRS Annals of the Photogrammetry. Remote Sensing and Spatial Information Sciences, 2*(5), 145.

Guy, S. J., Lin, M. C., & Manocha, D. (2010). Modeling collision avoidance behavior for virtual humans. In *Proceedings of the 9th International Conference on Autonomous Agents and Multiagent Systems* (vol. 2, pp. 575-582). International Foundation for Autonomous Agents and Multiagent Systems.

Hai, H., Lo, W. H., Ng, H. H., Brailsford, T., & O'Malley, C. (2018). Enhancing reflective learning experiences in museums through interactive installations. *Rethinking Learning in the Digital Age: Making the Learning Sciences Count, 2*(2), 776–783.

Halbwachs, M. (1992). *On collective memory*. University of Chicago Press.

Hammady, R., Ma, M., & Powell, A. (2018). User Experience of Markerless Augmented Reality Applications in Cultural Heritage Museums: 'MuseumEye'as a Case Study. In *International Conference on Augmented Reality, Virtual Reality and Computer Graphics* (pp. 349–369). Springer. 10.1007/978-3-319-95282-6_26

Han, D. I., Jung, T., & Gibson, A. (2013). Dublin AR: implementing augmented reality in tourism. In Information and communication technologies in tourism 2014 (pp. 511-523). Springer International Publishing. doi:10.1007/978-3-319-03973-2_37

Han, K., Shih, P. C., Rosson, M. B., & Carroll, J. M. (2014). Enhancing community awareness of and participation in local heritage with a mobile application. In *Proceedings of the 17th ACM conference on Computer supported cooperative work & social computing* (pp. 1144-1155). ACM. 10.1145/2531602.2531640

Handayani, B. (2017). *Going to the dark sites with intention: Construction of niche tourism*. Academic Press.

Handayani, B., & George, B. (2017a). An Analysis of Online User Reviews of the Death sites. In *Gazing at Death: Dark Tourism as an Emergent Horizon of Research*. Nova Science Publishers.

Handayani, B., & Korstanje, M. E. (2016a). Isle of the Dead: A Study of Trunyan Cemetery. Bali: Academic Press.

Handayani, B., & Korstanje, M. E. (2016b). *Place Brand Authenticity in Social Media Interaction: A Postmodern Perspective*. Academic Press.

Handayani, B., & George, B. (2017b). Dark Tourism as Quasi-Suicide: A Case Study of The Sea of Trees. In *Gazing at Death: Dark Tourism as an Emergent Horizon of Research, 2017*. Nova Science Publishers.

Handayani, B., Ivanov, S., & Korstanje, M. E. (2017). Smart tourism for dark sites: The sacred site of the dead, Trunyan cemetery. In *Gazing at Death: Dark Tourism as an Emergent Horizon of Research, 2017*. Nova Science Publishers.

Handwerk, B. (2006). *Google Earth, Satellite Maps Boost Armchair Archaeology*, Available at: http://news.nationalgeographic.com/news/2006/11/061107-archaeology.html

Hanson, W. S. (2014). Aerial reconnaissance for archaeology. The West of Scotland, Glasgow Museums.

Harding, D. W. (1994). Charles Francis Christopher Hawkes 1905-1992. *Proceedings of the British Academy*, *84*, 323–344.

Harris, E. (1997). *Principles of Archaeological Stratigraphy. Third print.* London: Academic Press.

Harrison, L. (2003). *Introduction to 3D Game Engine Design Using DirectX 9 and C.* Berkeley, CA: Apress. doi:10.1007/978-1-4302-0821-1

Harris, R. (1986). *Selling Hitler: The Extraordinary Story of the Con Job of the Century* (1st ed.). New York: Pantheon.

Hart, S. G., & Staveland, L. E. (1988). Development of NASA-TLX (Task Load Index): Results of empirical and theoretical research. *Advances in Psychology*, *52*, 139–183. doi:10.1016/S0166-4115(08)62386-9

Hassenzahl, M., Burmester, M. Koller, F. (2006) AttrakDiff: Ein Fragebogen zur Messung wahrgenommener hedonischer und pragmatischer Qualität. *Mensch & Computer 2003*, 187-196.

Hatala, M., & Wakkary, R. (2005). Ontology-Based User Modeling in an Augmented Audio Reality System for Museums. *User Modeling and User-Adapted Interaction*, *15*(3-4), 339–380. doi:10.100711257-005-2304-5

Hatch, J. A. (2002). *Doing qualitative research in education settings*. Suny Press.

Haydar, M., Roussel, D., Otmane, S., & Mallem, M. (2011). Virtual and augmented reality for cultural computing and heritage: a case study of virtual exploration of underwater archaeological sites. *Virtual Reality*, *15*(4), 311–327. doi:. hal00636621 doi:10.100710055-010-0176-4

He, H., Jin, J., Xiong, Y., Chen, B., Sun, W., & Zhao, L. (2008, December). Language feature mining for music emotion classification via supervised learning from lyrics. In *International Symposium on Intelligence Computation and Applications* (pp. 426-435). Springer Berlin Heidelberg. 10.1007/978-3-540-92137-0_47

Hein, A., & Kilikoglou, V. (2012). ceraDAT-Prototype of a web-based relational database for archaeological ceramics. *Archaeometry*, *54*(2), 30–243. doi:10.1111/j.1475-4754.2011.00618.x

Hendrix, J. C. (2010). *Checking Out the Future: Perspectives from the Library* Community *on Information Technology and 21st Century Libraries*. ALA Office for Information Technology Policy Brief, No. 2. Available at: www.ala.org/ala/aboutala/offices/oitp/publications/policybriefs/ala_checking_out_the.pdf

Hewett, T. T., Baecker, R., Card, S., Carey, T., Gasen, J., Mantei, M., . . . Verplank, W. (1996). *ACM SIGCHI Curricula for Human-Computer Interaction*. Retrieved from http://old.sigchi.org/cdg/cdg2.html#2_1

Hidden Creative. (2010). *The Future of Augmented Reality*. Retrieved 27 November 2016, from https://www.youtube.com/watch?v=tnRJaHZH9lo&spfreload=10

Higgett, N., Chen, Y., & Tatham, E. (2015). A User Experience Evaluation of the use of Augmented and Virtual Reality in Visualising and Interpreting Roman Leicester 210AD (Ratae Corieltavorum). *Athens Journal of History*, *2*(1), 7–22. doi:10.30958/ajhis.2-1-1

Hinsinger, D., & Neyret, F. (2002). Interactive animation of ocean waves. *Proceedings of ACM SIGGRAPH/Eurographics symposium on computer animation*, 161-166.

Hirschmuller, H. (2011). Semi Global Matching – Motivation, Developments and Applications. Photogrammetric Week, 173-184.

Ho, W. C., & Dautenhahn, K. (2008). Towards a Narrative Mind: The Creation of Coherent Life Stories for Believable Virtual Agents. Lecture Notes in Computer Science, 5208, 59-72.

Hoffler, T. N., & Leutner, D. (2007). Instructional animation versus static pictures: A Meta-analysis. *Learning and Instruction*, *17*(6), 722–738. doi:10.1016/j.learninstruc.2007.09.013

Hofstein, A., & Lunetta, V. N. (2004). The Laboratory in Science Education: Foundations for the Twenty-First Century. *Science Education*, *88*(1), 28–54. doi:10.1002ce.10106

Hofstein, A., & Mamlok-Naaman, R. (2007). The laboratory in Science education: The state of the art. *Chemistry Education Research and Practice*, *2*(8), 105–107. doi:10.1039/B7RP90003A

Hong, G., Luo, M. R., & Rhodes, P. A. (2001). *A study of digital camera colorimetric characterisation based on polynomial modelling*. Academic Press.

Honoré, C. (2009). *In praise of slow: How a worldwide movement is challenging the cult of speed.* Vintage Canada.

Horne, J. H. (2003). A Tasseled Cap Transform for IKONOS Images. *ASPRS Annual Conference Proceedings.*

Hsi, S. (2002). The Electronic Guidebook: A study of user experiences using mobile web content in a museum setting. *Proceedings of the IEEE International Workshop on Wireless and Mobile Technologies in Education.* 10.1109/WMTE.2002.1039220

Hsu, Y. S., & Thomas, R. A. (2002). The impacts of a web-aided instructional simulation on science learning. *International Journal of Science Education*, *24*(9), 955–979. doi:10.1080/09500690110095258

Huang, C. H., & Huang, Y. T. (2013). An annales school-based serious game creation framework for taiwanese indigenous cultural heritage. *Journal on Computing and Cultural Heritage*, *6*(2), 9. doi:10.1145/2460376.2460380

Huang, C., Wylie, B., Yang, L., Homer, C., & Zylstra, G. (2002). Derivation of a tasselled cap transformation based on Landsat 7 at-satellite reflectance. *International Journal of Remote Sensing*, *23*(8), 1741–1748. doi:10.1080/01431160110106113

Huang, Z., Gong, G., & Liang, H. (2015). Physically-based smoke simulation for computer graphics: A survey. *Multimedia Tools and Applications*, *74*(18), 7569–7594. doi:10.100711042-014-1992-4

Hurtak, J. (1986). *Subsurface morphology and geoarchaeology revealed by spaceborne and airborne radar.* The Academy For Future Science. Retrieved October 2016, from http://www.affs.org/html/geoarcheology.html

Huvila, I. (2013). The Unbearable Complexity of Documenting Intellectual Processes: Paradata and Virtual Cultural Heritage Visualisation. *Human IT*, *12*(1), 97–110.

Hu, X., & Downie, J. S. (2010, June). Improving mood classification in music digital libraries by combining lyrics and audio. In *Proceedings of the 10th annual joint conference on Digital libraries* (pp. 159-168). ACM. 10.1145/1816123.1816146

Hu, X., Ho, E. M., & Qiao, C. (2017). Digitizing Dunhuang Cultural Heritage: A User Evaluation of Mogao Cave Panorama Digital Library. *Journal of Data and Information Science*, *2*(3), 49–67. doi:10.1515/jdis-2017-0014

Hu, Y., Chen, X., & Yang, D. (2009, August). *Lyric-based Song Emotion Detection with Affective Lexicon and Fuzzy Clustering Method.* ISMIR.

ICOMOS. (1964). *International charter for the conservation and restoration of monuments and sites.* Retrieved on September 25, 2019 from http://www.icomos.org/charters/venice_e.pdf

ICOMOS. (2008). *Charter for the Interpretation and Presentation of Cultural Heritage Sites*. Retrieved on September 25, 2019 from http://icip.icomos.org/downloads/ICOMOS_Interpretation_Charter_ENG_04_10_08.pdf

ICOMOS. (2013). *Charter for Places of Cultural Significance*. Retrieved on September, 25, 2019 from http://australia.icomos.org/publications/charters/

ICOMOS. (2013). *The Burra Charter*. Retrieved on September 25, 2019 from http://portal.iphan.gov.br/uploads/ckfinder/arquivos/The-Burra-Charter-2013-Adopted-31_10_2013.pdf

Ieronutti, L., & Chittaro, L. (2007). Employing virtual humans for education and training in X3D/VRML worlds. *Computers & Education*, *49*(1), 93–109. doi:10.1016/j.compedu.2005.06.007

Ijaz, K., Bogdanovych, A., & Trescak, T. (2016). Virtual worlds vs books and videos in history education. *Interactive Learning Environments*, 1–26.

International Organization for Standardization. (2003). *ISO 19115: Geographic information - Metadata*. Retrieved June, 2015, from ftp://podaac.jpl.nasa.gov/misc/outgoing/ed/pre_2013/GHRSST_metadata/ISO%2019115%20.pdf

Internet Safety 101. (2019). *Enough Is Enough: Pornography*. Retrieved October 15, 2019, from Internet Safety 101 website: https://enough.org/stats_porn_industry

Iones, A., Krupkin, A., Sbert, M., & Zhukov, S. (2003). Fast, Realistic Lighting for Video Games. *IEEE Computer Graphics and Applications*, *23*(3), 54–64. doi:10.1109/MCG.2003.1198263

ISO 9241. Ergonomics of Human-System Interaction. International Organization for Standardization.

Jacobs, Q. J. (2013). *Ancient Monuments Placemarks*. Available at: http://www.jqjacobs.net/archaeo/sites/

Jacobson, J., & Gillam, R. (2012). The Egyptian Oracle; Recreating Egyptian Religious Ceremony in Mixed Reality. *ACM Journal of Computing and Cultural Heritage*.

Jakubowski, K., Farrugia, N., & Stewart, L. (2016). Probing imagined tempo for music: Effects of motor engagement and musical experience. *Psychology of Music*, *44*(6), 1274–1288. doi:10.1177/0305735615625791

Jalmain, D. (1963). Cinq années de prospection aérienne sur la Basée. In *Archéologie Aérienne, Colloque International, 31/8-3/9/1963, S.E.V.P.E.N.* (pp. 125-130). Academic Press.

Jati, A. (2014). Using Adele's "Someone Like You" to Teach Verbs Tenses and Passive Forms. *PAROLE: Journal of Linguistics and Education, 3*(2), 76-83.

Jenkins, H. (2006). *Convergence Culture: Where Old and New Media Collide*. New York: NY University Press.

Jenkins, H. (2009). *Confronting the Challenges of Participatory Culture: Media Education for the 21st Century*. Cambridge, MA: MIT. doi:10.7551/mitpress/8435.001.0001

Jeong, J. H., & Lee, K. H. (2006). The physical environment in museums and its effects on visitors' satisfaction. *Building and Environment*, *41*(7), 963–969. doi:10.1016/j.buildenv.2005.04.004

Jia, P., & Nie, Y. (2009). *Remote sensing technique application in the research of ancient cities. A Case Study in Changhua Ancient City of Hainan Province*. Paper presented at the 30th Asian Conference on Remote Sensing, Beijing, China.

Jikes, N. (2013). *Lets Fly Away*. Retrieved 15 July 2015, from https://www.musixmatch.com/lyrics/JIKES-feat-Nori-Jikes-Nori/Lets-Fly-Away

Jim, X., Xiadong, F., & Wegman, J. (1999). Real-time simulation of dust behavior generated by a fast traveling vehicle. *ACM Transactions on Modeling and Computer Simulation*, *9*(2), 81–104. doi:10.1145/333296.333366

Joachim Gauck. (2019). *Altbundespräsident wirbt für "erweiterte Toleranz in Richtung rechts."* Retrieved October 15, 2019, from https://www.zeit.de/politik/deutschland/2019-06/joachim-gauck-nationalismus-toleranz

Jones, C. E. K., Theodosis, S., & Lykourentzou, I. (2019). The Enthusiast, the Interested, the Sceptic, and the Cynic: Understanding User Experience and Perceived Value in Location-Based Cultural Heritage Games Through Qualitative and Sentiment Analysis. *Journal on Computing and Cultural Heritage, 12*(1), 6. doi:10.1145/3297716

Jonghyun, K., Jae-Hyun, J., Changwon, J., & Byoungho, L. (2013). Real-time capturing and 3D visualization method based on integral imaging. *Optics Express, 21*(16), 18742–18753. doi:10.1364/OE.21.018742 PMID:23938790

Julier, S., Lanzagorta, M., Baillot, Y., Rosenblum, L., Feiner, S., Hollerer, T., & Sestito, S. (2000). Information filtering for mobile augmented reality. In *Augmented Reality, 2000.(ISAR 2000). Proceedings. IEEE and ACM International Symposium on* (pp. 3-11). IEEE. 10.1109/ISAR.2000.880917

Juslin, P. N., & Sloboda, J. A. (2001). *Music and emotion: Theory and research.* Oxford, UK: Oxford University Press.

Jylhä, A., Hsieh, Y. T., Orso, V., Andolina, S., Gamberini, L., & Jacucci, G. (2015). A Wearable Multimodal Interface for Exploring Urban Points of Interest. In *Proceedings of the 2015 ACM on International Conference on Multimodal Interaction* (pp. 175-182). ACM. 10.1145/2818346.2820763

Kabassi, K., & Martinis, A. (2017) Multi-Criteria Decision Making in the Evaluation of the Thematic Museums' Websites", Springer Proceed. *Proceedings of the 4th International Conference on "Innovative Approaches to Tourism and Leisure: Culture, Places and Narratives in a Sustainability Context".*

Kabassi, K. (2016). Evaluating websites of museums: State of the art. *Journal of Cultural Heritage.*

Kabassi, K. (2017a). Evaluating Websites of Museums: State of the Art. *Journal of Cultural Heritage, 24*, 184–196. doi:10.1016/j.culher.2016.10.016

Kabassi, K. (2017b). Evaluation of Personalised Software in Cultural Heritage: An Exploratory Study. *International Journal of Computational Methods in Heritage Science, 1*(1), 41–57. doi:10.4018/IJCMHS.2017010103

Kabassi, K. (2019). *Evaluating Museum Websites Using a Combination of Decision-Making Theories. Journal of Heritage Tourism.* Taylor & Francis Online. doi:10.1080/1743873X.2019.1574301

Kadobayashi, R., Kochi, N., Otani, H., & Furukawa, R. (2004). Comparison and evaluation of laser scanning and photogrammetry and their combined use for digital recording of Cultural Heritage. Int. Arch. of PRS&SIS, 35(5).

Kadobayashi, R., Nishimoto, K., Sumi, Y., & Mase, K. (1998). Evaluation of mediating agents that personalize museum exhibitions. *Proceedings of the Ninth International Workshop on Database and Expert Systems Applications* 10.1109/DEXA.1998.707447

Kaimaris, D. (2006). *Photogrammetric processing of digital images in the service of archaeological research: the localization of Via Egnatia from Amphipolis to Philippi* (Doctoral Thesis). Interdisciplinary Postgraduate Studies Program Protection, preservation and restoration of cultural monuments, Aristotle University of Thessaloniki, Greece.

Kaimaris, D. (2006). *Photogrammetric processing of digital images in the service of archaeological research: the localization of Via Egnatia from Amphipolis to Philippi* (Ph.D. thesis). Aristotle University of Thessaloniki, Greece.

Kaimaris, D., Geogoula, O., Karadedos, G., & Patias, P. (2009). *Aerial and Remote sensing Archaeology in eastern Macedonia, Greece.* Paper presented at the conference of the CIPA XXII Symposium, Kyoto, Japan.

Kaimaris, D., Georgoula, O., Patias, P., & Stylianidis, E. (2011). Comparative analysis on the archaeological content of imagery from Google Earth. *Journal of Cultural Heritage, 12*(3), 263–269. doi:10.1016/j.culher.2010.12.007

Kaimaris, D., Karadedos, G., Georgiadis, Ch., & Patias, P. (2018). Locating and Mapping the Traces of the Covered Ancient Theater of Amphipolis (Eastern Macedonia, Greece). *Heritage, 1*(1), 306–319. doi:10.3390/heritage1020020

Kaimaris, D., & Patias, P. (2014). A low-cost image acquisition system for the systematic observation of traces of buried archaeological structures. *GEOMATICA, 68*(4), 299–308. doi:10.5623/cig2014-404

Kaimaris, D., & Patias, P. (2015). Systematic observation of the change of marks of known buried archaeological structures: Case study in the plain of Philippi, Eastern Macedonia, Greece. *Mediterranean Archaeology and Archaeometry, 15*(20), 129–142.

Kaimaris, D., Patias, P., & Tsakiri, M. (2012). Best period for high spatial resolution satellite images for the detection of marks of buried structures. *The Egyptian Journal of Remote Sensing and Space Sciences, 15*(1), 9–18. doi:10.1016/j.ejrs.2011.12.001

Kamar, A. (2003). *Mobile tourist guide (m-ToGuide).* Deliverable 1.4, Project Final Report. IST2001-36004.

Karaman, S., Bagdanov, A. D., Landucci, L., D'Amico, G., Ferracani, A., Pezzatini, D., & Del Bimbo, A. (2016). Personalized multimedia content delivery on an interactive table by passive observation of museum visitors. *Multimedia Tools and Applications, 75*(7), 3787–3811. doi:10.100711042-014-2192-y

Karoulis, A., Sylaiou, S., & White, M. (2006). Usability Evaluation of a Virtual Museum Interface. *Informatica, 17*(3), 363–380.

Kasapakis, V., Gavalas, D., & Galatis, P. (2016). Augmented reality in cultural heritage: Field of view awareness in an archaeological site mobile guide. *Journal of Ambient Intelligence and Smart Environments, 8*(5), 501–514. doi:10.3233/AIS-160394

Kasap, Z., & Magnenat-Thalmann, N. (2008). Intelligent virtual humans with autonomy and personality: State-of-the-art. In *New Advances in Virtual Humans* (pp. 43–84). Springer Berlin Heidelberg. doi:10.1007/978-3-540-79868-2_2

Katifori, A., Karvounis, M., Kourtis, V., Kyriakidi, M., Roussou, M., Tsangaris, M., ... Pujol, L. (2014). Chess: personalized storytelling experiences in museums. In A. Mitchell, C. Fernández-Vara, & D. Thue (Eds.), *Interactive Storytelling* (pp. 232–235). Springer International Publishing.

Katsianis, M., Tsipidis, S., Kotsakis, K., & Kousoulakou, A. (2008). A 3D digital workflow for archaeological intra-site research using GIS. *Journal of Archaeological Science, 35*(3), 655–667. doi:10.1016/j.jas.2007.06.002

Katsouri, I., Tzanavari, A., Herakleous, K., & Poullis, C. (2015). Visualizing and assessing hypotheses for marine archaeology in a VR CAVE environment. *Journal on Computing and Cultural Heritage, 8*(2), 10. doi:10.1145/2665072

Kauth, R. J., & Thomas, G. S. (1976). The Tasselled Cap -- A Graphic Description of the Spectral-Temporal Development of Agricultural Crops as Seen by LANDSAT. *LARS Symposia.*

Kazakis, N. A., & Tsirliganis, N. C. (2015). Provenance of ceramics: Methods and Practices. In A. Sarris (Ed.), *Best Practices of GeoInformatic Technologies for the Mapping of Archaeolandscapes* (pp. 241–252). Oxford, UK: Archaeopress.

Kazhdan, M., Bolitho, M., & Hoppe, H. (2006). Poisson surface reconstruction. *SGP '06 Proceedings of the fourth Eurographics symposium on Geometry processing*, 61-70.

Kennedy, S., Fawcett, R., Miller, A., Dow, L., Sweetman, R., Field, A., ... Allison, C. (2013, October). Exploring canons & cathedrals with open virtual worlds: The recreation of st andrews cathedral, st andrews day, 1318. In *Digital Heritage International Congress (DigitalHeritage)*, 2013 (Vol. 2, pp. 273-280). IEEE. 10.1109/DigitalHeritage.2013.6744764

Kiourt, C., Koutsoudis, A., Arnaoutoglou, F., Petsa, G., Markantonatou, S., & Pavlidis, G. (2015a). The 'Synthesis' Virtual Museum–an open virtual exhibition creation tool. *International Workshop on Virtual Archaeology: Museums & Cultural Tourism.*

Kiourt, C., Koutsoudis, A., Arnaoutoglou, F., Petsa, G., Markantonatou, S., & Pavlidis, G. (2015b). *A dynamic web-based 3D virtual museum framework based on open data.* Granada, Spain: Digital Heritage. doi:10.1109/DigitalHeritage.2015.7419589

Kiourt, C., Koutsoudis, A., & Pavlidis, G. (2016). DynaMus: A fully dynamic 3D virtual museum framework. *Journal of Cultural Heritage*, *22*, 984–991. doi:10.1016/j.culher.2016.06.007

Kiourt, C., & Markantonatou, S. (2018). Intertwining Culture With Education Through Gamified Storytelling: The Case of "Myth Trek". *International Journal of Computational Methods in Heritage Science*, *2*(1), 8–22. doi:10.4018/IJCMHS.2018010102

Kiourt, C., Pavlidis, G., Koutsoudis, A., & Kalles, D. (2017). Realistic Simulation of Cultural Heritage. *International Journal of Computational Methods in Heritage Science*, *1*(1), 10–40. doi:10.4018/IJCMHS.2017010102

Kirakowski, J., & Corbett, M. (1993). SUMI: The software usability measurement inventory. *British Journal of Educational Technology*, *24*(3), 210–212. doi:10.1111/j.1467-8535.1993.tb00076.x

Kirshenblatt-Gimblett, B. (2004). Intangible Heritage as Metacultural Production1. *Museum International*, *56*(1–2), 52–65. doi:10.1111/j.1350-0775.2004.00458.x

Kivy, P. (1991). *Music alone: Philosophical reflections on the purely musical experience.* Cornell University Press.

Koh, A. (2015, April 19). A Letter to Humanities: DH Will Not Save You. *Hybridpedagogy.*

Kolivand, H., El Rhalibi, A., Tajdini, M., Abdulazeez, S., & Praiwattana, P. (2018). Cultural Heritage in Marker-Less Augmented Reality: A Survey. In D. Turcanu-Carutiu & R.-M. Ion (Eds.), Advanced Methods and New Materials for Cultural Heritage Preservation. Academic Press. doi:10.5772/intechopen.80975

Kollöffel, B., & de Jong, T. (2013). Conceptual understanding of electrical circuits in secondary vocational engineering education: Combining traditional instruction with inquiry learning in a virtual lab. *Journal of Engineering Education*, *102*(3), 375–393. doi:10.1002/jee.20022

Kontogianni, A., Kabassi, K., & Alepis, E. (2018a). Designing a Smart Tourism Mobile Application: User Modelling through Social Networks' User Implicit Data. *Springer Lecture Notes in Computer Science series*, 148-158.

Kontogianni, A., Kabassi, K., Virvou, M., & Alepis, A. (2018b). Smart Tourism through social network user modeling: a literature review. *9th International Conference on Information, Intelligence, Systems and Applications.* 10.1109/IISA.2018.8633633

Korstanje M (2014). Conceptual discussion of dark tourism: suffering, egoism and the depersonalization of death. *Globalization of tourism, opportunities and challenges.*

Korstanje, M. (2012). Reconsidering cultural tourism: An anthropologist's perspective. *Journal of Heritage Tourism*, *7*(2), 179–184. doi:10.1080/1743873X.2011.639883

Korstanje, M. E. (2011). Influence of history in the encounter of guests and hosts. *Anatolia*, *22*(2), 282–28. doi:10.1080/13032917.2011.597991

Korstanje, M. E. (2016). *The Rise of Thana Capitalism and Tourism.* Abingdon, UK: Routledge. doi:10.4324/9781315457482

Korstanje, M. E., & George, B. (2015). Dark Tourism: Revisiting Some Philosophical Issues. *Ereview of Tourism Research*, *12*, 127–136.

Korstanje, M. E., & Handayani, B. (2016). Gazing at Death. *Dark Tourism as an Emergent Horizon of Research.*

Kotler, P., Armstrong, G., Saunders, J., & Wong, V. (1999). *Principles of marketing* (2nd ed.). Editura Prentice Hall.

Kounavis, C. D., Kasimati, A. E., & Zamani, E. D. (2012). Enhancing the tourism experience through mobile augmented reality: Challenges and prospects. *International Journal of Engineering Business Management*, *4*, 10. doi:10.5772/51644

Koutsabasis, P. (2017). Empirical Evaluations of Interactive Systems in Cultural Heritage: A Review. *International Journal of Computational Methods in Heritage Science*, *1*(1), 100–122. doi:10.4018/IJCMHS.2017010107

Koutsabasis, P., & Vosinakis, S. (2016). Adult and Children User Experience with Leap Motion in Digital Heritage. In *The Cycladic Sculpture Application. In Euro-Mediterranean Conference* (pp. 350-361). Springer International Publishing.

Koutsabasis, P., & Vosinakis, S. (2016). Adult and Children User Experience with Leap Motion in Digital Heritage: The Cycladic Sculpture Application. In *Euro-Mediterranean Conference* (pp. 350-361). Springer International Publishing. 10.1007/978-3-319-48496-9_28

Koutsabasis, P., & Vosinakis, S. (2018). Kinesthetic Interactions in Museums: Conveying Cultural Heritage by Making Use of Ancient Tools and (re-) Constructing Artworks. *Virtual Reality (Waltham Cross)*, *22*(2), 103–118. doi:10.100710055-017-0325-0

Koutsoudis, A., Ioannakis, G., Arnaoutoglou, F., & Chamzas, C. (2015). Using noise function-based patterns to enhance photogrammetric 3D reconstruction performance of featureless surfaces. *Journal of Cultural Heritage*, *16*(5), 664–670. doi:10.1016/j.culher.2015.01.008

Koutsoudis, A., Makarona, C., & Pavlidis, G. (2012). Content-based navigation within virtual museums. *Journal of Advanced Computing Science and Technology*, *1*(2), 73–81. doi:10.14419/jacst.v1i2.135

Koutsoudis, A., & Pavlidis, G. (2011). Content-based search and retrieval within complex 3d scenes - an application to cultural heritage. *16th International Conference on Cultural Heritage and New Technologies.*

Koutsoudis, A., Stavroglou, K., Pavlidis, G., & Chamzas, C. (2012). 3dsse–a 3d scene search engine: Exploring 3d scenes using keywords. *Journal of Cultural Heritage*, *13*(2), 187–194. doi:10.1016/j.culher.2011.09.001

Koutsoudis, A., Vidmar, B., Ioannakis, G., Arnaoutoglou, F., Pavlidis, G., & Chamzas, C. (2014). Multi-image 3D reconstruction data evaluation. *Journal of Cultural Heritage*, *15*(1), 73–79. doi:10.1016/j.culher.2012.12.003

Kozinets, R. V. (2015). The Post-Human Future of Brands. *Strong Brands, Strong Relationships*, 149-158.

Krentzman, A. R. (2013). *What Is Spirituality?* Retrieved 15 July 2015, from University of Minnesota, Center for Spirituality and Healing and Charlson Meadows website: http://www.takingcharge.csh.umn.edu/enhance-your wellbeing/purpose/spirituality/what-spirituality

Kress, G. R., & Van Leeuwen, T. (1996). *Reading images: The grammar of visual design.* Psychology Press.

Kucukkaya, G. A. (2004). Photogrammetry and remote sensing in archeology. *Journal of Quantitative Spectroscopy & Radiative Transfer*, *88*(1-3), 83–88. doi:10.1016/j.jqsrt.2003.12.030

Kuflik, T., Stock, O., Zancanaro, M., Gorfinkel, A., Jbara, S., Kats, S., Sheidin, J. & Kashtan, N. (2011). A Visitor's Guide in an "Active Museum": Presentations, Communications, and Reflection. *ACM Journal of Computing and Cultural Heritage*, *3*(3) article 11.

Kuflik, T., & Poteriaykina, K. (2009). User Model on a Key. *Hypertext, 2009*, 371–372.

Kuzma, L., Hanzelyova, E., Rajtar, J., & Tlrpak, J. (1996). New results in aerial archaeology in Slovakia: Experience with reconnaissance, geophysical measurement and follow-up excavations. *Archaeological Prospection, 3*, 71-79.

Kwon, Y. M., Kim, I. J., Ahn, S. C., Ko, H., & Kim, H. G. (2001). Virtual heritage system: Modeling, database & presentation. Proceedings - 7th International Conference on Virtual Systems and Multimedia, VSMM 2001, 137–146. 10.1109/VSMM.2001.969665

Kyoungah, C., & Impyeong, L. (2011). A UAV based close-range rapid aerial monitoring system for emergency responses. *Proceedings of the International Archives of the Photogrammetry, Remote Sensing and Spatial Information Sciences.*

Kyriakou, P., & Hermon, S. (2019). Can I Touch This? Using Natural Interaction in a Museum Augmented Reality System. *Digital Applications in Archaeology and Cultural Heritage, 12*, e00088. doi:10.1016/j.daach.2018.e00088

Lake, M. W. (2014). Trends in Archaeological Simulation. *Journal of Archaeological Method and Theory, 21*(2), 258–287. doi:10.100710816-013-9188-1

Lanir, J., Kuflik, T., Zolantz, I., & Lanzet, U. (2013). Personalized video summary of a museum visit. AI* HCI@ AI* IA.

Lanir, J., Kuflik, T., Wecker, A. J., Stock, O., & Zancanaro, M. (2011). Examining proactiveness and choice in a location-aware mobile museum guide. *Interacting with Computers, 23*(5), 513–524. doi:10.1016/j.intcom.2011.05.007

Lasaponara, R., & Masini, N. (2012). Satellite Remote Sensing, A new tool for Archaeology. Springer Science & Business Media B.V. DOI doi:10.1007/978-90-481-8801-7

Lash, S. M., Urry, S. L. J., & Urry, J. (1993). *Economies of signs and space* (Vol. 26). London: Sage.

Laugwitz, B., Held, T., & Schrepp, M. (2008). Construction and evaluation of a user experience questionnaire. In *Symposium of the Austrian HCI and Usability Engineering Group* (pp. 63-76). Springer. 10.1007/978-3-540-89350-9_6

Laurier, C., Grivolla, J., & Herrera, P. (2008, December). Multimodal music mood classification using audio and lyrics. In *Machine Learning and Applications, 2008. ICMLA'08. Seventh International Conference on* (pp. 688-693). IEEE. 10.1109/ICMLA.2008.96

Lavie, T., & Tractinsky, N. (2004). Assessing dimensions of perceived visual aesthetics of web sites. *International Journal of Human-Computer Studies, 60*(3), 269–298. doi:10.1016/j.ijhcs.2003.09.002

Leachtenauer, J. C., Malila, W., Irvine, J., Colburn, L., & Salvaggio, N. (1997). General image-quality equation: GIQE. *Applied Optics, 36*(32), 8322–8328. doi:10.1364/AO.36.008322 PMID:18264373

Lee, S., Carlson, G., Jones, S., Johnson, A., Leigh, J., & Renambot, L. (2010). Designing an expressive avatar of a real person. *Lecture Notes in Computer Science, 6356*, 64–76. doi:10.1007/978-3-642-15892-6_8

Lennon, J. J., & Foley, M. (2000). *Dark tourism.* London: Cengage Learning EMEA.

Lepouras, G., & Vassilakis, C. (2004). Virtual museums for all: Employing game technology for edutainment. *Virtual Reality (Waltham Cross), 8*(2), 96–106. doi:10.100710055-004-0141-1

Lévi Strauss, C. (1962). *La pensée sauvage*. Paris: Plon.

Lévy, P. (1995). *Qu'est-ce que le virtuel?* Paris: Editions La Découverte.

Lewis, C., & Rieman, J. (1994). *Task-eentered User Interface Design: A Practical Introduction.* Boulder, CO: University of Colorado.

Lewis, M., & Jacobson, J. (2008). Game engines in scientific research. *Communications of the ACM*, *45*(1), 27–31.

Liang, H., Deng, S., Chang, J., Zhang, J. J., Chen, C., & Tong, R. (2016). Ontology-based interactive animation/game generation for Chinese shadow play preservation. In *2016 8th International Conference on Games and Virtual Worlds for Serious Applications (VS-GAMES)* (pp. 1-9). IEEE.

Liarokapis, F., & Sylaiou, S. (2010). Experiencing Personalized Heritage Exhibitions through Multimodal Mixed Reality Interfaces. In *Proceedings, of the 5th International Workshop on Ubiquitous and Collaborative Computing (iUBICOM '10), In conjunction with the 24th BCS Conference on Human Computer Interaction (HCI 2010)*. University of Abertay.

Liarokapis, F., Sylaiou, S., & Mountain, D. (2008). Personalizing Virtual and Augmented Reality for Cultural Heritage Indoor and Outdoor Experiences. *Proceedings of the 9th International Symposium on Virtual Reality, Archaeology and Cultural Heritage*, 55-62.

Lichti, D. D., Gordon, S. J., Stewart, M. P., Franke, J., & Tsakiri, M. (2002). Comparison of digital photogrammetry and laser scanning. In *Proc* (pp. 39–44). International Society for Photogrammetry and Remote Sensing.

Lim, C. K., Cani, M. P., Galvane, Q., Pettre, J., & Talib, A. Z. (2013). Simulation of past life: Controlling agent behaviors from the interactions between ethnic groups. In *Digital Heritage International Congress (DigitalHeritage)*, 2013 (Vol. 1, pp. 589-596). IEEE. 10.1109/DigitalHeritage.2013.6743800

Lim, C. K., Tan, K. L., Zaidan, A. A., & Zaidan, B. B. (2019). A proposed methodology of bringing past life in digital cultural heritage through crowd simulation: A case study in George Town, Malaysia. *Multimedia Tools and Applications*, 1–37.

Lim, M. Y., & Aylett, R. S. (2007). Feel the difference: A Guide with Attitude! In *IVA 2007, LNAI 4722* (pp. 317–330). Berlin: Springer-Verlag. doi:10.1007/978-3-540-74997-4_29

Linaza, M. T., Marimón, D., Carrasco, P., Álvarez, R., Montesa, J., Aguilar, S. R., & Diez, G. (2012). Evaluation of mobile augmented reality applications for tourism destinations. In *Information and Communication Technologies in Tourism 2012*. Wien: Springer-Verlag. doi:10.1007/978-3-7091-1142-0_23

Liritzis, I., Volonakis, P., Vosinakis, S., & Pavlidis, G. (2015). Cyber-archaeometry from cyber-archaeology: new dynamic trends in archaeometric training and research. In *Virtual Archaeology (Methods and benefits). Second International Conference held at the State Hermitage Museum* (pp. 38–40). Saint Petersburg: The State Hermitage Publishers.

Liritzis, I. (2009, Nov.). Archaeometry-Archaeometria a review. *History (London)*, 16–23.

Liritzis, I., Al-Otaibi, F. M., Volonakis, P., & Drivaliari, A. (2015). Digital technologies and trends in cultural heritage. *Mediterranean Archaeology and Archaeometry*, *15*(3), 313–332. doi:10.5281/zenodo.33832

Löcker, K., Nau, E., Neubauer, W., & Hinterleitner, A. (2009). Magnetic surveys of Early and Middle Neolithic settlements in Austria. *ArcheoSciences, revue d'archéométrie, 33*, 101-104.

Loizides, F., El Kater, A., Terlikas, C., Lanitis, A., & Michael, D. (2014). Presenting cypriot cultural heritage in virtual reality: A user evaluation. In *Euro-Mediterranean Conference* (pp. 572-579). Springer International Publishing. 10.1007/978-3-319-13695-0_57

Lorenzini, C., Carrozzino, M., Evangelista, C., Tecchia, F., Bergamasco, M., & Angeletaki, A. (2015). *A Virtual Laboratory An immersive VR experience to spread ancient libraries heritage. In 2015 Digital Heritage* (Vol. 2, pp. 639–642). IEEE.

Lowe, D. G. (2004). Distinctive Image Features from Scale-Invariant Keypoints. *International Journal of Computer Vision*, *60*(2), 91–110. doi:10.1023/B:VISI.0000029664.99615.94

Loyall, A. B., & Bates, J. (1997) Personality-rich believable agents that use language. *Proceedings of the First International Conference on Autonomous Agents*, 106–113. 10.1145/267658.267681

Luck, E., & Eisenreich, M. (1999). Geophysical Prospection of Archaeological Sites in Brandenburg, Germany. *Archaeological Prospection*, *6*(3), 125–133. doi:10.1002/(SICI)1099-0763(199909)6:3<125::AID-ARP111>3.0.CO;2-U

Luck, M., & Aylett, R. (2000). Applying artificial intelligence to virtual reality: Intelligent virtual environments. *Applied Artificial Intelligence*, *14*(1), 3–32. doi:10.1080/088395100117142

Luginbuhl, T., Delattre, L., & Gagalowicz, A. (2011). Towards the automatic generation of 3D photo-realistic avatars using 3D scanned data. Lecture Notes in Computer Science, 6930, 192–203.

Lund, A. M. (2001). Measuring usability with the USE questionnaire. *Usability Interface*, *8*(2), 3–6.

MacCannell, D. (1976). *The tourist: A new theory of the leisure class*. Berkeley, CA: University of California Press.

MacDonald, C. M., & Atwood, M. E. (2013). Changing perspectives on evaluation in HCI: past, present, and future. In CHI' 13 Extended Abstracts on Human Factors in Computing Systems (pp. 1969-1978). ACM. doi:10.1145/2468356.2468714

MacDonald, L., Hindmarch, J., Robson, S., & Terras, M. (2014). Modelling the appearance of heritage metallic surfaces. *The International Archives of the Photogrammetry, Remote Sensing and Spatial Information Sciences*, *40*(5), 371–377. doi:10.5194/isprsarchives-XL-5-371-2014

Machidon, O. M., Duguleana, M., & Carrozzino, M. (2018). Virtual humans in cultural heritage ICT applications: A review. *Journal of Cultural Heritage*, *33*, 249–260. doi:10.1016/j.culher.2018.01.007

Machidon, O.-M., Tavčar, A., Gams, M., & Duguleană, M. (2019). CulturalERICA: A conversational agent improving the exploration of European cultural heritage. *Journal of Cultural Heritage*. doi:10.1016/j.culher.2019.07.010

Mackie, J. (2016). *Microsoft HoloLens Review, mind blowing Augmented Reality?* Retrieved 15 July 2015, from https://www.youtube.com/watch?v=ihKUoZxNClA

Madsen, J. B., & Madsen, C. B. (2016). Handheld visual representation of a castle chapel ruin. *Journal on Computing and Cultural Heritage*, *9*(1), 6.

Magnenat-Thalmann, N., & Kasap, Z. (2009). Modelling socially intelligent virtual humans. *International Conference on Virtual Reality Continnum and its Applications in Industry VRCAI.*

Magnenat-Thalmann, N., Kim, H. S., Egges, A., & Garchery, S. (2005) Believability and Interaction in Virtual Worlds. In *Proceedings of the 11th Intl. Multimedia Modelling Conference (MMM'05)*. IEEE Computer Society. 10.1109/MMMC.2005.24

Magnenat-Thalmann, N., & Papagiannakis, G. (2010). Recreating Daily life in Pompeii. *Virtual Archaeology Review*, *1*(2), 19–23. doi:10.4995/var.2010.4679

Magnenat-Thalmann, N., Seo, H., & Cordier, F. (2004). Automatic modeling of virtual humans and body clothing. *Journal of Computer Science and Technology*, *19*(5), 575–584. doi:10.1007/BF02945583

Maiezza, P. (2019). As-Built Reliability in Architectural HBIM Modeling. *The International Archives of the Photogrammetry, Remote Sensing and Spatial Information Sciences*, *42*(W9), 461–466. doi:10.5194/isprs-archives-XLII-2-W9-461-2019

Maina, J. K. O., & Suleman, H. (2015, December). Enhancing Digital Heritage Archives Using Gamified Annotations. In *International Conference on Asian Digital Libraries* (pp. 169-179). Springer International Publishing. 10.1007/978-3-319-27974-9_17

Ma, J., & Nickerson, J. V. (2006). Hands-on, simulated, and remote laboratories: A comparative literature review. *ACM Computing Surveys*, *38*(3), 7, es. doi:10.1145/1132960.1132961

Makransky, G., Thisgaard, M. W., & Gadegaard, H. (2016). Virtual simulations as preparation for lab exercises: Assessing learning of key laboratory skills in microbiology and improvement of essential non-cognitive skills. *PLoS One*, *11*(6), 1–11. doi:10.1371/journal.pone.0155895 PMID:27253395

Malegiannaki, I., & Daradoumis, T. (2017). Analyzing the educational design, use and effect of spatial games for cultural heritage: A literature review. *Computers & Education*, *108*, 1–10. doi:10.1016/j.compedu.2017.01.007

Mallick, S. P., Zickler, T. E., Kriegman, D. J., & Belhumeur, P. N. (2005, June). Beyond lambert: Reconstructing specular surfaces using color. In *Computer Vision and Pattern Recognition, 2005. CVPR 2005. IEEE Computer Society Conference on* (Vol. 2, pp. 619-626). IEEE.

Manhita, A., Dias, C., Martins, S., Costa, J., Teixeira, D., Costa, M., & Rocha, L. (2016). A new look into the archaeological materials from the Museum of Évora, Portugal–the case study of the Zambujeiro Dolmen. In *XIII CONFERENCIA INTERNACIONAL Antropologia* (pp. 212–228). Instituto Cubano de Antropologia.

Mann, T. (1992). *Confessions of Felix Krull, confidence man: The early years*. Vintage.

Manovich, L. (2001). *The Language of New Media*. Cambridge, MA: The MIT Press.

Marco, J. (2011). A history of NASA remote sensing contributions to archaeology. *Journal of Archaeological Science*, *38*(9), 2003–2009. doi:10.1016/j.jas.2010.09.017

Margetis, G., Papagiannakis, G., & Stephanidis, C. (2019). Realistic natural interaction with virtual statues in x-reality environments. *The International Archives of the Photogrammetry, Remote Sensing and Spatial Information Sciences*, *42*(W11), 801–808. doi:10.5194/isprs-archives-XLII-2-W11-801-2019

Marimon, D., Sarasua, C., Carrasco, P., Álvarez, R., Montesa, J., Adamek, T., & Gascó, P. (2010). *MobiAR: tourist experiences through mobile augmented reality*. Barcelona, Spain: Telefonica Research and Development.

Marshall, M. T., Petrelli, D., Dulake, N., Not, E., Marchesoni, M., Trenti, E., & Pisetti, A. (2016). Audio-based narratives for the trenches of World War I: Intertwining stories, places and interaction for an evocative experience. *International Journal of Human-Computer Studies*, *85*, 27–39. doi:10.1016/j.ijhcs.2015.08.001

Marshmello. (2016). *Alone*. Retrieved 27 November 2016, from http://www.azlyrics.com/lyrics/marshmello/alone.html

Martin, J., & Fowler, F. (2013). Declassified Intelligence Satellite Photographs. In W. S. Hanson & I. A. Oltean (Eds.), Archaeology from Historical Aerial and Satellite Archives (pp. 47–66). Springer.

Martínez, B., Casas-Yrurzum, S., Vidal-González, M., Vera, L., & García-Pereira, I. (2018). TinajAR: An Edutainment Augmented Reality Mirror for the Dissemination and Reinterpretation of Cultural Heritage. *Multimodal Technologies and Interaction.*, *2*(33). doi:10.3390/mti2020033

Martin, K., & Mauriello, D. (2013). Motion and embodiment: 3D simulations for historic fashion. In *Digital Heritage International Congress (DigitalHeritage)*, 2013 (Vol. 2, pp. 329-332). IEEE. 10.1109/DigitalHeritage.2013.6744773

Marton, F., Rodriguez, M. B., Bettio, F., Agus, M., Villanueva, A. J., & Gobbetti, E. (2014). IsoCam: Interactive visual exploration of massive cultural heritage models on large projection setups. *Journal on Computing and Cultural Heritage*, *7*(2), 12. doi:10.1145/2611519

Marty, P. F. (2011). My lost museum: User expectations and motivations for creating personal digital collections on museum websites. *Library & Information Science Research*, *33*(3), 211–219. doi:10.1016/j.lisr.2010.11.003

Matsui, Y., Gidding, A., Levy, Th. E., Kuester, F., & DeFanti, T. A. (2012). ArchaeoSTOR Map: Publishing Archaeological Geodata on the Web. *COM.Geo '12 Proceedings of the 3rd International Conference on Computing for Geospatial Research and Applications*. 10.1145/2345316.2345355

Maye, L. A., McDermott, F. E., Ciolfi, L., & Avram, G. (2014). Interactive exhibitions design: what can we learn from cultural heritage professionals? In *Proceedings of the 8th Nordic Conference on Human-Computer Interaction: Fun, Fast, Foundational* (pp. 598-607). ACM. 10.1145/2639189.2639259

McCaffery, J., Miller, A., Vermehren, A., & Fabola, A. (2015). *The Virtual Museums of Caen: A case study on modes of representation of digital historical content. In 2015 Digital Heritage* (Vol. 2, pp. 541–548). IEEE.

McCamy, C. S., Marcus, H., & Davidson, J. G. (1976). A color-rendition chart. *Journal of Applied Photographic Engineering*, *2*(3), 95–99.

McCrae, R. R., & John, O. P. (1992). An introduction to the five-factor model and its applications. *Journal of Personality*, *60*(2), 175–215. doi:10.1111/j.1467-6494.1992.tb00970.x PMID:1635039

McGookin, D., Tahiroğlu, K., Vaittinen, T., Kytö, M., Monastero, B., & Vasquez, J. C. (2019). Investigating tangential access for location-based digital cultural heritage applications. *International Journal of Human-Computer Studies*, *122*, 196–210. doi:10.1016/j.ijhcs.2018.09.009

Menninger, K. A. (1938). *Man against himself.* New York: Harcourt, Brace.

Merriam, A. P., & Merriam, V. (1964). *The anthropology of music*. Evanston, IL: Northwestern University Press.

Meyers, O. C. (2007). *A mood-based music classification and exploration system* (Doctoral dissertation). Massachusetts Institute of Technology.

Micle, D., Torok-Oance, M., & Maruia, L. (2009). The morpho-topographic and cartographic analysis of the archaeological site Cornes, ti "Iarcuri", Timis, County, Romania, using computer sciences methods (GIS and Remote Sensing techniques). *Anale. Computer Science*, *7*, 249–262.

Mihalcea, R., & Strapparava, C. (2012, July). Lyrics, music, and emotions. In *Proceedings of the 2012 Joint Conference on Empirical Methods in Natural Language Processing and Computational Natural Language Learning* (pp. 590-599). Association for Computational Linguistics.

Milgram, P., & Kishino, F. (1994). A taxonomy of mixed reality visual displays. *IEICE Transactions on Information and Systems*, *E77-D*, 12, 1321–1329.

Miřijovský, J., Martínek, J., & Brus, J. (2011). Reconstruction of historical paths with using of small format aerial photography. *Proceedings of XXIIIrd International CIPA Symposium CTU.*

Mirti, P., Casoli, A., & Calzetti, L. (1996). Technology of production of fine pottery excavated on a western Greek site investigated by scanning electron microscopy coupled with energy-dispersive X-ray detection. *X-Ray Spectrometry*, *25*(3), 103–109. doi:10.1002/(SICI)1097-4539(199605)25:3<103::AID-XRS151>3.0.CO;2-V

Mitchell, W. J. (1996). *City of Bits*. Cambridge, MA: MIT Press.

Miyashita, T., Meier, P., Tachikawa, T., Orlic, S., Eble, T., Scholz, V., ... Lieberknecht, S. (2008). An augmented reality museum guide. *Proceedings of the 7th IEEE/ACM International Symposium on Mixed and Augmented Reality*, 103–106.

Moher, D., Cook, D. J., Eastwood, S., Olkin, I., Rennie, D., & Stroup, D. F. (1999). Improving the quality of reports of meta-analyses of randomised controlled trials: The QUOROM statement. *Lancet*, *354*(9193), 1896–1900. doi:10.1016/S0140-6736(99)04149-5 PMID:10584742

Mommsen, H. (2001). Provenance determination of pottery by trace element analysis: Problems, solutions and applications. *Journal of Radioanalytical and Nuclear Chemistry, 247*(3), 657–662. doi:10.1023/A:1010675720262

Mommsen, H. (2004). Short note: Provenancing of pottery-The need for an integrated approach? *Archaeometry, 46*(2), 267–271. doi:10.1111/j.1475-4754.2004.00156.x

Monaco, J. (2000). *How to read a film: the world of movies, media, and multimedia: language, history, theory.* Oxford University Press.

Moriarty, S. (2005). Visual semiotics theory. Handbook of visual communication: Theory, methods, and media, 8, 227-241.

Mori, M. (1970). The Uncanny Valley. *Energy, 7*(4), 33–35.

Moropoulou, A., Bakolas, A., & Bisbikou, K. (1995). Thermal analysis as a method of characterizing ancient ceramic technologies. *Thermochimica Acta, 269-270,* 743–753. doi:10.1016/0040-6031(95)02570-7

Mortara, M., Catalano, C. E., Bellotti, F., Fiucci, G., Houry-Panchetti, M., & Petridis, P. (2014). Learning cultural heritage by serious games. *Journal of Cultural Heritage, 15*(3), 318–325. doi:10.1016/j.culher.2013.04.004

Moscatelli, M., & Vallone, R. (2013). GIS as Tool for Cultural Heritage Management. Susteinable Tourism as driving force for cultural heritage sites development

Müllensiefen, D., & Baker, D. J. (2015, October). Music, Brands, & Advertising: Testing What Works. In Audio Branding Yearbook 2014/2015 (pp. 31-52). Nomos Verlagsgesellschaft mbH & Co. KG.

Müllensiefen, D., Davies, C., & Dossman, L. (2013, May). Implicit and Explicit Effects of Music on Brand Perception in TV Ads. In Audio Branding Academy Yearbook 2012/2013 (pp. 139-155). Nomos Verlagsgesellschaft mbH & Co. KG. doi:10.5771/9783845243559-139

Munnelly, G., Hampson, C., Lawless, S., & Conlan O. (2013). The CULTURA Portal - Exploring Cultural Treasures. *TPDL Workshops*, 155-158.

Muntean, R., Antle, A. N., Matkin, B., Hennessy, K., Rowley, S., & Wilson, J. (2017). Designing cultural values into interaction. In *Proceedings of the 2017 CHI Conference on Human Factors in Computing Systems* (pp. 6062–6074). ACM. 10.1145/3025453.3025908

Murphey, T. (1992). *Music and Songs.* Oxford, UK: Oxford University Press.

Murphy, M., McGovern, E., & Pavia, S. (2011). Historic building information modelling - adding intelligence to laser and image based surveys. *The International Archives of the Photogrammetry, Remote Sensing and Spatial Information Sciences, 38*(W16).

Murray, J. (1997). *Hamlet on the Holodeck. The Future of Narrative in Cyberspace.* Cambridge, MA: The MIT Press.

Murray, J. H. (1997). *Hamlet on the Holodeck.* Cambridge, MA: The MIT Press.

Murray, J. H. (2012). *Inventing the Medium. Principles of Interaction Design as a Cultural Practice.* Cambridge, MA: The MIT Press.

Musílek, L. (2015). Archaeometry – an example of interdisciplinarity in engineering education. *Proceedings of 43rd SEFI Annual Conference 2015.*

Myers, A. (2010). Field work in the age of digital reproduction: A review of the potentials and limitations of Google Earth for archaeologists. *The SAA Archaeological Record, 4,* 7–11.

Myers, A., & Camp, D. (2010). Google Earth and the ethics of remote sensing in archaeology. *World Archaeology*, *42*(3), 455–467. doi:10.1080/00438243.2010.498640

Nareyek, A. (2004). AI in computer games. *Queue*, *1*(10), 58. doi:10.1145/971564.971593

Nelson, A. G., & Cohn, S. (2015). Data Collection Methods for Evaluating Museum Programs and Exhibitions. *Journal of Museum Education*, *40*(1), 27–36. doi:10.1080/10598650.2015.11510830

Neto, J. N., Silva, R., Neto, J. P., Pereira, J. M., & Fernandes, J. (2011). Solis' Curse-A Cultural Heritage game using voice interaction with a Virtual Agent. In *Games and Virtual Worlds for Serious Applications (VS-GAMES), 2011 Third International Conference on* (pp. 164-167). IEEE.

Neuhofer, B., Buhalis, D., & Ladkin, A. (2015). Smart technologies for personalized experiences: A case study in the hospitality domain. *Electronic Markets*, *25*(3), 243–254. doi:10.100712525-015-0182-1

Neumüller, M., Reichinger, A., Rist, F., & Kern, C. (2014). *3D printing for cultural heritage: Preservation, accessibility, research and education. In 3D Research Challenges in Cultural Heritage* (pp. 119–134). Springer Berlin Heidelberg. doi:10.1007/978-3-662-44630-0_9

Ngulube, P. (2015). Qualitative data analysis and interpretation: systematic search for meaning. In Addressing Research Challenges: Making Headway for Developing Researchers. Mosala-MASEDI Publishers & Booksellers.

Nguyen, D. Q., Fedkiw, R., & Jensen, H. W. (2002). Physically based modeling and animation of fire. *Transactions on Graphics*, *21*(3), 721–728. doi:10.1145/566654.566643

Nicholson, S. (2012). Strategies for meaningful gamification: Concepts behind transformative play and participatory museums. *Meaningful Play 2012*, (1999), 1–16.

Nicholson, S. (2012). Strategies for meaningful gamification: Concepts behind transformative play and participatory museums. Presented at Meaningful Play 2012, Lansing, MI.

Nicholson, S. (2011). Making gameplay matter: Designing modern educational tabletop games. *Knowledge Quest*, *40*(1), 60–65.

Nicholson, S. (2011). Making the Gameplay Matter: Designing Modern Educational Tabletop Games. *Knowledge Quest*, *40*(1), 60–65.

Nicolucci, F. (2012). Setting Standards for 3D Visualization of Cultural Heritage. In *Paradata and Transparency in Virtual Heritage* (pp. 23–36). Farnham: Ashgate Publishing.

Nielsen, J. (1994). *Usability Engineering*. Elsevier.

Nikolov, I., & Madsen, C. (2016, October). Benchmarking Close-range Structure from Motion 3D Reconstruction Software Under Varying Capturing Conditions. In *Euro-Mediterranean Conference* (pp. 15-26). Springer International Publishing. 10.1007/978-3-319-48496-9_2

Nofal, E., Elhanafi, A. M., Hameeuw, H., & Vande Moere, A. (2018). Architectural Contextualization of Heritage Museum Artifacts Using Augmented Reality. *Studies in Digital Heritage*, *2*(1), 42–67. doi:10.14434dh.v2i1.24500

Nofal, E., Reffat, R., Boschloos, V., Hameeuw, H., & Moere, A. (2018). The Role of Tangible Interaction to Communicate Tacit Knowledge of Built Heritage. *Heritage*, *1*(2), 414–436. doi:10.3390/heritage1020028

Noh, Z., Sunar, M. S., & Pan, Z. (2009). A review on augmented reality for virtual heritage system. In *International conference on technologies for E-learning and digital entertainment* (pp. 50-61). Springer. 10.1007/978-3-642-03364-3_7

Not, E., Cavada, D., Maule, S., Pisetti, A., & Venturini, A. (2019). Digital augmentation of historical objects through tangible interaction. *Journal on Computing and Cultural Heritage*, *12*(3), 18. doi:10.1145/3297764

Not, E., & Petrelli, D. (2018). Blending customisation, context-awareness and adaptivity for personalised tangible interaction in cultural heritage. *International Journal of Human-Computer Studies*, *114*, 3–19. doi:10.1016/j.ijhcs.2018.01.001

Novick, D., Rodriguez, L., Pacheco, A., Rodriguez, A., Hinojos, L., Cartwright, B., ... Ponce, E. (2017). The Boston Massacre history experience. In *Proceedings of the 19th ACM International Conference on Multimodal Interaction* (pp. 499-500). ACM.

O'Keefe, B., & Benyon, D. (2015). Using the blended spaces framework to design heritage stories with schoolchildren. *International Journal of Child-Computer Interaction*, *6*, 7–16. doi:10.1016/j.ijcci.2016.02.001

O'Sullivan, L., Picinali, L., Feakes, C., & Cawthorne, D. (2014). Audio tactile maps (atm) system for the exploration of digital heritage buildings by visually-impaired individuals-first prototype and preliminary evaluation. Forum Acusticum, Krakow, Poland.

Ohdake, T., & Chikatsu, H. (2005). 3d modelling of high relief sculpture using image-based integrated measurement system. *The International Archives of the Photogrammetry, Remote Sensing and Spatial Information Sciences*, *36*(5), W17.

Oh, H., Assaf, A. G., & Baloglu, S. (2014). Motivations and goals of slow tourism. *Journal of Travel Research*, *55*(2), 205–219. doi:10.1177/0047287514546228

Okura, F., Akaguma, T., Sato, T., & Yokoya, N. (2014). Indirect augmented reality considering real-world illumination change. *Proceedings of the 2014 IEEE International Symposium on Mixed and Augmented Reality*. Retrieved September 10–12, 2014 10.1109/ISMAR.2014.6948453

Olsen, L., & Chiddo, C. (2008). *Directory Interchange Format (DIF) Standard*. Retrieved June, 2015, from https://earthdata.nasa.gov/files/ESDS-RFC-012v1.pdf

Ontiveros, M. A. C., Macias, J. M., Berni, P., & Reynolds, P. (2014). lrcw.net: A web site with a virtual laboratory for the study of coarse and cooking wares in the late antique Mediterranean (http://www.lrcw.net/). In N. Poulou-Papadimitriou, E. Nodarou, & V. Kilikoglou (Eds.), *LRCW 4 Late Roman Coarse Wares, Cooking Wares and Amphorae in the Mediterranean: Archaeology and archaeometry. The Mediterranean: a market without frontiers* (Vol. 1, pp. 617–622). Publishers of British Archaeological Reports.

Oreni, D., Brumana, R., Della Torre, S., Banfi, F., Barazzetti, L., & Previtali, M. (2014). Survey turned into HBIM: The restoration and the work involved concerning the Basilica di Collemaggio after the earthquake (L'Aquila). *ISPRS Annals of the Photogrammetry. Remote Sensing and Spatial Information Sciences*, 2(5), 267–273.

Ortony, A. (2003). On making believable emotional agents believable. In R. P. Trapple, P. (Ed.), Emotions in humans and artefacts. Cambridge, MA: MIT Press.

Ortony, A., Clore, G. L., & Collins, A. (1990). *The cognitive structure of emotions*. Cambridge University Press.

Otegi, A., Agiree, E., & Clough, P. (2014). Personalized PageRank for Making Recommendations in Digital Cultural Heritage Collections. *Proceeding JCDL '14 Proceedings of the 14th ACM/IEEE-CS Joint Conference on Digital Libraries*, 49-52.

Padeletti, G., & Fermo, P. (2010). A scientific approach to the attribution problem of renaissance ceramic productions based on chemical and mineralogical markers. *Applied Physics. A, Materials Science & Processing*, *100*(3), 771–784. doi:10.100700339-010-5689-x

Pagano, A., Pietroni, E., & Cerato, I. (2017). User experience evaluation of immersive virtual contexts: the case of the virtual museum of the Tiber Valley project. *International Conference on Education and New Learning Technologies*, 3–5. 10.21125/edulearn.2017.1735

Paliokas, I., & Sylaiou, S. (2016). The Use of Serious Games in Museum Visits and Exhibitions: A Systematic Mapping Study. In *Games and Virtual Worlds for Serious Applications (VS-Games), 2016 8th International Conference on* (pp. 1-8). IEEE. 10.1109/VS-GAMES.2016.7590371

Palmer, R. (2005). Google Maps. *AARGnews*, *31*, 38–39.

Panayiotou, S., & Lanitis, A. (2016). Paintings Alive: A Virtual Reality-Based Approach for Enhancing the User Experience of Art Gallery Visitors. In *Euro-Mediterranean Conference* (pp. 240-247). Springer International Publishing. 10.1007/978-3-319-48974-2_27

Pang, W. C., Wong, C. Y., & Seet, G. (2018). Exploring the use of robots for museum settings and for learning heritage languages and cultures at the chinese heritage centre. *Presence (Cambridge, Mass.)*, *26*(4), 420–435. doi:10.1162/PRES_a_00306

Panou, C., Ragia, L., Dimelli, D., & Mania, K. (2018). An Architecture for Mobile Outdoors Augmented Reality for Cultural Heritage. *ISPRS International Journal of Geo-Information*, *7*(12), 463. doi:10.3390/ijgi7120463

Panzoli, D. (2010). A level of interaction framework for exploratory learning with characters in virtual environments. *Intelligent Computer Graphics*, *2010*, 123–143.

Papadimitriou, N. (2012). Multiple Intepretations, Technological Applications and Public Interaction in Archaeological Museums in Europe. In M. Vaudetti, V. Minucciani, & S. Canepa (Eds.), *The Archaeological Musealization* (pp. 39–50). Torino, Italy: Multidisciplinary Intervention in Archaeological Sites for the Conservation, Communication and Culture.

Papastamatiou, N., Alexandridis, T., Tsergoulas, K., Michopoulos, A., & Karadimas, N. (2010). Virtual reality applications with user interface for dynamic content development. *CEA'10 Proceedings of the 4th WSEAS international conference on Computer engineering and applications*, 201-206.

Paradiso, A., & Landay, A. (2009). Guest editors' introduction: Cross-reality environments. *IEEE Pervasive Computing*, *8*(3), 14–15. doi:10.1109/MPRV.2009.47

Parkin, S. (2019). The rise of the deepfake and the threat to democracy. *The Guardian, 22*. Retrieved from https://www.theguardian.com/technology/ng-interactive/2019/jun/22/the-rise-of-the-deepfake-and-the-threat-to-democracy

Parry, R. (Ed.). (2010). *Museums in a Digital Age*. Abingdon, UK: Routledge.

Partarakis, N., Antona, M., & Stephanidis, C. (2016a). Adaptable, Personalizable and Multi User Museum Exhibits. Curating the Digital, Springer Series on Cultural Computing, 167-179

Partarakis, N., Antona, M., Zidianakis, E., & Stephanidis, C. (2016b). Adaptation and content personalization in the context of multi user museum exhibits. *Proceedings of the 1st Workshop on Advanced Visual Interfaces for Cultural Heritage (AVI*CH 2016)*, 1621.

Paternò, F., & Mancini, C. (1999). Designing web user interfaces adaptable to different types of use. *Proceedings of the International Conference for Culture and Heritage Online 1999 on Museums and the Web*. Retrieved from http://www.archimuse.com/mw99/papers/paterno/paterno.html

Pavlidis, G., Koutsoudis, A., Arnaoutoglou, F., Tsioukas, V., & Chamzas, C. (2007). Methods for 3D digitization of cultural heritage. *Journal of Cultural Heritage*, *8*(1), 93–98. doi:10.1016/j.culher.2006.10.007

Pavlidis, G., Makarona, C., Arnaoutoglou, F., Koutsoudis, A., & Chamzas, C. (2008). Museums In The Virtual World. *International Symposium Information and Communication Technologies in Cultural Heritage*, 16-18.

Pavlidis, G., Markantonatou, S., Donig, S., & Koumpis, A. (2018). Ten Challenges for Digital Humanities and the Way Forward. *International Journal of Computational Methods in Heritage Science*, *2*(1), 1–7. doi:10.4018/IJCMHS.2018010101

Pavlidis, G., Tsiafakis, N., Provopoulos, G., Chatzopolos, S., Arnaoutoglou, F., & Chamzas, C. (2006). Momi: A dynamic and internet-based 3d virtual museum of musical instruments. *Third International Conference of Museology*.

Paxinou, E., Karatrantou, A., Kalles, D., Panagiotakopoulos, C., & Sgourou, A. (2018a). *A 3D Virtual Reality Laboratory as a Supplementary Educational Preparation Tool for a Biology Course*. Retrieved from http://www.eurodl.org/?p=current&sp=brief&abstract=777

Paxinou, E., Zafeiropoulos, V., Sypsas, A., Kiourt, C., & Kalles, D. (2018b). Assessing the Impact of Virtualizing Physical Labs. *27th EDEN Annual Conference*, 151-158.

Paxinou, E., Panagiotakopoulos, C., Karatrantou, A., Kalles, D., & Sgourou, A. (2019). Implementation and evaluation of a 3D virtual reality biology lab vs conventional didactic practices in lab experimenting with the photonic microscope. *Biochemistry and Molecular Biology Education*. doi:10.1002/bmb.21307

Pechenizkiy, M., & Calders, T. (2007). A Framework for Guiding the Museum Tours Personalization. *Proceedings of the Workshop on Personalized Access to Cultural Heritage (PATCH'07)*, 11-28.

Pekarik, A. J., Doering, Z. D., & Karns, D. A. (1999). Exploring satisfying experiences in museums. *Curator (New York, N.Y.)*, *42*(2), 152–173. doi:10.1111/j.2151-6952.1999.tb01137.x

Pelechano, N., Allbeck, J. M., & Badler, N. I. (2008). Virtual crowds: Methods, simulation, and control. *Synthesis Lectures on Computer Graphics and Animation*, *3*(1), 1–176. doi:10.2200/S00123ED1V01Y200808CGR008

Pensyl, W. R., Jernigan, D. K., Qui, T. C. T., Fang, H. P., & Ping, L. S. (2008). Large area robust hybrid tracking with life-size avatar in mixed reality environment: for cultural and historical installation. In *Proceedings of The 7th ACM SIGGRAPH International Conference on Virtual-Reality Continuum and Its Applications in Industry* (p. 9). ACM. 10.1145/1477862.1477874

Pereda, J. (2019). A TUI To Explore Cultural Heritage Repositories on The Web. In *Proceedings of the Thirteenth International Conference on Tangible, Embedded, and Embodied Interaction* (pp. 259–267). ACM. 10.1145/3294109.3301000

Perlin, K., & Goldberg, A. (1996). Improv: A System for Scripting Interactive Actors in Virtual Worlds. *Proceedings of the 23rd Annual Conference on Computer Graphics and Interactive Techniques - SIGGRAPH '96*, (212), 205–216. 10.1145/237170.237258

Perry, R. (2003). Foreword. Digital Heritage: Agora and Agility. In E. Ch'ng, V. Gaffney, & H. Chapman (Eds.), *Visual Heritage in the Digital Age* (pp. v–vii). New York: Springer-Verlag.

Pescarin, S. (2016). Digital Heritage into Practice. *SCIRES-IT*, *6*(1), 1–4.

Petrelli, D., & Not, E. (2005). User-centred design of flexible hypermedia for a mobile guide: Reflections on the hyperaudio experience. *User Modeling and User-Adapted Interaction*, *15*(3–4), 303–338. doi:10.100711257-005-8816-1

Petrelli, D., & Not, E. (2019). Empowering cultural heritage professionals with tools for authoring and deploying personalised visitor experiences. *User Modeling and User-Adapted Interaction*, *29*(1), 64–120. doi:10.100711257-019-09224-9

Petrelli, D., Not, E., Sarini, M., Stock, O., Strapparava, C., & Zancanaro, M. (1999). HyperAudio: Location-Awareness +Adaptivity. *Proceeding of Conference on Human Factors in Computing Systems*, 21-22.

Petrelli, D., Not, E., Zancanaro, M., Strapparava, C., & Stock, O. (2001). Modelling and adapting to context. *Personal and Ubiquitous Computing*, *5*(1), 20–24. doi:10.1007007790170023

Petrescu, F. (2007). *The use of GIS technology in Cultural Heritage*. In *XXI International CIPA Symposium*, Athens, Greece.

Petrie, H., & Bevan, N. (2009). The Evaluation of Accessibility, Usability and User Experience. In C. Stephanidis (Ed.), The Universal Access Handbook, (pp. 10-20). Boca Raton, FL: CRC Press.

Petrucco, C., & Agostini, D. (2016). Teaching our cultural heritage using mobile augmented reality. *Je-LKS: Journal of e-Learning and Knowledge Society, 12*, 115-128. doi:10.20368/1971-8829/1180

Philbin-Briscoe, O., Simon, B., Mudur, S., Poullis, C., Rizvic, S., Boskovic, D., … Skarlatos, D. (2017). A serious game for understanding ancient seafaring in the Mediterranean sea. In *2017 9th International Conference on Virtual Worlds and Games for Serious Applications (VS-Games)* (pp. 1–5). IEEE.

Pieraccini, M., Guidi, G., & Atzeni, C. (2001). 3D digitizing of cultural heritage. *Journal of Cultural Heritage*, *2*(1), 63–70. doi:10.1016/S1296-2074(01)01108-6

Pierrot-Deseilligny, M., & Paparoditis, N. (2006). A multiresolution and optimization-based image matching approach: An application to surface reconstruction from SPOT5-HRS stereo imagery. *The International Archives of the Photogrammetry, Remote Sensing and Spatial Information Sciences*, *36*(1), w41.

Pietroni, E., & Antinucci, F. (2010). The Approval of the Franciscan Rule. Virtual Experience among the Characters of Giotto's Work. *Proceedings of the 11th International Symposium on Virtual Reality, Archaeology and Cultural Heritage VAST.*

Pietroni, E., & Adami, A. (2014). Interacting with virtual reconstructions in museums: The Etruscanning Project. *Journal on Computing and Cultural Heritage*, *7*(2), 9. doi:10.1145/2611375

Poel, M., Heylen, D., Nijholt, A., Meulemans, M., & Van Breemen, A. (2009). Gaze behaviour, believability, likability and the iCat. *AI & Society*, *24*(1), 61–73. doi:10.100700146-009-0198-1

Pollalis, C., Minor, E. J., Westendorf, L., Fahnbulleh, W., Virgilio, I., Kun, A. L., & Shaer, O. (2018). Evaluating learning with tangible and virtual representations of archaeological artifacts. In *Proceedings of the Twelfth International Conference on Tangible, Embedded, and Embodied Interaction* (pp. 626–637). ACM. 10.1145/3173225.3173260

Pollard, A. M., & Bray, P. (2007). A bicycle made for two? The integration of scientific techniques into archaeological interpretation. *Annual Review of Anthropology*, *36*(1), 245–259. doi:10.1146/annurev.anthro.36.081406.094354

Popovici, D. M., Bogdan, C. M., Polceanu, M., & Querrec, R. (2011). Applying of an ontology based modeling approach to cultural heritage systems. *Advances in Electrical and Computer Engineering*, *11*(3), 105–110. doi:10.4316/aece.2011.03017

Power, C., Lewis, A., Petrie, H., Green, K., Richards, J., & Eramian, M. (2017). Improving archaeologists' online archive experiences through user-centred design. *Journal on Computing and Cultural Heritage*, *10*(1), 3. doi:10.1145/2983917

Principles of Seville. (2012). Retrieved on September 25, 2019 from http://smartheritage.com/seville-principles/seville-principles

Principles of Seville. (2012). Retrieved on September, 25, 2019, from http://smartheritage.com/seville-principles/seville-principles

Proctor, N., & Tellis, C. (2003). *The State of the Art in Museum Handhelds in 2003, Museums and the Web*. Retrieved from http://www.archimuse.com/mw2003/papers/proctor/proctor.html

Puig, A., Rodríguez, I., Arcos, J. L., Rodríguez-Aguilar, J. A., Cebrián, S., Bogdanovych, A., ... Piqué, R. (2019). Lessons learned from supplementing archaeological museum exhibitions with virtual reality. *Virtual Reality (Waltham Cross)*. doi:10.100710055-019-00391-z

Pujol, L., Katifori, A., Vayanou, M., Roussou, M., Karvounis, M., Kyriakidi, M., . . . Ioannidis, Y. (2013). From personalization to adaptivity - Creating immersive visits through interactive digital storytelling at the Acropolis Museum. In J.A. Botνa & D. Charitos (Eds.), *Workshop Proceedings of the 9th International Conference on Intelligent Environments*. (pp. 541-554). Academic Press.

Pujol-Tost, L. (2019). Did We Just Travel to the Past? Building and Evaluating With Cultural Presence Different Modes of VR-Mediated Experiences in Virtual Archaeology. *Journal on Computing and Cultural Heritage*, *12*(1), 2. doi:10.1145/3230678

Purini, F. (2003). Digital divide. In L. Sacchi & M. Unali (Eds.), *Architettura e cultura digitale* (pp. 87–96). Milano: Skira.

Ramkissoon, H., & Uysal, M. (2014). Authenticity as a value co-creator of tourism experiences. *CABI*, 113-124.

Ramsay, S. (2013). Who's In and Who's Out. In M. Terras, M. Nyhan, & E. Vanhoutte (Eds.), *Defining Digital Humanities* (pp. 239–241). Farnham: Ashgate.

Ravyse, W. S., Blignaut, A. S., Leendertz, V., & Woolner, A. (2016). Success factors for serious games to enhance learning: A systematic review. *Virtual Reality (Waltham Cross)*, 1–28.

Read, J. C. (2008). Validating the Fun Toolkit: An instrument for measuring children's opinions of technology. *Cognition Technology and Work*, *10*(2), 119–128. doi:10.100710111-007-0069-9

Reeves, T. C. (1993). Evaluating technology-based learning. In G. M. Piskurich (Ed.), *The ASTD Handbook of Instructional Technology* (pp. 15.1–15.32). New York: McGraw-Hill.

Reeves, W. (1983). Particle Systems— A Technique for Modeling a Class of Fuzzy Objects. *ACM Transactions on Graphics*, *2*(2), 91–108. doi:10.1145/357318.357320

Refsland, S. T., Ojika, T., Addison, A. C., & Stone, R. (2000). Virtual Heritage : Breathing New Life into Our Ancient Past. *IEEE MultiMedia*, *7*(2), 20–21. doi:10.1109/MMUL.2000.848420

Reitmayr, G., & Drummond, T. (2006). Going out: Robust model-based tracking for outdoor augmented reality. *Proceedings of the 2006 IEEE/ACM International Symposium on Mixed and Augmented Reality*.

Reitmayr, G., & Schmalstieg, D. (2004). Collaborative augmented reality for outdoor navigation and information browsing. *Proceedings of symposium location based services and telecartography*.

Remondino, F., Barazzetti, L., Nex, F., Scaioni, M., & Sarazzi, D. (2011). UAV photogrammetry for mapping and 3D modeling: current status and future perspectives. *Proceedings of the International Archives of the Photogrammetry, Remote Sensing and Spatial Information Sciences*.

Remondino, F., El-Hakim, S., Gruen, A., & Zhang, L. (2008). Development and performance analysis of image matching for detailed surface reconstruction of heritage objects. *IEEE Signal Processing Magazine*, *25*(4), 55–65. doi:10.1109/MSP.2008.923093

Rennick-Egglestone, S., Brundell, P., Koleva, B., Benford, S., Roussou, M., & Chaffardon, C. (2016). Families and mobile devices in museums: Designing for integrated experiences. *Journal on Computing and Cultural Heritage*, *9*(2), 11. doi:10.1145/2891416

Reunanen, M., Díaz, L., & Horttana, T. (2015). A holistic user-centered approach to immersive digital cultural heritage installations: Case Vrouw Maria. *Journal on Computing and Cultural Heritage*, *7*(4), 24. doi:10.1145/2637485

Rice, P. M. (1987). *Pottery Analysis: A Sourcebook*. Chicago: The University of Chicago Press.

Richards, D. (2012). Agent-based museum and tour guides: applying the state of the art. In *Proceedings of The 8th Australasian Conference on Interactive Entertainment: Playing the System* (p. 15). ACM. 10.1145/2336727.2336742

Richards, J. A. (2013). *Remote Sensing Digital Image Analysis. An Introduction* (5th ed.). Springer Verlag Berlin Heidelberg. doi:10.1007/978-3-642-30062-2

Rickly-Boyd, J. M. (2012). Authenticity & aura: A Benjaminian approach to tourism. *Annals of Tourism Research*, *39*(1), 269–289. doi:10.1016/j.annals.2011.05.003

Rizvić, S., & Skalonjić, I. (2015). *Reconstructing cultural heritage objects from storytelling. In 2015 Digital Heritage* (Vol. 2, pp. 221–226). IEEE.

Robertson, D. P., & Cipolla, R. (2009). *Structure from motion, Practical image processing and computer vision*. John Willey and Sons Ltd.

Robinson, J. (2014). *How Music Grabs the Emotions*. Retrieved 27 November 2016, from Emotion Researcher ISRE's Sourcebook for Research on Emotion and Affect, website: http://emotionresearcher.com/how-music-grabs-the-emotions/

Roes, I., Stash, N., Wang, Y., & Aroyo, L. (2009). A Personalized Walk through the Museum: The CHIP Interactive Tour Guide. *CHI*, *2009*, 3317–3322.

Rogers, A. (1996). *Teaching Adults*. Buckingham, UK: Open University Press.

Rojas, S. L., Oppermann, L., Blum, L., & Wolpers, M. (2014, November). Natural Europe educational games suite: using structured museum-data for creating mobile educational games. In *Proceedings of the 11th Conference on Advances in Computer Entertainment Technology* (p. 6). ACM. 10.1145/2663806.2663841

Rose, G. (2016). *Visual methodologies: An introduction to researching with visual materials*. London: Sage Publication.

Roth, J. (2002). Context-aware web applications using the pinpoint. In *IADIS International Conference WWW/Internet 2002*. IADIS Press.

Rousou, M., Katifori, A., Pujol, L., Vayanou, M., & Rennick-Egglestone, S. (2013). A Life of Their Own: Museum Visitor Personas Penetrating the Design Lifecycle of a Mobile Experience. *CHI 2013 Extended Abstracts*, 547-552.

Roussou, M. (2008). The components of engagement in virtual heritage environments. *New Heritage: New media and cultural heritage*, 225-241.

Roussou, M., & Drettakis, G. (2003). Photorealism and Non-Photorealism in Virtual Heritage Representation. In A. Chalmers, D. Arnold, & F. Niccolucci (Eds.), *International Symposium on Virtual Reality, Archeology and Cultural Heritage* (p. 10). Brighton, UK: Academic Press.

Roussou, M., & Katifori, A. (2018). Flow, staging, wayfinding, personalization: Evaluating user experience with mobile museum narratives. *Multimodal Technologies and Interaction*, *2*(2), 32. doi:10.3390/mti2020032

Rubin, J., & Chisnell, D. (2008). *Handbook of Usability Testing: How to Plan, Design, and Conduct Effective Tests*. John Wiley and Sons.

Rubino, I., Barberis, C., Xhembulla, J., & Malnati, G. (2015). Integrating a location-based mobile game in the museum visit: Evaluating visitors' behaviour and learning. *Journal on Computing and Cultural Heritage*, *8*(3), 15. doi:10.1145/2724723

Rüther, H., Mtalo, G., & Mngumi, E. (2003). 3D modelling of heritage sites in Africa. A case study in the world heritage site of Kilwa Kisiwani, Tanzania. *Proceedings CIPA XIXth International Symposium*, 175–180.

Rutledge, L., Aroyo, L., & Stash, N. (2006). Determining user interests about museum collections. *Proceedings of the 15th International Conference on World Wide Web (WWW'06)*, 855–856. 10.1145/1135777.1135912

Rutten, N., Van Joolingen, W. R., & Van Der Veen, J. T. (2012). The learning effects of computer simulations in science education. *Computers & Education*, *58*(1), 136–153. doi:10.1016/j.compedu.2011.07.017

Saaty, T. L. (1980). *The analytic hierarchy process*. New York, NY: McGraw-Hill.

Sanders, D. H. (2008). *Why do Virtual Heritage?* Retrieved from https://archive.archaeology.org/online/features/virtualheritage/

Sansonetti, G., Gasparetti, F., Micarelli, A., Cena, F., & Gena, C. (2019). Enhancing cultural recommendations through social and linked open data. *User Modeling and User-Adapted Interaction*, *29*(1), 121–159. doi:10.100711257-019-09225-8

Santoši, Ž., Budak, I., Stojaković, V., Šokac, M., & Vukelić, Đ. (2019). Evaluation of synthetically generated patterns for image-based 3D reconstruction of texture-less objects. *Measurement*, 147.

Santos, M. E. C., Taketomi, T., Sandor, C., Polvi, J., Yamamoto, G., & Kato, H. (2014). A usability scale for handheld augmented reality. In *Proceedings of the 20th ACM Symposium on Virtual Reality Software and Technology* (pp. 167-176). ACM. 10.1145/2671015.2671019

Satyanarayanan, M. (2001). Interview on Mobile and Pervasive Computing. *IEEE Distributed Systems Online*, *2*(6).

Sauro, J. (2012). *10 things to know about the Single Ease Question (SEQ)*. Retrieved from Measuring U: https://measuringu.com/seq10/

Sauro, J., & Lewis, J. R. (2012). *Quantifying the User Experience: Practical Statistics for User Research*. Elsevier.

Savage, H. S., Levy, E. T., & Jones, W. I. (2012). Prospects and problems in the use of hyperspectral imagery for archaeological remote sensing: A case study from the Faynan copper mining district, Jordan. *Journal of Archaeological Science*, *39*(2), 407–420. doi:10.1016/j.jas.2011.09.028

Schafer, D. P. (2014). *The Age of Culture*. Rock's Mills Press.

Schaper, M.-M., Santos, M., Malinverni, L., Berro, J. Z., & Pares, N. (2018). Learning about the past through situatedness, embodied exploration and digital augmentation of cultural heritage sites. *International Journal of Human-Computer Studies*, *114*, 36–50. doi:10.1016/j.ijhcs.2018.01.003

Scherp, A., & Boll, S. (2004). Generic support for personalized mobile multimedia tourist applications. *ACM Multimedia 2004 - proceedings of the 12th ACM International Conference on Multimedia*, 178-179.

Schmidt, S., Bruder, G., & Steinicke, F. (2018). *Effects of Embodiment on Generic and Content-Specific Intelligent Virtual Agents as Exhibition Guides*. ICAT-EGVE.

Schnädelbach, H., Koleva, B., Flintham, M., Fraser, M., Izadi, S., Chandler, P., ... Rodden, T. (2002). The Augurscope: a mixed reality interface for outdoors. *Proceedings of the SIGCHI Conference onHuman Factors in Computing Systems*, 9-16. 10.1145/503376.503379

Schönberger, J. L., & Frahm, J. M. (n.d.). Structure-from-Motion Revisited. *The IEEE Conference on Computer Vision and Pattern Recognition (CVPR)*.

Schröttner, M., Havemann, S., Theodoridou, M., Doerr, M., & Fellner, D. W. (2012). A generic approach for generating cultural heritage metadata. *EuroMed'12 Proceedings of the 4th international conference on Progress in Cultural Heritage Preservation*. 10.1007/978-3-642-34234-9_23

Schwartz, O. (2018). You thought fake news was bad? Deep fakes are where truth goes to die. *The Guardian*. Retrieved from https://www.theguardian.com/technology/2018/nov/12/deep-fakes-fake-news-truth

Scollar, I. (1963). Physical conditions tending to produce crop sites in the Rhinelad. In *Archéologie Aérienne, Colloque International, 31/8-3/9/1963, S.E.V.P.E.N.* (pp. 39-47). Academic Press.

Scopigno, R., Callieri, M., Cignoni, P., Corsini, M., Dellepiane, M., Ponchio, F., & Ranzuglia, G. (2011). 3D models for Cultural Heritage: beyond plain visualization. IEEE Computer, 44(7), 48-55. Doi:10.1109/MC.2011.196

Seaborn, K., & Fels, D. I. (2015). Gamification in theory and action: A survey. *International Journal of Human-Computer Studies*, *74*, 14–31. doi:10.1016/j.ijhcs.2014.09.006

Sénécal, S., Cadi, N., Arévalo, M., & Magnenat-Thalmann, N. (2017). Modelling life through time: cultural heritage case studies. In *Mixed Reality and Gamification for Cultural Heritage* (pp. 395–419). Cham: Springer. doi:10.1007/978-3-319-49607-8_16

Seo, B., Kim, K., Park, J., & Park, J. (2010). A tracking framework for augmented reality tours on cultural heritage sites. *ACM SIGGRPAH Conference*, 169-174. doi:10.1145/1900179.1900215

Sequeira, L. M., & Morgado, L. (2013). Virtual Archaeology in Second Life and OpenSimulator. *Journal of Virtual Worlds Research*, *6*(1), 3–7. doi:10.4101/jvwr.v6i1.7047

Shih, J. L., Jheng, S. C., & Tseng, J. J. (2015). A simulated learning environment of history games for enhancing players' cultural awareness. *Interactive Learning Environments*, *23*(2), 191–211. doi:10.1080/10494820.2014.997249

Shin, J., Park, H., & Woo, W. (2017). Connecting the dots: Enhancing the usability of indexed multimedia data for AR cultural heritage applications through storytelling. In *Proceedings of the 15th International Workshop on Content-Based Multimedia Indexing* (p. 11). ACM. 10.1145/3095713.3095725

Shi, Y., Ying, F., Chen, X., Pan, Z., & Yu, J. (2014). Restoration of traditional Chinese shadow play-Piying art from tangible interaction. *Computer Animation and Virtual Worlds*, *25*(1), 33–43. doi:10.1002/cav.1530

Shneiderman, B., & Pleasant, C. (2009). *Designing the User Interface* (5th ed.). Pearson Education.

Siekański, P., Michoński, J., Bunsch, E., & Sitnik, R. (2018). CATCHA:Real-Time Camera Tracking Method for Augmented Reality Applications in Cultural Heritage Interiors. *ISPRS International Journal of Geo-Information*, *7*(479). doi:10.3390/ijgi7120479

Silberman, N. (2008). Chasing the Unicorn? The Quest for Essence in Digital Heritage. In Y. E. Kalay, T. Kvan, & J. Affleck (Eds.), *New Heritage* (pp. 81–91). Abington, UK: Routledge.

Silberman, N. (2016). Heritage places: Evolving conceptions and changing forms. In W. Logan, M. N. Craith, & U. Kockel (Eds.), *A Companion to Heritage Studies*. London: Wiley-Blackwell.

Silberman, N., & Purser, M. (2012). Collective memory as affirmation: People-centered cultural heritage in a digital age. In E. Giaccardi (Ed.), *Heritage and Social Media: Understanding heritage in a Participatory Culture* (pp. 13–29). Abingdon, UK: Routledge.

Silberman, N., & Purser, M. (2012). Collective memory as affirmation: People-centered cultural heritage in a digital age. In E. Giaccardi (Ed.), *Heritage and Social Media: Undestanding heritage in a Participatory Culture* (pp. 13–29). Abingdon, UK: Routledge.

Sillaurren, S., & Aguirrezabal, P. (2012). 3d publish: A web-based solution for building dynamic 3d virtual museums. *International Journal of Heritage in the Digital Era*, *1*(1_suppl), 147–152. doi:10.1260/2047-4970.1.0.147

Simeone, D., Cursi, S., Toldo, I., & Carrara, G. (2014). B(H)IM – Built Heritage Information Modelling. Extending BIM to historical and archaeological heritage representation. In E. Mine Thompson (Ed.). *Fusion, Proceedings of the 31nd International Conference on Education and research in Computer Aided Architectural Design in Europe:* Vol. 1. *eCAADe: Conferences 1* (pp. 613-622). Newcastle upon Tyne, UK: Northumbria University.

Skoll, G. R., & Korstanje, M. (2014). Urban heritage, gentrification, and tourism in Riverwest and El Abasto. *Journal of Heritage Tourism*, *9*(4), 349–359. doi:10.1080/1743873X.2014.890624

Skowronski, M., Wieland, J., Borowski, M., Fink, D., Gröschel, C., Klinkhammer, D., & Reiterer, H. (2018). Blended Museum: The Interactive Exhibition Rebuild Palmyra? In *Proceedings of the 17th International Conference on Mobile and Ubiquitous Multimedia* (pp. 529–535). ACM. 10.1145/3282894.3289746

Sloan, R. J. S., Cook, M., & Robinson, B. (2009). Considerations for believable emotional facial expression animation. In *Visualisation, 2009. VIZ'09. Second International Conference in* (pp. 61-66). IEEE. 10.1109/VIZ.2009.28

Sloboda, J. A. (1999). Music: Where cognition and emotion meet. *The Psychologist*, *12*, 450–455.

Sookhanaphibarn, K., & Thawonmas, R. (2009). A content management system for user-driven museums in second life. *International Conference on CyberWorlds*, 185–189. 10.1109/CW.2009.58

Spagnesi, G. (1984). Autonomia della Storia dell'architettura. In G. Spagnesi (Ed.), *Storia e restauro dell'architettura* (pp. 7–10). Roma: Istituto della Enciclopedia Italiana Treccani.

Spasojevic, M., & Kindberg, T. (2001). Evaluating the CoolTown User Experience. *Ubicomp'01 Workshop: Evaluation Methodologies for Ubiquitous Computing*. Retrieved from http://zing.ncsl.nist.gov/ubicomp01/papers/Exploratorium-UbicompPosition.pdf

Spring, D. (2015). Gaming history: Computer and video games as historical scholarship. *Rethinking History*, *19*(2), 207–221. doi:10.1080/13642529.2014.973714

Stanjek, H., & Fassbinder, J. (1995). Soil Aspects Affecting Archaeological Details in Aerial Photographs. *Archaeological Prospection*, *2*, 91–101.

Sterba, J. H., Mommsen, H., Steinhauser, G., & Bichler, M. (2009). The influence of different tempers on the composition of pottery. *Journal of Archaeological Science*, *36*(7), 1582–1589. doi:10.1016/j.jas.2009.03.022

Stock, O., Zancanaro, M., Busetta, P., Callaway, C., Krüger, A., Kruppa, M., ... Rocchi, C. (2007). Adaptive, intelligent presentation of information for the museum visitor in PEACH. *User Modeling and User-Adapted Interaction*, *17*(3), 257–304. doi:10.100711257-007-9029-6

Stokes, J. (2012). *How to do media and cultural studies.* Sage Publications.

Stone, R. J. (1999, Nov.). Virtual heritage. *UNESCO World Heritage Magazine*, 18-20.

Stone, P. (2006). A dark tourism spectrum: Towards a typology of death and macabre related tourist sites, attractions and exhibitions. Tourism: An Interdisciplinary. *International Journal (Toronto, Ont.)*, *54*(2), 145–160.

Stone, P., & Sharpley, R. (2008). Consuming dark tourism: A thanatological perspective. *Annals of Tourism Research*, *35*(2), 574–595. doi:10.1016/j.annals.2008.02.003

Strasser, C., Kunze, J., Abrams, S., & Cruse, P. (2014). DataUp: A tool to help researchers describe and share tabular data. *F1000 Research*, *3*, 6. doi:10.12688/f1000research.3-6.v2 PMID:25653834

Střelák, D., Škola, F., & Liarokapis, F. (2016). *Examining User Experiences in a Mobile Augmented Reality Tourist Guide*. doi:10.1145/2910674.2935835

Střelák, D., Škola, F., & Liarokapis, F. (2016). Examining User Experiences in a Mobile Augmented Reality Tourist Guide. In *Proceedings of the 9th ACM International Conference on PErvasive Technologies Related to Assistive Environments* (p. 19). ACM.

Su, D., & Fung, P. (2013, October). These words are music to my ears: Recognizing music emotion from lyrics using AdaBoost. In *Signal and Information Processing Association Annual Summit and Conference (APSIPA), 2013 Asia-Pacific* (pp. 1-4). IEEE.

Sundar, S., Go, E., Hyang-Sook, K., & Zhang, B. (2015). Communicating Art, Virtually! Psychological Effects of Technological Affordances in a Virtual Museum. *International Journal of Human-Computer Interaction*, *31*(6), 385–401. doi:10.1080/10447318.2015.1033912

Swartout, W. R., Gratch, J., Hill, R. W., Hovy, E., Marsella, S., Rickel, J., & Traum, D. (2006). Toward Virtual Humans. *AI Magazine*, *27*(2), 96–108.

Sylaiou, S., Mania, K., Liarokapis, F., White, M., Walczak, K., Wojciechowski, R., . . . Patias, P. (2015). Evaluation of a Cultural Heritage Augmented Reality Game. Cartographies of Mind, Soul and Knowledge.

Sylaiou, S., Mania, K., Paliokas, I., Pujol, L., Kilintzis, V., & Liarokapis, F. (2016). Exploring the educational impact of diverse technologies in online Virtual Museums. *International Journal of Arts and Technology.*

Sylaiou, S., Liarokapis, F., Kotsakis, K., & Patias, P. (2009). Virtual museums, a survey and some issues for consideration. *Journal of Cultural Heritage*, *4*, 520–528.

Sylaiou, S., Liarokapis, F., Kotsakis, K., & Patias, P. (2009). Virtual museums, a survey on methods and tools. *Journal of Cultural Heritage*, *10*(4), 520–528. doi:10.1016/j.culher.2009.03.003

Sylaiou, S., Mania, K., Karoulis, A., & White, M. (2010). Exploring the relationship between presence and enjoyment in a virtual museum. *International Journal of Human-Computer Studies*, *68*(5), 243–253. doi:10.1016/j.ijhcs.2009.11.002

Sypsas, A., Kiourt, C., Paxinou, E., Zafeiropoulos, V., & Kalles, D. (2019). The Educational Application Of Virtual Laboratories In Archaeometry. *International Journal of Computational Methods in Heritage Science*, *3*(1), 1–19. doi:10.4018/IJCMHS.2019010101

Tahoon, D. (2017). Simulating Egyptian Cultural Heritage by Augmented Reality Technologies. Case Study: Pyramids and Giza Plateau cultural heritage site, Egypt. *1st BUE Annual Conference & Exhibition - BUE ACE1-"Sustainable Vital Technologies in Engineering & Informatics"*.

Tamborrino, R. (Ed.). (2014). *Digital Urban History: Telling the History of the City in the Age of ICT Revolution*. Roma: Croma.

Tan, J., & Fan, X. (2011). Particle System Based Snow Simulating in Real Time. *3rd International Conference on Environmental Science and Information Application Technology ESIAT 2011*, 1244-1249. 10.1016/j.proenv.2011.09.199

Tapete, D., & Cigna, F. (2016). (in press). Trends and perspectives of space-borne SAR remote sensing for archaeological landscape and cultural heritage applications. *J. Archaeol. Sci. Rep.*

Terras, M., Nyhan, J., & Vanhoutte, E. (Eds.). (2013). *Defining Digital Humanities: A Reader*. Farnham: Ashgate.

Terrenghi, L., & Zimmerman, A. (2004). Tailored Audio Augmented Environments for Museums. *IUI '04 Proceedings of the 9th international conference on Intelligent user interfaces*, 334-336.

Thalmann, D., Maïm, B., & Maïm, J. (2014). Geometric Issues in Reconstruction of Virtual Heritage Involving Large Populations. In 3D Research Challenges in Cultural Heritage (pp. 78-92). Springer Berlin Heidelberg. doi:10.1007/978-3-662-44630-0_6

Thalmann, D. (2014). Populating 3D Cities: A True Challenge. *Proceeding of the Electrical Engineering Computer Science and Informatics*, *1*(1), 1-10.

The Cinematic Orchestra. (2007). *To build a home*. Retrieved 27 November 2016, from http://www.azlyrics.com/lyrics/cinematicorchestra/tobuildahome.html

The London Charter. (2009). Retrieved on September 25, 2019 from http://www.londoncharter.org/

The London Charter. (2009). Retrieved on September, 25, 2019, from http://www.londoncharter.org/

Third Eye Blind. (2016). *Company of Strangers*. Retrieved 27 November 2016, from http://www.azlyrics.com/lyrics/thirdeyeblind/companyofstrangers.html

Thomas, D., Kidd, F., Nikolovski, S., & Zipfel, C. (2008). The archaeological sites of Afghanistan in Google Earth. *AARGnews*, *37*, 22–30.

Tielden, F. (1957). *Interpreting Our Heritage*. Chapel Hill, NC: University of North Carolina Press.

Tite, M. S. (2008). Ceramic Production, Provenance and Use-A Review. *Archaeometry*, *50*(2), 216–231. doi:10.1111/j.1475-4754.2008.00391.x

Tolani, D., & Badler, N. I. (1996). Real-time inverse kinematics of the human arm. *Presence (Cambridge, Mass.)*, *5*(4), 393–401. doi:10.1162/pres.1996.5.4.393 PMID:11539377

Trescak, T., Bogdanovych, A., & Simoff, S. (2014). City of Uruk 3000 BC: Using genetic algorithms, dynamic planning and crowd simulation to re-enact everyday life of ancient Sumerians. *Proceedings of the Simulation of the Past to Understand Human History Conference.*

Tröndle, M., Greenwood, S., Kirchberg, V., & Tschacher, W. (2014). An integrative and comprehensive methodology for studying aesthetic experience in the field: Merging movement tracking, physiology, and psychological data. *Environment and Behavior*, *46*(1), 102–135. doi:10.1177/0013916512453839

Trundle, K. C., & Bell, R. L. (2010). The use of a computer simulation to promote conceptual change: A quasi-experimental study. *Computers & Education*, *54*(4), 1078–1088. doi:10.1016/j.compedu.2009.10.012

Tsichritzis, D., & Gibbs, S. (1991). Virtual Museums and Virtual Realities. *International Conference on Hypermedia and Interactivity in Museums*, 17–25. Retrieved from http://dblp.uni-trier.de/rec/bibtex/conf/ichim/TsichritzisG91

Tsichritzis, D., & Gibbs, S. (1991). Virtual museums and virtual realities. *International Conference on Hypermedia and Interactivity in Museums*, 17-25.

Tussyadiah, I. P. (2017). Technology and Behavioral Design in Tourism. In *Design Science in Tourism* (pp. 173–191). Springer International Publishing. doi:10.1007/978-3-319-42773-7_12

Tussyadiah, I. P., Wang, D., & Jia, C. H. (2017). Virtual Reality and Attitudes Toward Tourism Destinations. In *Information and Communication Technologies in Tourism 2017* (pp. 229–239). Cham: Springer. doi:10.1007/978-3-319-51168-9_17

Tzanelli, R. (2016). *Thanatourism and Cinematic Representations of Risk: Screening the End of Tourism* (Vol. 176). Abingdon, UK: Routledge. doi:10.4324/9781315624105

U.S. Geological Survey. (2008). Declassified intelligence satellite photographs. *U.S. Geological Survey Fact Sheet*, 2008–3054.

U.S. Geological Survey. (2016). Landsat-Earth observation satellites (ver. 1.1, August 2016). *U.S. Geological Survey Fact Sheet*, 2015–3081.

Uchiyama, H., & Marchand, E. (2012). Object detection and pose tracking for augmented reality: Recent approaches. *18th Korea-Japan Joint Workshop on Frontiers of Computer Vision (FCV).*

Ulicny, B., & Thalmann, D. (2001). Crowd simulation for interactive virtual environments and VR training systems. In *Computer Animation and Simulation 2001* (pp. 163–170). Springer Vienna. doi:10.1007/978-3-7091-6240-8_15

UNESCO. (1954). *Convention for the Protection of Cultural Property in the Event of Armed Conflict.* Retrieved on September 25, 2019 from http://portal.unesco.org/en/ev.php-URL_ID=13637&URL_DO=DO_TOPIC&URL_SECTION=201.html

UNESCO. (1972). *Convention Concerning the Protection of the World Cultural and Natural Heritage.* Retrieved on September 25, 2019 from http://whc.unesco.org/en/conventiontext/

UNESCO. (1972). *Recommendation concerning the Protection at National Level, of the Cultural and Natural Heritage.* Retrieved October 1, 2016, from http://whc.unesco.org/en/conventiontext/

UNESCO. (1976). *Recommendation concerning the Safeguard and Contemporary Role of Historic Areas.* Retrieved on September 25, 2019 from http://portal.unesco.org/en/ev.php-URL_ID=13133&URL_DO=DO_TOPIC&URL_SECTION=201.html

UNESCO. (1994). *The Nara Document on Authenticity.* Retrieved on September 25, 2019 from whc.unesco.org/document/9379

UNESCO. (1994). *The Nara Document on Authenticity.* Retrieved on September, 25, 2019, from whc.unesco.org/document/9379

UNESCO. (2003). *Charter on the Preservation of the Digital Heritage.* Retrieved on September, 25, 2019, from http://portal.unesco.org/en/ev.php-URL_ID=17721&URL_DO=DO_TOPIC&URL_SECTION=201.html

UNESCO. (2003a). *Charter on the Preservation of the Digital Heritage.* Retrieved on September 25, 2019 from http://portal.unesco.org/en/ev.php-URL_ID=17721&URL_DO=DO_TOPIC&URL_SECTION=201.html

UNESCO. (2003b). *Convention for the Safeguarding of Intangible Cultural Heritage.* Retrieved on September 25, 2019 from https://ich.unesco.org/en/convention

UNESCO. (2009). *World Heritage Cultural Landscape.* Retrieved on September 25, 2019 from http://whc.unesco.org/en/culturallandscape/

UNESCO. (2009). *World Heritage Cultural Landscape.* Retrieved on September, 25, 2019, from http://whc.unesco.org/en/culturallandscape/

UNESCO. (2011). *Recommendation on the Historic Urban Landscape.* Retrieved on September 25, 2019 from http://whc.unesco.org/en/activities/638

UNESCO. (2015). *Operational Guidelines for the Implementation of the World Heritage Convention.* Retrieved on September 25, 2019 from http://whc.unesco.org/en/guidelines/

van der Vaart, M., & Damala, A. (2015). *Through the loupe: visitor engagement with a primarily text-based handheld AR application. In 2015 Digital Heritage* (Vol. 2, pp. 565–572). IEEE.

Van Dijk, B., Lingnau, A., & Kockelkom, H. (2012). Measuring Enjoyment of an Interactive Museum Experience. ICMI' 12.

Van Dijk, B., Lingnau, A., Vissers, G., & Kockelkom, H. (2014). Individual and Collaborative Personalization in a Science Museum. In Playful User Interfaces, Gaming Media and Social Effects. Springer Science+Business Media Singapore.

Van Eck, R. (2006). Digital game-based learning: It's not just the digital natives who are restless. *EDUCAUSE, 41*(2), 16–30.

Van Hage, W. R., Stash, N., Wang, Y., & Aroyo, L. (2010). Finding Your Way through the Rijksmuseum with an Adaptive Mobile Museum Guide. In ESWC 2010: The Semantic Web: Research and Applications. Springer-Verlag Berlin Heidelberg

Van Krevelen, R., & Poelman, R. (2010). A Survey of Augmented Reality Technologies, Applications and Limitations. *International Journal of Virtual Reality, 9*(1).

Van Welbergen, H., Nijholt, A., Reidsma, D., & Zwiers, J. (2006). Presenting in virtual worlds: An architecture for a 3d anthropomorphic presenter. *IEEE Intelligent Systems, 21*(5), 47–53. doi:10.1109/MIS.2006.101

Van Zaanen, M., & Kanters, P. (2010, August). Automatic Mood Classification Using TF* IDF Based on Lyrics. In ISMIR (pp. 75-80). Academic Press.

Vaughan-Nichols, S. J. (2009). Augmented Reality: No Longer a Novelty? *Computer (Long Beach, Calif.), 42*(12), 19–22.

Vayanou, M., Katifori, A., Karvounis, M., Kourtis, V., Kyriakidi, M., Roussou, M., ... Pujol, L. (2014). Authoring personalized interactive museum stories. In A. Mitchell, C. Fernández-Vara, & D. Thue (Eds.), *Interactive Storytelling* (pp. 37–48). Springer International Publishing.

Verhoeven, G., Taelman, D., & Vermeulen, F. (2012). Computer vision based orthophoto mapping of complex archaeological sites: The ancient quarry of Pitaranha (Portugal-Spain). *Archaeometry, 54*(6), 1114–1129. doi:10.1111/j.1475-4754.2012.00667.x

Viinikkala, L., Yli-Seppälä, L., Heimo, O. I., Helle, S., Härkänen, L., Jokela, S., . . . Seppälä, K. (2016). Reforming the representation of the reformation: Mixed reality narratives in communicating tangible and intangible heritage of the protestant reformation in Finland. In *2016 22nd International Conference on Virtual System & Multimedia (VSMM)* (pp. 1-9). IEEE.

Vila, P. (2014). *Music and Youth Culture in Latin America.* Oxford, UK: Oxford University Press. doi:10.1093/acprof:oso/9780199986279.001.0001

Vines, T. H., Albert, A. Y., Andrew, R. L., Debarre, F., Bock, D. G., Franklin, M. T., ... Rennison, D. J. (2014). The availability of research data declines rapidly with article age. *Current Biology, 24*(1), 94–97. doi:10.1016/j.cub.2013.11.014 PMID:24361065

Vlahakis, V., Karigiannis, J., Tsotros, M., Gounaris, M., Almeida, L., Stricker, D., . . . Ioannidis, N. (2001). Archeoguide: first results of an augmented reality, mobile computing system in cultural heritage sites. *VAST '01 Proceedings of the 2001 conference on Virtual reality, archaeology, and cultural heritage*, 131-140.

Vlahakis, V., Karigiannis, J., Tsotros, M., Gounaris, M., Almeida, L., Stricker, D., ... & Ioannidis, N. (2001). Archeoguide: first results of an augmented reality, mobile computing system in cultural heritage sites. *Virtual Reality, Archeology, and Cultural Heritage, 9.*

Vlahakis, V., Ioannidis, M., Karigiannis, J., Tsotros, M., Gounaris, M., Stricker, D., ... Almeida, L. (2002, October). Archeoguide: An augmented reality guide for archaeolog sites. *IEEE Computer Graphics and Applications*, *22*(5), 52–60. doi:10.1109/MCG.2002.1028726

Vlahakis, V., Karigiannis, J., Tsotros, M., Gounaris, M., Almeida, L., Stricker, D., ... Ioannidis, N. (2001). Archeoguide: First results of an augmented reality, mobile computing system in cultural heritage sites. *Proceedings of the 2001 Conference on Virtual Reality, Archeology, and Cultural Heritage, VAST '01*, 131. 10.1145/584993.585015

Vorderer, P., Wirth, W., Gouveia, F. R., Biocca, F., Saari, T., Jäncke, F., ... Klimmt, C. (2004). *MEC spatial presence questionnaire (MEC-SPQ): Short documentation and instructions for application.* Report to the European community, project presence: MEC (IST-2001-37661), 3.

Vosinakis, S., & Panayiotopoulos, T. (2001). SimHuman: A platform for real-time virtual agents with planning capabilities. In *International Workshop on Intelligent Virtual Agents* (pp. 210-223). Springer Berlin Heidelberg. 10.1007/3-540-44812-8_17

Vosinakis, S., & Avradinis, N. (2016). Virtual Agora: Representation of an Ancient Greek Agora in Virtual Worlds using Biologically-Inspired Motivational Agents. *Mediterranean Archaeology and Archaeometry*, *16*(5), 29–41.

Vosinakis, S., Avradinis, N., & Koutsabasis, P. (2018). Dissemination of Intangible Cultural Heritage using a Multi-Agent Virtual World. In *Advances in Digital Cultural Heritage* (pp. 197–207). Cham: Springer. doi:10.1007/978-3-319-75789-6_14

Vosinakis, S., Koutsabasis, P., Makris, D., & Sagia, E. (2016). A Kinesthetic Approach to Digital Heritage using Leap Motion: The Cycladic Sculpture Application. *8th International Conference on Games and Virtual Worlds for Serious Applications (VS-GAMES).* 10.1109/VS-GAMES.2016.7590334

Vourvopoulos, A., Liarokapis, F., & Petridis, P. (2012). Brain-controlled serious games for cultural heritage. In *Virtual Systems and Multimedia (VSMM), 2012 18th International Conference on* (pp. 291-298). IEEE. 10.1109/VSMM.2012.6365937

Wagner, G. A. (1998). *Age Determination of Young Rocks and Artifacts – Physical and Chemical Clocks in Quarternary Geology and Archaeology.* Berlin: Springer.

Wakkary, R., & Hatala, M. (2006). ec(h)o: Situated play in a tangible and audio museum guide. *Proceedings of the 6th Conference on Designing Interactive systems*, 281–290. 10.1145/1142405.1142448

Wakkary, R., Hatala, M., Muise, K., Tanenbaum, K., & Budd, J. (2009). Kurio: a museum guide for families. *Proceedings of 3rd International Conference on Tangible and Embedded Interaction*, 215–222.

Wallis Filtering Implementation. (n.d.). Retrieved October 20, 2019 from the website: https://photogrammetric-vision.weebly.com/download-page.html

Wallis, R. (1976). An approach to the space variant restoration and enhancement of images. *Proc. of symp. on current mathematical problems in image science, naval postgraduate school,* 329-340.

Wang, L., Guo, J. W., Yang, C. L., Zhao, H. S., & Meng, X. X. (2010). O3D-based game learning environments for cultural heritage online education. In *International Conference on Technologies for E-Learning and Digital Entertainment* (pp. 417-428). Springer Berlin Heidelberg. 10.1007/978-3-642-14533-9_43

Wang, C. Y., Wu, H. K., Lee, S. W. Y., Hwang, F. K., Chang, H. Y., Wu, Y. T., ... Lo, H. (2014). A Review of Research on Technology-Assisted School Science Laboratories. *Journal of Educational Technology & Society*, *17*(2), 17, 307–320.

Wang, K., Torkhani, F., & Montanvert, A. (2012). A fast roughness-based approach to the assessment of 3D mesh visual quality. *Computers & Graphics*, *36*(7), 808–818. doi:10.1016/j.cag.2012.06.004

Wang, L., & Champion, E. (2012). *Chinese culture approached through touch*. Virtual Systems in the Information Society.

Wang, X., Khoo, E. T., Nakatsu, R., & Cheok, A. (2014). Interacting with traditional Chinese culture through natural language. *Journal on Computing and Cultural Heritage*, *7*(3), 18. doi:10.1145/2597183

Wang, Y., Stash, N., Aroyo, L., Gorgels, P., Rutledge, L., & Schreiber, G. (2008). Recommendations based on semantically enriched museum collections. *Journal of Web Semantics*, *6*(4), 283–290. doi:10.1016/j.websem.2008.09.002

Wang, Y., Stash, N., Sambeek, R., Schuurmans, Y., Aroyo, L., Schreiber, G., & Gorgels, P. (2009). Cultivating Personalized Museum Tours Online and On-Site. *Interdisciplinary Science Reviews*, *34*(2–3), 139–153. doi:10.1179/174327909X441072

Ware, C. (2000). *Information Visualization: Perception for Design*. San Francisco, CA: Morgan Kaufmann.

WebGuide. (2001). *WebGuide: A City Guide for the internet. European Media Lab*. Retrieved from http://www.eml.org/english/research/deepmap/deepgis/webguide.html

Weibelzahl, S. (2005). Problems and pitfalls in evaluating adaptive systems. In Adaptable and Adaptive Hypermedia Systems, (pp. 285–299). IRM Press.

Weller, J. M. (2004). Simulation in undergraduate medical education: Bridging the gap between theory and practice. *Medical Education*, *38*(1), 32–38. doi:10.1111/j.1365-2923.2004.01739.x PMID:14962024

Werner, P. (2018). Review of Implementation of Augmented Reality into the Georeferenced Analogue and Digital Maps and Images. *Information*, *10*(12). doi:10.3390/info10010012

Westermann, C. F. (2008). Sound Branding and Corporate Voice–Strategic Brand Management Using Sound. In *Usability of Speech Dialog Systems* (pp. 147–155). Springer Berlin Heidelberg. doi:10.1007/978-3-540-78343-5_7

Westoby, M. J., Brasington, J., Classer, N. F., Hambrey, M. J., & Reynolds, J. M. (2012). Structure-from- Motion photogrammetry: A low-cost, effective tool for geoscience applications. *Geomorphology*, *179*, 300–314. doi:10.1016/j.geomorph.2012.08.021

What, I. A. B. (2016a). *Audio Branding Academy*. Retrieved 27 November 2016, from http://audio-branding-academy.org/aba/knowledge/what-is-audio-branding/

What, I. A. B. (2016b). Retrieved 27 November 2016, from http://www.soundbranding.com/

Wikipedia. (2016). *Larissa*. Available at: https://en.wikipedia.org/wiki/Larissa

Wilhelmson, H., & Dell'Unto, N. (2015). Virtual taphonomy: A new method integrating excavation and postprocessing in an archaeological context. *American Journal of Physical Anthropology*, *157*(2), 305–321. doi:10.1002/ajpa.22715 PMID:25720527

Wilkinson, P. F. (2010). Review of "The darker side of travel: The theory and practice of dark tourism", by Sharpley and Stone. *e-Review of Tourism Research, 8*(1).

Wilson, G. (2004). Multimedia tour programmer at Tate Modern. *Proceedings of Museums and the Web*.

Wilson, A. L. (1978). Elemental Analysis of Pottery in the Study of its Provenance: A Review. *Journal of Archaeological Science*, *5*(3), 219–236. doi:10.1016/0305-4403(78)90041-9

Wither, J., Tsai, Y., & Azuma, R. (2011). Indirect augmented reality. *Comput. Graph*, *35*(4), 810–822. doi:10.1016/j.cag.2011.04.010

Witmer, B. G., & Singer, M. J. (1998). Measuring presence in virtual environments: A presence questionnaire. *Presence (Cambridge, Mass.)*, *7*(3), 225–240. doi:10.1162/105474698565686

Wojciechowski, R., Walczak, K., White, M., & Cellary, W. (2004). Building virtual and augmented reality museum exhibitions. *Proceedings of the ninth international conference on 3D Web technology*, 135-144. 10.1145/985040.985060

Wooldridge, M., & Jennings, N. R. (1995). Intelligent agents: Theory and practice. *The Knowledge Engineering Review*, *10*(02), 115–152. doi:10.1017/S0269888900008122

Wurzel, G., Kowarik, K., & Reschreiter, H. (Eds.). (2015). *Agent-based Modeling and Simulation in Archeology*. Cham: Springer. doi:10.1007/978-3-319-00008-4

Wu, Y., Bryan-Kinns, N., Wang, W., Sheridan, J. G., & Xu, X. (2017). Designing a Cross-Cultural Interactive Music Box through Meaning Construction. In *International Conference on Cross-Cultural Design* (pp. 241–257). Springer. 10.1007/978-3-319-57931-3_20

Xue, L., Manuel-Navarrete, D., & Buzinde, C. N. (2014). Theorizing the concept of alienation in tourism studies. *Annals of Tourism Research*, *44*, 186–199. doi:10.1016/j.annals.2013.10.001

Yang, D., & Lee, W. S. (2009, December). Music emotion identification from lyrics. In *Multimedia, 2009. ISM'09. 11th IEEE International Symposium on* (pp. 624-629). IEEE. 10.1109/ISM.2009.123

Yang, Y. H., Lin, Y. C., Cheng, H. T., Liao, I. B., Ho, Y. C., & Chen, H. H. (2008, December). Toward multi-modal music emotion classification. In *Pacific-Rim Conference on Multimedia* (pp. 70-79). Springer Berlin Heidelberg.

Yang, Y., & Marques, N. C. (2005). User group profile modeling based on user transactional data for personalized systems. Lect. Notes Comput. Sci., 3808, 337–347. doi:10.1007/11595014_34

Yang, D., & Lee, W. S. (2004, October). *Disambiguating Music Emotion Using Software Agents* (Vol. 4). ISMIR.

Yang, L., Dong, H., Alelaiwi, A., & El Saddik, A. (2015). See in 3D: State of the art of 3D display technologies. *Multimedia Tools and Applications*, *75*(24), 17121–17155. doi:10.100711042-015-2981-y

Yarbrough, L. D., Easson, G. & Kuszmaul J. S. (2005). QuickBird 2 tasseled cap transform coefficients: a comparison of derivation methods. *Pecora*, *16*.

Yaroslavsky, L. P. (1996, October). Local adaptive image restoration and enhancement with the use of DFT and DCT in a running window. In *SPIE's 1996 International Symposium on Optical Science, Engineering, and Instrumentation* (pp. 2-13). International Society for Optics and Photonics. 10.1117/12.255218

Yelmi, P., Kuşcu, H., & Yantaç, A. E. (2016). Towards a Sustainable Crowdsourced Sound Heritage Archive by Public Participation: The Soundsslike Project. In *Proceedings of the 9th Nordic Conference on Human-Computer Interaction* (p. 71). ACM. 10.1145/2971485.2971492

Yin, R. K. (2013). *Case study research: Design and methods*. Sage Publications.

Yngve, G., Obrien, J., & Hodgins, J. (2000). Animation explosions. In *Proceedings of ACM SIGGRAPH 2000 conference proceedings*. (pp. 29–36). ACM Press.

Yovcheva, Z., Buhalis, D., & Gatzidis, C. (2012). Overview of smartphone augmented reality applications for tourism. *e-Review of Tourism Research, 10*(2), 63–66.

Yu, X., Wang, R., & Yu, J. (2010). Real-time depth of field rendering via dynamic light field generation and filtering. *Computer Graphics Forum*, *29*(7), 2099–2107. doi:10.1111/j.1467-8659.2010.01797.x

Yu, Z., Zhou, X., Yu, Z., Hyuk Park, J., & Ma, J. (2008). iMuseum: A scalable context-aware intelligent museum system. *Computer Communications*, *31*(18), 4376–4382. doi:10.1016/j.comcom.2008.05.004

Zafeiropoulos, V., & Kalles, D. (2016). Performance Evaluation in Virtual Lab Training. In *Proceedings of the Online, Open and Flexible Higher Education Conference 2016* (pp. 455-468). Aarhus: EADTU.

Zamora-Musa, R., Vélez, J., & Paez-Logreira, H. (2018). Evaluating learnability in a 3D heritage tour. *Presence (Cambridge, Mass.)*, *26*(4), 366–377. doi:10.1162/PRES_a_00305

Zancanaro, M., Kuflik, T., Boger, Z., Goren-Bar, D., & Goldwasser, D. (2007). Analyzing museum visitors' behavior patterns. In C. Conati, K. F. McCoy, & G. Paliouras (Eds.), Lecture Notes in Computer Science: Vol. 451. *User Modeling* (pp. 238–246). Heidelberg, Germany: Springer.

Zangwill, N. (2004). Against emotion: Hanslick was right about music. *British Journal of Aesthetics*, *44*(1), 29–43. doi:10.1093/bjaesthetics/44.1.29

Zheng, F. (2015). Spatio-Temporal Registration. In *Augmented Reality*. Chapel Hill, NC: University of North Carolina.

Zimmerman, A., & Lorenz, A. (2008). LISTEN: A user-adaptive audio-augmented museum guide. *User Modeling and User-Adapted Interaction*, *18*(5), 389–416. doi:10.100711257-008-9049-x

Zimmerman, D. W. (1971). Thermoluminescent dating using fine grains from pottery. *Archaeometry*, *13*(1), 29–52. doi:10.1111/j.1475-4754.1971.tb00028.x

Zimmerman, J., Stolterman, E., & Forlizzi, J. (2010). An analysis and critique of Research through Design: towards a formalization of a research approach. In *Proceedings of the 8th ACM Conference on Designing Interactive Systems* (pp. 310-319). ACM. 10.1145/1858171.1858228

About the Contributors

Eros Agosto, Ph.D. in Survey and design for the safeguard of land and building Heritage at Turin Polytechnic. Post-doc researcher at Turin Polytechnic and ITHACA research center; Co-founder of the first Italian university spin-off in Geomatics; He took part as geospatial consultant at several EU-funded cooperation projects in Myanmar. His research interests concern both the integration of different survey techniques and the innovative management of geospatial data.

Paolo Ardissone graduated in Ancient Literature - archaeological studies at the University of Turin, PhD in Geomatics for Archaeology at the Politecnico di Torino. Expert in the field of archaeological survey and archaeological documentation management, database design and GIS. He worked for years with The Center for Archaeological Research and Excavations in the Middle East and Asia in Turin for the missions in Iran.

Fotis Arnaoutoglou received his BSc (Hons) Computer Studies (Visualisation) degree from the School of Maths and Computing from the University of Derby, UK in 1999 and since present days he is working as a freelance programmer and 3D visualization specialist. He is experienced in various computer science fields, ranging from 3D content creation to program development, but his main expertise lies in the field of real-time 3D computer graphics programming with OpenGL. His frequent cooperation with the Athena Research Centre has led to a several scientific publications from a plethora of research and development projects in the field of 3D visualisation

Leandro Bornaz, Civil Engineer at the Politecnico di Torino, PhD in geodesy and geomatics at the Politecnico di Milano. Expert in design, detection and processing of terrestrial and aerial laser scanner data. Expert photogrammetric survey, data integration and management. In 2005 he received the national award Autec (Associazione Universitari di Topografia e Cartografia) as best research work in Italy in the field of geomatics with the doctoral thesis: Laser scanner data analysis and elaboration.

Stefano Brusaporci is Associate Professor of Architectural Representation, Drawing and Survey at the University of L'Aquila (Italy) – Department of Civil, Construction-Architectural and Environmental Engineering. He is Ph.D. in "Conservation, Planning and Preservation of Settlements and Territorial Contexts of Elevated Environmental and Landscape Value". His research fields are surveying and historical-critical analysis of architecture and historical urban contexts; surveying and documentation of architectural heritage, also with integrated information systems; 3-D modeling and computer-based visualization for architectural and urban interpretation and presentation.

Christodoulos Chamzas received his Diploma Degree in Electrical and Mechanical Engineering from NTUA in 1974 and the M.S. and PhD from the PINY at Farmingdale. He was an Assistant Professor with the Department of Electrical Engineering at PINY (1979-82), and with AT&T Bell Laboratories (1982-90). Since 1990, he is with the Department of the Electrical and Computer Engineering at Democritus University of Thrace. During 2001-2003, he was the Department Head (www.ee.duth.gr) while from 1998-2012 he was the director of the Cultural and Educational Technology Institute (www.ceti.gr). He has been a major player in the definition, design and implementation of the CCITT/ISO (JBIG, JPEG, etc), standards for coding, storage and retrieval of images (color & bilevel) an area where he holds six (6) international patents. His primary interests are in cultural technologies, digital signal processing, 3D Digitization of Cultural objects and content retrieval. He is a member of the Technical Chamber of Greece, Sigma Xi, an Editor in the IEEE Transactions of Communications (1989-1996) a Distinguished Member of the Technical Staff of AT&T Bell Laboratories and a Senior Member of IEEE.

Simon Donig is a research assistant at the chair for Digital Libraries and Web Information Systems at the University of Passau. He has studied History and Political Science at the Universities of Hamburg and Konstanz. His monograph "Adel ohne Land – Land ohne Adel? Lebenswelt, Gedächtnis und materielle Kultur des schlesischen Adels nach 1945" (A Nobility without Estates - a Country without Nobility? Lifeworld, Memory and Material Culture of the Silesian Nobility after 1945) will appear with deGruyter – Oldenbourg in the autumn of 2019. Simon is also a parent to the Neoclassica project, developing methods, instruments and semantics for digital research in material culture from the era of Classicism (ca.1770-1840). His research interests involve methodological aspects of the Digital Humanities; the formalized representation of material culture as well as AI in research instruments with a focus on the study of multimodal artefacts.

Thomas Gees is founding director – together with Prof. Dr. Reinhard Riedl – of the Institute Digital Enabling at the Berner Fachhochschule. Thomas holds a Master Degree in History from the University of Berne, and also a doctorate degree in European Contemporary History from the Institute of European Global Studies of Basel (Dr. phil.). He is teaching Public Management, Political Processes an Philosophy of Science in the Bachelor and Master Programme at BFH Business School; he is coordinating the Center Digital Society that carries out transdisciplinary research from the Business School, the School for Engineering and Technology, the Healthcare School, the School for Social Work, the School of Fine Arts, and the School for Architecture, Wood, and Civil Engineering.

Charalampos Georgiadis is an Assistant Professor in the School of Civil Engineering, The Aristotle University of Thessaloniki, Greece. He holds a Diploma in Surveying Engineering (1997), The Aristotle University of Thessaloniki, MSc in Protection, Preservation, and Restoration and of Cultural Monuments (2000), The Aristotle University of Thessaloniki, PhD (2005) Department of Spatial Information Science and Engineering, University of Maine, USA. His Areas of expertise include Photogrammetry, GIS, Cartography, UAV, Mobile Mapping Systems, Remote Sensing, 3D modelling using laser scanners, Image Processing and Analysis, Cultural heritage. Scientific Reviewer to 7 Journals. He is a member of research groups with a total of 32 Research Projects funded by National, European, or USA Organizations. His published work includes 37 papers in journals and proceeding and 3 dissertations.

Bintang Handayani is has served as head of undergraduate study programme at Sekolah Tinggi Pariwisata Bali International, Indonesia; where she also serves as a Senior Researcher. Her previous appointments include working as a Senior Fellow at School of Business in President University, has served as Graduate Teaching Assistant at Universiti Utara Malaysia, and worked as Part time Lecturer in Private Universities in Jakarta. Her research focuses on Branding in Tourism and Hospitality; Technology Mediated-Communication in Tourism and Hospitality; Special Interest Tourism; Media-related Tourism, Personification of a nation.

George Alexis Ioannakis received his Ph.D. degree in the area of 3D object processing at the dept. of Electrical and Computer Engineering, Democritus University of Thrace, Greece. He received his MEng Diploma at the dept. of Rural and Surveying Engineering, Aristotle University of Thessaloniki, Greece. Since 2013 he is working as a Research Assistant at the dept. of Electrical and Computer Engineering, Democritus University of Thrace and the Athena Research and Innovation Centre, Multimedia dept. Among his research interests are the 3D mesh processing, 3D object retrieval, photogrammetry, image processing and machine learning.

Katerina Kabassi is currently an Associate Professor and Head the Department of Environment, Faculty of Environment, Ionian University (Greece). She received a first degree in Informatics (1999) and a D.Phil. (2003) from the Department of Information, University of Piraeus (Greece). She has authored more than 110 articles, which have been published in international/national journals, books and conferences. She has served as a member of Program Committees in more than 150 conferences and/or reviewer in more than 160 conferences. Additionally, she has served as reviewer in 27 international journals. Her current research interests are in the areas of Multi-Criteria Decision Making, Evaluation Experiments, Personalised Software, Knowledge-based Software Engineering, Human Computer Interaction, Web-based Information Systems and Educational Software.

Dimitris Kaimaris is Assistant Professor of Remote Sensing and GIS in the School of Spatial Planning and Development (Eng.), Aristotle University of Thessaloniki (AUTh), Greece. He graduated from the School of Rural & Surveying Engineering, AUTh (2000), and later obtained an MSc (2002) and a PhD (2006) in Photogrammetry, Remote Sensing and GIS. In 2010 he was elected as Faculty member at AUTh. Dr. Kaimaris teaches remote sensing, GIS, etc. He has participated in numerous research projects, national and international, on photogrammetry, remote sensing and GIS. He has been an instructor and organizer in national and international conferences, seminars and workshops. He has published more than 80 scientific articles in proceedings and peer reviewed journals, and two scientific books. He is associate editor of the South-Eastern European Journal of Earth Observation and Geomatics (SEEJoEOG).

Nikolaos Kazakis received his diploma in Chemical Engineering with honors from the Chemical Engineering Department of the Aristotle University of Thessaloniki, Greece in 2003. After his graduation, he continued his studies at the same Department, from where he received his 1st PhD Degree in Chemical Engineering in 2008 (grade excellent). The title of his Thesis was “Study of bubble column equipped with porous gas sparger”. In 2009, he worked as a Post-Doctoral Fellow at the Department of Chemistry of the Aristotle University of Thessaloniki for approximately a year. In 2010 he joined the Laboratory of Archaeometry and Physicochemical Measurements of R.C. “Athena” in Xanthi and worked there as an Adjunct Researcher and Post-Doctoral Fellow until early 2019. In 2018, he received his 2nd PhD Degree in Physics/Dosimetry (grade excellent) from the School of Physics of the Aristotle University of Thessaloniki, Greece. The title of his Thesis was "High-dose dosimetry with emphasis on the industrial sterilization and accidental radiation dosimetry". He serves as a Principal Researcher at the Athena-Research and Innovation Center in Information, Communication and Knowledge Technologies, Greece, since March 2019 with area of expertise "Dosimetry and analytical radiation methods". He has 2 book chapters, 28 research publications in international scientific journals (6 monographs), 20 presentations in scientific conferences and meetings and 4 publications to other journals and/or the web. The impact of his scientific work is reflected on more than 540 citations (h-index=8 from Scopus), while he also acts as a referee in 15 international scientific journals in physics, archaeometry, chemical engineering and medical statistics.

Chairi Kiourt is an Assistant Researcher at the ATHENA - Research and Innovation Centre in Information, Communication and Knowledge Technologies - Xanthi's Division, multimedia department since 2019. Also, as of 2018, heis Adjunct Faculty at the Computer Science Department, International Hellenic University, Greece. In 2007, he received his BSc degree in Electrical Engineering from the Electrical Engineering Department of the Eastern Macedonia and Thrace Institute of Technology, Greece. He also received an M.Sc. in System Engineering and Management in the specialty area: A. Information and Communication Systems Management from the Democritus University of Thrace, Greece. In 2017, received his PhD in Artificial Intelligence and Software Engineering from the Hellenic Open University. He has participated in several national and European research programs and co- authored to the writing of several scientific publications in international peer-reviewed journals and conferences with judges in the fields of collective artificial intelligence, multi-agent systems, reinforcement learning agents, virtual worlds, virtual museums and gamification.

Maximiliano Korstanje is editor in chief of International Journal of Safety and Security in Tourism (UP Argentina) and International Journal of Cyber Warfare and Terrorism (IGI-GlobalUS). Besides being Senior Researchers in the Department of Economics at University of Palermo, Argentina, he is a global affiliate of Tourism Crisis Management Institute (University of Florida US), Centre for Ethnicity and Racism Studies (University of Leeds), Now he co-edits almost 10 specialized journals in such themes as human rights, mobility, tourism and terrorism. Korstanje is subject to biographical records for Marquis Who`s Who in the World since 2009. He had nominated to 5 honorary doctorates for his contribution in the study of the effects of terrorism in tourism. In 2015 he was awarded as Visiting Research Fellow at School of Sociology and Social Policy, University of Leeds, UK.

Adamantios Koumpis, before joining the team at the Berner Fachhochschule, was Research Fellow at the University of Passau in Germany since June 2014, and before this at the Insight Centre for Data Analytics at the National University of Ireland, Galway since December 2012. Prior to this position, he headed the Research Programmes Division of ALTEC Software S.A. in Greece which he founded in 1996 (then as Unisoft of Northern Greece). He has successfully led more than 50 commercial and research projects for new technology development, technology adoption and user uptake, both at the European and the national level in several areas such as E-Commerce, public sector and business enterprise re-organisation and information logistics, involving the linking of data/information repositories with knowledge management and business engineering models.

Panayiotis Koutsabasis is an assistant professor of human-computer interaction at the Department of Product and System Design Engineering, University of the Aegean, Greece.

Anestis Koutsoudis works as a researcher in the ATHENA - Research and Innovation Centre in Information, Communication and Knowledge Technologies, where he holds a principal researcher position. He has participated in many research and development projects with emphasis on real time 3D graphics programming, 3D digitisation, content-based retrieval, multimedia and IT application in the cultural heritage domain.

Stella Markantonatou holds the position of Research Director at the Institute for Language and Speech Processing (ILSP) of the "Athena research institute. Her areas of interest are Lexical Semantics, Ontologies, the Development of lexical resources with hybrid methods and Standardization especially as regards cultural data. Stella Markantonatou holds the following degrees: Degree in Chemical Engineering (NTUA), Degree in Linguistics (University of Athens), MA in Knowledge Representation (University of Sussex), PhD in Linguistics (University of Essex). For the period 1992-1996 she belonged to the Essex Computational Linguistics Group and was the person mainly responsible for a number of CEC funded projects concerning grammar development and computational lexica specifications (LRE, MLAP). She has been a member of ILSP since 1998. For the period 1998-2008 she was the Head of the Machine Translation Department of ILSP / R.C. "Athena". She has coordinated both nationally funded (Schematopiisis, Proteus) and EU funded (METIS I and II) projects and has worked on thematic areas concerning controlled languages and hybrid statistical machine translation. She was a main participant in national and European research projects that employed ontologies to represent lexical knowledge (EKFRASIS) and knowledge about cultural objects (ML-Images!, byzantine icons – EIKONOGNOSIA, Corgialenion Historical Museum). She has taught in various Universities (University of Essex, University of Cyprus, University of Crete, University of Athens, NTUA) at both a graduate and a post-graduate level while the topics addressed include grammatical formalisms (LFG, HPSG), lexical and formal semantics and computational linguistics. She has been a co-organizer of a number of international conferences (LAGB 1995 (Fall), LREC2000, LFG2002) and she is a member of TEE, EETN, LAGB and TE21.

Vasiliki Nikolakopoulou is a researcher and PhD student with the department of Product and Systems Design Engineering, University of the Aegean, Greece.

Petros Patias is a Professor, Director of Laboratory of Photogrammetry & Remote Sensing and ex-chairman at the School of Rural and Surveying Engineering (2003-2007), The Aristotle University of Thessaloniki (AUTH), board member of the Department of Urban Planning, AUTH (2004-2012) and Vice Rector at the University of Western Macedonia (2010-2015), Greece. Eng. (1981) The Aristotle University, MSc (1985) and PhD (1987) both from the Dept. of Geodetic Science and Surveying, The Ohio State University, USA. Chairman of various ISPRS (International Society of Photogrammetry and Remote Sensing) WGs from 1992 onwards, ISPRS Commission V President (2000-2004), CIPA (international Committee for Architectural Photogrammetry) President (2003-2007) and Honorary President (2013-for life), ISPRS Fellow (2016-for life), President of the Hellenic Society of Photogrammetry and Remote Sensing (1992-1996). Visiting Professor at various European universities (TU Delft, ETH Zurich, Universidad del País Vasco). Editor-in-chief of the "South-Eastern European Journal of Earth Observation and Geomatics" e-Journal (http://ejournals.lib.auth.gr/seejeog), Scientific reviewer to 51

Journals. Reviewer/evaluation to numerous promotions/elections to all Greek universities. In addition, internationally, he served as evaluator to promotions at National Research Council, Canada (2004), State University of New York, USA (2011), University of Haifa, Israel (2012), Politecnico di Torino, Italy (2015, 2016). Evaluator to research proposals (besides Greece) to NSERC Discovery Grant Applications, Canada (2013), Research Promotion Foundation Grants, Cyprus (2013), External Evaluation of Higher Education Institutions, Cyprus (2013), Israeli Ministry of Science, Technology and Space Grants, Israel (2014, 2016), Italian Research and University Evaluation Agency (ANVUR) Grants, Italy (2004-2016), Italian Ministry of Education, University and Research (MIUR) Grants, Italy (2015-2016), Ministry of Education, science and Technological Development Grants, Serbia (2016). Supervised 101 undergraduate Diploma Theses, 73 MSc Theses and 34 PhD Dissertations. Published work includes 6 books, 11 chapters in international books and 249 papers in journals and proceedings. Scientific Responsible, Principal Researcher or member of Research Group to a total of 91 Research Projects funded by European or National Organizations.

Evgenia Paxinou is a PhD candidate in Educational Biology, in School of Science and Technology at the Hellenic Open University (HOU), in Greece. She is also a member of OnLabs Team in HOU (https://sites.google.com/site/onlabseap/team), a team that develops Virtual Reality and Augmented Reality Biology experiments. She designes and implements educational scenarios enriched with VR and AR activities and she develops methods to assess the gained experimental skills and the students' learning outcomes. She is currently participating is research projects co-financed by the E.E. (Horizon 2014-2020). She received her BSc in Chemistry from the University of Patras, in Greece in 1993. She successfully attended the oenology training Programme which was drawn up by the General Assembly of the Department of Chemistry of the University of Patras, Greece. She obtained her MSc from the Department of Pharmacy, University of Patras, Greece, in 2002. Between 1999 and 2001 she was a visiting scholar, firstly at the Division of Immunologic and Infectious Diseases (UPENN, USA) and then at Joseph Stokes Jr. Research Institute, at Children's Hospital of Philadelphia, USA. Her work was translated to 15 full manuscripts in highly prestigious journals, such as Proceedings of the National Academy of Science of U.S.A., Neuroscience, Biochemistry and Molecular Biology Education, etc, and she has received, until now, more than 600 citations (https://scholar.google.com/citations?user=kIIjIkoAAAA J&hl=el). She also co-authored 3 chapters in scientific books. She has been a chemistry tutor in many public and private high schools in the region of Patras, Greece, after 2001. Her native lanquage is Greek but she also speaks English, French and Italian. Her current fields of interest are: Learning Simulation; Virtual Reality; Augmented Reality; Distance Learning Education; Assessment.

Argyro Sgourou is an Assistant Professor on "Cell structure and function" at the Hellenic Open University (HOU), School of Science and Technology (SST) and Director of the Biology lab. PhD in "Molecular Biology and Genetics" obtained from Medical School, University of Patras, under the funding of the "States Scholarship Foundation" of Greece. Visiting researcher funded by two short term EMBO research fellowships to the Laboratory of Gene Structure and Expression National Institute for Medical Research, UK and the Dept. of Medical and Molecular Genetics, King's College, London. Postdoctoral studies on Gene Therapy Biotechnology issues at the Dept. of Medical and Molecular Genetics, King's College, London, funded by a Marie Curie Individual Fellowship. Published 28 original papers, 2 book chapters and over 40 papers in conference proceedings, of which 3 have been awarded.

Athanasios Sypsas is a PhD candidate at Hellenic Open University, School of Science and Technology, Greece. He studied computer Science and Telecommunications at the National & Kapodistrian University of Athens, Greece (2001). He received his MSc in Intergraded Systems of Hardware and Software from University of Patras, Greece (2004). His main scientific interests are learning simulation, machine learning, distance learning and programming. He has been working in Telecommunication Industry (INTRACOM S.A.) and as a scientific collaborator at TEI of Epirus. He is now working as a high school computer science teacher.

Helena Theodoropoulou holds a Diploma degree in Architecture from the Department of Architectural Engineering, School of Engineering, Democritus University of Thrace (DUTh), Xanthi, Greece and a M.Sc. degree in Information Systems from the School of Science and Technology, Hellenic Open University, Greece. She is a freelance Architect and currently works as a Research Associate at the Industrial Systems Institute (I.S.I.), Research Center Athena, Patras, Greece.

Nestor Tsirliganis received his Bachelor's Degree in Physics from the Aristotle University of Thessaloniki in 1986 and continued his studies, under a Fulbright Scholarship, at The University of Michigan - Ann Arbor (U.S.A.) from where he received a Master's Degree in Nuclear Science in 1987 and a Ph.D. Degree in the same field in 1995. He specialized in nuclear measurements with emphasis on instruments and methods for neutron detection and measurement. During his graduate studies (1986-1994) he held a Research Assistant Appointment at the Nuclear Data Laboratory and a Teaching Assistant Appointment at the Department of Nuclear Engineering and Radiological Sciences of The University of Michigan. During the 1996–1998 period he worked as an Associated Research Scientist in various projects regarding environmental dosimetry, at the Nuclear Engineering Laboratory of the Democritus University of Thrace. In 1999, as an external consultant, planned and organized the Archaeometry Laboratory of the Cultural and Educational Technology Institute–CETI (today Institute of Language and Speech Processing–ILSP/Xanthi Branch) in Xanthi. In 2002, he joined the Institute as Research Lecturer, Head of the Archaeometry Laboratory (today Archaeometry and Physicochemical Measurements Laboratory), position that holds till presently as Research Director, since 2007. In 2012, following the merge of CETI with ILSP he undertook the position of head of the Xanthi Branch/ILSP. His research interests include luminescence dating of ceramics and sediments, luminescence measurement techniques, luminescence properties of minerals, applications of electromagnetic radiation and nuclear measurements for the investigation, preservation and authentication of cultural objects and art, and applications of the information technologies in the study and dissemination of the cultural heritage. He has more than 60 publications in international refereed journals and more than 65 participations in international conferences with published proceedings. His work has more than 500 references.

Spyros Vosinakis is an Assistant Professor at the Department of Product and Systems Design Engineering, University of the Aegean with subject "Virtual Reality". He holds a BSc in Informatics, University of Piraeus, an MSc in Computer Graphics and Virtual Environments, University of Hull, UK and a PhD in Informatics, University of Piraeus with subject "Intelligent Agents in Virtual Environments". His research interests include: Virtual Worlds in Education, Collaborative Virtual Environments, Intelligent Virtual Agents, Adaptivity and Personalization in 3D environments, Virtual Museums.

Index

I

L

M

O

P

R

S

T

U

V

www.ingramcontent.com/pod-product-compliance
Lightning Source LLC
LaVergne TN
LVHW062121300926
849161LV00010B/2510

* 9 7 8 1 7 9 9 8 2 8 7 1 6 *